Legal Defence in Armed Forces Tribunal

Act-Rules-Judgements

Attention Authors

'We Convert Fighters into Writers.' That's the motto of Manas Publications since more than four decades. Our message to the world is that India can win the battle not only by the bullet but also by the pen. There is no dearth of intellectuals in our country, but their knowledge is confined to them only. No sincere effort has been made by any other publisher to channelise their knowledge in national interest. That is why the talent of a large number of intellectuals remains latent. An author transforms his knowledge into a manuscript and it is our job to spread his/her knowledge by converting it into a beautiful book. For over four decades, Manas has been motivating the intellectuals by publishing their manuscripts and would like to publish your manuscript too. So if you or your colleagues have any manuscript ready for publication or are working on it, kindly contact us with detailed synopsis and list of contents. We will transform your work into a valuable publication. If you wish, we can also suggest you the suitable subjects for writing the books related to your area of expertise. Manas is known for its publishing quality and commitments. We take utmost care in production and give wide publicity to the book as well as its author through our National and International distribution network.

Legal Defence in Armed Forces Tribunal

Act-Rules-Judgements

Wg Cdr (Dr) UC Jha

Manas Publications
(We Convert Fighters into Writers)
New Delhi-110002 (INDIA)

MANAS PUBLICATIONS
(We Convert Fighters into Writers)
(Publishers, Distributors, Importers & Exporters)
4402/5-A, Ansari Road (Opp HDFC Bank)
Darya Ganj, New Delhi-110 002 (India)
Off. ✆ 011-23260783, 23265523, Res. ✆ 011-23842660
Fax: 011-23272766
E-mail: manaspublications@gmail.com
manaspublications@yahoo.com
Website: www.manaspublications.in

ISBN 978-81-7049-476-8
Rs. 995/-

Designed at
Manas Publications

Printed in India at
R.K Offsets, Delhi
and published by Mrs Suman Lata for
Manas Publications, 4402/5-A, Ansari Road,
(Opp HDFC Bank),
Darya Ganj, New Delhi-110 002 (INDIA)

Contents

Table of Cases

A

A. Ramar v. Union of India, OA No. 1215 of 2011, AFT Chandigarh Bench, decided on 11 February 2013.

A K Bhardwaj (Ex Colonel) v. Union of India, TA No. 429 of 2010, AFT Lucknow Bench, decided on 3 May 2011.

Ajit Singh v. Union of India, TA No. 1292 of 2010, AFT Chandigarh, decided on 13 February 2012.

Akhila Bihar Singh v. Union of India, TA No. 134 of 2010, AFT Kolkata Bench, decided on 7 March 2012.

Arunima Baruah v. Union of India (2007) 6 SCC 120l.

AVM MS Brar v. Union of India 96 (2002) DLT 483.

AVM NM Vaishnavi v. Union of India, OA No. 300 of 2011, AFT PB, decided on 3 April 2012.

B

B. Ramu v. Union of India, TA No.183 of 2010, AFT Chennai, decided on 9 December 2010.

Baby v. Union of India, 2003 (3) KLT 362 (FB).

Baidaya Nath Ghosh v. Union of India TA No. 81 of 2009, AFT Jaipur Bench, decided on 11 November 2011.

Baljeet Singh v. Union of India, TA No. 602 of 2009, AFT PB, decided on 29 May 2012.

Bakhshish Singh v. Union of India OA No. 481 of 2010, AFT Chandigarh Bench, decided on 7 January 2011.

Beant Singh v. Union of India, TA No. 503 of 2009, AFT PB, decided on 2 May 2011.

Bharat v. State of Uttar Pradesh (1971(3) SCC 950.

Bikramjit Singh v. Union of India OA No. 354 of 2010, AFT Chandigarh Bench, decided on 7 January 2011.

Brig A K Bhutani v. Union of India, OA No 144 of 2011, AFT Chandigarh Bench, decided on 19 April 2012.

Brig L. Venkatachalam v. Union of India, WP No. 3913/86, Order dated 16 July 1987.

Brig LI Singh v. Union of India, OA No. 85 of 2013, AFT PB, decided on 21 March 2013.

Brig PS Gill v. Union of India, OA No. 147 of 2010, AFT PB, decided on 24 May 2011.

Brig SPS Baswani v. Union of India, 1993 (1) Simla, LC 373.

Brig Satinder Kumar Sud v. Union of India, OA No. 575 of 2011, AFT Chandigarh Bench, decided on 14 November 2011.

C

Capt Kanika Gupta, OA No. 195 of 2011, AFT PB, decided on 14 March 2012.

Capt P L Bhatia v. Union of India, TA No. 274 of 2009, AFT Jaipur Bench, decided on 5 March 2010.

Capt Tony George v. Union of India, TA No. 164 of 2010 AFT Kochi Bench, decided on 28 October 2010.

Cdr Alok Kumar Pathak v. Union of India, OA No. 579 of 2011, AFT PB, decided on 9 April 2013.

Cdr Naresh Chandro Sahu v. Union of India, TA No. 276 of 2010, AFT PB, decided on 6 August 2012.

Chairman, DA Rani Lakshmi Bai KG Bank v. JS Varshney, 2009 (4) SCALE 169.

Chaudhary M.R. Ex. Sepoy v Union of India CWP No. 563 of 1990 (HP).

Col A D Nargolkar v. Union of India, WP (C) 13360 of 2009 and WP (C) 13367 of 2009, decided by the Delhi High Court on 26 April 2011.

Col Debashis Mitra v. Union of India, TA No. 4 of 2010, AFT Kolkata Bench, decided on 20 July 2010.

Col H. C. Goswami (Retd) v. Union of India, OA No. 27 of 2011, AFT PB, decided on 23 April 2012.

Col Harjinder Singh Lamba v. Union of India, TA No. 633 of 2009, AFT PB, decided on 24 February 2011.

Col Harvinder Singh Kohli v. Union of India, TA No. 254 of 2009, AFT PB, decided on 11 January 2010.

Col Kamal Deep Singh v. Union of India, OA No. 93 of 2012, AFT PB decided on 1 May 2013.

Col NS Parmar v. Union of India, OA No. 15 of 2013, AFT PB, decided on 15 May 2013.

Col R. Jayaprasad v. Union of India 151 (2008) DLT 435(DB).

Col Rajesh Kapoor v. Union of India, OA No. 113 of 2009, AFT PB, decided on 30 May 2011.

Col Rakesh Sharma, SM v. Union of India, OA No. 113 of 2011, AFT PB, decided on 7 August 2012.

Col R. K. Nair (Retd) v. Union of India TA No. 34 of 2010, AFT Kochi Bench, decided on 25 March 2010.

Col S K Jain v. Union of India, OA No. 445 of 2010, AFT PB, decided on 1 June 2012.

Col Sanjeev Sehgal v. Union of India, OA No. 488 of 2011, AFT Chandigarh Bench, decided on 18 July 2011.

Commander Ravinder Singh v. Union of India, OA No. 421 of 2010, AFT PB, decided on 29 May 2012.

D

D.S. Nakara v. Union of India AIR 1983 SC 130; 1983(1) SCC 305.

Devi Lal Sahu v. Union of India 2009 (2) Service Cases Today 152 (Raj).

Dhirendra Kumar Singh v. The Chief of Naval Staff, TA No. 140 of 2010, AFT Kochi Bench, decided on 8 November 2010.

Dimple Singla v. Union of India, OA 108 of 2010, AFT Chandigarh Bench, decided on 25 July 2012.

Director General, BSF v. Vijoy, 2000 (2) KLT 509 (FB).

Divisional Forest Officer v Madhusudan Rao, JT 2008 (2) SC 253.

Duraibabu R. v. Union of India, WP No. 11525 of 1990 and WQA No. 794 of 1992 dated 9 April 1992 (Madras).

E

Ex Col A K Kadian v. Union of India TA No. 245 of 2010, AFT PB, decided on 1 June 2012.

Ex Cpl CL Kataria v. Union of India OA 162 of 2010, AFT Jaipur Bench, decided on 01 June 2011.

Ex Cpl Madan Kumar Singh v. Union of India, OA No. 144 of 2009, AFT PB, decided on 11 April 2011.

Ex Cpl Nitish Kumar v. Union of India, OA No. 184 of 2012, AFT PB, decided on 7 November 2012.

Ex Gnr Ghan Shyam Singh v. Union of India, TA No. 39 of 2010, AFT PB, decided on 18 February 2013.

Ex Hav Moharsingh v. Union of India, TA No. 309 of 2009, AFT Jaipur Bench, decided on 20 May 2010.

Ex Hav Mohinder Singh v. Union of India, TA No. 32 of 2011, AFT PB, decided on 10 April 2012.

Ex Hav Nancha Ram Jat v. Union of India, TA No. 649 of 2009, AFT PB, decided on 22 July 2010.

Ex Hav Prem Upreti v. Union of India TA No. 163 of 2010, AFT PB, decided on 4 May 2012.

Ex Hav Prithpal Singh v. Union of India 1984 (3) SLR 675 (J&K).

Ex Hav Rakesh Dhaka v. Union of India, TA No. 684 of 2009, AFT PB, decided on 2 July 2010,

Ex Hav Rampat Yadav v. Union of India, OA No. 135 of 2013, AFT PB, decided on 2 April 2013.

Ex L/Nk (DMT) Shyam Sunder Thakur, v. Union of India, OA No. 87 of 2009, AFT PB, decided on 19 October 2010.

Ex. Naib Subedar Suresh Kumar v. Union of India, OA No. 773 of 2010, AFT Chandigarh Bench, decided on 27 January 2011.

Ex Hav/Tech Comn Suresh Kumar v. Union of India, OA No. 04 of 2012, AFT PB, decided on 5 November 2012.

Ex Nk Birendra Kumar Singh v. Union of India, TA No. 563 of 2009, AFT PB, decided on 27 February 2012.

Ex. Nk Shri Bhagwan v. Union of India, OA No. 328 of 2011, AFT PB, decided on 4 July 2012.

Ex Col A. K. Kadian v. Union of India, RA No. 47 of 2011, in TA No. 245 of 2010, AFT PB, decided on 4 May 2012.

Ex Gnr Ghan Shyam Singh v. Union of India, TA No. 39 of 2010, AFT PB, decided on 18 February 2013.

Ex Gnr Krishan Kumar v. Union of India, TA No. 312 of 2009, AFT PB, decided on 19 October 2010.

Ex Hav Ashok M Rao v. Union of India, TA No. 391 of 2010, AFT PB, decided on 25 March 2011.

Ex Hav Suresh Kumar v. Union of India, TA No. 99 of 2009, AFT Jaipur Bench, decided on 2 July 2010.

Ex Lt Col B K Mall v. Union of India, TA No. 512 of 2009, AFT PB, decided on 22 September 2011.

Ex Lt Col Ranjodg Singh v. Union of India, TA No. 68 of 2010, AFT Lucknow Bench, decided on 5 October 2010.

Ex Lt Col S S Bedi v. Union of India TA No. 246 of 2010, AFT PB, decided on 30 May 2012.

Ex Major Rehman Hussain v. Union of India, TA No. 361 of 2010, AFT PB, decided on 8 November 2012.

Ex Major NR Ajwani v. Union of India 55 (1994) DLT 217.

Ex Major YS Nagar v. Union of India, TA No. 677 of 2009, AFT PB, decided on 25 February 2011.

Ex Naib Subedar Gobind Singh v. Union of India, OA No. 444 of 2011, AFT Chandigarh Bench, decided on 08 December 2011.

Ex Nb Sub Jai Lal v. Union of India, OA No. 55 of 2011, AFT Chandigarh Bench, decided on 11 November 2011.

Ex Nk Birendra Kumar Singh v. Union of India, TA No. 563 of 2009, AFT PB, decided on 27 February 2012.

Ex Nk Jawar Singh Chauhan v. Union of India, TA No. 475 of 2009, AFT PB, decided on 24 February 2011.

Ex Nk N A. Mithilesh Kumar v. Union of India, TA No. 747 of 2009, AFT PB, decided on 22 July 2010.

Ex. Naik P. Baskaran v. Secretary, Government of India, Ministry of Defence, TA No. 13 of 2009, AFT Chennai Bench, decided on 12 January 2010.

Ex Naik Ravindra Kumar Kushwaha v. Union of India, TA No. 146 of 2010, AFT Lucknow Bench, decided on 18 April 2011.

Ex-Naik Sardar Singh v Union of India 1991 (3) SCC 213.

E. P. Royappa v. State of Tamil Nadu 1974 (4) SCC 3.

Ex Rfn/WM Jagsir Singh v. Union of India, OA No. 235 of 2011, AFT PB, decided on 16 March 2012.

Ex Rfn Satbir Singh v. Union of India, TA No. 454 of 2009, AFT PB, decided on 24 February 2011.

Ex. Sep. Balakotaiah Mekala v. Union of India, OA No. 96 of 2012, AFT Chennai Bench, decided on 08 April 2013.

Ex Sep Balinder Pandey v. Union of India, TA No. 432 of 2010, AFT PB, decided 19 March 2012.

Ex. Sepoy Gnr Amarjit Singh v. Union of India, TA No. 189 of 2009, AFT PB, decided on 27 August 2012.

Ex Sepoy (PANK) Mahender Singh v. Union of India, in TA No. 239 of 2009, AFT PB, decided on 15 January 2010.

Sep Raj Bahadur Singh v. Union of India, TA No. 228 of 2009, AFT PB, decided on 27 January 2010.

Ex Sep P. R. Yadav v. Union of India, TA No. 22 of 2010, AFT Jaipur Bench, decided on 2 July 2010.

Ex-Sepoy Sasikumar K., v. Union of India OA No. 3 of 2010, AFT Chennai Bench, decided on 1 April 2011.

Ex Sep Umesh Singh v. Union of India, OA No. 38 of 2010, AFT PB, decided on 1 August 2012.

Ex Sep/Dvr Rakesh Kumar v. Union of India, OA No. 116 of 2010, AFT PB, decided on 25 February 2011.

Ex Sgt R.S. Dwivedi v. Chief of the Air Staff, TA 404 of 2010, AFT PB, decided on 19 October 2011.

Ex Signalman Rajesh Kumar v. Union of India, TA No. 426 of 2010, AFT PB, decided 5 February 2010.

Ex Signalman Vijay Kumar v. Union of India, TA No. 630 of 2009, AFT PB, decided on 24 February 2011.

Ex Sub Ram Kumar v. Union of India, OA No. 488 of 2011, AFT PB, decided on 28 August 2012.

G

G. Devanand v. Union of India, TA No.156 of 2010, AFT Chennai Bench, decided on 10 December 2010.

Ganesh Bhavan Patel v. State of Maharashtra AIR 1979 SC 135.

Gangeshwar Baitha (Ex-Havilder) v. Union of India, TA No. 92 of 2010, AFT Kolkata, decided on 10 January 2011.

Gautam Sanyal v. Union of India, TA No. 484 of 2010, AFT PB, decided on 19 April 2011.

Gopi K v. Union of India, TA No. 11 of 2009, AFT Kochi Bench, decided on 30 July 2010.

Gp Capt Ajit Singh, VSM v. Union of India, OA No. 117 of 2012, AFT PB, decided on 23 November 2011.

Gp Capt Atul Shukla v. Union of India, TA No. 385 of 2009, AFT PB, decided on 2 May 2013.

Gp Capt SPS Rajkumar v. Union of India, TA No. 122 of 2010, AFT PB, decided on 22 February 2011.

H

Harish Uppal v. Union of India, (1973) 2 SCR 1025.

Hav Amarjit Singh v. Union of India OA No. 64 of 2011, AFT PB, decided on 18 October 2011.

Hav Avinash U Pardeshi v. Union of India, OA No. 112 of 2011, AFT PB, decided on 07 May 2012.

Hav Manktu Ram v. Union of India, OA No. 67 of 2011, AFT Kochi Bench, decided on 21 March 2012.

Hav Parmanand Sahoo v. Union of India, OA No. 228 of 2010, AFT PB, decided on 21 May 2012.

Hav Pradhan Pandurang Wakoji v. Union of India, OA No. 455 of 2010, AFT PB, decided on 3 September 2012.

Hav Pratap Chandra Sahu v. Union of India, OA No. 191 of 2011, AFT PB, decided on 19 March 2012.

Hav Rajvir v. Union of India, OA No. 228 of 2011, AFT PB, decided on 4 April 2013.

Hav Ravindra Singh v. Union of India, OA No. 305 of 2010, AFT PB, decided on 17 April 2012.

Hav Shiv Kumar Joshi v. Union of India, OA No. 02 of 2009, AFT Lucknow Bench, decided on 16 March 2010.

Hav Surat Singh v. Union of India, OA No. 433 of 2011, AFT PB, decided on 20 March 2012.

Hav Vijay Kumar v. Union of India, OA No. 454 of 2010, AFT PB, decided on 3 September 2012.

Harbhajan Singh and others v. Union of India, OA No. 1844 of 2011, AFT Chandigarh Bench, decided on 21 November 2011,

Harish Chandra Joshi v. Union of India, TA No. 75 of 2010, AFT PB, decided on 24 February 2012.

Hazara Singh v. The Chief of the Air Staff 1982 SLR 521.

I

Inder Singh v. Union of India, OA No. 2054 of 2012, AFT Chandigarh Bench, decided on 9 August 2012.

Inderjit Singh v. Union of India, TA No. 585 of 2010, AFT Chandigarh Bench, decided on 27 January 2011.

Indeevarakshan Nair v. Union of India, TA No.17 of 2009, AFT Kochi Bench, decided on 16 July 2010.

J

Jai Bhagwan Sharma v. Union of India, OA No. 569 of 2010, AFT PB, decided on 24 November 2011.

Jai Narain Chhillar v. Union of India, OA No. 794 of 2010, AFT Chandigarh Bench, decided on 06 January 2012.

Jai Prakash Rana v. Union of India, TA No. 183 of 2010, AFT PB, decided on 1 December 2010.

Jasvendra Singh v. DG AFMS New Delhi, OA No. 56 of 2013, AFT PB, decided on 8 May 2013.

Jayendra Vishnu Thakur v. State of Maharashtra 2009 (7) SCC 104.

K

K Tirupathi v. The Chief of the Army Staff, TA No. 40 of 2009, AFT Chennai Bench, decided on 4 March 2010.

Kashmiri Singh v. State of Madhya Pradesh AIR 1952 SC 159.

Kerala State Electricity Board v. Hitech Electrothermics & Hydropower Ltd., JT 2005 (7) SC 485.

Kulawant Singh v. Union of India, TA No. 127 of 2010, AFT Chandigarh Bench, decided on 12 February 2013.

Kuldeep Singh v. State of Punjab 2002(6) SCC 757.

L

Lachhman Singh v. Union of India, TA No. 206 of 2009, AFT Jaipur Bench, decided on 7 May 2010.

L. Chandrakumar v. Union of India AIR 1997 SC 1125; (1997) 3SCC 261.

L/Nk Mirza Nazir Ahmed v Union of India WP No. 317 of 1981 Dated 30 January, 1988 (J&K).

Lance Naik V.P. Singh V. Union of India WP (C) 2511/1992, Delhi HC, decided on 25 January 2008.

Lance Nk Sanjeev Kumar v. Union of India in TA No. 413 of 2010, AFT PB, decided on 8 February 2010.

LEM H.S. Bind v. Union of India, TA No. 471 of 2009, AFT PB, decided on 1 August 2012.

Lt (SDW) R.P. Sharma v. Union of India, TA No.138 of 2010, AFT Chennai Bench, decided on 19 November 2010.

Lt Cdr Alok Ambastha v. Union of India, TA No. 84 of 2010, AFT PB, decided on 21 December 2012.

Lt Cdr Deepak Kanathey v. Union of India, TA No.178 of 2010, AFT PB, decided on 6 August 2012.

Lt Col Dharmender Singh Yadav v. Union of India, OA No. 107 of 2011, AFT Lucknow Bench, decided on 27 July 2011.

Lt Col G Himashree v. Union of India, OA No. 651 of 2010, AFT PB decided on 23 August 2012.

Lt Col Hardeep Sandhu v. Union of India, OA No. 15 of 2011, AFT PB, decided on 3 February 2012.

Lt Col Naveen Ahlawat v. Union of India, OA No. 170 of 2010, AFT PB, decided on 01 March 2011.

Lt Col G. R. Verma v. Union of India, TA No. 537 of 2009, AFT PB, decided on 6 July 2010.

Lt Col P. Ahluwalia v. Union of India, TA No. 266 of 2009, AFT PB, decided on 15 March 2010.

Lt Col Prasad Purohit v. Union of India OA No. 485 of 2010, AFT PB, decided on 9 March 2011.

Lt Col Prithi Pal Singh Bedi v. Union of India (1982) 3 SCC 140.

Lt Col Ranjodh Singh v. Union of India, OA No. 88 of 2012, AFT Lucknow Bench, decided on 16 March 2012.

Lt. Col. S.K. Goswami, SM v. Union of India, OA No. 279 of 2011, AFT Lucknow Bench, decided on 6 January 2012.

Lt. Gen. Avadhesh Prakash (retd.) v. Union of India, OA No. 66 of 2010, AFT PB, decided on 22 February 2010.

Lt Gen Gurjit Singh Dhillon v. Union of India, TA No. 195 of 2010, AFT Kochi Bench, decided on 26 November 2010.

Lt Gen (Retd) D.P. Singh v. Union of India, OA No. 973 of 2011, AFT Chandigarh Bench, decided on 3 November 2011.

Lt Gen S.K. Dahiya v. Union of India, Mil LJ 2007 Del 151.

M

M. Krishna Reddy v. State Deputy Superintendent of Police, Hyderabad 1992(4) SCC 45.

M. Vijayan Unni v. Union of India, OA No.15 of 2011, AFT Kochi Bench, decided on 9 February 2012.

Madhya Pradesh Industries Ltd. v Union of India, AIR 1966 SC 671.

Mafatlal Industries Ltd v Union of India, (1997) 5 SCC 536.

Major Arjun Singh Tomar v. General Officer Commanding-in-Chief, Eastern Command, Kolkata, OA No. 13 of 2010, AFT Kolkata, decided on 12 April 2012.

Major Birendra Singh Tomar (Retd.) v. Union of India, OA No. 29 of 2011, AFT New Delhi, decided on 8 October 2011.

Maj B. S. Kohli, SM (retd) v. Union of India, OA No. 376 of 2011, AFT PB, decided on 26 April 2012.

Major G S Sodhi v. Union of India 1992 (5) SLR 108.

Major Leena Gurav v. Union of India, OA No. 208 of 2010, AFT Lucknow Bench, decided on 18 April 2011.

Major Mahesh Bisht v. Union of India TA No. 766 of 2009, AFT PB, decided on 22 May 2012.

Major Manmohan Singh Battu v. Union of India, TA No. 371 of 2009, AFT PB, decided on 6 April 2010.

Major Nishant Gupta v. Union of India, OA No. 330 of 2011, AFT PB, decided on 14 March 2012.

Maj KP Dutta v. Union of India, TA No. 364 of 2009, AFT PB, decided on 5 October 2010.

Major Rabindra Singh v. Union of India, TA No. 37 of 2010, AFT Kolkata Bench, decided on 04 April 2011.

Major Radha Krishan v. Union of India, AIR 1996 SC 3091.

Major S S Chillar v. Union of India, TA No. 246 of 2009, AFT PB, decided on 1 April 2010.

Major Shiv Kumar v. Union of India, OA No. 357 of 2011, AFT PB, decided on 21 May 2012.

Maj Gen Devendra Nath Verma, AVSM (Retd.) v. Union of India, TA No. 255 of 2009, AFT PB, decided on 22 February 2010.

Maj Gen KTG Nambiar v. Union of India, TA No. 412 of 2010, AFT PB, decided on 29 May 2012.

Maj Gen Mrs. Usha Sikdar v. Union of India, TA No. 211 of 2010, AFT PB, decided on 30 March 2010.

Managing Director, ECIL, Hyderabad v. B. Karunakar, AIR 1994 SCC 1074.

Manoramyam Widow of Ex Sep (Dvr) N. Sarangapani v. Union of India, OA No. 53 of 2011, AFT Chennai Bench, decided on 21 December 2012.

Morris v. United Kingdom (2002) 34 EHHR 1253.

M. K. Harshan v. State of Kerala, AIR 1995 SCC 2178.

Mrs Charubala Rath v. Union of India, TA No. 168 of 2010, AFT Kolkata Bench, decided on 17 February 2012.

N

Nakhat Bharti v. Union of India, TA No. 48 of 2009, AFT PB, decided on 28 October 2009.

Naib Risaldar Vijay Pal v. Union of India, TA No. 476 of 2010, AFT PB, decided on 31 January 2011.

Naib Sub B.C. Barua v. Union of India, TA No.188 of 2010, AFT Kochi, decided on 29 October 2010.

Nb Sub Gulab Rao v. Union of India, OA No. 513 of 2011, AFT PB, decided on 4 April 2012.

Nb Sub Raju Thapa v. Union of India, OA No. 453 of 2010, AFT PB, decided on 3 September 2012.

NC (E) Chiranjeelal v. Union of India, OA No. 224 of 2011, AFT PB, decided on 27 November 2012.

Naik Dinesh Chand Sharma v. Union of India, TA No. 180 of 2010, AFT PB, decided on 26 July 2010.

Naik Yogendra Singh v. Union of India, TA No. 543 of 2010, AFT PB, decided on 16 September 2010.

Nk/SKT (Sepoy) Lalan Kumar v. Union of India, TA No. 42 of 2010, AFT Lucknow Bench, decided on 19 March 2012.

O

Oinam Doren Singh v. Union of India OA No. 01 of 2011, AFT Guwahati Bench, decided on 3 May 2011.

P

P. Purushottam v. Union of India TA No.113 of 2009, AFT Chennai Bench, decided on 19 March 2010.

Paul K. John v. Union of India, TA No. 65 of 2010, AFT Kochi Bench, decided on 7 February 2012.

Pradeep Kumar Singh v. The Chief of the Army Staff, TA No. 545 of 2009, AFT PB, decided on 3 April 2012,

Pramod Kumar Singh v. Union of India, TA No. 595 of 2010, AFT PB, decided on 8 August 2012.

Prithpal Singh v. Union of India, 1984 (3) SLR 675 (J&K).

Pritpal Singh v. Union of India OA No. 355 of 2010, AFT Chandigarh Bench, decided on 7 January 2011.

R

R.N. Pandey v. Chief of the Army Staff, TA No. 88 of 2009, AFT PB, decided on 1 December 2010.

Raj Kumar v. Union of India, TA No.252 of 2009, AFT PB, decided on 16 November 2009.

Rajesh U. Ex Naik v. Union of India, OA No. 47 of 2010, AFT Kochi Bench, decided on 1 March 2013.

Rakshak Ganga Ram Singh v. Union of India in OA No. 217 of 2012 AFT PB, decided on 8 March 2013.

Ramaswamy Ayyangar v. State of Tamil Nadu 1976(3) SCC 779.

Ranchod Mathur Wasawa v. State of Gujarat, AIR 1974 SC 1146.

Ranjit Thakur v. Union of India 1987 (4) SCC 611.

Ratna Bahadur Chetry v. Union of India, TA No. 19 of 2010, AFT Guwahati Bench, decided in February 2011.

Ravinder Singh v Union of India 97 (2002) DLT 756.

Reid v. Covert, 1 L Ed 2d 1148: 354 US 1 (1957).

Rfn Ram Pal v. Union of India, OA No. 712 of 2010, AFT PB, decided on 7 February 2012.

Rfn (Tailor) Bhupal Ram Okesa v. Union of India, TA No. 49 of 2010, AFT Guwahati, decided on June 2011.

Roshan Lal v. Union of India, OA No 279 of 2011, AFT PB (3 Member), decided on 06 September 2012.

R. S. Misra v. Union of India (2012) 8 SCC 558.

S

S C Patnaik v. Union of India, 1969 Cri LJ 930 (Ori).

S N Mukherjee v Union of India (1990) 4 SCC 594; 1990 (SC) SLR 8.

Sarabjit Rick Singh v. Union of India, 2008(2) SCC 417.

Sarjeet Singh through Smt Indrawati (wife) v. Union of India, TA No. 358 of 2010, AFT Chandigarh Bench, decided on 9 April 2013.

Satpal Singh v. Union of India, TA No. 536 of 2009, AFT PB, decided on 1 December 2010.

Secretary, Ministry of Defence v. A. V. Damodaran, 2009 (9) SCC 140.

Sep Joga Singh v. Union of India, TA No. 699 of 2009, AFT PB, decided on 24 February 2011.

Sep N. Baskaran v. Union of India, TA No. 201 of 2010, AFT Chennai Bench, decided on 11 April 2011.

Sepoy/Chef (U) Raj Kumar v. Union of India, TA No. 48 of 2009, AFT Luchnow Bench, decided on 21 January 2010.

Sep Puran Singh v. Union of India, TA No. 01 of 2009, AFT Chandigarh Bench, decided on 19 January 2010.

Sepoy Raghubir Singh Tomar v. Union of India, OA No. 142 of 2012, AFT PB, decided on 7 November 2012.

Sgt P Prem Kumar v. Union of India OA No.7 of 2010, AFT Kochi Bench, decided on 28 July 2010.

Sgt Shiva Murati v. Union of India, OA No. 126 of 2012, AFT PB, decided on 29 May 2012.

Sgt Tek Chand Sharma v. Union of India, TA No. 96 of 2010, AFT PB, decided on 19 February 2010.

Sheel Kr. Roy v. Secretary, Ministry of Defence, 2008(1) MLJ (Crl) 481.

Sh. Rabendra Singh v. Union of India, TA No. 134 of 2010, AFT PB, decided on 29 May 2012.

Shambu Murari Sinha v. Project & Development India JT 2000 (6) SC 358.

Shri Bhaskar Kishan v. Union of India, TA No. 133 of 2010, AFT Kolkata Bench, decided on 14 February 2012.

Shri Sat Pal v. The Chief of the Army Staff, 94 (2001) DLT 521.

Shri Shiv Murath Singh Yadav v. Union of India, TA No. 18 of 2010, AFT Guwahati Bench, decided on 10 November 2011.

Siemens Engineering & Manufacturing Co. Ltd. v. Union of India, AIR 1976 SC 1785.

Smitha Praveen, widow of Late Naik A Praveen v. Union of India, OA 119 of 2012, AFT Kochi Bench, decided on 4 March 2013.

Smt Kamala Rani v. Union of India, OA No. 504 of 2011, AFT Chandigarh Bench, decided on 12 February 2013.

Smt Mahuya Das v. Union of India, OA No. 469 of 2011, AFT PB, decided on 8 May 2013.

Smt. Navindra Devi v. Union of India, OA No. 972 of 2011, AFT Chandigarh Bench, decided on 8 December 2011.

Smt. Rajbala Saini v. Union of India, OA No. 202 of 2012, AFT PB, decided on 4 February 2013.

Smt Ram Sri v. Union of India, OA No. 397/2010, AFT PB, decided on 1 October 2010.

Som Datt Datta v. Union of India 1969 CrLJ 663.

Soma Chakravarty v. State through CBI, 2007(5) SCC 403.

Sqn Ldr Jyoti Kumar Dhan v. Union of India, OA No. 9 of 2011, AFT Guwahati Bench (3 Member), decided on 16 February 2012.

Sqn Ldr R Bhusal v. Union of India, TA No. 511 of 2010, AFT PB, decided on 15 May 2013.

SSVN Murthy v. Union of India, TA No.135 of 2010, AFT Chennai Bench, decided on 26 November 2010.

State of Bihar v. Lal Krishna Advani AIR 2003 SCC 3357.

State of Bihar v. Ramesh Singh 1977(4) SCC 39.

State of Himachal Pradesh v. Manoj Kumar 2008 (13) SCALE 82.

State of Uttar Pradesh v. M.K Anthony 1985(1) SCC 505.

Sub Maj J.S. Pundhir v. Union of India, OA No. 64 of 2010, AFT PB, decided on 19 July 2012.

Sub (GD) Rajbir v. Union of India, OA No. 28 of 2011, AFT PB, decided on 1 February 2013.

Sub/skt Nandlal Pandey v. Union of India, TA No. 09 of 2010, AFT PB, decided on 16 May 2012.

Sub Ved Prakash v. Union of India, OA No. 223 of 2011, AFT PB, decided on 12 March 2012.

Subhash P. Sonvare v. State of Gujarat (2002) 5 SCC 86.

Sukhdev Singh v. Union of India OA No. 303 of 2013, AFT Chandigarh Bench, decided on 13 February 2013.

Sunil Batra v. Delhi Administration (1979) 1 SCR 392.

Surendra Kumar Sahni v. Chief of Army Staff (Delhi) 2008(3) SLR.

Suresh Kumar Yadav v. Union of India, OA No. 121 of 2012, AFT Chandigarh Bench, decided on 13 January 2012.

Surinder Singh v. Union of India Misc. Petition No. 2323 of 1991 (MP).

T

The Chief of Army Staff v. Major Dharam Pal Kukrety, (1985) 2 SCC 412.

The Siemens Engineering & Manufacturing Co. of India Ltd. V. Union of India (1976) 2 SCC 981.

U

Uma Shankar Pathak v. Union of India 1989(3) SLR 405 (Allahabad).

Umesh Kumar Singh v. Union of India, TA No. 11 of 2011, AFT Chennai Bench, decided on 5 January 2012.

Union of India v. A.K. Pandey (2009) 10 SCC 552.

Union of India v. Deepak Kumar Santra 2009 7 SCC 370.

Union of India v. Maj Gen Arun Roye 2008 CWN 528.

Union of India v. Brigadier P. S. Gill, Supreme Court, Criminal Appeal No. 564 of 2012, decided on 23 March 2012.

Union of India v. Corporal A.K. Bakshi (1996) 3 SCC 65.

Union of India v. Ex. Major Sudershan Gupta (2009) 6 SCC 298.

Union of India v. Jaswant Singh, TA No. 1258 of 2010, AFT Chandigarh Bench, decided on 1 August 2012.

Union of India v. K.V. Jankiraman, AIR 1991 SCC 2010.

Union of India v. Major General Madan Lal Yadav (Retd), AIR 1996 SC 1340.

Union of India v. Neki Ram, AIR 2004 SC 1235.

Union of India v. P D Yadav (2002) 1 SCC 405.

Union of India v. Prafulla Kumar Samal 1979(3) SCC 4.

Union of India v. Rajesh Vyas, (2008) 3 SCC 386.

Union of India v. Tulsiram Patel, AIR 1985 SC 1416.

Union of India v. V N Singh 2010 (5) SSC 579.

V

Ved Prakash v. Union of India, OA No 1960 of 2012, AFT Chandigarh Bench, decided on 3 August 2012.

Vinod Kumar (Retired) v. Union of India, OA No. 639 of 2010, AFT PB, decided on 10 May 2012.

Virender Singh v. Union of India OA No. 42 of 2010, AFT Chandigarh, decided on 8 February 2010.

W

Yamuna Rai Yadav v. Union of India, TA No. 216 of 2010, AFT Kolkata Bench, decided on 18 May 2011.

Wg Cdr M S Mander v. Union of India, TA No. 14 of 2010, AFT PB, decided on 14 May 2010.

Wg Cdr M S Narsimha Rao v. Union of India, OA No.2 of 2010, AFT Chennai Bench, decided on 3 August 2010.

WO Ummed Singh Choudhury v. Union of India, TA No. 331 of 2010, AFT PB, decided on 8 February 2012.

Preface

Military law in India has been inherited from the British. The law, enacted by the colonial masters primarily to deal with a mercenary force, remained more or less static and any change was protested by the military authorities, who called it 'time-tested'. The first landmark judicial intervention occurred in 1982, when the Supreme Court, in Lt Col PPS Bedi's case, criticized the military justice system, calling it archaic and antiquated. The Supreme Court pointed out a glaring deficiency in the military law, viz the absence of the remedy of appeal against the orders of courts-martial. The government took almost twenty-five years to act on the Supreme Court's suggestion.

The Armed Forces Tribunal and its benches started functioning since mid-2009 and have decided more than 18,700 cases in the last four years. They have given relief to thousands of serving and ex-military personnel and their families who had been victims of the callous approach of the bureaucratic system. A few of the cases decided by the Tribunal highlight the callous, inhumane and perfunctory approach of the authorities while dealing with the military members of our society.

Jai Bhagwan Sharma was enrolled in the Navy in 1965 and served till 1973. He had also taken part in the 1971 Indo-Pak War. He received a head injury when a high-pressure steam pipe burst in the engine room of his ship in 1972. The disabled sailor was sanctioned disability pension with effect from 1975 by the Tribunal in 2011. Holding that the sailor was entitled to benefits for 20% disability for life, the Tribunal also ordered the pension authorities to pay the sailor interest on arrears since 1975 at the rate of 12% per annum.

The Tribunal, while expressing its ire over the attitude of the authorities and the manner in which the case was handled, observed that the departments concerned had made the sailor run from pillar to post for nearly 40 years, and ordered that he be adequately compensated for this callous delay.

In another landmark decision emphasizing that callousness towards human life would not be tolerated, the Chandigarh Bench of the Tribunal ordered an exemplary compensation of Rs 10 lakh along with special family pension to Navindra Devi, the widow of a soldier who died in 1998. The petitioner's husband, while posted near Bikaner, developed psychiatric problems for which he was given electric shocks in a civil hospital. Thereafter, he was sent on leave to recuperate. A few days after returning from leave, he walked out of the unit and went missing. He was found wandering near the Delhi railway station by the Government Railway Police (GRP) who requested the Army authorities to take him back to his unit. However, rather than sending a team to bring back the soldier, his unit in Bikaner and the military authorities in Delhi kept writing letters to each other in this regard.

The GRP let the soldier go when no one from the Army came to escort him. His body was found in a well. The Army unit then showed him on leave retrospectively from the date when he had wandered out of his unit. The mandatory court of inquiry was not conducted as the Bikaner and Delhi authorities kept shifting the blame. After three rounds of litigation, the Delhi High Court, finally ordered the authorities to convene an inquiry, which was held 11 years after the soldier's unnatural death. Holding the unit responsible for callousness, the Tribunal observed that there was extreme negligence in handling the issue since no care was taken to keep the soldier under medical supervision and to bring him back from the GRP. The Tribunal granted special family pension and appropriate compensation to the widow.

The Jaipur Bench of the Tribunal blamed the members of the Appeal Medical Board for their "inhuman approach and failure of performance of duty" in denying disability pension to Havildar Mohar Singh, who was diagnosed with a degenerative motor neuron disease. It asked the military authorities to pay Rs 1 lakh as cost to the Havildar, who was injured in an accident during a military operation. The Tribunal took a serious note of the Medical Board's dismissal of the application of disability pension on grounds that the disability suffered by Mohar Singh was 'nil' and was neither attributable to nor aggravated by military service. It directed that the three officers who constituted the Medical Board should be subjected to disciplinary action for their callous approach.

The Principal Bench of the Tribunal, in its decision in *Major S. S. Chillar v. Union of India* [WP(C) No. 2649 of 1989, TA No. 246 of 2009] of 1 April 2010, set aside a 1987 court-martial, and made the following observations:

> "Before parting with the case, we would like to observe that in conduct of Court Martial proceedings elementary mistakes are committed.

> Neither the Judge Advocate, who advises the Court, has, at any time, experience of conducting sessions trial, as a result of which he could not properly advise the Court Martial authorities nor are the prosecutors properly trained to conduct such criminal trials....We have seen a number of Court Martial cases.... and we find that most of the elementary mistakes were committed in conduct of the criminal trials under Court Martial proceedings. Now that a proper appeal lies against the Court Martial proceedings before this Tribunal, the Tribunal has to examine all the procedure as well as substance of the criminal trial like in Court of Appeal, including appreciation of the evidence, and our experience is that the trials in the Court Martial proceedings relating to civil offence[s] like murder or other penal code offences or offences under the other acts are not properly conducted like a regular criminal trial. The result is that they will turn into acquittal. Therefore, the matter requires a serious consideration of overhauling of the procedure."

The Tribunal has also given relief to a large number of military personnel who were punished by Summary Court Martial (SCM). This calls attention to serious lapses on the part of the military authorities who conduct SCM and those who review its proceedings. Unlike other court martial, the finding and sentence of SCM are not required to be confirmed, but are carried out forthwith. However, under Army Rule 139, every SCM proceeding is required to be reviewed by a senior officer of the Judge Advocate General Branch. The shortcomings brought out by various benches of the Tribunal exhibit that the task is not being performed with due diligence. One reason could be that those subjected to SCM are from the lowest ranks of the military and may not even be aware of their legal rights. The Lucknow Bench of the Tribunal in the case of *Ex Naik Ravindra Kumar Kushwaha v. Union of India*, TA No. 146 of 2010, awarded compensation of Rs 2 lakh to be paid to aggrieved party who was subjected to an unfair trial in a SCM.

Notwithstanding the good work done by the Tribunal so far, it suffers from a serious shortcoming. It lacks the power to get its orders executed by way of civil contempt. There have been a number of cases where the government has not implemented the Tribunal's orders granting relief to individuals, thus forcing the litigants to approach the Supreme Court, and defeating the purpose of the Tribunal. For instance, more than 2,000 cases decided by the Tribunal have been pending for execution. The Armed Forces Tribunal (Amendment) Bill, 2012 aiming to empower the Tribunal with civil contempt has been vehemently opposed by the military authorities on the ground that it would jeopardize their operational functioning. No judicial body can function effectively unless its orders are honoured. The military authorities in India are perhaps not aware of the changes incorporated in the military justice systems of other countries.

The military justice system of the US is in numerous ways superior to that of the civilian criminal justice system in matters of the rights of the convicted person. Depending upon the type of court-martial and the sentence approved by the convening authority, there are three levels of appellate forum: the Courts of Criminal Appeals (CCA), the United States Court of Appeals for the Armed Forces (USCAAF), and the United States Supreme Court. The accused is entitled to representation and the appellate defence counsel is provided free of charge. An accused may also hire a civilian lawyer at his or her own expense to operate alongside the military counsel. In the UK, a convicted person may appeal to the Court-Martial Appeal Court (CMAC) against a finding or sentence or both awarded by a court-martial. The CMAC is part of the judiciary and therefore independent of the government and of the Armed Forces. The Australian military justice system contains a hierarchy of service tribunals reflecting the civilian criminal standards and processes.

The redress of grievance (ROG) system of the three services remains faulty. The operation of the ROG system, rightly or wrongly, is often taken to be an indicator of the wider health and effectiveness of the military justice system. The right to make a complaint and have it dealt with expeditiously is certainly a significant element of the military justice system. It is of fundamental importance that the complaints system not only works properly, but is seen to work properly. The fact that an increasing number of persons are approaching the Tribunal indicates that military personnel may not have the confidence to pursue complaints through their chain of command.

The creation of an Armed Forces Tribunal is the first step in the civilianization of military law in India. The judicial review of administrative decisions provides an important form of control over arbitrariness in the administrative process. Many key elements of the Indian military justice system are controversial in a constitutional sense. The government must appoint an expert committee to bring about systematic reforms in the three services Acts and the Armed Forces Tribunal Act to assure those who don the uniform that a modern justice system based on the rule of law exists to protect their rights.

The first chapter of this book provides a detailed background of the military justice system and the Armed Forces Tribunal. The chapter includes few errors and shortcomings observed in the Armed Forces Tribunal Act, 2007. These have to be corrected by the legislature in the due course of time. The second chapter contains brief account of the judgements given by the Tribunal in the service matters and the third chapter covers the judgements of the Tribunal against the finding and sentences of courts martial. The book contains the Armed Forces Tribunal Act, 2007 and all the rules framed under it by the government. It also contains the Armed Forces Tribunal (Amendment) Bill, 2012 and an extract of the report made by the Parliamentary Standing Committee on Defence on the Bill.

I am grateful to the Parliamentary Standing Committee on Defence for giving me an opportunity to explain my point of view on the Armed Forces Tribunal Bill, 2005 and the Armed Forces Tribunal (Amendment) Bill, 2012.

My sincere thanks to Ratna, Medha, Chandana, and Aditya for their valuable suggestions and support.

Wg Cdr (Dr) UC Jha

1

Introduction

The British military justice system is the progenitor of the Indian military legal system. Before India attained independence, the defence forces were governed by the Indian Army Act, 1911, the Indian Navy Discipline Act, 1934 and the Indian Air Force Act, 1932. A need was felt for a general revision of these Acts even at that time as some of the provisions of these Acts had become outdated.

After independence, three separate Acts came into force for the governance of the three services – the Army Act, 1950[1], the Air Force Act, 1950[2] and the Navy Act, 1957[3]. The Army and Air Force Acts were virtually a continuation of the existing Indian Army Act, 1911, as no procedural or other reforms were made in these Acts. The Indian Navy had waited for the report of the Pilcher Committee[4] appointed in the UK to consider the Administration of Justice under the British Naval Code. The Navy Act adopted a few procedural reforms suggested by the Pilcher Committee.[5]

1. The Army Act, 1950, was passed by the Indian Parliament on 22 May 1950 and came into force on 22 July 1950.
2. The Air Force Act, 1950 (Act 45 of 1950), was passed by the Parliament in 1950 and came into force on 22 July 1950. SRO No. 123 dated 22nd July 1950, Gazette of India, Part II, Section 4, p.87.
3. The Navy Act, 1957, was finally passed by Parliament on 27 December, 1957, and came into effect from 1 January, 1958. SRO. No. 11-E Extra Ordinary Gazette of India dated 31st December, 1957, Part II, Section 4.
4. The Committee appointed to consider the Administration of Justice under the Naval Discipline Act (1949), commonly known as Pilcher Committee.
5. Consequently to the passage of the Navy Act, 1957, three earlier Acts were repealed. These were the Indian Navy (Discipline) Act, 1934 (XXXIV of 1934), the Indian Naval Reserve Forces (Discipline) Act, 1939, and the Naval Forces (Miscellaneous Provisions) Act, 1950.

1.1 Subordinate Legislations in the Army

The Army Rules, 1950 made under Section 191 of the Army Act of 1950 were subsequently replaced by the Army Rules, 1954. Army Rules are in the nature of procedural laws, somewhat like the Code of Criminal Procedure. The Regulations for the Army, 1962, were issued under the authority of the Government of India and replaced the Regulations for the Army in India (reprint 1945) and instructions by His Excellency the Commander-in-Chief (reprint 1945). The Regulations of 1962 were updated and replaced by the Regulations for the Army, Revised Edition, 1987. Certain provisions of the Regulations of 1987, especially procedures relating to statutory complaints contained in Para 364 have been amended in 1997.[6]

The Manual of Indian Military Law (MIML) was compiled by the Judge Advocate General of the Army in India in 1912. The Manual was divided into four parts:

- Part I contained a history of military law and chapters on the laws of evidence applicable to courts-martial, ordinary criminal offences and other legal matters a knowledge of which was considered essential for the officers and soldiers;
- Part II consisted of a reprint of the Indian Army Act, 1911 and statutory rules issued thereunder;
- Part III consisted of the text of certain Acts of the Indian legislatures which were referred to in the earlier parts of the manual; and
- Part IV contained all notifications issued by the Governor General in Council under the Indian Army Act, 1911.

The MIML was amended and updated in 1937, and was reprinted in 1961. The reprint incorporated the Army Act, 1950 and the Army Rules, 1954. Further reprints were brought out in 1967, 1971 and 1976. In 1983, the Government of India issued an updated and revised bilingual Manual of Military Law (MML) in three volumes:

- Volume I consists of eight chapters dealing with a brief history of military law in India (Chapter I), an outline of the Army Act (Chapter II), arrests and investigations of charges (Chapter III), courts-martial (Chapter IV), evidence (Chapter V), civil offences (Chapter VI), duties in aid of civil power (Chapter VII) and service privileges (Chapter VIII).
- Volume II contains the Army Act, 1950, and the Army Rules, 1954, with explanatory notes, forms and appendices.
- Volume III contains certain enactments which are referred to in earlier parts of the Manual. This volume also contains Gazette Notifications

---

6. For details of grievance procedure followed in the three services, kindly refer para 1.18 and 1.19 of this chapter.

issued under the Army Act by the Government of India and forms of warrants.

An updated version of the Manual of Military Law (MML) has been published in 2011. Volume III of the MML, besides earlier enactments, also contains the Armed Forces Special Powers Act, 1958, the Right to Information Act, 2005 and the Armed Forces Tribunal Act, 2007.

1.2 Subordinate Legislations in the Air Force

In the exercise of the powers conferred by the Air Force Act, 1950 [Section 21, sub-section (4) of Section 103 and Section 189 of the Air Force Act, 1950], the Central Government issued the Air Force Act Rules, 1950. These rules were further revised and amended, and the Air Force Rules, 1969, were issued under the provisions of Section 189 of the Air Force Act, 1950.[7]

The Regulations for the Air Force (Revised Edition), 1964, were issued under the authority of the Government of India and superseded the "Regulations for the Royal Indian Air Force (Rules)—Reprint 1942", and "Regulations for the Indian Air Force-- Instructions issued by Excellency the Commander-in-Chief of India—Reprint 1945". A 'Regulation Cell' formed at the Air Headquarters, New Delhi, in 1980s failed to bring out a revised edition of the Regulations. In 1988, the Judge Advocate General (Air Force) issued the Manual of Air Force Law under the authority of the Chief of the Air Staff. The manual, which is considered to be an authoritative commentary on the provisions of the Air Force Law, is in two volumes. Volume I contains the Air Force Act, 1950, while Volume II contains the Air Force Rules, 1969 and certain appendices containing extracts from the Constitution of India and other related legislations.

1.3 Subordinate Legislations in the Navy

Unlike the Army and the Air Force, the Indian Navy does not have its own rules. The Regulations for the Navy Part I was issued in 1991, under the authority of the Government of India and superseded the corresponding provisions of the Regulations for the Navy Part I, 1965 (non-statutory). The Regulations contain 44 Chapters on regulations of an administrative character. Part II of the Regulations is called the Navy (Discipline and Miscellaneous Provisions) Regulations, 1965 and is statutory in nature. These were issued by the government under the power conferred under Section 184 of the Navy Act, 1957. Part III of the Regulations is called the Naval Ceremonial, Conditions of Service and Miscellaneous Regulations, 1963, and is also statutory in nature. Part IV contains the Indian Naval Auxiliary Service Regulations, 1973.

---

7. Vide SRO 310, dated 24 September, 1969, published in the Gazette of India, Extraordinary, Part II, Sec. (iv).

The acts, rules and regulations governing the three services have not been updated in the last 60 years, except for a few minor changes made in the Army Act and the Navy Acts in 1992 and 2005, respectively.[8]

1.4 Action against a Military Offender

In the system of military law, a commander occupies an important position. Unlike a superior in a civilian government organization, a military commander exercises discretion in deciding whether an offence should be charged and how an offender should be punished. On of the most difficult decisions facing a commander concerns the manner in which to dispose of the case. An administrative or disciplinary action may be taken against a service person who fails to meet or uphold the service's standard of conduct. The fundamental purpose of administrative or disciplinary processes is to foster and promote discipline and the type of behaviour required for the maintenance of operational effectiveness. The commander has a number of options for the resolution of disciplinary problems. They are as follows:

a. **No Action.** The commander may choose to take no action. The circumstances surrounding an event may warrant that no adverse action be taken. The preliminary inquiry might indicate that the accused is innocent, that the only evidence is inadmissible, or the commander may decide that other valid reasons exist for not prosecuting the alleged accused.

b. **Administrative Action.** The commander may initiate administrative action against a military offender. He might decide that the best disposition for the offence and offender is to take administrative rather than punitive action.

c. **Minor Summary Punishment.** The commander may dispose of the offence summarily with a minor punishment. The trial is conducted by the commanding officer or a superior officer depending upon the rank of the accused. The maximum punishment depends on the rank of the commander imposing punishment and the rank of the service member being punished. The military accused does not have any right to appeal against the commander's decision.

d. **Court-martial.** The commander may dispose of the case with the help of a court-martial. If he decides that the offence is serious enough to warrant trial by court-martial, he may exercise the fourth option of preferring and forwarding charges. He may choose from four potential levels of court-

8. Certain amendments were incorporated in the Army Act and in the Army Rules in 1992 and 1993 respectively. The amendments were incorporated in the Army Act, 1950 vide Army Amendment Act 37 of 1992, and in the Army Rules vide S.R.O. 17E, dated 6 December 1993.

The Navy (Amendment) Act, 2005, amended sections 3 (16), 79, 94,133, 151, 176 and 184. It inserted a new section 163A (provisions relating to parole) and omitted Chapter XXII from the Act of 1957.

martial: summary, district, summary-general, or general. These courts -martial differ in the procedures, rights, and possible punishment that can be adjudged.

The military chain of command must use its powers appropriately in keeping with the context of the offence/misconduct and the operational circumstances. The existence of an administrative action regime does not prevent a commander from proceeding directly to disciplinary action where it is more appropriate. Conversely, good management practice may require that certain professional failings be dealt with without recourse to either regime. Such minor transgressions could be corrected more informally and immediately.

1.5 Provision for Appeal

The system of administration of justice in the Armed Forces provides for submission of statutory complaints against grievances relating to service matters and pre and post confirmation petitions to various authorities against the findings and sentences of courts-martial. However, there was no independent adjudicatory forum for hearing complaints of defence personnel relating to the service matters and appeals against the judgment of court -martial.

The need to provide the right to appeal against the decisions of a court -martial was raised in Parliament when the Army Act, 1950 and the Navy Act, 1957 were passed. The Government resisted the proposal to grant such right of appeal on the grounds that the Acts provide for judicial review of the proceedings of court-martial by the Judge Advocate General and his deputies[9] and the Chief of the Army Staff was empowered to make

---

9. The Navy Act, 1957, Chapter XV deals with the Judicial Review of Court-Martial Proceedings. Section 160 and 161 of this Chapter state:

Judicial review by the Judge Advocate General of the Navy

160. (1) All proceedings of trials by court martial or discipline courts shall be reviewed by the Judge Advocate General of the Navy either on his motion or on application made to him within the prescribed time by any person aggrieved by any sentence or finding and the Judge Advocate General of the Navy shall transmit the report of such review together with such recommendations as may appear just and proper to the Chief of the Naval Staff for his consideration and for such action as the Chief of the Naval Staff may think fit.

Consideration by the Chief of the Naval Staff

161. (1) On receipt of the report and recommendations if any, under section 160, the Chief of the Naval Staff shall in all cases of capital sentence and in all cases where the court-martial is ordered by the president, and may in other cases transmit proceedings and the report to the Central Government together with such recommendations as he may deem fit to make.

(2) Nothing in section 160 or this section shall authorize the Judge Advocate General of the Navy or the Chief of the Naval Staff to make any recommendation for setting

modifications of findings and remission or reduction of sentences awarded by court-martial.[10] It was also stated by the Government that all punishments in the armed forces must be comparatively swift in order to maintain discipline and the giving a right of appeal would mean long absence of persons concerned from their service stations. The issue, whether verdicts of court-martial should be subject to appeal or review by a judicial tribunal was again raised in Lok Sabha in April 1960 when the then Minister of Defence resisted the demand stating:

> "The general question of appeal to civil court from court-martial was not under contemplation at present, and indeed there is no occasion at the moment for agitating a question bristling with legal and constitutional complications and likely to provoke a conflict between the civil and military authorities such as arose during the viceroyalty of Lord Curzon."[11]

1.6 *Lt Col Prithi Pal Singh Bedi* v. *Union of India* (1982) 3 SCC 140

The Supreme Court of India in *Lt Col Prithi Pal Singh Bedi v. Union of India* pointed out a glaring deficiency in the Army Act, *viz,* the absence of the remedy of appeal against the orders of courts-martial. The court also pointed out the changes brought about by the UK and USA in the military justice system and observed that Parliament should pass similar legislation consistent with the changed value system. Further, the Court held that it would be desirable, for a court-martial to record reasons in support of its conclusions and orders.

The observations of the Court in paragraphs 44 and 45 of the said judgment are as follows.

> Reluctance of the apex court more concerned with civil law to interfere with the internal affairs of the Army is likely to create a distorted picture in the minds of the military personnel that persons subject to the Army Act are not citizens of India. It is one of the cardinal features of our Constitution that a person by enlisting in or entering the Armed Forces does not cease to be a citizen so as to wholly deprive him of his right under the Constitution. More so when this court held in *Sunil Batra v Delhi Administration* (1979) 1 SCR 392, 495 that even prisoners deprived of personal liberty are not wholly denuded of their fundamental rights. In the larger interest of national security and military discipline, Parliament

---

aside or the Central Government to set aside, an order of acquittal passed under this act.

The power of Naval Judge Advocate General is only recommendatory in nature and the Chief of Naval Staff or the Central Government are not bound by it. The Army Act, 1950 and the Air Force Act, 1950 do not have such provisions.

10. Joint Committee on the Navy Bill, 1957, Speech delivered by Sh. Krishna Menon, Minister of Defence in Lok Sabha on 22 and 23 July 1957.Cyclostyled debates (unpublished), p. 1457.
11. The Times of India, Editorial, 25 April 1960 (Bombay Ed.).

in its wisdom may restrict or abrogate such rights in their application to the Armed Forces but this process should not be carried so far as to create a class of citizens not entitled to the benefits of the liberal spirit of the Constitution. Persons subject to the Army Act are citizens of this ancient land having a feeling of belonging to the civilized community governed by the liberty-oriented Constitution. Personal liberty makes for the worth of human beings and is a cherished and prized right. Deprivation thereof must be preceded by an enquiry ensuring fair, just and reasonable procedure and trial by a judge of unquestioned integrity and wholly unbiased. A marked difference in the procedure for trial of an offence by the criminal court and court-martial is apt to generate dissatisfaction arising out of this differential treatment. Even though it is pointed out that the procedure of trial by court-martial is almost analogous to the procedure of trial in the ordinary criminal courts, we must recall what Justice William O'Douglas observed: "That civil trial is held in an atmosphere conducive to the protection of individual rights while a military trial is marked by the age-old manifest destiny of retributive justice. The very expression 'court-martial' generally strikes terror in the heart of the person to be tried by it. And somehow or other the trial is looked upon with disfavour." In *Reid v. Covert*, 1 L Ed 2d 1148: 354 US 1 (1957) Justice Black observed at page 1174 as under:

Courts-martial are typically ad hoc bodies appointed by a military officer among his subordinates. They have always been subject to varying degree of 'command influence'. In essence, these tribunals are simply executive tribunals whose personnel are in the executive chain of command. Frequently, the members of the court-martial must look to the appointing officer for promotions, advantageous assignments and efficiency rating – in short, for their future progress in the service. Conceding to military personnel that high degree of honesty and sense of justice which nearly all of them undoubtedly have, the members of a court-martial, in the nature of things, do not and cannot have the independence of jurors drawn from the general public or of civilian judges.

The absence of even one appeal with power to review evidence, legal formulation, conclusion and adequacy or otherwise of punishment is a glaring lacuna in a country where a counterpart civilian convict can prefer appeal after appeal to a hierarchy of courts. Submission that full review of finding and /or sentence in confirmation proceedings under Section 153 is provided for is poor solace. A hierarchy of courts with appellate powers each having its own power of judicial review has of course been found to be counter-productive but the converse is equally distressing in that there is not even a single judicial review. With the expanding horizons of fair play in action even in administrative decision, the Universal Declaration of Human Rights, and retributive justice being relegated to the uncivilized days, a time has come when a step is required to be taken for at least one review and it must truly be a judicial review as and by way of appeal to a body composed of non-military personnel or civil personnel. The Army is always on alert for repelling external aggression and suppressing internal disorder so that the peace-loving citizens enjoy a social order based on the rule of law; the same cannot be denied to the protectors of this order. And it must be realized that an appeal from Ceaser to Ceaser's wife – confirmation proceeding under Section 153 – has been condemned as injudicious and merely a lip sympathy to form. The core question is whether at least there should be one appeal to a body composed of non-military personnel and who would enjoy the right of judicial review both on law and facts as also determine the adequacy of punishment being commensurate with the gravity of the offence charged. A judicial approach by people well-versed in the objective analysis of evidence and trained by experience to look at facts and law objectively, fair play and justice cannot always be sacrificed at the altar of military discipline. Unjust decisions would be subversive of discipline. There must be a judicious admixture of both. And nothing revolutionary is being suggested. Our Army Act was more or less modelled on the UK Act. Three decades of its working with winds of change blowing over the world necessitates a second look so as to bring it in conformity with the liberty-oriented constitution and rule of law which is the uniting and integrating force in our political society. Even the UK has taken a step of far-reaching importance for rehabilitating the confidence of the Royal Forces in respect of judicial review of decisions of the court-martial. The UK had enacted a Court Martial (Appeals) Act of 1951 and it has been extensively amended in the Court Martial (Appeals) Act, 1968. Merely providing an appeal by itself may not be very reassuring but the personnel of the appellate court must inspire confidence. The Court Martial Appellate Court consists of the ex-officio and ordinary judges of the Court of Appeal, such of the judges of the Queen's Bench Division as the Lord Chief Justice many nominate after consultation with the Master of the Rolls, such of the Lords, commissioners of Justiciary in Scotland as the Lord Chief Justice generally may nominate, such Judges of the Supreme Court of Northern Ireland as the Lord Chief Justice of the Northern Ireland may nominate and such of the persons of legal experience as the Lord Chancellor may appoint. The Court Martial Appellate Court has power to determine any question necessary to be determined in order to do justice in the case before the court and may authorize a new trial where the conviction is quashed in the light of fresh evidence. The court also has power inter alia, to order the production of documents or exhibits connected with the proceedings, order the attendance of witnesses, receive evidence, obtain reports and the like from the members of the court martial or the persons who acted as Judge-Advocate, order a reference of any question to a Special Commissioner for enquiry and appoint a person with special expert knowledge to act as an assessor (Halabury's laws of England, 4th Edition, paragraphs 954-55, pp 458-459). Frankly the appellate court has power of full judicial review unhampered by any procedural claptrap.

Turning towards the USA, a reference to the Uniform Code of Military Justice Act, 1950, would be instructive. A provision has been made for the setting up of a court of military appeals. The Act contains many procedural reforms and due process safeguards not then guaranteed in civil courts. To cite one example, the right to a legally qualified counsel was made mandatory in general court martial cases 13 years before the decision of the Supreme Court in Gideon v Wainwright (372 US 335 (1963). Between 1950 and 1968 when the Administration of Justice Act, 1968 was introduced, many advances were made in the administration of justice by civil courts but they were not reflected in military court proceedings. To correct these deficiencies the Congress enacted the Military Justice Act, 1968, the salient features of which are: (1) a right to legally qualified counsel guaranteed to an accused before any special court martial; (2) a military judge can in certain circumstances conduct the trial alone and the accused in such a situation is given the option after learning the identity of the military judge of requesting for trial by the judge alone. A ban has been imposed on command interference with military justice, etc. Ours is still an antiquated system. The wind of change blowing over the country has not permeated the closed and sacrosanct precincts of the Army. If in civil courts the universally accepted dictum is that justice must not only be done but it must seem to be done, the same holds good with all the greater vigour in the case of a court-martial where the judge and the accused don the same dress, have the same mental discipline, have a strong hierarchical subjugation, and a feeling of bias in such circumstances is irremovable. We, therefore, hope and believe that the changes all over the English-speaking democracies will awaken our Parliament to the changed value system. In this behalf, we would like to draw pointed attention of the Government to the glazing anomaly that courts-martial do not even write a brief reasoned order in support of their conclusion, even in cases in which they impose the death sentence. This must be remedied in order to ensure that a disciplined and dedicated Indian Army may not nurse a grievance that the substance of justice and fair play is denied to it."

In 1983, consequent to the decision of the Supreme Court in Lt Col PPS Bedi's case the service headquarters were asked to examine the need for constitution of a court-martial appeal court. The three services were not in agreement as to the need of setting of an appeal court.[12]

In the year 1992, Parliament enacted the Army (Amendment) Act, 1992, and few provisions of the Army Act, 1950 were amended but no provisions were made for an 'appellate forum' as recommended by the Supreme Court in *Lt Col Prithi Pal Singh Bedi*.

---

12. Sharma OP. 1990. Military Law in India, Bombay: NM Tripathi Pvt Ltd, p. 203

1.7 The Law Commission Report

Since the government did not take any action on the recommendations of the Supreme Court in Bedi's case for the constitution of an appellate forum for the armed forces, the Law Commission suo motu submitted its report on the 'Amendment of the Army, Navy and Air Force Acts'. The Law Commission was of the view "....that while maintaining the discipline in the armed forces, the dignity of the individual must be respected" and that "Justice and discipline should go together".

The 169th Report of the Law Commission[13] had the following objective:

> The idea underlying this report, taken up suo motu, is that while maintaining the discipline in the Armed Forces, the dignity of the individual must be respected. It is necessary to ensure that the armed forces are not deprived of the services of the cream of the society and that the bright and courageous among them do not keep out on account of an inadequate machinery for getting justice in the armed forces, or for fear of being punished for no wrong done by them. It is equally necessary to ensure that punishment is not disproportionate to the offence and also to make military law more humane and dynamic to bring it in tune with the culture in the armed forces of the developed countries. It should be remembered that a soldier's life is not a comfortable one. Most of the time he is away from his family. It is the sense of pride in and sacrifice for the cause of the country's defence that sustains him. It would not be proper to deny him justice which is available to other citizens of the country. It must also be remembered that military discipline cannot be based only upon domination and implicit obedience to the orders of superiors. The superiors must continuously demonstrate their competence and technical ability in order to command respect and loyalty of those under them. Kccping this in mind, many democratic nations have felt it necessary to rewrite their military laws to provide greater protection against arbitrary action. It is not correct to say that in as much as the number of persons affected by military law and the courts martial are small or because the members of the armed forces have voluntarily submitted themselves to the existing system with all its defects, no reform of the law is called for. It should not be forgotten that the military justice system has evolved to enforce certain standards of behaviour, some of which are identical to the standards enforced in civilian life. The higher standards of conduct and discipline in the armed forces are called for not only to keep in readiness an efficient fighting machine but also to command public respect for the armed forces. Justice and discipline should go together.
>
> It should also be borne in mind that even today, interference by the high courts and the Supreme Court with the decisions and findings of courts martial are not totally excluded. Instead of each high court adopting its

13. 169th Report on "Amendments of Army, Navy and Air Force Acts", was forwarded to the Ministry of Law, Justice and Company Affairs on 3 May 1999.

> own approach in these matters, it would be desirable, and also conducive to better discipline, if a single appellate tribunal is created to hear the appeals against the findings, decisions and orders of the courts martial under all the three enactments. The Army Act and the Air Force Act were enacted in 1949-50 and are based mostly upon the British Acts. While the law in the United Kingdom has made several advances as indicated hereinbefore, the military law in India has remained more or less rooted in the past. This report is an attempt to rectify the situation in certain respects.

The Law Commission's Report highlighted the observations made by the Supreme Court in *Lt Col PPS Bedi's* case. It discussed the provisions of Chapter XII of the Army Act, 1950, comprising Sections 153 to 165, relating to the confirmation and revision of orders of the court-martial. The Report stated:

> *No existing right of appeal against the order of the courts-martial:* It is thus evident that in the case of a final finding or sentence awarded by the general courts-martial, district courts-martial and summary general courts-martial, the only remedy provided to the accused persons is the one provided in sub-section (2) of Section 164, as pointed out by the Supreme Court in *SN Mukherhee's* case. (The opportunity to make a representation to the confirming authority before confirmation is not a remedy but only an opportunity to make a representation before the final order is passed). The said remedy under Section 164(2) can be invoked only after the finding of the sentence has been confirmed by the confirming authority and not before the confirmation of the same. The power of revision and the power to alter the finding or sentence in certain cases, or for that matter, the power to annul the proceedings, provided by Sections 160, 163 and 165 are not so much remedies given to the accused persons but are really the powers of the various specified authorities. In sum, there is no right of appeal against the order of the court martial (i.e., where it has been confirmed as required by law or where it does not require such confirmation, as the case may be), or against an order passed under sub-section (2) of Section 164, with which the accused is aggrieved.

The Report also discussed the differences in the procedures in the Navy Act and the Army Act. The Navy Act, unlike the Army Act, does not require confirmation of the sentence or order recorded by the courts-martial. The only exception is where a sentence of imprisonment is awarded to an officer, in which case the sentence pronounced by the court-martial cannot be implemented until the same has been communicated to the Chief of the Naval Staff, who is entitled to pass such orders thereon as he may think fit. It is the responsibility of the convening authority to take the necessary steps to give effect to the sentence (Para 194 of the Regulations for the Navy Part-II). The Navy Act does provide for judicial review of the proceedings of a trial held by court-martial. The power of judicial review is vested in the Judge Advocate

General and can be exercised either *suo motu* or on an application made by the aggrieved person. The Law Commission made recommendations for setting up of two different kinds of tribunals for the armed forces.

1.7.1 Appellate Tribunal

The Law Commission concluded that it is necessary to provide an appropriate appellate forum to entertain appeals against the final orders passed by the courts-martial. As regards appellate tribunal's constitution and functioning, the recommendations contained in Chapter 5 of the Report were as follows:

> The appellate tribunal, in our opinion, should not be a totally civilian appellate tribunal, as has been provided in the United Kingdom, since it may not be conducive to the discipline of the armed forces. We think it more appropriate to create a tribunal headed by a civilian judge whose other members shall be drawn from the retired members of the Armed Forces and from among those who have acted as or worked in the Judge Advocate General's department. To be precise, it shall be a three-member tribunal consisting of (1) a retired judge of the Supreme Court or a retired chief justice of a high court who shall be the chairman for a term of 4 years, (2) a retired officer of the Army of the rank of Major General or above, or a retired officer of the Air Force of the rank of Air Vice Marshal or a retired officer of the Navy of the rank of Rear Admiral, and (3) a retired Judge Advocate General of the Army/Air Force/ Navy.
>
> The term of the president and members shall be four years. However, if an appeal is preferred by a person holding a rank higher than the rank held by the person appointed as member at the time of his retirement from category 2 above, the president of the tribunal will write to the Central Government to nominate a retired officer for the case as a member of the tribunal, who shall be of a rank not lower than that of the person who has preferred an appeal, in place of the members from category 2.
>
> The quorum for the tribunal shall be two, but no decision shall be rendered by the tribunal except with the participation of the president.
>
> The tribunal shall be common to the Army, Navy and Air Force. The seat of the tribunal shall be Delhi, but it shall be open to the tribunal to hold its sittings at such other places as it may decide in the interest of the convenience of all concerned.
>
> From the decision of the tribunal, a direct statutory appeal shall lie to the Supreme Court. This is not something new since such direct appeals are already provided by certain other enactments, for example, Section 130-E of the Customers Act, and Section 35-L of the Central Excises and Salt Act, 1944, or for that matter, Section 23 of the Consumer Protection Act, 1986. In view of the proposed statutory appeal to the Supreme Court, it is expected that no high court will entertain writ petition under Article 226 of the Constitution of India against the orders of the appellate tribunal. If such an appeal is provided, it would be appropriate to delete clause (2)

> of Article 136 of the Constitution which provides that the power to grant special leave to appeal conferred upon the Supreme Court by clause (1) of the said article shall not apply to any judgment, determination, sentence or order passed or made by any court or tribunal constituted by or under any law relating to the Armed Forces.

1.7.2 Service Tribunal for Disputes Relating to Conditions of Service

In Chapter VI of its Report, the Law Commission discussed the issue of disputes relating to the conditions of service of armed forces personnel. As hundreds of writ petitions were being filed every year in higher courts by members of the armed forces concerning service matters like seniority, promotion, pension and other conditions of service, the Law Commission was of the view that a separate 'service tribunal' for the Armed Forces be created. It suggested that this service tribunal should function more or less on the pattern of the administrative tribunals created under the Administrative Tribunals Act, 1985. In this regard, the Law Commission made the following recommendations:

> The Army, Navy and Air Force Acts should be amended providing for the creation of a tribunal to adjudicate disputes and complaints with respect to the conditions of service of persons appointed to the Army, Navy and Air Force. The amendments should further provide for statutory appeal to the Supreme Court against the final decisions and orders of such a tribunal. An appeal against the interlocutory order should be expressly barred. It is hoped that the high courts should give due regard to the legislative intention behind such a provision, concerned in the public interest of discipline in the Armed Forces. In this behalf, the observations of the Supreme Court in para 108 (x) of the decision in *Mafatlal Industries Ltd. v Union of India'* may be referred to:[14]
>
> "... So far as the jurisdiction of the high courts under Article 226 of the Constitution – or of this Court under Article 32 – is concerned, it remains unaffected by the provisions of the Act. Even so, the Court would, while exercising the jurisdiction under the said articles, have due regard to the legislative intent manifested by the provisions of the Act ...This is for the reason that the power under Article 226 has to be exercised to effectuate the regime of law and not for abrogating it. Even while acting in the exercise of the said constitutional power, the high court cannot ignore the law, nor can it override it. The power under Article 226 is conceived to serve the ends of law and not to transgress them."

It would be appropriate to provide further that every service matter should necessarily be decided by a bench of two members, one of whom shall be a judicial member. In case of difference of opinion between the members of the bench, the matter shall be referred to the bench of the three members, one of whom shall be a judicial member.

---

14. *Mafatlal Industries Ltd v Union of India*, (1997) 5 SCC 536 at p. 635.

In such a situation, it would be easier to convince the Supreme Court of the desirability of such a direct appeal mainly on the ground that the necessity of prompt disposal of service disputes in the armed forces and in the interest of the discipline therein justify such a course. While indiscipline in any pubic service is not desirable and every service dispute should be adjudicated promptly, the need is much more in the case of the armed forces. In this context, it must be remembered that the Armed Forces are treated as a separate class even by the Constitution; Article 33 provided that Parliament may, by law, determine to what extent any of the Fundamental Rights (in Part III) shall apply to the armed forces. Article 311, including clause (2) thereof, which contains very important protections to members of service, is made inapplicable to the defence forces; the article applies only to the civil services.

The service tribunal so created shall be common to all three services. There shall be four benches of the tribunal, i.e., at Delhi, Mumbai, Chennai and Calcutta, with the Delhi bench being treated as the principal bench. (The machinery provisions of the Administrative Tribunals Act, 1985 can be imported to the extent necessary for giving shape to this idea.) Such a course will undoubtedly contribute towards a more satisfactory and prompt adjudication of such disputes. But this has to be an independent service tribunal apart from and in addition to the appellate tribunal recommended in Chapter V of this Report. In case such a tribunal is created, the Parliament may also consider bringing other paramilitary services too under the jurisdiction of this tribunal.

Pending the amendment of the Army, Navy and Air Force Acts on the above lines, the proper thing to do to expedite disposal of petitions in high courts would be for the Central Government to make a request to all the chief justices of various high courts in the country to amend the respective high court rules and to provide that all service disputes concerning the Army, Navy and Air Force shall be entertained and adjudicated only by a division bench of the high court and that such disputes should be given priority over other matters as far as possible. In such a case, the High Court would mean only one stage of litigation where after an appeal may lie to Supreme Court by special leave under article 136 of the Constitution. This recommendation can be adopted straight away.

1.8 The Army Headquarters' Proposal

In 1999, the Army Headquarters had also made a proposal for an armed forces tribunal. It was proposed that the principal bench of the tribunal should be in Delhi and be headed by a chairman who should be a serving judge of the Supreme Court. Its four administrative members should be serving officers of the rank of Lieutenant General or equivalent from the Air Force and Navy. The two judicial members should be the officers of the Judge Advocate General (JAG) branch, of the rank of Colonel and above, having more than 10 years of service in the branch. The tribunal should have four other benches, located in metropolitan cities and consisting of two members each, one a serving high court judge and one a member of the JAG branch. The proposed tribunal should have original jurisdiction in all service matters, including postings, promotions and appointments, and appellate jurisdiction in all trials by courts-martial.

The shortcoming of the proposal were that: (i) it tried to accord judicial status to the officers of the JAG branch who otherwise function under the executive chain of command and do not carry out any judicial function; (ii) the composition of the proposed tribunal would be such that the military officers would have a greater say in the tribunal's decision; (iii) the tribunal's decision would be final and not subject to appeal in the Supreme Court; and (iv) the tribunal would try to bar the jurisdiction of all other courts (including the high courts and Supreme Court) and keep them away from entertaining suits or appeals in respect of matters in which it was empowered.[15]

1.9 Attempts by Various Committees

Emphasizing the need for setting up an independent adjudicatory forum for defence personnel, various Parliamentary Committees made the following recommendations.

(i) The Estimates Committee of the Parliament in its 19th Report presented to the Lok Sabha on 20th August, 1992 desired that the Government should constitute an independent statutory board or tribunal for service personnel.

(ii) The Standing Committee on Defence in its 20th Report presented to Lok Sabha on 19.8.2003, recommended that special court of appeal on the line of countries like France, Germany, Russia, Sweden and United Kingdom be constituted for redress of grievances of the service

---

15. The armed forces have been wary of the power exercised by the Supreme Court and the High Courts under the Writ Jurisdiction. This could be because military bureaucracy might not have understood of the importance of the judicial institution in a democratic set up following the rule of law. In a seminar held at the Vigyan Bhawan New Delhi on 26 February 1982, on the subject "The Relationship of Military Law and Discipline with the Judicial System of the Country", the recommendations were: (a) reappraisal of the existing judicial system in the Army so as to make it up to date and bring it in line with the more modern and progressive concepts in military justice, (b) there should be some kind of an Appellate Court or a Review Board to review courts-martial verdicts and an Administrative Tribunal to consider complaints relating to other service grievances, (c) in the event of setting up of the appellate bodies as aforementioned, desirability of suitably curtailing the Writ Jurisdiction of the civil courts in respect of matters which fall within the purview of such appellate bodies may be examined. Interestingly, the seminar was attended by the then senior serving and retired army officers as well as Mr Justice DM Sen, former Judge Advocate General (Army) and Judge of Guwahati High Court. USI Seminar Proceedings, Number 10. *"The Relationship of Military Law and Discipline with the Judicial System of the Country"*, United Services Institution of India, New Delhi.

personnel, where aggrieved personnel may appeal against the judgment of military court. In pursuance thereof, the Standing Committee on Defence (2004-05) in their 2nd Report presented on 25 April 2005 again stressed on the urgency of new mechanism to deal with the large number of cases pertaining to the Armed Forces.[16]

1.10 Proposal of the Ministry of Defence

The Ministry of Defence proposed for setting up of an Armed Forces Tribunal for adjudicating service matters excluding transfer and postings of the Armed Forces personnel, and appeals arising out of the verdicts of the courts-martial were approved by the Cabinet in its meeting held on 29th September, 2005. The Armed Forces Tribunal was proposed to be set up under Article 246 of the Constitution read with Entry 2 of List-1 (Union List) in the Seventh Schedule to the Constitution.

1.11 Armed Forces Tribunal Bill, 2005

The Government introduced the Armed Forces Tribunal Bill, 2005 in Parliament on 20 December 2005, for the establishment of an independent armed forces tribunal. The salient features were as follows:

1. There will be one tribunal to deal with service matters (original jurisdiction) and appeals from the verdicts of courts-martial (appellate jurisdiction). The numbers of benches will be determined by the Central Government after the appointment of chairperson.
2. The chairperson of the armed forces tribunal shall be either a retired judge of the Supreme Court or a retired chief justice of a high court.
3. The administrative member(s) shall be a serving or retired Major General or above in the Army or equivalent in the Navy or the Air Force, with three years of service in that rank.
4. The judicial members should be a serving or retired judges of high courts. However, serving or retired Judge Advocate Generals who are of the rank of Major General in the Army or equivalent in the Navy or Air Force can also be appointed.[17] The serving officers shall have to seek retirement before assuming such appointment.
5. One or more member(s) of the tribunal may be appointed as Vice-Chairperson(s) by the Central Government.
6. The chairperson and each member shall have a four-year non-extendable

---

16. Article 323A of the Constitution of India empowers Parliament to provide, by law, for the adjudication or trial by administrative tribunals. Under this Article, Parliament enacted the Administrative Tribunals Act, 1985. As a sequel thereto, the Central Administrative Tribunal (CAT) adjudicates service matters concerning Central Government employees. The Central Administrative Tribunal Act, 1985 does not apply to the personnel of the Armed Forces.
17. The Judge Advocate General (JAG) in the Indian Air Force and the Navy are of the rank of Air Commodore and Commodore respectively, one rank below the Major General.

tenure, and shall be of a maximum age of 70 years if he/she is a retired judge of the Supreme Court and 65 years if he/she is a retired chief justice of a high court.

7. The tribunal shall have powers to punish for its contempt.
8. The tribunal shall decide questions both of law and facts. The Central Government was to make rules to implement the provisions of the proposed tribunal.
9. All appointments to the armed forces tribunal were to be made in consultation with the Chief Justice of India.

1.11.1 The Parliamentary Standing Committee's Recommendations

The Armed Forces Tribunal Bill, 2005, was referred to the Standing Committee of Defence for comment and report. The Standing Committee made 14 recommendations, of which the Ministry of Defence accepted five without changes and two with some modifications. The committee was of the view that military laws should be strict enough to deal with military offences firmly and effectively to enforce discipline, but at the same time the law should not be oppressive to the extent of having a demoralizing effect on the defence personnel. The Standing Committee's Tenth Report was presented to the Lok Sabha on 23 May 2006.[18]

1.11.2 Discussion in Parliament

The Armed Forces Tribunal Bill, 2005, came for discussion before the Rajya Sabha on 3 December 2007. Shri AK Antony, Minister of Defence, moved the motion for the consideration of the Bill. At the conclusion of discussion the Minister of Defence made the following statement:

"Many hon. Members, while participating in the debate, gave very valuable suggestions. I am not rejecting them. There were many valuable suggestions. But today, if we try to restart the whole thing, it would be delayed. So, I assure you that we shall keep in mind some of the valuable suggestions given by the hon. Members and bring suitable amendments at the appropriate time. Let us first pass this Bill and try to operationalise this Bill as early as possible. I don't claim that it is a hundred per cent ideal Bill, but it is a major step towards redressing the long-pending grievances of our Armed Forces. This Bill is almost at par with the existing redressal machinery of the advanced countries such as UK, France, Canada, Australia and other countries. Let us always look for improvement; we shall do that gradually." Further, "Once it is operationalised, there will be need for more amendments. Once again, I assure you that at the proper time, after going into your important suggestions, the Government will bring more amendments at the earliest."[19]

---

18. The 10th Report is available at http://164.100.24.208/ls/CommiteeR/Defence/2report.pdf
19. http://164.100.24.167/Bullitensessions/sessionno/212/31207.pdf

The Armed Forces Tribunal Bill, 2005, could not be discussed in the Lok Sabha. It was put to vote by the Deputy Speaker on 05 December 2007 and received the nod of the Lok Sabha.

1.12 The Armed Forces Tribunal Act, 2007

The Armed Forces Tribunal Act, 2007, was passed by both the houses of Parliament in December 2007 and thereafter received the assent of the Hon'ble President.[20] The Government issued a notification under Section 1 (2) of the Act bringing it into force.

1.12.1 Rules

The following Rules have been made under the Armed Forces Tribunal Act, 2007.

1. The Armed Forces Tribunal (Procedure) Rules, 2008.
2. The Armed Forces Tribunal (Procedure for Appointment of Vice-Chairperson and other Members) Rules, 2008.
3. The Armed Force Tribunal (Procedure for Investigation of Misbehaviour or Incapacity of Chairperson and other Members) Rules, 2008.
4. The Armed Forces Tribunal (Financial and Administrative Powers) Rules, 2008.
5. The Armed Forces Tribunal (Salaries, Allowances and Conditions of Service of Chairperson and Members) Rules, 2009.
6. The Armed Forces Tribunal (Practice) Rules, 2009.
7. The Armed Forces Tribunal (Procedure) Amendment Rules, 2011.

1.12.2 Composition of the Tribunal and Benches

The Tribunal consists of a Chairperson, and such number of judicial and administrative members as the Central Government may decide. The principal bench of the Tribunal is headed by the chairperson, and has judicial and administrative members. A bench of the tribunal consists of one judicial member and one administrative member. The chairperson, in cases which having regard to the nature of the questions involved, are required to be decided by a bench composed of more than two members, may issue general or special orders for its composition. However, every bench constituted in pursuance of this clause shall include at least one judicial member and one administrative member.[21]

If the members of a bench differ in opinion on any point(s), the point shall be decided according to the opinion of the majority, if there is a majority, but if the members are equally divided, they shall state the point on which they differ and refer it to the chairperson. The chairperson shall either hear the

---

20. The Armed Forces Tribunal was set up under Article 246 of the Constitution read with Entry 2 of List-1 (Union List) in the Seventh Schedule to the Constitution.
21. Section 5, the Armed Forces Tribunal Act, 2007.

point himself or refer the case for hearing on such point(s) by one or more of the members of the tribunal. The point shall be decided according to the opinion of the majority of the members of the Tribunal who have heard the case, including those who first heard it.[22]

1.12.3 Number of Benches

A total of 15 benches have been created across India. A table indicating the number of benches and the locations follows.

SNo	Location	No of Benches
(i)	Delhi (Principal Bench)	3
(ii)	Chandigarh	3
(iii)	Lucknow	3
(iv)	Kolkata	1
(v)	Guwahati	1
(vi)	Mumbai	1
(vii)	Kochi	1
(viii)	Chennai	1
(ix)	Jaipur	1

For convenient disposal of all the matters the territorial jurisdiction of all the benches has been delineated. The Chandigarh Bench has jurisdiction to decide all the matters of Punjab, Haryana, Himachal Pradesh and Jammu & Kashmir. The Lucknow Bench has jurisdiction to decide the matters pertaining to UP, Madhya Pradesh and Chattisgarh; while Kolkata bench has jurisdiction to decide the matters pertaining to West Bengal, Bihar, Orissa, Jharkhand and Andaman & Nicobar Islands. The Guwahati Bench has jurisdiction to decide the matters arisen from Assam, Manipur, Nagaland, Meghalaya, Tripura, Mizoram and Arunachal Pradesh. Mumbai Bench has a territorial jurisdiction of Maharashtra, Goa and Gujarat, Kochi Bench has jurisdiction of Kerala and Karnataka States; Chennai Bench has jurisdiction of Andhra Pradesh, Tamil Nadu and the Union Territory of Puducherry. The Jaipur Bench has jurisdiction to all the cases arising from Rajasthan. A person who has any cause of action arising in this territorial jurisdiction has right to approach the respective bench of the Tribunal. Section 27 of the AFT Act provides that in case any person finds it difficult to approach the Tribunal bench of respective territorial jurisdiction, he can make an application to the Chairperson to transfer the case from one bench to another.

1.12.4 Additional Benches

If at any time the vice-chairperson of a bench is satisfied that circumstances exist which render it necessary to have a sitting of the said bench at any place

22. Section 28, the Armed Forces Tribunal Act, 2007.

falling within its territorial jurisdiction other than the place or places at which it ordinarily sits, he may, with the previous consent of the chairperson, direct that the additional bench shall hold its sittings at any such appropriate place.[23]

1.13 Jurisdiction

Original Jurisdiction: The Armed Forces Tribunal has original jurisdiction over service matters. The term 'service matters' is defined in section 3 (o) of the Act, and includes:

(i) remuneration, allowances, pension and retirement benefits;

(ii) tenure, including commission, appointment, enrolment, probation, confirmation, seniority, training, promotion, reversion, premature retirement, superannuation, termination of service and penal deductions;

(iii) summary disposal and trials where the punishment of dismissal is awarded.[24]

(iv) any other matter, whatsoever, but shall not include matters relating to–

  (i) orders issued under section 18 of the Army Act, 1950, sub-section (1) of section 15 of the Navy Act, 1957 and section 18 of the Air Force Act, 1950;

  (ii) transfers and postings including change of place or unit on posting whether individually or as a part of unit, formation or ship in relation to the persons subject to the Army Act, 1950, the Navy Act, 1957 and the Air Force Act, 1950;

  (iii) leave of any kind;

  (iv) summary court-martial except where the punishment is of dismissal or imprisonment for more than three months.

The Tribunal does not have jurisdiction in matters relating to (i) order of dismissal invoking the doctrine of Presidential pleasure (ii) transfers and postings, (iii) leave; (iv) summary trials, except where the punishment is of dismissal; and (iv) summary court-martial, except where the punishment is of dismissal or imprisonment for more than three months.

Appellate jurisdiction: The Tribunal has jurisdiction in relation to any appeal against order, finding or sentence passed by a court-martial.[25] The Tribunal shall allow an appeal against conviction by a court-martial where (a) the finding of the court-martial is legally not sustainable due to any reason whatsoever; or (b) the finding involves a wrong decision on a question of law;

---

23. Rule 3, The Armed Forces Tribunal (Financial and Administrative Powers) Rules, 2008

24. The term "summary disposals and trials" is defined in Section 3 (p) of the Tribunal Act meaning "summary disposals and trials held under the Army Act, 1950, the Navy Act, 1957 and the Air Force Act, 1950." The punishment of dismissal in a summary trial can be awarded only under section 93 (2) of the Navy Act.

25. Section 15, Armed Forces Tribunal Act, 2007.

or (c) there was a material irregularity in the trial resulting in miscarriage of justice.[26] In other cases, the Tribunal shall be empowered to dismiss the appeal where it considers that no miscarriage of justice is likely to be caused or has actually resulted to the applicant. While dismissing an appeal the Tribunal shall give reasons in writing.[27] It may allow an appeal against conviction and pass an appropriate order.[28]

1.14 Functioning of the Tribunal

The Tribunal decided its first case in August 2009[29] and in the last four years of functioning has given decision in more than 18,700 cases. The Tribunal is functioning as a court of record and has the power to punish for criminal contempt. It can exercise powers similar to those of a criminal court in respect of 'offences against justice' such as forgery, perjury and misrepresentation in the proceedings. For the purposes of trying an offence of criminal contempt, the provisions of sections 14, 15, 17, 18 and 20 of the Contempt of Courts Act, 1971 (70 of 1971) shall *mutatis mutandis* apply.[30] Parties aggrieved by the decisions of the Tribunal in 'criminal contempt' have the option of approaching the Supreme Court. The appeal should be filed in the Supreme Court within sixty days from the date of the order appealed against. Pending any appeal the Supreme Court may order that (a) the execution of the punishment or the order appealed against be suspended; or (b) if the appellant is in confinement, he be released on bail.[31]

The Tribunal, however, does not have any power to punish for 'civil contempt'. The Act in its present form does not contain any provision for the execution of the orders finally passed by the Tribunal. This has resulted in a situation where the authorities have not taken any action on the orders and decisions passed by the Tribunal and certain cases involving serious

---

26. Section 15 (4) (a), (b), and (c), Armed Forces Tribunal Act, 2007.
27. Section 15 (4), Armed Forces Tribunal Act, 2007.
28. Section 15 (5), Armed Forces Tribunal Act, 2007.
29. In exercise of the powers conferred by Section 4 of the Armed Forces Tribunal Act, 2007, the Central Government established the Armed Forces Tribunal with effect from the 10 August, 2009.
30. Section 19 (2), the Armed Forces Tribunal Act, 2007. For the purposes of trying an offence under this section, the provisions of sections 14, 15, 17, 18 and 20 of the Contempt of courts Act, 1971 (70 of 1971) shall mutatis mutandis apply, as if a reference therein to:

    (a) Supreme Court or High Court were a reference to the Tribunal;

    (b) Chief Justice were a reference to the Chairperson;

    (c) Judge were a reference to the Judicial or Administrative Member of the Tribunal;

    (d) Advocate-General were a reference to the prosecutor; and

    (e) Court were a reference to the Tribunal.
31. Section 30 (2) and (3), the Armed Forces Tribunal Act, 2007.

questions of law of public importance had to be taken to the Supreme Court for appropriate directions.[32] Civil contempt as defined in Section 2 (b) of the Contempt of Courts Act, 1971 means wilful disobedience to any judgment, decree, direction, order, writ or other process of a Court or wilful breach of an undertaking given to a Court. The lack of civil contempt power has greatly hampered the functioning of the Tribunal.

Due to the shortage of the judicial members, a number of benches of the Tribunal became non-functional in the last two years. This resulted in a huge backlog of cases at various benches of the Tribunal. For instance, as on 30 November 2012, there were more than 4,600 pending cases at various benches of the Tribunal. The list included AFT (PB) Delhi- 385 cases, AFT Lucknow- 1088 cases, AFT Chandigarh- 1565 cases, AFT Kochi- 334 cases, AFT Chennai- 81 cases, AFT Kolkata- 259 cases, AFT Jaipur- 94 cases, AFT Mumbai- 94 cases and AFT Guwahati- 14 cases.[33]

1.15 The Armed Forces Tribunal (Amendment) Act, 2012

In order to overcome two main obstacles in the functioning the Tribunal, the Armed Forces Tribunal (Amendment) Bill, 2012 was introduced in Rajya Sabha on 13 August 2012 for bringing amendments to the Armed Forces Tribunal Act, 2007. The first amendment related to the enhancement of term of office from four to five years for the Chairperson or a Member of the Tribunal and age of Judicial Member in case he has been Chief Justice of High Court from sixty-five to sixty-seven years. The reason given for the amendment was that it would avoid repeated selection of Members for short tenures so as to provide the Tribunal with stability and continuity. The second amendment was proposed for conferring of powers of civil contempt on the Armed Forces Tribunal.

It was informed by the Principal Bench of the Tribunal that the AFT Act, 2007, in its present form did not contain any provision for the execution of the order finally passed by the Tribunal. Even the arrangements made in Section 29 of AFT Act, 2007 which stated that "subject to the other provisions of this Act and the rules made thereunder, the order of the Tribunal disposing of an application shall be final and shall not be called in question in any court and such order shall be executed accordingly" did not operate as a string of caution unless powers were conferred to get its orders enforced. Further, there

32. The Armed Forces Tribunal expressed its anguish over lack of powers to get its orders executed. Many a time it found itself helpless as its orders were not implemented by the authorities. The Tribunal said: "orders were at mercy of the authorities; if they wish, they can execute and if they do not wish, they may not. We feel that we are handicapped because we do not power to issue civil contempt to get the orders of the Tribunal Executed." Armed Forces Tribunal throws up its hands, *The Hindu*, 02 February 2011.

33. The Parliamentary Standing Committee on Defence (2012-13) Eighteenth Report, page 38.

was no other provision in the Act to get its order complied with, in case of failure to do so. As the existing power to punish for contempt covers only for criminal contempt, this provision could not be used to enforce its orders.

While there was no disagreement on the first amendment relating the age and tenure of the Chairperson/Members, the three services unanimously rejected the proposal to accord the Tribunal with the power of "civil" contempt. The three services were of the opinion that the AFT Act was passed after having considered all the aspects including the functioning of the Armed Forces and there was need to let the system stabilize and review the matter after a reasonable period. The Chief of Staff Committee was of the view that some more time may be given and the issue may be revisited after five years and a decision may be taken based on the inputs from the three services and the serving/retired personnel.

In another step, aimed at making the ATF a strong and independent institution, and to avoid conflict of interest, the Standing Committee has recommended that the administrative control of the Tribunal should be with the Ministry of Law and Justice rather than the Ministry of Defence (MoD). The Punjab and Haryana High Court, in its decision in the public interest litigation, *Maj Navdeep Singh v. Union of India,* (2012) directed that the Armed Forces Tribunal be placed under the Law Ministry, and not the MoD, to ensure its independence and that keeping in view the separation of powers enshrined in the Constitution, the government should have a minimal say in its functioning.[34]

The Bill was referred to the Parliamentary Standing Committee on Defence by the Speaker for examination and report on 28 August, 2012. The Standing Committee's (2012-2013) Eighteenth Report on the Armed Forces Tribunal (Amendment) Bill, 2012, was presented to Lok Sabha on 20 March 2013. A copy of the Armed Forces Tribunal (Amendment) Bill, 2012 is at Appendix "H" and the extracts of the Eighteenth Report of the Standing Committee on Defence is placed at "I".

1.16 Errors in the Armed Forces Tribunal Act, 2007

1.16.1 Re-trial under Section 16

Section 16 of the Armed Forces Tribunal Act, 2007 is a copy of Section 18

34. The role played by the Ministry of Defence (MoD) is adversarial towards litigants. Petitioners are viewed as 'enemies of the system'. Even settled and covered matters are not conceded, government counsel not briefed fairly and all pleas are opposed as if it is state policy to increase litigation and live off the miseries of poor personnel. As the joke goes, if a person files a plea that Sun rises from the East, it would be opposed by the MoD stating that it rises from the West. Unwanted, forced and imposed multiple litigation up to the Supreme Court is the order of the day and shockingly most appeals filed by the MoD are against disabled soldiers. Navdeep Singh, Redeeming the Idea of Armed Forces Tribunal, available at: http://www.indianmilitary.info/2013/02/oped-in-tribune-on-armed-forces.html, accessed 11 June 2013.

and 19 of the British Court Martial (Appeals) Act, 1968. However, while copying this provision from the British Act, certain errors have occurred. These are as follow.

> *Retrial: Section 16 (2), Armed Forces Tribunal Act, 2007*
>
> The Tribunal shall have the power of quashing a conviction, to make an order authorizing the appellant to be retried by court-martial, but shall only exercise this power....

Section 16 deals with retrial. The language of this sub-section 16 (2) gives an impression that it deals with the two separate powers of the Tribunal in matters of appeal against court martial: to quash a conviction, and to make an order of retrial. The power of the tribunal has been dealt with in Section 15 of the Armed Forces Tribunal Act. Section 15 does not specifically mention about the power of 'quashing a conviction'. However, Section 15 (f) grants the Tribunal the power to "pass any other order as it may think appropriate"; and the power of 'quashing a conviction' could be exercised under this provision. The power to order retrial by a court-martial, can only be exercised after the Tribunal has quashed a conviction under Section 15.

In order to remove above error in the Act, the word 'of' appearing in the first sentence of Section 16 (2) need to be replaced with 'on'; and a comma (,) need to be inserted after the word 'power' in the first sentence to make it meaningful:

> The Tribunal shall have the power, on quashing a conviction, to make an order authorizing the appellant to be retried by court-martial, but shall only exercise this power....

1.16.2 Section 16 (3) Armed Forces Tribunal Act, 2007

While substituting the words in Section 19 (4) of the British Act, the text of Sub-section 16 (3) of the Armed Forces Tribunal Act has become confusing.

> *Section 16 (3), Armed Forces Tribunal Act, 2007*
>
> A person who is to be retried under this section for an offence shall, if the Tribunal or the Supreme Court so directs, whether or not such person is being tried or retried on one or more of the original charges, no fresh investigation or other action shall be taken under the relevant provision of the Army Act, 1950 or the Navy Act, 1957 or the Air Force Act, 1950, as the case may be, or rules and regulations made there under, in relation to the said charge or charges on which he is to be retried.

Sub-section 16 (3) may be replaced with the following:

> (3) During a retrial under Section 16 for an offence, no fresh investigation in relation to the alleged charge or charges will be undertaken.

1.16.3 Section 17 Armed Forces Tribunal Act

Section 17 of the Armed Forces Tribunal Act, 2007 deals with the powers of the Tribunal on appeal under Section 15.

> *Section 17: The Tribunal, while hearing and deciding an appeal under section 15, shall have the power:*

(a) to order production of documents...;

(b) to order the attendance of the witnesses;

(c) to receive the evidence;

(d) to obtain reports from court martial;

(e) order reference of any question for inquiry;

(f) appoint a person with special expert knowledge to act as an assessor; and

(g) to determine any question which is necessary to be determined in order to do justice in the case.

There are errors in the text of sub-section (e), (f) and (g) of this section. In Sub-section 17 (e) word 'to' needs to be inserted at the beginning of the text. The use of words "special expert knowledge" in Sub-section 17 (f) is superfluous. An expert is one who has devoted his time and study to a special branch of learning, and thus is especially skilled on those points on which he is asked to state his opinion. The Indian Evidence Act, Section 45 deals with the opinion of experts. In Sub-section 17 (f), word 'to' needs to be inserted at the beginning, and to be replaced with the following text: "to appoint an expert to act as an assessor; and." Further, the text of sub-section 17 (g) is incorrect/confusing and needs to be corrected. The existing sub-sections 17 (e), (f) and (g) need to be amended to read as:

(e) to order reference of any question for inquiry;

(f) to appoint an expert to act as an assessor; and

(g) to determine any question in order to do justice in the case.

1.16.4 Limitations: Section 22, Armed Forces Tribunal Act, 2007

In the first sentence, after 22, Sup-para number '(1)' needs to be inserted.

1.17 Shortcomings in the Act

1.17.1 Jurisdiction over Summary Court Martial

The Armed Forces Tribunal does not have jurisdiction in cases of summary court martial, where a punishment of imprisonment for three months or less (3rd punishment in the scale under Section 71 of the Army Act, 1950) has been awarded. However, in cases of other courts martial (i.e., General Court Martial, Summary General Court Martial or District Court Martial), an accused having been awarded the least severe punishment of 'stoppage of pay and allowances' (12th in the scale of punishment) is entitled to seek the intervention of the Tribunal.

One may argue that under section 376 of Cr PC, there is no right to appeal where a Court of Sessions or Metropolitan Magistrate awards a sentence of three months of imprisonment, so why should it be available in the case of summary court martial.

A trial in a Session's court cannot be equated with a summary court martial. An accused in a summary court martial cannot be represented by a defending officer or counsel and the commanding officer alone constitutes the court, and acts as prosecutor and judge. Moreover, only individuals of the rank of Havildar and below are tried by a summary court martial. The only solace is that an accused may avail of the services of a 'friend' who may suggest questions to be put to the witnesses. An accused cannot challenge his trial by the commanding officer on the grounds of bias or personal interest.

Summary court martial as it exists in the Indian Army was started by the British after the First War of Independence in 1857. It does not exist in the Indian Air Force of the Navy. The British never had this system of court martial in their country. Summary court martial are being used extensively, depriving a large number of army personnel of their livelihood and freedom. During the period of 1999 to 2004, an average 995 summary courts martial were held every year in the Indian Army. A large number of summary court martial trials have been criticised by the Supreme Court, the High Courts and the Armed Forces Tribunal.

1.17.2 Jurisdiction over Summary Trials

The military commanders at various levels are empowered to award minor punishments summarily to the officers and personnel below the officer rank (PBORs). The Tribunal is not empowered to entertain any petition against the award of minor punishments like forfeiture of seniority, severe reprimand awarded to the officers and JCOs or imprisonment/detention up to 42 days to the personnel below the rank of Naik in the Army (or equivalent rank in the Air Force or Navy). The only exception is the award of 'dismissal' through a summary trial under the Navy Act, 1957, where an affected person can approach the Tribunal [AFT Act, 2007, Section 3 (o) (iii) refers]. The aggrieved persons are forced to seek remedy through the writ jurisdiction of the high courts, which is contrary to the aims and objectives of the Tribunal.

The summary trials are conducted by the commanding officer/ senior military officers, and there are no rules of evidence, there are no right to counsel, there are no transcripts, and there are no right to appeal. The rule of law provides that interactions within society be governed by the principles of fairness according to which citizens are provided meaningful opportunities to be heard, and to have disputes resolved by impartial arbitrators. The degree of fairness and impartiality of the arbitrator is dependent upon the nature of the decision being made. For example, criminal proceedings, where the liberty of the accused may be at stake, require the highest degree of fairness and impartiality, while administrative processes, where the liberty of an accused is not at stake, do not have to meet as high a burden. These principles of fairness are guaranteed by the Indian Constitution to every citizen.

The punishments awarded under summary trials by the commanding officers and senior commanders have invariably deeply affected the career prospects of the serving personnel, it is recommended that summary disposals and trials must be brought under the purview of the Tribunal in order to ensure justice.

1.17.3 Power to Grant Bail

The Tribunal is empowered to grant bail to a 'military accused' under Section 15 (3) of the Act. Proviso to this sub-section, copied from Section 437 of the Cr PC, states: "provided that no accused shall be so released if there appears reasonable ground for believing that he has been guilty of an offence punishable with death or imprisonment for life." The Tribunal has no power to grant bail to a 'military convict'. The power of the Tribunal to grant bail to a military accused/ convict thus becomes even lower than that of the Sessions Court.

The issue was considered by the Standing Committee (2005-06). The Ministry of Defence's submission that "The Tribunal has been given the powers to grant bail, but not on people who have been sentenced with death or life imprisonment" was not convincing to the Committee. The Committee recommended that the matter may be reconsidered and the Tribunal may have discretion to grant bail to the Armed Forces personnel, as is being provided by the High Courts to the accused persons under section 437 of Cr PC.

The Army Act, 1950 is a copy of the Indian Army Act, 1911, made by the British to govern 'natives'. Its provisions are harsh and a large number of the offences provide for the punishment of death or life imprisonment. If the Tribunal, as an appellate forum, does not have the power to grant bail a military convict, a military accused/convict would be forced to approach the High Court under the Writ Jurisdiction. The provision relating to bail need to be amended to ensure that the Tribunal enjoys the powers of an appeal court under Section 389 Cr PC in granting the bail to a military accused or convict.

1.17.4 Legal Aid

Insufficiency of legal aid poses a serious handicap for the armed forces personnel approaching the Tribunal. The question of legal aid becomes more pertinent in the context of the armed forces because the fundamental rights of those serving in the forces have been abrogated by the Constitution. The democratic provision of equality before law strongly warrants the provision of legal aid for the armed forces personnel, especially below the officer rank.

1.18 Systems of Grievance Redressal

The armed forces world over have their own administrative and judicial systems which assist in maintaining discipline and in the dispensation of justice. In India, the fundamental rights of armed forces personnel are restricted by Article 33 of the Constitution to ensure the proper discharge of duties and maintenance of discipline among them. They do not have the right to be members of trade unions or associations, to attend political meetings and to communicate with the press.[35] The Government has, however, bestowed on them the right to make complaints seeking the redress of their grievances. This statutory right has been accorded exclusively to armed forces personnel and is

35. Section 21, Army Act, 1950.

not available to the members of the para-military forces.[36] The provision for the redress of grievances is contained in the Army Act, 1950, the Air Forces Act, 1950 and the Navy Act, 1957. The Regulations of the three services provide different procedures for the processing of complaints.[37]

1.18.1 Procedure for Redress of Grievances

Chapter V of the Army Act, which deals with service privileges, makes provision for the redress of the grievances of army personnel. Section 26 of the Army Act[38] provides that any person below the officer rank (PBOR) who deems himself wronged by any superior or other officer may complain to the commanding officer (CO) for the redress of his grievance. When the officer complained against is the officer to whom the complaint should be preferred, the aggrieved person may complain to the officer who is next in superiority to such officer. Section 27 of the Army Act[39] provides that any officer who deems himself wronged by his CO or any superior officer, and who on due application made to his CO does not receive the redress to which he considers himself entitled, may complain to the Central Government. Redress

---

36. The National Security Guard Act, 1985 (section 13) also make provision for submission of grievance applications.
37. The Army Act, 1950, sections 26 and 27; the Air Force Act, sections 26 and 27; and the Navy Act, Section 23 deal with the redress of grievance. The Regulations for the Army (1987), para 364 (as amended in 1992); the Regulations for the Air Force (1964), para 621 and 622; and the Regulations for the Navy (1991), Part II, para 238 to 240 prescribe procedure for submission and processing of the redress complaints.
38. 26. Remedy of aggrieved persons other than officers. (1) Any person subject to this Act other than an officer who deems himself wronged by any superior or other officer may, if not attached to a troop or company, complain to the officer under whose command or orders he is serving ; and may, if attached to a troop or company, complain to the officer commanding the same.

    (2) When the officer complained against is the officer to whom any complaint should, under sub-section (1), be preferred, the aggrieved person may complain to such officer's next superior officer.

    (3) Every officer receiving any such complaint shall make as complete an investigation into it as may be possible for giving full redress to the complainant; or, when necessary, refer the complaint to superior authority.

    (4) Every such complaint shall be preferred in such manner as may from time to time be specified by the proper authority.

    (5) The Central Government may revise any decision by the Chief of the Army Staff under sub-section (2), but, subject thereto, the decision of the Chief of the Army Staff shall be final.
39. 27. Remedy of aggrieved officers.---Any officer who deems himself wronged by his commanding officer or any superior officer and who on due application made to his commanding officer does not receive the redress to which he considers himself entitled, may complain to the Central Government in such manner as may from time to time be specified by the proper authority.

applications by the officers are to be addressed to the Central Government and by the PBORs to the Chief of the Army Staff (COAS).

Subject Matter of the Complaint. The complaint under Section 26 and 27 may relate to:

(a) Any matter relating to the conditions of service like promotion, appointment, postings, transfers, release, pension, leave of absence etc., where person subject to the Army Act deems himself wronged by his commanding officer or any superior officer.

(b) Any person subject to the Army Act against the decision of an authority disposing of a case under Sections 80, 83, 84 and 85 of the Army Act.

(c) An officer or JCO who deems himself wronged by the award of Censure.[40]

The complaints must be confined to a statement of facts. A joint complaint is not allowed as it amounts to 'mutiny'. It is also an offence against service discipline to make a complaint which is untrue to the knowledge of the complainant. Similarly, it is an offence to make a complaint which contains language or comments that are disrespectful or insubordinate or subversive of discipline. The right to complain can be exercised only once. However, a second complaint can be allowed if fresh facts and circumstances emerge necessitating reconsideration of the case.

1.18.2 Processing of Complaint

On receipt of the application, the CO is to investigate the case and, if possible, redress the grievance. If the CO is not in a position to redress the grievance, the application, together with a report from the CO, is to be forwarded to the next higher formation in the chain of command. The channel through which complaints must be preferred are specified in paragraph 364 of the Regulations for the Army. The application is to be continued to be forwarded to the next higher authority until it reaches the Army headquarters. The applicant is to be informed of the fact that his application has been forwarded to the next higher authority.

The intermediate authorities in the chain of command can interview the complainant and investigate the matter within their jurisdiction. They are empowered to withhold the complaint if it is incomplete; couched in discourteous, disrespectful or improper language; or contains any unauthorized official document. If they decide to withhold the complaint, they must inform the complainant and the next superior authority. Otherwise, the intermediate authorities are to forward the complaint, along with detailed paragraph-wise comments, to the next superior authority.

The PBOR's statutory right is exhausted after his application has been considered and a decision has been taken by the COAS. The Central Government is empowered to revise the decision of the COAS, but a PBOR

40. Para 364, Regulations for the Army, 1987, Part I.

has no statutory right to petition the government for such a revision. While relief to the petitioner may be given by the lower authority, the final rejection of the application can only be at the level of the COAS. The COAS cannot delegate this power to a subordinate authority. In the case of the officers, the decision of the Central Government is final. The provisions under the Air Force Act are similar to those for the Army.

In the case of naval personnel, too, if an officer or sailor thinks that he has suffered any personal oppression, injustice or other ill-treatment at the hands of any superior officer, he may make a complaint, though the procedure is slightly different. Navy Regulations also allow the complainant to take assistance for making his redress application. If the complainant is a junior officer or a sailor, he may request any officer in his ship to advise and assist him in making a complaint. If no such request is made, it shall be the duty of the Divisional Officer/ Commanding Officer to detail an officer or to give his assistance.

In the Indian Navy, the initial complaint is oral. If the CO refuses or is unable to redress the complaint, the complainant may ask to be allowed to make his complaint in writing, and on receiving such a request, the CO is obliged to take 24 hours to reconsider the matter. If the CO cannot redress the grievance, the written complaint, together with the CO's remarks, is to be sent to the next superior officer. If the complainant is not satisfied with the decision on his complaint, or does not get redress within a month of the date of submission, he may request that his complaint be forwarded to the next superior authority, up to the Chief of the Naval Staff (CNS), and finally, to the government.

1.18. 3 Time-frame for Processing

The Regulations of the three services state that the grievance applications are to be processed expeditiously; however, the time-frame for processing is different in the case of each service. In the case of the Army, when the complaint does not contain any accusation requiring investigation, it must reach the Army headquarters within 135 days. If the complainant has made an accusation requiring investigation, the complaint should reach the headquarters within 180 to 195 days. If the final decision on the statutory complaint, regardless of whether it contains an accusation against any superior officer, is not taken within a period of 12 months or 9 months, respectively, from the date of submission of the complaint, the complainant has a right to represent directly to the Army Headquarters or the Central Government. The Regulations do not provide any time-frame for the Army Headquarters or the Central Government to give its final decision in the matter.[41]

41. The Regulations for the Army do not provide any time-frame within which the Army Headquarter or the Central Government are bound to give the final order. In this regard, the Additional Secretary (I), Ministry of Defence vide ID No. 6891/ AS/(I) dated 17 October 2005 has conveyed view of the Raksha Mantri for timely disposal of statutory and non-statutory representations. The Ministry of Defence

The Air Force Act provides that complaints should reach the Chief of the Air Staff (CAS) within 45 days of the date of submission, and no intermediate authority should hold up the complaint for more than 10 days. In the event of a longer delay, a report indicating the reasons is required to be made to the next higher authority. In the Navy, the complainant can appeal directly to the next superior authority if he does not receive the final reply within a period of six months from the date of submission of his complaint. As in the case of Army, the Regulations for the Air Force and the Navy also do not provide any time-frame for the giving final decision in the matter.

1.19 Shortcomings in the System of Grievance Redressal

There has been an unusual increase in the filing of applications in the armed forces tribunal by the military personnel, which demonstrates a gradual erosion of faith in the system of governance as well as redress of grievance in the armed forces. The large number of cases that have come up before the benches of the Armed Forces Tribunal in recent years show that the grievance redress system of the defence forces has not only been moving at a very slow pace, but has also not been able to satisfy the aspirations of men in uniform. The recent judgments of the Tribunal have found the existing system of governance 'not in consonance with the liberal spirit of the Indian Constitution'. The unscrupulous processing of a grievance petition damages the effectiveness of a statutory right. Some of the flawed provisions of the grievance redress system are as follows.

1.19.1 Comments of Intermediate Authorities.

During the processing of a complaint, the complainant is not informed about the comments of the section commander/CO and intermediate authorities on his grievance application. Recently, in the case of *Union of India v. Maj Gen Arun Roye* 2008 CWN 528, the Calcutta High Court opined: "...non-furnishing of comments of the intermediate authorities to the complainant who lodged the statutory complaint is tantamount to violation of the principles of natural justice." The Court held, "This is because the comments that are furnished by the intermediate authorities to the Central Government are essential to the

---

letter states that "from the timethe statutory representation is received in the Service Headquarters to the time it is finally decided, the period should not exceed six months." [Additional Directorate General D&V, Adjutant General's Branch letter No. 62736/AG/DV-1 (P) dated 28 October 2005]. Therefore, keeping in view the RA para 364, and the Ministry of Defence letter, the time for disposal of a statutory representation could be a minimum of one year (135 to 180 days of transit period in addition to six months at the Army Headquarters/Ministry of Defence). The transitory period is mentioned in para 364 of the Regulations is minimum and wherever a complaint is delayed for any period exceeding the stipulated timeframe, the reasons for the delay could be explained on a separate sheet of paper. Jha U. C. 2013. *A Handbook of Military Law: Reference Manual*, New Delhi: Vij Book India Pvt Ltd, p. 108-109.

complainant, so as to enable that person to know what has been commented against him/her by the said military authority while forwarding the complaint to the Government." The authorities, therefore, must convey the comments of the intermediate authorities to the complainant.

1.19. 2 Timely Disposal of Grievance Applications

Undue delays in the processing and disposal of complaints are another source of problem. The Regulations for the Army provide that whenever the disposal of a complaint is delayed for any period exceeding the stipulated time-frame, the reasons for the delay need to be annexed. Often, the delay is justified under the pretext that the military chain of command is engaged in making investigations. There is also no fixed time-frame for the Army Headquarters or the Central Government to give its final decision in the matter. There have been cases where final decision on the grievances relating to promotions have been delayed until the complainant retires.The delay in the finalization of a complaint often frustrates the complainant, leading to dissatisfaction and demoralization.[42]

The Principal Bench of the Tribunal in the case of *Sepoy Mohan Chandra v. Union of India*, OA No. 607 of 2010, decided on 31 January 2011, expressed great displeasure the way the death sentences were taken up by the Army HQ. In this case the summary general court martial (SGCM) had awarded the incumbent the death penalty on 8 May 2008, but his pre-confirmation petition was not disposed of till January 2011. When questioned by the Tribunal, the government counsel gave vague justification of 'legal formalities' as the reason for delay. The Tribunal commended, "it seems there is a total slackness and insensitivity in dealing with death sentence matters." In fact there is absolute insensitivity in dealing with matters of grievance redress in the armed forces.

Section 21 of the Tribunal Act specifies the condition for not admitting an application unless other available remedies are exhausted. It also specifies the remedies available and the time limit for preferring the petition or representation.[43] Section 22 specifies the period of limitation for admitting or

---

42. The Delhi High Court in the case of *AVM MS Brar v. Union of India* CWP 2600/2002 decided in July 2002 has observed that while disposing of representation by the Air Force authorities, the petitioner has been deprived of his valuable rights, as he was not given a reasonable opportunity of hearing. The decision on the application for extension of service was given after the retirement of the petitioner. The Court imposed a penalty of Rs 50,000 on the Union of India.

43 21. (1) The Tribunal shall not ordinarily admit an application unless it is satisfied that the applicant had availed of the remedies available to him under the Army Act, 1950 or the Navy Act, 1957 or the Air Force Act, 1950, as the case may be, and respective rules and regulations made thereunder.

(2) For the purposes of sub-section (1), a person shall be deemed to have availed of all the remedies available to him under the Army Act, 1950 or the Navy Act, 1957 or the Air Force Act, 1950, and respective rules and regulations—

(a) if a final order has been made by the Central Government or other authority or

otherwise of an application and also to condone the limitation provided under this clause. The tribunal shall not admit an application unless the applicant has exhausted the remedies available under the Act/Regulations. Applications are required to be made to the tribunal within 6 months of the final order of the competent authority.[44] An aggrieved person can approach the tribunal if no order has been made by the competent authority within 6 months from the date of petition. The Regulations of the three services, therefore, need to be amended to ensure redress in less than 6 months.

1.19.3 Reasoned Order

The decision on an application is not required to be a "reasoned" order and it could be conveyed in a brief sentence, such as: "Your application has been rejected by the competent authority as being devoid of merit." Stereotype rejection orders reinforce the doubt that complaints are treated arbitrarily and against the principles of natural justice. The Supreme Court has recently held that failure to give reasons amounts to denial of justice. It held,

> Reasons substitute subjectivity by objectivity. The emphasis on recording reasons is that if the decision reveals the "inscrutable face of the sphinx", it can, by its silence, render it virtually impossible for the Courts to perform their appellate function or exercise the power of judicial review in adjudging the validity of the decision. Right to reason is an indispensable part of a sound judicial system, reasons at least sufficient to indicate an application of mind to the matter before Court. Another rationale is that the affected party can know why the decision has gone against him. One of the salutary requirements of natural justice is spelling out reasons for the order made, in other words, a speaking out. The "inscrutable face of a sphinx" is ordinarily incongruous with a judicial or quasi-judicial performance.[45]

The need of a reasoned decision could be justified on the following grounds:

(a) In case the individual affected by the decision desires to go for appeal, he must have the opportunity to study the reasons on which the original judgement was based, so as to be able to present his counter-arguments in appeal.

(b) The need to give reasons for a legal decision is closely linked to the

---

officer or other person competent to pass such order under the said Acts, rules and regulations, rejecting any petition preferred or representation made by such person;

(b) where no final order has been made by the Central Government or other authority or officer or other person competent to pass such order with regard to the petition preferred or representation made by such person, if a period of six months from the date on which such petition was preferred or representation was made has expired.

44. Section 22, Armed Forces Tribunal Act, 2007.
45. *State of Himachal Pradesh v Manoj Kumar* 2008 (13) SCALE 82.

character of law. A judgement which does not give reasons may not be, but certainly appears to be arbitrary.

(c) A judgement will normally have an adverse result for one of the parties. In order to make such a result acceptable, it is necessary to give convincing reasons. Without reasoning, a judgement is not justifiable.

(d) For reasons of transparency, a judgement must assure that appropriate care has been given to determining the result, and that outcome is not the result of improper motives.

(e) A reasoned decision would provide the necessary feed-back about the views of the authority on his arguments. It will also highlight that the authority had examined the arguments.

The reason given for a judgement plays a significant role in demonstrating that the person concerned has actually been heard. [46] The rejection of a grievance, in the absence of any reasoning, indicates either that the authority did not listen or that it took an arbitrary decision. A decision is arbitrary if it is not based on reasons and as such amounts to an interference with the principles of justice. The Supreme Court has held that access to justice is a human right. A person who has a grievance against the state, a forum must be provided for redress thereof. The right to a reasoned decision, therefore, may be viewed from the human rights concept of access to justice.[47] The effect of a failure to provide proper reason is that the decision is unlawful.[48]

1.19.4 Deletion of Coercive Provision

In the Army, if a complainant has made an accusation, he/she is required to render a certificate, "I undertake that any false statement or false accusation made by me in this complaint will render me liable for disciplinary action."[49] In cases of the use of abusive language, misbehaviour and sexual harassment, which may take place in private, it may not be possible for a victim to support his/her accusation with any documentary proof or witness. Then the victim would be liable to disciplinary action based on the certificate rendered with

---

46. The Madras High Court in *Brigadier L. Venkatachalam v. Union of India* WP No. 3913/86, order dated 16 July 1987, held that statutory complaint must be disposed of by a speaking order. It also held that Army HQ should not return the second complaint stating that it does not contain any fresh material. In fact, Army HQ is only a channel and is duty bound to forward the same for consideration of the Government.
47. *Arunima Baruah v. Union of India* (2007) 6 SCC 120l.
48. *R v Tower Hamlets LBC (1991) 23 HLR, 488. Also see Divisional Forest Officer v Madhusudan Rao, JT 2008 (2) SC 253; Madhya Pradesh Industries Ltd. v Union of India, AIR 1966 SC 671; Siemens Engineering & Manufacturing Co. Ltd. v Union of India,* AIR 1976 SC 1785. Even in respect of administrative orders Lord Denning M.R. in *Breen v. Amalgamated Engineering Union* (1971 (1) All E.R. 1148) observed "The giving of reasons is one of the fundamentals of good administration".
49. Paragraph 364.8, Regulations for the Army.

his/her petition. This often deters the victim from seeking redress and makes the statutory right meaningless.

1.19.5 Legal Help

All levels of the military hierarchy are entitled to seek legal advice on a complaint. However, the aggrieved person is not provided any legal help for preferring his complaint. The persons objected to may participate in disposing of the objection.[50] It is therefore necessary that the affected person is provided legal help by the service for preferring his complaint.

1.19.6 Social Security

If the grievance is against the CO or higher military authorities, the affected individual or his family may also face social seclusion and harassment. There have been allegations that those lodging complaints against their military superiors have been transferred to far-flung places, causing harassment to them and their family members. The impersonal approach in handling grievance cases, inordinate delay in processing and harassment may cause stress and dissatisfaction among the military personnel.

The service headquarters and the government must make the grievance redress system more transparent. The 2nd Administrative Reforms Commission Report, 2005, describes nine qualities of good governance. These are participation, rule of law, transparency, consensus orientation, equity, responsiveness, effective and efficient process, accountability and strategic vision of the leaders. The armed forces have to revamp their grievance redress process keeping in view the principles of good governance and system of grievance redress followed in the other democracies. The Recommendations are:

1. The three services must follow a uniform policy framework and timeframe for the redress of grievances. The final order must be made within 6 months of submission of a grievance.
2. Coercive provision contained in the Regulations for the Army (1987), Part I, Para 364.8 needs deletion.[51]
3. The service HQs may consider appointing an independent body outside the military chain of command for managing complaints and grievances. This body may have former officers and other ranks as members. It can function in addition to the CO's power to redress a grievance to ensure that the processing channel is pruned.
4. The final order for the redress of grievance petition must be a reasoned one, and in case an individual desires to appeal to the tribunal, he/she must have the opportunity to study the reasons so as to be able to present counter-arguments in appeal.

---

50. The Supreme Court in the case of *Lt Col PPS Bedi v. Union of India* AIR 1982 SC 1413 has observed that such practice leads to bias.
51. A false accusation or false statement made in preferring a complaint is punishable under section 56 of Army Act, 1950.

5. The redress system must be made more transparent and the authorities must be held accountable for undue delay.
6. The Regulations for the Army (1987) and the Regulations for the Air Force (1964) need revision. The revised Regulations must be laid before the Parliament as required under section. 193A of the Army Act, 1950; and s. 191A of the Air Force Act, 1950.

As the armed forces constitute the most powerful weapon of the executive, their internal management and other functional systems are required to be efficient, modern and in tune with the times. Military organizations and their management have undergone a sea change the world over. It is the fundamental obligation of government to create an efficient administrative and legal system for the armed forces that is worthy of respect and embodies the notions of justice. The existing grievance redress system needs to be strengthened further to ensure that the decisions can withstand judicial scrutiny by the Armed Forces Tribunal and the Supreme Court.

2

Judgements: Service Matters

I. Administrative Action

Non application of Army Rule 180

The AFT Principal Bench New Delhi in the case of *Col Kamal Deep Singh v. Union of India,* OA No. 93 of 2012 (with MA No. 152 of 2012), decided on 1 May 2013, considered a prayer for setting aside order of removal from service.

The applicant was commissioned in the Indian Army on 29 August 1981 and in due course of time he was promoted to the rank of Colonel. He was placed in Command of his parent unit in October 2004. On 05 December 2005, applicant was injured in a case of road rage at Hissar (Haryana). Consequently, a court of inquiry was ordered on 19 December 2005 to investigate the circumstances under which the applicant sustained injuries. The applicant also deposed in the court of inquiry along with other persons. Thereafter, another court of inquiry was ordered on 08 January 2006 to investigate the circumstances under which the applicant sustained injuries with same terms of reference. More than 60 witnesses including the applicant were examined before the court of inquiry. Then a third court of inquiry was convened to investigate the circumstances under which applicant sustained injuries on same terms of reference. Then another court of inquiry was ordered vide convening order dated 26 March 2006 to investigate the alleged sale of unit FOL (Fuel Oil & Lubricants) by personnel of 1 HORSE.

The inquiry was followed by a summary of evidence and finally a GCM found the applicant guilty. The applicant/accused was awarded punishment of forfeiture of four years of service for the purpose of pension and severe reprimand. The applicant filed a petition under section 164 of the Army Act and his case was remanded back to the GCM for reconsideration of the sentence. The Court in revision awarded forfeiture of five years service for the purposes of pension, severe reprimand and put under stoppage of pay and allowance until he has made good a sum of Rs. 20,000/- in respect of loss of property belonging to the government as mentioned in the first charge. The applicant's post confirmation petition was rejected on 19 November 2011. Thereafter, the petitioner was issued a show cause notice for taking administrative action against him. He filed a reply to the show cause notice. The Government passed a formal order of removal from service on 12 January 2012.

The Tribunal observed that in the present case the first and second court of inquiry was found to be inconclusive, because first court of inquiry was quashed for the reason that it was presided over by Colonel to investigate allegation against another Colonel. According to para 518 of the Army Regulations, the Presiding Officer should be senior to the officer who is being investigated. Second inquiry which was headed by a Brigadier remained inconclusive as no finding was given. Therefore, a need arose for third court of inquiry headed by another Brigadier and he completed the inquiry and found the petitioner blameworthy that he had given information of his said injuries received on 5 December 2005 in a case of road rage, whereas he was beaten up not on account of road-rage but by some unknown persons for having so called illicit relations with the wife of another officer.

The Tribunal observed that while recoding of statements, the court of inquiry violated Army Rule 180. The Army Rule 180 is very sacrosanct and it gives the full opportunity to the incumbent against whom it is invoked when military reputation and character was involved. In this case, the Tribunal observed that the rule was invoked against the petitioner right from the beginning and in that 14 witnesses were examined in presence of the petitioner but subsequently remaining witnesses i.e. up to 48 witnesses were examined when petitioner was asked to go out. The copies of statement of remaining witnesses were given to him for cross-examining those witnesses by calling them again. It is true that petitioner was given opportunity to cross examine these witnesses, but this conduct of court of inquiry of asking the person against whom Rule 180 has been invoked to go out and examine large number of witnesses in his absence is something unheard of. The participation throughout inquiry was a must. Therefore, this illegality in conducting of Court of Inquiry goes to the root of the matter and this renders the entire Court of Inquiry vitiated.

The Tribunal observed that the findings of court martial on charge number 1 and 2 relating to FOL were fully justified on the basis of the evidence on the record. However, the difficulty was that show cause notice which was given to the petitioner was based on the court of inquiry with regard to road rage and with regard to the misappropriation of the FOL. The order for the removal from the service was a composite order on two incidents; first, the road rage in which false statement was given by the applicant that he received the injuries by way of accident whereas he was beaten by other persons because his illicit relations with wife of another officer. In this court of inquiry no punishment was given but finding was that he was blamed for having illicit relations. In this inquiry, the Tribunal observed that it was not sustainable because it suffers from serious infirmities of conduct under Army Rule 180. Therefore, part of this order based on that finding on that court of inquiry was not sustainable. However, second part of show cause notice pertaining to misappropriation of fuel was concerned; the Tribunal observed that the petitioner was rightly found guilty in the court martial proceedings. The order of removal from service which has two elements (i) on account of court of inquiry and other (ii) on account of court-martial. The authorities combined both these issues and ultimately terminated the services. In the case two things have been combined together (i) one illegal finding, and (ii) another legal finding. Therefore, the tribunal remanded matter back to the Government to decide whether the administrative action against the petitioner for termination of the services could be sustained on account of the findings of the court martial or they may decide to grant an alternative punishment to him.

The Tribunal quashed the order dated 12 January 2012 and remanded this matter back to the authorities to take an appropriate action by giving fresh show cause notice to the applicant and by segregating two items or to proceed against petitioner in accordance of law.

II. Annual Confidential Report (ACR)

Non-forwarding of ACRs

The Armed Forces Principal Bench New Delhi in the case of *Lt Col G Himashree v. Union of India*, OA No. 651 of 2010, decided on 23 August 2012, considered a prayer for quashing annual confidential reports (ACR).

The petitioner was commissioned in the Army Medical Corps (AMC) on 01 December 1986. While posted at DIPAS, Delhi the petitioner submitted her ACRs for initiation pertaining to the period 1999-2000. She was unaware that the ACR for 1999-2000 and subsequent period were kept pending by her initiating officer (IO). The petitioner contended that DIPAS, being a civil organization and her initiating officer who happened to be a scientist, had very little idea about the procedure laid down by the respondents for such initiation of ACRs of the officers belonging to AMC. The petitioner was not aware of the status of her ACRs for the period from 1999 to 2004. When petitioner received orders for movement to a new unit, the initiating officer (IO) told her to complete the CR forms for the period from 1999 to 2004 afresh for initiation. The DIPAS vide letter dated 15 March 2005 forwarded five ACRs pertaining to the petitioner to higher authorities through the proper channel, which the petitioner later learnt as she had already left for a new place of posting.

The petitioner was not considered for the promotion to the rank of Colonel by the promotion board held in the year 2008. On account of non-empanelment to the rank of Colonel, the petitioner made a statutory complaint and the same was pending since more than 10 months. That respondents contested that the ACRs for the years 1999-2000, 2000-2001 & 2001-2002 could not be endorsed and the same remained unendorsed and were considered to be technically invalid ACRs. Therefore, the case of the petitioner for promotion from Lt Col to the rank of Colonel had not been considered on the basis of earlier ACRs in the absence of the ACRs for the years 1999-2000, 2000-2001 & 2001-2002.

The Tribunal observed that the reason given by the respondents for not treating the ACRs for the period in question were not sustainable in view of the two circulars of the respondents dated 25 June1993 and 26 May 1998. Further, the action of the respondents by rendering three ACRs invalid was not justified and they are the valid ACRs and should have been taken into consideration for promotion from the rank of Lt Col to Colonel of petitioner. The Tribunal directed that the respondents will take into consideration the ACRs for the years 1999-2000, 2000-2001 and 2001-2002 as valid ACRs and shall consider the case of the petitioner afresh by calling the selection board and consider her case for promotion from the post of Lt Col to Colonel and if she was found fit, then all consequential benefits be given to her.

Adverse Remarks in ACR

The AFT Principal Bench in the case of *Col Rajesh Kapoor v. Union of India*, OA No. 113 of 2009 with MA No. 128 and 129 of 2011, decided on 30 May 2011, considered a petition for the rejection of annual confidential report.

The petitioner joined the Indian Army in 1979. He did his post-graduate diploma in Gynaecology and Obstetrics in the year 1986. On 7 May 2005, the Promotion Board (Medical) No. 3 was held and the petitioner was considered for promotion to the post of Colonel. However, the petitioner could not make it to the post of Colonel. Aggrieved against non-selection, the petitioner filed a non-statutory complaint on 29 August 2005 praying for review of all his annual ACRs considered for promotion to the rank of Colonel and expunging of any inaccuracy/inconsistency. Then again on 23 December 2005, the Promotion Board (Medical) No. 3 met and the petitioner was not promoted. However, his non-statutory complaint was not disposed of for more than 14 months and he came know that his ACR for 1996-97 was adverse but the same was not communicated to him. The petitioner filed a supplementary non-statutory complaint in the light of the adverse remarks against him on 14 December 2006 and objected that his adverse ACR should have been communicated to him. Then again, next Promotion Board met on 28 December 2006 and the petitioner was not selected. Remarks of the Senior Reviewing Officer area came in his way. On 5 April 2007, the non-statutory complaint of the petitioner was disposed of and partial relief was given to him by expunging his ACR for 1996-97 on the ground of inconsistency.

The petitioner contended that despite realizing the fact that the ACR for 1996-97 was not subjective, the respondents only granted partial relief on the ground of inconsistency. Further, the partial relief given by the respondents was not proper and his statutory complaint was rejected. The petitioner prayed that the ACR for 1996-97 should be completely expunged and he should be considered for promotion to the post of Colonel by the Review Selection Board.

The respondents contested that the remarks given by the RO and SRO have been completely expunged but the remarks given by the IO have not been expunged completely; only the remarks given in Item No. 12(d), 12(l) and 12(r) have been expunged being inconsistent. It was also submitted that after modification of this ACR, his case was again considered for promotion to the post of Colonel but again he could not make it.

The Tribunal examined the ACR of the petitioner for 1996-97 and observed that the IO had completely changed the entire figurative assessment and tampered with the ACR. Not only this, he had also not put his full signatures while changing the figurative assessment. The Tribunal commented that this conduct of the IO was highly reprehensible and....and this kind of behaviour cannot be expected from an officer. This will lead to losing of faith in the institution if the ACRs are being tampered in this manner. The tampering done by the IO was not warranted and was absolutely against the principles of natural justice. The Tribunal directed that the ACR for 1996-97 should not be considered and the case of the petitioner be taken afresh without the ACR for 1996-97.

III. Allotment, Vacation of Accomodation

Unauthorized occupation

The AFT Principal Bench New Delhi in the case of *Col NS Parmar v. Union of India*, OA No. 15 of 2013, decided on 15 May 2013, considered a prayer for quashing an order for vacation of government accommodation.

The petitioner was commissioned in the Army on 09 June 1984 in Infantry and while posted in active counter insurgency area in the North East, he got badly injured in an encounter with militants. He was awarded Sena Medal for Gallantry and was given 60% disability which was categorised as Battle Casualty. He was permanently downgraded to low medical category and due to his employability restrictions; he was posted as Commanding Officer, NCC Bn at Delhi. He served in the unit from 2003 to 2006, during which he retained the accommodation allotted at Manekshaw Marg, Delhi Cantt, as per his entitlement. In 2006 the petitioner got posted to NCC, Hapur which was a non-family station and therefore, he was allotted an alternative separated family accommodation also located at Manekshaw Marg, Delhi Cantt. This was occupied by the petitioner till February 2008 when he requested for a change of the accommodation which was permitted by respondent and he was allotted accommodation at Pratap Chowk, Delhi Cantt., which he took over on 04 February 2008.

Thereafter, the petitioner was got posted to Gujarat which was also a hard non-military station and was allowed to retain the same family accommodation vide order dated 21 April 2009. After having been posted from Gujarat to Kolkata, the petitioner applied for retention of the said accommodation on 10 December 2010 on children education ground which was allowed vide order dated 22 December 2010, whereby the petitioner was permitted to retain the said accommodation till 31March 2011. The petitioner again made an application vide letter dated 26 December 2010 for retention of the said accommodation from 01 April 2011 to 31 July 2012 on the ground that his daughter was studying in class XII. Meanwhile, the petitioner also applied for grant of study leave at Delhi which was sanctioned on 09 June 2011 by which the petitioner was permitted to proceed on study leave for two years w.e.f. 01 August 2011 to 30 July 2013. The petitioner applied for the retention of present accommodation at Delhi during his study leave period. The request made by the petitioner was rejected vide letter dated 21 August 2011 and he was informed that his request for grant of retention of this accommodation was not acceded to but he will be allotted alternative lower scale accommodation. The petitioner was declared an unauthorized occupant of premises at Pratap Chowk, Delhi Cantt, and was charged Ceiling Rate of rent during the unauthorized period.

The petitioner contended that the respondents were under an obligation to provide an accommodation when he officer was on study leave, of the same status as far as possible, and in case it is not available, they can also provide a house of lower scale. The Tribunal held that since the petitioner came back to Delhi on study leave, he will have to pay the ceiling rate of rent for occupation of house for the aforesaid period, as he was not entitled to retain this accommodation during study leave. The petition was dismissed.

IV. Appeal To Supreme Court

Leave to appeal

The Supreme Court in the case of *Union of India v. Brigadier P. S. Gill*, criminal appeal 564 of 2012; and *K. K. Awasthi v. Union of India* civil appeal 3046 of 2012 considered the maintainability of an appeal before it against a final decision and/or order of the Armed Forces Tribunal. The appellants had claimed that an appeal against the final orders or decisions of the Armed Forces Tribunal lies to the Supreme Court as a matter of right; and is not subject to provisions of sections 30 and 31 of the AFT Act. The question considered by the Court was whether an aggrieved party can file an appeal against any final decision or order of the Tribunal under section 30 of the Armed Forces Tribunal Act before the Supreme Court without taking resort to the procedure prescribed under section 31 of the Act.

The Supreme Court held that the Parliament has made a clear distinction between cases where an appeal lies as a matter of right and others where it lies subject to the provisions of section 31 of the Act. A plain reading of section

30 shows that it starts with the expression "subject to the provision of section 31", which is not an "ornamental or inconsequential" provision. The right of appeal under section 30 can be exercised only in the manner and to the extent it is provided for in section 31 to which said right is made subject.

(i) Subject to provision of section 31: Section 31 of the Act specifically provides for an appeal to the Supreme Court but stipulates two distinct routes for such an appeal. The first route to the Supreme Court is sanctioned by the Tribunal granting leave to file such an appeal. Section 31(1) in no uncertain terms forbids grant of leave to appeal to the Supreme Court unless the Tribunal certifies that a point of law of general public importance is involved in the decision. This implies that section 31 does not create a vested, indefeasible or absolute right of filing an appeal to the Supreme Court against a final order or decision of the Tribunal. Such an appeal must be preceded by the leave of the Tribunal and such leave must in turn be preceded by a certificate by the Tribunal that a point of law of general public importance is involved in the appeal.

The second and the only other route to access the Supreme Court is also found in section 31(1) itself. The expression "or it appears to the Supreme Court that the point is one which ought to be considered by that Court" empowers the Supreme Court to permit the filing of an appeal against any such final decision or order of the Tribunal. A conjoint reading of sections 30 and 31 can lead to only one conclusion that there is no vested right of appeal against a final order or decision of the Tribunal to the Supreme Court other than those falling under section 30 (2) of the Act.

(ii) As a matter of right: A plain reading of section 30 (2) makes it clear that unlike other final orders and decisions of the Tribunal, those passed in exercise of the Tribunal's jurisdiction to punish for contempt are appealable as of right. Provided such appeals are filed in the Supreme Court within 60 days from the date of the order appealed against.

The only mode to bring up the matter to the Supreme Court in appeal is either by way of certificate obtained from the Tribunal that decided the matter or by obtaining leave of the Court under section 31 for filing an appeal depending upon whether the Supreme Court considers the point involved in the case to be one that ought to be considered by the Court.

The Supreme Court also considered an incidental question whether an application for permission to file an appeal under section 31 can be moved directly before the Supreme Court without first approaching the Tribunal for a certificate in terms of the first part of section 31(1) of the Act. The Court held that a careful reading of the section 31 shows that it not only stipulates the period for making an application to the Tribunal for grant of leave to appeal to the Supreme Court but also stipulates the period for making an application to the Court for leave of the Court to file an appeal against the said order sought to be challenged. The period stipulated for filing application to the Supreme Court starts running from the date the application is made to the Tribunal for grant of certificate is refused by the Tribunal. This implies that the aggrieved party cannot approach the Supreme Court directly for grant of leave to file an appeal under section 31(1) read with section 31(2) of the Act.

The Supreme Court observed that the scheme of section 31 being that an application for grant of a certificate must first be moved before the Tribunal, before the aggrieved party can approach the Supreme Court for the grant of leave to file an appeal. The purpose underlying the provision appears to be that if the Tribunal itself grants a certificate of fitness for filing an appeal, it would be unnecessary for the aggrieved party to approach the Supreme Court for a leave to file such an appeal. An appeal by certificate would then be maintainable as a matter of right in view of section 30 which uses the expression "an appeal shall lie to the Supreme Court.

It was observed by the Apex Court that there were several other statutes in which an appeal is provided to the Supreme Court but such provisions are differently worded. For example the Advocates Act, 1961, the Customs Act, 1962 and the Central Excise Act, 1944 provide that an appeal shall lie to the Supreme Court using words different from those that have been used in sections 30 and 31 of the Armed Forces Tribunal Act. It is one of the settled canons of interpretation of statutes that every clause of a statute should be construed with respect to the context and the other clauses of the Act, so far as possible to make a consistent enactment of the whole statute or series relating to the subject.

Leave to appeal, barred by limitation

The Armed Forces Tribunal Bench Chandigarh in *Dimple Singla v. Union of India*, in MA 798 and 799 of 2012 in OA 108 of 2010, decided on 25 July 2012, refused to grant the leave to appeal to the Supreme Court under section 31 of the Armed Forces Tribunal Act, 2007, as the applicant failed to move the petition within 30 days from the date of decision of the Tribunal. The Bench held that the application has been filed beyond that period, and was barred by limitation.

Leave to appeal; not of general public importance

The AFT Principal Bench New Delhi in the case of *Ex Lt Col S S Bedi v. Union of India* MA Nos. 266 and 265 of 2012 in TA No. 246 of 2010 [WP (C) No. 1824 of 1988 of Delhi High Court] decided on 30 May 2012 considered a prayer for the grant of leave to appeal before the Apex Court under section 31 of the AFT Act.

The Tribunal vide the final order dated 01 October 2010 upheld the conviction of the applicant on both the charges, but converted the punishment and sentence of cashiering into fine of Rs. 50,000. Feeling aggrieved by the said judgment and order the respondents preferred Civil Appeal No. 36276 /2011 before the Supreme Court, which was dismissed on the basis of the judgment passed in case of *Union of India v. Brigadier P.S. Gill* and permitted the applicant to approach the Tribunal for obtaining its permission under section 31 of the AFT Act, 2007 to file appeal before the Supreme Court.

The respondents contended that looking to the charges against the applicant; the Tribunal was not justified in setting aside the sentence of cashiering. The applicant, who had abused his position and committed the offences of outraging the modesty of wives of the army jawans did not required any leniency. He also submitted that the applicant was a doctor, who had betrayed the trust of patient. It was also contended that the observation of the Tribunal that the punishment of cashiering could not have been awarded for an offence under section 69 of the Army Act read with section 354 of the IPC was not correct, therefore, these issues are of general public importance and permission to file the appeal while condoning the delay may be granted.

The Tribunal, considering the scope of section 31 and the submissions made, was of the view that the issues raised by respondents were not of general public importance and rejected the petition along with the application for condonation of delay.

General public importance

The AFT Principal Bench New Delhi, Court No. 2 in the case of *Ex Col A K Kadian v. Union of India* MA Nos. 253 & 252 of 2012 in TA No. 245 of 2010 [WP (C) No. 830 of 2002 of Delhi High Court] decided on 1 June 2012 considered an application for granting permission to file appeal before the Supreme Court against the judgment dated 24 May 2011 passed by the Tribunal.

The applicant, during the course of submissions contended that the period of limitation in initiating general court martial (GCM) proceedings was not properly considered by the Tribunal as the GCM was time barred. He further contended that court of inquiry report was submitted on 14 August 1995 and GCM was convened on 08 September 1998, therefore, it is presumed that the competent authority had considered the court of inquiry and had knowledge of the offence. Counting the period from the presentation of the court of inquiry, the GCM was time barred. The applicant further contended that likewise, the Tribunal had not given due attention towards section 313 of the Cr PC *para materia* Army Rule 58 to explain the adverse material to applicant during GCM. Further, the Tribunal had not considered the appointment of Judge Advocate, who was junior to the applicant. He submitted that these points were not considered by the Tribunal which were pertaining to public importance. Therefore, considering these points as of general public importance, permission be granted to file appeal before the Supreme Court. He also contended that on the grounds stated in the application for condonation of delay, the period of delay in filing the application under section 31 of the AFT Act, may also be condoned.

The Tribunal examined the submissions made by the applicant as well as respondent and came to conclusion that no question of general public importance was involved in the judgement and for that there is no justifiable ground for the Tribunal to grant permission to file appeal before the Supreme Court.

V. Appeal To Armed Forces Tribunal

Excessive delay, Time barred

The AFT Principal Bench New Delhi, Court No. 2, in the case of *Hav Surat Singh v. Union of India*, OA No. 433 of 2011, decided on 20 March 2012, refused to condone the delay in filing OA under section 22 of the Armed Forces Tribunal Act, 2007. In this case the applicant was discharged in 1999 and he filed the application after nearly 22 years. The Tribunal held that the grounds stated in condonation of delay application were found not sustainable. The Tribunal in a similar case of *Sep. Bijendra Singh Kushwah v. Union of India* (OA No.154/2011) on 17 October 2011 had dismissed the application as time barred.

Time barred

The AFT Principal Bench New Delhi, Court No. 2, in *Sepoy Raghubir Singh Tomar v. Union of India*, OA No. 142 of 2012, decided on 7 November 2012, considered the reinstatement of the petitioner, based on acquittal by High Court of Madhya Pradesh.

The petitioner was enrolled on 29 October 1990. He was married in the year 1995. Unfortunately his wife died on 15 September 2000 for which he faced a charge of dowry death under Section 304-B, and was convicted by the Court of Additional Sessions Judge, Gwalior on 31 July 2001. Based on that conviction, on the same day, the army authorities passed an order, discharging the petitioner from service, stating that his services were no longer required due to the aforesaid conviction. It was communicated to the applicant through letter dated 18 March 2003. The petitioner challenged that conviction before the High Court, which acquitted him vide judgment dated 28 February 2008.

The petitioner thereupon approached the authorities for reinstatement, and he was informed vide letter dated 18 October 2008 that it was not feasible to reinstate him back in military service, as he had already completed his terms of engagement on 29 October 2007, *i.e.,* before issue of court order dated 22 February 2008 (17 years as a Sepoy) and that the judgment of High Court does not contain a direction to reinstate the petitioner back into Military service. In this connection, the petitioner relied on the judgment of the AFT Principal Bench in *Hav Deshpal v. Union of India* OA No. 74 of 2011, dated 09 January 2012. The petitioner also contended that after acquittal the respondents cannot come with the spacious ground of the petitioner being in jail with other criminals, as this aspect has also been settled by the Armed Forces Tribunal in *Lance Naik Binod Ray v. Union of India* OA No.118 of 2011.

The Tribunal observed that the petitioner has given no valid explanation for delay of almost two years in approaching the Tribunal and dismissed the petition as time barred.

VI. Boards and Court of Inquiry

Violation of Army Rule 180

The AFT Principal Bench New Delhi in the case of *Lt. Gen. Avadhesh Prakash (retd.) v. Union of India* OA No. 66 of 2010, decided on 22 February 2010, considered the rights of a military person under Army Rule 180.

The Tribunal held that the court of inquiry is only a preliminary inquiry,....nonetheless, the law has emphasized that the incumbent should be given full opportunity and should be present throughout.... that principles of natural justice are followed. The principles of natural justice depend upon variable factors and it also varies from situation to situation. But, the concept of the fair hearing is ingrained in our system, be it administration or in our judicial system. The attempt should be to promote justice and fair play in all adjudicatory functions.

The Tribunal referred to its earlier decision in *Lt. Gen. Surendra Kumar Sahni v. Union of India* [TA No. 34 of 2009] and the Delhi High Court's decision in the case of in *Lt. Gen. Surendra Kumar Sahni v. Chief of Army Staff* [2008 (3) SLR 39]. It concluded that Army Rule 180 clearly stipulates that throughout the court of inquiry full opportunity should be given to incumbent including the right to cross-examine or examine any witness. The requirement under Army Rule 180 is mandatory.

***

The AFT Principle Bench New Delhi, Court No. 2, in the case of *Ex Lt Col B K Mall v. Union of India*, TA No. 512 of 2009 [WP (C) No. 4539 of 1999], decided on 22 September 2011, considered a prayer for letter of termination from service.

The applicant was commissioned into the Army 22 December 69. On 27 August 1988 he was posted as the Station Staff Officer (SSO) in the rank of Major at Bhatinda. Col R C D Joshi was posted to the same place as the Administrative Commandant. As per the Standard Operating Procedure (SOP), the applicant was appointed as the Canteen Officer. One retired officer, Col Singla, who was re-employed, was attached to the Station HQ Bhatinda and he was deputed to look after the CSD Canteen and to assist the SSO. On 21 December 1990, the applicant was promoted as Lt Col Time Scale (TS).

On 5 May 1991, the applicant was posted to 116 GL Section and was relieved by Major K A Singh. During the handing/taking over, all the stocks in the Canteen were checked and found to be correct. It is revealed from the record that there were some allegations of financial irregularities in Canteen management.

On 30 July 1993, a court of inquiry was convened to investigate the same in which the applicant was called as a witness. Army Rule 180 was not applied. On completion of the inquiry in October 1994, the applicant, alongwith some others, was held responsible for the losses which were detected during the inquiry. Consequently, the applicant was directed to deposit vide order dated 29 September 1994 a sum of Rs. 41899.53, which was deposited by him. No further action was suggested at that time.

On 30 January 1996, consequent to the recommendations of the inquiry, a show cause notice was issued to the applicant asking him as to why his services should not be terminated. Paragraph 5 of the show cause notice stated: "In consideration of the fact that the case has become time barred for disciplinary action by way of Court Martial; and in view of your confirmed weak moral fibre and unreliability in financial matters, the Chief of the Army Staff has decided that your further retention in service is not desirable."

The applicant replied to the show cause notice on 23 May 1996 in which he agitated that he had already made up the deemed losses by depositing a sum of Rs. 41899.53 and therefore, he was already punished and thus, the show cause notice was irrelevant. In his reply, he also made an averment that he was in supervisory capacity which was consequent to his designation as the SSO and therefore, was not directly responsible for the deemed losses. He further stated in the reply that he had only one year left before he would superannuate on 30 June 1997. The respondents considered his reply to the show cause notice but did not find satisfaction and his services were terminated by the MOD vide their order dated 14 February 1997.

On 22 October 1997, another show cause notice was issued by the Ministry of Defence (MOD) to the applicant which sought reasons for why his pensionary benefits that were admissible to him, had he retired from the service on the same date in the normal course, should not be forfeited. The applicant replied to this second show cause notice on 07 November 1997 and made an averment that he had already deposited Rs. 41,899.53 with the Government in order to make up the deemed losses. Further, that his services were terminated w.e.f. 06 March1997 by the MOD vide their letter dated 14 February 1997, which did not mention forfeiture of pensionary benefits. In case the pensionary benefits were forfeited, the applicant would suffer three times penalty for the same cause of action. However, the Ministry of Defence vide letter dated 18 May 1998 ordered the forfeiture of entire pensionary benefits entitled to the applicant.

The applicant contended that the GOC-in-C had recommended in the court of inquiry for disciplinary action on 27 April 1994 which was besides the penal deduction in order to make good the losses. However, for the reasons best known to the respondents, no disciplinary action was taken. On the other hand administrative action was taken and his services were terminated after serving him the show cause notice. Para 5 of the show cause notice clearly showed that the reason for taking administrative action instead of disciplinary action was because the case was getting time barred. Further, the dismissal order issued by the Central Government on 14 February 1997 was not a speaking order and without having considered the averments and pleas made by the applicant in his reply to the show cause notice of 30 January 1996.

The applicant also contended that in the court of inquiry which was conducted in August 1993, the applicant was only called as a witness. Army Rule 180 was not applied and therefore, to call upon the applicant to deposit the money for the deemed losses and subsequently using the same material for issuing a show cause notice for dismissal of service was prejudicial and violative of laws laid down by the various courts. In support of their contention, the petitioner referred to the decisions of the Delhi High Court in *Lt Gen S.K. Dahiya v. Union of India*, Mil LJ 2007 Del 151 and *Surendra Kumar Sahni v. Chief of Army Staff* (Delhi) 2008(3) SLR, where in the Court had held that Army Rule 180 is mandatory in character due to the word 'must' used in the Rule; Court of Inquiry proceedings vitiated on account of violation of Rule 180; the compliance to the requirements of Rule 180 was mandatory. The language of the Rule is certain and unambiguous, capable of only one interpretation i.e. that to afford a full opportunity in terms of this provision is the responsibility of the competent authority.

The respondents contested that the Court of Inquiry was of a general nature to find about the losses that accrued in the CSD Canteen. The applicant was called by the Court of Inquiry just to give evidence. It was only on the conclusion of the Court of Inquiry that the authorities realized that the applicant was responsible for the losses to a certain extent by virtue of poor supervision/negligence. He further contested that the Show Cause Notice was issued which gave out the detailed gravamen of the charges against the applicant. The respondents in support of issuance of notice for forfeiting the pensionary benefits referred the decision of the Supreme Court in the case of *Union of India v. P D Yadav (2002) 1 SCC 405.*

The Tribunal observed that nature of the court of inquiry and the tasking for the inquiry was such that perhaps it would not have been possible at the initial stages to incorporate the names of all the people involved. The names emerged only during the deposition by the witnesses. It was, therefore, required that the Court should have summoned the individuals for compliance of Army Rule 180, in whose case character and military reputation was involved. The provisions of Army Rule 180 should have been complied with as and when individuals were named and involved. In this case during inquiry the name of the applicant came and he was found involved and at that stage Army Rule 180 should have been applied.

The Tribunal was of the opinion that though court of inquiry is a fact finding body and any discrepancy in its proceedings as long as substantial compliance has been carried out and the investigation does not prejudice the accused in the subsequent trial proceedings, the infirmities can be over-looked. However, in this case, the subsequent action of the respondents to punish the applicant has been based totally on the court of inquiry proceedings. Copy of the court of inquiry proceedings were also not supplied to the applicant alongwith the notice. It was evident that in the absence of the copy of court of inquiry, the applicant was not in a position to prepare his defence in a fair and adequate manner and thus he had been prejudiced. The Tribunal referred to the Delhi High Court decision in the case of *Major Harbhajan Singh v. Ministry of Defence*, All India Services Law Journal 1982 (2) page 120:

> ".....A highly commendable provision is made in Rule 180 to give full opportunity of being heard even in this fact finding proceeding. When a Court of Inquiry affects the character or military reputation or a person, he is given full opportunity (i) of being present throughout the inquiry, (ii) making any statement, (iii) giving of any evidence, (iv) cross examining any witnesses and (v) producing any witnesses in defence of his character or military reputation. The Presiding officer of the Court is obliged by the said Rule to make the delinquent officer "fully understand his rights" under this rule.....
>
> 15. I, therefore, hold that the findings of guilt against the petitioner recorded by Court of Inquiry are vitiated by the facts that the relevant witnesses were not procured by the Court for ascertaining the existence of relevant facts and by denying the opportunity of citing defence witnesses to the petitioner. The evidence of other witnesses for prosecution was found sufficient by the Court of Inquiry for holding that the prosecution case was proved but the legal infirmity is that the defence evidence was not allowed and assessment was one sided. 16. Since the findings of the Court of Inquiry are vitiated and since they form the basis of Show Cause Notice, the Show Cause Notice also stands vitiated for this reason.
>
> 18. For the reasons stated above, the writ petition is allowed, with costs."

The Tribunal quashed the proceedings of the court of inquiry and all consequent actions i.e., order of termination of service dated 14 February 1997 and order of forfeiture of pension dated 18 May 1998. The Tribunal ordered that the applicant will be deemed to be in service till his superannuation. All consequential benefits including pensionary benefits shall accrue. The respondents are, however, free to initiate the departmental action and/or disciplinary action as deemed fit without taking recourse to the said court of inquiry. They are also free to take departmental and/or administrative action against the applicant after having rectified the legal infirmities in the said court of inquiry. The exercise to pay the monetary dues to the applicant to be completed within 180 days failing which the amount will attract 12% interest till the date of payment.

***

The AFT Principal Bench New Delhi in the case of *Lt Col Prasad Purohit v. Union of India* OA No. 485 of 2010, decided on 9 March 2011, directed the respondents to reconvene the court of inquiry from the stage when the statements of the witnesses were recorded in absence of the appellant, and to afford opportunity to the applicant to cross examine the witnesses. The applicant had contended that he was not afforded a full and fair opportunity of being present throughout the recording of court of inquiry and to cross examine the witnesses, thereby violating Army Rule 180.

***

The AFT Regional Bench Kochi in the case of *Lt Gen Gurjit Singh Dhillon v. Union of India*, TA No. 195 of 2010 [WP (C) No. 25964 of 2009, High Court of Karnataka] decided on 26 November 2010, considered the convening order by which a court of inquiry was constituted.

In June 2008 a court of inquiry was assembled by the GOC-in-C, Western Command to investigate into the irregularities and illegalities in the registration of firms. The Convening Order was signed by an officer of the rank of Brigadier on behalf of the GOC-in-C, Western Command. The Petitioner, on receipt of intimation, appeared before the court of inquiry on 6 and 7 of October 2008 and was examined as witness No. 13. Thereafter the petitioner received intimation on 29 June 2009 to appear as a witness before the court of inquiry which was re-assembling at Delhi on 20 July 2009. The petitioner appeared before the court on the said date and was orally informed that provisions of Army Rule 180 were invoked against him. The petitioner filed a representation questioning the validity of the constitution of court of inquiry, contending that constitution of court was contrary to Army Rule 177(3), and in violation of the provisions of Para 518 of the Regulations for the Army, 1987.

The Tribunal observed that Army Rule 177(3) specifically provides that a court of inquiry should be assembled by an officer in command of the troops. Para 518 of the Regulations for the Army specifically provides that convening order should ensure that the court is be composed of the Presiding Officer who is senior in rank and Members at least of the equivalent rank to that of the person whose character and military reputation is likely to be a material issue. The petitioner was holding the rank of Lieutenant General (Substantive) with effect from 18 July 2008. The Presiding Officer of the court of inquiry was of the rank of Major General, one rank below that of the petitioner. The other members of the court were of the rank of Brigadier, two ranks below that of the petitioner.

The Tribunal further observed that the purpose of re-convening the court of inquiry was only to comply with the provisions of Army Rule 180. It held that the entire proceeding of the court of inquiry were illegal and unsustainable. The Tribunal set aside the court of inquiry proceedings with the direction that the competent authorities were free to re-consider the matter and proceed in accordance with law.

Cross examine in administrative inquiries

The AFT Principal Bench, New Delhi, Court No. 2 in the case of *Brig LI Singh v. Union of India*, OA No. 85 of 2013, decided on 21 March 2013, considered a prayer quashing a preliminary inquiry.

An inquiry was initiated against the petitioner for borrowing money from contractors of units and from subordinate officers. It was also alleged that he has taken away official property of the Flag Staff House prior to relinquishing his appointment. On the basis of the inquiry, which was initiated against the applicant, a decision was taken to hold court of inquiry against him. The Court of Inquiry was initiated in terms of Army Rule 180 and had been concluded. Consequently an order was passed on 25 February 2013 whereby the petitioner was attached to the HQ for the purpose of facing disciplinary proceedings.

The petitioner contended that the nature of complaint, which was referred to one man committee, was not disclosed to him. His further contention was that during the course of the court of inquiry, he did not have the occasion to cross examine the witnesses as the previous statement of these witnesses, which were recorded by one man inquiry committee were not made available to him. The petitioner has been prejudiced in this behalf as his right to cross examine the witnesses was denied to him on account of non availability of the previous statements made by the witnesses.

The Tribunal was of the view that there was no reason for the Tribunal to intervene with the order of holding disciplinary proceedings against the petitioner. Respondents had the right to initiate disciplinary action against the petitioner and the same cannot be scuttled at this stage. The only statutory provision which deals with the holding of an inquiry was under Army Rule 180. There was no statutory provision which provides for holding of a preliminary inquiry. The said preliminary inquiry, which according to the petitioner has been held is only administrative in nature and was intended to find out prima facie material for holding court of inquiry under Army Rule 180. The petitioner was entitled to the safeguards only in respect of the inquiry which were conducted under Army Rule 180. The Tribunal thus dismissed the petition.

VII. Commission

Grant of permanent commission

The AFT Principal Bench New Delhi in the case of *Sqn Ldr R Bhusal v. Union of India,* TA No. 511 of 2010 [WP (C) 8037 of 2002], decided on 15 May 2013, considered a prayer for the grant of permanent commission.

The petitioner joined the Air Force as a Trainee Pilot in helicopters in October 1991 after qualifying in the competitive examination, with an option that he will be considered for permanent commission when his short service commission term was over. On 20 February 1993, the petitioner was commissioned after successfully completing his training and ranked as Pilot Officer and subsequently as Fg Offr and Flt Lt in 1997.

On 17 May 2000, the petitioner was on an aerial mission of "Search & Rescue" Operation of another crashed Helicopter, when his Helicopter also developed some snag and crashed. This was attributed to engine failure due to overheating and failure of turbine blades. The petitioner sustained injury i.e.

compression fracture of the spine and was placed in Low Medical Category. The matter was investigated by a court of inquiry and on 26 December 2000, the Chief of the Air Staff absolved him of any responsibility for the crash and held that no one could be blamed for the accident and the injuries received by the petitioner were attributable to service.

On 11 April 2002, while the petitioners release order from service was issued, his contemporaries, similarly situated, were given permanent commission. The petitioner was medically examined on 24 July 2002 by a Release Medical Board. Thereafter, petitioner filed an appeal against the order dated 17 August 2002 for denial of permanent commission. The petitioner, on 26 August 2002 was given promotion to the rank of Squadron Leader (Acting) in Low Medical Category (T).

The petitioner filed an appeal against the denial of permanent commission, which was rejected by the respondent. The petitioner thereafter filed writ petition before the Delhi High Court against his denial of permanent commission. The Delhi High Court held that SSC Officers are treated at par with Permanent Commission officers in all respects as per terms and conditions dated 13 July 1990 issued by Government of India and it held that the criteria of 6.5 marks is not sustainable in law, not being in conformity with para 915 of the Regulations for the Air Force, 1964. The writ petition was allowed and release order was quashed, with the directions that the respondent's to grant permanent commission to the petitioner. The operative portion of order read:

> "We fail to understand that on the one hand petitioner was promoted to the post of Squadron Leader on the basis of grading of 5 and above in August 2002 but he has been denied permanent commission on the basis of a policy which we have already said cannot be construed to be a policy in terms of rules and regulations framed under the Air Force Act. In the circumstances, we quash the orders dated 11 April 2002 as well as 23 December 2002 of the respondents, and direct the respondents to grant the petitioner a permanent commission. However, it is left open to the respondents to provide alternate employability in their own discretion, keeping in view the medical fitness of the petitioner."

Against this decision, a SLP was filed before the Supreme Court. The operative portion of the order of the Supreme Court read:

> "High Court's consideration of the writ petition filed by the respondent and conclusions arrived at were beyond the pleadings. The High Court acted on certain materials and purported concession without examining whether that concession was well founded and whether the appellant got an opportunity to clarify the position as regards the applicability of the regulations which according to the High Court had application. The basic challenge in the writ petition was that the medical deficiency found by the appellant was not properly assessed. In the counter, affidavit, the specific stand of the appellant-Union of India was that the medical deficiency was only one of the factors while assessing suitability for

permanent commission. The Union of India's specific stand was that the performance criteria fixed under the applicable policy regulations was not fulfilled by the respondent. In the rejoinder affidavit filed, there was no specific challenge as to the applicability of the either criteria or policy regulations. Therefore, we find no substance in the plea of learned counsel for the respondent that though the High Court apparently travelled beyond the pleadings, its conclusions are justified in law. In the fitness of things, the High Court should re-hear the matter. We make it clear that we have not expressed any opinion on the acceptability of the plea raised by the respondent in the writ petition. If the High Court so feels, it may permit the parties to place further materials in respect of their respective stand. Learned counsel for the appellant submits that by virtue of interim order the respondent is continuing in service. Keeping that in view, we request the High Court to explore the possibility of disposing of the writ petition within a period of four months from the date of receipt of our order."

The WP came back before the Delhi High Court which was subsequently amended and prayers were modified. The main grievance of petitioner was denial of Permanent Commission in Indian Air Force. The interim order of stay by the Delhi High Court remained in force, and after the WP was transformed to the Tribunal.

The petitioner contended that a number of officers who were downgraded from flying duties were given extension and permanent commission, while the opportunity was denied to him.

Further, the injury received by him was attributable to military service. He was suitable to be transferred to any other branch.

The respondents contested that the petitioner was commissioned as a Short Service Commission Officer (helicopter pilot) on 20 February 1993 for an initial tenure of ten years, this ended on 19 February 2003. Petitioner's case was considered for grant of permanent commission in February, 2001 along with his course mates by a duly constituted Board of Officers, headed by an Air Commodore. For grant of permanent commission, petitioner was assessed on demonstrated performance and medical fitness. Since the petitioner did not meet the minimum performance criteria specified for grant of Permanent Commission, both in terms of average AR grading and grading in one of the mandatory qualities, he was therefore, recommended to be released.

The Tribunal did not find any irregularity in the release of the appellant by the Air Force. So far as grant of alternative employment was concerned, the Tribunal observed that it was a social measure but has to be governed by rules and applied uniformly. However, despite the government not granting him any alternative employment, the petitioner had remained in service by virtue of the stay order granted by the Delhi High Court, which was still in force. The petitioner was still in service and had already put in more than 20 years service and was holding the rank of Squadron Leader.

The Tribunal directed that the appellant be released from Air Force and pensionary benefits be given to him as he had already completed more than 20 years of service.

VIII. Disability Pension

The AFT Principal Bench New Delhi in the case of *Jai Bhagwan Sharma v. Union of India*, OA No. 569 of 2010, decided on 24 November 2011, considered a prayer for the sanction of disability pension. The Petitioner was enrolled in Navy in 1965 and had taken part in Indo Pak War in 1971. He served in the Navy till 1973. During the service, the petitioner suffered a head injury when there was a sudden burst of high pressure steam pipe in the engine room of the ship. Over a period of time, he started suffering from frequent bout of severe headaches which led to Neurological complications. He was hospitalized for a long time during 1972-1973 and was finally boarded out of the Navy in Medical Category EEE w.e.f. 04 June 1973. At the time of discharge, he was diagnosed as "Neurosis" and his disability was assessed at 20% attributed to Military Service. He was granted disability pension of Rs. 59/- per month from 05 June 1973 to 07 March 1975 and Rs. 50/- per month from 08 March 1975 for life was sanctioned in 1973. He was hospitalized twice in 1974 and 1975 and had frequent attacks of cerebral seizures. Then he got himself examined at Senior Neurologist who treated him and saved his life. After his medical condition stabilized, he was referred to AIIMS, New Delhi for clinical investigations and treatment. At AIIMS, the petitioner was examined on 06 September 1990 and was found handicapped to the extent of 75%. He was under the treatment for life time. His vision had also become very weak.

The petitioner contended that when he visited the Pension Distribution Officer, Delhi for yearly identification in June 2002, he discovered that the disability pension had two elements i.e. disability element and service element and that the payment of disability element of his pension had been discontinued since 08 March 1975 without any reason and any intimation to him. Since, the petitioner did not receive any response for payment of disability element from 1975, he filed a writ before the Delhi High Court of Delhi in December, 2002 for the payment of arrears and reassessment of the disability percentage.

The writ petition was disposed of on 20 December 2002 and the respondents were directed to decide the representations of the Petitioner within a period of three months. That order was not adhered to then Petitioner sent a legal notice dated 26 August 2003 seeking compliance of the order. Petitioner received a letter from the Navy on 12 September 2003, stating that all the medical documents had been traced and forwarded to the Base Hospital, Delhi Cantonment for a fresh opinion by the Medical Board and was directed to report to the Base Hospital accordingly. His medical however, never reached the base Hospital. Ultimately, on 12 January 2004 he was admitted to a ward of the Base Hospital, Delhi Cantonment but the staff of the hospital did not confirm whether his medical documents had been received or not. He was kept in hospital for 48 hours but no examination or tests were conducted and he was discharged on 14 January 2004, without any Re-Survey Medical Board having been held. The Petitioner received a communication from respondent on 24 March 2005 informing him that he was granted disability element pension of Rs. 310/- from 14 January 2004 for life. He made several representations for increase in disability pension but without any result.

The Tribunal made adverse remarks on the functioning of the respondents for not sending petitioner's medical documents in to the Base Hospital. It held that the petitioner was entitled to interest @12% from 1975 when disability was diagnosed till he was released revised PPO i.e. 23 November 2011. It directed that the amount should be calculated by the respondents and released within a period of three months from the date of the order. For the pension from 1975 to till date, the Tribunal directed that the petitioner was entitled to 20% disability element of pension from 1975 for life and all the arrears to be paid to him within three months with an interest @12% from 1975 when disability was diagnosed.

Battle Casualty: disability pension

The AFT Principal Bench in the case of *Hav Rajvir v. Union of India*, OA No. 228 of 2011, decided on 4 April 2013, considered a prayer for declaring injury as battle casualty.

The petitioner was enrolled in the Indian Army on 28 August 1990 and on 06 July 1999 during the Operation Vijay i.e. Kargil Operation, while transporting the casualties from Pimple Complex, Mashkoh Valley, he received a knee injury. He immediately reported to the MI Room and he was given certain medical treatment and thereafter he was sent to the rear area. The injury was diagnosed as "Tear Medial Menicus (Lt) Knee". He was treated and necessary medical treatment was administered to him. Thereafter, he was transferred to Lucknow where he again felt pain in the knee and a court of inquiry was held. In the court of inquiry, it was opined that he sustained the injury during the Operation Vijay and the injury was attributable to military service in field. Part-II order of the unit was also published. Thereafter, he was declared as a medical category A-3(permanent) but his injury was not declared a battle casualty. He made a representation to the higher authorities but without any result.

The respondents contested that the battle casualty was guided by the parameters laid down in the Army Order 1/2003 and since the petitioner did not meet the parameter No. 2(viii), therefore, he could not be treated as a battle casualty as there is no parallel connection between the date of casualty and date of reporting of casualty. The petitioner's case for treating his injury as a battle casualty was rejected by order dated 10 December 2010.

The petitioner contended that the Army Order 1/2003 had no relevance far his case as it was issued in 2003 whereas he received the injury on 06 July 1999. The relevant circular applicable in his case was SAO 8/S/85 and para 4(iv) of the order defined the battle casualty as: "(iv) Accidental injuries and deaths which occur in action in an operational area will be treated as battle casualties."

The Tribunal held that the applicant sustained the injury in operational area, therefore, this injury to be treated as a battle casualty. The Tribunal directed that a certificate to this effect may be issued to the petitioner and published in Part-II Order; and consequential benefits to be paid to the petitioner within three months.

Disability attributable to service

The AFT Bench Chandigarh in *Ved Prakash v. Union of India, OA No 1960 of 2012*, decided on 3 August 2012, considered a bunch of applications involving a common question of law. The applicants were retired, superannuation, or discharged military personnel; and at the time of discharge, they were carrying disability, attributable to or aggravated by military service, and to the extent of not less than 20 per cent. Some of the individuals in the petition were discharged prior to 01 January 1996, while others were discharged after 01 January 1996. These individuals claimed to be entitled to the benefit of "rounding off" or "broad-banding", as introduced by the Government of India vide letter dated 31 January 2001.

The Tribunal observed that in terms of the letter dated 31 January 2001, it applied to only those persons, who were in service as on or after 01 January 1996, and did not apply to others, which gave rise to a spate of litigation all around, which litigation finally culminated in favour of the individuals, by concluding, that the benefit is available to all individuals, irrespective of the fact that they were in service on 01 January 1996 or not. The Bench held that in view of the judgments rendered by the Supreme Court; the Government of India vide letter dated 29 February 2012, had extended the benefit of the letter dated 31 January 2001 to all persons alike, irrespective of the individual(s) being in service or not as on 01 January 1996. The concept of "broad banding" envisages disability assessed at 20% to below 50% to be taken as 50%, 50% to below 75% as 75% and 75% and above as 100% for all consequent benefits.

The controversy involved in the cases was, as to whether this benefit of "broad-banding" was available to all such persons, who have been discharged in whatever circumstances, with attributable or aggravated disability, or is available to only those individuals, who have been discharged with attributable or aggravated disability, not below the specified extent, but in particular specified, limited set of circumstances only?

The benefit of broad-banding was not made available to such individuals, who retired voluntarily or were discharged on request, or who were discharged on completion of service limits, or on completion of term of engagement, or on attaining the prescribed age of retirement. In other words, though these expressions were not used in so many words, and may not be the precise or correct expressions, yet to put it loosely, the benefit of broad-banding was sought to be given only to those persons, whose tenure of service was "cut-short" on account of the disability, and is not made available to others.

The Bench referred to the three decisions of the Supreme Court:

1. *Lt Col (Retd) P.K. Kapur v. Union of India*, Civil Appeal No. 4356 of 2006, decided on 01 February 2007, wherein the petitioner was said to have not been "invalided out", and, therefore, it was held that he was not entitled to the benefit of concept of invalidment and broad banding.
2. *K.J.S. Buttar v. Union of India*, Civil Appeal No. 5591 of 2006, decided on 31 March 2011, wherein, after considering the provisions of Regulation 53 of the Pension Regulations the Supreme Court held, that a person who was discharged by retirement on completion of terms of service with a disability, was held to be "invalided out", and was held entitled to the benefit of "broad-banding".

   There was thus is a direct conflict between the two judgments of the Supreme Court, one rendered in P.K. Kapur's case, and the other one rendered in K.J.S. Buttar's case.
3. The Supreme Court, in the case of *Union of India v. Nk Narikar*, Civil Appeals No. 8433 and 8434 of 2009, decided on 25 April 2012; considered the judgment relating to the benefit of "broad-banding" given by the judgment of Delhi High Court. The judgment of the Delhi High Court was set aside, by referring to, rather quoting, a paragraph from the judgment from P.K. Kapur's case, and by holding, that in Narikar's case also, as the individual had completed his tenure in the Army service, and retired, his case was squarely covered by the judgment in P. K. Kapur's case, and, therefore, is not entitled to the relief granted by the High Court.

The Bench adjudicated on the direct conflict of opinion between the two judgments rendered by the Supreme Court in P.K. Kapur's case and K.J.S. Buttar's case. It held that "Broad-Banding" was never intended or desired to be confined to any particular category or categories of persons only. It was intended for universal application across the spectrum. It held that that the view taken by the Supreme Court in K.J.S. Buttar's case addresses the issue comprehensively and is required to be followed by us. The Bench also granted leave to the Government of India for appeal to the Supreme Court under section 31 of the Armed Forces Tribunal Act, 2007 as issue was related to the two conflicting judgments, and also involved the substantial questions of general importance required to be finally adjudicated by the Supreme Court.

Disability pension: injury sustained during annual leave

The AFT Regional Bench Kolkata, in the case of *Akhila Bihar Singh v. Union of India*, TA No. 134 of 2010, decided on 7 March 2012, considered a prayer for the sanction of disability pension.

The petitioner was enrolled in the Army on 21 January 1974. The petitioner while on annual leave from 8 January 1979 to 12 March 1979 met with an accident with a two-wheeler. He was evacuated to a government hospital and was treated for fracture of his leg from 5 March to 26 March 1979. He was later shifted to the Command Hospital Calcutta and remained under treatment from 27 March to 28 September 1979 and then sent on sick leave till 24 November 1979. He continued in service and was placed in permanent low medical category for 'fracture tibia fibula' in left leg (OPTD). In 1981, he was subjected to release medical board at HM Meerut which assessed his disability as 40% for duration of 2 years, but opinion on attributability/aggravation due to military service was left vague.

He was discharged from the service w.e.f. 28 May 1981 after rendering approximately 7 years of service on account of being in the low medical category under Army Rule 13 (iii) (v). The petitioner was not sanctioned any pension for not having put in minimum pensionable service and was also denied disability pension. His appeal submitted on the authorities, on the orders of the Orissa High Court, was also rejected by the government on 20 May 1996 on the grounds that he sustained the injury while on annual leave in a motor cycle accident. Being aggrieved, the appellant once again approached the Orissa High Court.

The petitioner contended that the contention of the respondent authorities was not judicious and hence the impugned order be quashed and he should be sanctioned disability pension @ 40% as awarded by the medical board. He also urged for quashing of Army Group Insurance letter 25 May 1983, which had denied disability cover under the Army Group Insurance Scheme on the grounds that he was not invalidated out of service on medical grounds but was discharge from the service.

The Tribunal observed that no inquiry was held to ascertain as how the petitioner sustained injury on 5 March 1979. Therefore, it was difficult to ascertain as to how the authorities concluded that the individual was not entitled to any disability pension. Further, the medical board had mentioned that "attributability to be decided by the CDA(P) in the absence of injury report." In paragraph 21 of Part IV of the release medical board proceeding on from AFMS16 dated 31 March 1981, the board had clearly mentioned that the petitioner was recommended for the disability pension.

The Tribunal was of the opinion that the injury sustained by the petitioner which ultimately resulted in him being placed in low medical category and eventually caused him being discharged under the Army Rules was on account of circumstances that had some casual connection with military duty. In that event the accident as a result of which the individual sustained injury in circumstances that were attributable to his military duty, the Army Group Insurance authorities should reconsider his case appropriately. The Tribunal quashed the order of the government and held that the petitioner's injury be considered as attributable to military service. The Tribunal ordered that the petitioner should be awarded disability pension at the rate of 40% for a period of two years with effect from 28 May 1981. The petitioner should be immediately called for review medical board for re-ascertaining the percentage of his disability. The percentage of disability pension should be rounded off to 50% in terms of exant rules.

Disability: direction for employment

The AFT Principal Bench New Delhi in the case of *Major Mahesh Bisht v. Union of India* TA No. 766 of 2009 [WP(C) No. 4535 of 2002] decided on 22 May 2012 considered a prayer to declare Notification No. 16-27/2001-N1.1 dated 28 March 2002 issued by the Ministry of Social Justice and Empowerment, Government of India as null and void.

The petitioner was commissioned in the Indian Army on 13 June 1987 and at the time of incident was in the rank of Major. Unfortunately on 24 March 2000, the petitioner met with a road traffic accident near Barog, Solan in Himachal Pradesh while returning back to his unit in course of performing military duty. The petitioner was travelling in a military vehicle being driven by Naik T P Gurung, who was killed in said accident, while the petitioner sustained serious spinal cord injuries which resulted in the disability of paraplegia which disabled him practically. He was treated for 50 days at Commnd Hospital, Chandimandir at Chandigarh from where he was shifted to Military Hospital, Kirkee, Pune.

After completion of treatment of petitioner, the respondents, on 15 October 2000, held a medical board proceedings with a view to invalidate the petitioner out of service. A show cause notice dated 15 October 2000 was served upon the petitioner. In reply to the said notice, the petitioner submitted his representation dated 29 October 2000. However, the respondents vide their order dated 10 January 2002 rejected the representation of the petitioner and accepted the medical board proceedings. They also passed the impugned invalidment order dated 20 February 2002 ordering release of the petitioner from service w.e.f. 01 March 2002. The petitioner's appeal against his release was rejected.

The petitioner, due to the disability of paraplegia, was not able to make use of his legs but was otherwise fully fit to do any kind of sedentary job by sitting for long hours on a chair or wheelchair. The petitioner's unit submitted a statement of case dated 15 July 2000 referring s. 47(1) of the Persons with Disabilities (Equal Opportunities, protection of Rights and Full Participation) Act, 1995 for his retention in service. The case was strongly recommended by his superiors.

The petitioner contended that the Persons with Disabilities (Equal Opportunities, protection of Rights and Full Participation) Act, 1995 (Act of 1995) was a social legislation and according to section 47 of the Act of 1995, he was entitled to be given an employment suitable to his physical condition and he should not have been discharged from service. Section 47 of the Act of 1995 intends to advance the cause of social justice. However, a proviso is added that the appropriate Government may, having regard to the type of work carried on in any establishment, by notification and subject to such conditions, if any, as may be specified in such notification, exempt any establishment from the provisions of this section. Pursuance to this exemption provision, the Government had issued a notification dated 28 March 2002 (Published in the Gazette of India dated 13 April 2002) which exempt all categories of posts of combatant personnel of the Armed Forces from the provision of the said section.

The respondents contested that on completion of petitioner's treatment and rehabilitation, his condition was reviewed and he was found to have complete paralysis of both legs with loss of sensation over left leg and had no control over his bowel and bladder. Since, petitioner had been observed for adequate period and there was no scope of his being fit in future, he was declared unfit for further military service and was recommended invalidment in medical category A-5, P-5 as per paragraph 4 of AO 513/71 and paragraph 424 RMSAF-1983 by Sr. Adv. Surgery and Orthopaedic. The Medical Board held at Military Hospital, Kirkee on 15 October 2000 agreed with the recommendation and accordingly. The Invaliding Medical board proceedings were approved by the Chief of the Army Staff on 08 February 2001 and the same were submitted to the Ministry of Defence who approved it on 10 January 2002. The Invaliding Medical Board proceedings were accepted by DGMS (Army) on 8 February 2002.

The Tribunal observed that the petitioner met with an accident on 24 March 2000 and this exemption notification of s. 47 of the Act of 1995 was issued on 28 March 2002 and it was published in the Gazette on 13 April 2002. Therefore, this exemption notification has no applicability so far as the present case was concerned. The Tribunal rejected the contentions of the respondents that the notification may be treated to be declaratory and to have effect from the date the Act came into force. The Tribunal rejected the submission and held that it is a principle interpretation of Statute that no notification or provision of the Act could be read retrospectively unless it is specifically intended to do so.

The Tribunal came to conclusion that that petitioner got the disability due to an accident which occurred prior to the notification coming into force, therefore, the benefit accrued under s. 47 of the Act of 1995 cannot be denied to him. It set aside the Invalidating Medical Board proceedings dated 15 October 2000; invalidment order dated 20 February 2002 ordering release of the petitioner from service and directed the respondents to explore possibility for rehabilitation of petitioner at proper place after examining him by a fresh medical board. It ordered that in case the medial board finds the petitioner fit for discharging sedentary duties then he should be given all benefits pertaining to the post. Petitioner would also be entitled for all consequential benefits in view of setting aside of his invalidment from service. The process, as far as possible, should be completed within three months from the date of the order.

Disability not attributable to service

The AFT Chandigarh Bench in the case of *Brig Satinder Kumar Sud v. Union of India*, OA No. 575 of 2011, decided on 14 November 2011, considered the issue of the grant of disability of pension to the petitioner. The petitioner during tenure of service was posted at Andaman & Nikobar Islands from October 2001 to 2004 which has been considered as uncongenial climatic area. In 2005 he suffered heart attack and was admitted in Military Hospital, Jodhpur and was placed under low medical category. Ultimately, he was discharged from the service on 31 August 2007 after completion of 33 years of service. Prior to that, he was brought before the Release Medical Board. He was found to be suffering from the disease, "coronary artery disease (anterior wall MI)" and his disability was assessed as 40% for life. His claim for grant of disability element of disability pension was rejected on the ground that the disability suffered by him was found neither attributable to nor aggravated by military service. His subsequent appeals against that rejection did not found any favours from the government.

The Tribunal held that the petitioner was found medically fit when he was enrolled in the Army service in the year 1974. No note with regard to the aforesaid disease was recorded by the Medical Authority at that time. The disability was suffered in the year 2005 after rendering of 31 years of service. It is clear that onset of the aforesaid disease has occurred in course of service. Having regard to these facts and in accordance with entitlement rules, the presumption would be that the disease which occurred during course of military service is deemed to be attributable to or aggravated as a result of stress and strain of military service.

The Tribunal noted that in the Medical Board opinion given in review medical board proceedings dated 26 April 2007, the petitioner's disability has been clearly shown as attributable to military service. The Bench held that the disability claim has been rejected without giving and valid reason holding the disability as neither attributable to nor aggravated by service. The Bench held that the ischemic heart disease (IHD) is one of the classified diseases, which normally arises as a result of stress and strain of the military service. The Bench held that the petitioner is entitled to disability element of disability pension under Regulation 48 of the Pension Regulations for the Army, 1961. He was also entitled to the same @ 50% disability after giving the benefit of "rounding off" from the date of his discharge i.e. 31 August 2007. The petitioner is also entitled to arrears, restricted to a period of three years prior to filing of this application with interest @ 10% per annum.

Disability after retirement

The AFT Chandigarh Bench in the case of *Lt Gen (Retd) D.P. Singh v. Union of India*, OA No. 973 of 2011, decided on 3 November 2011, directed the government to conduct medical examination of the retired officer to ascertain disability of the officer, and release the disability element in case the findings are found positive by the competent medical authority.

In this case the petitioner was in Medical Category SHAPE-1 at the time of his retirement. He claimed that during his last tenure from 2003 to 2005 at the Infantry School he first experienced marked hearing deficiency after exposure to field and classification range firing which involved firing of small arms, mortars, anti-tank weapons and missiles routinely. The diminishing hearing was duly reported to the medical authorities, but his medical category was not down-graded by the authorities. After retiring from the Army, the petitioner with the time felt that his disability which had basis in his exposure had further deteriorated which is duly reported to Ex-servicemen Contributory Health Scheme (ECHS) Centre which after examination referred him to a Hearing Care Centre where he was put on a hearing aid.

It was also submitted that in view of Rule 8 (a) of the Entitlement Rules 2008 read with Regulation 54 of the Pension Regulations for the Army, 1961, and government policy the petitioner has a right to be examined by the competent medical authority as to know whether the disability is a delayed manifestation of a pathological process set in motion by service conditions occurring prior to discharge. The petitioner had approached the competent authority twice, but his prayer for re-assessment of disability/examination by the medical authority for the purpose of post-retirement benefits was rejected.

Disability pension: arbitrariness in date

The AFT Regional Bench Jaipur in *Capt P L Bhatia v. Union of India*, TA No. 274 of 2009 (WP (C) 1168 of 2005), decided on 5 March 2010, considered discriminatory provisions contained in Government of India, Ministry of Defence Letter No. 1(2)/97/1/D(Pen-C)dated 31 January 2001.

The applicant was commissioned in the Indian Army on 9 February 1964 as an Emergency Commissioned Officer. Whilst in service, he met with an accident on 20 October 1997, in which, he lost his right leg. Since the accident occurred while the applicant was on military duty, the same was attributable to service and disability was assessed as 60 percent. The petitioner was invalided out of service on 30 September 1969 with 60 percent disability attributed to military Service. Since he had not completed his pensionable service, he was sanctioned disability pension with effect from the date of his invalidation. The applicant continued to receive disability pension.

The Ministry of Defence issued a letter No. 1(2)/97/1/D(Pen-C) dated 31 January 2001, wherein, certain liberalization was carried out as regards the broad banding of disability but the same was applicable only to those retiring, invaliding or dying in harness on or after 1 January 1996. Para 7.2 of the letter categorically stated that when an armed forces personnel is invalided out, the extent of disability or functional incapacity shall be determined in the following manner for the purposes of computing the disability element:

Percentage of disability as assessed by invaliding Medical Board	Percentage to be reckoned for computing of disability element
Less than 50	50
Between 50 and 75	75
Between 76 and 100	100

The applicant had applied for enhancement of disability element from 60 to 75 percent with effect from 1 January1996; however, it was informed to him that the provisions of the letter were valid only for those, who were retiring invaliding or dying in harness on or after 1 January 1996. Since the applicant had been invalided out on 30 September 1969, the provisions of the above letter were not applicable to him and his disability will continue to be treated as 60 percent only.

The Tribunal considered the Constitutional Bench of the Supreme Court in D.S. Nakara v. Union of India AIR 1983 SC 130; 1983(1) SCC 305: "when a State considers it necessary to liberalize a pension scheme, it could not grant the benefit of liberalization only to those who retired subsequent to the specified date and denied the same to those who had retired prior to that date. The division which classified the pensioners into two classes on the basis of specified date was devoid of any rational principle and was both arbitrary and unprincipled and was violative of Article14 of the Constitution of India."

The Tribunal ordered that the applicant's disability to be assessed as 75 percent with effect from 1 January 1996 and the arrears of enhanced disability pension be paid within a period of three months with interest at the rate of 6 percent per annum.

Disability Pension; Discrimination

Disability pension: injury sustained on leave

The AFT Regional Bench Chandigarh in the case of *Ex. Naib Subedar Suresh Kumar v. Union of India*, OA No. 773 of 2010 decided on 27 January 2011 considered petition under section 14/15 of Armed Forces Tribunal Act, 2007 for grant of disability pension at the rate of 75% disability against 50% by giving the benefit of rounding off.

The petitioner while on annual leave sustained injuries in a road accident on 23 November 2004. The petitioner was admitted to PGI, Rohtak and subsequently shifted to Base Hospital Delhi Cantt for treatment of the injuries. An injury report was initiated and the Medical Board held on 01 April 2005 downgraded him to low medical category A-2 (Permanent). His injuries were not found to be aggravated by the Military Service by the Medical Board. A Court of Inquiry was held on 25 June 2005 and as per findings, since the petitioner sustained injuries during annual leave, the same were held to be not attributable to military service. However, the Commanding Officer declared that the individual sustained injuries under the circumstances beyond his control and he cannot be blamed for the same. Ultimately the petitioner was discharged from service in low medical category with effect from 31 October 2006. At the time of discharge, the petitioner was brought before the Release Medical Board, which assessed the disability of the petitioner as 50%. However, the same was declared as neither attributable to nor aggravated by military service. The claim of the petitioner for grant of disability pension was rejected.

The respondents were of the view that disability pension has rightly been denied by the competent authority as the disability suffered by the petitioner was found as neither attributable to nor aggravated by military service. He was not entitled to disability pension as he does not fulfill the conditions of paragraph 173 of Pension Regulations for the Army, 1961.

The Tribunal observed that in number of decisions of the High Court as well as the Supreme Court including a recent decision of Chandigarh Bench dated 15 December 2010 (*Ex. Nk Raj Pal v. Union of India*, TA No. 237 of 2010) it has been held that if an individual receives any injury as a result of accident not due to his negligence in course of authorized leave and his act is not inconsistent with military service, the same is deemed attributable to military service and the individual is entitled to get disability pension to the extent of disability suffered by the individual as per paragraph 173 of Pension Regulations for the Army, 1961.

The Tribunal held that the petitioner was entitled to get disability element of disability pension for 75% disability for life by giving the benefit of rounding off from the date of his discharge. The respondents were directed to assess and release the disability pension in favour of the petitioner after giving the benefit of rounding off from the date of discharge within six months from the date of receipt of the order. The petitioner was also entitled to arrears of disability pension with interest of 10% per annum.

***

The AFT Regional Bench Chennai in the case of *Ex-Sepoy Sasikumar K.v. Union of India* OA No. 3 of 2010, decided on 1 April 2011 considered the case relating to disability pension. The applicant, while on annual leave, met with a motor accident on 05 July 2004 and was admitted in Christian Medical College Hospital, Vellore, and was subsequently treated at Command Hospital (Air Force), Bangalore. He was discharged from service on 05 December 2005 and at the time of discharge, he had completed 8 years 7 months and 6 days of military service. His claim for disability pension and subsequent appeals were rejected by the government.

The respondents claimed that the appellant was examined by a Classified Specialist (Ortho & Surgical) at Command Hospital (Air Force), Bangalore, who recommended that the applicant to be invalided out of service in medical category A5. Finally the applicant was brought before invaliding Medical Board and as per the opinion of the Medical Board dated 17 October 2005, for the diagnosis 'Fracture shaft (LT) Femur with Sciatic Palsy", he was invalided out of service, which was also approved by the DDMS, HQ, ATNK & K Area, Chennai, on 11 November 2005. The Court of Inquiry had opined that the multiple injuries sustained by the applicant was due to road traffic accident while on annual leave at native place and it has further opined that the injury sustained on annual leave was not attributable to military service. The respondents further contended that the applicant was not entitled to the disability pension as per the Regulation 173 of the Pension Regulations for the Army 1961, Part-I, since he had sustained the disability while on annual leave.

The Tribunal referred the decision of the Division Bench of the Punjab and Haryana High Court in *Siri Krishan v. Union of India*, 1997 (1) SLR 607 and Ex-Sepoy Balwant Singh v. Union of India, 1999(3) Service Cases Today 55, wherein the ratio decidendi was that even when an Army personnel is on a long leave or casual leave, such person is entitled to the benefit of disability pension irrespective of the fact that he suffers the disability while on annual leave or casual leave. The relevant observation of the Punjab and Haryana High Court is note worthy and reproduced:

> "After considering the rival contentions of the parties, I am of the considered opinion that the submissions raised by the counsel for the respondent is devoid of any merit. In the opinion of this Court, casual leaves, annual leave, furlough or medical leave etc. are the incidents of service and these types of leaves are permissible to the government employees. In these circumstances, the defence of the respondents appears to be without any basis when it was argued by the learned counsel for the respondents that the petitioner suffered the injury/disability when he was on annual leave.
>
> While in annual leave the petitioner has never severed his relationship with his employer, who granted the annual leave to the petitioner according to rules. The leave will remain as a leave and casual leave, long leave, medical leave and furlough are the different branches of leave. This view of this Court can be looked into from other angle. Supposing an Army personnel while on long leave/casual leave/furlough commits an offence, is it not governed by Army rules? The answer is in the affirmative. Supposing after availing annual leave such employee does not return to his unit, can he not be prosecuted departmentally? Again the answer is in the affirmative. If such situations are there, how it can be said that Army personnel when on long leave suffers disability that disability is not attributable to the Army Service."
>
> Aggrieved by the said decision of the Punjab and Haryana High Court, the Union of India, respondents therein, preferred an Appeal before the Supreme Court under Civil Appeal No.5356 of 2002. The Apex Court dismissed the appeal preferred by the Union of India, confirming the judgment of the Punjab and Haryana High Court referred to above, on 01 April 2009.

The Tribunal, relying on the observations of the Punjab and Haryana High Court in *Gurmit Singh Butter v. Union of India* 2000(3) RSJ 327, confirmed by the Supreme Court in C.A. No. 5356 of 2002, held that the rejection of disability pension on the ground that the disability sustained while availing the annual leave cannot be attributable to or aggravated by military service, is against all cannon of principles of natural justice. The Tribunal held that the applicant was entitled to the disability pension due to him under Rules and directed the respondents to sanction the disability pension due to the applicant from the date of his discharge within three months. Further, failure of compliance would entail the applicant 6% per annum interest for arrears.

Disability Pension: arbitrary action by PCDA

The AFT Regional Bench Chandigarh in *Inderjit Singh v. Union of India* TA No. 585 of 2010 (arising out of CS No. 32 of 2009) decided on 27 January 2011, considered the entitled for grant of disability pension.

The petitioner joined Indian Army on 26 February 1976 in a medically fit condition and was discharged from the service on 31 July1991 on low medical category with more than 30% disability. The PCDA (P) granted disability pension to the petitioner from August 1992 to August 1997 and it was discontinued thereafter. However, on the basis of Review Medical Board opinion, it was restored, but w.e.f. March 2008. The petitioner made all efforts to persuade the authorities concerned for restoration of the disability element w.e.f. August 1997 to March 2008, but no effect. He did not receive any reply to the legal notice sent to the government.

The Tribunal observed that the petitioner has filed the suit for grant of disability element of disability pension for the period August 1997 to 25 March 2008. The admitted fact is that during the period, the plaintiff's disability was found to be 20% by the Re-survey Medical Board, but on the order of PCDA (P), it was reduced to less than 20% and accordingly no disability element was granted to the plaintiff for that period.

The Tribunal held that it is well settled principle of law that the PCDA (P) has no power or authority to reduce the percentage of disability assessed by the Medical Board with physical examination of the individual. In this case, the PCDA has reduced the percentage of the disability from 30% to less than 20% arbitrarily and that too without physical examination of the plaintiff and hence it is not tenable in the eyes of law. The petitioner was entitled to get disability element of disability pension for the percentage of disability as given by the Re-survey Medical Board.

The Tribunal directed the respondents restore the disability element in favour of the petitioner from the date of discontinuation for 20% disability within a period of six months from the date of receipt of the order. The petitioner was also entitled to get arrears, restricted to a period of three years prior to restoration of his disability element with effect from 26 March 2008 with interest @ 10% per annum.

Liberalised Disability Pension

The AFT Chandigarh Bench in the case of *Sep Puran Singh v. Union of India*, TA No. 01 of 2009 [CW (P) 21863 of 2008], decided on 19 January 2010, considered a prayer for liberalised disability pension.

In this case, the petitioner, while travelling on the duty with another soldier, was attacked by anti social elements and sustained serious injuries. A court of inquiry was ordered to the investigate the circumstances under which the petitioner sustained severe injuries. The petitioner was placed in low medical category in February1992, which was reviewed from time to time. Finally, he was invalided out of service on 10 March 2001 and was granted disability pension. The petitioner had claimed liberalized disability pension in term of the instructions contained in the Government of India letter.

The Tribunal directed the competent authority to release the liberalized disability pension in terms of the Central Government letter and also to pay the arrear of pension to the petitioner within two months from the date of the order. It further ordered that the payment of the arrear of liberalized disability pension shall be confined to a period of three years from the date of filling of this application. In case the competent authority fails to release the disability pension and pay the arrears within the stipulated period of two months, the petitioner shall be entitled to interest on the arrears @ 18% per annum till the date of payment.

Disability pension: discharged as case of neurosis

The AFT Regional Bench Chennai in the case of *SSVN Murthy v. Union of India*, TA No.135 of 2010 [WP (C) No. 13952 of 2000, High Court of Andhra Pradesh], decided on 26 November 2010, considered a petition for the award of disability pension.

The petitioner joined the Indian Naval service as a Combatant Member on 2 January 1989 and was found fit medically at the time of joining the service. The petitioner served in the Indian Navy for a period of about 8 years and 9 months and was discharged on medical ground 'Neurosis' on 3 September 1997. The service medical authorities lowered the petitioner's medical category due to the disability (Neurosis) occurred to him while in service and found him unfit for military duties. The petitioner had made several representations to the authorities concerned but the disability pension has been denied to him. The petitioner had contested that the rejection of the disability pension was illegal, arbitrary and against the principles of natural justice.

The Tribunal examined the AFMSF-16 relating to the petitioner. It observed that the petitioner had served from 19 July 1992 to 25 May 1993 in the field area wherein the actual onset of the disease 'Neurosis' had occurred. The Tribunal referred to the Entitlement Rule 5 incorporated in the Navy Pension Regulations 1964: "In deciding on the issue of entitlement all the evidence, both direct and circumstantial, will be taken into account and the benefit of reasonable doubt will be given to the claimant. This benefit will be given more liberally to the claimant in field service cases."

The Tribunal further noted that while rejecting the claim of disability pension of the petitioner, the competent authorities have failed to look into the above said Entitlement Rule 5 incorporated in Navy Pension Regulations 1964. The disease has been aggravated only due to the stress and strain the petitioner had undergone in the Naval service. Due to the disease, the petitioner had gone to an extreme step of committing suicide in 1993 and also in 1996 by consuming overdose of sleeping pills and rat poison respectively. The Tribunal held that the petitioner was entitled for the disability pension as per the Rules.

Disability Pension: discharged on his own request on compassionate grounds

The AFT Regional Bench Chandigarh in the case of *Suresh Kumar Yadav v. Union of India*, OA No. 121 of 2012, decided on 13 January 2012, considered a petition for the grant of disability pension.

The petitioner was enrolled on 21 May 1975, and was discharged on his own request on 30 November 1999, in Low Medical Category, for the disability "Osteo-Arthritis." The Medical Board assessed the disability at 30%, and opined it to be aggravated by military service. The petitioner was aggrieved that his claim for disability pension was rejected vide communication dated 24 November 2011, on the ground that he was discharged on his own request on compassionate grounds.

The Tribunal referred the judgment of Delhi High Court in *Mahavir Singh Narwal v. Union of India*, dated 05 May 2004, passed in CWP No. 2967 of 1989, which was up-held by the Supreme Court vide order dated 04 January 2008, passed in SLP (Civil) No. 24171 of 2004. The Tribunal further observed that in OA No. 329 of 2010, *Lt Gen Vijay Oberoi v. Union of India*, decided on 04 August 2010, it was held that even discharged on own request in Low Medical Category, does tantamount to invaliding out.

The Tribunal held that the petitioner was entitled to get disability pension on the basis of the disability assessed by the Medical Board, along with the benefits of rounding off. It directed the respondents to make necessary calculations and make payment to the petitioner, within a period of three months, failing which the amount would carry interest at the rate of 10 per cent per annum.

Disability Pension: discharged as case of unspecified psychosis

The AFT Regional Bench Chandigarh in the case of *Jai Narain Chhillar v. Union of India*, OA No. 794 of 2010, decided on 06 January 2012, considered a petition for grant of disability pension.

The petitioner was enrolled on 26 March1985, and was invalided out on 31 March 2009, with disability "unspecified psychosis." The disability was assessed at 40 per cent, and was opined by the Release Medical Board to be neither attributable to nor aggravated by Military Service, rather not related to service conditions. The on-set of disability was in November, 2006 in Modified Field Area, Sri Ganganagar.

The petitioner has contended that the initial Categorization Medical Board dated 20 February 2007 had opined the disability to be attributable to military service, and subsequent Medical Boards of 28 August 2007, 05 February 2008, and 18 July 2008, consistently opined in accordance with the Medical Board's Proceedings dated 20 February 2007. Further, the final Medical Board (RMB) had opined it to be not attributable to military service, which is contrary to the consistent opinion of the Medical Boards, apart from the fact that it could not be changed by Release Medical Board, and in the abstract of Medical Board, given to him and produced before the Tribunal, there has been a cutting made on the aspect of attributability.

The respondents contended that Medical Boards opinion is required to be given due weightage and referred to judgment of the Supreme Court in the case of *Secretary, Ministry of Defence v. A. V. Damodaran*, 2009 (9) SCC 140, which had been relied upon in the Invaliding Medical Boards proceedings. The Tribunal observed that nothing was said by the respondents, as to how and why the cutting was made, and under what circumstances, much less under what legal authority.

The Tribunal perused the initial Categorization Medical Board dated 20 February 2007, and observed that in paragraph No.19, the disability was clearly opined to be attributable to military service. However, the column contemplates reasons for the opinion, which was not mentioned. He Tribunal also observed a few cuttings, over writings, and alterations in the release medical board proceedings. The tribunal was of the opinion that, since the cutting does show that the opinion given in favour of attributability, has been cut, and has been replaced by negative opinion, under the signatures of said Lt Col J. Joshi on 29 December 2008, this obviously, has to be taken to be without any authority of law.

The Tribunal held that the disability of the petitioner should be taken to be attributable to military service, and the petitioner was entitled to disability element of pension, with the benefits of rounding off, in view of the judgment of the Tribunal in *Lt Gen Vijay Oberoi v. Union of India* OA No. 329 of 2010, decided on 04 August 2010. The respondents were directed to make payment to the petitioner, within a period of three months, from the date of receipt of certified copy of the order, failing which the amount shall carry interest at the rate of 10 per cent per annum.

Disability pension: psychiatric cases

The AFT New Delhi Principal Bench in the case of *Nakhat Bharti v. Union of India*, TA No. 48 of 2009 [WP(C) No. 6324 of 2007 Delhi High Court] with TA Nos. 5 of 2009, 106 of 2009 and 36 of 2009 [WP (C) Nos. 7447/2009, 886/2009 and 889/1991 Delhi High Court], decided on 28 October 2009, considered four petitions involving identical question of law.

The petitioner was enrolled in Army on 3 October 1998. At the time of entry into service the petitioner was subjected to a thorough medical examination conducted by a board of doctors and when he was found medically fit in all respects he was enrolled in the Army. He was again put through medical examination at the Artillery Centre and he was found fit. After successful training, the petitioner was attested as a soldier on 21 August 1999.

The petitioner was posted to new unit in September 1999, which was located on in Sambha sector of Jammu & Kashmir. The area was infested with terrorists and counter insurgency operations were carried out frequently. This operational environment caused tremendous mental stress and strain on petitioner as the fear of the unknown always lurked at the back of his mind. The petitioner was posted as a Sentry on ammunition guard in a solitary area. On 22 September 1999 the petitioner first exhibited sign of mental disease.

The petitioner was admitted to Command Hospital at Udhampur on 23 September, 1999 and he was treated there for more than five months but his medical condition did not improve after treatment. The medical authorities after treatment recorded that 'no evidence of any organic basis could be detected for his invaliding psychiatric disability clinically'. Thereafter he was brought to Invaliding Medical Board on 7 March 2000. The Medical Board found disability to the extent of 40% for five years and further observed that it was neither attributable to nor aggravated by the military service. It was found that the psychiatric disorder was not connected with service. The petitioner was placed in low medical category (EEE) and invalidated out from service on 18 March 2000.

The petitioner's his claim for disability pension was rejected by the PCDA (P) Allahabad order dated 30 July 2001. The petitioner's statutory appeals as well as petitions in Defence Pension Adalat were rejected. Thereafter, petitioner filed a writ petition in Delhi High Court challenging the order denying disability pension.

The petitioner referred to three provisions for his disability claim: (i) Rule 14 (b) of Entitlement Rules of 1982 for casualty pensionary award, (ii) Regulation 173 of Pension Regulations for the Army-1961, Part-I, and (iii) Regulation 423(c) of Regulations for Medical Services for Armed Forces 1983. A combined reading of these three provisions makes it clear that when an incumbent is discharged from service it has to be examined that whether his discharge is attributable to army service or aggravated by the army service. Two expressions "contributed"/"aggravated" has been used in Regulation 173 of Pension Regulations for the Army-1961. It clearly contemplates that medical authority has to state that the disease was present at the time of enrolment and could not have been detected on medical examination prior to acceptance for service.

The Tribunal observed that in case it is found that the incumbent was suffering from a disease, prior to his acceptance in service, at the time of discharge on medical ground, the authorities has to record the reason that why the disease, which was present at the time of acceptance of service could not detected. If such cogent reason does not find in the finding of medical board then a presumption has to be drawn that disease seems to have arisen during the course of service. Similar presumption was also mentioned in the Regulation 423 (c):

> ".......disease which has led to an individual's discharge or death, will ordinarily be deemed to have arisen in service if no note of it was made at the time of individual's acceptance for service in the Armed Forces."

But, it further puts rider that medical board, which recommended for discharge, has to record a reason that why this disease could not be detected on medical examination prior to acceptance in service. In case, such a reason is given, then presumption will stand rebutted. The Tribunal observed that in all the cases under appeal, no categorical reason had been mentioned that why the disease like 'psychosis' or so called 'schizophrenia' could not be detected at the time of induction in the army service [except in case of *Naresh Kumar v. Union of India* TA 106 of 2009]. The medical board had, only in some cases, stated that it was due to constitutional disorder or psychosomatic. Such a non-speaking explanation cannot be good substitute for a reason. The expression "reason" means a speaking detailed order showing the application of mind that why this disease, which may be having embryo at the time of induction in service, could not be detected.

The Tribunal was of the view that the induction in the army and the training was very rigorous and sometimes people can stand it and sometimes people may not stand it. The Tribunal referred to para 54 of the Guide to Medical Officers for Military Pension, 2008:

> "54. Mental & Behavioural (Psychiatric) Disorders: Psychiatric illness results from a complex interplay of endogenous (genetic/biological) and exogenous (environmental, psychosocial as well as physical) factors. This is true for the entire spectrum of psychiatric disorders (Psychosis & Neurosis) including substance abuse disorders.
>
> The relative contribution of each, of course, varies from one diagnostic category to another and from case to case. The concept of attributability or aggravation due to the stress and strain of military service can be, therefore, evaluated independent of the diagnosis and will be determined by the specific circumstances of each case.
>
> (a) Attributability will be conceded where the psychiatric disorder occurs when the individual is serving in or involved in:
>
> (i) Combat area including counterinsurgency operational area.
>
> (ii) HAA service.
>
> (iii) Deployment at extremely isolated posts.
>
> (iv) Diving or submarine accidents, lost at sea.
>
> (v) Service on sea.

(vi) MT accidents involving loss of life or flying accidents (both as flier and passenger) in a service aircraft or aircraft accident involving loss of life in the station.

(vii) Catastrophic disasters particularly while aiding civil authorities like earthquake, cyclone, tsunami, fires, volcanic eruptions (where one has to handle work in proximity of dead or decomposing bodies).

(b) Attributability will also be conceded when the psychiatric disorder arises within one year of serious multiple injuries (e.g. amputation of upper/lower limb, paraplegia, quadriplegia, severe head injury resulting in hemiplegia of gross neurocognitive deficit which area themselves considered attributable to military service. This includes Post Traumatic Stress Disorder (PTSD).

(c) Aggravation will be considered in Psychiatric disorders arising within 3 months of denial of leave due to exigencies of service in the face of:

(i) Death of parent when the individual is the only child/son.

(ii) Death of spouse or children.

(iii) Henious crimes (e.g.murder, rape or dacoity) against members of the immediate family.

(iv) Reprisals or the threat of reprisals against members of the immediate family by militants/terrorists owing to the fact of the individual being a member of the Armed Forces.

(v) Natural disasters such as cyclones/earthquakes involving the safety of the immediate family.

(vi) Marriage of children or sister when the individual is the only brother thereof and specially if their father is deceased.

(d) Aggravation will also be conceded when after being diagnosed as a patient of psychiatric disorder with specific restrictions of employability the individual serves in such service environment which worsened his disease because of the stress and strain involved like service in combat area including counterinsurgency operations, HAA, service on board ships, flying duties.

(e) Attributability may be granted to any psychiatric disorder occurring in recruits and results in invalidment from service only when clearly identifiable severe stressors including sexual abuse or physical abuse are present as causative factor /factors for the illness."

In the Tribunal's opinion, these causes which lead to aggravation or attributability, in case of mental disorder or psychiatric disorder, may occur when individual involved in a combat area including counterinsurgency or deployment at extremely isolated posts or on the high seas or seeing the accidents involving loss of people as a result of such accident, sometimes in seeing a disasters particularly earthquake and cyclone. Such kind of harrowing scenes can cause mental disorder. It is very difficult to assess at the time of induction in service, but it can develop during the course of the service on happening of such unfortunate events.

The Tribunal observed that the reasons given by the medical board like constitutional or psychosomatic; was not a sufficient reason to show that why this disease could not be detected at the time of induction in service. It held that in the three cases, *viz., Nakhat Bharti v. Union of India, N.K. Sisram v. Union of India and Manmohan Singh v. Union of India*, no proper reasons were given. However, in the case of *Naresh Kumar v. Union of India*, detailed reason had been given with reference to the guidelines contained in para 54 of the Guide to Medical Officers for Military Pension, 2008.

The Tribunal ordered that in three cases the incumbent shall be entitled to disability pension as per rules: *Nakhat Bharti v. Union of India* [TA No. 48 of 2009], *N.K. Sisram v. Union of India* [TA No. 36 of 2009] *and Manmohan Singh v. Union of India* [TA No. 5 of 2009]. The Tribunal rejected the case of *Naresh Kumar v. Union of India*, TA No. 106 of 2009, as the cogent reason had been provided in the case.

Disability pension; boarded out due to psychiatric reasons

The AFT Regional Bench Kochi in the case of *Indeevarakshan Nair v. Union of India* TA No.17 of 2009 [WP (C) No.1327 of 2004 The High Court of Kerala] decided on 16 July 2010, The TA No. 17 of 2009 was heard along with TA Nos. 35 of 2009, 112 of 2009 and 18 of 2010.

The petitioner was enrolled in the Army on 31 March 1979. At the time of enrolment, medical examination was conducted and he was sent for training to Gaya (Bihar). While undergoing training, the petitioner became sick and was admitted in Military Hospital, Dhanpur. He was transferred to Military Hospital, Jabalpur and underwent treatment for six months. The petitioner was placed in low medical category 'E' and was examined by the Release Medical Board. It was found that petitioner was suffering from 'Catatonic Schizophrenia'. He was discharged from service on 20 September 1980. The petitioner's claim for disability pension was rejected. His first as well as the second appeal were also dismissed.

The petitioner filed an OP No.12593 of 1993 before the High Court of Kerala. The High Court allowed the claim of the petitioner and directed payment of disability pension. That order was challenged by the respondents in WA No.1028 of 1999. The Division Bench relying on the decision in *Director General, BSF v. Vijoy*, 2000 (2) KLT 509 (FB) set aside the order of the Single Judge and gave an opportunity to the petitioner to disprove the medical report. It was also directed that petitioner may make a representation to discharge the burden, in the event of which the same will be considered by the appropriate authority and will pass appropriate orders at the earliest. The disability claim was again rejected. Challenging that order, the WP was filed contending that the principle laid down in *Vijoy's case* was re-considered in *Baby v. Union of India*, 2003 (3) KLT 362 by another Full Bench and the case of the petitioner is to be re-considered in the light of the subsequent decision.

The respondents contested that the petitioner was only an ex-recruit and he was not holding any rank in the Army and so the benefit of ex-servicemen cannot be claimed by the petitioner. Further, that disease of the petitioner might have existed prior to his entry in service and the same might not have been detected by the recruiting medical officer at the time of enrolment, since the same was not always apparent in nature. Petitioner was suffering from Schizophrenia and on account of that illness he was invalided out of service. The Invaliding Disease (ID) - Schizophrenia, was not a disease either attributable or aggravated by military service and hence the petitioner was not entitled to any relief.

TA No. 35 of 2009: The petitioner was enrolled in the Army on 29 October 1994 after passing written examination, interview, mental and physical test and medical examination. While undergoing training in Secunderabad, he fell down and sustained head injury. He became unconscious and was taken to Military Hospital, Secunderabad. After undergoing treatment for a week, he was transferred to Command Hospital, Pune for further treatment. He was examined by an Invaliding Medical Board which placed him in the lowest medical category. He was discharged on 9 April 1996. The petitioner's claim for disability pension was rejected on the ground that his Invaliding Disease was 'Unspecified Psychosis', which is neither attributable to nor aggravated by military service. Petitioner filed two appeals and the both were dismissed.

The petitioner filed OP No.17567 of 2000 before the High Court of Kerala claiming disability pension. The High Court after considering the contentions raised by the respondents set aside the order rejecting disability pension and directed the respondents to consider the case in accordance with the principles laid down in *Baby v. Union of India.* The government, without considering any point, again rejected the claim for disability pension.

The petitioner contended that there is no history of mental illness in his family. His father was a Havildar in EME, who had served the Army for 21 years. His brother was also serving in the EME and his sisters were working as teachers. It is also contended that petitioner was a holder of Orange Belt in Kung-Fu, which was considered to be an advanced position in Kung-Fu.

The respondents contested that the petitioner was invalided out of service with effect in low medical category 'EEE' due to his disability 'Unspecified Psychosis'. It was also contested that Invaliding Medical Board held that the Invaliding Disease of the petitioner was neither attributable to nor aggravated by military service and the same was a constitutional disorder and not connected with service factors. Hence the claim for disability pension was rejected.

TA No.112 of 2009: The petitioner was enrolled in the Indian Navy on 10 September 1987 after a thorough medical examination and physical and mental tests. He completed strenuous military training successfully and he was posted in regular Naval Units. While the petitioner was serving in the Missile Boat Unit (INS) Vipul during the year 1993, he developed mental illness and was admitted in INHS, Asvini. He was placed in the low medical category and was discharged from the hospital. He was again admitted in INHS Asvini during October, 1994. He was examined by an Invaliding Medical Board and subsequently, by a Release Medical Board. He was placed in the lowest medical category S5A5(S) PMT and invalided out of service with effect from 2 February 1995. The claim of the petitioner for disability pension was rejected. An appeal was filed through his father, who was an ex-serviceman, however, that appeal was also dismissed.

The petitioner filed an OP No.24191 of 2000 before the High Court of Kerala challenging the rejection of disability pension claim. The High Court set aside the order passed by the respondents and directed the respondents to re-consider the same in accordance with the principles laid down in *Baby v. Union of India*. The disability pension claim was again rejected.

The petitioner contended that there was no history of mental illness in his family. His father is an ex-serviceman and his mother is also very healthy. The respondents contested that the petitioner was invalided out from service on 2 February 1995 as he was suffering from invaliding disease –"Neurotic Depression [ICD 310(d)]." The petitioner had rendered only 7 years, 4 months and 22 days of service. The Invaliding Medical Board examined the petitioner and found that the invaliding disability of the petitioner was neither attributable nor aggravated by the Naval service and was a constitutional disease. Further, the Principal Controller of Defence Accounts (Pension), Allahabad had re-considered the matter and rejected the same by a speaking order.

TA No.18 of 2010: The petitioner was enrolled in the Indian Air Force as non-combatant on 12 October 1987 and he worked as Laskar for five years. Thereafter, on 20 March 1992, he was selected and enrolled as Airman (Combatant) in the Indian Air Force. He underwent nine months of training at Avadi and after the training he was posted at various places. After completion of 15 years of service, some symptoms of mental disorder were found in the petitioner and he was treated in the Military Hospital during January, 2002. His invaliding disease was diagnosed as 'Schizophrenia' and he was placed in low medical category with effect from April, 2002. The petitioner was discharged with effect from 10 November 2004 with 30% disability. The claim for disability pension put forward by the petitioner was rejected by the stating that invaliding disease was neither attributable nor aggravated by Air Force Service.

The petitioner contended that the disease was caused him due to the hazardous nature of work and the stress and strain occurred to him due to service conditions. The respondent contested that the petitioner had psychic breakdown in January 2002 with delusions of reference and persecution, 2nd person auditory hallucinations, anxiety and disturbed bio drives. He was Treated in Command Hospital (Air Force), Bangalore in April 2002 and discharged after a week. He had a relapse in July 2004. The Psychiatrist at Command Hospital, Air Force, Bangalore, recommended his invalidment on account of relapse. The Invaliding Medical Board which examined petitioner found that the invaliding disease of the petitioner was neith attributable to nor aggravated by the Air Force service and was a constitutiona one and hence, he was not entitled to any disability pension.

The Tribunal observed that all the four petitioners were suffering from mental illness which developed after enrolment. In all cases the claim for disability pension is resisted contending that the invaliding disease is neither attributable to nor aggravated by the service in the Armed Forces and the same was a constitutional one. In all these cases, invalidment factor was a disease and not injury.

The common contention raised by the petitioners was that, in all these cases, petitioners were enrolled in the Armed Forces after thorough medical examination and no abnormality was detected or noted by the Recruitment Medical Board at the time of their enrolment and the petitioners developed the invaliding disease on account of the stress and strain of the service in the Armed Forces and as such it ought to have been found that it is either attributable to or aggravated by the stress and strain in the service and the individuals ought to have been paid disability pension. The petitioners relied on the decision of the Single Judge in *Ramachandran Nair v. C.D.A.* ILR 1996 (1) Ker. 168; a Bench decision of the High Court of Kerala in *Ravi v. Union of India* 1998 (1) KLT 56, and the Full Bench decision in *Baby v. Union of India*, 2003 (3) KLT 362 (FB) and also the decision of the Supreme Court in *Union of India v. Neki Ram*, AIR 2004 SC 1235.

The respondents contested that there was absolutely no material available on record to hold that the invaliding disease arose on account of the stress and strain of service and the competent medical authority had found that illness, in all these cases, was constitutional and neither attributable nor aggravated due to the service in the Armed Forces. It was also contested that the burden was on the petitioners to establish that the injury ordisease was on account of the military/naval/air force service or aggravated on account of it. It was also contested that in all these cases the Medical Boards have elaborately considered the matter and recorded that the Invaliding Disease suffered by the petitioners is a constitutional one and this Tribunal cannt sit in judgment over the opinion of the experts.

The respondents relied on a Full Bench decision of the High Court of Kerala in *Director General, BSF v. Vijoy*, 2000 (2) KLT 509 (FB); and the decisions of the Supreme Court in *Ex Sapper Mohinder Singh v. Union of India* (Civil Appeal No.164 of 1993 arising out of SLP (C) No. 4233 of 1993 decided on 14.1.1993; *Union of India v. Baljit Singh* (1996) 11 SCC 315; *Union of India v. Dhir Singh China, Colonel (Retd.)*, (2003) 2 SCC 382; *CDA (Pension) v. Balachandran Nair*, (2005) 13 SCC 128; *Union of India v. Keshar Singh*, (2007) 12 SCC 675; *Union of India v. Surinder Singh Rathore* (2008) 5 SCC 747, and *Secretary, Ministry of Defence v. AV Damodharan* (2009) 9 SCC 14.

It was also contested that the Tribunal was bound by the decisions rendered by the Supreme Court as binding precedents. Further, the judicial discipline commands that the Tribunal should follow the decision of the Supreme Court in letter and spirit. Reliance was placed on Article 141 of the Constitution to argue that the Tribunal was not entitled to distinguish or ignore the decision of the Supreme Court.

The Tribunal observed that a substantial change was brought in the year 1973 when Regulation 173 of the Pension Regulations for the Army was amended. After going through various documents related to the issue, the Tribunal held:

TA No. 17 of 2009: The decision of the respondents that the petitioner was not entitled to disability pension was correct and does not call for any interference. The TA was dismissed.

TA No. 35 of 2009: The petitioner was entitled to disability pension in accordance with the rules. The Tribunal directed the respondents to calculate the disability pension due to the petitioner from 1 January 2000 onwards, i.e. the year on which OP No.17567 of 2000 was filed, in accordance with the rules and disburse the same within four months from the date of the order.

TA No. 112 of 2009: The petitioner was entitled to disability pension from 1 January 2000 onwards, i.e. the year on which the petitioner filed OP No. 24191 of 2000 before the High Court of Kerala. The respondents were directed to calculate the disability pension due to the petitioner in accordance with the rules and disburse the same within four months from the date of the order.

TA No. 18 of 2010: The petitioner was entitled to get the disability pension from the date of his discharge. It directed the respondents to calculate the disability pension due to the petitioner from the date of his discharge and disburse the same within four months from the date of the order.

While considering petitions, the Tribunal highlighted two issues for consideration by the Ministry of Defence and the Service Headquarters. First, a duty is cast upon the Union of India as well as the Armed Forces to evolve a scheme to rehabilitate service personnel who are discharged on account of mental illness and has not completed 10 years of service. This could be in the form of ex-gratia monthly payment and medical aid for life at least for the individual. The second issue was the ignorance or the lack of understanding of the matter by the counsels. It was very unfortunate that a person who has dedicated his life for the country was not getting his due on account of the fact that applicable rules are not brought to the notice of the Court or the Tribunal. Further, an updated or amended copy of the Pension Regulations for the Army, Navy and Air Force was not available. Hence, it was essential that in the interest of justice, the exact provision as applicable to a particular person was clear and well known to one and all. The matters which need clarity are rules and regulations on; Ordinary Family Pension, Special Family Pension, Liberalized Family Pension, Disability Pension and Invalid Pension.

Disability pension: callousness of medical board

The AFT Regional Bench Jaipur in the case of *Ex Hav Moharsingh v. Union of India*, TA No. 309 of 2009 [WP (C) No. 4831 of 2008], decided on 20 May 2010, considered a prayer for disability pension. The opening paragraph of the judgment read:

> A shockingly bizarre incident reflects inhuman treatment which had crossed all boundaries of humanity by superior responsible Armed Forces Medical Officers, whose actions when resulted into injustice forced the applicant to seek his legal remedy in the form of the present application for grant of disability pension.

The applicant was enrolled in the Army on 9 March 1988. On 26 February 2002 when the applicant was traveling in an army truck during Operation Falcon, Tawang (Arunachal Pradesh), the truck overturned resulting into multiple injuries on head and various parts of the body. He was admitted in the Hospital on the same day, where multiple injuries were detected. After the treatment, he was discharged on 4 March 2002. He told to the Doctor about the cause of accident as steering failure and the Doctor narrated the facts in his report. Thereafter, he was hospitalized in Pune from 30 May 2003 to 3 November 2003, where on 9 June 2003, the Neurologist diagnosed the 'Motor Neuron disease'. The MRI on 8 October 2003 suggested neuro degenerative disorder. The Command Hospital Lucknow on 2 August 2004 after complete examination suggested for Invaliding Medical Board.

The Invaliding Medical Board of the applicant was held on 28 September 2004 and it found the disability of 'Motor Neuron Disease', which was assessed as 80% for life long and was held to be aggravated by military service. The applicant was discharged from service on 19 November 2004. The case of the applicant for grant of disability pension was forwarded to the Principal Controller of Defence Accounts (Pension) [PCDA (P)], Allahabad, which described the disability suffered by the applicant as constitutional in nature and not related to his military service and rejected the claim of the applicant for grant of disability pension vide order dated 20 July 2005.

Thereafter, an appeal was preferred by the applicant. The Appeal Medical Board of the applicant was held on 26 February 2007, which described the percentage of disability suffered by the applicant as NIL and held that the disability suffered by the applicant is neither attributable to nor aggravated by his military service. In these circumstances, the applicant preferred a Writ Petition (C) No.4831 of 2008 before the High Court of Rajasthan, Bench at Jaipur.

The Tribunal summoned the petitioner and looking at his pathetic condition wherein he was brought in on a stretcher, it ordered the Commandant of the Military Hospital, Jaipur, to medically examine him. The medical board assessed his disability as 100 per cent and attributed it to military service. The medical expert opined that Hav Moharsingh was suffering from a progressive, degenerative neurological disorder with no specific treatment. Observing that the report of the Appeal Medical Board was not only contrary to that of two other boards, but also did not mention the reasons for assessing disability as 'Nil', the Tribunal held that Appeal Medical Board was grossly incorrect and deserved to be deprecated.

The Tribunal set aside the order dated 31 August 2005 passed by the PCDA (P) Allahabad and order dated 22 March 2007 passed on the appeal filed by the applicant. It directed the respondents to grant the disability pension to the applicant from the date of his discharge from service i.e. 19 November 2004. The arrears of disability pension be paid to the applicant within a period of three months from the date of the judgment with interest @ 6% per annum. The Tribunal imposed the costs of Rs.100,000/-, to be paid to the applicant by the non-applicants but shall be recovered in equal ratio from Air Commadore D P Joshi, Lt Col Shobana Das and Col S B Singh from their salary. The Tribunal directed the Secretary, Ministry of Defence to initiate disciplinary action against all the three erring officers immediately after the receipt of copy of the Judgment.

Disability pension: case of diabetes mellitus

The AFT Regional Bench Jaipur in the case of *Ex Cpl CL Kataria v. Union of India* OA 162 of 2010, decided on 01 June 2011, considered a prayer for disability pension.

The applicant was enrolled in the Indian Air Force on 4 July 1984 and was invalided out of service on 31 March 1986. Before invaliding him out of service, the applicant was subjected to Invaliding Medical Board, which found him medically unfit for further service in the Indian Air Force. The Invaliding Medical Board found that the applicant was suffering from the disabilities, i.e. diabetes mellitus with 100% disability for two years, attributable to service; Rt ear total deafness with 20% disability, aggravated by service; and Rt CP angle tumour with 20% disability for two years, neither attributable to nor aggravated by service. However, the composite disability of the applicant was assessed at 100%.

The applicant's claim for grant of disability pension was forwarded to the Principal Controller of Defence Accounts (Pension) [PCDA (P)], Allahabad, who opined that the disability suffered by the applicant was neither attributable to nor aggravated by service, as such, rejected the claim for grant of disability pension. Thereafter, the applicant preferred an appeal, which was also dismissed. A second appeal was also preferred and the applicant was subjected to Appeal Medical Board on 21 May 2007. The appeal medical board found the disability diabetes mellitus as static and did not consider it as either attributable to or aggravated by service. As regards the disability Rt CP angle tumour, it was considered as neither attributable to nor aggravated by service. However, the disability total deafness Rt. Ear was assessed at

40% for life, aggravated by service. The Appeal Medical Board considered composite disability at 50%, as such, the applicant was granted disability pension considering the composite disability at 50%.

The applicant contended that since his composite disability was considered at 100% by the Invaliding Medical Board, as such, he should have been granted disability pension considering his composite disability at 100%. Further, the rejection of his claim b y the PCDA (P) Allahabad without any cogent and valid reasons was totally unjust, illegal and arbitrary. The applicant placed reliance on the decision of the Tribunal in *Lachhmansingh v. Union of India* (TA No. 206 of 2009, decided on 7 May 2010) and *Samunder Singh v. Union of India* (TA No. 208 of 2009, decided on 26 February 2010), wherein it was observed that if there are two different and contrary opinions expressed by two different experts, in such case, opinion which was beneficial to the incumbent should be given due weightage. The respondent contested that the appeal medical board was the final authority and it has every right to differ with the opinion of the Invaliding Medical Board and the decision of the appeal medical board should be considered as final.

The Tribunal was of the opinion that pension is not a bounty but a legal right is vested in an individual. It there were two different and contrary opinions expressed by two different experts, in such case, the opinion which was benevolent to the incumbent should be given due wieghtage. Further, the case was covered by the decision of the Tribunal in *Samunder Singh's* case.

The Tribunal held that after considering the opinion of the Release Medical Board that disease/disabilities No.1 and 3 were aggravated by military service and are compositely assessed at 100%, the applicant was entitled to receive disability pension with effect from the date he was invalided out of service i.e. from 31 March 1996. Since the applicant was granted 50% disability pension with effect from 21 May 2007, the arrears of the disability pension be paid to the applicant within a period of three months from the date of the order adjusting the amount of disability pension already paid to him with interest at the rate of 8% per annum.

Disability pension: disability not attributable to military service

The AFT Regional Bench Jaipur in the case of *Lachhman Singh v. Union of India*, TA No. 206 of 2009, decided on 7 May 2010, considered a prayer for disability pension.

The applicant Lachhman Singh was initially enrolled in the Indian Army on 12 June 1962 and was discharged from service on 1 July 1977. He was granted service pension with effect from 1 July 1977. Thereafter, he was re-enrolled in DSC on 25 February 1984. He was discharged from DSC service on 30 June 1998 under Army Rule 13 (3) (iii) on attaining the age of 55 years with pension. He was placed in low medical category CEE (Permanent) with effect from 13 May, 1994 and was brought before the Release Medical Board held on 16 March, 1998 at Military Hospital, Ahmedabad. The Release

Medical Board assessed his all disabilities together 40% (Permanent). It was opined by the Medical Board that the disability suffered by the applicant was not attributable to military service but is aggravated by his military service. The claim of the applicant for grant of disability pension was rejected by the Principal Controller of Defence Accounts (PCDA) stating that both the disabilities are constitutional in nature and neither attributable to nor aggravated by military service. The first appeal preferred by the applicant was rejected by the Ministry of Defence on 20 July 2001.

The applicant preferred a second appeal and appeal medical board of the applicant was held on 2 April 2007 at Base Hospital, Delhi Cantt and it re-examined all the service and medical documents, physically examined the applicant and opined that both the disabilities suffered by the applicant are neither attributable to nor aggravated by military service. Thus, based on the opinion rendered by the appeal medical board, the second appeal filed by the applicant was rejected. As regards grant of second service pension, it was held that the applicant has rendered 14 years and 126 days of service in DSC, which did not entitle him for the second pension.

The applicant that there contended that there were two different medical opinions: one given by the Release Medical Board and the other given by the Appeal Medical Board. The Release Medical Board had opined that the disabilities suffered by the applicant were aggravated by military service whereas the Appeal Medical Board has opined that the disabilities suffered by the applicant were neither attributable to nor aggravated by military service. The only reason given by the appeal medical board was that the applicant continued to serve in peace station from onset of the disabilities in 1993 till his Release Medical Board was held and there was no other ground, which could have differed from the opinion of the Release Medical Board. The disability of hypertension was found to be an idiopathic disorder whereas the disability of angina was found to found to be due to atherosclerosis of blood vessels.

The respondents contested that since the applicant had not completed the requisite qualifying service of 15 years for the purpose of grant of regular pension, he was not entitled for regular pension and since the disabilities suffered by him were held to be not attributable to or aggravated by military service, the applicant was not entitled to disability pension also.

The Tribunal was of the opinion that it is well settled principle of law that if there are two different and contrary opinions expressed by two different experts, in such case, opinion which is beneficial to the incumbent should be given due weightage. The Tribunal referred to its earlier decision in the case of *Samunder Singh v. Union of India,* TA No. 208 of 2009, decided on 26 February 2010. The Tribunal held that the applicant was entitled to receive disability pension with effect from the date of his discharge from DSC service. The arrears of the disability pension to be paid with interest @ 6% per annum.

Disability pension: stab injury sustained on leave

The AFT Regional Bench Chandigarh in the case of *Union of India v. Jaswant Singh*, TA No. 1258 of 2010 [RSA No. 2805 of 2004], decided on 1 August 2012, considered challenge to the judgments and decrees of the two courts.

The appeal was filed before the High Court of Punjab and Haryana, which was admitted vide order dated 23 December 2005, on the questions enumerated in Para 11 of the Grounds of Appeal. After establishment of the Tribunal, the matter was transferred and was taken up for hearing.

The plaintiff-respondent was enrolled into Army in February, 1963, and was invalided out, through Invaliding Medical Board, upon being placed in Medical category `CEE', and the disability was accepted at 40%, for life, which was accepted as attributable to military service, and disability pension was sanctioned was sanctioned vide PPO dated 19 December 1969, which was received up to June, 1975, and was discontinued with effect from 25 June 1975, for no cause or reason, and without intimation to the plaintiff. It was contended, that the CCDA had no right to discontinue the disability pension, without affording any order of discontinuation, and without giving any opportunity to appeal.

The defendants contested that the plaintiff was invalided out because he developed minimal tremer of extended fingers insidiously, and developed tumer of both hands. He also received stab injury in abdomen, when he tried to mediate quarrel between the two civilians at his home town, when he was on leave. It was contested that the invaliding disease was assessed at 20% for two years capable of improvement and second disability was assessed as Nil, and he was granted disability pension taking disability at 20% for two years. The Re-Survey Medical Board of the plaintiff was held on 03 June 2005 and the Medical Board assessed the previous disability at Nil percentage and the stab-injury disability was assessed at 30%. Since the disability resulting from stab-injury was already found to be not attributable to Military service and since the disability 'hysterical tumer' was assessed at Nil percentage, the disability pension was discontinued. The plaintiff was communicated the discontinuance of disability pension. Then appeal was preferred by him, which was also dismissed. The second appeal was not filed.

The plaintiff filed a replication that under Pension Regulations, the CCDA has no power to reduce the degree of disablement, as accepted by the Medical Board, and that the "degree of disablement was 50% composite 40%". It was also pleaded that the order of CCDA was never conveyed to the plaintiff. Regarding the stab injury received in the abdomen, it was pleaded in the replication, that the abdomen injury was caused while saving one's life, and in such cases the injury is deemed to be attributable to Military service, in accordance with the provisions laid down in Appendix-II to the Pension Regulations for Army, 1961.

The Tribunal observed that during trial, the plaintiff examined himself by recording his oral statement on 22 August 2001, and a close reading of the entire statement showed, that he had not said anything about the circumstances in which he received stab injury in the abdomen. He had admitted to have been brought before Re-Survey Medical Board, and disability pension to have been stopped since 1975. He maintained the stand of having not received any communication of rejection of disability pension claim or rejection of the appeal.

The Tribunal noted that the trial Court vide judgment dated 30 March 2002 decreed the plaintiff's suit in part, holding the plaintiff entitled to disability pension, regarding injury No.2 (stab injury of abdomen), by discussing the matter in Para No. 11 of the judgment, finding that the injury was received by the plaintiff while on annual leave, and relying upon a judgment of Punjab and Haryana High Court in the case of *Gurmeet Singh Butter v. Union of India*, 2000(3) RSJ 327, found him entitled to disability pension for this injury. Regarding first disability the trial Court held that the legally constituted Medical Board assessed the disability to be less than 20% and, thus, he was not entitled to disability pension as per rules. Against this judgment, upholding discontinuance of disability pension for disability No.1, no appeal was filed by the plaintiff, nor even any cross-objections were filed in the appeal filed by the Union of India, with the result that the question of entitlement to get disability pension or any part thereof for the first disability became a closed chapter with the decision of the trial Court.

The defendants filed appeal to challenge the grant of disability pension for the second disability, and the Lower Appellate Court, vide judgment dated 24 November 2003, maintained the decree granted by the trial Court, again relying upon the judgment in *Gurmeet Singh Butter's* case. In para No.21 it was also observed, that the plaintiff was on annual leave when he intervened in a fight to pacify the parties, and in that process he received stab injury on his abdomen. Nothing was elicited from the witness by the plaintiff even by directing any cross-examination on that aspect.

The Tribunal considered that question as to whether the Lower Appellate Court and the Trial Court were right in holding the plaintiff to be entitled to get disability pension for the second disability, being stab injury in the abdomen, received by him at his home while on annual leave, by relying upon the judgment of Punjab and Haryana High Court in Gurmeet Singh Butter's case.

The Tribunal referred to the recent judgments of the Supreme Court in *Jagtar Singh v. Union of India*, Civil Appeal No. 1988 of 2011 decided on 13 March 2012; in *Union of India v. Talwinder Singh*, Civil Appeal No. 3686 of 2012 decided on 20 April 2012, and in *Union of India v. Jujhar Singh*, Civil Appeal No. 4281 of 2006 decided on 15 July 2011, which clearly held that in such circumstances plaintiff was not entitled to get disability pension, as the injury could not be said to be attributable to Military service. The Tribunal set aside the judgments and decrees of the lower Appellate Court and the Trial Court and the plaintiff's suit was dismissed.

IX. Discharge From Service

Discharge: four red-ink entries

The AFT Regional Bench Chandigarh in the case of *Kulawant Singh v. Union of India*, TA No. 127 of 2010, decided on 12 February 2013, considered a prayer for re-instatement in the service.

The petitioner was enrolled in the Army on 14 February1995. The petitioner was promoted to the rank of Acting Lance Dafedar in Jun 2001 and Lance Dafedar in Jan 2004. In his 11 years 8 months service the petitioner earned four red ink entries in his conduct sheet awarded by various commandants under s. 80 of the Army Act after adhering to the provisions of Army Rule 22. He was discharged on 28 October 2006 under Army Rule 13 (3) (III) (v) as services of the petitioner were no longer required as he was found to be an undesirable and inefficient soldier.

The petitioner contended that his discharge from service was illegal and unconstitutional. The red ink entry punishments were awarded without holding any inquiry or following the proper procedure. Moreover the petitioner was not medically examined by any medical officer at the time of passing order for discharge from service. He was neither provided an opportunity to explain his position nor provided the copy of the proceedings. In fact the defendants have passed the order of discharge without any jurisdiction, in violation of provisions of the Army Act and Army Rules.

The respondents contested in detail the reasons and procedure followed in the case of the petitioner's discharge under section 13 (3) item III (v); and in support cited the decision of the AFT Chandigarh Bench in the case of Singhara Singh v. Union of India OA No. 362 of 2011, decided on 07 January 2013.

The Tribunal while dismissing the petition made following observations:

(a) Disciplinary awards resulting in red ink entries in the service record may be challenged or represented against at the relevant time as provided by the statute, rules and regulations. They cannot be the subject of agitation at the time of notice of discharge being contemplated under Army Rule 13(3) Item III(v).

(b) The number of red ink entries alone was not the criteria for discharge under Army Rule 13(3)III(v). Four red ink entries are only a guideline. The disciplinary conduct of the individual as reflected in the service record and the requirement of maintaining discipline would decide if services are no longer required.

(c) Discharge under Army Rule 13(3) Item III (v) for services being no longer required was a consequence of unsatisfactory service record. It cannot be taken as a punishment.

(d) Discharge under Army Rule 13(3) Item III(v) is an administrative action resulting from an unsatisfactory record of service and was not a second punishment.

(e) Policy guidelines can supplement statutory provisions and rules, these cannot supplant them. As long as the statutory provisions and rules are adhered to no injustice can be claimed on grounds of non compliance of a policy guideline which supplants these provisions or rules.

Revocation of voluntary discharge

The AFT Principal Bench in the case of *Ex Hav Rampat Yadav v. Union of India*, OA No. 135 of 2013, decided on 2 April 2013, considered a request for quashing the order for discharge and reinstatement in service.

The petitioner was enrolled on 16 February 1977 in the Indian Army. He served in the Army till 1992. Thereafter, on superannuation he joined the Defence Security Corps (DSC) on 19 October 1992 in the rank of Sepoy. From 1992 he served in the various units of DSC. In January 2001, the applicant was posted to 221 DSC Platoon attached to the AFCC Gurgaon and assigned with duty to check the guards. In the night of 10/11 April 2011, while the applicant was carrying out checks of guards on duty, found one guard sleeping at Post. When the applicant woke him up and questioned as to why he was sleeping, the guard misbehaved with him and started beating the applicant with rifle butt due to which the applicant sustained injuries.

The applicant reported the matter to his Platoon Commander and also to the Security Officer who advised the applicant to go to unit Medical Inspection Room and get treatment. The applicant thereafter repeatedly requested the Security Officer to take action against the guard, however, no action was taken. The applicant sought interview of the Station Commander, which was denied to him. The Security Officer developed a grudge against the applicant and forced him to submit an application on 16 April 2011 for premature discharge from service on compassionate ground that his wife was falling frequently ill. He moved an application and discharge was sanctioned on 29 July 2011 to be effective 31 January 2012. Thereafter, the applicant sent a telegram dated 01 August 2011 for revocation of premature discharge and cancellation of his discharge order. However, no action was taken for revocation of voluntary discharge. Despite his repeated requests for revocation of voluntary discharge he was discharged on 31 January 2012, though the applicant wanted to continue till completion of his term of engagement up to 20 November 2013.

The Tribunal observed that that the authorities acted upon the request for premaster discharge and finally passed discharge order on 29 November 2011 but before he could be discharged i.e. on 31 January 2012, he has revoked the same by sending a telegram on 01 August 2011 and followed with a written request on 26 August 2011. The authorities should have taken necessary steps in the matter and revoked the discharge order when he had withdrawn his request for voluntary discharge. The authorities had no right to act upon his offer after the same had been revoked before it could be acted upon. In the case of *Balram Gupta v. Union of India* 1987 (Supp) SCC 228, in an identical situation a person sought voluntary retirement but he withdrew the same before it could be acted upon and the Lordship has laid down that, "there was no valid reason for withholding the permission by the respondent. Therefore, the appellant was entitled to put back to his job with all the consequential benefits being treated as in the job from 31 March 1981." In the case of *Shambu Murari Sinha v. Project & Development India* JT 2000 (6) SC 358 also a similar view was taken by the Supreme Court that, "the resignation, in spite of its acceptance, can be withdrawn before the "effective date."

The Tribunal quashed the discharge order and directed that the petitioner to be reinstated till he attains the age of superannuation. However, he shall have to return all the money which was paid to him (retirement benefits) back to respondent with interest.

Discharge after 6 red/black entries: not punitive

The AFT Regional Bench Kochi, in the case of *Rajesh U. Ex Naik v. Union of India*, OA No. 47 of 2010, decided on 1 March 2013, considered a prayer for reinstatement with back wages in the Army.

The applicant joined the Indian Army on 17 November 1988 as a Clerk in AMC at Lucknow. During the service, he was awarded five red and one black ink entries. The respondents found him as an undesirable soldier and decided to dispense with his services. Accordingly a notice dated 11 June 1999 was served on him to show cause as why his service should not be terminated as an undesirable soldier.

The applicant submitted his reply on 28 June 1999 to the show cause notice. The respondents considered the applicant's reply and ultimately decided to discharge him from service. The applicant questioned the order of discharge before the Kerala High Court vide OP No.198 of 2000, which was disposed of on 2 July 2004 with a direction to the concerned authority to pass appropriate order on the representation to be given by the applicant. Accordingly, the Chief of Army Staff considered the applicant's representation and passed the reasoned order dated 14 November 2004, whereby he rejected the applicant's representation. The Chief of Army Staff was of the view that the applicant's discharge from service was legal, just and appropriate.

Against the said order, the applicant preferred a Revision Petition before the Government of India, Ministry of Defence on 20 January 2005, which had been kept pending without any decision by the Government of India. The applicant, thereafter, filed WP (C) No. 23502 of 2008 before the High Court of Kerala, which was disposed of on 4 September 2008 with a direction to the Ministry of Defence to consider and pass orders on the applicant's Revision Petition expeditiously within three months from the date of the judgment, after affording an opportunity of being heard to the applicant.

The respondents filed Review Petition No. 558 of 2009 for modification of the order dated 4 September 2008. The Review Petition was dismissed with the observation that appeal could be filed against the judgment. Accordingly, the respondents filed WA No. 1396 of 2009 before a Division Bench of the

Kerala High Court, which was decided on 6 July 2009. The Division Bench concluded the matter with the observation that the direction issued by the Single Judge will not be taken as a direction to the Defence Secretary for personal hearing and disposal of the applicant's revision petition, which was only a direction to the Central Government. The Division Bench further observed that the decision could be taken in the matter as per the Rules of Business governing such decisions by the Government. In view of the direction of the Division Bench of the Kerala High Court, the Government of India, Ministry of Defence considered the Revision Petition and passed the speaking order dated 11 November 2009 dealing with all the relevant aspects of the matter. Not satisfied with the order the petitioner filed the instant Original Application.

The petitioner contended that the red as well as black ink entries were recorded against him by way of punishment, therefore, the same could not be taken as a ground to pass another punishment order in the form of discharge from the Army. The discharge from the Army on the basis of the aforesaid entries was virtually a second punishment with regard to the same misconduct, which was not legally permissible in law.

The respondents contested that the discharge from the service was not a punishment. In view of the antecedents of the applicant, he had become a liability to the Army as he was an undesirable soldier therefore; his discharge was not only in the interest of the Army but also in the interest of maintaining discipline in the Army. The applicant's discharge from the Army has been made under Army Rule 13(3) III (v), according to which, the Brigade or Sub Area Commander was the competent authority to discharge a person from the Army but before doing so, he has to give an opportunity to the person, whose discharge was contemplated, to show cause against the contemplated discharge. Further, the explanations and points raised by the applicant were given due consideration by the authorities.

The Tribunal considered the decision of the Supreme Court in the case of *Union of India v. Rajesh Vyas*, (2008) 3 SCC 386: "the purpose of the policy to discharge was to weed out undisciplined personnel by discharging them simpliciter and it was not a punitive action." The Tribunal thus dismissed the petition.

Discharge on compassionate grounds

The AFT Regional Bench Kochi in the case of *Sgt P Prem Kumar v. Union of India* OA No.7 of 2010, decided on 28 July 2010, considered a prayer for discharge on compassionate grounds.

The applicant was enrolled in the Indian Air Force on 7 September 1993 and his term of engagement was to expire on 6 September 2013. He had submitted an application on 4 December 2008 for discharge from the Air Force on compassionate grounds to look after his aged and ailing father. It was averred that the first applicant was the only son of his parents and there was no one else to look after his aged and ailing parents suffering from chronic ailments. As per the Air Force Order No. 16 of 2008, airmen were permitted to apply and seek discharge from service on compassionate grounds before expiry of their regular engagement. Illness of parents was one of the grounds for discharge. The application for discharge was recommended by the Commanding Officer, but was rejected by the higher authorities. No order rejecting his request was intimated to the applicant. He came to know about that fact from the website. The father of the applicant also made a representation before the respondents seeking discharge of the first applicant. He received a communication from the respondents stating that the application submitted by the first applicant has not been approved by the respondents, since he has not completed his initial term of engagement of 20 years. The applicant and his father together filed WP (C) No.12229 of 2009 before the High Court of Kerala alleging that two other airmen were discharged on getting civil employment. The respondents contended that due to shortage of manpower, the applicant could not be discharged.

The High Court observed that the Airmen of the same trade were discharged during the relevant period and there was no reason to adopt a different stand as far as the applicant was concerned. The High Court vide their judgment dated 20 October 2009 directed the respondents to reconsider the request made by applicant for compassionate discharge. The applicants filed a petition to initiate contempt of court action against the respondents. In that proceeding, an affidavit was filed on behalf of the respondents stating that the case was reconsidered and rejected again on 7 January 2010. The High Court closed the contempt case with an observation that if the petitioner was aggrieved he could seek relief against the order of 7January 2010.

The applicant contended that presently there was no shortage of manpower for missile fitter tradesmen as one airman of this trade was discharged from service on compassionate grounds with effect from 18 February 2009, and two were discharged from service for taking civil employment. Also a number of airmen personnel belonging to critical trades were employed in various duties not related to their trade.

The respondents contested that if the petitioner was discharged, it would adversely affect the posting, logistics and preparedness of the defence forces. It was also contended that petitioner was working and residing outside the territorial jurisdiction of this Tribunal and the OA was to be dismissed on the ground of lack of territorial jurisdiction. It was contended that territorial jurisdiction of the Tribunal was only what was being exercisable immediately before the date of its constitution and the Tribunal cannot wrest or exercise jurisdiction over subject matter, which is a primary concern of a Tribunal under whose jurisdiction the applicant was presently working.

The respondents also contested that applicant alone [The father of the applicant was the second petitioner in the case before the Tribunal] can be treated as the person aggrieved by the order impugned and not his father, the second applicant. Only a person aggrieved could approach the Tribunal of the zone where was working. The fact that second applicant received a communication does not confer the Tribunal jurisdiction to consider the Original Application. What the High Court was not permitted to do, this Tribunal may not entertain.

The Armed Forces Tribunal (Procedure) Rules, 2008 indicate the place of filing of application. As per Rule 6, the application should have been filed either before the Registrar of the Bench within whose jurisdiction the applicant was posted for the time being or was last posted or attached, or where the cause of action wholly or in part has arisen. Only a person who had ceased to be in service can approach the Bench at the place where he was ordinarily residing at the time of filing the application. The first applicant alone had a cause of action. He was posted at Jodhpur for the time being. The final order was passed and issued from New Delhi. The mere fact that certain letters were received in Kerala will not clothe the Tribunal with jurisdiction. The cause of action was either at Jodhpur or at New Delhi. The mere fact that the second applicant was residing in Kerala will not clothe this Tribunal with jurisdiction to entertain this Original Application. Further, the applicant was not discharged only because the rules did not permit it.

The petitioner contended that Rule 6 of the Armed Forces Tribunal (Procedure) Rules, 2008 stipulates that application 'shall ordinarily' be filed by the applicant where he was posted for the time being or was last posted or attached; or where the cause of action wholly or in part, has arisen. It was contended that the word used is 'ordinarily' which means that there can be some alternate place of jurisdiction also, depending upon the facts and circumstances of each case. Further, the part of cause of action has arisen in Kerala. Since Union of India is made a party, this Tribunal was having jurisdiction. The respondents were having an office at Kochi and were defending the case through the office at Kochi.

The Tribunal considered three points: (1) whether the Tribunal was having territorial jurisdiction to entertain the OA; (2) Whether the order passed by the respondents rejecting discharge was legal and proper; and (3) Whether the request of the petitioner for discharge on compassionate ground was allowable.

The Tribunal observed that since the applicants was posted to a unit c/o 56 APO, he was prohibited by the law to disclose the location of the unit. Further 56 APO starts from Kerala, Karnataka and extends up to Jammu and Kashmir. The respondents themselves had produced documents before the High Court of Kerala. When an airman was prohibited from disclosing the place where he was working, it was not at all just and proper to deny the relief on the ground that he did not disclose the place where he was working. The Tribunal held since Kerala falls under the jurisdiction of c/o 56 APO, the Bench of the Tribunal can exercise jurisdiction over the matter.

The Tribunal further held that the action of the respondents rejecting the request of the applicant to discharge him on the compassionate ground after allowing the request of other three persons and also deputing eight persons to non public fund institutions was not sustainable. The applicant was entitled to discharge on compassionate ground. The Tribunal set aside the respondent's letter dated 7 January 2010 and directed them to discharge the applicant on compassionate grounds in accordance with rules as expeditiously as possible, at any rate within three months from the date of the order.

Irregularity in discharge under habitual offender policy

The AFT Regional Bench Kochi in the case of *Paul K. John v. Union of India*, TA No. 65 of 2010, AT No. 21 of 2011 [TA No.24 of 2010 of AFT, Jaipur Bench and WP (C) No.2588 of 2001 of the High Court of Rajasthan], decided on 7 February 2012, considered a prayer challenging the order of discharge from the service.

The applicant was enrolled in the Indian Air Force on 12 October 1987 for a term of engagement for 20 years and was allotted the trade of ADSO with a reserve liability. The applicant before arriving on posting at No.505 Signals Unit had two minor punishment entries of 'Admonition' and 'Severe Reprimand' (i.e. two Black and one Red Ink entry) during his career of more than 9 years of service. However within the short span of nearly 1 year and six months service at his new unit, No. 505 SU the applicant had incurred four more minor punishment entries under s. 82 of the Air Force Act, 1950 due to personal grudge and the mala fides of his commanding officer and another superior officer. The applicant had made various representations in the form of ROG (Redressal of Grievances) under s. 26 of the Air Force Act.

During the year 1984 a policy with regard to the discharge of Airman under Air Force Rule 15 read in conjunction with sub-rule 2(g)(ii) of the Air Force Rules, 1969 was issued by the Air HQ which was duly modified vide Air HQ letter No. Air HQ/C 23406/685/PS dated 18 December 1986, giving the background, criteria, guidelines etc., prescribing the procedure for issue of warning letter, show cause notice and fresh show cause notice, movement of Airmen on posting and procedure for issuing a fresh show cause notice due to change of command and action at various levels including the ROG applications in relation to punishment entries, *etc*.

The applicant was issued with a warning letter for potential habitual offender by his commanding officer vide letter No.505SU/C451/9/P1 dated 14 October 1999 and was also cautioned. The applicant was awarded another punishment severe reprimand on 3 July 2000 and subsequently was issued with a show cause notice vide HQ CAC, IAF, Allahabad dated 18 August 2000 to show cause as to why he should not be discharged from service under Rule 15(2)(g)(ii) of Air Force Rules, read in conjunction with s. 22 of the Air Force Act, 1950. The applicant was also asked to submit a reply to the said show cause notice to his Commanding Officer within 10 days of the receipt of the show cause notice, failing which it shall be assumed that the applicant has nothing to urge in his defence against his discharge from the service and further action would be taken accordingly. The applicant submitted a detailed and comprehensive reply dated 13 September 2000 and explained not only the circumstances under which he was victimised but also invited the attention with regards to the unjust punishments awarded to him. The applicant was, however, posted out from No. 505 SU to AF Station Nal, under the jurisdiction of HQ WAC, IAF

The HQ CAC, intimated their counterpart at HQ WAC vide letter dated 21 November 2000 that since the applicant has been routed to new unit under HQ WAC, the documents relating to the applicant together with the recommendations and data sheet were forwarded for their further necessary action. The HQ WAC promptly returned the documents/papers stating that the Airman in his reply had made various allegations, which can be suitably replied and analysed by only his previous unit/command. Further, for the processing of the case at their HQ and the Airman will be attached to 505 SU till finalisation of the case. The applicant was subsequently issued a discharge order vide letter No.RO/2510/1/RW(Dis) dated 22 June 2001 under Air Force Rule 15(2)(g)(ii) 'his service no longer required – unsuitable for retention in the Air Force and to be SOS from the IAF with effect from 12 July 2001.'

The applicant contended that his grievance applications submitted under s. 26 of the Air Forces Act, 1950 were not considered by the competent authorities. Further, the procedure prescribed under AFO 341/67 about processing of the Redressal of Grievances applications was never followed. He further contended that the discharge order issued to him was non-speaking; illegal, void and unconstitutional and to be quashed and set aside by the Tribunal.

The respondents contested that the applicant was discharged from Air Force with effect from 12 July 2001 after following the procedures contemplated under law. The applicant was punished with black as well as red ink entries in the service book. The red ink entry recorded in the service was taken as a serious concern. The applicant was cautioned by the Station Commander vide communication dated 14 October 1999. However, despite warning the applicant again indulged in an act of indiscipline and consequently he was punished with "severe reprimand" on 3 July 2000.

The Tribunal considered whether the discharge of the applicant under Rule 15 (2)(g)(ii) of the Air Force Rules, 1969 is in conformity with the rules and procedures prescribed under Air Head Quarters Policy Letter No. C 23406/685/PS dated 18 December 1996. The Tribunal observed that after transfer from 505 SU AF to AF Station Nal, no fresh show cause notice was issued to him as contemplated under Air HQ letter No. C23406/685/PS dated 18 December, 1996, which was flagrant violation of the mandatory requirement of the rules.

The Tribunal also observed that the applicant had already completed 13 years and 9 months of Air Force Service as on 3 July 2000. Even though as per the dictum in *Union of India v. Corporal A.K. Bakshi* (1996) 3 SCC 65, the respondents were entitled to discharge the Air Force personnel under Rule 15(2)(g)(ii) of the Air Force Rules, 1969, in the case of the applicant since the respondents have failed to follow the mandatory rule of issuing second show cause notice after his transfer from 505 SU AF to AF Station Nal, the impugned order of discharge under challenge was vitiated and liable to be vacated. The Tribunal set aside the order of discharge against the applicant and ordered that applicant shall be deemed to have been discharged from service after completion of the required qualifying service for pension and consequently will be entitled to all monetary benefits.

Irregular discharge

The AFT Principal Bench New Delhi in the case of *L/Nk Sanjeev Kumar v. Union of India* in TA No. 413 of 2010 [WP(C)No. 5793 of 2007 of Delhi High Court], decided on 8 February 2010, set aside the order of discharge and reinstated the petitioner with all back wages.

The petitioner alleged that he was threatened by his commanding officer and forced to write an application for premature discharge from service. When he refused to do so, the commanding officer threatened with a trial by court martial. The petitioner submitted an application for pre-mature discharge under threat on the false ground of old age of his parents. Based on his application, he was actually discharged on 31 March, 2006 from his Unit. Petitioner was also asked to file an affidavit before civil courts that he is voluntarily submitting the letter of discharge and he will not agitate the matter in any court. The petitioner was detained at military station Bareilly from 6 March 2006 to 31 March 2006.

During his stay at Bareilly petitioner was forced to go on three days leave from 14 March to 16 March 2006 to his home for obtaining the signature of his wife on certain documents. However, petitioner filed an application for revocation of discharge and he gave a long telegram also but without any result. His name was finally struck off from the strength of Army. His statutory complaint dated 13/14 March 2006 was also rejected on 15 March 2007. Aggrieved against this order petitioner filed a Writ Petition before Delhi High Court, which was transferred to the Tribunal on its constitution.

The Tribunal observed: "Chief of the Army Staff has only disposed of the petition in a mechanical way without proper application of mind. When the petitioner is making assertion that his request for voluntary discharge was extracted under the pressure then, in that case, the proper course was to investigate the matter by a proper enquiry. This kind of casual disposal of the statutory complaint is not at all warranted. If the statutory complaints are disposed of in the light hearted fashion, then purpose of filing the complaint would loose its significance. So far as law is concerned, it is well settled by series of decisions of apex court that in case a person voluntarily gives letter for resignation, but, before it can be acted upon, it is revoked, then, in that case, the request for resignation cannot be implemented."

The Tribunal held that the action of the respondent is prima facie bad in law and the disposal of the statutory complaint by the Chief of the Army Staff on 15 March 2007 was wrong. The Tribunal set aside the order of discharge, and reinstated the petitioner with all back wages.

Discharge: unlikely to become an efficient Airman

The AFT Regional Bench Chennai in the case of *G. Devanand v. Union of India*, TA No.156 of 2010 [WP No. 25440 of 2003, High Court of Andhra Pradesh] decided on 10 December 2010, considered a petition against the discharge from the India Air Force. The petitioner, an air craftsman (under training) was discharged from Air Force service under Rule 15(2)(j) of the Air Force Rules on the ground 'unlikely to become an efficient Airman.'

The Tribunal after considering the achievements of the petitioner in sports and other activities set aside the order of discharge, with a direction to the respondents to reinstate the petitioner and give him an opportunity to complete the prescribed examination. The order also stated that the petitioner will not be entitled to any back wages for the interregnum period i.e., from the date of discharge till the date of reinstatement. If the petitioner was not reinstated within three months of the order, he would be entitled to claim wages with all monetary benefits as per Rules.

Cancellation of discharge and extension of service

The AFT New Delhi Principal Bench, Court No. 2, in the case of *Nb Sub Gulab Rao v. Union of India*, OA No. 513 of 2011, decided on 4 April 2012, considered a prayer for the cancellation of discharge order and extension of service.

The applicant was enrolled in the Indian Army on 30 January 1986. In the course of his service, he got promoted to Nb Sub. While was posted as Havildar at Udhampur, on 04 July 2009 he was admitted to the Command Hospital and his medical category was downgraded to P-3(T-24) w.e.f. 09 January 2010 for having been diagnosed as a case of HBV related cirrhosis of liver. The applicant was again reviewed by the Medical Board on 25 June 2010 in which he was upgraded to P-2(T-24) w.e.f. 16 August 2010 and with his next review board on 30 January 2011. Despite being low medical category (LMC) since he was within acceptable limits, he was promoted to the rank of Nb Sub on 01 January 2011. The applicant was again admitted in the Command Hospital on 22 January 2011 from where he was transferred to Army Hospital (R&R), New Delhi where he underwent deceased donor liver transplantation on 29 January 2011. It was also detected that the applicant had post transplant diabetes mellitus and was advised continuation of treatment by the Senior Advisor (Medicine and Gastroenterology). On 24 May 2011, a Medical Board was convened and his medical category was converted to P-2(P) w.e.f. 30 January 2011 with the next date of review being 30 January 2013.

On 5 May 2011, the applicant was posted to COD Delhi Cantt. on medical grounds to facilitate his treatment as advised by the Army Hospital. He reported to the new unit on 18 July 2011. Here he was informed that the respondents have issued discharge order in respect of the applicant dated 09 July 2011 and directed his previous unit to add the name of the applicant at Serial No.34, after Serial No.33 in the Appendix to the discharge order already issued on 04 January 2011 for discharge w.e.f. 31 January 2012. The applicant was informed by the unit in August 2011 that he was required to report to AOC Centre, Secunderabad on 04 January 2012 for discharge drill as he was to discharged w.e.f. 31 January 2012 since he was LMC P-2(P) w.e.f. 30 January 2011 before commencement of the extension period and therefore, as per existing policy at that time he was not eligible for extension of service and hence the discharge order was to be enforced on 31January 2012.

It was contended by the applicant that meanwhile, the Army HQ issued a revised policy regarding screening for extension dated 20 September 2010. Vide this policy, the parameters for LMC personnel to be granted extension were made similar to that of promotion policy dated 10 October 1997 that a LMC(P) army personnel is entitled to extension within acceptable medical category. Therefore, the applicant considered himself as being eligible for extension of service. It was contended that the applicant was told that the applicability of the policy is from 01 April 2011. Since the discharge order was issued on 09 July 2011, apparently it was not as per revised policy of 20 September 2010.

It was also contended that the applicant has left with just two years of service in the present rank and due to retire on 31 December 2013, it was only a matter of time that he was finally superannuate. But it was important that he received treatment in the Army Hospital which has been recommended by the Doctor and for that he was posted to Delhi. The applicant requested that his discharge order be set aside.

After considering the revised policy letter for screening, the Tribunal was of the view that the applicant should be governed by the revised policy of 20 September 2010. As such, he being P-2(P) was eligible for extension of service by two years from 31 January 2012 to 31 January 2014. The Tribunal directed that the applicant be deemed to be reinstated in service w.e.f. 31 January 2012 and would be entitled to continue in service with all consequential financial benefits. The respondents were directed completed the process within a period of 90 days from the date of the order.

Illegal discharge in low medical category

The AFT Principal Bench, New Delhi in the case of *Ex Sep Umesh Singh v. Union of India*, OA No. 38 of 2010, decided on 1 August 2012, considered a prayer for quashing discharge order.

The petitioner was enrolled in the Army on 29 December 1994 in the Army Medical Corps as an Ambulance Assistant. He was medically fit in all respects when he entered service. In the month of June 2005, the petitioner fell ill and it was detected that he was been suffering from 'Acute Hepatitis (Non B, Non C)' with 'Unconjugated Hyperbilurubinenza' (Gilbert's Syndrome). He was placed in temporary low medical classification S1H1A1P2(T-24)E for a period of six months by the Medical Board held at Army Hospital R&R, Delhi on 27 June 2005. He was again brought before the Medical Board in December, 2005 at Military Hospital for re-categorisation, which placed the petitioner in permanent low medical classification S1H1A1P-2(P)E1 w.e.f. 03 December 2005 for two years.

The military authorities issued a disposal order for low medical category persons on 21 August 2006 relating to the petitioner with a direction to the unit that he be discharged from service w.e.f. 01 February 2007. Thereafter a show cause notice was issued to the petitioner on 09 September 2006 to which he replied on 16 September 2006. Thereafter respondents passed a detailed speaking discharge order dated 27 October 2006 and finally his services were terminated w.e.f. 01 February 2007, on medical ground under the Army Rules 13. The petitioner's Writ Petition No. 3604 of 2007 of 16 January 2007 was dismissed by the Allahabad High Court for want of territorial jurisdiction on 24 January 2007.

The petitioner relied on the decision of the Supreme Court in the case of *Union of India v. Rajpal Singh* (2009) 1 SCC 216, wherein the Court had held that persons who have been downgraded to unacceptable low medical category status can only be discharged by holding Invalidating Medical Board (IMB) under Army Rule 13 (3) (iii). The Court also held that if a particular action is required to be taken in a particular manner then it should be taken in that manner only and not in any other way. The petitioner also submitted the reasons for delay in application and pleaded for condonation. Looking to the facts of the case, the Tribunal observed that the petitioner had made out a good case for condonation of delay under s. 22 of the Armed Forces Tribunal Act, 2007 and condoned the delay while exercising power under s. 22(2) of the Armed Forces Tribunal Act, 2007.

The Tribunal observed that the petitioner had been discharged on the basis of Release Medical Board (RMB) and not by the IMB. Therefore, in view of above judgment of Supreme Court, discharge orders passed on the basis of RMB dated 21 August 2006 and 27 October 2006 were held to be illegal and same were accordingly set aside.

Keeping in view that the petitioner had illegally been discharged by RMB in 2006, the Tribunal ordered that the petitioner will be deemed to have completed his qualifying service of 15 years i.e. up to 28 December 2009 and he would be entitled for service pension. Petitioner would also be paid arrears of the service pension. It was made clear that petitioner will continue to get the disability pension besides service pension and the decision given in the case of *Subedar (SKT) Puttan Lal v. Union of India* decided on 20 November 2008 will not come in his way as he has already agitated the matter before the Allahabad High Court at the relevant point of time.

Discharge: unsuitable in training

The AFT Principal Bench, New Delhi in the case of *Pramod Kumar Singh v. Union of India*, TA No. 595 of 2010, [WP (C) No.1252 of 2009 of Bombay High Court] decided on 8 August 2012, considered a prayer for setting aside an order for discharge.

The petitioner was enrolled into the Navy as Matric Entry Recruits (MER) for 2/2002 Batch. He initially reported at INS Netaji Subhas, Kolkata and was thereafter sent to INS Chilka, Orissa for the necessary training course for a period of six months. After completing the training, the petitioner was allotted Medical Care Department and was posted on 02 August 2002 as Medical Assistant (MER) at INS ASVINI, Colaba, Mumbai The petitioner after having appointed as a Medical Assistant was required to clear specific course being MA-II 'Q' Course.

The petitioner reported at the School of Medical Assistants, Mumbai on 30 March 2003. He was unable to clear the said course in the first attempt held in October 2003 and also in re-examination held in April 2004. Since the petitioner was not able to clear the said course, he requested for a change of branch from MER (Medical Assistant) to NMER (Steward/Cook), as a number of people were permitted to change the branch earlier. Para 278 (i) (a) of Regulations for Navy Part III makes a provision that if a sailor due to reason of incompetency was unable to perform the duties of the lowest rate in his branch, may volunteer for transfer to a different rate and the Commanding Officer shall then forward the application for such change of branch in accordance with Regulation 273.

The petitioner's case for the change of branch was also recommended but he was not permitted to change from MER to NMER and was discharged from the service. His writ petition before the High Court of Patna was dismissed on 12 February 2007 on account of lack of territorial jurisdiction. Then, the petitioner then filed a writ petition bearing No. 2407 of 2007 before the Bombay High Court. The said writ petition was disposed off by the order dated 16 January 2008 with the direction that the petitioner may file an appropriate representation and the same may be disposed off expeditiously. The petitioner filed a representation before the Naval authorities and the same was rejected on 15 May 2009. Thereafter, the petitioner filed the petition before the Bombay High Court challenging that order.

The respondents in their reply pointed out that the petitioner failed in MA-II 'Q' Exam and thereafter he was given another opportunity but he could not succeed, therefore, as per Regulation 278 (4) he was found 'unsuitable', and his services were discharged. So far as his representation with regard to giving him alternative appointment like Steward/Cook was concerned, it was considered but was not agreed. Therefore, the petitioner could not be offered an alternative appointment.

After going through the Regulation 273 as well as Naval Order 8 of 2001, the Tribunal was of the opinion that there was no prohibition in all these Regulations for offering an appointment for a lower grade to the incumbent if he was not found 'suitable' for the post for which he had been recruited. The Tribunal observed that it was true that in case the person who has failed to qualify for the post for which he has been selected during the training period, then only the option is to discharge him from the service. The authorities can consider the matter sympathetically but the petitioner as a matter of right cannot seek an alternative appointment, if he was not found suitable during the training. The Tribunal desired that the authorities may take a sympathetic approach in the matter and if they found fit, the services of the petitioner can be utilised for any post like Steward.

Discharge: five red-ink entries

The AFT Principal Bench New Delhi in the case of *Ex Nk Birendra Kumar Singh v. Union of India*, TA No. 563 of 2009 [WP (Civil) No. 6577 of 1998], decided on 27 February 2012, considered a prayer for setting aside an order of discharge from the service.

The petitioner was enrolled in Indian Army Sepoy on 11 January 1984 and he became Naik in 1992. On 25 November 1995 a show cause notice was issued to him on account of earning more than four red ink entries and he was asked to give a reply till 28 November 1995. The petitioner did not submit any reply and wanted to meet the issuing authority i.e. his commanding officer and the permission for same was not granted. On 29 November 1995 he was discharged from service. He filed a writ petition in the Patna High Court which was rejected because of lack of territorial jurisdiction. Thereafter, he filed a writ petition in in the Delhi High Court in 1998.

The petitioner contended that he was served with a show cause notice only on 27 November 1995 and he was asked to file a reply by 28 November 1995, and therefore, he did not get sufficient opportunity to reply. Further, the Army HQ letter dated 28 December 1988 contained a detailed procedure for removal of undesirable and inefficient JCO, Warrant Officer and Other Ranks and in that it is mentioned that how a person with more than four red ink entries should be dealt with by the commanding officer. The petitioner contended that the said procedure was not followed in his case.

The respondents contested that the petitioner had earned five red ink entries during the tenure of 11 years and 9 months of service. In view of these five red ink entries the documents were forwarded to the Brigade Commander and a show cause notice was given to the petitioner in front of two accused and his reply was sought but he refused to accept the show cause notice. The petitioner was given a show cause notice on 25 November 1995 and it was sought to be served on 25 November 1995 but he declined to accept it. The respondents also referred the decision of the Supreme Court in *Union of India v. Deepak Kumar Santra* 2009 7 SCC 370 in which the Court has held that once the Army Rule provides that the commanding officer is competent to discharge a person then in that case any circular issued by the authorities will be of no significance. Further, the Delhi High Court has followed the decision of the Supreme Court in the case of *Sepoy Islam Khan v. Union of India* (WP (C) 5023 of 2011 decided on 12 September 2011).

The Tribunal dismissed the petition and held that in view of the fact that incumbent has earned five red ink entries, the commanding officer under Army Rule 13(3) was fully competent to discharge a person and the petitioner has been rightly discharged from service.

Irregularity in discharge on medical grounds

The AFT Principal Bench New Delhi in the case of *Rfn Ram Pal v. Union of India*, OA No. 712 of 2010, decided on 7 February 2012, considered a prayer for reinstatement in the service.

Petitioner vide this petition has prayed that respondents may be directed to allow the petitioner to join duty at the Rajputana Rifles Centre immediately. It is also prayed that respondents may be directed to treat the petitioner absent without leave only for the period from 22 February 2009 to 24 May 2009 and to regularize this period.

The petitioner was enrolled in the Indian Army on 21 September 2001 and was assigned to Rajputana Rifles. After successful completion of training, he was posted to Raj Rif. He was sent on deputation to Mtn Bde located in field area where he performed his duties with complete dedications from May 2005 to September 2008. Because of stressful environment in Mtn Bde, petitioner developed psychiatric problem but it was initially dormant. He was posted back to his parent unit in September 2008. Since the petitioner was suffering from "varicose veins", he was operated in Military Hospital (MH) Mhow in October/November, 2008. As a result of operation/hospitalization, he developed a high blood pressure and the disease was diagnosed as primary hypertension. The petitioner also developed psychiatric problems and was treated in MH Jabalpur and was placed in medical category P-3 and S-3 and was discharged from hospital on 21 February 2009.

On arrival to unit, the petitioner again got mentally disturbed and, therefore, requested for 15 days leave as he had entire leave for 2009 to his credit but the request of the petitioner was denied by the authorities. Because of depressed and desperate condition, petitioner went home to meet his family on 22 February 2009 without authorized leave. Then after his mental condition stabilized, the petitioner reported to Raj Rif Centre at 1230 hrs on 25/26 May, 2009. His name was entered in the Register kept at Kargil Gate. Hav Narender, the RP Hav took the petitioner to Centre Sub Maj who took him to Centre Adjutant. After consultation with the Deputy Commandant, the Adjutant ordered Sub Maj that the petitioner will not be allowed to join duty and he be pushed out of Centre's gate. Thereafter petitioner went to his unit and reported at 1230 hrs on 09 July 2009. He could not pick up courage earlier to go to his unit and, therefore, went to his unit along with Rfn Jagdeep of the same unit. At the gate, he met Rfn Mukesh of the regimental police (RP) who took the petitioner to Sub Maj Mahender Singh. Thereafter, petitioner was sent to Adjutant Maj Akhelesh Kumar duly escorted. The Adjutant spoke to the commanding officer who ordered that the petitioner be thrown out of unit immediately. He filed certain representations but without any result. The petitioner has also contended that he has not been paid his salary w.e.f 01 December 2008 and his arrears on account of pay and allowance were approximately Rs 1,25,000/-. The respondents contested that the petitioner never reported to the Centre or to the Unit.

In order to verify the contentions of the petitioner, the Tribunal vide order dated 03 February 2012 directed the respondents to produce the relevant register kept at the entry gate of the Centre and Unit. The respondents after scrutinizing the register pointed out that on 26 May 2009 petitioner did report at Raj Rif Centre at Kargil Gate and there was a corresponding entry to this effect in the register. Though in the reply filed by the respondents, it is mentioned that petitioner never reported to Centre or his Unit. The Tribunal observed that the reply was not filed with due diligence.

The Tribunal commented that when petitioner reported to Raj Rif Centre on 26 May 2009 then at least he should have taken on the roll and a proper inquiry should have been instituted to find out the cause of his absence and accordingly, respondents could have taken a proper action in accordance with law. The Tribunal, therefore, directed the respondents to take petitioner back in service and proper action may be taken in accordance with law. The amount due to the petitioner should also be paid to him in accordance with rules.

***

The AFT Principal Bench New Delhi in the case of *Rakshak Ganga Ram Singh v. Union of India* in OA No. 217 of 2012 with MA No. 304 of 2012 and OA No. 186 of 2012 with MA No. 255 of 2012, decided on 8 March 2013, considered a common question of law and facts.

The petitioner was enrolled in the Territorial Army (TA) on 01 April 1997. He had put in 9 years and 281 days of military embodied service in the TA, when in the year 2010 an advertisement cum proposal was received in the unit for volunteers who want to go to Defence Security Corps (DSC) on permanent transfer. Petitioner, looking to the bright prospects in the DSC service, opted for DSC service and his bio data was sent to DSC records on 30 March 2010. The DSC records verified the same and gave a call letter after which the petitioner put up a request for voluntary discharge from service and he was discharged on 30 March 2010. The petitioner reported to DSC centre for training and was re-enrolled on 31 March 2010. On 29 June 2010 the DSC realized that the petitioner had three red ink entries in his service record, therefore, he was not eligible to be enrolled in the DSC service. There was a lot of correspondence between DSC records and the TA. On 29 June

2010 the petitioner was issued a show cause notice proposing to discharge the petitioner from the service. The petitioner replied to the same on 06 July 2010 and he was discharged from service on 25 July 2010.

The respondents contested the petition and pointed out that as per the policy of Ministry of Defence letter Nop.62502/Rtg-5(OR)A dated 13 September 2007 any individual opting for DSC should not have incurred more than two red ink entries during the entire previous service and not more than one red ink entry during the last five years prior to the date of discharge from the previous service for re-enrolment into DSC. The petitioner had incurred three red ink entries during his former service, therefore, he was not eligible for re-enrolment into DSC and was accordingly discharged as per provisions of Rule 13(3), item (iv) of Army Rule 1954.

The Tribunal observed that the Chief Record Officer, 114 Infantry Bn, TA should not have forwarded the application of the petitioner when they very well knew that he had three red ink entries and was ineligible for DSC service. Further, the DSC should not have entertained the petitioner without going through the records forwarded along with the application. Both the departments, the TA and the DSC have faulted in not properly examining the records of the petitioner and acted in a most irresponsible manner. The petitioner had been on the receiving end and was suffering because he had lost his job. Neither the DSC was going to take him back or the TA, because the TA has already accepted his voluntary discharge from service. However, in the present case initial mistake has been committed by TA. Therefore, it was the responsibility of the 114 infantry battalion TA Jat Regiment to take him back in service and give him all benefits as the primary mistake was committed by them.

The Tribunal in the case of *Sepoy Amit Kumar v. Union of India,* OA 186 of 2012 observed that the same mistake was committed by the Dogra Regiment and therefore, Dogra Regiment was responsible and petitioner to be taken back by Dogra Regiment and he will also be entitled to salary for the interim period of his discharge from DSC and reinstatement. This period will be counted for his pension also. The Tribunal ordered that both petitioners to be reinstated in service within three months of the order.

X. Dismissal

Administrative dismissal

The Armed Forces Tribunal, Principal Bench (Court No. 2), in the case of *Ex Sgt R.S. Dwivedi v. Chief of the Air Staff,* TA 404 of 2010 [WP (C) No. 9959 of 2009], decided on 19 October 2011, held that punishment of dismissal awarded under section 20 (3) of the Air Force Act, 1950 read with Rule 18 of Air Force Rules of 1969, was 'little' severe, keeping in view the conduct of the delinquent and his unblemished record. The Bench referred the cases of *Bhagat Ram v. State of Himachal Pradesh* (1983) 2 SCC 442 and *Nk Sardar Singh v. Union of India* (1991) 3 SCC 213 where the Supreme Court had laid down that the punishment should be proportionate to the gravity of misconduct and further it should be tempered by the past conduct of the delinquent.

The Tribunal held that considering the length of service put in by the applicant, and the facts and circumstances of the case; the punishment given to the applicant be moderated so that he remained entitled to pension. The Tribunal remanded the case back to the Competent Authority for reconsideration of the punishment of dismissal, to be decided preferably within a period of 120 days.

Violation of principle of natural justice

The AFT Principal Bench, New Delhi in the case of *R.N. Pandey v. Chief of the Army Staff*, TA No. 88 of 2009 [WP (C) No. 3034 of 1994], decided on 1 December 2010, considered a case of dismissal under AA s. 20 read with Army Rule 17.

The appellant joined the Indian Army as a Sepoy on 26 October 1959. In 1989, he became a Junior Commissioner Officer. When there were barely five months left for him to superannuate, the appellant was dismissed from service, based on a complaint levelled against him by the widow of one Sepoy, who had committed suicide on 15 August 1995. The widow had also filed a complaint before the civil police, which was investigated, but dropped as baseless.

The military authorities, based on the applications of the widow ordered a court of inquiry which held the appellant blameworthy on the following account: (a) failed in duties by not exercising proper command and control that ultimately resulted in the suicide of Sepoy Kumar; (b) failed in duties in the absence of superior to arrange immediate and expert medical aid to the deceased; (c) failed to provide a guard immediately on occurrence of the incident resulting in total loss of important evidences; (d) attempted to steal affection of a subordinate's wife and making advances to her, the honour of whom it was the sacred duty to uphold; (e) used abusive language to subordinates and causing harassment to the deceased; and (f) indulged in obscene and unnatural acts with a subordinate. Based on the findings of court of inquiry, the appellant was given a show cause notice under section 20 (1) of the Army Act read with Army Rule 17. Having found no substance in the grounds put forth by the appellant, he was dismissed from service.

It was contended by the appellant that by not following the provisions under the Army Act and the Rules, the military authorities violated the principles of natural justice, equity and fairness. Further the court of inquiry was illegal. He was denied a fair opportunity to defend his case, as copy of the court of inquiry proceedings was not given to him. In its absence, the appellant did not know on what grounds he had to defend himself. In addition, the findings of the court of inquiry and the proceedings under section 20 (1) of the Army Act read with Army Rule 17 are contrary to the final report given by the civil police.

The Tribunal observed that the military authority failed to furnish any of the documents referred to in the show cause notice to the appellant. This deprived him of an opportunity to defend his case. Non adherence to the Army

Rules had vitiates the impugned order.

The Tribunal made reference to the decision of the Supreme Court in *Arivazhagan v. State* (AIR 2000 SC 1198), wherein it was observed by the Court that "it is essential that the rules of procedure designed to ensure justice should be scrupulously followed and the court should be jealous in saying that there is no breach of them." Further, in *Uma Nath Pandey v. State of U.P.* (AIR 2009 SC 2375), the Supreme Court held:

> "16. Natural justice has been variously defined by different Judges. A few instances will suffice. In *Drew v. Drew and Lebura* (1855(2) Macg. 1.8, Lord Cranworth defined it as 'universal justice'. In *James Dunber Smith v. Her Majesty the Queen* (1877-78(3) App. Case 614, 623 JC) Sir Robert P. Collier, used the phrase 'the requirements of substantial justice', while in *Arthur John Specman v. Plumstead District Board of Works* (1884-85(1) App. Case 229, 240), Earl of Selbourne, SC preferred the phrase 'the substantial requirement of justice'. Lord Esher, MR defined natural justice as 'the natural sense of what is right and wrong'. While deciding *Hookings v. Smethwick Local Board of Health* (1890(24) QBD 712), Lord Fasher, instead of using the definition given earlier by him in Vionet's case chose to define natural justice as 'fundamental justice'. In *Ridge v. Baldwin* (1963(1) WB 569, 578), Harman LJ, in the Court of Appeal countered natural justice with 'fair-play in action' a phrase favoured by Bhagawati, J. in *Maneka Gandhi v. Union of India* (1978(2) SCR 621)."

The Tribunal observed that the non-furnishing of the papers to the appellant amounted to denial of full opportunity to appellant to explain the adversities appearing against him. The appellant had put in 27 years of service and was dismissed without following due procedure. Such action on the part of the respondents is against the principles of natural justice. The Tribunal set aside the order of dismissal and directed that the appellant shall be deemed to have been discharged from service from the date of his dismissal entitling him for all pensionary benefits.

Dismissal converted to discharge

The AFT New Delhi Principal Bench, Court No. 2, in the case of *Hav Avinash U Pardeshi v. Union of India*, OA No. 112 of 2011, decided on 07 May 2012, considered the legality of the order of court martial.

The applicant was enrolled in the Indian Army on 01 January 1995 in the trade of musician. He was charged for abetment of offence committed by L/Nk M. Suresh Babu in respect of sale of five passports prepared for visit to Germany to a civilian. He was also charged for visiting Embassy of Germany without proper authority and clearance, in contravention of existing orders.

After a court of inquiry was held to investigate the matter, the applicant was served with a show cause notice on 23 June 2010 by the GOC, HQ Delhi Area under section 20(3) of Army Act read with Army Rules 17. The applicant responded to the show cause notice on 26 August 2010 and denied all the charges as also the evidence recorded in the court of inquiry and subsequently in the summary of evidence. In his reply, the applicant stated that he has not been supplied with the findings of the court of inquiry and therefore, was unable to reply completely to the charges made against him. He further contended that there is no evidence to prove the charges against him. The service of the applicant was terminated by the orders of GOC HQ Delhi Area on 08 September 2010 who considered both the show cause notice as also the reply submitted by the applicant to the show cause notice dated 26 August 2010. At the time of dismissal, the applicant had put in almost 16 years of unblemished service.

The applicant contended that there has been violation of Army Rule 180 and 184; therefore, the applicant was prejudiced in preparation of his defence. The Army Rule 180 was not invoked in its letter and spirit and therefore, the court of inquiry was vitiated and thus no action should have been initiated based on only the court of inquiry. The applicant further contended that the show cause notice was based on the court of inquiry, which itself was vitiated and therefore, the entire action was the colourable exercise of power by the administrative authorities. The applicant also contended that the punishment of dismissal awarded to him was too harsh especially, in view of the fact that the there was no evidence whatsoever even remotely connected to the applicant in the case. He was a very senior Havildar and was on the verge of earning his pension and had maintained exemplary.

In support of contentions, the applicant cited the case of *Managing Director, ECIL, Hyderabad v. B. Karunakar* AIR 1994 SCC 1074, wherein the Supreme Court had observed: "Delinquent is entitled to copy thereof before disciplinary authority takes decision regarding guilt or innocence. Refusal to furnish a copy amounts to denial of reasonable opportunity for defence."

The respondents contested that the court of inquiry had found the applicant guilty of abetment of offence committed by L/Nk Suresh Babu with respect to sale of five passports to a civilian, and twice visiting Embassy of Germany without proper authority. Since the trial of the applicant by Court Martial was felt to be inexpedient and impracticable as he had retracted from his earlier admissions during the summary of evidence, it was decided by the GOC Delhi Area to take administrative action under section 20(3) of the Army Act read with Army Rule 17. After considering the reply of the applicant to the show cause notice, a speaking order was passed whereby the services of the applicant were directed to be terminated w.e.f. 08 September 2010. Further the documents that were supplied to the applicant were the proceedings of the court of inquiry less the recommendations and opinion and there was no violation of Army Rule 184.

The Tribunal observed that in the present case the applicant has not able to establish the facts that how he has been prejudiced by non-supply of complete court of inquiry proceedings. On the contrary, evidence collected during the inquiry and summary of evidence has been supplied and he was aware of the allegations levelled against him. The contentions raised in this regard were not sustainable. Further no prejudice has been caused to the applicant in preparation of his defence.

The Tribunal was of the view that considering the charges against the applicant and also taking into account his unblemished service for 15 years and 8 months, the punishment of dismissal is rather harsh. Furthermore, the CBI having interrogated him had not filed any case against him as has been done in the case of L/Nk M. Suresh Babu. The Tribunal held that in the interest of justice interference is needed in the dismissal order. It ordered that the dismissal be treated as "discharge" with consequential benefits.

Dismissal under section 20 not bad in law

The AFT Principal Bench, Court No. 2, in the case of *Ex Hav Prem Upreti v. Union of India* TA No. 163 of 2010 [WP (C) 23738 of 2005], decided on 4 May 2012, considered a prayer for quashing of the order of dismissal.

A General Court Martial (GCM) was ordered against applicant by the GOC Delhi area on 12 December 2001. There were allegations against the applicant that he was involved in an offence prejudicial to the safety or interest of the state i.e. in espionage activities, and a criminal case was pending in civil court filed by the civil police. In view of legal infirmities of jurisdiction with regard to GCM proceedings, the applicant filed a WP (C) No. 4212 of 2002 and the Delhi High Court passed a stay order on the further proceeding of the GCM which remained operative for two and a half years. On 11 December 2004, the Army Authorities issued a show cause notice under section 20 of the Army Act read with Army Rule 17 for taking administrative action against him. The applicant submitted a reply to the show cause notice on 25 December 2004 denying all the allegations. On 28 December 2004, vide impugned order the services of the applicant were terminated.

The applicant contended that on 23 November 2004, the respondents conceded and cancelled the GCM and confirmed to the Delhi High Court that the case would be transferred to the Court of Civil Judge (Judicial) Roorkee for trial as criminal case was pending before the said Court. While on the other hand they issued a show cause notice on 11 December 2004. The applicant also contended that since the case was subjudice, the show cause notice and further action should not have been taken. This action of the respondents was bad in law and his termination of service should be quashed. In support of his contentions, the applicant cited the case of *Ex Sgt Avimanyu Panda v. Union of India* 78 (1999) DLT 47 in which the Court had observed that issuing a show cause notice after dropping court martial proceedings is arbitrary exercise of powers.

The Tribunal observed that the applicant was found involved in espionage activities. After an inquiry was made by the Army in the facts and circumstances of case, the decision not to retain the applicant in service does not seem without any basis. Referring to the cases of *Union of India v. Harjeet Singh Sandhu*, JT 2001(4) SC 597, *The Chief of Army Staff v. Major Dharam Pal Kukrety*, (1985) 2 SCC 412, and *Union of India v. J. S. Sivia*, MLJ 1996 SC, the Tribunal held that the action of respondent authorities was not arbitrary or malafide. It dismissed the petition.

Reduction to rank, punishment quashed.

The AFT Regional Bench Lucknow, in the case of *Nk/SKT (Sepoy) Lalan Kumar v. Union of India*, TA No. 42 of 2010, decided on 19 March 2012, considered a prayer for quashing the order of reduction to ranks.

The applicant was enrolled in the Indian Army on 04 July 1991 and was promoted to the rank of Naik. He was made NCO in-charge of the Butchery along with Subedar, JCO in-charge of Butchery and the Officer Commanding. In the night of 3/4 April 1997 some carcasses slaughtered in the night were found insufflated. A court of inquiry was held in which it was found that the applicant as also the Subedar, the veterinary officer, officer commanding, and the contractor had defaulted. A show cause notice dated 26 January 2003 was issued to the applicant alleging that the applicant had neglected to obey technical instructions 9/89 of Headquarters Central Command, ST Branch by not being present in the Buchery for entire duration from slaughtering to issue of the meat thus, resulting in insufflation of 11 carcasses. He also failed to report to his officer commanding regarding shortage of water and electricity thereby causing delay in the slaughter and late setting-in of the meat.

The applicant submitted his reply to the show cause notice. The Commandant, Punjab Regimental Centre, by an order dated 04 February 2003, ordered that the applicant to be reduced to the rank of Sepoy under section 20 (4) of the Army Act, as the reply of the applicant was found unsatisfactory. The applicant filed a statutory complaint which was rejected by an order dated 17 November 2004. He then filed a WP No. 312 of 2005 in the Allahabad High Court, which was transferred to the Tribunal.

The applicant contended that during the course of slaughtering, the electricity supply and water supply were disconnected for a period of half an hour and he had gone to MES complaint cell to have the water supply restored. The water supply was restored within short time and therefore, the applicant cannot be blamed. He also contended that other than him, no other official was present in the butchery. Also he could not report about the failure of the electricity and shortage of water to the commanding officer as there was no telephone within the butchery premises and no one from staff was present there apart from him. The applicant also contended that he has been made a scapegoat and action has been taken against him whereas other defaulting officers and contractor had been let off liberally or without any punishment.

The Tribunal examined the court of inquiry proceedings and observed that none of the witnesses had stated anything to falsify the explanation given by the applicant in his statement before the inquiry. There was no material to indicate that explanation given by the applicant was false. Further no material had been filed nor any inquiry was made from the MES staff whether there had been failure of water and electricity supply.

The Tribunal observed that no action was taken against the officer commanding, and Subedar JCO in-charge of the butchery. A show cause notice was issued to veterinary officer and he was awarded severe displeasure (recordable). There was nothing to show that any action was taken against the contractor. Further, Article 14 of the Constitution of India applies also in the matter of award of punishment and where it is found that the persons equally responsible or more responsible for the default have been let off with no punishment or lighter punishment the punishment awarded to a person who has been singled out cannot be sustained. Referring the decision of the Supreme Court in *Bongaigaon Refinery & Petrochemicals Ltd v. Girish Chandra Sarma* (2007) 7 Supreme Court Cases 206, the Tribunal quashed the order of punishment of reduction of rank with consequential benefits.

XI. Extension of Service

Failure to grant extension, fault of the organization

The AFT Principal Bench New Delhi, Court No. 2 in the case of *Hav Parmanand Sahoo v. Union of India*, OA No. 228 of 2010, decided on 21 May 2012, considered a prayer for setting aside the retirement order.

The applicant joined the Indian Army in EME Corps on 01 October 1983. In due course, he became a Havildar. The applicant was posted from EME Battalion to 17 Horse on 02 September 2007 and subsequently to HQ Armd Brigade on 17 May 2008. The movement was duly informed to the EME Record Office vide Part-II order. On 06 October 2008, the EME Records issued a letter detailing the applicant for promotion cadre course from Havildar to Nb Subedar. Unfortunately, the intimation of the cadre promotion course never reached the applicant's unit as it was sent to the previous unit of the applicant. Hence the applicant was unable to attend the said course. The applicant was issued with the retirement order in the rank of Havildar w.e.f. 01 October 2009 and was also informed on 19 March 2009 by the respondents that he has been superseded since he was not qualified on the promotion cadre course.

The unit of the applicant immediately took up the case with the officer in-charge EME Records vide letter dated 09 July 2009 informing that the unit was never informed that the applicant has been detailed for the promotion cadre course. A similar letter was also sent by the unit on 11 July 2009 to the higher formations. Looking at the urgency of the case, the DDG EME also wrote a letter dated 13 July 2009 addressed to the EME Records stating that the applicant was not at fault and he should not be penalised for organisational lapses. The EME Records replied on 14 July 2009 to the unit, admitting the fault of the previous unit of the applicant but declined to give any relief to the applicant stating policy constraints. The applicant submitted a non-statutory complaint dated 05 August 2009 and again on 07 September 2009 seeking redressal for promotion to the rank of Nb Subedar which was not disposed off at the time of filing of the present OA. The applicant finally retired on 30 September 2009.

The applicant contended that this was a clear case of lapse and mismanagement by the Record Office. The Record Office was always aware of the location of the individual as the Part-II Order of his movement was published on 21 July 2008 immediately after his arrival to the new unit on 17 May 2008.

The respondent contested that since the applicant could not attend the said course, he was declared absent on the course. Thereafter, the applicant could not be detailed again for the subsequent promotion cadre course as per Government of India letter dated 04 May 1999 wherein there was a restriction on the age for promotion to the rank of Nb Subedar which was normally below 44 years of age or those who have not completed more than 26 years of service. In the instant case, the applicant's date of birth was 22 March 1965 and he had crossed the upper age limit of 44 years for promotion to the rank of Nb Subedar on 22 March 2009.

The respondents further contested that while going on the UN Mission, the applicant has submitted "Adverse Career Certificate". On his de-induction from UN Mission, the applicant did not ever represented for undergoing promotion cadre course and his promotion prospects. He did not even make a representation even after the issuance of discharge order. Therefore, the applicant was discharged on 30 September 2009 on completion of his 26 years of service as per terms and conditions applicable to his rank.

The Tribunal observed that looking at the dates and the time available, the Record Office cannot absolve itself from not having despatched the letter to the correct unit of the applicant about promotion cadre course. Further, the other excuses submitted by the respondent were also baseless. It was obligatory duty of the respondents to intimate the applicant for cadre course, and they utterly failed in discharging their duty; for that the applicant cannot be blamed and made sufferer. The correspondence on record clearly showed that the organisation was at fault for not intimating the applicant for cadre test, resulted in deprivation of promotion and financial loss thereon and for extension of period of service.

The Tribunal referred to its judgment in *Vinod Kumar (Retired) v. Union of India* OA No. 639 of 2010 decided on 10 May 2012; and the Supreme Court judgement in *Govt. of A.P. v. M. Adbuta Rao* (2005) 12 SCC 258; where in the petitioners were compensated against the wrongs committed by the respondents. Making note that the applicant cannot be promoted even notionally to the rank of Nb Subedar as he was lacking of mandatory promotion criteria, the Tribunal awarded compensation of Rs. 50,000/- to the applicant to meet the ends of justice. The amount was to be paid within 90 days of the order, failing which interest @12% would be chargeable on the amount to be paid from the date of the order.

Arbitrary extension policy

The AFT Regional Bench Jaipur in the case of *Baidaya Nath Ghosh v. Union of India* TA No. 81 of 2009 [WP (C) No. 2566 of 2007, decided on 11 November 2011, considered a prayer for quashing of the order by which two years extension granted to him was cancelled.

The applicant was enrolled in the Indian Army on 27 June 1979 and in the due course was promoted to the rank of Subedar. Consequent to the change in terms and conditions of service, the applicant was considered for extension of his service beyond two years i.e. from 28 to 30 years and was screened by a Board constituted for this purpose. The Board extended the service of the applicant by two years till 26 June 009 vide order dated 5 September 2005. However, by an order dated 20 March 2006, the extension granted to the applicant was cancelled on the ground that he did not meet the discipline criteria as laid down for extension of service. The letter stated, that a punishment under section 39(b) of the Army Act, 1950 was awarded to the applicant on 7 April 1982 when he was Sepoy and the said punishment, debarred him from grant of further extension. Accordingly, the retirement order of the applicant was issued a fresh on 9 July 2006, by which he retired on 30 June 2007 without having been granted extension of two years service.

Being aggrieved by the denial of extension, the applicant filed a writ petition in the Rajasthan High Court at Jaipur. During pendency of the said writ petition, the Army Headquarters modified the policy and the discipline criteria for grant of extension of two years to Junior Commissioned Officers (JCOs). As per this new policy issued on 13 June 2007, the discipline criteria was amended and bar for extension was only in case a punishment under sections 39(a) (b) and 45 of the Army Act, 1950 was awarded to an individual while serving as JCO. Thus, the applicant became eligible for grant of extension w.e.f. 13 June 2007 after issuance of the said letter but was retired on 30 June 2007 without granting him any extension.

In applicant contended that a duly constituted Board had approved his extension after going through the policy letters and thus, it was not understood as to how the policy could be changed once the extension had been granted to him. The applicant also questioned the validity of letter dated 22 November 2005 which was quoted whilst cancelling the extension.

The respondents contested that the criteria for screening personnel below officer rank for further extension in service had been laid out vide Army Headquarters letter No. B/33098/AG-PS-2(c) dated 21September 1998. The said letter amplifies the procedure whereby after obtaining willingness of the personnel concerned, various medical, ACR and discipline criteria have been laid down to be adhered by the Board before screening an individual for extension of service. The discipline criterion for grant of extension was laid out in Para 2(e) of Appendix "A" to the said Army Headquarters letter. The applicant was debarred under discipline criteria as laid out in Para 2(e) (ii), which said that an individual who has been convicted or awarded red-ink entry for an offence as indicated in the Annexure on the date of screening will not be eligible for extension and will be discharged in accordance with the existing Rules on the subject. This Annexure includes an offence under section 39(b) of the Army Act, 1950 i.e. without sufficient cause, overstaying leave granted to him. The applicant was punished under section 39(b) of the Army Act, 1950 on 7 April 1992 when he was Sepoy and thus, he was debarred from any extension of service. Therefore, the applicant was rightly denied extension of service and retired on due date after completing 28 years.

The Tribunal observed that a new policy letter on procedure and criteria for screening of personnel below officer rank was issued by the Adjutant General Branch, Integrated Headquarters (Army) on 13 June 2007 vide their letter No. B/33098/AG-PS-2(c). As per paragraph 3 of the said letter, the JCOs who were convicted under these offences, i.e. sections 39(a), (b) and 45 of the Army Act, 1950 during service as JCO only would be debarred for extension. Thus, any conviction in the lower rank under the above mentioned offences would not debar a JCO from grant of extension provided other requisite criteria are met. Para 4 of the said Revised Policy letter also said that this policy would be effective from the date of issue of this letter.

The tribunal observed that from reading of the revised policy letter, which was issued on 13 June 2007, it was very clear that the applicant fully met all the criteria for grant of extension of service to him. Despite this, he was retired from service on 30 June 2007 and struck off strength on 1 July 2007. The applicant was in service when the revised policy came into vogue and he deserved to be given benefit of this revised policy and granted extension of two years service.

The Tribunal quashed the letter dated 23 February 2006 denying extension to the applicant and retirement order dated 9 July 2006 issued in respect of the applicant. It ordered two years of extension of service w.e.f. 1 July 2007 to 30 June 2009 to the applicant for pensionary benefits only.

Extension of service, meaning of term 'past case'

The AFT Regional Bench Kochi in *Naib Sub B.C. Barua v. Union of India*, TA No.188 of 2010 [WP(C) No. 10090 of 2009 The High Court of Karnataka), decided on 29 October 2010, considered a statutory complaint filed under section 26 of the Army Act and the extension of service for two years.

The petitioner was enrolled in the Indian Army on 10 June 1983, and in the due course was promoted to the rank of Naib Subedar. He was entitled to the extension of service for two years. In the year 1992, the petitioner while in the rank of Havildar, was tried by a SCM under section 39(b) of the Army Act for the overstayed annual leave for 22 days and was awarded punishment of severe reprimand. It was a red ink entry punishment. His claim for extension for two years as Naib Subedar was disallowed by the Screening Board because of red ink entry as stipulated in the policy letter No. B-33098/AG/PS-2(c) dated 21 September 1998. Subsequently the policy was changed as per letter No. B-33098/AG/PS-2(c) dated 13 June, 2007. But the petitioner was denied the benefit only on the ground that the decision was taken that cases prior to 13 June 2007 were not to be considered for the grant of extension.

It was contested by the respondents that claim for extension was denied only on the ground that the petitioner's case was considered by the Screening Board on 24 May 2007 in accordance with the policy in vogue at that time and the new policy came into effect only on 13 June 2007.

The Tribunal observed that as per the changed policy extension was denied to a Naib Subedar only if he earned the red entry in that rank. The petitioner was claiming a benefit conferred by a subsequent policy letter dated 13 June 2007, which came into force while he was in service. The Tribunal further observed that the relevant portion of policy letter dated 13 June 2007 reads: "Revised policy will be effective from the date of issue of this letter. It was also clarified that "no past case will be re-opened."

For meaning of the words 'past case' used in the policy letter, the Tribunal relied on the decision of the Delhi High Court of Delhi in *Naib Subedar Gurmeet Singh v. Union of India* [WP(C) No.4894/07] decided on 14 January 2008. It was held that the words 'past case' means that persons who had already retired would not be entitled to seek re-opening of their case, but if only papers have been processed earlier and persons are still in service then new policy will apply. This decision was challenged before the Supreme Court by filing Special Leave Petition by the respondents. That SLP was also dismissed. The principle laid down in that decision has been followed by the Delhi High Court in WP (C) No.8556 of 2008 and in a number of other cases.

The Tribunal held that the persons who had already retired prior to 13 June 2007 would not be entitled to get their case re-opened. The Tribunal set aside the discharge order issued to the petitioner with the directions that the government to consider the case of the petitioner for extension of service for two years in the post of Naib Subedar and the decision communicated to him within a period of one month from the date of the order. The petitioner will also be entitled to the consequential benefits for the period for which he was discharging the duties in the rank of Naib Subedar.

Extension of service, notional increase

The AFT Principal Bench New Delhi in the case of *Major Shiv Kumar v. Union of India*, OA No. 357 of 2011, decided on 21 May 2012, considered a prayer for the of notional increase of service by two years with consequential benefits.

All the petitioners were enrolled in the Army as Sepoys between the period 1975-1979 and in due course they attained the ranks of JCOs. The Government of India introduced a special commission designated as Regimental Commission vide Army Instruction (AI) 18/84. The retirement age prescribed under para 17 of this AI was 48 years of age or 10 years of service. This AI was further amended by AI 32/89. Retirement age for all categories of officers of the Army was increased by 2 years across the board by Central Government vide their notification dated 03 September 1998. As per latest instructions and notification, the service conditions of Regimental Commission Officers (RCO) now stood as 12 years of service or 52 years of age, whichever was earlier. However, commissioning through RC entry ceased after May 1998 vide AI 10/98.

The Central Government appointed Ajay Vikram Singh Committee (AVSC) for suggesting changes in terms and conditions of service officers in the Army. After considering all aspects, AVS Committee gave its recommendation to grant substantive ranks of Capt at 2 years, Maj at 6 years and Lt Col at 13 years of service and other recommendations were also given by AVS Committee. The Central Government accorded approval for implementing the recommendations of AVS Committee and same was promulgated by Army HQ, MS Branch vide letter issued in December 2004, however, the RCOs were excluded from the ambit of this Committee.

The petitioners contended that they made several representations, however matter remained pending with the Government for one reasons or the other. It was brought to the notice of the Tribunal that a writ petition was filed in the Kolkata High Court on the same issue for grant of 2 years extension of service. The writ petition was transferred to the Kolkata Regional Bench of Armed Forces Tribunal. The Kolkata Regional Bench vide its order dated 04 April 2011 partially allowed the petition filed by Maj Rabindra Singh with the following directions:

"(a) The retirement orders of the applicant shall remain in vogue, as the application has been retired in accordance with rules on the subject and was well aware of the terms and conditions of his service. Therefore, we do not wish to interfere with the same.

(b) The petitioner shall be granted a notional increase of service by two years, as was proposed by the Respondents but could not reach the Cabinet.Being a notional extension of service, he shall not be paid any arrears or monetary advantage in Pay and allowances.

(c) However, we direct that the petitioner shall be notionally promoted to the rank of Lt. Col. (Time Scale) on completing of 13 years of such assumed service, only after fulfilling all other criteria, except length service, as required for promotion to the rank of Lt Col (Time Scale); and, only if the applicant is found suitable in all respects after holding a selection board by the Military Secretary's Branch. Such notional promotion shall only be for carrying the rank and for pension as entitled in that rank.

(d) The applicant shall get pension of a Major till he is promoted notionally to the rank of Lt Col. On such notional promotion to Lt Col, his pay in that rank shall be re-fixed and pension shall accordingly be fixed again in the rank of Lt Col to which he shall remain eligible."

Against the above said order dated 04 April 2011 passed by the AFT Regional Bench Kolkata, the respondents preferred a SLP before the Supreme Court and the same was dismissed. The Tribunal's attention was also drawn to a decision passed by the AFT Regional Bench Lucknow in the case of *Major Birendra Singh Tomar (Retd.) v. Union of India*, OA No. 29 of 2011, decided on 8 October 2011, wherein Bench had followed the decision passed by the Kolkata Regional Bench dated 04 April 2011. In view of the directions given by the Kolkata Regional Bench in the case of *Major Rabindra Singh v. Union of India* (TA No. 37/2010) on 04 April 2011, the Tribunal directed the respondents to grant reliefs to the petitioners within 3 months from the date of the order.

Extension of service : New Policy

The AFT Principal Bench (Three Member) New Delhi in the case of *Roshan Lal v. Union of India* OA No 279 of 2011, considered a bunch of 21 petitions having a common question of law. The bunch of matters was considered by the larger Bench pursuant to the order passed by the Regular Bench in OA No. 279 of 2011 on 06 September 2012. It was submitted that the Principal Bench had taken one view with regard to the policy dated 20 September 2010, as against this, Allahabad Bench and Kochi Bench had taken a separate view.

The Tribunal considered three judgments being those of the Principal Bench and the Lucknow and Kochi Benches of the Tribunal: (1) The judgment of the Principal Bench in *Nb. Subedar Gulab Rao v. Union of India* OA 513/2011 passed on 04 April 2012. (2) The judgment of Lucknow Bench *Sub Brijesh Kumar Shukla v. Chief of the Army Staff*, OA No. 234 of 2010 passed on 15 February 2012. (3) The judgment of the Kochi Bench in *Hav Manktu Ram v. Union of India*, OA No. 67 of 2011 passed on 21 March 2012. After going through these decisions, the Tribunal was of the opinion that in substance the matter involved was about interpretation of policy dated 20 September 2010 and also about the validity of the cut-off date fixed in the above policy.

The Tribunal observed the judgment of Lucknow Bench considered the validity of policy dated 20 September 2010 on the grounds that the policy being for the welfare of the personnel of Indian Army, the implementation of the same ought to have been made with immediate effect and not on a subsequent date. In other words fixing of dates regarding implementation of the policy was contended to be manifestly illegal, arbitrary and offended Article 14 of the Constitution. The Lucknow Bench after going through the matter and relying upon the judgment of the Supreme Court came to the conclusion firstly, that the cut of date fixed being 01 April 2011 was neither arbitrary nor illegal nor offended Article 14 of the Constitution and thus was held to be valid. Further the Delhi Principal Bench also observed that even otherwise it did not find any ground to interfere in the policy.

In the judgment of Kochi Bench, the denial of extension of service to the applicants therein was challenged as arbitrary and illegal and the applicants claimed to be entitled to further extension of service as per provisions of the policy. The Kochi Bench noticed the contention of the respondents therein that the controversy was identical to be one raised before the Lucknow Bench and therefore, the matter should be decided in the light of the prepositions laid down by Lucknow Bench. In the judgment of the Principal Bench in Gulab Rao's case, the individual was for the first time screened on 09 July 2011 i.e, after the cut-off date fixed in the policy dated 20 September 2010, being 01 April 2011.

All the persons being the petitioners in these matters were the persons who were to retire or to be discharged on completion of their colour service or original terms of engagement, on or before 31 March 2013. All these persons had already been screened by the Screening Board in accordance with the requirements of the earlier policy being dated 21 September 1998 and were to be discharged either on account of having not been found entitled to extension of service for two years or having been found entitled on screening but because of drop in performance or medical category criteria before commencement of the period of extension they were not allowed to avail the extension and some of the persons were those who became disentitled to complete the extension period after having started to avail it, on account of the reasons or conditions incorporated in the policy of 21 September 1998.

The petitioners contended that since all of them were in actual service "within original terms of engagement or colour service", on or after 01 April 2011 or were availing the extended period as on the date on or after 01 April 2011, they were entitled to the benefit of policy the dated 20 September 2010 as this policy was a beneficial policy to the employees. In view of the Tribunal, the new policy did not simply water down the earlier policy nor did it simply liberalize parameters, rather it had laid down different parameters in which process some parameters were liberalized still some parameters were made more stringent, the petitioners are neither entitled to invoke compassion nor sympathy nor can it be said that there would be any violation of the Article 14 of the Constitution. The Tribunal further held that the new policy was not a policy laid down only to ameliorate the conditions of the individual but was a new policy laying down different parameters. It thus dismissed the petitions.

Extension of service in low medical category

The AFT Regional Bench Guwahati in the case of *Sqn Ldr Jyoti Kumar Dhan v. Union of India*, OA No. 9 of 2011, decided on 16 February 2012, considered a petition for the extension of the service while in the low medical category.

The appellant was granted Short Service Commission (SSC) in the Indian Air Force on 9 January 2001 in the rank of Flt Lt in Army Medical Branch (AMC). As per the prevailing rules, the initial engagement of the appellant was for a period of 5 years which is further extendable for another period of

5 years. In consideration of the satisfactory service rendered by the appellant and upon completion of his initial period of 5 years, the service of the appellant was extended for another period of 5 years vide order dated 9 January 2006. The appellant successfully completed the extended period of service also. Meanwhile the Central Government formulated and adopted a policy dated 2 November 2007 to allow total tenure of Short Service Commission in respect of AMC, AD Corps and MNS from 10 years to 14 years.

The appellant being eligible to continue his service up to 14 years by further extension made an application on 17 June 2010 for the second extension. The said application was duly recommended and forwarded by the commanding officer of his Unit. While the appellant was continuing his service he was informed by a letter dated 2 August 2006 that as per the information of the Air Force Medical Board, he had been diagnosed as suffering from 'Takayasu's Arteritis' and he was placed in medical category A4G2(P) w.e.f 2 March 2004, during the initial period of his service. The disease having no impact on the service required to be rendered by the appellant, he was granted the first extension of service on 9 January 2006, although during this period also the appellant was suffering from the said disease.

An order was issued by Air Headquarters, New Delhi on 04 January 2011 informing that the appellant that approval was given for his release from service w.e.f. 9 January 2011 as he was not granted extension of service for failing to meet the eligibility criteria for grant of such extension, without disclosing as to in which respect the appellant was deficient. The said order was challenged before the Guwahati Bench of the Tribunal in OA No. 6 of 2011 which was disposed of on 01 March 2011 allowing the appellant to file appropriate application/complaint in terms of s. 27 of the Air Force Act, allowing him to raise all the grounds in support of his prayer of extension enclosing therewith necessary documents and till disposal of the appeal status-quo in regards to the service of the appellant till then prevailing was allowed to be continued.

The appellant submitted his application of 8 March 2011 in compliance with the order of the Tribunal, which was rejected/dismissed vide order dated 27 April 2011 by the Under Secretary to the Govt of India and resultantly the appellant was released from his service with immediate effect vide order dated 9 May 2011. The order dated 9 May 2011 was again challenged before the Tribunal by OA No. 5 of 2011. The appeal was allowed by the Tribunal vide order dated 30 June 2011, in which all consequential orders were set aside and allowing the appellant to continue in his service primarily on the ground that the impugned order had not disclosed any reason and did not address the points so raised by the appellant in his appeal. The matter was remanded back to the respondent authority for passing an appropriate speaking order keeping in mind the discussions made in the order addressing the points raised by the appellant. The respondent authorities vide order dated 12 August 2011 intimated the appellant that his appeal was examined by the respondents and rejected. The appellant again challenged the order in a fresh appeal.

There was a difference of opinion between two Members of the Bench while disposing of the appeal. The matter was referred to the Chairperson under section 28 of the Armed Forces Tribunal Act. The third Member set aside and quashed order dated 12 August 2011 and directed the respondents to pass appropriate order within 30 days, granting second extension to the appellant in terms of existing provisions.

XII. Maintenance Allowance

After due process

The AFT Regional Bench Chandigarh in the case of *A Ramar v. Union of India*, OA No. 1215 of 2011, decided on 11 February 2013, considered a prayer for the grant of maintenance allowance.

The petitioner was enrolled in the Army as Driver Mechanical Transport on 26 September 1993. He married Ms. J. Sudha on 18 February 2005. The couple was blessed with a daughter on 02 December 2005. However due to an ongoing marital discord, which started immediately after marriage, the couple were staying separately since last six years. The wife of the petitioner submitted an application dated 7 August 2010 to President AWWA, IHQ of Ministry of Defence and Commandant Artillery Centre, Nasik Road Camp for grant of maintenance allowance on the grounds that the petitioner was willfully staying separately and failing to look after her and her daughter. The competent authority issued show cause notice to the petitioner asking him to explain the reasons as to why maintenance allowance should not be granted to his wife. Based on the reply of the show cause notice by the petitioner the competent authority, under the provisions of AO 2/2001, directed that maintenance allowance @ 16-1/2% (11% for wife and 5.5% for the child) be deducted from the pay and allowances of the petitioner w.e.f. 7 August 2010 and paid to his wife. The wife had also filed a petition in the civil court for maintenance allowance under section 9 of Hindu Marriage Act.

The petitioner contended that he always wanted to bring his wife and daughter to the duty station and bear the responsibilities of a husband and a father but Smt. J. Sudha at her end had not given him a chance to prove his commitment. In August 2008, when the married accommodation was allotted to him at the new station, he went home to get his family. On her refusal to accompany him the petitioner made several attempts to resolve the issues including pleading before the local panchayat and elders at her village. Further, when his wife wrote to the Commanding Officer asking for maintenance allowance, he had sent Rs 5,000 for three months continuously to his wife through money order. In spite regularly giving money to his wife and never neglecting or ignoring her and child towards maintenance, he was served with a legal notice wherein he was called upon to live with his wife and child failing which legal proceeding would be initiated.

The petitioner further contended the order for maintenance was passed in complete contravention of various grounds and parameters which are to be satisfied and considered before passing any order of grant of maintenance allowance as given in the relevant regulations of the Army Orders. The petitioner was not been given any remedy of appeal or petition against the administrative order causing him financial loss. Also the order for maintenance allowance was a non-speaking order and the averments made by the petitioner the reply to the show cause notice were not been taken into consideration.

The respondents contested that the case of maintenance allowance was considered on its merit by the competent authority and all the parameter for grant of maintenance allowance and the circumstances of the case and the evidence available was duly considered before passing the orders for grant of maintenance allowance to the wife of the petitioner which she was legally entitled.

The Tribunal observed that the maintenance allowance cannot be deducted from the pay and allowances of the petitioner without complying with the provisions contained in section 90(i) of the Army Act, Army Rule 193 as well as in AO 2/2001 which gives a detailed procedure for disposing of the application of the wife for grant of maintenance allowance to her and the children. It is the responsibility of the competent authority to satisfy itself about the prima-facie genuineness of the complaint as submitted by the wife. It is imperative for the competent authority to ensure the following:

(i) The petitioner is the legally wedded wife of the person, or his legitimate/ illegitimate child.

(ii) The person complained against is neglecting to maintain the petitioner.

(iii) The wife is unable to maintain herself and dependent children.

Further, para 4(a) of the Army Order No. 2 of 2001 lays down that the wife will be asked to intimate by means of an affidavit whether she was employed, and if so, indicate her emoluments. She will also be asked to intimate details of any independent source of income and movable/immovable property she may possess and any income there from. The Tribunal observed there was nothing in the impugned order dated 27 July 2011 to show that any affidavit was called for from the wife and if so how the affidavit of the wife and the reply of the petitioner in response to the show cause notice was dealt with by the competent authority and whether any order sanctioning maintenance allowance was passed by the authority concerned. The letter dated 27 July, 2011 cannot by any stretch of imagination be treated as an order. In fact, it was merely a communication of the fact that the GOC-in-C has accorded sanction for grant of maintenance as aforesaid. It was evident that the competent authorities dealing with the petitions regarding maintenance allowance were exercising quasi-judicial functions and they were supposed to dispose them off by passing a speaking order.

The Tribunal also referred the decision of the Supreme Court in the case of *The Siemens Engineering & Manufacturing Co. of India Ltd. V. Union of India* (1976) 2 SCC 981:

> "6. ....If courts of law are to be replaced by administrative authorities and tribunals, as indeed, in some kinds of cases, with the proliferation of Administrative law, they may have to be so replaced, it is essential that administrative authorities and tribunals should accord fair and proper hearing to the persons sought to be affected by their orders and give sufficiently clear and explicit reasons in support of the orders made by them. Then alone administrative authorities and tribunals exercising quasi-judicial function will be able to justify their existence and carry credibility with the people by inspiring confidence in the adjudicatory process. The rule requiring reasons to be given in support of an order is, like the principle of audi alteram partem, a basic principle of natural justice which must inform every quasi-judicial process and this rule must be observed in its proper spirit and mere pretence of compliance with it would not satisfy the requirement of law."

The Tribunal set aside that order dated 27 July 2011 regarding sanction of the maintenance allowance and its deduction from his pay and allowances of the petitioner; and remitted the matter back to the competent authority to decide it afresh by passing a speaking order dealing with the contentions of both the parties. The Tribunal allowed an interim maintenance of Rs. 3000 pm to the wife and the daughter with effect from 01 March 2013 till the matter was decided by the competent authority.

Maintenance allowance, reasoned order

The AFT Regional Bench Kolkata in the case of *Major Arjun Singh Tomar v. General Officer Commanding-in-Chief, Eastern Command, Kolkata*, OA No. 13 of 2010, decided on 12 April 2012, considered the application preferred against the order of maintenance allowance.

The applicant had contended that his wife intentionally and without any just excuse, preferred to leave the matrimonial house and was staying with her parents with the child. Subsequently, the applicant came to know that his wife has made a complaint with the military authority stating that the applicant was ill-treating her and also failed and neglected to maintain her. On the basis of the said complaint, the Commanding Officer of the applicant issued a show cause notice to the applicant. The applicant in his reply denied the allegations, as made against him, and also stated that his wife left the matrimonial house without any reason and as such, she was not entitled to get any maintenance. He also stated that his wife was employed in the capacity of an executive in a private firm, she had no sufficient reason for living separately with her parents and since she is earning, no maintenance amount should be allowed in her favour. However, the General Officer Commanding-in-Chief, Eastern Command, Kolkata by an order dated 4 May 2010, granted maintenance allowance in favour of his wife to the extent of 22% of the salary of the applicant and 5.5% of the salary was allowed in favour of the minor child towards maintenance. It was further directed that the applicant should pay the arrear amount with effects from 28 November 2009. The applicant alleged that the impugned order was passed without giving any opportunity of hearing to the applicant, which is in clear violation of the principle of natural justice.

The respondents contested that after considering the reply of the applicant, the order of maintenance was passed by the competent authority under section 90(i) of the Army Act read with Rule 193 of Army Rules. The maintenance allowance was granted in favour of applicant's wife and son as he failed to maintain them.

The Tribunal observed that no reasoning has been given as to why 22% and 5.5% was to be deducted from the salary of the applicant towards maintenance of the wife and the child. The amount so fixed by the competent authority must bear good reasoning. There was no doubt that the competent military authority is empowered under the rules to grant maintenance allowance in favour of the wife and the child to the maximum extent, but in doing so, he must give some reasoning as to why he was in favour of granting such amount and not a lesser amount. The order issued by the General Officer Commanding-in -Chief, does not speak anything about such grant of maintenance allowance in favour of the wife and the child. It is the settled position of law that the authority exercising powers under section 90(i) of the Army Act must act reasonably and fairly, apart from giving a reasonable opportunity to the army personnel concerned. The Tribunal set aside the maintenance order passed by the competent authority, being in violation of the principle of natural justice; except the maintenance allowance of 5.5% as granted in favour of child.

The Tribunal further ordered that General Officer Commanding-in-Chief, Eastern Command, Kolkata, must give opportunity of hearing to both the sides and pass a reasoned order as to whether any maintenance allowance should at all be passed in favour of the wife or not and if so, then, what will be the amount. So long as the claim of maintenance of the wife was not settled, he was authorized to deduct a sum of Rs. 5000/- only from the salary of the applicant towards interim maintenance for the wife, in addition to the amount of maintenance that has already been allowed in favour of the child.

Military authorities v. civil court

The AFT New Delhi Principal Bench, in the case of *Hav Ravindra Singh v. Union of India*, RA No. 12 of 2012, in OA No. 305 of 2010, decided on 17 April 2012, considered a petition for reviewing its order dated 24 January 2012. The petitioner approached the Tribunal for reviewing its order whereby the OA No. 305 of 2010 filed by the petitioner was dismissed and order passed by the Army authorities dated 18 August 2009 was maintained.

The petitioner contended that in an earlier case of *Lt Col Naveen Ahlawat v. Union of India,* OA No. 170 of 2010, disposed of by the Tribunal vide order dated 01 March 2011, a view was taken that whenever there is a conflict between the order passed by the civil court and the Army authority, the order passed by the civil court will have precedence over the Army order. However in the case of petitioner (Hav Ravindra Singh), a different view has been taken that Army authority will process the case to supplement the maintenance allowance within limit of ceiling prescribed therein. The civil court order will not be treated as a prohibition on the powers exercised by Army authority. Army order can be given effect to subject to the order passed by the civil court.

The Tribunal observed that in the present case, while passing the order of maintenance allowance by the Army authority, the order of civil court was taken into consideration and maintenance allowance was extended up to 27.5% as per Army Order 2/2001. It was further observed that Army order was not contradictory to the civil court's order rather it supplements the civil court order by granting maintenance allowance up to the prescribed limit under the Army Order 2/2001.

In the case of Lt Col Naveen Ahlawat, the Tribunal had observed that once a civil court has passed the order, then civil court order will have precedence and no Army authority can sit over the matter. It was also observed that a judicial order can only be set aside or over ruled by superior court, which is the basic structure of the Constitution. Therefore, the order passed by the civil court always has precedence and there is no option with the Army authorities to sit over that order of civil court.

The Tribunal held that there was no contradiction in the decisions. In the case of Hav Ravindra Singh, the Tribunal had observed that civil court order will have precedence over the order of Army authorities. The same view was taken in the case of Lt Col Naveen Ahlawat. A consistent view taken in both the cases was that order passed by the civil court will have precedence; therefore, there is no apparent contradiction between the two decisions. The Tribunal reiterated that order of civil court will always have precedence over the order passed by the Army authorities under AO 2/2001. The Army order is always an administrative order whereas the maintenance order passed by the civil court is a judicial order; therefore, the judicial order will have precedence over the Army order.

In order to resolve contradiction, the Tribunal laid down the proposition that if such application for grant of maintenance allowance is moved before the Army authorities under AO 2/2001, the Army authorities shall always ask the party concerned that whether any matter is pending in the civil court or not. If matter is pending with the civil court, then Army authorities shall advise the party concerned to approach the civil court in terms of AO 2/2001. That will enable the civil court to extend the limit of maintenance allowance up to 22% of the salary to be paid to the wife and 5.5% for each child. This will avoid the confrontation between the Army order and civil court order. However, whenever there is no matter pending before the civil court, then it will be open for the Army authorities to exercise their powers as per AO 2/2001 and pass the maintenance order. This proposition is not going to put ceiling on the powers of the civil court. The civil court has powers to grant maintenance allowance more than the limit fixed as per AO 2/2001 and even less amount. That is the discretion of the civil court.

The Tribunal disposed of the review application with the following order. For the benefit of the parties, it set aside the order passed by the Army authorities dated 18 August 2009 and fixed the maintenance allowance as Rs. 4,000 per month as an interim measure. The arrears of the maintenance allowance will be subject to this order. It would be open for both the parties to approach the Appellate court for increasing or decreasing the maintenance allowance fixed by the Tribunal and it would be open for the civil court to pass appropriate order in accordance with law after hearing both the parties.

XIII. Minor Punishment

Lack of jurisdiction

The AFT Principal Bench New Delhi in the case of *Sgt Tek Chand Sharma v. Union of India*, TA No. 96 of 2010 [WP (C) No. 815 of 2004], decided on 19 February 2010, refused to consider the prayer where the applicant was awarded a minor punishment.

The applicant had contended that he was discriminated and harassed by the authorities who failed to afford him a fair opportunity to ventilate his grievance and awarded the punishment of admonition and reprimand on 04 December 2002 and 11 March 2003. The respondent contested that the petition was not maintainable as the punishment of admonition and reprimand cannot be questioned before the Tribunal as the Tribunal had no jurisdiction to entertain such petition in view of the section 3(o)(iii) of the Armed Forces Tribunal Act, 2007.

The Tribunal observed that the definition in Section 3(o)(i)(ii)(iii) of the Act was in the nature of substantive law and conferred jurisdiction to the Tribunal. However, Section 3 (o)(iii) restricts the jurisdiction in the matter of Summary disposal only where the punishment of dismissal is awarded. This provision is clear and unequivocal. No other meaning can be attributed to it. The Tribunal remitted the case back to the Delhi High Court.

The AFT Principal Bench New Delhi in the case of *Maj Manmohan Singh Battu v. Union of India,* TA No. 371 of 2009 [WP (C) No. 621 of 1990] decided on 6 April 2010, refused to entertain the application, where the petitioner was awarded punishment of severe reprimand in a summary trial.

The petitioner contended that the harmonious interpretation of Section 3(o)(iii) would lead only to the conclusion that all service matters are to be entertained by the Tribunal except those specifically excluded under the Act. Further, four categories of service matters have been excluded by the legislature as was clear from Section 3(o)(iv). This case does not fall within that exclusion clause and this Tribunal alone had the jurisdiction. The respondent contested that the severe reprimand was awarded to the petitioner in a summary trial and in view of Section 3(o)(iii) of the Armed Forces Tribunal Act, 2007, the Tribunal had no jurisdiction.

The Tribunal observed that Section 3(o)(iii) of the Act restricts the jurisdiction in the matter of Summary disposal only, where punishment of dismissal is awarded. This provision is clear and unequivocal. No other meaning can be attributed to it nor is any aid required from other provisions of this Act to interpret it. Referring to the decision of the Supreme Court in the case of *Oil and Natural Corporation Ltd. V. Saw Pipes Ltd.* 2003(5) SCC 705, and *Tek Chand Sharma's* case (TA No. 96 of 2010), the Tribunal remitted the matter back to the Delhi High Court.

XIV. Pay and Allowances

Back wages

The AFT Principal Bench New Delhi in the case of *Ex Ris Chanda Singh v. Union of India*, OA No. 307 of 2012, considered a prayer for back wages and promotion.

The petitioner was enrolled in the Indian Army on 21 April 1969 and was discharged on 24 October 1993 prematurely. The order of discharge was challenged by filing a WP No. 3169 of 1994 before the Delhi High Court. The said WP was transferred to the Tribunal as TA No. 95 of 2009 and was disposed of on 20 November 2009 whereby the Tribunal set aside the order of discharge dated 24 October 1993 of the Competent Authority and remitted the matter to the authorities for fresh consideration in accordance with law. In pursuance of this, the respondents passed the order on 27 April 2011 and reinstated the petitioner notionally w.e.f. 30 April 1997 on completion of term of engagement of 28 years in the rank of Risaldar in compliance of the order of the Tribunal dated 20 November 2009. However, he was not given the back wages for the period of reinstatement based on the principle of "No Work No Pay" and this was communicated vide order dated 01 June 2011. Therefore, the petitioner filed the a new petition seeking the arrears of pay from the order of discharge till reinstatement.

The petitioner relied on the decisions of the Supreme Court in *Union of India v. K.V. Jankiraman*, AIR 1991 SCC 2010; *J. N. Srivastava v. Union of India* (1998) 9 SCC 559; and *R. S. Misra v. Union of India* (2012) 8 SCC 558. In all these cases, reinstatement was granted and the benefit of arrears of pay was given and the principle of "No Work No Pay" was not followed.

The respondents contested that looking at the past performance of the petitioner; his bevaviour was not in keeping with service norms. During the period of 1973 to 1993, the petitioner was punished on six occasions for misconduct, quarrelling, the use of insubordinate language, disobeying the lawful command etc., Therefore, though technically, the petitioner succeeded before the Tribunal as the order of discharge was not a speaking order, and the same was set aside; but looking to his conduct he was not entitled to any back wages. The respondents referred the decision of the Supreme Court in the case of *State of U.P. v. Ved Pal Singh* (1997) 3 SCC 483, where in the Court held: "....In the light of the confidential reports indicating doubtful integrity, we are of the view that it is not expedient to direct payment of back wages, though he was acquitted by the criminal court may be on technical grounds or no merits, he is not entitled to back wages."

The Tribunal commented that a person who incurs four red ink entries can be discharged from service on account of his inefficiency in the service. But in the present case, the petitioner had six entries which warranted his discharge from service. We would have condoned it, had it been for a minor and not pertaining to disciplinary matter. But the Army depends on discipline and if a soldier acts in an undisciplined manner, such soldier was not entitled to any benefit. The Tribunal held that it would be just and proper to reduce the back wages to the extent of only 50%.

Revision of compensation after pay commission award

The AFT Principal Bench in the case of *Col Rakesh Sharma, SM v. Union of India*, OA No. 113 of 2011, decided on 7 August 2012, considered a prayer for the award of commuted value of the war injury pension as lump sum compensation.

The petitioner was commissioned in the Indian Army and was serving in J&K.On 05 December 1995, he became victim of the militant's bullets and sustained multiple gunshot injuries. He was hospitalised and released from Hospital on 23 June 1997 as Low Medical Category (Permanent). On 27 January 1998, the petitioner requested for claiming disability compensation under the provisions of existing rules and asked for the Medical Board to assess his disability at an early date. On his request, a Medical Board was convened on 23 March 1998 and on 28 July 1998, the Medical Board gave his recommendation that incumbent has a disability to the extent of 80%. The petitioner was asked for the option whether he would like to have the compensation lump sum or will claim the same at the time of release from service. He opted to pay the compensation at lump sum on 25 September 1998 and the compensation was sanctioned on 10 March 1998 to the extent of 80% and thereafter the final payment was made on 10 December 1999.

The petitioner contended that he was paid the compensation which was prevalent at the time when he had received the injury. In the meanwhile the Fifth Pay Commission has come into force w.e.f. 01 January 1996 and therefore, the petitioner was entitled to the rates of compensation as recommended by the Fifth Pay Commission and accepted by the Government from 01 January 1996. The respondents contested that since the petitioner has received the injury on 05 December 1995, therefore, the compensation may be determined with reference to the provisions and rules which were prevalent at the time when the injury took place.

The Tribunal was of the opinion that till the Medical Board gives its ruling that how much disability the incumbent has suffered, it cannot be decided whether the compensation should be paid in lump sum or he should wait till the completion of his tenure. The above option only arises when the Medical Board decides that whether the petitioner has received injury more than 20% or not. In the present case, the petitioner's disability was decided by the Medical Board for the first time on 28 July 1998. Then alone the whole process of asking the option whether he want to encash the compensation in lump sum or to wait till he completed his tenure of service. Therefore, the crucial date was when the Medical Board has said that whether he is entitled to compensation at all or not. Had it been the case that petitioner received less than 20% disability, perhaps he would not have been entitled to any disability pension. It is only more than 20% disability, which entitles a person to disability pension.

The Tribunal further held that the Fifth Pay Commission came into force w.e.f. 01 January 1996 and the purpose of the Pay Commission was to ameliorate the service conditions of the employees. The very purpose of the Pay Commissions is to ameliorate the service conditions of the employees and therefore, the Tribunal held that the petitioner was entitled to the benefit of the Fifth Pay Commission, which has revised the rates of such cases from 01 January 1996. Further, the argument of the respondents that petitioner wais entitled for disability compensation at the rates which were prevalent on 05 December 1995 at the time of injury was totally negative approach.

The Tribunal directed that the petitioner was entitled to lump sum compensation on the basis of the rates recommended and accepted by the Government as per the Fifth Pay Commission. The amount should be determined and whatever payment has already been made, be deducted and remaining deficient amount should be released to the petitioner within a period of three months.

Special Compensatory (Counter-Insurgency) allowance to personnel posted in BRO/GREF

The AFT Bench Chandigarh in the case of *Brig A K Bhutani v. Union of India*, OA No 144 of 2011, decided on 19 April 2012, considered a petition for the grant of the Special Compensatory (Counter-Insurgency) Allowance.

The Special Compensatory (Counter-Insurgency) Allowance was stopped in 2007 to the personnel posted to BRO/GREF based on an objection by the Comptroller and Auditor General (CAG) that the applicants were not actually employed in Counter-Insurgency Operations.

The Bench observed that the government was paying the said allowance to personnel of Army Postal Service and Judge Advocate General staff who were performing normal secure duties in proper built up area in Srinagar but are not paying the same to the applicants who were in the midst of counter-insurgency operations. Even personnel of the Territorial Army who were part-time volunteers and not regular employees of the government were paid the said allowances even when attached to the units of the BRO/GREF. The Bench referred to the Supreme Court decision in *State of Karnataka v. Karnataka State Patels Sangha* 2007 (2) SCT 191 SC that when two officers are discharging similar duties and when the Government has treated two posts as equal, then there can be no discrimination in pay and allowances.

The Tribunal ordered for the release the Special Compensatory (Counter-Insurgency) Allowance to the applicants (posted in BRO/GREF) with 10% interest per annum, till the time they remain posted in designated areas where the said risk-related allowance was authorized to personnel posted in other Army units and establishments.

The Bench commented: "we expect the respondents to base their actions on the touch-stone of judiciousness and fairness while determining such issues which can have far-reaching consequences on the morale of the troops operating in difficult conditions. The approach should not be highly legalistic or ultra-technical but in tune with the practical realities and in consonance with the actual spirit behind the policy, the primary aim of which was to boost the morale and motivation of the men and women in uniform who ensure our internal and external security in trying and difficult conditions day in and night out".

ACP, junior receiving higher pay

The AFT Principal Bench New Delhi in the case of *NC (E) Chiranjeelal v. Union of India*, OA No. 224 of 2011, decided on 27 November 2012, considered a prayer for fixation of pay.

The petitioner was enrolled as NC (E) Trade Lascar on 02 September 1983 in Indian Air Force. He was promoted to the rank of Tindal on 11 December 2002 and his position was shown as per the ACP scheme in the Pay Band of Rs. 7880/-; Grade Pay 1800/-; NCA, GCB + Class pay Rs. 1000/-; DA,TPT Allowance Rs. 4356/- HRA + L/Fee + DA 2320/- FLY/PJI Allowance Rs.150/-, GAL Awards Rs.266/- and the total credits were Rs. 18,014/-.

The petitioner contended that the persons junior to him were getting more pay and gave example of an individual who was enrolled on 06 October 1983 in the same trade of Lascar and was promoted on 01 January 2004 to the rank of Tindal and his pay scale was shown in the Pay Band of Rs. 8180/-; Grade Pay Rs. 1800/- ; NCA, GCB + class pay Rs. 1000/- DA; TPT allowance Rs. 4491/-; HRA + L/Fee + DA Rs. 2320/-; Comp Allowances Rs. 2994/-; FLY/PJI Allowance Rs. 150/-; LRA Rs. 266/- Mic. Credits Rs. 5066 and total credits Rs. 26267. Further, he made a representation which was supported by Air Force Record Office requesting the government to do away with the anomaly but the same was rejected by the government referrring to clause 6 of the ACP Scheme which reads as under:

> "6. The financial up gradation under the ACP Scheme shall be purely personal to the service personnel and shall have no relevance to his seniority, position or rank. As such there shall be no additional financial up gradation for the senior personnel on the ground that the junior personnel in the rank has got higher pay scale under ACP Scheme."

The respondents contested that the ACP scheme clearly states that financial up gradation under the ACP Scheme shall be purely personal to the service personnel and shall have no relevance to his seniority, position or rank.

The Tribunal observed that the scheme does creates bad feeling specially in the organization like armed forces where a there is hierarchical set up and where the rank makes lot of difference. In the present case, the petitioner was promoted on 01 December 2002 and another individual was promoted on 01 January 2004. Still petitioner was getting lesser pay, it was bound to create heart burning. However, looking into the nature of the scheme, which has larger application and it affects large number of persons, it will not be conducive to interfere with the Scheme. The Rule 22 of the FR may be invoked in the present case but the Ministry of Defence after consulting Ministry of Finance had intimated that Rule 22 of the FR was not applicable to such cases.

The Tribunal observed that there was a definite discrimination in operation between two persons i.e. petitioner and another individual that one person who is junior getting higher pay grade than the senior. The Tribunal directed the Government to consider such hardship cases and do justice so that the discrimination was avoided.

XV. Pension, Special Family Pension and Ex-gratia

Special family pension

The AFT Regional Bench Chandigarh, in the case of *Smt. Navindra Devi v. Union of India*, OA No. 972 of 2011, decided on 8 December 2011, considered a prayer for the release of special family pension. The husband of the petitioner had joined the Indian Army on 15 September 1984 and died while in service on 06 June 1998. He was serving with Field Workshop Company based near Bikaner. Towards the end of 1997, the late husband of the petitioner showed signs of depression due to which the authorities at Military Hospital referred him for treatment and admission in Medical College and Hospital, Bikaner where he was taken under military escort and was admitted in the said hospital for a few days and was also given electric shocks. Thereafter the petitioner's late husband was returned to the unit. He was later sent home to recuperate on annual leave from 09 March 98 till 09 May 98 after which he duly reported back to his unit.

The military authorities failed to detail escort for the petitioner's husband. Due to his bad psychiatric state and carelessness on part of his unit, he wandered out of unit location on 18 May 1998. A telegram was then sent to the petitioner to advise her husband to report back to the unit. The petitioner was shocked at the development since the respondents were assuming that her husband was at home with her. On receiving the telegram she immediately contacted the unit and questioned them as to why was he allowed to be alone or leave the unit lines when he was under psychiatric treatment but no satisfactory answer was given. She then personally visited the unit location alongwith her brother-in-law where the unit authorities expressed their apologies for not keeping an eye on her husband but did not provide any other reasonable answer as to what steps were being taken by them to trace him.

Petitioner then learnt from the unit that her late husband had been found wandering by the Govt Railway Police (GRP) in Delhi. However, rather than sending a team to bring back the soldier, his parent unit in Bikaner and the military authorities in Delhi kept writing to each other. No attempt was made by the unit to detail someone from 26 May 1998 till 4 June 1998 to personally visit Delhi Railway Station and take over the said soldier who was in a bad psychiatric and mental state. The petitioner herself visited GRP Delhi and was informed that her husband had indeed been kept by them but was allowed to go when no one turned up from the Army to escort him.

When the petitioner again contacted the unit requesting them to send someone to personally visit Delhi Railway Station, they informed her that her husband was not on duty when found wandering by the GRP but was on annual leave and hence they did not have any jurisdiction or responsibility for what had happened to him on leave. When the petitioner confronted them with their telegram to her dated 20 May 98 in which they had stated that he was 'absent without leave' the unit informed her that as far as they were concerned he was on annual leave. It was at a later stage that it was discovered that in order to palm of their responsibility, the respondents had illegally shown the petitioner's husband on 'annual leave' so that they may not be held responsible for their lack of supervision over the mentally ill soldier. The dead body of the petitioner's husband was found floating in the village well on 5 June 1998 and the death of her husband remained a mystery and the cause or reason could never be established though he died due to drowning.

The petitioner contended that the claim for Special Family Pension was rejected declaring the death to be neither attributable to, nor aggravated by service by the administrative authorities without even a Court of Inquiry which could have actually commented upon the attributability on the death.

The petitioner then approached the Delhi High Court vide Writ Petitioner No 4925 of 2002 and the Court directed the respondents to decide the representation of the petitioner. The petitioner's representation was rejected and she challenged the same through a fresh Writ Petition No 4980 of 2006 on which orders were passed on 01 August 2008 to hold Court of Inquiry within two months as is mandatory under the Regulations. The court of inquiry brought out that the late soldier as on advance of annual leave at the time of death.

The petitioner relying on the decision of Supreme Court in the case of

Charanjit Kaur v. Union of India (1994) 2 SCC contended that in case a defence personnel under medical treatment dies if he is left unattended, then the death is to be considered 'attributable to military service' and the widow would be entitled to Special Family Pension.

The respondents contested that though the husband of the petitioner had died while he was a Deserter/ Absent Without Leave, his commanding officer had shown mercy and compassion to the petitioner and converted his Desertion/Absent Without Leave to advance of annual leave for the year 1999 w.e.f. 18 May 98 to 16 Jun 98 and cancelled their earlier apprehension roll issued vide letter dated 11 June 1998. This was done to enable the petitioner to get Ordinary Family Pension/financial help and other service/death benefits of her late husband. Therefore, the death under such circumstances is not in any way related to duties of military service, and consequent upon his death, legitimate dues were paid to the petitioner being legally wedded wife. Special Family Pension is sanctioned only to those personnel whose death is caused due to disease or injury which is sustained while performing the bonafide military duties. In the instant case the petitioner was found dead in a well at his home town during Desertion/ Absence Without Leave period which was later converted into advance of annual leave. Hence the petitioner was granted ordinary family pension and her appeal for Special Family Pension was rejected due to the death being neither attributable to nor aggravated by military service.

The Tribunal observed glaring lapses of the part of military authorities in dealing with the case. It observed that the military authorities showed negligence in handling a psychiatric patient/soldier. Further, the mandatory court of inquiry as required vide para 520(c) of the Regulations for the Army 1987 into the death of Nk Rajpal Singh was not held. The court of inquiry was held after 11 years in 2009 on directions of the Delhi High Court. The findings of the court of inquiry further brought out serious lapses/negligent actions on the part of Unit of Nk Rajpal Singh/Army Authorities. Nk Rajpal Singh was initially shown to have absented himself without leave. His absence was converted to 30 days advance of annual leave with effect from 18 May retrospectively to cover up the negligent action/omission in allowing a psychiatric patient to wander out of the Unit. The military authorities also failed in collecting and escorting Nk Rajpal Singh from GRP.

The Tribunal relied on the decision of the Supreme Court in the case of *Charanjit Kaur v. Union of India*, where it was held that the death of a patient in care of the Army caused by acts of omission and commission was considered as attributable to and aggravated by military service. It considered the death of Nk Rajpal Singh as attributable to and aggravated by military service and allowed the petitioner Special Family Pension from the date of death of her husband i.e., 05 June 1998. The petitioner was also entitled to get arrears with effect from the same date with interest @10% per annum. In addition, the Tribunal directed that a compensation of Rs. 10 Lac be paid to the petitioner for the acts of omission and commission of the respondents.

Missing person declared deserter, family pension allowed

The AFT Regional Bench Chennai in the case of *Manoramyam Widow of Ex Sep (Dvr) N. Sarangapani v. Union of India*, OA No. 53 of 2011, decided on 21 December 2012, considered a prayer for grant of pension.

The applicant's husband Ex Sepoy N. Sarangapani was enrolled in the Indian Army on 22 October 1965. He came home on annual leave and after spending the leave at home, he left for joining duty on 24 July 1977 and thereafter he joined his duty after arrival at the working place. He had also written a letter on 28 July 1977 informing his safe arrival and reporting for duty and also sent a money order to the applicant. However, the applicant was informed by her father-in-law that he had received an intimation from the unit stating that her husband was absent from the unit without leave from 17 August 1977. The applicant had enquired the matter with the unit through her letters, dated 30 August 1977 and 14 September 1977, but they were not responded. The applicant had also requested the respondents by sending reminders to investigate and find out about her husband. On 12 September 1977, the unit intimated the applicant that her husband was still absent from the unit and his whereabouts would be informed to her as soon as he was located. Thereafter, no information reached the applicant regarding her husband.

In the year 1980, the applicant received the Discharge Certificate of her husband Ex Sepoy N. Sarangapani dated 29 November 1980 wherein her husband was shown as discharged from the Army as a deserter with effect from 15 October 1980. Thereafter, the husband of the applicant never came home nor she heard about him till date and he should therefore be presumed to be dead. The applicant had also lodged a police complaint on 30 April 1997 with Police Station, Old Washermenpet, Chennai-600021 and the efforts taken by the applicant were also not fruitful.

The petitioner contended that the proceedings which declared her husband as a 'deserter' from the Army were not conducted in accordance with law and therefore, they were not sustainable. Her husband should have been declared a missing person, but, on the contrary, he was declared as a deserter. Her request for the grant of family pension was unlawfully rejected by a hasty and merciless decision of the respondents. The petitioner also contended that her husband was perhaps missing from the unit while performing his duty and therefore, he ought to have been declared as a missing person as per the instructions of Government of India, Ministry of Defence letter No. 12(16)86/D Pens/(Sers), dated 3 June 1988 and the applicant should have been paid family pension as being done in several other cases.

The respondents contested that the husband of the applicant while serving with the ASC Battalion had absented himself without leave on and from 16 August 1977. A Court of Inquiry was held at the unit on 16 September 1977 and the individual was declared as a deserter with effect from 16 August 1977. An Apprehension Roll was issued to the District Collector and District

Superintendent of Police, Madras through a letter No.1565/A Coy/ST-12, dated 22 August 1977. The applicant's husband was neither apprehended nor joined voluntarily and therefore, he was discharged from service with effect from 15 October 1980. The accounts of the applicant's husband were finalized and the benefits payable on the dismissal of the deserter to the next of kin was paid at Rs. 2,436/- towards AFPP Fund and Rs. 95/- towards AGI Maturity Benefit. An individual dismissed under the provisions of Army Act was not eligible for pension and gratuity for the past service under para 113(a) of Pension Regulation for the Army 1961 (Part-I) as the individual was not entitled to any service pension. Therefore, the applicant was not entitled for the grant of family pension.

The Tribunal considered two issues in the matter (1) Whether the order of discharge of Ex Sep N. Sarangapani by the Army authorities under Army Rule 13(3)(III)(v) as deserter was unconstitutional? (2) Whether the applicant was entitled for the grant of eligible family pension and benefits, as prayed for with interest at 12% per annum till the date of payment?

On a careful perusal of the Apprehension Roll, the Tribunal observed that a copy of the Roll was endorsed to the applicant. Therefore, it was quite clear that no intimation was given to the applicant by the respondents regarding the missing of her husband at the time when the Apprehension Roll was issued to police and District Collector. The Tribunal after going through the provisions of Army Rule 183 (4) observed that when the absentee's kin were also not notified regarding the proceedings conducted by the Court of Inquiry under section 106 of Army Act and no opportunity was given to the applicant or other kin of absentee N. Sarangapani to adduce their evidence under Army Rule AR 183(4), the findings of the Court of Inquiry cannot be considered as legally sustainable.

Also the procedure before Court of Inquiry had not been followed properly to adjudicate a person as absented from the unit willfully. The declaration made thereafter as a deserter and the consequent order of discharge based upon the illegal proceedings cannot be sustained. The Tribunal was of the view that the applicant's husband Ex Sep N. Sarangapani should not have been declared as a deserter even though his whereabouts were not found by the respondents or the applicant. Therefore, the order passed by the army authorities that the declaration of the applicant's husband Ex Sep N. Sarangapani as a deserter was certainly not in accordance with law.

The Tribunal further noted that the government letter dated 3 June 1988 for the purpose of grant of family pension would not be applicable in the case as para-6 of the letter states that the provisions would take effect from 29 June 1986. According to section 108 of Evidence Act, the various steps taken by the applicant and the non-hearing of the said N. Sarangapani would lead to a presumption of his death. Therefore, the said N. Sarangapani should have been deemed to be dead as per the provisions of section 108 of the Evidence Act. In the said circumstances, the applicant's husband N. Sarangapani should have been deemed to have been in service till 16 August 1984, the date of deemed death of N. Sarangapani, i.e., after the lapse of 7 years of unheard of him. Upon the said circumstance, when the service period is calculated till 16 August 1984, the said N. Sarangapani should have completed more than 15 years, the minimum requirement of service period for grant of pension. Therefore, the said N. Sarangapani who was not seen from 16 August 1977 was entitled to service element pension for the service period commencing from 22 October 1965 to 16 August 1984, on the basis of the death of the said N. Sarangapani, presumed to have taken place on 16 August 1984. Therefore, the applicant was entitled to family pension as on 16 August 1984, in accordance with the pension procedures.

The Tribunal further observed that the applicant did not ask for the grant of family pension for all these years, but had raised the plea of pension only recently. The principle laid down by the Supreme Court in *Union of India v. Tarsem Singh* (2008) 8 SCC 648 were applicable to the present case. According to the said principles, family pension payable to the applicant could be allowed for a period of three years prior to the filing of the present application. Keeping in view the date of OA, the petition was presented on 23 August 2011, the tribunal held that the applicant would be entitled to the family pension with effect from 23 August 2008 only.

The Tribunal directed that the family pension to be paid to the applicant from 23 August 2008 for the service rendered by her husband from 22 October 1965 to 16 August 1984 and the future family pension to be paid in accordance with pension rules. The arrears of pension to be paid within a period of three months, and in default to pay the said amount, the applicant would be entitled to interest at 12% per annum.

Family pension while on bail

The AFT Regional Bench Chandigarh in the case of *Smt Kamala Rani v. Union of India*, OA No. 504 of 2011, decided on 12 February 2013, considered a prayer for restoration of family pension.

The husband of the petitioner was enrolled in the Army on 24 April 1971 and discharged from service on 23 February 1987 on his own request on extreme compassionate ground under Army Rule 13 III (ii) after rendering more than 15 years of service. He was in receipt of service pension w.e.f. 15 February 1987 through DPDO Pathankot. Family pension in respect of Smt Kamla Rani, widow of the deceased was also notified under Joint Notification Schedule.

Hav Buta Ram and his wife Smt Kamla Rani were imprisoned with effect from 24 November 2006 in Central Jail Gurdaspur under case FIR 37 dated 13 August 2006 under ss. 304-B, 498-A, and 34 IPC at police station Narot Jaimal Singh. A petition dated 15 September 2009 was received from the petitioner informing the authorities that herself and her husband had been imprisoned w.e.f. 21 September 2006 and her husband, Hav Buta Ram had expired on 24 January 2009 while still being in jail. The Jail Superintendent Central Jail vide his letter of 23 October 2009 intimated that the petitioner and Hav Buta Ram were not convicted and the Hav Buta Ram had died in jail as under-trial.

The Additional Sessions Judge, Gurdaspur (Punjab), by an order dated 15 January 2010 convicted the petitioner and her son Sunil Kumar and sentenced them to undergo 7 years RI and a fine of Rs 1000/- each. An appeal was preferred by the petitioner before the High Court of Punjab & Haryana at Chandigarh against the order of Additional Sessions Judge. The appeal was heard on 23 April 2010 and the petitioner was granted bail. On getting out of prison on 28 April 2010 the petitioner applied for restoration of ordinary family pension to DPDO Pathankot, which was rejected.

The petitioner contended PCDA's clarification that the family pension cannot be restored as the petitioner was in judicial custody and thereafter out on bail after being convicted pending appeal in High Court. Further, the family pension can only be restored on order of higher authority if the petitioner was acquitted of charges on pronunciation of verdict of the court was not correct. According to petitioner, for restoration of the family pension it was sufficient to be released from jail and not acquittal. The petitioner also contended that the show cause notice, as envisaged at para 73.1 of Pension Payment Instructions 2005 was been served upon the pensioners prior to withholding family pension. Being a widow of 50 years of age with four dependent children she was struggling to survive.

The respondents contested that the deceased soldier had never disclosed about his imprisonment and continued to draw his monthly pension till August 2008. The deceased had neither appeared for his annual identification after August 2007 nor sent any life certificate to DPDO and therefore his pension was stopped in August 2008. Subsequently the petitioner and her son Sunil Kumar were "convicted and sentenced to undergo 7 years RI and to pay a fine of Rs 1000/- each." In the instant case the petitioner was released on bail from Central Jail, Gurdaspur on 28 Apr 2010 and she was not acquitted from the charges. No provision exists to restore pension to the petitioner during bail period. More over the High Court of Punjab & Haryana at Chandigarh vide order dated 23 April 2010 had not given any directions regarding grant of family pension to the petitioner during the bail period. The respondent during his arguments brought out that while interpreting the law under para 82 (a) and (b) of pension regulations for the Army, the term "release" relates to acquittal of the pensioner.

The Tribunal examined Para 82 (a) and (b) of Pension Regulations for the Army 1961(Part-II):

> "82 (a). If a pensioner is sentenced to imprisonment for a criminal offence, his pension shall be suspended from the date of his imprisonment and the case will be reported to the Controller of Defence Accounts

(Pension), Allahabad for the orders of the competent authority. In case, where a pensioner is kept in police or jail custody as an under-trial prisoner and is eventually sentenced to a term of imprisonment for a criminal offence, the suspension of pension shall take effect from the date of imprisonment only.

82 (b). Restoration of Pension withheld- A pension withheld in whole or in part may be restored in full or in part by the competent authority in consultation with the State Government or Administration concerned in political cases and with the Controller of Defence Accounts (Pensions) and the civil authorities, if necessary, in other cases. In the case of a pensioner undergoing imprisonment, any action under this Regulation shall only be taken on his application after release but in no case, shall pension be sanctioned for the period of imprisonment in jail for a serious crime."

The Tribunal observed that a conjoint reading of Para 82(a) and (b) makes it clear that the pension during the period of imprisonment will not be available. However, the pension may be restored after the release of the pensioner from custody. The word used in the Regulation is "Release" and not "acquittal". If the word "release" is equated with the word "acquittal" then it would mean that if the hearing of the appeal remains pending for 20 years, the petitioner will not get the pension for 20 years till her acquittal. That cannot be the intention of the frames of the regulations.

The Tribunal held that the argument of the respondents that the pension can be released only on acquittal was fallacious. In the Tribunal's opinion, the petitioner was entitled to family pension from the date of her release from jail i.e., 28 April 2010. The Tribunal directed that the respondents to work out and commence payment of family pension to the petitioner along with arrears due within 3 months of the order, failing which the outstanding amount will carry interest @ 8% per annum.

Pension: discharged on medical ground as case of schizophrenia (paranoid)

The AFT Regional Bench Kolkata in the case of *Shri Bhaskar Kishan v. Union of India*, TA No. 133 of 2010 [WP (C) No. 1077 of 2008], decided on 14 February 2012, considered a prayer for quashing of discharge order.

The applicant was enrolled in the Army (Bihar Regiment) on 13 March 2001. While performing his duty at Bhuj, he was admitted in the Military Hospital in August 2003 and treated for "Schizophrenia (paranoid)". He was discharged from the MH in Medical category S3 on 23 July 2004 and was later upgraded to S2 (Permanent) while he was posted in Jammu & Kashmir. Finally the applicant was discharged from the service under Army Rule 13 (3) III, read with AR 13 (2A), on 1 April 2007, but was not given any disability for the above ailment. His disability was considered neither attributable nor aggravated by military service and the quantum of disability was assesses as

20% for life.

The petitioner contended that he could have been given sheltered appointment and urged that the discharged order be quashed and he should be reinstated in the service. In case the same was not feasible, he should be granted the disability pension as his disability was attributable and aggravated on account of military service. The disease "schizophrenia" which led to his discharge had casual connection to non-congenial service conditions, i.e., stress and strain. He should also be granted the status of ex-servicemen so that he could get some meaningful employment and other facilities entitled to an ex-serviceman.

The applicant was re-examined by a fresh appeal medical board on 5 September 2011 and awarded the disability as 40% for life. The First Appellate Committee in its order dated 19 October 2001 ordered that the applicant is deemed to have been invalided out of service in terms of Regulation 173A of PRA (Pt-1)-1996 and was entitled to disability pension @ 50% for life with effect from 5 September 2011.

The Tribunal held that it was inappropriate for the government to limit the applicability of the order only from 5 September 2011. It directed that the pension shall be applicable from 01 April 2007, i.e., the date when the applicant was discharged from the service and shall also be entitled to arrears of pension with 6% interest.

Pension of Naib Subedar, rank granted after retirement.

The AFT Regional Bench Chandigarh in the case of *Harbhajan Singh and others v. Union of India*, OA No. 1844 of 2011, decided on 21 November 2011, considered six petitions for grant of pension of Naib Subedar to the individuals having been granted the rank of honorary Naib Subedar after retirement, and prior to 01 January 2006.

The Tribunal relied on its earlier decision of 08 February 2010 on the issue, passed in the case of *Virender Singh v. Union of India* OA No. 42 of 2010, which was subsequently affirmed by the Supreme Court. The Tribunal opined that in the case of Virender Singh directions in general nature were issued and were required to be complied within the time frame. The Tribunal granted the same relief, i.e. the petitioners No. 1, 2, 3, 5 and 6, be paid the pension of Naib Subedar and the petitioner No. 4 be paid the pension of Naib Subedar to the individual till he survived, and thereafter, his family will be entitled to family pension. The Tribunal directed that necessary verifications to be made by the respondents, and after verification, necessary calculations and actual payments be made to the petitioners within a period of three months from the date of the order, failing which the respondent No.1 would be liable to pay costs of Rs. 10,000/- to be deposited in the Tribunal.

Pension of Naib Subedar

The AFT Regional Bench Chandigarh in the case of *Inder Singh v. Union of India*, OA No. 2054 of 2012, decided on 9 August 2012, directed for grant of pension of Naib Subedar to petitioner having been granted the rank of Honorary Naib Subedar after retirement and prior to 01 January 2006. The Tribunal also pointed out that the grant of pension to Naib Subedar was passed by the same bench in Virender Singh v. Union of India OA No. 42 of 2010 dated 8 February 2010, which has subsequently been followed by the Tribunal consistently apart from the fact that it has been affirmed by the Supreme Court. Concerned with the delay, the Tribunal directed that actual payment be now made to the petitioner with a period of three months from the date of receipt of copy of the order, failing which the Union of India shall be liable to pay costs of Rs.10,000/- to be deposited in the Tribunal.

War injury pension

The AFT Bench Chandigarh in the case of *Ex Nb Sub Jai Lal v. Union of India*, OA No. 55 of 2011, decided on 11 November 2011, considered a prayer for war injury pension.

The petitioner was enrolled in the Army on 11 May 1968. While deployed in operation he sustained shell wound injury in the left thigh on 16 December 1971. He was admitted in Military Hospital, Pathankot on 18 December 1971, then was transferred to Base Hospital, Delhi Cantt, and then to Command Hospital, Pune. He was discharged from the hospital in low medical category on 08 March 1972. He was admitted for re-categorization in Military Hospital, Nasirabad on 18 December 1972, then transferred to Command Hospital, Pune. He was discharged from service on 31 May 1994. The petitioner's claim for grant of "War Injury Pension" was forwarded to CCDA(P) Allahabad. He was sanctioned disability pension in other rank (OR) category taking 50% disability. Then Re-survey Medical Board declared the disability at 50% final and for life.

The petitioner contended that at the time of release, he was in the rank of JCO and, therefore, he was entitled to "War Injury Pension" in the rank of JCO. The respondents contested that the Release Medical Board assessed the petitioner's disability at 30% for two years, and opined as "injury sustained due to enemy action" and lastly, his disability was assessed at 50% by the Re-survey Medical Board. The claim for conversion of disability pension into "War Injury Pension" was contested on the ground of delay, though regarding rank in which he was entitled, a stand was taken that matter has already been taken up with the authorities and he will be informed accordingly on receipt of directions from them. The respondents also contested the rounding off, stating that injury was sustained in the year 1971 therefore MoD letter dated 31 January 2001 was not applicable to him. Further, in view of paragraph 179 of the Pension Regulations for the Army, 1961 grant of benefit in the rank of JCO was incorrect.

The Tribunal observed that paragraph 179 of the Pension Regulations for the Army, 1961 provided: "The disability element....shall be assessed on the accepted degree of disablement at the time of retirement/discharge on the basis of the rank held on the date on which the wound/injury was sustained or in the case of disease on the date of first removal from duty on account of that disease."

Referring to the decision of the Supreme Court in the case of *K.J.S. Buttar v. Union of India* dated 31 March 2011 passed in Civil Appeal No. 5591 of 2006, the Tribunal held that the petitioner was entitled to "rounding off". The Tribunal ordered that the petitioner was entitled to 'War Injury Pension' taking the disability to be 50% to be rounded off to the extent provided in the letter 31 January 2001. The respondents were directed to make necessary calculations and make payment to the petitioner within three months from the date of the order, failing which the amount shall carry interest at the rate of 10% per annum.

Pension to ex-servicemen convicted by the court

The AFT Regional Bench Chandigarh in the cases of *Pritpal Singh v. Union of India* OA No. 355 of 2010, *Bikramjit Singh v. Union of India* OA No. 354 of 2010, and *Bakhshish Singh v. Union of India* OA No. 481 of 2010, decided on 7 January 2011, considered the issue of continuation of pension to retired military personnel convicted by the courts.

In all the three cases, the petitioners were retired Army personnel, and after discharge from the service they were involved in a criminal case. They were convicted by the trial court for offences including the offence under section 302 of IPC, and sentenced to life imprisonment. Appeals were filed in the High Court and in Pritpal Singh's case and Bikramjit Singh's case, which were pending in the High Court, while in Bakhshish Singh's case, the conviction had been affirmed by the High Court, and the same was under challenge before the Supreme Court. However, all the three petitioners were undergoing sentence in jail. Consequent upon conviction, their pensions have been stopped under order of the PCDA by addressing a communication to the Disbursing Authority (Banks).

The petitioners contended that the communication by the PCDA to stop their pension has been addressed without giving any 'show cause notice' or any opportunity of hearing to them. Further, according to Para 3 (a) (b) and (c) of Regulation 4 of the Pension Regulations for the Army, 1961 (Part I) provides that the Competent Authority before passing an order under Para 1, ordering withholding or withdrawing a pension or part thereof, whether permanently or for a specified period, in case the pensioner is convicted of a serious crime, or is found guilty of grave misconduct, is required to serve upon the pensioner specifying the action proposed to be taken against him, and the grounds on which it is proposed to be taken, calling upon him to submit, within 15 days of receipt of the notice, such representation as he may wish to make against the proposed action, then to take into consideration the representation if submitted, and then pass an order, in writing, which is appealable to the President of India. It was contended that in view of this provision, since no 'show cause notice' has been given to the petitioners, the pension could not be stopped. Referring the judgements of the Tribunal in the case of *Kesar Singh v. Union of India* TA No. 291 of 2009, decided on 2 August 2010, and in *Jarnail Singh v. Union of India* OA No. 138 of 2010, decided on 15 July 2010, wherein in identical circumstances the order of stopping pension was quashed, the petitioners prayed for quashing the order of the PCDA.

The respondents relying upon Para 74 of part II of Pension Regulations contested that the provision makes it clear that the pensioner being sentenced to imprisonment for criminal offence his pension shall be suspended from the date of imprisonment. Further, whether the offence for which he is convicted is serious one or not, is to be decided by the Competent Authority, in consultation with CDA. In cases where the pensioner was in jail, show cause notice was not required to be given. Referring to the two cases cited by the petitioners, the respondents contested that in these cases, the individuals were on bail, while in the present case, they were in jail and undergoing sentence.

The Tribunal examined provisions of Regulation 4 as well as Para 74 of the Pension Regulations for the Army, 1961. In the opinion of the Tribunal, there was no distinction in the continuation of pension on the basis of the individual being in custody or at liberty. The Tribunal observed that the provisions of Regulation 4 confers a right upon the Competent Authority to withhold or withdraw a pension, or part thereof, whether permanently or for a specified period, if the pensioner is convicted of a serious crime or is found guilty of grave misconduct. From a reading of the two provisions, it was clear that this was to be done by the Competent Authority by an order in writing, and at the same time, before passing such an order in writing, the procedure prescribed in sub para (3) of Regulation 4, was required to be followed. So far as, Para 74 was concerned, on the face of it, it appears to be operative in a different field, viz. it talks suspension of pension, and does require the CDA to report the matter for orders by the Competent Authority, and then, the Competent Authority is to decide, in consultation with CDA, and if necessary, with civil authority also whether the offence was serious one, and if so, he is entitled to order removal of the name of the pensioner from the pensioners' list from the date of commencement of imprisonment. Further, Para 76 permits restoration of pension withheld. The order of withdrawal of pension, either whole or in part or whether permanently or for a specified period, is required to be made by the Competent Authority in writing after following the prescribed procedure.

The Tribunal held that in the present case the PCDA has arrogated to itself the power of withdrawing the pension only because the petitioner has been convicted. In these cases, since no show cause notice was given to the petitioners, the order for withdrawing the pension cannot be passed without following the procedure prescribed in sub-para (iii) of Regulation 4, apart from the fact that it has to be by an order in writing by the Competent Authority.

The Tribunal directed that the order passed by the PCDA stopping the pension, to be treated an order suspending the pension passed by the PCDA, and the matter is assumed to have been reported to the Competent Authority. The Competent Authority was directed to give show cause notice to all the three petitioners respectively within a period of four weeks from the date of the order, and the petitioners to submit their representations within the time to be given by the Competent Authority. After the representation is submitted (if submitted), the Competent Authority is to take appropriate decision objectively, dispassionately, and keeping in mind the letter and spirit of the provisions of Regulation 4 of Pension Regulations for the Army, 1961. Such decision should be taken within a period of two weeks from the date of receipt of representation, if filed, or expiry of the period provided to the petitioners for submitting representation. In case the Competent Authority fails to take decision within the time-frame as given, it shall be assumed that the suspension was no longer valid and the petitioners will start getting pension prospectively.

Pension to honorary commissioned officer

The AFT Principal Bench New Delhi in the case of *Sub Maj J.S. Pundhir v. Union of India*, OA No. 64 of 2010, decided on 19 July 2012, considered a prayer for grant of pension admissible to the rank of Honorary Captain.

The petitioner was commissioned as Naib Subedar in the Territorial Army on 20 January 1986. He became Subedar on 15 July 1989 and Subedar Major on 01 February 2001. He was granted the rank of Hony Lt w.e.f. 15 August 2004 and Hony Capt w.e.f. 26 January 2005. He retired as Hony Captain on 31 January 2005. The petitioner contended that despite the fact that he was granted Hony ranks of Lt and Capt before his retirement; he was still in receipt of pension of a Sub Maj.

The respondents contested that the petitioner had not completed mandatory service to get pension of commissioned rank as per provision laid down vide Para 136 of Pension Regulations for the Army 1961 and Government of India, Ministry of Defence letter dated 03 February 1998. Therefore, he was granted pension for the rank of Sub Maj w.e.f. 01 February 2005 and PCDA(P), Allahabad recovered a sum of Rs. 58,513/- from the pay of the petitioner as he was erroneously granted retirement gratuity as applicable for Hony Rank which was not applicable to him.

The Tribunal referred to Correction Slip No. 1/2011 in respect of amendment to Territorial Army Regulations, 1948 (Revised) 1976 which read:

> "AMENDMENT TO TERRITORIAL ARMY REGULATIONS 1948 (REVISED) 1976 C.S. No. 1/2011 1. Regulations for the Territorial Army 1948 (1976 Edition) are amended as under:-
>
> In Para 172(c) For Junior Commissioned Officers holding Honorary ranks of Captains and Lieutenants will be paid in accordance with the rank they held prior to being granted the honorary ranks.

> Read Junior Commissioned Officers granted honorary commission of Captain and Lieutenants while in service will continue to be entitled to same pay and allowance that is paid to their equivalent Honorary Commissioned Officers in Regular Army.
>
> However, Junior Commissioned Officers granted honorary ranks of Captain and Lieutenants on retirement will be paid in accordance with the rank they held prior to being granted the honorary rank.
>
> Case No. 47144/GS/TA-3/561/US/(GS-III)/2011 This issues with the approval of MoD/Fin diary No 710/FIN/GS/11 dt 8 July 2011. (V Rajaram) Under Secretary to the Government of India"

In the Tribunal's view, according to the amendment, Junior Commissioned Officers granted honorary commission of Captain and Lieutenants while in service will continue to be entitled to same pay and allowance that is paid to their equivalent Honorary Commissioned Officers in Regular Army. However, Junior Commissioned Officers granted honorary ranks of Captain and Lieutenants on retirement will be paid in accordance with the rank they held prior to being granted the honorary rank. The petitioner got both honorary ranks while in service. As per the amendment, he was entitled for the benefits for the rank of Hony Captain.

The Tribunal ordered the respondents to release pension for the rank of Hony Captain from the date of the retirement with all other benefits. The recovery effected by the respondents of Rs. 58,513/- was absolutely illegal and it was directed that same be refunded to the petitioner. Petitioner would also be entitled for interest @ 12% per annum on the arrears.

Condonation of deficiency of service

The AFT Principal Bench New Delhi in *Ex. Nk Shri Bhagwan v. Union of India*, OA No. 328 of 2011, decided on 4 July 2012, considered a prayer for condonation of deficiency of service and grant of pension.

The petitioner was enrolled in the Army on 11 July 1988 and was posted to Rashtriya Rifles (RR). While posted at RR, the petitioner started taking alcohol during non-duty period for which he was repeatedly awarded severe reprimand three times within a period of six months. He was sent back to his parent unit where he was promoted to the rank of Naik. He was again awarded severe reprimand under section 48 of Army Act, 1950 for intoxication. He was discharged on 08 April 2002 from service as per the policy of Army Headquarters dated 28 December 1988 for being awarded four red ink entries.

The petitioner filed a Writ Petition (C) No. 1930 of 2003 before the Delhi High Court against his discharge. The Delhi High Court vide judgment dated 02 May 2008 allowed the writ petition. However, he was not allowed to rejoin duty despite order of the High Court, therefore, he filed a Contempt Petition No. 425 of 2009 before the Delhi High Court. The respondent authorities requested for extension of time for implementing the court order, therefore, the said contempt petition was withdrawn vide order of the High Court dated

11 May 2009. Meantime, the respondents instead of implementing the order of High Court filed the Special Leave Petition before the Supreme Court which was also dismissed. The petitioner again filed a Contempt Petition No. 728 of 2009 before the Delhi High Court and finally petitioner was allowed to rejoin duty on 23 February 2010. The petitioner was discharged from service on completion of terms of engagement on 31 July 2010 vide discharge order dated 05 April 2010. The Delhi High Court while allowing the writ petition moved by the petitioner observed that the intervening period from the date of discharge i.e. 08 April 2002 to the date of judgement (02 May 2008) was not to be considered for the benefit of pay and allowances and pensionary benefits.

The petitioner contended that the period from the date of judgment i.e. 02 May 2008 till 23 February 2010 when petitioner was actually allowed to rejoin duty should be computed for the purpose of pay and allowances and retirement benefits. However, respondent authorities have not accepted his plea and vide their letter dated 05 March 2011 rejected the appeal of the petitioner for grant of pension. It was also contended that as per Government of India, Ministry of Defence letter dated 14 August 2011, there was a provision for condonation of deficiency of service up to one year.

The petitioner further contended that despite the judgment of the Delhi High Court dated 02 May 2008, petitioner was not allowed to rejoin duty which led to filing of two contempt petitions. Ultimately, petitioner was allowed to rejoin duty w.e.f. 23 February 2010. Therefore, petitioner should be treated notionally in service from the date of decision of the High Court i.e. 02 May 2008 till he was allowed to rejoin duty on 23 February 2010 as petitioner was ready and willing to rejoin duty after the decision of the High Court, but the respondents who did allow the petitioner to rejoin duty. The petitioner also submitted that if this period (1 year and 10 months) is computed to the account of petitioner then his total service would come to about 16 years and he will be entitled for pensionary benefits.

The respondents contested that the petitioner has physically rendered 14 years, 02 months and 02 days of qualifying service for pension whereas as per Para 132 of Pension Regulations for the Army 1961, a minimum of 15 years of qualifying service is required to earn service pension. The petitioner was falling short of 09 months and 29 days of qualifying service for grant of minimum service pension. Further the period from 02 May 2008 to 23 February 2010 cannot be counted as the petitioner did not physically serve during this period.

The Tribunal observed that it was the respondents who did not allow the petitioner to rejoin and showed defiance of the order of the High Court which led to filing of two contempt petitions by the petitioner before the Court. Respondents also approached the Supreme Court by filing SLP against the order of the Delhi High Court which was also dismissed. Ultimately, petitioner was allowed to rejoin his duty on 23 February 2010. Therefore petitioner was to be notionally treated in service for the period from the date of decision of the Delhi High Court i.e. 02 May 2008 till he was allowed to rejoin duty by the respondents i.e. 23 February 2010.

The Tribunal set aside the impugned order dated 05 March 2011 and directed the respondents to release all the pensionary benefits to the petitioner from the date of discharge i.e. 31 July 2010 and all the arrears to be worked out and paid to the petitioner along with interest at the rate of 12% per annum. Respondents were further directed to release pay and allowance for the period from 02 May 2008 to 23 February 2010 along with interest at the rate of 12% per annum, if not paid earlier.

Reservist Pension

The AFT Regional Bench Kochi in the case of *M. Vijayan Unni v. Union of India*, OA No.15 of 2011, decided on 9 February 2012, considered a prayer from 75-years-old Ex Corporal for pension.

The applicant was enrolled in the Air Force on 6 October 1953 as an Airman. His term of engagement was 9 years regular and 6 years reserve service. In accordance with the applicant's terms of engagement, he was discharged from the Indian Air Force on 6 October 1965 after completion of 9 years of regular service. He was transferred to reserve service after 6 October 1962. Later, on 30 September 1965 the applicant was discharged from reserve service after completion of 2 years and 360 days of service. Total colour and reserve service has become 11 years and 360 days.

The applicant was not given any pension after his discharge. He was granted service gratuity for his regular period and half of the reserve service. The applicant had approached the competent authority pointing out the discrepancies made in discharge certificate stating that the reserve service of the applicant was not mentioned in the said certificate. But the applicant was informed that only active service will be reflected in the certificate.

The applicant contended that in an identical case, the High Court of Kerala at Ernakulam had sanctioned reservist pension for the applicant in OP No. 7713 of 1996 who was an Airman in the Indian Air Force who had completed 9 years of colour service, but was discharged from service before completing the service. The Writ Appeal No. 1392 of 1997 preferred against the judgment in OP No. 7713 of 1996 was also dismissed by a Division Bench. In another case of similar nature in WP (C) No. 29497 of 2004 in which the petitioner had served in the Air Force for 9 years and discharged with reserve liability, was called during the emergency and after the emergency he was discharged. But he was not kept in reserve after discharge from reserve service. However, the High Court had allowed the said WP and directed the respondents to pay reservist pension. The Writ Appeal preferred against the verdict in WP No. 29497 of 2004 was appealed under WA No.1439 of 2006; but the same was dismissed by a Division Bench.

In response to his application, the Air Force Record Office (AFRO) vide letter No.RO/2704/2/P&WW(RES) dated 30 October 2007 informed that he was not entitled to reservist pension as per Regulation 136 of the Pension Regulations for the Air Force. The main objection raised by the respondent was that the applicant had not served for 15 years and that he had received gratuity. The applicant further contended that his discharge from the reserve was not on any request of his own and the gratuity paid was service gratuity and not lump sum gratuity. Thereafter, the applicant received another letter No. RO/2801/Corr/C-05/PW(SP) dated 5 June 2008 under which the AFRO admitted that the gratuity received by the applicant was service gratuity, but rejected the claim of the applicant for reservist pension on the ground that the applicant was short of qualifying service.

The respondents contested that there was no entry in the long roll with regard to the discharge of the petitioner from the reserve. However, as per Air Head Quarters letter No. Air HQ/31/31783/212747/Res.3 dated 16 October 1965 the individual was discharged from the reserve on 30 September 1965 under the clause "services no longer required", before completion of his term of engagement in the regular Air Force Reserve. Further, at the time of discharge, the applicant had total service of 11 years and 360 days (9 years in the regular and 2 years and 360 days in the reserve). As per Regulation 121 of the Pension Regulation for the Air Force, 1961 (Part-I), the minimum qualifying service to earn service pension was 15 years and as per Regulation 136 to earn reservist pension one should have combined service of 15 years in the colour and reserve service. Since the applicant had only 11 years and 360 days inclusive of his regular and reserve service, he was not qualified either for service pension or reservist pension. The applicant was paid service gratuity for his service of 11 years and 360 days. The service documents/records of the applicant have been destroyed after retaining them for the stipulated period.

The respondents further contested that the applicant has come forward after an inordinate delay of 47 years, for which no explanation was forthcoming from the applicant. It is a well settled law that a litigant should not be benefitted by lodging a late appeal and he should not stand to benefit by virtue of delay. In a similar case, OA No. 84 of 2010 the Tribunal had rejected the claim of reservist pension on 16 May 2011. Hence the application was liable to be dismissed.

The Tribunal observed that the applicant after completing the terms of engagement of 9 years of regular service, continued in the reserve service only for 2 years and 360 days and thereafter he was discharged from service on the ground that his "service is no longer required". An Airman who had combined service of 15 years colour and reserve service was entitled to reservist pension. An individual discharged from reserve for any cause other than own request was entitled for reservist pension.

Further, the applicant had not opted for voluntary discharge from reserve service and even after serving for 2 years and 360 days in the reserve service in spite of his wish to continue in the reserve service to complete his term of engagement, the respondents without assigning any reason discharged him on the ground "his service were no longer required" for which the applicant was in no way responsible and the denial of reservist pension on the said ground was illegal.

The Tribunal referred to a similar case decided by the Principal Bench of the AFT New Delhi (TA No. 564 of 2010 WP (Civil) No. 6458 of 2009) relying on several dictums of the Supreme Court in *Deokinandan Prasad v. State of Bihar* (AIR 1971 SC page 1409), *Union of India v. Anglo (Indo) – Afghan Agencies Ltd.* (AIR 1968 SC 718), *Motilal Padampat Sugar Mills v. State of Uttar Pradesh AIR* (1979 SC 621), *Bakul Cashew Co. v. STO* (1986) SCC 365) and *State of S.P. Dubey v. MPSRTC* (AIR 1991 SC 276). The Court came to a definite conclusion that once it is found that the applicant was in no way responsible for the discharge during his reserve service, it is to be treated that he has completed the terms of engagement and he was entitled to the reservist pension. The important observation in the above said order runs as follows:

> "As a matter of fact, in the initial appointment given to the petitioner it was clearly mentioned that petitioner will have to serve 9 year as regular service and 6 years as reserve service. Subsequently the respondents cannot reverse the situation that since the appointment has been terminated, therefore, they are not entitled to count 6 years reserve service. The respondents are bound by principle of promissory estoppels, that once they made a representation and asked the other party to act on it and petitioner has served for 9 years as regular service and kept him in reserve service for 6 years, they cannot wriggle out of this on the moral ground that subsequently after China War their services were terminated also. This is clear breach of terms of conditions of appointment. Once respondents availed the services of petitioners for 9 years as active service and kept them on reserve service for 6 years they cannot go back."

The Tribunal observed that the said principle was reiterated by the Supreme Court in *Motilal Padampat Sugar Mills v. State of Uttar Pradesh* (AIR 1979 SC 621), which reads:

> "....where one party has by his words or conduct made to the other a clear and unequivocal promise which is intended to create legal relations or affect a legal relationship to rise in the future, knowing or intending that it would be acted upon by the other party to whom the promise is made and it is in fact so acted upon by the other party, the promise would be binding on the party making it and he would not be entitled to do back upon it, if it would be inequitable to allow him to do so having regard to the dealings which have taken place between the parties, and this would be so irrespective whether there is any pre-existing relationship between the parties or not.
>
> It is elementary that in a republic governed by the rule of law, no one, howsoever high or low, is above the law. Everyone is subject to the law as fully and completely as any other and the Government is no exception. It is indeed the pride of constitutional democracy and rule

of law that the Government stands on the same footing as a private individual insofar as the obligation of the law is concerned: the former is equally bound as the latter. It is indeed difficult to see on what principle can a government, committed to the rule of law, claim immunity from the doctrine of promissory estoppels? Can the Government say that it is under no obligation to act in a manner that is fair and just or that it is not bound by considerations of "honesty and good faith?" Why should the Government not be held to a high "standard of rectilinear rectitude while dealing with its citizen?"

The doctrine of promissory estoppel against the Government has been laid down in the judgment of the Supreme Court in *Bakul Cashew Co. v. STO* (1986) SCC 365 as under:

> "Three principles are evolved in order to protect the applicability of doctrine of promissory estoppel against the government. They are (i) that there was a definite representation by the Government, (ii) that the person to whom the representation or promise was made, in fact altered their position by action upon such representation and (iii) that he has suffered some prejudices sufficient to constitute an estoppel."

The Tribunal held that under such circumstances, the discharge of the applicant after he had completed the colour service of 9 years and while he was in the midst of his reserve service of 2 years and 360 days the respondents after entering into a contract of engagement with the applicant for 9 years colour service and 6 years reserve service cannot discharge him on the ground "his services are no longer required", without assigning any substantial reason.

The Tribunal, relying upon the decision of the Supreme Court in *Union of India v. Tarsem Singh*, (2008) 8 SCC 648, ordered that applicant would be entitled to reservist pension from three years prior to the date of filing of the application i.e., 20 January 2008. The respondents were given a time of three months for compliance, failing which the applicant would be entitled to 9% interest per annum for the arrears.

Damages for delay in pension

The Armed Forces Tribunal Principal Bench New Delhi in the case of *Ex Hav Mohinder Singh v. Union of India*, TA No. 32 of 2011, [Suit No. 529/06/04 of District Court, Delhi] decided on 10 April 2012, considered a suit seeking decree of Rs. 75,000/- against the Union of India for delay in the payment of pensionary benefits.

The petitioner retired from Indian Army as Havildar on 31 December 1998 and furnished his bank account details to the respodents i.e. Punjab & Sind Bank, for the remission of retirement benefits and pension. He was entitled to the retirement dues and PPO in this regard was sent to the bankers, Punjab & Sind Bank vide ASC Records Letter No. 13863068 L/SP 4507/Pen dated 31 December 1998. The petitioner contended that the said PPO was incomplete and invalid as the same was not duly signed by the concerned officer and it was unsigned. The bankers did not honour this PPO and returned the same to the Union of India for signature and for sending it back to the Bank after being signed. The process of sending unsigned PPO and its returning for signature and again sending the same to the Bank took a period of 7 months, therefore, the payment to the plaintiff was delayed by 7 months as a result of which plaintiff suffered hardship, humiliation, mental torture, agony and harassment despite no fault of his. He could only get his retirement dues on 29 July 1999 whereas he was entitled to get the same on 31 December 1998.

The petitioner further contended that the payment was delayed due to the negligence and carelessness on the part of defendants, so he was claiming the interest @ 18% per annum on the sum of Rs. 201,292/- for the period of 7 months amounting to Rs. 25,000/-as well as damages of Rs. 50,000/- for harassment, mental agony and torture caused to him. Further, the petitioner submitted that all the defendants are jointly and severally liable to pay the suit amount of Rs. 75,000/- to him as they all are responsible for withholding the dues.

The defendant Bank contended in their reply that it could not honour the PPO sent by the defendant, Union of India as it was unsigned, therefore, the delay occurred. They received the signed PPO in July, 1999 and immediately credited the amount in petitioner's account on 29 July 1999, therefore, they were not liable to pay any interest or damages to the petitioner.

The Tribunal observed that the defendants were trying to shift the liability from one shoulder to other and tried to persuade the Tribunal that delay in making the pensionary benefits to the petitioner was a bonafide mistake and was not a malafide one. The Tribunal held that there was contributory negligence on the part of defendant Bank as well as Union of India. Due to this negligence on the part of defendant bank, petitioner suffered great financial hardships and mental trauma. The Tribunal recorded its serious displeasure with the functioning of Punjab & Sind Bank as acted in most negligent manner and they have to be saddled with the consequences to this kind of negligence at their end.

The Tribunal held that the petitioner was entitled to the interest @12% on the sum of Rs. 2,01,292/- for the period from 31 December 1998 to 29 July 1999 amounting to Rs. 14,090/-, in addition to damages of Rs. 20,000/- on account of harassment and mental trauma suffered by him. The Tribunal directed that both, the interest and damages to be borne by the defendants, Union of India and Punjab & Sind Bank equally and the amount to be released to the petitioner within a period of one month from the date of the order.

Death during military operation, liberalized family pension

The AFT Regional Bench Kolkata, in the case of *Mrs Charubala Rath v. Union of India*, TA No. 168 of 2010 [WP (C) 15218 of 2008], decided on 17 February 2012, considered a prayer for the sanction of liberalized family pension.

The applicant's husband late Nb Sub Himadri Kumar Rath was serving in the Army. While he was deployed in the desert sector of Rajasthan as part of "OP PARAKRAM", his tank transporter caught fire on 20 September 2003 and the JCO died on the spot. The petitioner Mrs. Charubalal Rath, wife of the deceased JCO, was in receipt of special family pension with effect from 21 September 2003, which was admissible to the widow of those who die on duty and the said death was attributable to the military service. She also received entitled DCRG and ex-gratia payment of Rs. 5 lakh.

The petitioner contended that she should be authorized liberalized family pension which she was entitled to, as her husband had died in circumstances that would classify his death as a case of "Battle casualty (BC)". Her claim was rejected by the CDA (P) stating that her husband had died as a result of vehicle accident while on bonafied military service in peace. The petitioner further contended that after the accidental death of her husband a court of inquiry was held. Further her husband had died on 20 September 2003 while on duty in operational area during OP PARAKRM and it was a battle casualty. A Part II Order for battle casualty was also published by the Record Office.

The responded conceded that the husband of the petitioner died due to massive burns on account of an accident with his vehicle loaded with tank (T-55) of Armoured Regiment. Further, at the time of accident he was in "OP PARAKRAM", and the court of inquiry subsequently declared that the death was attributable to Military Service in Operational Area and was a battle casualty.

The Tribunal observed that the JCO was indeed performing operational duty while engaged in "OP PARAKRAM". It involved a large scale mobilization, induction and de-induction of heavy military equipments. He was performing an operational duty when he met with the fatal accident that charred him to death. Therefore the death of the JCO was indeed a battle casualty. The Tribunal ordered the respondents to sanction liberalized family pension to the petitioner with effect from 21 September 2003 with all other consequential benefits.

Second pension

The Armed Forces Tribunal Principal Bench New Delhi in the case of *Smt. Rajbala Saini v. Union of India*, OA No. 202 of 2012, decided on 4 February 2013, considered a prayer for family pension.

The petitioner was the wife of deceased Petty Officer who was enrolled on 17 September 1969 and continued in service till he was discharged on 30 November 1984. Thereafter he was reemployed in the RBI on 04 March 1987; but unfortunately expired on 08 August 2007. The petitioner, widow of the deceased was denied family pension after his death for the Navy service, but was regularly drawing family pension from RBI for the service rendered by her husband in RBI.

The petitioner contended that she was denied family pension of the service rendered by her late husband in the Navy. The respondent clarified that the Government has rectified the anomaly and issued a circular dated 17 January 2013 that the incumbents, who had put in pensionable service in the Armed Forced and thereafter re-employed in the civil side shall be held entitled to the pensions, both, the defence pension as well as civil pension w.e.f. 24 September 2012. The petitioner's claim was rejected on 24 April 2012. Since the anomaly has been sorted out by the Government, the petitioner was entitled to the pension from the Navy also.

The Tribunal held that petitioner was entitled to pension from 24 September 20012 along with arrears with interest @ 12% per annum. The Tribunal also awarded a cost of Rs.10,000.

Retirement benefits and pension

The AFT Regional Bench Guwahati in the case of *Ratna Bahadur Chetry v. Union of India*, TA No. 19 of 2010, decided in February 2011, considered a prayer for the grant the retirement benefits including pension.

The appellant was recruited in the Army on 30 January 1971 as Sepoy in the Assam Regiment. He was promoted to the rank of Naik in the year 1985. The wife of the appellant was ill since three years preceding her death on 18 January1987 necessitating the appellant to make request to the authorities on 01 June 1986 for the discharge from service on extreme compassionate ground, as there was nobody to look after his ailing wife and three minor children. The said application was received by the Respondent authorities. Prior to that, the wife of the appellant also filed an application on 09 October 1985 addressed to the Commanding Officer, Assam Regiment requesting the authority to discharge her husband (the appellant) from service to facilitate her treatment and to look after the domestic affairs. Not getting any favourable action on such request made by the appellant's wife, the appellant submitted another application on 01 June 1986 repeating his request for allowing him to go on voluntary retirement on extreme compassionate ground, which was duly received and forwarded on 06 June 1986 by the applicant's superior for necessary action. The Commanding Officer recommended the prayer of the appellant in writing on the application itself as "a very genuine case strongly recommended" vide endorsement dated 02 June 1986. The wife of the appellant unfortunately breathed her last on 01 July 1986 leaving behind three minor daughters. The Respondents did not take any decision on the applicant's request for discharge. The appellant again submitted another application for release from service, but without any response.

The appellant availed leave with effect from 19 January 1988 to 19 February 1988, but after expiry of the leave the petitioner could not report immediately leaving the three minor daughters without any guardian. Under the circumstances beyond his control, as nobody was there to look after his minor children, he had to overstay. On 19 March 1988 the appellant informed the Commanding Officer about the situation faced by him and the reasons for not joining and requesting him to allow him to go on voluntary retirement/

discharge. The appellant also filed another application on 27 March 1987 which was strongly recommended to the higher authorities. To add to the miseries of the appellant, his father, who, somehow was looking after his minor daughters after the death of appellant's wife, also expired in the month of September, 1988.

However, the respondents on 16 March 1990 acknowledged receipt of the application dated 13 February 1990 and directed the appellant to report to the unit immediately. On receipt of the said letter, the appellant attended the unit along with his three minor daughters, but no action was taken by the authorities to release him from service. In such a situation the appellant could not attend his further duties. Thereafter, the appellant made several correspondences requesting for payment of retirement benefits including pension, but the authorities neither favoured the appellant with such payment nor an effective order was passed to discharge the appellant from service as requested by him. On the contrary, the respondent included the name of the appellant in the list at Serial No.1 of dismissed persons vide Order No.26 dated 23 November 1991 and 27 November 1991. In the said list the appellant was shown to be dismissed as deserter under s. 20(3) of the Army Act. He was refused retirement benefits. The appellant approached the Guwahati High Court by filing WP (C) No. 6100 of 2002, which was transferred to the Tribunal.

The Respondents contested the claim of the appellant stating that the appellant was advised to report the Unit for consideration of his prayer for discharge since he was already declared a deserter. But the appellant did not return and as such he was dismissed from Army service with effect from 20 February 1991. The respondents further contested that the appellant ever applied for discharge from service on extreme ground and that the appellant availed leave from 18 January 1988 to 19 February 1988 and thereafter he did not return to the Unit for re-joining after expiry of leave and as such he was declared deserter with effect from 20 February 1991. The respondents maintained that the appellant was not entitled to get pensionary benefit; inasmuch as, he was dismissed as deserter and whatever amount payable to him under the admissible Rules have already been paid to the appellant.

The Tribunal observed that technically, there was no doubt as to the fact that the appellant deserted from service, firstly because he overstayed his leave and secondly he expressed his intention or inability to rejoin service after about 30 days of overstayal. The finding of desertion cannot, therefore, be legally faulted. In the Armed Forces, personnel cannot be allowed to remain absent without leave at their will and thereafter request for discharge.

The Tribunal further noted that the appellant has produced two applications, one by his wife, and the other by himself, which were submitted by him and strongly recommended by his commanding officer for the discharge of the appellant in view of the family circumstances. Whilst the respondents acknowledged receipt of the application from the wife and stated that it was not entertained as it was unsigned, but have denied about the appellant having ever submitted an application for discharge on extreme compassionate ground. The Respondents also denied any intimation to this effect from the appellant. Only other application that the respondents accepted and received from the appellant was dated 19 February 1990, which was more than two years after his desertion from the Army. It was with reference to this application, the respondents advised the appellant to report to the unit so that his discharge could be considered. The respondents, however, claimed that the appellant did not report back for duty.

Further, the respondents have shown ignorance about the fate of application dated 1 June 1986, produced before the Tribunal, wherein the commanding officer had strongly recommended the case for discharge. In the absence of any denial from the Respondents on this issue, the application dated 01 June 1988 was taken to be true. The Tribunal was of the opinion that the respondents failed to take a reasonable stand on the request for discharge on extreme compassionate ground as made by the appellant and his wife. Even if the Rules did not permit any unsigned application to be taken cognizance of, the Respondents could, in the least, have checked with the appellant who was serving with them as regards genuineness of the application/ facts and circumstances stated therein. The respondents clearly failed to do this. Same goes for the application purported to have been made by the appellant and strongly recommended by the then Commanding Officer in June, 1986. Proper processing of these applications could well have lead to timely discharge of the appellant in view of the compelling circumstances. The Respondents clearly defaulted in this regard and thereby practically forced the appellant into staying at home without leave as there was really speaking no choice available to the appellant on account of there being no one else to look after the three minor daughters after the death of his wife.

The Tribunal was of the opinion that failure on the part of the respondents to properly consider the application for discharge as submitted by the appellant and his wife, resulted in forcing the appellant to overstay his leave and, therefore, he remain absent. Accordingly, the Tribunal quashed the order declaring the dismissal of the appellant on the ground of desertion and directed the respondents to accept the prayer of the appellant for voluntary discharge from service as prayed by him and to grant the necessary pension as required under the law, considering that the petitioner had already rendered the minimum required number of pensionable service. The Tribunal directed that the action be the respondents to be completed within 45 days from the date of the order.

Death on duty: payment of ex-gratia

The AFT Regional Bench Kochi in the case of *Smitha Praveen, widow of Late Naik A Praveen v. Union of India*, OA 119 of 2012, decided on 4 March 2013, considered a prayer for the award of ex-gratia payment.

The applicant's husband, Ex Naik A. Praveen was enrolled in the Madras Regiment of the Indian Army on 20 February 1995. While serving with Madras

Regiment, he died due to snake-bite on 5 May 2008 in exercise area during formation level exercise. The Court of Inquiry proceedings dated 14 August 2008 found that cause of death of Naik Praveen was attributable to military service as he was sleeping after completion of his part of training while the battalion was deployed in exercise at District Una, Himachal Pradesh, where poisonous snakes and other creatures were found. Accordingly, the applicant was sanctioned Special Family Pension.

However, her claim for ex-gratia payment of Rs. 10 lakhs in accordance with the terms and conditions provided by the Government of India, Ministry of Defence Letter No.20 (1)/98/D (Pay/Service) dated 21 October 2008 was denied by the Principal Controller of Defence Accounts (Pension), Allahabad. According to the said letter, a sum of Rs. 10 lakhs was payable as ex-gratia lump sum compensation to the next of kin of the deceased defence personnel if their death occurs in accidents in the course of duties. Further, the death of the applicant's husband did not fall within the purview of the Government Letter dated 21 October 2008 as the individual was not actually performing the bonafide military duty at the time of death. The PCDA (P) by the subsequent letter dated 7 September 2011 had informed the applicant that the death of her husband was due to snakebite. The PCDA (P) further informed the applicant that the basic condition to be satisfied as stipulated in the Government Letter dated 21 October 2008 was that there should be a casual connection between the death and actual performance of bonafide military duty, which did not exist in the matter of the death of applicant's husband. So, she was denied ex-gratia payment.

The Tribunal observed that Record Office of the Madras Regiment had sent another letters dated 25 November 2008 and 26 February 2009 to the PCDA (P), Allahabad, clarifying that the cause of death of the individual was attributable to military service and the accidental death of this particular individual should not be treated as "death occurred while sleeping". The above request of the Record Office of the Madras Regiment was turned down by the PCDA (P) vide letter dated 8 April 2011 stating that the death of applicant's husband did not fall within the purview of Government of India, Ministry of Defence Letter No. 20(1)/98/D/(Pay/Ser) dated 21 October 2008 as the individual was not actually performing the bonafide Military duty at the time of death.

The Tribunal was of the view that the stand of the PCDA (P) Allahabad was not correct in law. There was a casual connection between the duty of the applicant's husband and his death. Had he not been deployed there for the aforesaid training programme, he would not have died due to snakebite, especially when he was not permitted to leave the place and had to stay there. The Tribunal also mentioned that the Integrated Headquarters of the Ministry of Defence (Army) had issued a letter dated 20 April 2010 to the PCDA (P), Allahabad conveying that the President was pleased to decide that the death of late Naik A. Praveen should be regarded as attributable to military service, but surprisingly, the PCDA (P), Allahabad, who was not the appropriate authority to decide the question of attributability, overruled the opinion of the President without any justification.

The Tribunal held that the death of the applicant's husband took place while on duty in the exercise area, which was attributable to military service; and directed the respondents to sanction and pay the lump sum ex-gratia compensation of Rs. 10 lakhs to the applicant within four months from the date of the order, failing which the unpaid amount will carry a simple interest at 8% per annum to be paid by the respondents to the applicant.

Pension and ex-gratia, death while on leave

The AFT New Delhi, Principal Bench in the case of *Smt Ram Sri v. Union of India*, OA No. 397/2010, decided on 1 October 2010, considered the case of grant special family pension and ex-gratia to the applicant where her husband was killed in a road accident during casual leave.

A court of inquiry was held to investigate the matter, and the death was declared attributable to military service as per Regulations of the Army, 1987. However, her claim of death benefits and subsequent appeals were rejected by PCDA (P), Allahabad. The PCDA was of the view that claim of applicant was not maintainable as death of her husband was neither attributable nor aggravated by Military Service.

The Tribunal held: "Normally finding of Station Commander and Brigade Commander under Regulation 520 of the Army Regulations, 1987 and section 8 of the Army Act read with recommendations of the Fifth Central Pay Commission dated 07.02.2001, shall be final and not the PCDA (P), Allahabad. In the present case, PCDA (P) tried to split hair...But, the findings of the PCDA (P), Allahabad is erroneous."

The Tribunal directed that applicant's husband to be treated on duty at the time of accident/death and applicant shall be entitled to special family pension. Applicant being the widow of the deceased will also be entitled to ex-gratia payment in accordance with rules bearing on the subject. The Bench also directed the government to release special family pension along with arrears with interest @ 12% from the date of death of her husband along with admissible ex-gratia payment.

Ex-gratia

The AFT Principal Bench New Delhi in the case of *Smt Mahuya Das v. Union of India*, OA No. 469 of 2011, decided on 8 May 2013, considered a case for the grant of ex-gratia payment.

The petitioner's husband, late Sep S C Das was enrolled in the Army on 27 June 2002. Thereafter, he was posted to Transport Company on 27 August 2007 and was working as a Sahayak to an officer who was posted at Integrated HQ, Ministry of Defence (MOD) at New Delhi. On 14 August 2010, while the deceased was cleaning the accommodation of his officer at the 9th floor of

Arjun Apartments, Dwarka, New Delhi, he accidently fell down and died. The Court of Inquiry was ordered to investigate the matter reached an opinion that the death of Sep S C Das was attributable to military service. Accordingly the case for family pension was taken up sanctioned.

The petitioner contended that she should also be granted (i) ex-gratia payment of Rs. 10 lakhs, and (ii) the officer for whom her late husband was working as sahayak be directed to pay Rs. 10 lakhs as compensation. The petitioner further contended that she was entitled to the ex gratia payment, as her husband had died after falling from the 9th floor and that his death was attributable to military service.

The Tribunal observed that the letter dated 22 September 1998 issued by the Government of India, for grant of ex-gratia payment laid down certain guidelines for grant of ex-gratia lump sum compensation to families of the defence services personnel who die in harness. The circular stated that families of defence service personnel who die in harness in performance of their bona fide official duties shall be paid Rs. 5 lakhs as ex-gratia lump sum compensation. This amount was increased by the subsequent notification dated 03 September 2009 to Rs.10 lakhs, with other conditions being the same.

The respondents strenuously contested that there are certain guidelines for granting ex-gratia lump sum and such contingency was not covered in the list appended to this communication, wherein it had been mentioned that death should have occurred while on duty, in an accident while travelling, or by terrorist attack or while discharging of duties in aid to civil authorities or in a cyclone or any such situations, and the present case was not covered by any of the contingencies mentioned in the guidelines which have been given by the authorities.

The Tribunal observed that while it was true that these are illustrative examples, they cannot be exhaustive and a contingency. What has happened in the present case was peculiar and very rare. General broad guidelines have been given by the government but those general guidelines cannot be exhaustive, therefore, they have left it to the discretion of the administrative authorities and it has been clearly mentioned in the guidelines itself that these powers have been delegated to the administrative ministries to sanction ex-gratia payment under these orders. Further, these guidelines have to be interpreted more benevolently so as to advance the cause of social justice. In this case a young widow, who hardly had a marital life of one year, had to meet such an unfortunate accident of losing her husband has undergone a very traumatic experience, therefore, granting of ex gratia compensation of Rs. 10 lakhs was fully justified. The Tribunal directed that the respondents should release the ex-gratia payment of Rs. 10 lakhs within three months.

On the question of compensation against the officer, the Tribunal observed that it was not possible because petitioner's husband was not a private employee of the officer. He was attached because of his official position and he was working for him. The government has already compensated for his discharge of duties as a Sahayak to the officer. The Tribunal held that the officer cannot be held personally liable for any compensation; therefore, the prayer for grant of compensation against the officer was over-ruled.

XVI. Posting

Outside the jurisdiction

The AFT Regional Bench Chandigarh in the case of *Sukhdev Singh v. Union of India* OA No. 303 of 2013, decided on 13 February 2013, considered a case for compensation.

The petitioner was enrolled in the Army as Naib Subedar on 01 July 1989 in the Engineering Branch of the Army. He was promoted to the ranks of Subedar on 20 August 1996 and to Subedar Major on 08 April 2004. He retired from the service on 30 April 2008 after completion of 19 years of service. On representation, the petitioner was given last leg posting in situ, however, due to differences with AGE B/R-2, who was officiating as AGE B/R (P) Barnala the petitioner was transferred to Chief Engineer Bathinda. On refusal of request for cancellation of the posting by the OIC records the petitioner approached the High Court vide CWP No. 18127 of 2007 which was disposed of with a direction that the petitioner may file representation through proper channel and if any such representation is made, the authority concerned shall forward the same to the higher authority for proper action, who shall consider the same in a sympathetic manner. Pursuant to the High Court order, he made a representation to the authorities concerned.

The Chief Record Officer vide its letter dated 18 March 2008 dealing with cancellation of posting of the petitioner from GE AF Halwara to CE Bathinda Zone held that JCO had already reported to his new unit i.e. CE Bathinda Zone. While he was due for retirement wef 1 May 2008 he was required to report to STB (D) at BEG and Centre Roorkee during the first week of April 2008 and it would not be technically in order to cancel posting order which had already been implemented and it was not in organization interest.

The petitioner was charge-sheeted on two charges under sections 39 (a) and 63 of the Army Act i.e. an act prejudicial to good order and military discipline for impropriety of sitting on 'Dharna' outside the office of GE AF Halwara. In the trial be GCM the petitioner was held 'not guilty' of the first charge but he was held 'guilty' of the second charge. He was sentenced to 'forfeit one year's past service for the purpose of pension and to be 'severely reprimanded'. He made pre- confirmation petition to the competent authority. Thereafter, he filed representation praying for early decision in his Pre-Confirmation petition and the confirmation of the sentence awarded by the GCM. The confirming authority being not satisfied with the findings of the GCM ordered the revision by the GCM. The GCM upheld its previous findings in the review. The petitioner filed an appeal which has yet not been decided.

The petitioner contended that with only eight months of service remaining, he was transferred from GE Air Force Station, Halwara to Bathinda without any reason and was neither afforded any time to handover the official charge to someone else nor allowed to approach the higher authorities against the arbitrary posting. This led to the absence of the petitioner for which he was charge-sheeted and later convicted by a GCM. During the long period of the GCM the petitioner received a number of civil appointments which he could accept leading to financial loss to him. He was denied civil appointments due to the illegal and arbitrary action of the respondents. The provisions of s. 123 of the Army Act were ignored by the concerned authorities and thus the petitioner was entitled for compensation. He also contended that the respondents be directed to take disciplinary action against respondents No. 3 to 6, who were responsible for his harassment, humiliation and financial loss and further to compensate him to the tune of Rs. 20 lakh by way of liquidated damages.

The Tribunal observed that being a matter of differences arising due to posting, and subsequent compensation for the harassment, humiliation and financial loss, the matter was not covered under the definition of service matters as given in s. 3(o) (iv) of the AFT Act 2007. The Tribunal dismissed the petition with liberty to file afresh at appropriate court.

XVII. Promotion

Notional promotion

The AFT Principal Bench New Delhi in the case of *Maj Gen Devendra Nath Verma, AVSM (Retd.) v. Union of India*, TA No. 255 of 2009 [WP (C) No. 4800 of 995 of Delhi High Court], decided on 22 February 2010, considered a prayer for quashing of the order of retirement and reinstatement and promotion to the rank of Lt. Gen.

The petitioner was promoted to the rank of Maj Gen in 1991 and contended that he was considered by a Promotion Board held on 4 January 1994, but was found unsuitable for promotion. He was surprised when he was told that he did not make the grade as he lacked experience in Staff Appointments. The petitioner submitted that he was qualified, had held staff appointments and was also recommended by his superiors. The petitioner retired in the rank of Maj Gen on 30 September 1995.

The Tribunal after going through the promotion policies and the list of officer promoted, observed that the extension granted to an officer had set forth a chain of events which eventually denied promotion to the petitioner, who was otherwise fully eligible to become a Lt Gen in his own Corps. The Tribunal was of the opinion that the treatment meted out to the petitioner was malafide and unfair. The Tribunal quashed the impugned order of retirement dated 30 September 1995. Since the petitioner had retired, the Tribunal ordered that he may be granted notional promotion to that of a Lt Gen w.e.f. 01October 1995 and would be entitled to the financial consequences had he been in service, including that of pensionary benefits.

Promotion in JAG branch

The AFT Regional Bench Lucknow, in the case of *Major Leena Gurav v. Union of India*, OA No. 208 of 2010, decided on 18 April 2011, considered a petition for grant of permanent commission in the JAG branch of the Army. The applicant, a short service commissioned officer (WSECO Scheme) was aggrieved by two orders passed by the military authorities. The MS Branch in its order dated 1 September 2010 refused to grant her promotion to the rank of Lt Col on the grounds that she had not cleared the JAG Departmental Examination; further the JAG department vide its letter 13 August 2010, asked her to appear in the JAG Departmental Examination so that she could be considered for grant of permanent commission.

The applicant contended that she was granted exemption from appearing in the JAG Departmental Examination and was granted permission to appear directly in the JAG Department Promotion Examination. The tribunal observed that the promotion to the substantive rank of Major and Lt Col by selection could be granted only on clearance of an examination known as the JAG Department Promotion Examination provided under Regulation 82(e) of the Regulations for the Army, 1987. The Tribunal quashed the letters dated 1 September 2010 and13 August 2010 and directed the military authorities to consider the result of selection board in respect of the applicant who would be entitled to promotion to the rank of Lt Col in due turn. Further, the case was unique and its decision not to be treated as a precedent for other cases.

Promotion granted

The AFT Regional Bench Chandigarh in the case of *Ajit Singh v. Union of India*, TA No. 1292 of 2010, decided on 13 February 2012, considered a prayer for promotion to the rank of Nb Risaldar.

The appellant was enrolled into the Army on 24 January 70 and promoted to the rank of Dafadar in 1985. On 01 April 1992, an individual junior to the appellant was promoted to the rank of Nb Risaldar ignoring the claim of the appellant. He subsequently retired on 31 January 2004 in the same rank as no other vacancy was available for promotion. The appellant filed a petition in 1994 for declaration that he was entitled to the promotion of Nb Risaldar w.e.f. 01 April 2002. The petition was dismissed vide judgment dated 7 June 2002. An appeal against the judgement was also dismissed on 31 May 2005. The second appeal was transferred to the Tribunal.

The Tribunal observed that as the appellant was senior in the service, he should have been promoted on the date the vacancy arose, i.e., 01 April 1992. The Tribunal after going through the relevant policy letters relating to the promotion set aside the Judgment and Decree dated 31 May 2005 passed by the Addl District Judge Hoshiarpur and held that the appellant shall be deemed to be promoted to the rank of Nb Risaldar w.e.f. 01 April 1992. Since the appellant had already retired since 31 January 1994, in light of the principles of 'no work no pay' [as decided by the Supreme Court in its judgment reported in *State of Haryana v. OP Gupta* (1996) 7 SCC 533], the appellant would not be entitled for any pay and allowances but would be entitled to pension in the rank of Nb Risaldar w.e.f. 31 January 1994. The Tribunal directed the respondents are to work out and grant the revised pension in the rank of Nb Risaldar to the appellant w.e.f. 01 February 1994 with arrears within 3 months of the order, failing which the outstanding amount would carry interest @ 8% per annum.

Promotion on amalgamation of trades

The AFT Principal Bench New Delhi in the case of *Ex Hav/Tech Comn Suresh Kumar v. Union of India*, OA No. 04 of 2012 decided on 5 November 2012, considered a prayer for promotion.

The petitioner was enrolled as a Sepoy in Corps of EME in the trade of Tele Communication Mechanic (Radio) [TMC (RO)] and in due course of time, was promoted to the rank of Hav on 1 August 1997. From this date the petitioner was senior most Hav in his trade and was qualified for promotion to the rank of Nb Sub. As per policy decisions dated 30 January 2009 and 24 April 2009, trades of TCM (RO) and TCM (Line) were merged into a new trade called Technician Communication (Tech Comm). This policy was executed by the government by letter dated 24 April 2009. A total of 26 JCOs in the trade of Tech Comm superannuated from service between 1 July 2009 and 30 August 2010. Accordingly, 26 chain vacancies in the rank of Nb Sub were created but the Petitioner was not promoted though he was placed at serial No. 1 in the seniority list of Hav Tech Comm Trade.

The petitioner contended that one Hav Binu was promoted to the rank of Nb Sub on 8 November 2009 though he was junior to the Petitioner. No explanation justifying supersession was communicated to the petitioner. The petitioner also contended that the policy letters dated 30 January 2009 and 24 April 2009 were arbitrary, unreasonable and inequitable and therefore be set aside. He should be reinstated in service and be promoted to the rank of Nb Sub from the date first vacancy was available in TCM (RO) trade or Tech Comn trade. Further, under the Modified Assured Career Progression (ACP) Scheme introduced by the Ministry of Defence on 14 January 2010, he was eligible to promotion to the rank of Nb Sub as he had stagnated in the rank of Hav for 13 years but was deprived of this benefit without assigning any reason.

The respondents contested that by the letter dated 24 April 2009, the Integrated HQ of MoD had introduced a new trade/category named Tech (Computer) and 550 persons from the erstwhile trade of TCM (Line), who were qualified in Class III and Class II, were selected for re-mustering into the new trade Tech (Computer). The remaining persons in the category of TCM (RO) had been merged into Tech (Comm) after fixing their inter-se-seniority in common roster as indicated by the aforesaid letter. The existing strength of both the trade (i.e. TCM (RO) re-designated as Tech (Comm) and remaining person in TCM(L) have been added and held against the existing authorization only of Tech (Comm) and no additional authorization in existing authorization has been released to the newly merged trade.

Further, the holding strength of JCOs in the erstwhile traders of TCM (RO) and TCM (L) have also been added up therein. It was also argued that due to this merging, and no release of any additional JCO vacancies, the holding strength of JCOs had become surplus by 26 in the newly merged trade i.e. Tech (Comm), and as such the surplus vacancies were liquidated in a phased manner against the ensuing monthly wastage. As a result of this, promotion in this category remained stagnant till October 2010, which consequently debarred the Petitioner to come up for promotion to the rank of Nb Sub in the newly merged trade Tech (Comm). Further the petitioner could not be promoted due to the non-availability of vacancies in the erstwhile trade.

The respondents also contested that so far as the promotion of Hav Binu was concerned, he was given promotion in accordance with rules against sports quota being an outstanding sportsman. The respondents also submitted a clarification on MACP has been issued from MoD on 13 June 2011 and the matter is already under consideration and he is eligible for benefit of this MACP from 1 September 2008.

The Tribunal ordered for the grant of MACP to petitioner and directed that the exercise should be done expeditiously and completed in three months.

Empanelment for higher rank

The AFT Regional Bench Lucknow in the case of *Lt Col Dharmender Singh Yadav v. Union of India*, OA No. 107 of 2011, decided on 27 July 2011, considered a prayer for non-empanelment to the rank of colonel. The Tribunal set aside the order of the Central Government dated 14 March 2011. Further the portion of the ACR for the year 2003-04 relating to the potential for promotion qualities given by the IO and RO was also quashed. The Tribunal directed that the case of the petitioner be considered without reference to the age bar and in case the applicant is selected to the rank of colonel, he would be given his due seniority.

Implementation of Dynamic Assured Career Progression Scheme/ AMC officer

The AFT Regional Bench Chandigarh in the case of *Col. Sanjeev Sehgal v. Union of India*, OA No. 488 of 2011, decided on 18 July 2011, considered a prayer for implementation of Dynamic Assured Career Progression Scheme (DACP) as approved by the Central Government.

The petitioner was a serving officer of Army Medical Corps (AMC), with more than 20 years of commissioned service. The 6th Pay Commission recognized the Army Medical Corps as one of the Medical Services under the Central Government along with others such as Central Health Services, Indian Railway Medical Services etc. The Pay Commission recommended that a DACP Scheme should be implemented in all organized and unorganized medical services under the Government of India which implied four time-bound movements and progressions into higher grade pay till 20 years of service.

The petitioner contended that while the first 3 grade pays of the pay hierarchy has already been implemented in AMC like most of the other Doctors, the 4th pay progression has not yet been implemented which was to be given on completion of 20 years of service. The DACP Scheme for all medical and dental officers under the Central Government had already been approved by the Union Cabinet and notified by the Central Government. The same was also accepted in the case of Army Medical Officers, however, in spite of lapse of about 2 and a half years of the Notification the said scheme had not yet been implemented and the petitioner was denied the benefit available to him under the DACP Scheme.

The respondent submitted that the matter was under consideration and would be decided by 31 December, 2011. Further, the military authorities were examining the issue holistically and analyzing the issue in depth before implementing the DACP Scheme.

The Tribunal directed the respondents to issue instructions for the implementation of the DACP Scheme within three months from the date of the order.

Substantive rank of Major: SSC officers

The AFT Principal Bench New Delhi in the case of *Major Nishant Gupta v. Union of India*, OA No. 330 of 2011, decided on 14 March 2012, considered a prayer grant of substantive rank. Two petitions bearing OA No. 330 of 2011 (*Major Nishant Gupta*) and OA No. 195 of 2011 (*Capt Kanika Gupta*) were involved in similar disputed question, and were decided together.

The petitioner was commissioned on 01 September 2001 as a Short Service Commissioned officer. He was approved for Permanent Commission on 24 May 2006 but because of his low medical category status, he could not be granted Permanent Commission and was discharged on 31 August 2011. The main contention of the petitioner was that he has retired as Acting Major and not as a Substantive Major, which disentitled him to the benefits of a Major thereby subjecting him to loss of status and finances. The Ministry of Defence (MoD) had issued a clarification on 28 May 2005 by which the Permanent Commission officers was given substantive rank that should also be given to the Short Service Commission.

The respondents contested that a new notification has been issued modifying the terms and conditions for Short Service Commission officers and it has been modified by the circular dated 20 July 2006. Under this circular, the persons who have been recruited as Short Service Commission officers their terms and conditions have been revised. It has been laid down that persons who are recruited as Short Service Commission officers will be given a rank of Capt on completion of 2 years reckonable commissioned service, Major on completion of 6 years reckonable commissioned service and Lt Col on completion of 13 years reckonable commissioned service but an option has been asked from all the officers who are already serving in the Army. They have been asked to give their option whether they are willing to be governed by the revised terms and conditions or by the old terms and conditions.

The Tribunal observed that the petitioner had opted for revised terms on 23 November 2006. Thereafter he cancelled his earlier option for the revised terms and opted for the existing/old terms on 24 February 2007. Thereafter he again change his mind and gave his option third time for revised scheme on 13 April 2009.

The Tribunal was of the opinion that once the petitioner had given his option for old scheme and that has been accepted by the respondents and on that basis all actions have been taken, therefore, it was not open for the petitioner to change his option from old scheme to new one. Hence, arguments of learned counsel for the petitioner that petitioner may be allowed to govern under the revised scheme were not sustainable. As petitioner was inducted in service by virtue of Army Instruction (AI) No. 1/93, therefore, his services will be governed by that AI.

The Tribunal was also informed by the respondent that matter of granting substantive rank of Major was already under consideration with Army HQ. The clarification was sought by the Army HQ from the Ministry of Defence; and the Ministry had informed on 28 October 2005 that all those persons (men and women) who were recruited as Short Service Commissioned officer will be given substantive rank as given to the Permanent Commission officer.

The Tribunal directed that the respondents to grant substantive rank to the petitioners and to the other similarly situated persons as given to the Permanent Commissioned officer so as to avoid flood of litigations by filing separate petitions before the Tribunal.

Arbitrariness in promotion/appointment

The AFT Regional Bench Chennai in the case of *P. Purushottam v. Union of India* TA No.113 of 2009 (WP (C) No.18124 of 2008) decided on 19 March 2010, set aside the impugned order of the Engineer-in-Chief Branch of the Army Headquarters, with the direction that the petitioner be inducted in DCRE service against the original year of 2001-02 with effect from 01 April 2003, with requisite seniority and fixation of wages and all entitlements.

Promotion and financial benefits

The AFT Principal Bench, Court No. 2 in the case of *Harish Chandra Joshi v. Union of India*, TA No. 75 of 2010 [WP (C) No. 6602 of 2003 of Delhi High Court] decided on 24 February 2012, considered a prayer challenging the denial of promotion.

The applicant was enrolled in the Army on 28 February 1978 and was posted to 4 Kumaon on completion of his training. While attached to the Garh Rif under 25 Infantry Division, the applicant became a case of Battle Casualty due to mine blast. He was placed in permanent medical category CEE, and continued to serve to the best of his ability both in field and peace stations. The applicant was awarded the "Army Commander's Commendation Card" for his gallantry act.

The applicant was promoted to the rank of Acting/paid Havildar by the Unit w.e.f. 01 April 1995. At that time he had not passed the "Map Reading Standard One" on the presumption by the respondent authority that Map Reading Standard One was not applicable to battle causality. As such he was also not detailed to attend "Map Reading Standard One" class as the unit was under the impression that Map Reading Standard One is not applicable to battle causalities. The applicant was made substantive Havildar w.e.f. 01 April 1995.

After completion of one year, the Record Office observed that the promotion of the applicant was irregular since he had not passed "Map Reading Standard One" exam. For about 8 months, the unit corresponded with the Record Office but the Record Office prevailed and the applicant was directed to pass the "Map Reading Standard One" exam which he did so on 07 May 1997 at first attempt. On representation, the Commanding Officer of the applicant assured him that his seniority would not be affected.

However, the record office cancelled the seniority of the applicant and a fresh date of seniority was given from 07 May 1997 i.e., the date he passed the Map Reading Standard One Exam. The applicant appealed to the Commanding Officer from time to time through normal channels but to no avail.

The applicant was detailed for promotion cadre from Havildar to Nb Subedar during September-December 2002 based on his fresh seniority i.e. 07 May1997. He successfully completed the cadre and qualified in the Havildar to Nb Subedar cadre. Consequent to this cadre, all those seven candidates who qualified, except for one who was overage, the other five were promoted in their turn. The applicant was not promoted being shown junior. Another promotion cadre was run by the unit between February to April 2003 and some more Havildars who were not eligible for promotion cadre earlier became eligible to attend the cadre and qualified. Thus, they all became senior to the applicant.

The applicant contended that his seniority could have been saved had the Unit and the Record Office acted promptly. In his case the Unit and the Record Office took nearly two years to decide as to whether the applicant should be directed to do "Map Reading Standard One" or not. Further, there was no comprehensive promotion policy in the Unit and promotions are made in an arbitrary manner. Also the Record Office failed to inform the unit in time the discrepancy and objections to the promotion until one year after the promotion was made by the unit. The CO gave him false assurances about the retention of the original seniority. The applicant continued to wear the badges and rank of Havildar and he was never asked to wear the badges of rank of Naik despite the applicant not having done the Map Reading Standard One.

The applicant further contended that he was denied promotion due to ACR criteria, but detail of ACRs were never given. In fact the respondent informed that the ACR in question have been destroyed. The respondents also failed to provide the DPC proceedings in case the ACRs were not available. The respondents have also been unable to produce the DPC proceedings though they have made an averment that the individual did not meet the ACR criteria for being considered for promotion to Nb Subedar. He further contended that the respondents have also not produced any evidence to show that the proceedings of DPC or ACR were destroyed. Since the applicant retired on 28 February 2004 and the case was already sub-judice by then, it was difficult to comprehend that the records have been destroyed. It amounted to contempt of court. As such, the applicant stressed that adverse inference should be taken.

In support of his contentions, the applicant cited the following decisions: *Lt. Col. Mukul Dev v. Union of India* 145(2007) DLT 53 (DB); *Union of India v. Ex. Major Sudershan Gupta* (2009) 6 SCC 298; *L/Hav Ran Singh v. Union of India* TA No. 407 of 2009 decided by the AFT Principal Bench on 05 May 2010; *Hav Bhagmal v. Union of India* TA No. 516 of 2009 decided by the AFT Principal Bench on 06 September 2011; and *Hav Amarjit Singh v. Union of India* OA No. 64 of 2011 decided by the AFT Principal Bench on 18 October 2011.

The respondents contested that the applicant was promoted to the rank of paid acting Havildar w.e.f. 01 April 1995 before his passing Map Reading Standard One exam on the "assumption" that the applicant was exempted from passing "Map Reading Standard One" being Battle Casualty case. The applicant came up for promotion to the rank of Nb Subedar alongwith personnel with seniority of 01 january1998. However, he could not be promoted because he was lacking ACR criteria.

The Tribunal observed that the present petition was first filed in the Delhi High Court in 2003 challenging the denial of promotion. The case pertains to the year 2001. Therefore the contention of the respondents that the records pertaining to ACRs have been destroyed in spite of the fact that the case was pending in the Court was inconceivable. Since the records were not available, the Tribunal commented that it could not ascertain the veracity of the averment made by the respondents as regards the fact that the applicant was lacking in ACR criteria. In addition there was no allegation of any disciplinary proceedings against the applicant, no warning letter in respect of any ACR was stated to have been issued nor was any adverse report communicated.

The Tribunal, guided by the view taken by the Supreme Court in the case of *Union of India v. Major Sudershan Gupta* (2009) 2 SCC (L&S) 197, took an adverse inference from the statements of the respondents that the applicant was fit for promotion. The Tribunal held that the applicant would be deemed to have been promoted to the rank of Naib Subedar w.e.f. October

2003 i.e. the date when he became eligible to be considered for JCO with the seniority of Havildar w.e.f. 07 May 1997 with all financial benefits from the date when any junior to him in the said rank was promoted to the rank of Naib Subedar. The applicant will further be deemed to be superannuated in the rank of Naib Subedar as applicable in the rules and also will be entitled to financial benefits. However, he will not be entitled to further promotion to the rank of Subedar as he has not worked in that rank. The Tribunal ordered that this exercise should be completed within a period of 120 days from the date of the order failing which the applicant would be entitled for interest @12% p.a. on the amount due.

Compensation

The AFT Principal Bench New Delhi, Court No. 2, in the case of *Vinod Kumar (Retired) v. Union of India*, OA No. 639 of 2010, decided on 10 May 2012, considered a prayer for promotion with all consequential benefits.

The applicant was enrolled in the Indian Army on 31 January 1977 as a Direct Entry Havildar. On 19 February 1991, the applicant was summarily tried under section 41(2) of the Army Act and was awarded severe reprimand. This summary punishment barred him from promotion for three years only and this period was completed on 19 February 1994. The applicant was due for his promotion to the rank of Nb Sub on 01 April 1997 but the respondents did not ask the applicant's Unit for timely submission of his ACR and thereby ACR was initiated very late and resulting in delay for granting promotion to the applicant.

The records of the applicant were reviewed after lapse of seven years. The punishment entry of severe reprimand dated 19 February 1991 was found to be illegal and respondents on their own in terms of ss. 87 and 88(b) of the Army Act read with para 442 of the Regulations for the Army, expunged the aforesaid punishment vide their Review Order dated 26 December 1997. It was communicated to the applicant vide letter dated 10 August 1998. The applicant submitted a non-statutory complaint on 28 December 1998 regarding his promotion to higher rank of Nb Sub as he was due for promotion on 01 April 1997 and his punishment entry had been cancelled.

The respondent on 29 December 2001 informed the applicant that the sanction of the Chief of the Army Staff has been obtained for relaxation of age in respect of the applicant for the promotion to the rank of Nb Subedar. The applicant was promoted to the rank of Nb Subedar on 10 December 2001 with seniority effective from 01 November 2001. The applicant was actually due for promotion to the rank of Nb Subedar on 01 April 1997 as he was fully eligible and there was no requirement of relaxation of age and he was also fully qualified. Aggrieved by the non-grant of retrospective seniority in the rank of Nb Subedar w.e.f. 01 October 1996, the applicant submitted a statutory complaint on 19 September 2002 which was rejected by the Army HQ on 15 October 2003. Aggrieved by the rejection of the statutory complaint, the applicant filed a CWP No. 658 of 2004 before the High Court of Delhi.

His petition was partly allowed vide order dated 05 July 2007. The Court directed that the applicant be considered for grant of promotion to the rank of Nb Subedar from the date he was otherwise due for promotion with financial benefits.

On 12 March 2008, the respondents passed an order giving effect to the directions of the High Court of Delhi and promoted the applicant with retrospective effect from 01 April 1997 with entitled pay and allowances. On 25 March 2008, the Records Office further directed PAO (OR) AEC that financial dues consequent to his promotion w.e.f. 01 April 1997 be issued to the applicant.

The applicant on 23 April 2008 submitted a representation praying for promotion to the rank of Subedar in the year 2003 as he had fulfilled all the criteria. The applicant had passed the Junior Leadership Proficiency Test on 27 November 2002 which was essential for promotion to the rank of Subedar. On 02 May 2008, the respondents informed the applicant that the legitimate benefits as ordered by the High Court had already been extended and thus his representation was rejected. The applicant filed a contempt petition (Civil) before the Delhi High Court on 5 November 2008, which was dismissed by the Single Judge on the grounds that no contempt has been committed by the respondents.

The applicant contended that as per the orders dated 05 July 2007 passed by the Delhi High Court in his favour, he was entitled to all consequential benefits but the respondents have considered the consequential benefits only up to the rank of Nb Subedar. Further, the respondents have changed their stance twice, once during the affidavit presented by them in CWP No. 658 of 2004 and secondly in civil contempt petition CAS (C) No. 702 of 2008 which was filed on 21 April 2010 before the Delhi High Court. After perusing both the affidavits, it was quite clear that the punishment entry against the applicant was suo moto expunged from his records being unsustainable and illegal. Therefore, the applicant was entitled to full benefits.

The Tribunal observed that after expunging the award of "severe reprimand" on 26 December 1997, the applicant was eligible for all consequential benefits including promotion with ante dated seniority as per his original batch, but he was denied his legitimate right of ante dated seniority. In this case the applicant was forced to submit the statutory complaint in 1998 based on which he was promoted on 10 December 2001. Even thereafter, there was adequate time for the respondents to detail the applicant to the mandatory ADP (Fundamental) course or any other criteria course as his batch mates had apparently attended the same already.

The Tribunal was of the opinion that the respondent authorities were responsible for not detailing the applicant to ADP (fundamental) or other criteria course. For that their failure resulted in deprivation of promotion and loss of monetary benefit to the applicant. The applicant submitted another statutory complaint before he was considered for the promotion to the rank of Subedar based on ante dated seniority. In both his petitions, he has never agitated for permission to attend the ADP (Fundamental) course or other mandatory criteria course. Implications of not having attended the same would have been known to the applicant. On the other hand, the respondents have also not been able to produce any evidence to show the reasons why the applicant was not detailed on these courses.

The Tribunal observed that since the applicant has already been superannuated, therefore, he cannot be directed to be detailed for the said courses. Thus, there was no other alternative except to compensate the applicant by way of monetary benefits in order to meet the ends of justice. Taking into account the lapses on the part of the respondents and other facts of the case, the Tribunal held that the ends of justice would meet by awarding compensation of Rs. 50,000/- to the applicant.

Contempt petition

The AFT Principal Bench New Delhi, Court No. 2 in the case of *Sub/skt Nandlal Pandey v. Union of India*, CA No. 17 of 2011 in TA No. 09 of 2010 decided on 16 May 2012, considered an application for implementation of the judgment and order passed by the Tribunal on 08 September 2010.

The Tribunal had passed a judgment and order in favour of the applicant. The operative portion of the judgment dated 08 September 2010 was as under:

> "In view of the foregoing, we quash the order vide Signal of Army Headquarters (ST-12) dated 15 October 1998. Consequently, we direct that his application for relaxation dated 15.05.1998 be again considered without influence by earlier order and if relaxation is granted for the ACR for 1994 then the applicant should be reconsidered by a Board of Officers for promotion to the rank of Subedar Major based on the ACRs of 1995, 1996, 1997 and 1998 by taking into account the point system as laid down in the policy letter of 10th October, 1997. If the applicant thus qualifies in the merit list, he shall be entitled to all consequential benefits. The application is partially upheld. No order as to costs."

The applicant submitted that the respondents did not act and proceed in true spirit of the judgment. In implementation of the Tribunal's order, the officer in-charge ASC Records passed a speaking order dated 18 February 2011. The reasons for non-compliance of the AFT orders were given in Para 7 of the order as under:

"In view of the above, the application dated 15 Sep 1998 of the JCO does not fall under the spirit and ambit of Para 8 and 12 of the IHQ of MoD (Army) letter No. B/33513/AG/PS-2(c) dated 10 Oct 1997, hence the application is hereby rejected being devoid of merit and not in consonance with the policy on promotion."

Based on observations made in the Court on 20 April 2011, the COAS passed the order dated 01 July 2011 in which again reasons for non-compliance were stated at para 7, as under:

"In view of the above, the application dated 15 Sep 1998 of the JCO does not fall under the spirit and ambit of Para 8 and 12 of the IHQ of MoD (Army) letter No.B/33513/AG/PS-2(c) dated 10 Oct 1997, hence the application is hereby rejected being devoid of merit and not in consonance with the policy on promotion."

The applicant contended that respondents be directed to calculate the ACR part of the OAP on the basis of 4 ACRs of 1995, 1996, 1997 and 1998 and other OAP points already calculated in 1998 for other aspects totalling 15 points as per policy letter dated 10 October 1997 and quash the speaking orders passed by the authorities concerned dated 18 February 2011 (OIC AEC Records) and 01 July 2011 (COAS) and further prayed that respondents be directed to hold the promotion board based on the orders dated 08 September 2010 passed by the Tribunal.

After considering the respondents contention, the Tribunal quashes and set aside the orders dated 18 February 2011 passed by the officer in-chage ASC Records as also order dated 01 July 2011 passed by the Chief of the Army Staff as they had not proceeded in right perspective and directions given in the judgment dated 08 September 2010. A cost of Rs.10,000/- was further imposed on the respondents.

The Tribunal directed the respondents to reconsider the applicant for promotion to the rank of Subedar Major by the DPC going by 1998 norms by considering the "last five reports" with the ACR of 1994 having been dispensed with under Para 12 of the Policy letter dated 10 October 1997 in compliance of the judgment of the Tribunal; and complete this exercise within a period of 90 days from the date of the order. All consequential benefits shall accrue to the applicant based on the result of the DPC.

Promotion and fixation of pay

The AFT Principal Bench New Delhi (Court No. 2) in the case *WO Ummed Singh Choudhury v. Union of India*, TA No. 331 of 2010 [WP (C) No. 5887 of 2002 of Delhi High Court] decided on 8 February 2012, considered a prayer for promotion.

The applicant was enrolled in the Indian Air Force as an Airman on 04 July 1969 and became Junior Warrant Officer (JWO) in 1987. He was promoted as Warrant Officer in 1998 with seniority from 01 December 1996. On 30 March 1992, the applicant was posted at Air NCC Sqn Trichy. On 06 August 1992 he caught one JWO stealing certain items from the store. On reporting the said matter to the authorities, he faced harassment from all concerned. From 31 December 1993 till 21 July 1995 he continued representing against the harassment but received no response.

The applicant was superseded for promotion to the rank of Warrant Officer due to poor ARs from 1992 to 1994. On 21 August 1997 he was also not granted extension and was directed to be discharged in July 1998 upon completing normal terms of engagement. Thereafter, the applicant approached the High Court of Gauhati (Shillong Bench) and filed WP

Nos. 119 of 1997 and 208 of 1997 challenging his denial of promotion and extension. The High Court vide its order dated 24 March 1998, allowed the writs of the applicant and consequently he was promoted on 30 June 1998 with seniority w.e.f. December 1996. But financial benefits were not given. Thereafter, the applicant made several representations for grant of increments. However, the respondents vide their letter dated 22 December 1998 though confirmed granting seniority but denied the financial benefits of higher rank. His representation for grant of increments on 08 March 1999 was also rejected by the respondents on 30 May 99. In order to harass the applicant, he was sent for on a long temporary duty. On return from the temporary duty, the applicant applied for 20 days leave and proceeded on leave. When he returned back from leave, he was informed that his leave was not sanctioned. He was charged for absent without leave for 20 days and was punished.

The respondents contested that the seniority of the applicant was from December 1996 but he could not be promoted to next higher rank as he did not make the minimum grade for promotion to the rank of WO. Further, in terms of the orders of the High Court of Guwahati dated 24 March 1996, his case was referred to the Competent Authority who in pursuance to the High Court's order, as a special case promoted the applicant vide order dated 11 February 1998. There was no provision to grant promotion from retrospective date, as the individual was required to work in acting unpaid capacity for 28 days in terms of para 16 of AFI 12/S/48. Therefore, the applicant cannot claim arrears with retrospective date, since he has not served in that rank for that period. However, his seniority had been protected from the retrospective date for the future promotion, the advantage of which was given to him when he was considered for his next promotion as Warrant Officer.

The Tribunal was of the opinion that the applicant had been given a fair chance for consideration for promotion and also for extension by the authorities consequent to the orders of the High Court of Guwahati. The Tribunal, however, observed that the respondent authorities have not given due weightage in letter and spirit of the judgment of the High Court and had denied increments. The High Court in its order had also directed: "This existing fact of supersession by juniors to the writ petitioner shall be taken into account while reviewing the case of the writ petitioner for the purpose of his promotion and extension of his services."

The Tribunal directed that it was essential that his fixation of pay in the rank of Warrant Officer needs to be done as per his batch i.e. at the same level as his immediate junior has been drawing as on 11 February1998. That would imply that the applicant would not be considered junior to his batch in terms of pay and other allowances from the date he was promoted on 11 February 1998. The Tribunal ordered that the exercise of granting increments from 1996 at par with juniors be completed within a period of 90 days from the date of the order or else interest of 12% p.a. would be levied on the amount so found due.

Policy changes not informed

The AFT Principal Bench New Delhi, in the case of *LEM H.S. Bind v. Union of India*, TA No. 471 of 2009 [WP (C) 8149 of 2009] decided on 1 August 2012, considered a prayer for promotion to the rank of Petty Officer Engineering Mechanic.

The petitioner was enrolled on 18 January 1993 as a Sailor in the Navy. He was promoted to the rank of Leading Engineering Mechanic. The petitioner was intimated of his promotion to the rank of Petty Officer Engineering Mechanic on 15 December 2006 with the ante date seniority of 1 July 2006. However, he could not avail such promotion as he did not have two years of residual service which was the criteria in vogue as per IHQ MOD (Navy) letter dated 11 April 2005. Since petitioner did not have two years residual service, therefore, he did not avail this promotion and declined the same by communication dated 30 July 2007. But the policy dated 11 April 2005 was subsequently amended on 17 May 2007 which was not known to the petitioner. According to the revised policy, the two years embargo was set aside. The petitioner came to know about this when persons junior to him were promoted and these persons also did not have the requisite two years residual service.

The petitioner took up the case of his promotion and the commanding officer vide letter dated 28 November 2007 recommended the matter to the higher authorities for promotion as the embargo of the residual service of two years has already been removed. The petitioner contended that application was not accepted and he was not promoted to the post of the Petty Officer Engineering Mechanic.

The Tribunal observed that the change of policy perhaps was not intimated to the petitioner and even the commanding officer of was not aware of it and it was only subsequently that he came to know of it. Had the Commanding Officer known about the change of policy, which was under contemplation, that the embargo of two years had been scrapped then he would have informed the petitioner and petitioner would not have declined his promotion. But because of the lack of communication at the hand of the respondents, the petitioner under bonafide impression did not feel persuaded to avail the promotion as he felt that he did not have two years residual service. Therefore, the mistake was with the respondents and not with the petitioner. It was an equal responsibility of the respondents to have correctly apprised the petitioner that embargo of two years is no more there.

The Tribunal held that the employer has the responsibility to inform changes which have been brought about in the rules from time to time. Therefore, the petitioner was entitled to benefit of the mistake committed by the respondents and petitioner will be deemed to have been promoted and the training which is required to undergo is dispensed with under the special circumstances of the case. The Tribunal directed that the petitioner be promoted to Petty Officer Engineering Mechanic and all the benefits coming from that promotion be given to him. Since the petitioner had already retired and discharged from service he could not be given benefit of reinstatement, but he was given the benefit of promotion as per the order dated 15 December 2007 and monetary benefits arising out of this promotion.

Revocation of promotion

The Armed Forces Principal Bench New Delhi in the case of *Ex Sub Ram Kumar v. Union of India*, OA No. 488 of 2011, decided on 28 August 2012, considered a prayer for the continuance of the petitioner in the rank of Subedar with all consequential benefits.

The petitioner was enrolled in the Indian Army on 27 December 1982 as a Sepoy and in the due course of time; he was promoted to the rank of Subedar and retired from service w.e.f. 31 December 2010. The petitioner remained physically fit throughout his service. The promotion orders were issued on 31 January 2010 for promotion to the rank of Subedar w.e.f. 01 April 2010 and the name of the petitioner was placed at Sl. No.112.

Unfortunately the petitioner met with a road accident and was hospitalised due to which he could not be granted promotion in time. The petitioner was placed on low medical category. The promotion order of the petitioner was cancelled on 17 April 2010 as he was placed in low medical category (A-3) w.e.f. 08 April 2010. In the meantime, the Release Medical Board of the petitioner was held on 17 August 2010 and the respondents issued a notice on 23 August 2010 asking the petitioner to give his willingness/unwillingness to continue in service. The petitioner vide his representation dated 23 August 2010 submitted that he was performing his trade work and administrative work well and was willing to continue in service in low medical category. The respondents, thereafter, issued an order on 17 September 2010 for promotion of the petitioner to the rank of Subedar and his promotion was shown w.e.f. 01 October 2010. The petitioner took the charge of Subedar and thereafter retired on 31 December 2010.

The petitioner contended that the respondents revoked the his promotion order of the rank of Subedar vide order dated 21 October 2011 almost after 10 months of his retirement without issuing any show cause notice in gross violation of the principles of natural justice.

The respondents contested that the grant of extension and its continuation during extension period was subject to the individual remaining in acceptable medical category. This clarification was issued on 18 June 2001. Thus in view of the clarification read with original policy order [Army HQ Letter No. B/33098/AG/PS-2 (C) dated 21 September 1998], the promotion and continuation of the petitioner was not warranted. Therefore, the order of revocation was passed and the same was as per the rules on the subject.

The Tribunal observed that the policy decision was known to the authorities at the time when the promotion order of the petitioner was issued. Despite that, the petitioner was allowed the promotion during the extended period. It was only in 2011 when the person had already superannuated and retired after availing the full extended period of the rank of Subedar, the authorities woke up after 10 months that mistake had been committed and they revoked the promotion order of the petitioner without giving any show cause notice to the petitioner. The Tribunal noted that the policy was not properly enforced by the respondents. It held that the respondents were responsible for committing this mistake and allowing the promotion to the petitioner during the extended period when he was low medical category (permanent). The petitioner has served the extended period up to 31 December 2010. The order of revoking the promotion of the petitioner at this belated stage was harsh and breach of principles of natural justice and against the equity also.

The Tribunal held that the order dated 21 October 2011 revoking the promotion of the petitioner cannot be sustained on principles of natural justice as well as equity. It quashed the order dated 21 October 2011 and directed the respondents that the petitioner be treated as retired as a Subedar and all his retirement benefits should be worked out and paid to him within a period of three months.

Acquitted by court martial, seniority in promotion

The AFT Principal Bench New Delhi in the case of *Sh. Rabendra Singh v. Union of India*, TA No. 134 of 2010 [WP (C) No. 3650 of 2004], decided on 29 May 2012, considered a prayer for promotion after acquittal by the court martial.

The petitioner was enrolled as a Sepoy in the Indian Army on 19 July 1979 and with the passage of time he was promoted to the rank Havildar on 01 February 1994. During his posting, while he was performing his duties of Canteen NCO, some discrepancies were found. The matter was investigated by a court of inquiry, followed by the recording of summary of evidence. The petitioner was tried by a District Court Martial (DCM) but was acquitted of all the charges on 24 January 2003. After his acquittal, the petitioner approached the respondents to consider him for promotion to the rank of Nb Sub as persons junior to him were already promoted. However, his request was not considered by the respondents.

The respondents contested that promotions can be considered only if there exists any vacancy in the unit and in February, 2003, at the time of acquittal of the petitioner, there was no vacancy of Nb Sub in the unit. Even if there had been any vacancy, his proposal for promotion could have been forwarded only after completion of annual confidential reports (ACR) for the year 2001 and 2002 which could not be initiated as per Army Order 1/2002/ MP till finalization of the case. The petitioner lacked with two ACRs as on 01 February 2003 and was also overage. Further, the Unit had forwarded the proposal of the petitioner for promotion with anti-date seniority on 01 May 2003 but the same was rejected by the Records, Jat Regiment for the reason being that petitioner was overage at the time of consideration.

The Tribunal observed that the reply of the respondents was not satisfactory and as per the law. The petitioner was acquitted of all the charges on 24 January 2003 and he became overage for promotion to the post of Nb Sub on 01 February 2003, however the persons junior to petitioner were promoted by this time. Once petitioner has been acquitted of all the charges then he is relegated to the same position as he was as if there was nothing against him. When the petitioner has been acquitted of all the charges then his position should have been restored back in his unit with his seniority and he should have been given promotion to the rank of Nb Sub which has been given to the persons junior to him.

The Tribunal further observed that person junior to petitioner was promoted in July, 2001 then the case of the petitioner for promotion should have been considered vis-a-vis that person subject to petitioner has acquired all necessary qualification for promotion to the rank of Nb Sub. Reply of the respondents that petitioner's case could not be considered because he became overage or there was no vacancy, was ad in law. The Tribunal held that it was for the respondents to ensure that once the petitioner has been acquitted is restored back to his original position and he should be considered for promotion vis-a-vis persons junior to him. Petitioner has already gone through the drill of court of inquiry, summary of evidence and DCM and has been found not guilty then as a matter of right, he should have been considered for promotion.

The Tribunal ordered that the respondents to consider the case of the petitioner for promotion to the rank of Nb Sub from the date person junior to him was promoted i.e. on 01 July 2001 and in case, he meets all requisite criteria then all consequential benefits following thereof be given to him. Since the petitioner has retired on 31 July 2003 as Hav, he would be entitled for all notional benefits to the rank of Nb Sub. The Tribunal ordered that this exercise to be completed by the respondents within three months from date of the order.

Discriminatory promotion policy

The AFT Principal Bench New Delhi in the case of *Baljeet Singh v. Union of India*, T A No. 602 of 2009 [WP (C) No. 2755 of 2008], decided on 29 May 2012, considered a prayer for promotion to the rank of Nb Sub with consequential benefits.

The petitioner was enrolled in the Indian Army on 10 July 1984 and in due course was promoted to the rank of Nb Sub in 2008. He duly passed the promotion cadre test for the rank of Nb Sub in 2003 but he could not be promoted for the said rank in 2006. He moved an application dated 08 August 2006 to the Commandant, CAMS, Delhi Cantt, duly recommended for promotion to the rank of Nb Sub. It was replied by the respondents vide letter dated 31 August 2006 that two vacancies were allotted by the letter of AHQ dated 05 June 2006 and the same have been utilized as one vacancy against surplus and another one was promoted vide letter dated 31 July 2006. The petitioner contended that the utilization of vacancies by way of letter dated 31 July 2006 was absolutely discriminatory, arbitrary and illegal. The petitioner's statutory complaint dated 29 March 2007 was rejected by the COAS vide order dated 18 March 2008.

The Tribunal observed serious contradictions in the promotion/transfer of vacancy, which had seriously affected the career of the petitioner. The Tribunal directed the respondents to examine the case of the petitioner for promotion to Nb Sub against one of the vacancies allotted vide AHQ letter dated 05 June 2006, and if he was found deserving in all respects then he be granted notional benefit, since he has already been promoted to the rank of Nb Sub since 01 May 2008.

Promotion and consequential benefits

The AFT Principal Bench Delhi, Court No. 3, in the case of *Naib Risaldar Vijay Pal v. Union of India*, TA No.476 of 2010 & MA No.106 of 2010 [WP (C) No.7173 of 2009 of Delhi High Court] decided on 31 January 2011, considered the case of promotion to the rank of Subedar.

The applicant was enrolled on 29 January 1983 and rose to the rank of Naib Risaldar. During his service the applicant was medically downgraded to H2 (P) and as a result of which he was discharged for the first time on 29 February 2008. He was, however, reinstated on 19 January 2009 as a sequel to the Delhi High Court order dated 20 November 2008 given in Putan Lal case. A few days after rejoining, the applicant was discharged for the second time on 31 January 2009 on attaining the age of superannuation in the rank of Naib Subedar vide letter dated 23 January 2009.

The applicant contended that during the period of his absence on discharge from 29 February 2008 to 19 January 2009, juniors to him were promoted. He referred the judgment in the case of *Naib Subedar Kalu Ram*, WP (C) No. 579 of 2009, in which the ruling was: "had the petitioner been in service he would also have been promoted to the post of Risaldar before his date of discharge …., which in turn would have entailed the benefit of an extension of service of two years besides other monetary benefits." The respondents stated that the applicant could not be promoted since promotions were ordered against clear vacancies and when the applicant reported for duty, after his reinstatement, on 20 January 2009, there were no vacancies available in his unit; thus the petition be rejected.

The Tribunal relying upon the judgment of the Delhi High Court in Naib Risaldar Kalu Ram, WP (C) No. 579 of 2009, directed that the petitioner be considered for promotion to the rank of Subedar. If approved for promotion, the order of his discharge w.e.f. 31 January 2009 not to come in his way and the applicant would also be entitled to all consequential benefits.

Notional promotion with consequential benefits

The AFT New Delhi Principal Bench, in the case of *Col H. C. Goswami (Retd) v. Union of India*, OA No. 27 of 2011, decided on 23 April 2012, considered a case for promotion.

The petitioner had joined the Indian Army on 30 June1963. In the year 1989, he was tried by a General Court Martial (GCM) and cashiered. He challenged the trial by GCM and subsequent punishment before the Delhi High Court by filing a writ petition. The High Court of Delhi vide order dated 28 May 1992 quashed the court martial proceedings and subsequent orders of punishment against the petitioner. The Union of India challenged the order of the Delhi High Court in the Supreme Court by filing SLP. The Supreme Court vide its order dated 28 April 1999 dismissed the appeal preferred by the respondents.

The petitioner contended that the respondents without any reason disqualified him for being selected for the rank of Brigadier as intimated to him vide their letter dated 25 October 1999. Petitioner filed a petition in the Delhi High Court (No. 7391 of 2000) contending that order of the Delhi High Court dated 28 May 1992 had not been complied with by the respondents. The Delhi High Court vide its order dated 07 August 2008 directed that the petitioner's case be considered afresh reference to the officers of 1963 batch to which the petitioner belonged. Against the said order of the Delhi High Court dated 07 August 2008, respondents preferred an appeal before the Supreme Court which was ultimately dismissed by the Court vide its order dated 13 July 2009.

The petitioner thereafter moved an application dated 18 September 2009 to the Central Public Information Officer, Indian Army (RTI Cell) seeking certain information regarding his consideration for the rank of Brigadier. The concerned authority vide their letter dated 06 October 2009 informed the petitioner that meeting of the Board was held on 30 March 2009 to reconsider his case for promotion to acting rank of Brigadier and the competent authority had intimated to MS Branch by Ministry of Defence on 06 July 2009. Respondents challenged the order dated 30 September 2009 of the Central Information Commission before the Delhi High Court and the said order dated 30 September 2009 was confirmed by the Delhi High Court vide its order dated 30 September 2009. The petitioner filed SLP bearing No. 8863 of 2010 against the order dated 06 October 2009 before the Supreme Court which was dismissed as withdrawn on 08 July 2010. The petitioner thereafter approached the Tribunal for the grant of notional promotion as Brigadier with all consequential benefits.

The respondents contended that record pertaining to the petitioner for promotion from Colonel to Brigadier had been destroyed; however they have somehow retrieved some records. They pointed out that in the petitioner's batch of 1963, 22 persons were approved for promotion out of which record of 19 persons are available with them and among 19 persons, lowest percentage of marks were obtained by Col S.S. Chauhan who was found fit for promotion.

The Tribunal after examining the old record directed the respondents to consider the case of the petitioner within three months of the issue of the order. If the petitioner was found suitable, he would be entitled to all consequential benefits.

Compensation for denial of promotion

The AFT Principal Bench New Delhi in the case of *Sub (Now Nb Sub) (GD) Rajbir v. Union of India*, OA No. 28 of 2011, decided on 1 February 2013,considered a prayer for quashing an order of discharge from the service.

The petitioner was enrolled in the Army on 07 June 1983 and became Nb Subedar on 01 April 2008. On 06 July 2008, the petitioner was performing the duties of Road Opening Party in the field area and developed some medical problem in lower-back side of the body. During July to August 2008, the petitioner was considered for grant of two years extension based on the policy of respondents and was granted extension with effect from 07 June 2009 to 06 June 2011 after having been found fit in all respects for such extension. During April 2009, the old back problem of the petitioner resurfaced. The petitioner was admitted to MH Udhampur from 06 July 2009 to 25 July 2009 for such lower-back problem.

During 05 September 2009 to 26 November 2009, the petitioner was again admitted to MH Ambala for the same problem. On 24 November 2009, due to hospitalization of the petitioner, he was downgraded to the temporary medical category (P-3). On 01 December 2009, the petitioner having completed all requisite promotion criteria was due for his promotion based on his seniority after vacancy for such promotion arose consequent to the retirement of Sub Umed Singh. However, the petitioner was not promoted to the post of Subedar as per his turn. The petitioner was again admitted in the hospital on 16 August 2010 for the purpose of review of his medical category and his category was upgraded to P-2(P) category. The petitioner was issued discharge the orders vide letter dated 13 September 2010 by which the petitioner was to retire from service with effect from 31 January 2011.

The petitioner contended that the discharge order dated 13 September 2010 was issued back dated as the petitioner never learnt about issuance of discharge order. The petitioner further contended that according to the para 4 (b) of policy letter of 10 October 1997, personnel placed in medical category 'BEE' (P-2) would be eligible for promotion to the next higher rank. This will include both temporary and permanent low medical categories. Therefore, once the petitioner had been granted promotion as per the policy, there was no reason for the respondents to recall the promotion order and discharge the petitioner from the service.

The respondents contested that the petitioner was downgraded to low medical category (permanent) on 14 August 2010 which was published in the Regiment DO Part II order dated 18 September 2010 received at Records Office on 14 October 2010. On down gradation to low medical category (permanent) during extended period of service that commenced with effect from 07 June 2009, the JCO was not eligible for promotion to the rank of Subedar. The JCO was well aware of his ineligibility of his promotion to the rank of Subedar being low medical category (permanent) during extended period of service. Therefore, the contention of the JCO that Arty Records had issued the promotion order and the unit has deprived him of the benefit of the rank of Subedar was baseless as he was not eligible for promotion to the rank of Subedar being placed in low medical (permanent) during extended period of enhanced service in the rank of Nb Subedar.

The Tribunal, vide its order dated 05 October 2012 directed the respondents to file an affidavit that when DPC for the post of Subedar was convened and when petitioner became eligible for consideration for the post of Subedar and how the promotion of the Subedar was processed at various levels. The respondents, in pursuance of this direction, filed an additional affidavit and explained that the petitioner was in low medical category (temporary) up to 13 August 2010 and as such he was not eligible for promotion to the rank of Subedar as per the policy. However, on review, he was placed in low medical category (permanent) w.e.f. 14 August 2010 and as such in terms of letter dated 10 October 1997, he became eligible for consideration for the next promotion of Subedar. However, on being placed in low medical category (permanent) during the currency of enhanced service as started from 07 June 2009 to 18 June 2010, in terms of Ministry of Defence letter dated 18 June 2001, he would have been discharged under the existing rules and his promotion during the discharge drill after becoming low medical category (permanent) during the extended period was not in order.

The Tribunal was of the opinion that there has to be some compensation for loss of face for the petitioner because the promotion order was issued by the respondents knowing fully-well that the petitioner has become medical category in August 2010 and they issued a promotion order on 14 November 2010. The same was recalled by back dated letter of 24 October 2010 vide signal dated 27 October 2010. The petitioner had to undergo this humiliation as he had put the rank of Subedar but same was withdrawn back from him. In Army, putting of rank is a matter of prestige. Once a person bears a rank and the same was withdrawn, it causes more humiliation. The Tribunal therefore awarded compensation of Rs 10,000, to be paid to the petitioner within three months.

XVIII. Reinstatement in the Service

Violation of Principles of Natural Justice

The Armed Forces Principal Bench New Delhi in the case of *Lt Cdr Deepak Kanathey v. Union of India*, TA No.178 of 2010 and *Cdr Naresh Chandro Sahu v. Union of India*, TA No. 276 of 2010, decided on 6 August 2012, considered prayer for the reinstatement in particular arm of the service.

The first petitioner (Lt Cdr Deepak Kanathey) was Commissioned in the Navy on 01 January 1987. He joined the Submarine arm in December 1990. In due course, he was posted to INS Sindhukesari in 1998 as Second-in-Command (EXO). The Submarine was sent for major repair-cum-modernisation from 1999-2001. On return the Submarine was deployed in May 2002 where an incident took place leading to ingress of sea water into Torpedo. On return to the shore, the petitioner was transferred to INS Vajrabahu on 24 March

2002. In October 2002, a board of inquiry (BOI) was ordered in which the petitioner was summoned as a witness. Subsequently, based on this BOI, which did not implicate or blame the petitioner, a show cause notice dated 23 February 2003 was given to the petitioner in which certain allegations were made on his professional conduct and the performance of duty. The petitioner submitted a reply to this show cause notice vide his letter dated 03 March 2003. Thereafter, the FOC-in-C vide letter dated 23 June 2003 awarded the punishment of 'Displeasure' for the lapse. On 7 April 2004, a letter was received by the petitioner removing him from the Submarine arm and thereby also withdrawing his Submarine Badge w.e.f. 07 April 2004.

The petitioner contended that para 205 of the Regulation was not applied despite the fact that it was clearly mentions in the Convening Order dated 27 September 2002 that provisions of para 205 of Regulations for Navy Part-II will be invoked as and when character or military reputation of an individual was involved. The petitioner also contended that BOI findings and recommendations do not implicate him in any manner and therefore, it was incorrect for the convening authority or the FOC-in-C to invoke the findings of the BOI and initiate administrative proceedings against the petitioner.

The petitioner referred the decisions of the Supreme Court in the cases of *Lt Col P P S Bedi v. Union of India* (1982) 3 SCC 140; *R P Shukla v. General Officer Commanding-in-Chief, Lucknow* 1996 MP 233; *Lt Governor, Delhi v. Narinder Singh* (2004) 13 SCC 342; and *State of Bihar v. Lal Krishna Advani* AIR 2003 SCC 3357 and contended that an essential provision of the Navy Regulations para 205 (=Army Rules 180) was violated in his case. Therefore the award of 'displeasure' was against the law. The petitioner further cited AFT order in TA No. 244 of 2010 decided on 17 September 2010 wherein the Tribunal observed that no notice was given to the petitioner for withdrawal from the Submarine arm and thus the principles of natural justice in taking the administrative action was violated.

The respondents conceded that the proceedings of BOI did not implicate the petitioner nor did it recommended any action against him, but during the analysis of the proceedings of the BOI, the Convening Authority felt that there was a case of negligence on the part of the petitioner, therefore, it decided to award him a minor punishment. The respondents also contested that FOC-in-C before awarding 'Displeasure' to the petitioner had observed that as the EXO/ Principal Control Officer, he was culpable of negligence in the performance of his duties. The authority of awarding 'censure' to the Officers is contained in Navy Order 04/02 in which a letter of Displeasure can be awarded to an officer for offences of a minor nature.

Further the decision to remove the petitioner from the Submarine arm was taken by the Submarine Cadre Management and Training Conference (SCMTC) which is held once a year at Naval HQs. The case for removal of the petitioner from Submarine arm was taken up by the Western Fleet HQs on having analysed the BOI proceedings, as also the consequences of punishment of 'Displeasure' awarded to the petitioner. The respondents cited the judgment of the AFT in *Commander Vinod Kumar Jha v. Union of India* TA No. 395 of 2009 in which the Tribunal had held that since it was a general inquiry, there was no requirement of invoking para 205 of the Regulation at the onset of inquiry against any individual.

The Tribunal observed that the petitioner had not been blamed by the BOI but the Convening Authority in his own wisdom, on detailed analysis of the BOI proceedings had came to the conclusion that there had been a lapse on the part of the petitioner who was the EXO at that point of time. As such, they issued a show cause notice. Since the Convening Order did not specifically implicate the petitioner in any manner, therefore, it was not essential for the BOI to invoke Regulation 205 during the recording of the proceedings. The petitioner was examined as a witness and the recommendation of the BOI did not implicate the petitioner in any manner. However, the Convening Authority had the liberty to come to the conclusion that despite the fact that the proceedings of BOI do not implicate the petitioner, it was a lapse on the part of the petitioner which could have been avoided had the petitioner been more alert in his duties. Therefore, it was evident that the BOI proceedings were in order as also the action taken by the Convening Authority and the Regulation 208(9) are within the powers of the Convening Authority. As such, no infringement of natural justice had taken place.

As regards the removal of the petitioner from the Submarine arm and depriving him of Submarine Badge retrospectively, the Tribunal observed that the recommendation for removal from the Submarine arm was initiated by the Head Quarter Western Command on 14 February 2003. Further, the SCMTC should have called for a detailed report or at least give a notice before they decided on the removal of the petitioner from the Submarine arm. The tribunal also observed that the removal had been done retrospectively which was not in order because during the intervening period, the petitioner had been drawing his special pay and it cannot be now refunded back. As such, the withdrawal order was incorrect.

The Tribunal held that the principles of natural justice in the administrative action were not followed. It quashed the orders dated 18 May 2004 along with GENFORM dated 07 April 2004, with the order that the petitioner shall be reinstated into Submarine arm w.e.f. 07 April 2004 and will be entitled to wear his Submarine Badge with consequential benefits. The respondents were at liberty to take a view and it was left open for them to pass fresh orders in accordance with law.

In the second case, the petitioner (Cdr Naresh Chandro Sahu) was posted as Commanding Officer of Indian Naval Submarine Sindhukesari. While the ship was deployed for operations, the sea water leaked into the Torpedo on 25 June 2002. The petitioner reported the matter verbally on 21 June 2002 to COMCOS (West). On 14 September 2002 the said Torpedo was removed to workshop. Based on the report of the workshop, a BOI was ordered and on

27 April 2003 the petitioner was posted out from his command. The BOI had implicated the petitioner for which he was given a 'censure' by FOC-in-C. He was subsequently removed from submarine arm. The Petitioner contested his removal from the submarine arm.

The Tribunal observed that principles of natural justice had not been followed while removal of the petitioner from Submarine arm. The Tribunal, guided by their order in *Cdr Alok Kumar Pathak v. Union of India* TA No. 244 of 10 dated 17 September 2010, quashed the orders for removal of the petitioners from the Submarine arm w.e.f. 07 April 2004 with the order that the respondents were free to undertake fresh action keeping in view the laws of natural justice.

Re-instatement in service, acquitted by civil court

The AFT Regional Bench Chandigarh in the case of *Ex Naib Subedar Gobind Singh v. Union of India*, OA No. 444 of 2011, decided on 08 December 2011, considered a petition for reinstatement in service with consequential benefits.

The petitioner has contended that after an incident of indiscipline at the place of work, he was summoned in the unit where he narrated the complete facts of the incident to his commanding officer. On 26 July 2010, a prepared application in Hindi was placed before him in the office of his commanding officer; the applicant was not allowed to read it and was forced to sign it. He was informed that his premature discharge from service at his request had been sanctioned w.e.f. 01 October, 2010.

The petitioner contended that he was discharged from service prematurely by obtaining application for premature discharge forcibly which was withdrawn prior to the date fixed for discharge by following a procedure unknown to law. No Show Cause Notice was issued and no proper procedure had been adopted to discharge him from service.

The respondents contended that the petitioner had submitted an application dated 17 Aug 2010 to commanding officer for seeking premature discharge from service on compassionate grounds at his own request. The commanding officer recommended his discharge application and forwarded to Records the Rajput Regiment to consider premature discharge on compassionate grounds and on receipt of the same along with complete set of pension documents, his premature discharge from service on compassionate grounds was sanctioned under Army Rule 13(3)I(i)(b) w.e.f. 01 Oct 2010. The petitioner was locally discharged from service before completion of service tenure at his own request.

The Tribunal observed that before the actual discharge order were to take effect, the applicant submitted application dated 21 Sep 2010 for withdrawal of his request for premature discharge to the commanding officer, OIC Records and the Commander 32 Infantry Brigade but the same was not acceded to and the petitioner proceeded on discharge w.e.f. 01 Oct 2010. The general principle is that in the absence of a legal, contractual or constitutional bar, a prospective resignation can be withdrawn at any time before it becomes effective.

The Tribunal set aside the order of discharge and ordered that the petitioner should be reinstated in service with effect from the date of his discharge within 15 days of the receipt of copy of the order. The petitioner could take the order by hand and report to RAJPUT Regimental Centre or his unit for immediate reinstatement. He would be entitled to all pay and allowances and consequential benefits from the date of his discharge including extension of service and promotion subject to his qualification and conditions laid down.

***

The AFT Regional Bench Chennai in the case of *Ex. Sep. Balakotaiah Mekala v. Union of India*, OA No.96 of 2012, decided on 08 April 2013, considered a case for reinstatement in the service, where the applicant was acquitted by the civil court.

The applicant was enrolled as a Sepoy in the Army on 23 February 1996. While he was casual leave at his native village, due to some enmity in the village, a false case was instituted against him and seven others with the Police under sections 147, 148, 324, 307 and 302 read with 34 of the IPC. The case was investigated and was committed to Sessions Court in 2005. The case was tried by the said Court and in a judgment dated 5 July 2007, the applicant was sentenced to the life imprisonment. In pursuance of the conviction and sentence passed against the applicant, the military authorities invoked the provisions of section 20(3) of Army Act read with Army Rule 17, and dismissed him from service. However, the applicant and other accused preferred a criminal appeal against the conviction and sentence passed by the Sessions Court before the High Court of Andhra Pradesh. The High Court set aside the conviction and sentence passed by the District and Sessions Judge, Markapur, in its judgment dated 9 September 2009. Consequently, the applicant, made an application to the superior authorities on 26 November 2009 requesting them to reinstate him into service. Similarly placed accused, namely Kotaiah, the second accused in the said case was reinstated into service by the Commanding Officer 12 Madras on 24 July 2010. However, the applicant was not reinstated.

The applicant relied on the decision of the Delhi High Court in the case of *Shri Sat Pal v. The Chief of The Army Staff*, 94 (2001) DLT 521, wherein it was held that once the Criminal Court has come to a conclusion that the individual was not guilty of the offences charged against him and the individual was dismissed from service for the reason that the individual was involved in a criminal case, the reinstatement is consequential with all the back wages and benefits.

The Tribunal considered the decision of the Supreme Court in the case of *Union of India v. Tulsi Ram Patel* A1986 SC 1416. In paragraph 126 of the said decision it was held that the court has the power under Article 226 of the Constitution to consider whether the petitioner is an accused in the criminal case and if it is found by the court that the petitioner is not the person convicted the order of dismissal is to be set aside and an order is to be passed for his reinstatement. The Tribunal also observed that the co-accused, namely Kottaiah, was reinstated on the same ground or reason even as early as on 24 July 2010. It held that under the given circumstances, the request of the applicant for reinstatement and for other reliefs was quite genuine, reasonable, legal and acceptable. The Tribunal directed that the applicant be reinstated in service with back wages and allowances from 5 July 2007 till the date of reinstatement with all monetary benefits as well as promotion and seniority. In default to comply with the said direction, the applicant would be entitled to 9% interest on the quantum of arrears of pay and allowances from the date of default till the date of payment.

XIX. Release From Service

Civil employment: critical trade

The AFT New Delhi Principal Bench in *Sgt. Shiva Murati v. Union of India*, OA No. 126 of 2012, decided on 29 May 2012, considered a petition for immediate discharge from service for civil employment.

The Petitioner was enrolled in Indian Air force on 18 November 1996. Since the Petitioner was completing 15 years of service in November 2011 and was entitled to seek discharge by joining any other government service, he in response to the advertisement published by Uttar Pradesh Middle Education Service Selection Board in the news paper of 15 January 2009 applied for the post of Trained Graduate Teacher (TGT) through proper channel. The petitioner obtained proper permission of his commanding officer in accordance with Air Force Order No. 14 of 2008 and the application of the Petitioner was forwarded for further action.

The petitioner appeared in the written examination in March 2010 and was finally selected for the post of TGT on 11 January 2012. Then petitioner applied for premature release from service on 19 January 2012. His application for release/discharge from service duly supported with the documents and recommended by the commanders in chain was returned on 1 March 2012 on the ground that the petitioner belongs to critical trade and that he had not obtained no objection certificate (NOC) before submitting application for discharge on being selected for the post of TGT. Petitioner tried to seek release from service through all efforts but he failed.

The respondents contested the trade of the Radio Fitter, to which the petitioner belonged, had gone into a critical trade. Further, the 'criticality of trade', *i.e.* shortage of manpower in individual trades of IAF is worked out twice in a year by Air Force Record Office and relevant data is forwarded to all the Units with instructions to scrutinize applications submitted by Airmen seeking permission for civil employment and to forward their applications to prospective employer only after ascertaining their eligibility in terms of AFO

14/2008. It is also contested that NOC to the Airmen for civil employment is invariably issued by Air HQ. For the said purpose, the individual was to apply afresh through proper channel for grant of NOC after receiving call letter for appearing in the interview/verification of documents or after the result of written test where selection is based on success in written test only. The NOC is issued after ascertaining the criticality of the trade of the individual at the time of considering such application. Request for NOC was liable to be rejected out rightly in the cases wherein the individual has either not obtained prior permission of his Commanding Officer for applying for the civil post or the Commanding Officer has erroneously granted the said permission in contravention to the provisions of this AFO. The respondents also stated that in the present case the petitioner was earlier permitted to apply for the post by his parent Unit and later on his request for grant of NOC and discharge was rejected on the ground of criticality of service exigencies as his trade is facing critical manpower deficiency and that obtaining NOC is a prerequisite for discharge from service.

The Tribunal observed that the petitioner was under an obligation to serve the IAF for a period of 20 years but his pensionable service was 15 years. Therefore he had no right to seek a discharge for promoting his individual interest. The paramount consideration is the consideration of the institution and of the nation. When the incumbent was trained in a particular speciality and when his services are required at that time he cannot be permitted to go because he owes a greater responsibility and duty towards nation.

Keeping in view that the petitioner may not get such an opportunity of employment in civil service again, the Tribunal ordered that the matter should be considered by the authorities sympathetically; and decided possibly within three months.

XX. Retirement

Retirement age for Group Captain (TS)

The AFT Principal Bench New Delhi in the case of *Group Captain Atul Shukla v. Union of India,* TA No. 385 of 2009 [WP (C) No. 7811 of 2009], with TA No. 386 of 2009 [WP (C) No. 9772 of 2009] and OA No. 99 of 2009 decided on 2 May 2013, considered a common question of law relating to the age of superannuation of the officers.

The petitioner was commissioned in the Indian Air Force on 13 June 1974 in the logistic branch. He became Group Captain (Time Scale) on 16 December 2004. His date of retirement in existing position as per the age of superannuation i.e. 54 years was 30 June 2009. Whereas according to petitioner, he was entitled to continue till the age of 57 years and he should be retired on 30 June 2012.

The petitioner contended that he was considered for the promotion to the rank of Group Captain for the three successive years but he could not be empanelled even though he was fit in all respects. During these years the retirement age of Central Government Employees was increased from 58 years to 60 years by the government then in power. Thereafter, this was again reduced to 58 years. Normally three courses, one of each year, are considered for promotion together i.e. in 2000 the courses considered will be 1999, 2000 and 2001 & so on. However, during this period the age of retirement being increased and then subsequently decreased resulted in bunching up of as many as seven courses at a time for the limited amount of vacancies.

On 16 December 2004, the government implemented the AV Singh Committee recommendation regarding improvement of the career prospect of the officers of the Armed Forces by introducing, for the first time, the Rank of Group Captain (Time Scale) after completion of 26 years of service for those officers who could not be promoted in the select rank of Group Captain due to competitive merit or lack of vacancy.

On the basis of the recommendation of AV Singh Committee to abolish the rank of Wg Cdr (Time Scale) which was granted to those officers prior to promulgation of AV Singh Committee recommendations, who could not be promoted to the rank of Wing Commander on completion of 21 years of service with same retirement of age as that of select grade Wing Commander based on the said Committee. However, every officer who had completed 13 years of service was made eligible for promotion to the rank of substantive Wing Commander after implementation of the AV Singh Committee report.

The Air Headquarter Human Resource issued a policy dated 12 January 2009 on the recommendations of the AV Singh Committee report. As per the report, a detailed policy was laid down for consideration for promotion and laid down reckonable period of commission service for each post like Flt Lt - 2 years, Sqn Ldr - 6 years, Wg Cdr – 13 years and Gp Capt – 26 years. They laid criteria for promotion of Wing Commander to Group Captain (Time Scale) for which they were required to consider 3 years report and age of superannuation was mentioned – "The age of superannuation for Gp Capt (TS) would be same as it is for the rank of Wg Cdr in respective branches. Therefore, there was no change in the retirement age of a Wg Cdr on being promoted to the rank of Gp Capt (TS) i.e., 54 years. The petitioner could not be promoted in selection to the post of Gp Capt and he was informed by communication dated 16 June 2008 that he will be retiring from service on completion of 54 years of age whereas normal age in respect of Gp Capt was 57 years.

Petitioner was made substantive Gp Capt (TS) on 10 January 2006 published in the Gazette dated on 05 August 2006. It was pointed out that Gp Capt (TS) are identical to Gp Capt (Select) the financial powers given to Gp Capt (Select) are also vested with Gp Capt (TS). The duty discharged by both Gp Capt (Select) and Gp Capt (TS) were identical. The Pay Scale

& Grade Pay of both i.e. Gp Capt (Select) & Gp Capt (TS) was same after 6th Pay Commission. The incumbent by rank Gp Capt (TS) discharges all administrative functions as Gp Capt (select). The Gp Capt (TS) was getting same pay scale, grade pay & wears same rank but he has been discriminated in matter of age of superannuation. Gp Capt (TS) was to retire at the age of 54 years and Gp Capt (Select) was to retire at the age of 57.

The petitioner, a Gp Capt (TS), contended that the retirement at the age of 54 was discriminatory and violative of Article 14 and 16 of the Constitution of India. The petitioner challenged the order dated 06 June 2008 whereby he was informed that his date of superannuation will be 30 June 2008 at the age of 54 years may be quashed and similarly the policy laid down vide letter dated 12 January 2009 whereby this two ages of retirement has been prescribed be also struck down being violative of Articles 14 and 16 of the Constitution.

The respondent contested that in line of the AV Singh Committee proposal for the Air Force, the Gp Captain (TS) rank was granted to Air Force Officers on completion of 26 years of service. This rank was granted to officers who were superseded in the first select grade rank three times and who met the minimum performance criteria. Further, it was also made clear that this category of officers that they would be junior to Gp Capt (Select Grades). Thus, a new category of officers was created – that of Gp Capt (TS). As per government letter No. 2(2)/US(L)/D(Air-III)/04 dated 12 March 2005, which created this rank, the retirement age of GP Capt (TS) was be the same as the age at which the Wing Commander retires in that branch.

Therefore, if a flying branch Wing Commander retired at 52, so would the Gp Capt (TS) and likewise for ground duty branches Gp Capt (TS) at the age of 54. The respondents further contested that the objective behind the institution of GP Capt (TS) rank was to make every young officer stay motivated, even though he may not have made it to GP Capt (select) rank. It was felt that the rank of GP Capt has a great relevance and importance in the social fabric of society.

The Tribunal, however, observed that no rationale was brought out by the respondents for prescribing two dates of retirement for officers of the same rank. When both the persons wear the same rank, draw the same salary and they get the same grade pay and then to say that one Gp Capt (TS) will retire at the age of 54 years and the other Gp Capt (Select) at the age of 57 years. The Tribunal commented that, this distinction which is sought to be made has no rational basis whatsoever.

The Tribunal set aside the notification dated 12 June 2009 to the extent which laid down the ages of retirement for the Gp Capt (TS) at the age of 54 years and directed that all the persons who are in the rank of Gp Capt (TS) will be entitled to continue up to the age of 57 years. The order of the petitioner by which he was to retire at the age of 54 years dated 5 December 2008 was quashed and petitioner was entitled to all benefits up to the age of 57 years.

His pension and other emoluments to be worked out and he should be also entitled to arrears of the salary till he attains the age of 57 years.

Premature retirement

The AFT Principal Bench, New Delhi (Court No. 2) in the case of *Lt Col Hardeep Sandhu v. Union of India*, OA No. 15 of 2011, decided on 3 February 2012, considered a prayer for pre-mature retirement from the service.

The OA No. 15 of 2011 was filed in the Armed Forces Tribunal on 11 January 2011. It was dismissed by the Tribunal vide its order dated 13 January 2011. Against the said order, the applicant approached the Delhi High Court and obtained the order dated 25 May 2011 whereby the High Court remitted back the case to the Tribunal. Further, the High Court also issued a stay order to the transfer/posting of the applicant from the present place of posting. As per the directions of the High Court, the case was again taken up for hearing in the AFT to its original number.

The applicant was commissioned in the Army on 07 December 1996. He got married on 08 November 2002. On 12 April 2006 the applicant sought pre-mature retirement (PMR) from the service. On 18 March 2006, the applicant applied for resignation on the grounds that he had ancestral property which he was required to look after since his parents were aged. His application was rejected by the competent authority on 09 October 2006 with the reason that there was a shortage of officers and he could not be permitted to go on PMR.

On 10 January 2009, the applicant again applied for PMR on the grounds that his parents were ailing and being the only son he was required to look after them. This application was rejected vide order dated 08 April 2009 stating that "based on the merit of the case and the laid down criteria in this regard, request of the officer has been rejected by the competent authority." The applicant once again applied for PMR on 14 January 2010 on grounds that his parents were of old age. He had agricultural land and also that his conjugal rights were being affected because of his services with the Army. This application was once again rejected on 12 March 2010 for the reasons "based on the merit of the case and the laid down criteria in this regard, request of the officer has been rejected by the competent authority." Meanwhile, the applicant had applied for posting on compassionate grounds on 12 January 2008 which was granted by the respondents.

The applicant preferred a statutory complaint on 10 January 2010, highlighting that his PMR applications were declined on the grounds of shortage of officers which was incorrect. He also alluded to certain facts and figures which give out as to how the officers were being managed in terms of employment and that he should have been declared surplus to the establishment and permitted to go on PMR. This complaint was rejected by the respondents on 10 June 2011 with the comments: "....it emerges that the officer's applications for premature retirement have been considered by the Army HQ as per policy on the subject and rejected due to remaining service liability up to 22 May 2010 on account of the Engineer Officers Degree in Engineering (EODE) course and deficiency of officers. As service liability is now over the officer is advised to file an application for PMR with the Army HQ, if he so desires." The applicant was there after posted out from New Delhi.

The applicant contended that the action of the respondents by not to accept the application for PMR be declared as unjust, arbitrary and against the fundamental rights guaranteed under the Constitution. The applicant further prayed to quash and set aside the impugned orders which dealt with the letter of resignation and PMR. He further prayed that his resignation dated 07 March 2011 and resubmitted on 15 March 2011 be directed to be accepted and orders passed on those be quashed and set aside. He has also sought that his release be granted from the present place of posting, *i.e.* New Delhi.

In support of his contentions, the applicant cited the decisions of the Delhi High Court in *Major Rahul Shukla v. Union of India* (1995) DLT 573 (DB); *Major S.K. Jain v. Union of India* 2000 (54) DRJ; *Colonel R. Jayaprasad v. Union of India* 151 (2008) DLT 435(DB); and *Captain (Mrs.) Krishna v. Union of India* WP (C) No.166 of 2010 decided on 08 October 2010. He also cited the decision of the High Court of Bombay given in writ petition No. 289 of 2011 in the matter of *Major Yogesh Chandra Madhav Sayanakar v. The Chief of Army Staff* decided on 25 March 2011.

In support of their contentions, the respondents cited the judgment of the High Court of Delhi given in WP (C) No. 4646 of 2005 in the matter of *Sqn Ldr S. Tyagi v. Union of India*, wherein the Court had held that "In any case, this is not a case where this Court while exercising powers under Article 226 of the Constitution of India should interfere in the decision of the authorities as no case of malice, bias or discrimination has been made out by the petitioner in the challenge to the rejection of the plea of the petitioner for premature discharge." Further, the respondents also cited the decision of the AFT Principal Bench passed in *Maj Sumit Sharma v. Union of India* OA No. 423 of 2010.

The Tribunal examined the policy letter dated 20 January 1975, issued by the Ministry of Defence on PMR. The Tribunal remanded the case back to the respondents for consideration, with the direction that the applicant was at liberty to apply afresh for PMR or his resignation within two weeks of the order. The Tribunal also directed that the case to be decided in the light of its observations and directions of the Government of India dated 10 June 2011 and the application should be disposed off within 90 days of the receipt of the application by the respondents. Further, till disposal of PMR issue, the applicant will continue to be posted in Delhi.

Retirement orders

The AFT Bench Kolkata in the case of *Major Rabindra Singh v. Union of India*, TA No. 37 of 2010, (WP No. 23369(W) of 2006 Calcutta High Court) decided on 4 April 2011, considered a prayer for setting aside the retirement orders issued by the Military Secretary's Branch, Army Headquarters.

The petitioner was a Regimental Commissioned Officer (RCO) in the Indian Army, in Corps of Signals. The petitioner felt that he, being a RCO, had been subjected to discriminatory treatment by the authorities committing deliberate lapses by not revising his retirement age/ service upwards as was done for other entries amongst commissioned officers in the Army, post implementation of Ajay Vikram Singh Committee (AVSC) Report in December 2004.

The petitioner contested that he, like all other RCOs, was after all a "regular commissioned officer" working shoulder to shoulder with them in all regimental assignments. Terms of engagement of all officers were so amended after December 2004 (post AVSC) to ensure that none retired at a rank below that of Lt Col, if he was qualified; even Short Service Commissioned Officers (SSCO), both men and women, who could not be selected to get regular commission, were allowed to serve longer by increasing their terms from 10 to 14 years, so that they could become Lt Col. The petitioner felt that he was discriminated against amongst similarly placed officers.

The Tribunal held that since the applicant has already retired from service, the retirement orders of the applicant shall remain in vogue. It ordered that the petitioner shall be granted a notional increase of service by two years, without any arrears or monetary advantage in pay and allowances. The petitioner shall be notionally promoted to the rank of Lt Col (Time-Scale) on completion of 13 years of such assumed service, only after fulfilling all other criteria, except length service, as required for promotion to the rank of Lt Col (Time Scale), after holding a selection board by the Military Secretary's Branch. Such notional promotion shall only be for carrying the rank and for pension as entitled in that rank. The applicant shall get pension of a Major till he is promoted notionally to the rank of Lt Col. On such notional promotion to Lt Col, his pay in that rank shall be re-fixed and pension shall accordingly be fixed again in the rank of Lt Col to which he shall remain eligible

XXI. Reversion

The Principal Bench of the Armed Force Tribunal in the case of *Hav Pratap Chandra Sahu v. Union of India*, OA No. 191 of 2011, decided on 19 March 2012, considered a bunch of 46 petitions where the petitioner contested their en masse reversion back to the Engineer Group.

The petitioners was enrolled in the Corp of Engineers, and were in the due course were transferred to MES in various ranks with due seniority. In 2009, the IHQ (Army) AG's Branch Policy letter dated 05 Jan 2009, read with IHQ (Army) E in C Branch letter dated 15 March 2011, rationalized the trades in the Indian Army by regrouping, merger or deletion of various trades. As a result of this policy the petitioners who were serving in the MES were required to be sent back to their respective parent units. It was contested that as a result of repatriation the petitioner's career was going to suffer as many persons there in original units have been promoted to the higher post and petitioners will be reverted back to their post and given a lower position. The petitioners therefore challenged the validity of the policy of rationalisation of trades and merger and re-mustering being arbitrary and violative of Article 14 and 16 of the Constitution of India.

The Tribunal observed that there is no illegality in rationalizing the trade and the Government can always laid down a policy looking to the exigencies of service and can amend it from time to time. The policy decision is not violative of Article 14 and 16 of the Constitution of India and the Government can abolish the post and create the post. It is their absolute right. As regard, the seniority of repatriated individual, the Court held in case any person junior to these repatriated persons has been promoted to a higher rank then the case of these persons will be considered vis-a-vis such junior person and if they are found suitable then they will be given their due promotion and their seniority will be restored. The Tribunal also directed that the decision would be applicable to all the MES personnel and not only to those who have filed the present petitions. It will be unanimously applicable to all MES personnel who are being sought to be repatriated to their parent unit.

XXII. Summary Punishment

Lack of jurisdiction

The AFT New Delhi Principal Bench in *Raj Kumar v. Union of India*, TA No. 252 of 2009 [WP (C) Delhi High Court] decided on 16 November 2009, referred the petition back to the Delhi High Court, where it had no jurisdiction.

The writ petition was transferred from the Delhi High Court to the Armed Forces Tribunal under section 34 of the Armed Forces Tribunal Act, 2007. The Tribunal by order dated 16 November 2009, held that since the punishment awarded to the petitioner was a summary punishment of reduction in rank, therefore, under s. 3 (o)(iii), the Armed Forces Tribunal had no jurisdiction to hear the matter where the punishment awarded is other than dismissal. The WP was sent back to the Delhi High Court by order dated 3 February 2010.

Retrial

The AFT Regional Bench Chennai in the case of *B. Ramu v. Union of India*, TA No.183 of 2010 [WP (C) No.19060 of 2009, High Court of Andhra Pradesh), decided on 9 December 2010, considered a prayer for victimization in summary trial.

The petitioner had joined the Indian Navy as Sailor and in the due course was promoted to LRO (Leading Radio Operator, Telegraphic). He was due for his next promotion as Petty Officer in the year 2003. A lady, the neighbour of the petitioner, lodged a complaint at Town Police Station, Peda Waltair, Vishakapatnam on 24 November 2003, alleging that the petitioner had blackmailed and cheated her posing as a Sub-Inspector of Police and also demanded an amount of Rs. 2,000/-.Without registering the complaint, the civil police forwarded the complaint to the Naval authorities. The petitioner was taken into custody of the Naval Police and released subsequently. He was summarily tried for the said offence under the Navy Act, 1957 and the Regulations 25 to 34 of the Regulations for the Navy, Part-II (Statutory). He was sentenced to 90 days Rigorous Imprisonment, dismissal from Naval Service, reduction in rank and deprivation of good conduct badges. He was sent to the Central Jail at Visakhapatnam for imprisonment.

The petitioner contended that summary trial was conducted without following the procedures contemplated under Rules and Regulations and he was victimised. He was not given any opportunity to appeal under the provisions of section 23 of the Navy Act, 1957 to the Naval Command. Further, even before he was sent to prison to undergo the rigorous imprisonment of 90 days as per the Punishment Warrant, he was not furnished with a copy of the Punishment Warrant, to enable him to prefer an appeal against the decision of the Commanding Officer.

The respondent contended that the petitioner had filed WP No.3056 of 2004 questioning the summary trial, but the same was dismissed on 30 April 2004 on the ground that the complaint was withdrawn by the lady upon the request of the petitioner, and not voluntarily.

The Tribunal observed that the mandatory provisions contemplated under the Regulations for the Navy, Part-II, Statutory, have not been followed by the Commanding Officer, who had passed the order dated 20 May 2004 in Warrant No. 4/2004. The Tribunal further observed that there was no material on record to show that paragraphs 29(3) or 29(4) of Regulation have been complied with by the Commanding Officer before passing the order dated 20 May 2004. Further, the Commanding Officer had signed in the punishment warrant on 23 March 2004 itself. There respondents were not able to explain as to why said punishment warrant was sent for approval of the Chief of Naval Staff after an inordinate delay of two months.

The Tribunal further observed that in the letter dated 23 March 2004 addressed to the Flag Officer Commanding in Chief, Eastern Naval Command, from the Commanding Officer, for approval of the Chief of the Naval Staff (CNS), the original statements of the two important two witnesses were not sent to the CNS. Under such circumstances, it was highly doubtful whether the CNS had any opportunity to satisfy himself before giving his approval in Punishment Warrant against the petitioner without going through the original statements of two important witnesses in the complaint against the petitioner.

The Tribunal held that in the interest of justice the petitioner must be given an opportunity to go through the summary trial again. It ordered that the petitioner shall appear before naval authorities on or before 15 February 2011 and the summary trial shall be completed within one month thereafter. If the petitioner does not appear before Naval authorities as directed the petition shall deem to have been dismissed.

XXIII. Termination From Service

Civil offence

The AFT New Delhi Principal Bench in the case of *Ex Rfn/WM Jagsir Singh v. Union of India*, OA No. 235 of 2011, decided on 16 March 2012, considered the petition for quashing and setting aside of the order of termination from service with all consequential benefits and compensation.

The applicant was enrolled in the Indian Army and was posted to Rajputana Rifles as Rifleman/Washerman (Rfn/WM). It was contended by the applicant that his wife has filed a false complaint at the civil police station under sections 494 and 498-A of the IPC read with section 120-B alleging that the applicant has contracted plural marriage. In due course, the applicant was arrested and was also released on bail by the civil court. The Army, based on the complaint filed by the wife of the applicant, without conducting any inquiry or rendering any opportunity to the applicant to explain his case, terminated his services in an arbitrary manner under section 20 (3) of the Army Act 20(3) read with Army Rule 17 and Para 333(c) of the Regulations for the Army on the grounds of contracting plural marriage without prior sanction. The applicant was struck of the strength vide the impugned order dated 03 June 2006 and no discharge order was issued.

The applicant further contended that the Civil Court of Addl. Chief Judicial Magistrate, Ferozepur vide its order dated 11 February 2011 exonerated him from all the charges levelled against him by his wife and disposed off the case. The applicant immediately moved to the Unit at Jammu along with the court order but the unit refused to entertain him and advised him to report to Regimental Centre and Record Office at New Delhi. The applicant reported to the Record Office at New Delhi and made another representation but no action was taken by them.

The Tribunal observed that in this case a 'show cause notice' for plural marriage was issued by the GOC-in-C based on an independent investigation through the District Sainik Welfare Officer, Ferozepur confirming plural marriage by the applicant. The Tribunal examined the provisions of Para 333(c) of the Regulations for the Army: "In cases where cognisance has been taken by civil court of competent jurisdiction the matter should be treated as subjudice and the decision of the court awaited before taking any action." The Bench held that it was incorrect and illegal on the part of the Army authorities to have terminated the services of the applicant under section 20 of the Army Act and Army Rule 17 read in conjunction with Para 333(c) of the Regulations for the Army, 1987. The Tribunal set aside the order for termination of the services of the applicant dated 12 April 2006. Since the applicant had already served for about 11 years, he was deemed to have retired on that day accordingly and entitled to all pensionary benefits.

Arbitrary termination from service

The AFT Regional Bench Chennai in *Ex. Naik P. Baskaran v. Secretary, Government of India*, Ministry of Defence, TA No. 13 of 2009, [WP No. 18531 of 2004], decided on 12 January 2010, considered the arbitrary termination of the appellant after completing service of 14 years 3 months, making him ineligible for pension and other benefits.

The applicant had served at insurgency areas such as Manipur, Nagaland and Jammu & Kashmir operational area at Sri Lanka and other Field area to the entire satisfaction of his Superior Officers. The applicant had incurred four Red Ink entry punishments in his record of service and Allahabad Sub Area Commander had terminated his service from Army based on the recommendation of the commanding officer, without due consideration to past 14 years 3 months and 9 days service rendered by him. All the appeals made by the applicant to his commanding officer as well as to the higher authorities proved futile.

The Tribunal considered the Additional Director General, Personnel Services (PS-2), Army Headquarters, letter No. A/13210/159/AG/PS-C dated 28 December 1988 and observed that the concerned authorities failed to consider the provisions contained in the letter: "......In such cases the commanding officer must consider the nature of the offences for which each red ink entry has been awarded and not be harsh with the individual, especially when they are about to complete the pensionable service. Due consideration should be given to the long service, hard stations and difficult living conditions that the OR has been exposed to during his service., and the discharge should be ordered only when it is absolutely necessary in the interest of service. Such discharge should be approved by the next higher Commander."

The Tribunal relied on the Supreme Court decision in the case of *Sheel Kr. Roy v. Secretary, Ministry of Defence,* 2008(1) MLJ (Crl) 481: "Once it is held that arbitrariness of the Commanding Officer in the matter of holding the appellant and awarding punishment upon him is apparent on the face of the record, the impugned order must be held to be wholly unsustainable." The Tribunal was of the view that the termination order against the applicant was tainted with bias: (i) the applicant was not transferred to another unit once he was punished with severe reprim228and twice, (ii) the applicant was not discharged on medical grounds even after he was referred to a medical board, and (iii) the respondents could not tolerate the applicant for another 9 months to enable him to get his full service pension since he had served for 14 years 3 months 9 days in the Army both in peace area and field area, including in insurgent area.

The Tribunal ordered that the Army authorities to waive 9 months period of service to the applicant to enable him to get the full pension including the service pension, gratuity and other related benefits. It further ordered that the case should not be treated as a precedent for other cases.

Show cause notice quashed

The AFT Regional Bench Kolkata in the case of *Col Debashis Mitra v. Union of India*, TA No. 4 of 2010 [WP 9693(W) of 2009 High Court Calcutta] decided on 20 July 2010, considered the legality of a trial by the GCM.

The petitioner was tried by a GCM on 9 August 2006. It was presided over by one Brigadier, four Colonels and assisted by a Judge Advocate of the rank of Lt Col. The petitioner was arraigned on 12 charges levelled against him on the basis of the allegations of sexual harassment as made by a lady officer of the Army. However, the GCM did not find him guilty on any of the charges. The confirming authority returned back the said finding to the GCM for revision and directed it to rehear and to reconsider the earlier decision. On the basis of the said revision order the members of the GCM reassembled and held sitting from February 2007 to March 2007. After considering the entire evidence on record the GCM, on revision, held the petitioner "guilty" of the fifth charge and passed the sentence of reprimand subject to confirmation.

The petitioner preferred a post confirmation petition on 20 October 2007 under the provision of section 162 (2) of the Army Act before the Defence Secretary, Ministry of Defence, praying for setting aside the finding of "guilty" so far as the fifth charge was concerned and to confirm the finding of "not guilty" in relation to other charges as framed in the GCM. However, the petitioner did not receive any reply to his petition submitted to the defence Secretary.

On 28 January 2009, the petitioner received an order whereby he was transferred to Kolkata. On 4 April 2009, the petitioner received a show cause notice under section 19 of the Army Act read with Army Rules 14. The charges which were levelled against him in this 'show cause notice', were the same on which he was arraigned in the GCM. The petitioner submitted a reply to the said show cause notice claiming that the charges were not sustainable in the eye of law, as the same had already been considered by the GCM and as such the show cause notice, as served upon him should be quashed.

The petitioner contended that the decision of the confirming authority to return back the proceedings for revision was against the law. The petitioner also claimed that he was not informed about the decision of the confirming authority in writing, but he was informed verbally that the sentence of reprimand was confirmed. However, no decision of the confirming authority in respect of the finding of "not guilty" concerning the other charges was received from the confirming authority. He further contended that the issuance of show cause notice under section 19 of the Army Act read with Army Rules 14 was not only unwarranted in the facts and circumstances of the case but wholly without jurisdiction as this provision can be availed of when the Central Government and Chief of the Army Staff are satisfied that the trial of the officer by a Court Martial is inexpedient or impractical. He contested that the charges were already considered and decided by the GCM, therefore on the same grounds a further show cause notice cannot be issued as it is not only impermissible but also against ethics.

The respondents contested that the 'show cause notice' was issued mainly on the allegation of sexual harassment as was made against the petitioner. Since allegations, as made against the petitioner appears to be serious in nature, so the authority decided to issue such show cause notice against the petitioner to consider whether further retention of the petitioner in service will be justified or not. It has further been contended by the respondent that there was no bar to issue fresh show cause notice although a person has faced a GCM proceeding on the basis of earlier allegations. Further there was no bar for the Chief of the Army Staff or the Central Government to take action under section 19 of the Army Act read with Army Rules 14(2) in dismissing an unwanted officer even though he was found not guilty in the GCM.

The Tribunal held that the issuance of the show cause notice by the authority against the petitioner was nothing but colourable exercise of power in order to frustrate the decision of the court martial. There is reason to believe that the authority was bent upon to get rid of the petitioner from the service by any means whatsoever. The Tribunal quashed that show cause notice dated 4 April 2009 issued under section 19 of the Army Act read with Army Rules 14, against the petitioner and restrained the respondents from taking any action against the petitioner on the basis of such show cause notice.

XXIV. Transfer

Lack of jurisdiction

The AFT Regional Bench Lucknow Court No. 2, in the case of *Lt. Col. S.K. Goswami, SM v. Union of India*, OA No. 279 of 2011, decided on 6 January 2012, considered a prayer for cancellation of the order relating to change of the regiment.

The applicant was commissioned in the Indian Army on 09 December 1995, and thereafter he was empanelled for PARA (SF)/PARA duties in October 1997 and joined 9 PARA (SF). By an order of the Chief of the Army Staff, the Regiment of the applicant was changed from PARA (SF) to 5 Gorkha Rifles and he was posted as Joint Director, National Cadet Corps.

The applicant contended against the change of his Regiment by the military authorities as arbitrary. The respondent contested that the instant petition was not maintainable before the Tribunal as the impugned order amounts to transfer of applicant from one Regiment to another Regiment. Further, under s. 3(o) of the Armed Forces Tribunal Act, 2007, the Tribunal does not have jurisdiction to adjudicate the present dispute as 'transfers and postings' including the change of place or unit on posting are not within the domain of this Tribunal to adjudicate upon. Also, according to paragraph 64 (c) of the Regulations for the Army, 1987 transfers of officers within regular army will be carried out under the order of the Chief of the Army Staff whereas in the event the officer himself intends to get him transferred to another Regiment or place or Unit he will have to make an application which upon consideration appropriate orders will be passed by the competent authority.

Since under the order passed by the Chief of the Army Staff, the Regiment of the applicant was changed from PARA (SF) to 5 Gorkha Rifles and he was posted as Joint Director, National Cadet Corps, therefore, the said order comes within the exclusion clause of s. 3(o) as such the Tribunal had no jurisdiction in the matter.

The Tribunal referred to s. 3(o) of the Armed Forces Tribunal Act, and paragraph 64 of the Regulations for the Army, 1987; and came to the conclusion that the issue was related to the provisions contained in paragraph 64 of the Regulations. The Tribunal also examined the policy letter dated 10 April 2003 dealing with the Terms and Conditions of Service for Officers of PARA and PARA (SF) Battalions. Paragraph 5 of the policy contemplated that the PARA and PARA (SF) battalion officers of other Arms and Services will have the option of permanent transfer to the PARA Regiment or being reverted to their parent Arms or Services.

The Tribunal concluded that a conjoint reading of paragraph 64 of the Regulations for the Army, 1987 and paragraph 5 of the Policy states that in the event an officer is shifted from one Regiment to another Regiment it would amount to 'transfer'. Since by the impugned order the applicant was shifted from PARA (SF) to 5 Gorkha Rifles and had been directed to be posted as Joint Director, National Cadet Corps, therefore, the same would fall within the ambit of word 'transfer' as defined under s. 3(o) of the Armed Forces Tribunal Act, 2007. Since the Tribunal did not have jurisdiction to delve upon the issue of 'transfer', it dismissed the application.

XXV. Miscellaneous

Military Nursing officer as par with other commissioned officers

The AFT Principal Bench New Delhi in the case of *Maj Gen Mrs. Usha Sikdar v. Union of India,* TA No. 211 of 2010 [WP (C) No. 4485 of 2005 of Delhi High Court], decided on 30 March 2010, considered a prayer for restoring the status of Nursing Officers at par with other officers of the Indian Army.

The petitioner, a military nursing officer, alleged that as Additional Director General of Military Nursing Services (ADGMNS) when she visited a hospital of the Indian Navy, she was humiliated and insulted by the Commanding Officer of the hospital by denying her authorized staff car i.e. a car with star plate signifying her rank and a flag signifying her appointment. The matter was reported to the DGAFMS and DGMS (Army) immediately after the conclusion of her visit and representation was put up to the Army Headquarters. The Adjutant General's Branch, Army Headquarters issued a letter dated 28 April 2004 asking her not to display stars and fly flag on her official vehicle. The Adjutant General Branch again issued a letter on 30 April 2004 and disseminated the same to all concerned unit. The highlights of the order were that the Indian Military Nursing Officers were not covered under the definition of "Officer" as given in Section of Army Act 3(XVIII) Army Act, 1950. It was also mentioned that Military Nursing Service (MNS) was raised vide Indian Military Nursing Ordinance 1943, in that, MNS officers are appointed as "officers of Indian Military Nursing Service" implying that officers of MNS were not part of the Armed Forces/Regular Army and therefore, not at par with rest of the officers of the Indian Army and under the provisions of existing Army orders/Regulations for the Army, Nursing officers were not authorized to fly flags or display star plates.

Aggrieved by this discrimination and denying the status of officers of Indian Army she sought personal interview with the Chief of Army Staff (COAS), who assured her that all grievances of the MNS officers would be looked into and all the privileges which had been arbitrarily withdrawn would be restored. The Petitioner contended that the assurance given by the COAS was not adhered to.

The respondents contested that the petitioner was not recruited under Army Act and Rules and she has been recruited under Indian Military Nursing Ordinance 1943 and she cannot be treated to be part of Regular Army. As such she cannot be considered at par with officers who are regularly recruited under Army Act.

The Tribunal observed that the provisions of the Indian Army Act, 1911 were applicable to the officers of the Nursing Services as if they were Indian commissioned officers and the provisions of the Army Act shall apply to officers of the Nursing Services as if they were officers of the Regular Forces. With regard to relative Rank, the Tribunal noted that clause (b) of para 733 of Chapter XVII of Regulations for the Army provides: "Women officers serving in the Army Medical Corps and officers in the Military Nursing Service will rank equally with male officers of the same titular rank e.g., a captain (woman officer) in the Army Medical Corps, will rank equally with a captain in the Artillery or Engineers." Further, the Army Order 353/73 under the heading of "Saluting MNS Officers" provided: "Military Nursing Service Officers are required to salute and are entitled to salutes in the same manner as other commissioned officers." The Tribunal ordered that the petitioner was entitled to be treated as a commissioned officer and as a part of the regular force, she was authorized to all entitlements which are authorized to the regular recruited officers of the Indian Army.

Re-medical examination

The AFT Principal Bench New Delhi in the case of *Jasvendra Singh v. DG AFMS New Delhi*, OA No. 56 of 2013, decided on 8 May 2013, considered a prayer for medical check-up of the applicant by an independent medical board.

The petitioner was born on 10 December 1993 and had submitted an application for selection as an Airman in 'X' Group against the vacancy advertisement published by Central Airmen Selection Board, Delhi Cantt. He passed written examination on 27 August 2012 and subsequent physical and trade-proficiency tests. The applicant was asked to appear for medical test on 29 August 2012 at the same venue. During the medical test, the applicant was informed by the respondents that there is some wax accumulated in his right ear and he was asked to get it removed and to appear again for the medical test. According to the petitioner, because of paucity of time he could not get the wax removed from any private ENT specialist. He re-appeared on 29 August 2012 before the Medical Officer at the same venue and he was given Red Card wherein it was written that he was unfit due to Retracted TM (RT) and Lumbar Lordosis. He was also given an Appeal Form to make an appeal which he filled and sent by post to the respondents along with Rs.40/-. He was medically examined again. Being dissatisfied with his rejection he went to Sawai Mansingh Medical College and Hospital, Jaipur where ENT Professor & Unit Head Deptt of ENT observed that both the tympanic membranes of the applicant were normal.

In response to the appeal he was called at Air Force Station, Gwalior on 30 October 2012 for re-medical examination by the Appeal Medical Board. He was again examined and found that he was unfit for the Tympanic Membranes as there was blood in his right ear and as such he was medically unfit. Since the petitioner was found to be unfit on account of the ear problem by the Medical Board as well as the Appeal Medical Board, he was not inducted into the Indian Air Force.

The respondents contested that the petitioner was first examined and he was not found fit because of the Tympanic Membranes and Lumbar Lordosis. However, in the Appeal Medical Board he was cleared by the Surgeon for Lumbar Lordosis but the ENT Specialist again found the petitioner unfit for Tympanic Membranes. Respondents denied that the petitioner was asked to go and get the wax cleaned from his ear.

The Tribunal, keeping in view the petitioner's young age and eagerness to join the air force, directed that he should be given one more opportunity and may be examined by a Medical Board at the Research & Referral Hospital, Delhi. This should be done as far as possible within a period of three months.

Note: *The Tribunal apparently had no jurisdiction to entertain an application from the individual. Section 2 of the Armed Forces Tribunal Act, 2007 provides a list of persons on whom the provisions of the Act would be applicable.*

Non-compliance of the orders of the Tribunal

The AFT Regional Bench Chandigarh in the case of *Sarjeet Singh through Smt Indrawati (wife) v. Union of India* MA (E) No. 117 of 2012 in TA No. 358 of 2010, decided on 9 April 2013, expressed its displeasure about non-compliance of its orders by the authorities.

TA No. 358 of 2010 arising out of CWP No. 20146 of 2006 was decided by the Tribunal on 05 September 2011 and the petition was allowed. The order having not been executed, MA No. 117 of 2012 was filed by the petitioner and notice was issued to the respondents on 27 March 2012 to inform about the compliance of the order. No compliance having been reported on 27 April

2012, the matter was listed for 02 July 2012. On that date too, there being no compliance, cost of Rs. 30,000/- was imposed on the respondents. On 07 August 2012, the PPO was finally handed over to the petitioner through her counsel. However, cost imposed for non compliance of the order was not deposited. Further time was sought and was granted for depositing the pending cost of Rs 30,000/, subject to another cost of Rs.15,000/- to be deposited with the Registry. On 25 September 2012, the case was listed solely for confirming payment of previous cost of Rs. 45,000/- and the cost still not having been deposited, the matter was again listed for 05 November 2012 with a clear direction that if the costs were not deposited before that date, additional cost will be imposed. On 05 November 2012, compliance was not reported. Then on 26 November 2012, compliance still having not been made with respect to cost, further cost of Rs. 30,000/- was imposed.

On 08 January 2013, the cost so far imposed still having not been deposited, further time was allowed on payment of another cost of Rs. 50,000/- and then the matter was listed for 9 April 2013 for reporting compliance.

The Tribunal on 9 April 2013 observed that the costs had not been deposited and further time has been sought. Further time was again granted subject to payment another cost of Rs. 60,000/- to be deposited with the Registry and the matter be listed on 09 September 2013. The Tribunal also observed that in Mani Ram v. Union of India OA No. 680 of 2011, decided on 23 May 2011, costs amounting to Rs 1.70 lakh was imposed for failing to deposit costs of Rs 15,000/- (imposed for compliance of the order) was pending compliance.

The Tribunal commented that the inability to execute orders of the Tribunal results in unwarranted expenditure being imposed on the respondents and such a state of affairs cannot be allowed to continue without redress. The Tribunal also noted that as on date, to ensure compliance of costs imposed to be deposited amounting to Rs. 44,95,000/-, further costs amounting to Rs. 60,45,000/- imposed on the respondents were pending payment. In other words, the cost imposed to ensure compliance of costs imposed themselves amounts to much more than the former.

The Tribunal was of the view that the matter needs to be addressed at the highest level by the respondents to streamline procedures to ensure prompt compliance of orders of the Tribunal. It directed that a copy of the order be sent by name to the Chief of the Army Staff and the Secretary, Ministry of Defence. The Secretary, Ministry of Defence was also directed to appraise the Raksha Mantri on the above facts and directions.

Withdrawal of submarine badge

The AFT New Delhi Principal Bench in the case of *Cdr Alok Kumar Pathak v. Union of India*, OA No. 579 of 2011, decided on 9 April 2013, considered a petition against the withdrawal of submarine badge.

In this case a final order was passed by the Tribunal setting aside the order dated 18 May 2004 of the Naval authorities, with a liberty to pass fresh order after complying with the principle of natural justice. In pursuance of that a show-cause notice was issued on 24 December 2010 and a reply was filed by the applicant. Respondents after considering the reply passed finally order dated 31 March 2011 and by this order it has been ordered in Para 10 which reads as under: "in view thereof, the earlier decision of the competent authority to withdraw you from the Submarine Cadre on grounds of professional incompetence w.e.f. 07 April 2004 needs no interference and is being maintained."

The Tribunal observed that the order which has been passed by the respondents is ex-facie illegal. Once the Tribunal had already set aside the order of 18 May 2004 which was passed in breach of principle of natural justice, though we gave them liberty to proceed afresh, that did not mean that the petitioner's earlier order of 18 May 2004 withdrawing the Submarine Badge with effect from 07 April 2004 will be revived. Once the original order of 18 May 2004 was quashed, the Tribunal gave the liberty to the petitioner to pass a proper order after complying with the principle of natural justice. Therefore, a show-cause notice was issued to the applicant on 24 December 2010 and after receiving the reply the naval authorities should have passed the order if they wanted to reiterate the same position. But that order will be effective from the date it is passed. It cannot be made a retrospective. This was against the principle of legal jurisprudence. Once the order which had been declared by the Tribunal void; it cannot be revived back. All the orders which are passed in breach of principle of natural justice are void. Therefore, the order of withdrawing the Submarine Badge from 07 April 2004 was void and cannot be revived back. It was open for the respondents to pass a fresh order, which they did on 31 March 2011.

The Tribunal held that the order of withdrawing submarine badge will only be effective from the date the order was passed i.e. 31 March 2011. The petitioner would be entitled to all the benefits which flow after quashing of the order of 18 May 2004.

Priority in investigation

The AFT Principal Bench New Delhi in the case of *Sub Ved Prakash v. Union of India* OA No. 223 of 2011, decided on 12 March 2012, considered a prayer for quashing the attachment order.

The petitioner was enrolled in the Indian Army in Army Service Corps (ASC) as Sepoy on 02 June 1982 and in the due course was promoted to the rank of Subedar. On 04 March 2006, he joined the Unit on permanent posting from Jhansi. During his posting as Head Clerk in the new unit and thereafter in different capacities, he came to know that certain procedural as well as financial irregularities were being committed which were detrimental and against the interest of the Army. He brought these irregularities to the notice of the local authorities. However, instead of plugging the loopholes in the system and procedures, petitioner was advised to be flexible in implementation of rules and follow oral instructions given by the OC. Since the malpractices were of serious nature, some of them being in gross violation of well established procedures and rules of Army, petitioner did not agree to follow illegal instructions.

The petitioner preferred a complaint on 31 May 2008 under Para 317 of the Regulations for the Army mentioning financial and procedural irregularities in the functioning of the Unit. Another complaint under Para 317 was sent on 10 June 2008 against the then officer commanding and was sent to the Chief of Army Staff through the station commander, with a request that the allegations need to be investigated by holding a fair and impartial inquiry. He was, however, advised by station commander to withdraw both the complaints otherwise he would be facing consequences.

A court of inquiry was ordered to investigate these complaints on 21 June 2008 and the court found the petitioner blameworthy on 17 July 2008 and 28 October 2009. Subsequently an attachment order for taking disciplinary action against the petitioner was issued. This was challenged by the petitioner by filing a petition before the Tribunal vide OA No. 108 of 2010. The Tribunal after considering the allegations quashed the court of inquiry vide order dated 09 March 2010:

> "We, therefore, direct that the Court of Inquiry be set aside and a fresh Court of Inquiry be convened, wherein Army Rule 180 to be applied against any person whose character or military reputation is affected. Based on such fresh Court of Inquiry, the authorities are at liberty to take whatever action they deem appropriate."

Thereafter a review application was moved by Lt Col D.D. Manik [MA No. 121 of 2010] being the respondent no. 5. The MA was also considered by the same bench of the Tribunal and thereafter a detailed order was passed on 04 June 2010. The Tribunal observed in the case:

> "Considering the above circumstances, the Court of Inquiry does not inspire any confidence with regard to the application of Army Rule 180. While it is evident that Army Rule 180 has not been applied against the petitioner, the applying of such rule against Respondent No. 5 was also selective. It is, therefore, for the authorities to decide the outcome and utility of this Court of Inquiry. However, we hold that this Court of Inquiry cannot form the basis to initiate disciplinary proceedings against the petitioner. Should any disciplinary proceedings be contemplated against the petitioner, a fresh court of inquiry should be constituted for such purpose, wherein the petitioner should be entitled to protection of Army Rule 180 as mandated by law. The petition is accordingly disposed of."

After the disposal of the above review application, a fresh court of inquiry was ordered on 28 September 2010 but because certain officers were posted out, again a fresh court of inquiry was convened on 26 July 2011 which commenced its proceedings on 08 August 2011. The respondents submitted that the findings of Court of Inquiry have been concluded and directions have been issued for initiating disciplinary proceedings against the petitioner. The proceedings of court of inquiry were, however, in a sealed cover and had not been supplied to the petitioner.

The Tribunal considered that whether under these circumstances, the order of attachment dated 28 October 2009 was justified or not. The tribunal observed that once the court of inquiry was quashed then there was no justification to retain the petitioner for such a long time. However, he was retained. Since the court of inquiry has already concluded, the Tribunal ordered that all relevant papers pertaining to the disciplinary action and the court of inquiry and statements of all witnesses be supplied to the petitioner forthwith and the action should be completed within a period of two months from passing of the order as petitioner was due to retire on 30 June 2012.

Canteen facilities

The AFT Regional Bench Kolkata in the case of *Yamuna Rai Yadav v. Union of India,* TA No. 216 of 2010 [OJC No. 4775 of 2000], decided on 18 May 2011, considered a prayer for availing military canteen facilities.

The petitioner was enrolled in the Territorial Army (TA) and served in 120(TA) Battalion at Bhubneswar in the rank of a Sepoy from 28 April 1965 to 30 April1980. He had to put in 15 years of service in the TA and was thus entitled to avail facilities from canteen stores department (CSD) i.e. "unit run canteens" in the Army. He was issued with a canteen card after his retirement in 1980. This card was valid till 30 December 1977. The Military Station Headquarter, Bhubneswar, however, refused to renew this canteen card and denied him the facility of canteen services.

The petitioner represented against such refusal to renew and the instructions were issued from Quarter Masters General Branch, Army Headquarter on 31 August 1999 to Station Headquarter Bhubneswar to renew the petitioner's canteen card. In the said correspondence it has been clarified that the Ex-Territorial Army personnel with 15 years of embodied service were entitled to the canteen facilities. The petitioner contended that due to whimsical attitude of the authorities in Station Headquarter Bhubneswar, he was being denied his legal right.

The Tribunal observed that the case was filed in the year 2000 in the Orissa High Court, but there was no counter-affidavit filed by the respondent. Even after the case was listed with the Tribunal, since 21 December 2010, the respondents have failed to file any counter-affidavit in spite of repeated directions by the Bench. In the absence of the counter-affidavit, despite repeated reminders, the Tribunal relied on available documents and submissions made by the counsels. It also perused the Army HQ letter No. 96003/Q/DDGCS dated 24 March 2006 on rules for entitlement of canteen service that allows canteen facilities to those who had served for five years in the Army.

The Tribunal directed that the Station Commander, Bhubneswar, after ascertaining all facts and rules shall give directions with regards to issue of canteen card to the petitioner. In case, such canteen card is denied to him, a reasoned order shall be communicated to him after giving him a personal hearing apprising him in detail the reasons for which he was not entitled to such canteen facilities. This action was to be completed within three months of the order. The Station Commander would submit a report of compliance to his Area and Sub-Area Commanders.

Honours and awards

The AFT New Delhi Principal Bench, in the case of *Maj B. S. Kohli, SM (retd) v. Union of India*, OA No. 376 of 2011, decided on 26 April 2012, considered a petition for the change of grant of status in Sena Medal from 'distinguished service' to 'gallantry'.

The petitioner was commissioned in the Indian Army on 09 June 1979. On 24 May1984, the petitioner displayed exceptional courage and was able to save life of 10 civil policemen who were surrounded by a mob of about 500 personnel anti-social elements. For this act of bravery, he was awarded Sena Meda. After completing 10 years of service, petitioner got released from Army on 02 November 1989.

The petitioner has contended that recently the Army HQ had made a distinction of Sena Medal (Gallantry) and Sena Medal (Distinguished Service). Based on this distinction, one Sepoy Balwinder Singh was granted a Sena Medal (Gallantry) for the same bravery act whereas petitioner who was the leader of patrol team and showed the same bravery continued to have Sena Medal (Distinguished Service). The matter was taken up his father through proper channel as the petitioner; that the petitioner should also be granted Sena Medal (Gallantry) as he performed the same bravery and valour as was performed by Sepoy Balwinder Singh who has been granted Sena Medal (Gallantry). The petitioner's grievance was that his case had been rejected by the Military Secretary vide letter dated 16 March 2010.

The Tribunal was of the view that to grant or not to grant awards is the privilege of the Government as they are better advised and well versed on the subject; therefore, they are the competent authority to do this exercise. This cannot be subject matter of an appeal before the Tribunal. However, in the present case since the petitioner was the leader of the petrol team, he led the team and charged into the crowed and hit ring leaders and then grappled with two more rioters. This act of the petitioner encouraged the other member of the petrol team in which Sepoy Balwinder Singh was one of them and he displayed bravery emulating his leader/petitioner. Both petitioner and Sepoy Balwinder Singh performed bravery in the same incident, however petitioner's case for granting Sena Medal (Gallantry) has been rejected by the authority whereas Sepoy Balwinder Singh has been granted the same. The decision of the military authorities was considered illogical by the Tribunal.

The Tribunal held taking any decision in the said matter was the privilege of the Selection Committee. The Tribunal remitted the case back to the authority to reconsider the case of the petitioner for grant of Sena Medal (Gallantry) expeditiously.

Refund of outstanding dues

The AFT Regional Bench Kochi in the case of *Col R. K. Nair (Retd) v. Union of India* TA No. 34 of 2010 [WP (C) No. 30636 of 2005 The High Court of Kerala], decided on 25 March 2010, ordered for refund of house rent amounting to Rs. 17,270/- with interest to the petitioner. This amount was paid by the petitioner as house rent for a period from 15 June 1991 to 22 June 1992. The Tribunal directed the respondents to dispense with the Board proceedings, sanction of GOC-in-C Command in original, the pre-scrutiny of the claim by AAO BSO and disburse Rs. 17,270/- with 9% interest to the petitioner, as early as possible, at any rate, within four months from the date of receipt of a copy of the order. After expiry of four months, the Station HQ Pangode, Trivendrum was to file a statement before the Tribunal about the action taken in the matter.

Review petition

The AFT Principal Bench New Delhi, Court No. 2, in the case of *AVM NM Vaishnavi v. Union of India* RA No. 13 of 2012 in OA No. 300 of 2011, decided on 3 April 2012, considered a request for review of the judgment and order dated 23 January 2012.

The applicant contended that the Promotion Board-2011 was held prematurely and there was an organisational bias against the applicant. The respondents stated that applicant was seeking rehearing of the case under the garb of review. He argued that review can only be justified if some contentions have wrongly been noted or new facts have come to knowledge, which were not raised earlier due to unawareness.

Keeping in mind the limited scope of review, the Tribunal held that it was not permissible to rehear a matter decided earlier. It referred the judgment of the Supreme Court in *Kerala State Electricity Board v. Hitech Electrothermics & Hydropower Ltd.*, JT 2005 (7) SC 485 wherein the Court had observed that "in review petition it is not open to the court to re-appreciate the evidence and reach a different conclusion even if that be possible, permitting review petitioner would amount to converting a review petition into an appeal in disguise. Therefore, the review petition was not maintainable". The Tribunal did not find any error apparent on the face of the record and dismissed the review application.

Writ Petition against the order of the Tribunal

The Delhi High Court in the case of *Col A D Nargolkar v. Union of India*, WP (C) 13360 of 2009 and WP (C) 13367 of 2009, decided on 26 April 2011; while considering a bunch of 35 Writ Petitions, dwelled upon the issue whether the Writ Petitions against the decisions/orders passed by the Armed Forces Tribunal are maintainable in the High Court.

The Court noted that a simple revenue matter, pertaining to an entry in the record of rights, commences with a claim before the tehsildar whose decision is amenable to a challenge by way of an appeal either before the Revenue Assistant or an Additional Collector and a further forum of a Revision before the Financial Commissioner. Exhausting the channel of forums available before the Revenue Authorities, an aggrieved party can approach the High Court under its Writ or Supervisory Jurisdiction under Article 226 or Article 227 of the Constitution of India, which writ is heard by a learned Single Judge of the High Court. Further forum of a Writ Appeal or a Letters Patent Appeal is available before a Division Bench and at the top of the pyramid would be a Petition for Special Leave to Appeal before the Supreme Court.

The Delhi High Court commented:

> "The problem of judicial delays resulting from a pyramidical structure of adjudicatory forums has its roots in the concept of the Rule of Law having a feature of independent Judges, free from the control of the Executive, to decide disputes between the State and its citizens. The problem is the result of two conflicting values which society cherishes and has nurtured over the years. The first conflicting value is to secure, in the shortest possible time, the right conferred by law upon the citizen of the State and the second conflicting value is a say, in the adjudicatory process, by an independent Judge.
>
> Whereas the State beckons us, in the instant writ petitions, to sacrifice the value of an independent Judge having a say in the adjudicatory process to resolve a conflict between a member of an Armed Force, subject to the Army Act, the Navy Act and the Air Force Act, and the Force and leave it to the Tribunal constituted under the Armed Forces Tribunal Act 2007 to do the needful; the result being a speedy adjudication of claims, stated to be necessary to maintain discipline in Armed Forces. The protagonists i.e. the writ petitioners state that it would be too heavy a price to pay i.e. speedy justice, if they have to sacrifice an independent Judge having a say in the adjudicatory process."

The High Court considered the question: Whether a writ of error/certiorari or any other writ of the like nature would lie under Article 226 of the Constitution of India against a decision of the Tribunal constituted under the Armed Forces Tribunal Act 2007 and additionally whether a High Court can exercise the power of superintendence over said Tribunal, a power of the High Court under Article 227 of the Constitution of India.

The Court highlighted that neither Article 323A nor Article 323B of the Constitution of India specifically refers to an Armed Force Tribunal, but entry 2 under List-I read with entry 97 of said list would be the safe source of the legislative power to create an Armed Force Tribunal. The Armed Forces Tribunal Bill received the assent of the President of India on the 20 December

2007 and came on the Statute Book as The Armed Forces Tribunal Act, 2007 (Act No. 55 of 2007). In the Statement of Objects and Reasons, the necessity of the legislation was traced to the observations of the Supreme Court in the case of *Prithi Pal Singh Bedi v. Union of India* AIR 1982 SC 1414.

The AFT Act aims to provide, for the adjudication or trial, by Armed Forces Tribunal, of disputes and complaints with respect to commission, appointment, enrolment and conditions of service in respect of persons subject to the Army, Navy and Air Force Act and additionally to provide for appeals arising out of orders, findings or sentences of court martial held under the said three acts. In other words, the Tribunal exercises an appellate jurisdiction (under s. 15 of the AFT Act) with respect to orders, findings or sentences of court martial and exercises original jurisdiction (under s. 14 of the AFT Act) with respect to service disputes.

Further, vide s. 23 of the Act, the Tribunal is not bound by the procedure prescribed by the Code of Civil Procedure 1908 and is free to be guided by its own procedures. Chapter-V, having 2 sections i.e. ss. 30 and 31, deals with Appeals to the Supreme Court. Besides s. 33 of the AFT Act provides for exclusion of jurisdiction of civil courts and reads: " Exclusion of jurisdiction of civil courts - On and from the date from which any jurisdiction, powers and authority becomes exercisable by the Tribunal in relation-to service matters under this Act, no Civil Court shall have, or be entitled to exercise, such jurisdiction, power or authority in relation to those service matters."

The Court observed that the right to file an appeal before the Supreme Court created vide s. 30 of the Act is subject to s. 31 of the Act and this means that the right to appeal to the Supreme Court is not a matter of right but is a matter of discretion to be exercised by the Tribunal upon an application to be filed seeking leave of the Tribunal to file an appeal to the Supreme Court. Further, the discretion of the Tribunal to grant leave is not with respect to every point of law which may have arisen for consideration before the Tribunal, but is limited to a point of law of general public importance. Of course, under s. 31 a power has been vested in the Supreme Court to grant leave to appeal if the Supreme Court would be satisfied that the point raised before it is one which ought to be considered by the Supreme Court. In other words the right to appeal conferred by the Act is a very narrow right and is not akin to a statutory right of appeal, as a matter of right, understood in law.

The High Court considered the issue whether it can exercise jurisdiction under Article 226 and/or Article 227 of the Constitution of India with respect to decisions pronounced by the Armed Forces Tribunal constituted under the Armed Forces Tribunal Act 2007.

The Court observed that the drafters of the Constitution clearly understood that historically, jurisprudence in civilized democracies recognized power of judicial review over decisions and sentences of Court Martial and notwithstanding insertion of Clause 4 in Article 227 of the Constitution of India, the Constituent Assembly recognized the power of judicial superintendence over Court Martial. The High Court referred to the decision of the Supreme

Court in the case of *S N Mukherjee v. Union of India*, AIR 1990 SC 1984, wherein para 41 the Supreme Court observed:

> "Before referring to the relevant provisions of the Act and the Rules it may be mentioned that the Constitution contains certain special provisions in regard to members of the Armed Forces. Article 33 empowers Parliament to make law determining the extent to which any of the rights conferred by Part III shall, in their application to the members of the Armed Forces, be restricted or abrogated so as to ensure the proper discharge of their duties and the maintenance of discipline amongst them. By clause (2) of Article 136 the appellate jurisdiction of this Court under Article 136 of the Constitution has been excluded in relation to any judgment, determination, sentence or order passed or made by any Court or tribunal constituted by or under any law relating to the Armed Forces. Similarly clause (4) of Article 227 denies to the High Courts the power of superintendence over any Court or tribunal constituted by or under any law relating to the Armed Forces. This Court under Article 32 and the High Courts under Article 226 have, however, the power of judicial review in respect of proceedings of courts-martial and the proceedings have resulted in denial of the fundamental rights guaranteed under Part III of the Constitution or if the said proceedings suffer from a jurisdictional error or any error of law apparent on the face of the record."

The Court observed that the Constitutional Bench decision of the Supreme Court reported in *Keshwananda Bharti v. State of Kerala* 1973 (4) SCC 225 laid down the principle of the basic structure of the Constitution being inviolable. Further, the High Court commented that the Rule of Law is essentially a part of the basic structure and the judicial review has been held to be an integral part of the Constitution.

The High Court also observed the historical source of power of supervisory jurisdiction by superior courts in India contained in the decision of the Supreme Court in the case of *Suryadev Rai v. Ram Chandra Rai* 2003 (6) SCC 675. Dealing with the amendment to s. 115 CPC by Act No.46 of 1999 and its impact on the jurisdiction of the High Court under Article 226 and Article 227 of the Constitution of India, the Supreme Court held that the power of the superior court to issue a writ of error was historically treated as the inherent power of superior courts in common law countries. In para 29 of the decision it was held:

> "The Constitution Bench in *L. Chandra Kumar v. Union of India* dealt with the nature of power of judicial review conferred by Article 226 of the Constitution and the power of superintendence conferred by Article 227. It was held that the jurisdiction conferred on the Supreme Court under Article 32 of the Constitution and on the High Courts under Articles 2226 and 227 of the Constitution is a part of the basic structure of the Constitution, forming its integral and essential feature, which cannot be tampered with much less taken away even by constitutional amendment, not to speak of a parliamentary legislation."

The decision in Suryadev Rai's case brings out another interesting facet of the growth of jurisprudence with respect to the power conferred by Article 226 of the Constitution vis-à-vis the power conferred under Article 227 of the Constitution of India. It can be safely said that proceedings under Article 226 are in the exercise of the original jurisdiction of the High Court, proceedings under Article 227 of the Constitution are not original but supervisory proceedings.

In order to summarize the issues, the High Court observed that the position would be that the Armed Forces Tribunal, being manned by personnel appointed by the Executive, albeit in consultation with the Chief Justice of India cannot be said to be truly a judicial review forum as a substitute to High Courts which are constitutional courts and the power of judicial review, being a basic feature of the Constitution, under Article 226 and Article 227 of the Constitution of India is unaffected by the Constitution of the Armed Forces Tribunal. Further, Article 227(4) of the Constitution of India takes away only the administrative supervisory jurisdiction of High Court over the Armed Forces Tribunal and does not impact the judicial supervisory jurisdiction over the Armed Forces Tribunal. Thus, decisions by the Armed Forces Tribunal would be amenable to judicial review by High Court under Article 226 as also Article 227 of the Constitution of India. The Delhi High Court also referred to the similar view taken in the matter by the Division Bench of the Kerala High Court in *Joby Varghese v. Armed Forces Tribunal* 2010 (4) KLT 611.

The Delhi High Court held that the writ petitions against the decisions/ orders passed by the Armed Forces Tribunal are maintainable in the High Court.

3

Judgements: Court Martial

I. Court Martial and General Court Martial

Remission of Punishment

The AFT New Delhi Principal Bench in the case of *Ex Major Rehman Hussain v. Union of India*, TA No. 361 of 2010 [CW (P) No. 4726 of 2007], decided on 8 November 2012, considered a prayer for quashing the proceedings of General Court Martial (GCM).

The applicant was commissioned in the Indian Army on 09 December 1995. In due course, he was posted to Rashtriya Rifles (RR) in Kupwara District of Jammu & Kashmir. On the night of 6-7 October 2004, an incident took place and applicant was charged under ss. 376 (I), 354, 352 of the Ranbir penal Code and section 63 of the Army Act. The GCM found him not guilty of the first and second charge and guilty of third and fourth charge. He was sentenced to be "dismissed from service" on 31 January 2005. The confirming authority by an order dated 31 December 2007 reinstated the petitioner with a loss of five years of seniority for promotion and pension. The applicant also filed a CM No. 8826 of 2007 in the High Court for condonation of delay for filing the writ petition which was accepted by the Court.

The applicant contented that the entire case against him was concocted and therefore, findings and sentence was required to be set aside.

The Tribunal after examining the evidence opined that the GCM had correctly found the applicant/accused guilty of the second charge. On charge No.4 and 5, the Tribunal observed that the applicant had not followed the Standard Operation Procedure (SOP) as laid down by the Army. The SOP mandated that if any raid or search is to be conducted by the Quick Reaction Team, there was a requirement to have an independent witness, preferably a police man or police woman as available, and in the absence of that, a village elder who will witness the proceedings that take place during the search/raid.

The Tribunal was of the opinion that the GCM correctly found the petitioner guilty for charge No. 4 and 5.

Taking into consideration the period of service of the applicant on the date of incident and his record of service before the incident, the Tribunal was of the opinion that the sentence awarded to the applicant was harsh. In order to meet the ends of justice, the Tribunal remitted part of the sentence from five years of loss of seniority for promotion and pension to that of two years of loss of seniority for promotion only.

Severe Punishment

The AFT Principal Bench New Delhi in the case of *Ex Lt Col S S Bedi v. Union of India*, TA No. 246 of 2010 [WP (C) N0. 1824 of 1988], decided on 1 October 2010, considered a prayer against the findings and sentence awarded by the GCM.

The appellant was commissioned in the Army Medical Corps in July 1966. On 3 April 1984, the appellant was posted as medical Specialist at base Hospital, Lucknow. Based on the complaints dated 29 November 1986 made by two women the appellant was given a charge sheet. He was found guilty of having committed an offence under section 69 of the Army Act read with section 354 of the Indian Penal Code. The appellant pleaded not guilty to both the charges. However, the GCM found the appellant guilty of the charges and sentenced him to be cashiered.

The appellant contended that the entire case against him was fabricated. He was convicted merely on conjectures and surmises. The GCM had not appreciated the fact that it was a conspiracy hatched by the nursing staff to falsely implicate the appellant in the plot. The evidence of both the prosecutrix did not inspire confidence since the complaints were lodged after a long gap of alleged incidents, which would imply that it was concocted at the instigation of the nursing staff to falsely implicate the appellant. The procedures as provided in rules right from the stage of attachment of the appellant till the conclusion of the proceedings were not adopted. At the time of attachment of the appellant, no disciplinary proceedings were pending against him and, therefore, such attachment was in utter violation to Army Instruction No. 106/1960. The appellant was deprived of a fair trial as the Centre Commandant, who initiated investigation on the basis of the complaints made by the husbands of the victim women, had no authority to convene the GCM. Further, it being a civil offence, the GCM had no jurisdiction to try the appellant.

The respondents contested that there was ample evidence to prove the culpability of the appellant. Both the victim women made categorical narration of the incidents. They had complained to the higher authorities with regard to the misbehaviour of the appellant on the respective dates when the incident took place. There was no reason to disbelieve the testimony of the victim women. The appellant was not able to prove in what way he was prejudiced from the date of his attachment till the conclusion of the GCM proceedings.

The Tribunal after going through the evidence observed that the evidence of both PWs 2 and 3 remained intact. They had made a categorical narration of the entire incident, as to how the appellant examined them. The facts and the given circumstances proved the manner in which the appellant examined the patients and his motive was apparent as his touching the the private parts of the patients was unnecessary and was not part of the examination. Their testimony did not require any corroboration, as held by the Supreme Court in *Bharwada Bhoginbhai Hirjibhai v. State of Gujarat* (1983(3) SCC 217). The testimony of PWs 2 and 3 lend support to the prosecution version.

The Tribunal relied on the decisions of the Supreme Court in *State of Maharashtra v. Chandraprakash Kewalchand Jain* (1990(1) SCC 550), Karnel Singh v. State of M.P. (1995(5) SCC 518) and Sri Narayan Saha v. Statc of Tripura (2004) 7 SCC 775. In Chandraprakash's case the Supreme Court had held:

> "19. It is time to recall the observations of this Court made not so far back in *Bharwada Bhoginbhai Hirjibhai* (1983(3) SCC 217 at page 224 para 9):
>
> 'In the Indian setting, refusal to act on the testimony of a victim of sexual assault in the absence of corroboration as a rule is adding insult to injury. Why should the evidence of the girl or the woman who complains of rape or sexual molestation be viewed with the aid of spectacles fitted with lenses tinged with doubt, disbelief or suspicion? To do so is to justify the charge of male chauvinism in a male dominated society. We must analyse the argument in support of the need for corroboration and subject it to relentless and remorseless cross examination. And we must do so with a logical, and not an opinionated, eye in the light of probabilities with our feet firmly planted on the soil of India and with our eyes focused on the Indian horizon. We must not be swept off the feet by the approach made in the western world which has its own social milieu, its own social mores, its own permissive values, and its own code of life. Corroboration may be considered essential to establish a sexual offence in the backdrop of the social ecology of the western world. It is wholly unnecessary to import the said concept on a turnkey basis and to transplant it on the Indian soil regardless of the altogether different atmosphere, attitudes, mores, responses of the Indian society, and its profile. The identities of the two worlds are different. The solution of problems cannot therefore be identical.'
>
> Proceeding further the Court said: (SCC pp. 225-26, para 10):
>
> 'Without the fear of making too wide a statement, or of overstating the case, it can be said that rarely will a girl or a woman in India make false allegations of sexual assault....The statement is generally true in the context of the urban as also rural society. It is also by and large true in the context of the sophisticated, not so sophisticated, and unsophisticated society. Only very rarely can one conceivably come

across an exception or two and that too possibly from amongst the urban elites. Because (1) A girl or a woman in the tradition-bound non-permissive society of India would be extremely reluctant even to admit that any incident which is likely to reflect on her chastity had ever occurred. (2) She would be conscious of the danger of being ostracized by the society or being looked down by the society including by her own family members, relatives, friends and neighbours. (3) She would have to brave the whole world. (4) She would face the risk of losing the love and respect of her own husband and near relatives, and of her matrimonial home and happiness being shattered. (5) If she is unmarried, she would apprehend that it would be difficult to secure an alliance with a suitable match from a respectable or an acceptable family. (6) it would almost inevitably and almost invariably result in mental torture and suffering to herself. (7) The fear of being taunted by others will always haunt her. (8) She would feel extremely embarrassed in relating the incident to others being overpowered by a feeling of shame on account of the upbringing in a tradition-bound society where by and large sex is taboo. (9) The natural inclination would be to avoid giving publicity to the incident lest the family name and family honour is brought into controversy. (10) The parents of an unmarried girl as also the husband and members of the husband's family of a married woman, would also more often than not, want to avoid publicity on account of the fear of social stigma on the family name and family honour. (11) The fear of the victim herself being considered to be promiscuous or in some way responsible for the incident regardless of her innocence. (12) The reluctance to face interrogation by the investigating agency, to face the court, to face the cross examination by counsel for the culprit, and the risk of being disbelieved, acts as a deterrent.'"

The Tribunal observed that that the burden of establishing the mala fide was very heavy on the person who alleges it. Here, though the allegation of mala fide was made, the appellant has not been able to prove it. Referring to section 149 of the Army Act, the Tribunal was of the opinion that the irregularities at the pre-trial stage would not vitiate the trial. Further, the appellant/accused was rightly convicted under section 69 of the Army Act read with section 354 IPC.

The Tribunal observed that the appellant/accused had served the Army for about 20 years as a Medical Specialist. There was no other complaint in the past of a similar nature against him and his conduct was not exposed to activities of similar nature. Both the victims had made allegations only at a subsequent stage, long after the alleged incidents, when they had come for check up again. Their silence mitigated the seriousness of the allegations. No cogent and convincing reason had been stated as to their silence. In the given circumstances, the punishment of cashiering from service was not only excessive and disproportionate, but is also one which was not to be imposed under section 69 of the Army Act read with section 354 IPC. The Tribunal confirmed the conviction, but converted the sentence of cashiering from service into fine of Rs. 50000/- for the offences. The appellant was directed to deposit the fine before the GCM within four weeks and in default, to undergo RI for ten days. The Tribunal ordered that the appellant/accused would be deemed to be discharged from the date of his cashiering and shall be entitled to pension and other retirement benefits.

Prosecution based on unreliable evidence

The AFT Principal Bench New Delhi in the case of *Col Harjinder Singh Lamba v. Union of India*, TA No. 633 of 2009 [WP (C) No. 2626 of 2000], decided on 24 February 2011, considered a prayer to set aside the findings and sentence of the GCM.

The appellant joined the Army Service Corps (ASC) on 12 January 1969. In January 1992, while he was posted to ASC Battalion, a complaint against the appellant and one of his subordinate for alleged misuse of government transport was made. The appellant and another officer were attached to HQ Military Brigade for disciplinary action. The GCM did not find him guilty of any charge. However, the convening officer during the revision of GCM proceedings remanded the case for fresh consideration of charges 1 to 3. The GCM, on revision held the appellant guilty of having committed the offence under section 52 (f) Army Act read with section 34 of the Indian Penal Code and sentenced him (i) to forfeit five years service for the purpose of pension and (ii) to be severely reprimanded. The appellant's post confirmation petition was rejected by the Central Government on 8 March 1996.

The respondents contested the appeal and submitted that the service transports were illegally used to carry fresh rations and meat for troops in contravention to the conditions provided in the short term agreement and in the agreement of supply order, which caused loss to the Government. Further, the appellant ordered adjustment of fresh rations issued to the units and made payment to the contractor at higher rates with mala fide intention. The punishments awarded to the appellant were commensurate with the gravity of the offence.

The Tribunal, before examining the evidence, considered the legal position with regard to "common intention" to find out whether the appellant was vicariously liable for the offence charged against him. The term common intention implies a pre-arranged plan. The Tribunal referred to the case of *Ramaswamy Ayyangar v. State of Tamil Nadu* (1976(3) SCC 779), where it was observed by the apex Court that the essence of s. 34 IPC is simultaneous consensus of the minds of persons participating in the criminal action to bring about a particular result. It is true that to attract s. 34, no overt act is needed on the part of the accused if he shares the common intention with others anticipating in respect of the ultimate criminal act, which may be done by any one of the accused sharing such intention. Further, in *Dani Singh v. State of Bihar* 2004(13) SCC 203, the apex Court observed:

> "20. 'Common intention' implies pre-arranged plan and acting in concert pursuant to the prearranged plan. Under this section a pre-concert in the sense of a distinct previous plan is not necessary to be proved. The common intention to bring about a particular result may well develop on the spot as between a number of persons, with reference to the facts of the case and circumstances of the situation. Though common intention may develop on the spot, it must, however, be anterior in point of time to the commission of offence showing a prearranged plan and prior concert."

The Tribunal observed that the evidence was vague and from the statements of a few witnesses, connivance of the appellant could not be construed. Further, there were discrepancies of material nature which did not only affect the core of the prosecution case, but affected the trustworthiness of these witnesses. With regard to the credibility of the witnesses, the Tribunal referred the decision of the Supreme Court in *State of Uttar Pradesh v. M.K Anthony* 1985(1) SCC 505:

"10. While appreciating the evidence of a witness, the approach must be whether the evidence of the witness read as a whole appears to have a ring of truth. Once that impression is formed, it is undoubtedly necessary for the court to scrutinise the evidence more particularly keeping in view the deficiencies, drawbacks and infirmities pointed out in the evidence as a whole and evaluate them to find out whether it is against the general tenor of the evidence given by the witness and whether the earlier evaluation of the evidence is shaken as to render it unworthy of belief. Minor discrepancies on trivial matters not touching the core of the case, hyper-technical approach by taking sentences torn out of context here or there from the evidence, attaching importance to some technical error committed by the investigating officer not going to the root of the matter would not ordinarily permit rejection of the evidence as a whole. If the court before whom the witness gives evidence had the opportunity to form the opinion about the general tenor of evidence given by the witness, the appellate court which had not this benefit will have to attach due weight to the appreciation of evidence by the trial court and unless there are reasons weighty and formidable it would not be proper to reject the evidence on the ground of minor variations or infirmities in the matter of trivial details. Even honest and truthful witnesses may differ in some details unrelated to the main incident because power of observation, retention and reproduction differ with individuals. Cross-examination is an unequal duel between a rustic and refined lawyer."

The Tribunal set aside the findings and sentence awarded by the GCM and ordered that appellant would be entitled to all pensionary benefits taking into account his total period of service.

Disproportionate punishment

The AFT Principal Bench New Delhi in the case of *Gp Capt SPS Rajkumar v. Union of India*, TA No. 122 of 2010 [WP (C) No. 2015 of 2004, Delhi High Court], decided on 22 February 2011, considered the quantum of punishment awarded by the GCM.

The appellant joined the Air Force as a commissioned officer in the logistics branch. In 1998, certain allegations of large scale impropriety were made against the appellant. A charge sheet containing nine charges was issue to the appellant and all the charges pertained to improper purchase procedure and financial impropriety. He was tried by a GCM, which found the appellant guilty of four charges and sentenced him to forfeiture of two years seniority and severe reprimand. By order dated 13 April 2000, the convening authority, on review, ordered for re-assembly of the GCM for the purpose of revision of sentence. Thereafter, the GCM re-assembled and passed a fresh sentence of dismissal and revoked the earlier sentence. The Chief of Air Staff confirmed the findings and sentence. The Central Government rejected the post confirmation petition under s. 161(2) of the Air Force Act, 1950.

When challenged, a Division Bench of the Delhi High Court quashed the GCM proceedings on the ground that the Judge Advocate was junior in rank. Ultimately, the matter was brought before the Supreme Court in civil appeal by both sides. While allowing the appeal filed by the Government, the Supreme Court observed that the High Court was not justified in interfering with the conclusions of the GCM and set aside the order. The civil appeal of the appellant was dismissed, without deciding on the issue of sentence.

The Tribunal observed that the charges in which the guilt of the appellant was established, pertained to (i) improperly effecting purchase of various items, (ii) improperly directing a subordinate to sign Inspection Note knowing well that a junior warrant officer was not authorised to sign the said note, (iii) with intent to cause wrongful loss to Air Force to the extent of approximately Rs.7.6 lakhs, issued directions for return of two trucks of consignment as "wrongly received hence returned back", without ensuring that the corresponding entries in the consignor's copies of the said note were also deleted, leading to full payment to the supplier, and (iv) failure to ensure that proper local purchase procedure, as stipulated in IAP 1501 and Command Staff Instructions (Logistics) 1/98 of inviting quotations was being followed by Local Purchase Section. However, no allegations were attributed against the appellant of having misappropriated any amount or taken the benefits while effecting such purchases. The allegations were of improperly exercising his powers.

The Tribunal commented that the question of sentence has to be determined not with reference to the volume or character of evidence adduced by the prosecution in support of its case, but with reference to the fact whether there are any extenuating circumstances which can be said to mitigate the enormity of the crime. If the Court was satisfied that there are such mitigating circumstances, only then it would be justified in imposing lesser sentences provided by the law. In other words, the nature of the proof has nothing to do with the character of punishment. The nature of the proof can only bear the question of conviction. In this case, there is no dispute with regard to the fact that the conviction of the appellant was upheld by the Supreme Court.

The Tribunal relied upon the decision of the Supreme Court in the case of *Vadivelu Thevar v. State of Madras* (AIR 1957 SC 614). In the absence of the allegation of having the appellant committed any misappropriation or embezzlement, no severity can be attached. The sentence must commensurate with the gravity of the offence. In judging the adequacy of a sentence, the nature of the offence, the circumstances of its commission, the age and character of the offender, injury to individual or the society, effect of punishment on offender, are some amongst many other factors which should be ordinarily taken into consideration by the courts (*R. Venkatakrishnan v. Central Bureau of Investigation,* AIR 2010 SC 1812).

The Tribunal also referred the decision of the Supreme Court in *Ranjit Thakur v. Union of India* 1987(4) SCC 611, where in it was observed by the Court:

> "Judicial review, generally speaking, is not directed against a decision but is directed against the "decision-making process". The question of choice and quantum of punishment is within the jurisdiction and discretion of the court-martial. But the sentence has to suit the offence and the offender. It should not be vindictive or unduly harsh. It should not be so disproportionate to the offence as to shock the conscience and amount in itself to conclusive evidence of bias. The doctrine of proportionality, as part of the concept of judicial review, would ensure that even on an aspect which is, otherwise, within the exclusive province of the court martial, if the decision of the court even as to sentence is an outrageous defiance of logic, then the sentence would not be immune from correction. Irrationality and perversity are recognised grounds of judicial review. In the present case the punishment is so strikingly disproportionate as to call for and justify interference. Therefore, the impugned proceedings of the summary court-martial and the consequent order and sentence are quashed. The appellant is entitled to and shall be reinstated with all monetary and service benefits."
>
> The Tribunal observed that since no motive was proved against the appellant in making the purchase orders, the GCM was not justified in reviewing its earlier order. Further, no mala fide intentions were attributed against the appellant in regard to exercising his powers. In the given circumstances, the sentence awarded by the GCM was commensurate to the guilt proved against the appellant and that would meet the ends of justice.

The Tribunal sentenced the appellant for the offence under section 65 of the Air Force Act (a) to forfeit three years service for the purpose of pension; (b) to forfeit seniority in the rank for two years; and (c) to be severely reprimanded;

with the order that the appellant shall be entitled for the pensionary benefits from the date of the impugned order of the GCM.

No interference in punishment

The AFT New Delhi Principal Bench in *Col Harvinder Singh Kohli v. Union of India*, TA No. 254 of 2009 [WP (C) No. 7827 of 2009], decided on 11 January 2010, declined to interfere with the sentence of dismissal awarded to the petitioner by GCM.

In this case, five charges were levied against the petitioner for having committed civil offence i.e. criminal conspiracy whereby false reporting of an encounter for the purposes of bringing laurels to his unit and also making false statement about that killing, an offence under section 57(a) Army Act, read with section 34 IPC. It was alleged that the petitioner also sent false report to senior officers about the killing which was prejudicial to the good order and military discipline. The petitioner pleaded guilty to all the five charges and was awarded punishment of dismissal from service by the GCM. His statutory petition under section 164 (2) of the Army Act was rejected by the government.

The petitioner contended that while his unit was engaged in anti-insurgency operations, the Brigade Commander pressurised him to show few encounter killing so as to boost the image of the commander and also to bring laurels to the unit. The petitioner further stated that under extreme pressure from his superior, a fake encounter was designed. A false report about the five encounter killing was submitted to ensure the compliance of the directions of his superiors. Based on the anonymous complaint about fake encounter, the petitioner was made scapegoat whereas the entire scheme was hatched by his brigade commander. Further the statutory Army Rule 57 (a) and 63 was not complied during his trial by GCM.

The Tribunal held that, "such act on the part of the petitioner was inconsistent with the interest of military service and not befitting the status, position and dignity of the Commanding Officer. Whether he ensured false encounter on the instructions of senior officers, would be immaterial....The petitioner in the capacity of Commanding Officer, did not maintain absolute integrity, devotion to duty and did an act complained of bears forbidden quality or character.... He being the Commanding Officer was accountable for his acts or omissions and not to have been swayed by the wrongful command of his seniors. He was also under obligation not to succumb to the illegal command of senior to prepare forge papers showing killing of five militants....He cannot take the plea that he was faithfully discharging the orders of his superiors."

The Tribunal further held that the punishment of dismissal awarded by the GCM cannot be characterized as disproportionate and shocking.... undue sympathy to impose inadequate sentence would do more harm to the military discipline and justice system....Moreover the petitioner being the

Commanding Officer he was required to be more honest towards his duties and the personnel attached with him. He cannot claim parity with his senior or the subordinate for the said offence in which they are said to be involved. They were not on equal pedestal and so he cannot be treated at par with them in the award of sentence. The Tribunal dismissed the petition.

Evidence in GCM

The AFT Principal Bench New Delhi in the case of *Lt Col P. Ahluwalia v. Union of India*, TA No. 266 of 2009 [WP (C) No. 6577 of 2003], decided on 15 March 2010, considered an appeal under section 15 of Armed Forces Tribunal Act. The appellant contended that he was falsely framed in the case. and prayed for quashing the findings and sentence of the GCM including the orders passed by the GOC-in-C, HQs Western Command, confirming the sentence.

The petitioner was admitted to Base Hospital Delhi Cantt for treatment of dysentery where he was also found having mild hypertension. A Medical Classification Board was held and he was place in low medical category and discharged from the hospital. The petitioner was tried under section 45 of the Army Act for offering gratification as a motive for destruction of his (petitioner's) medical board proceedings, placing him in low medical category.

The Tribunal relied upon the opinion of the Supreme Court as to what extent a court can rely upon the evidence of an approver. The Tribunal held: "In the facts and circumstances of this case, the GCM erred in accepting the testimony of both the witnesses without corroboration." The Tribunal set aside the orders of the GCM and the confirmation order of the convening authority. It ordered that the appellant shall be deemed to be in service from the date of his dismissal till he attains the age of superannuation. He will be entitled for all back wages for interregnum period as well as pensionary benefits.

Joint trial: confession of co-accused not admissible as evidence

The AFT New Delhi Principal Bench in *Ex Sepoy (PANK) Mahender Singh v. Union of India*, in TA No. 239 of 2009 [WP (C) No. 3134 of 1989], decided on 15 January 2010, considered the challenge against the order passed by the GCM.

It was contended by the petitioner that the case against him was fabricated to implicate him in a conspiracy to allow a smuggler to cross the international border. He was convicted be the GCM without any evidence against him. The testimony of a co-accused was accepted as evidence which is not acceptable under the law. The accused cannot appear as a witness in the same case, where he was jointly tried with the co-accused. His position in such a situation would not be that of an approver. Further, procedural requirements as envisaged under Army Rules 22 and 97(2) were not adhered to by the Commanding Officer. He was not given legal assistance by providing the service of a civil lawyer. On the other hand, the prosecution was represented by a competent civil lawyer and the trial was thus unfair.

The Tribunal held that under Army Rule 35, it is the discretion of the GCM to amalgamate the cases against the accused persons if they relate to the same incident, provided their interest is not inconsistent with each other. The only requirement that the GCM has to satisfy is that the accused is not prejudicially affected and that it is expedient to amalgamate the cases. The Tribunal also considered the instruction issued by the Army for the guidance of the officers convening court martial, wherein joint trial of the co-accused, who has conflicting interest both as a witness and as an accused in the same trial, has been disapproved. The guidelines read as follows:

> "4. If in any case two or more persons are suspected of complicity in an offence, and it is found necessary to call one of these as a witness for the prosecution against the other or others charged in connection with the offence, one of two courses must be taken, either –
>
> (a) Proceedings against him must be abandoned and any charge therein already preferred against him dismissed; or
>
> (b) Steps must be taken to ensure that the case against him is disposed of summarily or tried by court martial, before the trial of persons concerned against whom he is to give evidence, and that he is, only tendered as a witness when he has already been acquitted or convicted.
>
> In all such cases the circumstances and the course proposed should be fully set out in a covering letter to the convening officer."

The Tribunal observed that one of the co-accused had made a confessional statement and disclosed the name of the petitioner. If that is read as evidence, it would materially affect the interest of the petitioner. Moreover, a co-accused cannot appear as a witness against his own cause.

The Tribunal observed that in a joint trial of all the three accused and one appeared as a witness against another. The testimony of the accomplice was taken into account by the GCM. At the very threshold, it suffers from the infirmity as they are also facing trial in the case. It causes certain doubts as to the truthfulness and such statement of the accomplice would not lend support so far as guilt against the co-accused is concerned. The testimony of the accomplice cannot be admissible unless there are other circumstances or evidence from an independent source lending assurance to the mind of the GCM that the evidence adduced by the accomplice is true as against another accused and it would be safe to act on the testimony of the accomplice. No independent witness was examined by the prosecution. Therefore, such a statement made by the accomplice cannot be read in evidence.

The Tribunal relied upon the Supreme Court's decision in *Kashmiri Singh v. State of Madhya Pradesh* AIR 1952 SC 159: "confession of a co-accused is not substantive evidence against other accused persons at the trial, but could be used for lending assurance if there is other substantive evidence to be utilised or acted upon." The Tribunal also commented on the right of a fair trial to an accused. During the trial by the GCM, the prosecution was assisted by a competent civil lawyer. On the other hand, the petitioner was not given a fair trial by providing a civil lawyer to defend him. The Tribunal referred to the observation made by the Supreme Court in *Ranchod Mathur Wasawa v. State of Gujarat*, AIR 1974 SC 1146: "indigent should never be a ground for denial of equal justice. Attention should be paid to appoint competent advocates equal to holding the complex cases – not patronizing gestures to raw entrants to the war."

The Tribunal set aside the order of GCM and ordered that the petitioner shall be deemed to have been reinstated in service from the date of his dismissal and will be entitled to all back wages till he attained the age of superannuation and the period of interregnum shall be counted for pensionary benefits.

Inadequate legal assistance

The AFT Regional Bench Lucknow in the case of *Ex Lt Col Ranjodg Singh v. Union of India*, TA No. 68 of 2010, decided on 5 October 2010, considered two connected cases relating to trial by GCM.

The appellant was tried by a GCM on three separate charges under s. 69 of the Army Act read with s. 120B of the IPC, for taking illegal gratification form a civilian. The second charge was under s. 69 of the Army Act read with s. 7 of the Prevention of Corruption Act, 1988 for attempting to obtain illegal gratification of Rs One lakh. The third charge was also under s. 69 of the Army Act read with s. 7 of the Prevention of Corruption Act, 1988 for attempting to obtain illegal gratification of Rs Fifteen thousands from Hav V Kumar. The appellant was convicted by the GCM and awarded sentence of five years RI and cashiering. The pre- and post-confirmation petitions filed by him were rejected. The appellant had filed a WP in the High Court of Uttarakhand, which were transferred to the Tribunal under s. 34 of the AFT Act and converted as an appeal.

The appellant contested that the GCM was not properly constituted, and out of five members constituting the court, two of them were holding the rank of Major, whereas the appellant was holding the rank of substantive Lt Col, thus in violation of Army Rule 40. The appellant placed his reliance of the Gazette Notification dated 23/29 September 2009, by which he was promoted to the rank of Lt Col. During the pendency of the case, the entry in the said Gazette notification relating to the appellant was cancelled.

The Tribunal observed that court martial was prejudiced for want of suitable defending officer or lawyer and consequently witness could not be cross examined. Further, the match with the prosecution represented by a practicing lawyer and the appellant by an unqualified defending officer was unequal.

The Tribunal held that in this case though irregularities have been conducted, the evidence is available and the prosecution witnesses can be recalled for cross examination. Thus, retrial would not be a futile exercise.

The Tribunal set aside the conviction and sentence awarded by the GCM, and authorized re-trial of appellant by court martial subject to the conditions in the proviso to sub-section 2 of s. 16 of the AFT Act. It further directed that in view of the fact that the conviction and sentence was set aside, the appellant would be reinstated in the service with consequential benefits admissible in law. However, it would be open to the respondent to suspend the appellant in accordance with law.

Violation of Army Rule 150

The AFT Regional Bench Kochi, in *Capt Tony George v. Union of India*, TA No. 164 of 2010 [WP (C) No. 6522 of 2001 of High Court Delhi and TA No. 736 of 2009 of AFT New Delhi], decided on 28 October 2010, considered challenges to the proceedings and punishment awarded by the GCM.

The petitioner was found guilty of an offence of perjury punishable under s. 60 of the Army Act and convicted. The GCM awarded a sentence of cashiering which was commuted as dismissal by the confirming authority. The petitioner had challenged the convening order of GCM, charge sheet under Army Rule 37 and the conviction and penalty imposed on him by the GCM as confirmed by the competent authority on 16 April 1987. It was also contended that the convening order of the GCM was not signed by the General Officer Commanding, but by a junior officer, of the rank of Major and hence there is violation of mandatory provisions contained in section 109 of the Army Act read with Army Rules 37. The petitioner sought reinstatement in service with full service benefits and compensation for malicious prosecution, loss of promotion, etc.

The Tribunal observed that the facts and circumstances stated in the case clearly showed that the GCM against the petitioner was held without any valid order or a report as provided under Army Rule 150 or any order by the competent Military Authority and that was the reason why the respondents were finding it shy to fight out this case on merits.

The procedure to take action for offence under section 60 of the Army Act is provided under Army Rule 150. It is clear that the Court Martial has to form an opinion that there is ground for enquiring into the offence specified in section 60. Even if the court martial finds that a witness has given false evidence, it is not mandatory that it should recommend action against that person. The Rule confers discretion on the GCM either to proceed as provided in the rules or to drop further proceedings. A reading of sub-rule (1) of Rule 150 shows that the discretion to the military authority is only in which manner such a person shall be proceeded. The military authority may proceed under sections 80, 83, 84, 85 or proceed with his trial by a court martial. There is absolutely nothing in the rule to indicate that apart from court martial any other authority is conferred with the power to recommend action against a witness for giving false evidence. The provisions of sub-rule (3) of Rule 150 are also relevant. Sub-rule (3) deals with the case of a witness who is not subjected to Army Act, Air Force Act or Navy Act; and in such a case, a written complaint is to be filed before the nearest Magistrate by the presiding officer of the Court Martial.

The Tribunal referred to the general principles laid down by the Supreme Court in *Patel Laljibhai Somabhai v. State of Gujarat*, (1971) 2 SCC 376, *Santokh Singh v. Izhar Hussain*, (1973) 2 SCC 406, and *Surjit Singh v. Balbir Singh*, (1996) 3 SCC 533, relating to section 195 of the Cr PC, which is applicable while interpreting Army Rules 150.

The Tribunal observed that the plain meaning of Army Rule 150 is clear. It is only the court martial in which a person gave false evidence can form an opinion as to whether the evidence given is false or not and forward a report to the military authority. So, there is absolutely no merit in the contention raised by the respondents that any authority can make or pass an order to prosecute a witness for giving false evidence in a court martial. We hold that the provisions of Rule 150 are mandatory and the military authority can initiate action for giving false evidence only on receipt of a report forwarded by the Court Martial before which the person was examined as witness, as contemplated under Rule 150 of the Army Rules. In this case, no such report was forwarded by the GCM and hence the convening order to court martial the petitioner for giving false evidence is without jurisdiction and illegal. The Tribunal also observed that there was violation of mandatory provisions contained in section 109 of the Army Act and Army Rules 37 and trial of the petitioner by the GCM has vitiated.

The respondent in support of their argument placed reliance on a common order dated 2 July 2010 by the Armed Forces Tribunal Regional Bench Jaipur in *Ex. Hav Suresh Kumar Yadav v. Union of India and others* (T.A.No.99 of 2009). The Jaipur Bench has held that when Army personnel convicted by a Court Martial file an appeal under s. 164(2) of the Act before the competent authority and the authority decides the appeal, he cannot file an appeal under s. 15 of the Armed Forces Tribunal Act.

The Tribunal did not agree with the above view taken by the Jaipur Bench. It endorsed:

> In the book, "Armed Forces Tribunal" by Wing Commander, Dr. UC Jha, at page 78, the learned author has stated as follows: "Remedies available before confirmation and after confirmation in Section 164 of the Army Act do not afford any right to an affected person. In fact, Section 164 defines the powers of military authorities in relation to a court martial proceeding. The absence of even one appeal with power to review the findings and sentence of a court martial has been a lacuna in the Indian military legal system until recently."
>
> We also agree with the view expressed by the learned author.

The Tribunal set aside the finding and sentence awarded by the GCM. The Tribunal observed that it was not possible to order reinstatement, as even if the petitioner continued in service without any break, by this time he would have retired. It therefore ordered that the petitioner to be treated on duty throughout without any break or suspension, and paid the salary and other allowances admissible to a person who is on actual duty till superannuation He would also be entitled to the arrears of pension from the date of superannuation. The arrears of salary, allowances and pension after adjusting the amounts, if any, already disbursed shall be paid to the petitioner within six months from the date of receipt of a copy of this order failing which each month's arrears shall carry interest @ 9% p.a. from the date on which it fell due till the date of payment.

Mitigation of punishment

The Armed Forces Tribunal New Delhi Principal Bench in the case of *Beant Singh v. Union of India*, TA No. 503 of 2009 [WP (C) No. 772 of 2004, Delhi High Court], decided on 2 May 2011, considered a prayer where two equally placed individuals were awarded different punishments for similar offence.

The petitioner challenged the GCM proceedings, whereby he was held guilty of having committed the offence under section 52(f) of the Army Act on nine counts for placing supply orders with intent to defraud, in contravention to the Standard Operating Procedures (SOP) issued by the CWE, Agra and sentenced to (i) undergo rigorous imprisonment for one year and (ii) to be cashiered. Both his pre- and post-confirmation petitions ended in rejection. The writ petition was transferred to the AFT and treated as an appeal under section 15 of the Armed Forces Tribunal Act, 2007.

The appellant contended that he was falsely implicated into the charges for violating the Standard Operating Procedures (SOP) dated 26 June 1996. Further, the findings of the court martial were without appreciating the evidence on record. The court martial was in violation of the principles of natural justice, in that the appellant was not provided a defending officer of his choice thereby violating Army Rule 95, denied the opportunity of being represented by a counsel of his choice in terms of Army Rule 97 and denied the mandatory "fair trial" as envisaged under Article 21 of the Constitution.

The respondents contested that the appellant, while posted as GE (East) Agra, manipulated the laid down instructions in the SOP in such a manner so as to place supply orders for procurement of stores on DGS&D rate contract without the approval of the competent authority with intent to defraud. The appellant was provided full opportunity to defend his case. No objection, whatsoever, was made by him with regard to the appointment of the defending officer.

The Tribunal observed that in identically placed circumstances, GE (West) was favoured by awarding minor punishment, whereas and the appellant, GE (East), was given severe punishment. Mitigating circumstances being similar, the appellant also should have been awarded only a minor punishment as was done in the case of GE (West). While awarding sentence, the GCM should have taken into account the mitigating circumstances viz. (i) the SOP dated 26 June 1996 was not strictly adhered to by GE (West); (ii) only a minor punishment was awarded to GE (West), who had also violated the SOP; (iii) in the facts and circumstances of the case, when CWE had lifted all restrictions imposed on the power of making supply orders, the appellant placed supply orders; and (iv) on objection, the appellant cancelled the supply orders.

The Tribunal cited the decision of the Supreme Court in *Bachan Singh v. State of Punjab* 1980(2) SCC 684 relating to the mitigating circumstances which should be given weight in the determination of sentence:

"209. There are numerous other circumstances justifying the passing of the lighter sentence; as there are countervailing circumstances of aggravation. 'We cannot obviously feed into a judicial computer all such situations since they are astrological imponderables in an imperfect and undulating society.' Nonetheless, it cannot be overemphasised that the scope and concept of mitigating factors in the area of death penalty must receive a liberal and expansive construction by the courts in accord with the sentencing policy writ large in Section 354(3). ...."

The Tribunal remanded the case to the government to reconsider the mitigating circumstances, including the sentence awarded to GE (W) Agra, while awarding the sentence to the appellant.

Harsh punishment

The AFT New Delhi Principal Bench in *Ex Major Rehman Hussain v. Union of India* TA No. 361 of 2010 [CWP No. 4726 of 2007, Delhi High Court], decided on 8 November 2012, considered the proceedings of a GCM.

The petitioner, while posted to Rashtriya Rifles (RR) was charged for civil offence relating an incident which took place on the night of 6-7 October 2004. The charges related to the offence of rape, using criminal force to a woman with intent to outrage her modesty, using criminal force, and act prejudicial to good order and military discipline. The GCM in its findings found him not guilty of the first and second charge and guilty of third and fourth charge. He was sentenced to be "dismissed from service" on 31 January 2005. However, on 31 December 2007, the Confirming Authority reinstated the petitioner with a loss of five years of seniority for promotion and pension.

The Tribunal was of the opinion that the GCM correctly found the petitioner guilty for charges, and therefore declined to interfere in the same. However, taking into consideration the period of service of the petitioner on the date of incident as also his record of service before the incident, the Tribunal was of the opinion that the sentence awarded to him was harsh. Under the powers of s. 15(6) of the Armed Forces Tribunal Act, 2007, it held that ends of justice would be met by remitting part of the sentence from five years of loss of seniority for promotion and pension to that of two years of loss of seniority for promotion only. The Tribunal accordingly directed that the punishment of the petitioner be reduced to two years loss of seniority for promotion only.

Inadequate evidence

The AFT Regional Bench Kochi in the case of *Dhirendra Kumar Singh v. The Chief of Naval Staff*, TA No. 140 of 2010 [WP No.24469 of 2000, AP High Court] decided on 8 November 2010, considered challenges to the order of the Court Martial.

On 04 June 1988 at about 1920 hours, the Branch Manager of Andhra Bank Extension Counter situated at Utility Complex of INS Virbahu closed the Bank transactions of the day. While he was settling accounts along with Cashier, he noticed two person entered into the Bank armed with country-made pistol wearing coloured helmet by lifting half closed shutter one of them entered stating that he wanted to open an account in the bank. The third person entered later and the three accused threatened the Manager and the Cashier of Andhra Bank Extension Counter, INS Virbahu, at gun point and got the Iron safe opened and put the money in their bag and locked up the bank officials in the safe room and escaped on unnumbered metallic blue scooter. The total amount of the loot as reported by the bank was Rs. 2.54 lakhs.

A FIR was lodged by the bank at police station. The Bank Manager made a statement before the Police that he could not see the identity of the person by reason of the helmets and masks. In the FIR also except for general description there were no clues as to the identity of the accused. The matter was investigated by the civil as well the naval police. The petitioner was finally handed over to the civil police on 12 August 1998. Thereafter, the petitioner was remanded to the judicial custody by the Metropolitan Magistrate. After the cognizance of the offence was taken by the magistrate, and the charge-sheet was filed, the Commissioner of Police wrote to the Flag Officer to take over the case.

The petitioner was tried by a Court Martial on 6 July 2000 for offences under section 392 of the Indian Penal Code read with section 77(2) of the Navy Act 1957, section 342 IPC read with section 77(2) of the Navy Act 1957, and under section 60(a) of the Navy Act, 1957. He was convicted and sentenced to 10 years RI and dismissal from service. The petitioner preferred a judicial review under the Navy Act, and the respondent while confirming the conviction, reduced the sentence to 96 calendar months of RI and also confirmed the order of dismissal and other punishments like forfeiture of pay and allowance for 29 days and reduction in rank to Sea-1.

The Petitioner contended that the transfer of the case from the civil court to the Court Martial was not in accordance with law. In addition, the identification parade conducted by the Magistrate was not in accordance with law. Further the court martial was not constituted according section 97(11) of the Navy Act 1957 and the prosecution has not been able to prove his guilt.

The Tribunal observed that the court martial was constituted properly. The Tribunal examined the evidence and set aside the conviction and sentence against the petitioner by the Court Martial. The Tribunal ordered the acquittal of the petitioner with the direction that the period of arrest till the date of sentence by the Court Martial shall be counted for the qualifying service to enable the petitioner to get his pension. The petitioner will not be entitled to any monetary benefits for the said interregnum period except the same is counted for qualifying service for getting pension. The petitioner was deemed to have been retired from service with effect from 3 May 2004 on completion of qualifying service required for pension. The amount of Rs. 5,000/- recovered from the petitioner, which was deposited in Canara Bank, Kamadhenu Deposit Account was to be returned to the petitioner with accrued interest after the appeal time is over.

Co-accused

The AFT Regional Bench Chennai in the case of *Umesh Kumar Singh v. Union of India*, TA No. 11 of 2011 [WP No. 21810 of 2000, High Court of Andhra Pradesh], decided on 5 January 2012, considered an appeal against the conviction by the Court Martial.

The applicant joined the Navy as Radio Operator (Special), First Class, at INS Circars, Visakhapatnam. He got married at the age of 23 years in May 1997. Under the Naval Regulations, the applicant was not entitled to have his spouse along with him till he attains the age of 25 years. The applicant was suffering from fits. The applicant while undergoing treatment as an in-patient in INS Kalyani Hospital was discharged on 24 July 1998 at the instance of the Naval Police. The applicant was handed over to the Civil Police. He was beaten and ill-treated while in custody of the Police both Civil and Naval. He was shown as arrested on 30 July 1998 by the Civil Police and was produced before the Magistrate and was lodged in Central Jail, Visakhapatnam and was under remand till 01 January 1999.

The Commissioner of Police, Visakhapatnam by letter dated 28 October 1998 advised the Flag Officer, Commanding-in-Chief, Eastern Naval Command, Visakhapatnam, the applicant and other two accused could be tried by Court Martial. A preliminary charge sheet in the case was filed on 26 September 1998 before the VIII Metropolitan Magistrate, Visakhapatnam. No part of the amount of Rs. 2.54 lakh was recovered from the applicant and the identity of the applicant as one of the accused in the alleged Bank robbery could not be established.

The applicant was issued with a charge sheet dated 29 June 1999. The Charge sheet stated that the applicant along with accomplices namely Dhirendra Kumar Singh and Ajay Kumar Singh duly armed with a country made pistol committed robbery of cash amounting to Rs. 2.54 lakh from Andhra Bank Extension Counter situated at INS Virbahu, Visakhapatnam, thereby committed an offence punishable under section 392 of the IPC read with section 77(2) of the Navy Act, 1957.

The charge sheet contained three more charges under section 342 of the IPC read with section 77(2) of the Navy Act, 1957, section 25(1-A) of the

Arms Act 1959 read with section 77(2) of the Navy Act 1957, and under section 51 of the Navy Act 1957. In the court martial, charges 1, 2 and 4 were held proved. The applicant was sentenced to 8 years Rigorous Imprisonment and also dismissal with disgrace with mulct of 14 days pay and allowance. The applicant filed an application under section 162 of the Navy Act 1957. The Chief of the Naval Staff by order dated 06 July 2000 reduced the period of Rigorous Imprisonment to 6 years from 8 years.

The applicant contended that the Court Martial was not in accordance with the provisions of the Navy Act. The composition of the Members was defective, causing serious prejudice to the applicant. Material evidence was not produced and the important witnesses were not examined resulting in serious miscarriage of justice. The seizures and recoveries alleged to have been made were in gross violation of mandatory procedure and action taken was procedurally ultra vires. The Investigating Officer was also the Prosecution Officer and he was not examined. The trial by the Court Martial was conducted in violation of principles of natural justice resulting in violation of the fundamental rights of the applicant. Further, while awarding sentence the competent authority has failed to take into account the period already undergone under trial as provided under section 155 of the Navy Act.

The applicant also contended that soiled currency notes, which were not mentioned anywhere in the FIR by Bank Manager, said to have been recovered by Provost Marshal and his staff and also by Civil Police, were not produced before the Court. The currency notes said to have been recovered by the Naval Police from one of the suit cases, which had been seized from D.K. Singh's (co-accused) residence and was opened by Naval Police by themselves without calling any independent civilian witnesses. This was in violation of para 25 of Regulations for the Navy, Part-II, which direct the investigating authorities to keep Divisional Officer of the Sailors throughout the investigation. The witnesses for recovery and confession were also not examined before the Court Martial. Most of the witnesses were from Naval Provost Branch and prosecutor being senior provost officer had definite influence over these witnesses who work or worked earlier under him.

The respondents contested that after a fair trial the Court Martial has convicted and sentenced the applicant on the basis of the oral and documentary evidences. The Court Martial has been constituted in terms of the provisions of the Naval Act.

The Tribunal after examining the entire evidence observed that as far as the Charge No. 4 was concerned, it was under section 51 of the Navy Act for having absented without leave for 334 hours, which had no bearing with regard to other charges levelled against the applicant/accused, which are relating to the charges under section 392 IPC and section 342 IPC read with section 77(2) of the Navy Act. The Court Martial should not have clubbed the charge, which was under section 51 of the Navy Act 1957, with other charges, which related to the crime, which had taken place on 04 June 1998 at Andhra

Bank Extension Counter. The Tribunal held that the clubbing of Charge No. 4 with the other charges was illegal.

As regard Charges 1 and 2 which were proved against the accused, the Tribunal observed that out of the 29 witnesses examined in the case, 12 witnesses had deposed against the applicant/accused. Out of them, the most important witness was PW15 through whom finger print report relating to the applicant/accused was produced. The evidence of PW15 coupled with report leads to a conclusion that the charges under sections 392 and 342 IPC read with section 77(2) of the Navy Act have been proved beyond any reasonable doubt against the accused.

The Tribunal further observed that soon after the occurrence on 04 June 1998, the accused had deposited a sum of Rs. 81,600/- in Central Bank of India, Azamgarh Branch, Uttar Pradesh, in his Account No. 8206. This fact was proved by the oral evidence of PW 29 coupled with documentary evidence like pay-in-slip, through which the applicant/accused had deposited the amount of Rs. 81,600/- under his signature. There was no material placed by the applicant/present accused to show from where he got this amount of Rs. 81,600/-. So, from which source the applicant/accused had got this amount of Rs. 81,600/- remained a mystery.

On the point of punishment, the Tribunal commented that the other co-accused A.K. Singh (Appellant in TA No.139 of 2010) was awarded 5 years RI, which was subsequently reduced to 2 years RI by the Chief of the Naval Staff (CNS). Whereas, the applicant/accused, who was also the co-accused to the same crime was awarded 8 years RI by the Court Martial, which was subsequently reduced to 6 years RI by the CNS. The respondents were unable to explain why the same yardstick which was applied to the co-accused A.K. Singh (Appellant in TA No.139 of 2010) was not applied to the applicant/accused. The applicant/accused was also under incarceration for more than 1 year 4 months after the verdict of the Court Martial. Under such circumstances, the Tribunal was of the considered opinion that it was not fair to send the accused behind the bars after a lapse of a decade. It would be just, in the interest of justice to apply the principles of set-off towards imprisonment in this case. The Tribunal, while confirming the conviction, modified the punishment of 6 years RI awarded by the court martial to that of the period already undergone by the accused. The amount of Rs. 81,600/-which was under the attachment was ordered to be confiscated to the Central Government.

Insufficient evidence

The AFT Principal Bench New Delhi in the case of *Lt Col G. R. Verma v. Union of India*, TA No. 537 of 2009 [WP (C) No. 6698 of 1999], decided on 6 July 2010, considered the challenges the GCM proceedings.

The appellant joined the Army on 9 October 1963. In 1993, while he was posted at Composite Platoon ASC at Ranchi, a bank robbery was took place, allegedly involving a Sepoy of his unit, who managed to escape from

Army custody on 31 March 1993. The appellant was tried on six charges under section 52 (f) and 63 of the Army Act. The GCM found the appellant not guilty of charge no. 1 and guilty of charge no. 2 to 6 and sentenced him to be dismissed from service. The post confirmation petition submitted by the appellant was also rejected.

The appellant contested that the entire case was fabricated and his conviction by the GCM on charges 2 to 6 was not based on convincing evidence and he had only carried out the instruction of his superior officers. Further the punishment of dismissal from service was disproportionate to the gravity of offence alleged to have been committed by him. The respondents contended that the case against the appellant was prima facie established by a court of inquiry. The appellant was given adequate opportunity under Army Rule 23 to defend his case. Further, the findings of the GCM were on the basis of the evidence.

The Tribunal scrutinized the entire evidence adduced against the appellant in the case. The Tribunal referred to the case of *State of Maharashtra v. Som Nath Thapa* (1996(4) SCC 659), wherein the Court explained the meaning of the word 'presume' referring to the dictionary meaning of the said word and held that on the basis of the materials on record, Court has to complete the prima facie conclusion of the commission of the offence. The observations of the Supreme Court read:

> "31. Let us note the meaning of the word 'presume'. In Black's Law Dictionary it has been defined to mean 'to believe or accept upon probable evidence'. In Shorter Oxford English Dictionary it has been mentioned that in law 'presume' means 'to take as proved until evidence to the contrary is forthcoming', Stroud's Legal Dictionary has quoted in this context a certain judgment according to which 'A presumption is a probable consequence drawn from facts (either certain, or proved by direct testimony) as to the truth of a fact alleged'.
>
> 32. The aforesaid shows that if on the basis of materials on record, a court could come to the conclusion that commission of the offence is a probable consequence, a case for framing of charge exists. To put it differently, if the court were to think that the accused might have committed the offence it can frame the charge, though for conviction the conclusion is required to be that the accused has committed the offence. It is apparent that at the stage of framing of a charge, probative value of the materials on record cannot be gone into; the material brought on record by the prosecution has to be accepted as true at that stage."

The Tribunal considered that it was necessary to define the word 'illegal', as is given in s. 43 of the Indian Penal Code, which reads:

> "43. 'Illegal', 'Legally bound to do': The word 'illegal' is applicable to everything which is an offence or which is prohibited by law, or which furnishes ground for a civil action; and a person is said to be 'legally bound to do' whatever it is illegal in him to omit."

For proving illegality, three essential conditions must be fulfilled: (i) an action which is prohibited by law; (ii) an action which is a ground for civil action; and (iii) an action which is legally bound is omitted to do. The Tribunal also relied on the decision of the Supreme Court in *E. P. Royappa v. State of Tamil Nadu* (1974 (4) SCC 3), which read:

> "The only question before us is whether the action taken by the respondents includes any component of mala fides; whether hostility and malus animus against the petitioner were the operational cause of the transfer of the petitioner from the post of Chief Secretary.... we must not also overlook that the burden of establishing mala fides is very heavy on the person who alleges it. The allegations of mala fides are often more easily made than proved, and the very seriousness of such allegations demands proof of a high order of credibility....In this context it may be noted that top administrators are often required to do acts which affect others adversely but which are necessary in the execution of their duties. These acts may lend themselves to misconstruction and suspicion as to the bona fides of their author when the full facts and surrounding circumstances are not known. The Court would, therefore, be slow to draw dubious inferences from incomplete facts placed before it by a party, particularly when the imputations are grave and they are made against the holder of an office which has a high responsibility in the administration. Such is the judicial perspective in evaluating charge of unworthy conduct against....high authorities, not because of any special status which they are supposed to enjoy, nor because they are highly placed in social life or administrative set up – these considerations are wholly irrelevant in judicial approach – but because otherwise, functioning effectively would become difficult in a democracy. It is from this standpoint that we must assess the merits of the allegations of mala fides made by the petitioner against the second respondent."

The Tribunal was of the view that the prosecution has failed to establish charge nos. 2 to 6 against the appellant. It set aside the findings and punishment awarded by the GCM. It directed that the respondent shall consider restoration of the withheld pension of the appellant.

Sentence of dismissal modified to discharge

The AFT Regional Bench Chennai in the case of *Wg Cdr M S Narsimha Rao v. Union of India*, OA No.2 of 2010, decided on 3 August 2010, considered a prayer for quashing the proceedings of GCM.

The petitioner had joined the Indian Air Force and in due course he was promoted to the rank of Wing Commander. In the year 2004, while he was working at Allahabad, he was issued with a charge sheet dated 19 November 2004 by the Station Commander Signal Unit, Allahabad, for disobeying a lawful command given by his superior officer and refusing to accept the clearance form and refusing to collect the railway warrant for the journey from Allahabad to Pune on posting. A GCM tried the petitioner on four charges under sections 41(2) and 65 of the Air Force Act, 1950. He was convicted under Charge No. 2 and 3, both under section 65 of the Act. He was acquitted from Charge No.1 framed under section 41(2), and Charge No. 4 framed under section 65 of the Act. He was awarded the punishment of dismissal from the service.

The petitioner contended that the charge sheet was issued by the authorities having no jurisdiction in the matter. He also challenged the order of conviction and sentence under Charge Nos. 2 and 3, which resulted in his dismissal from service. Further, the confirmation of dismissal order was not communicated to the petitioner, which was against the provisions of Para 766(a) of Regulations for the Indian Air Force, 1964. The petitioner has also contended that the salary for the interregnum period till the date of posting is to be disbursed to him and after setting aside the impugned order of the GCM, he should be reinstated into service as Wing Commander.

The respondents contested that the findings and sentence of the GCM, duly confirmed by the confirming authority i.e., the Chief of Air Staff were promulgated to the petitioner on 23 August 2005 by the Station Commander duly witnessed by an independent Officer. However, the petitioner declined to sign the promulgation certificate. He was struck of the strength (SOS) of the IAF with effect from 24 August 2005. Therefore, the petitioner was not entitled for posting order, salaries, consequential and other benefits as prayed by him. Further, the cause of action for the petitioner arose only at Allahabad and the bench of the Tribunal has no jurisdiction to try the case.

The Tribunal considered whether the charge Nos. 2 and 3 levelled against the applicant before the GCM have been proved beyond any reasonable doubt. The Tribunal came to conclusion that the Charge No. 2 levelled against the applicant under section 65 of the Air Force Act, 1950 has been proved beyond any reasonable doubt, and does not warrant any interference. However, as regard charge No. 3, the Tribunal was of the view that it has not been proved against the petitioner. The Tribunal ordered that the order of the GCM in respect of Charge No. 2 as proved to be confirmed and the order of the GCM in respect of Charge No. 3 to be set aside. The Tribunal while confirming the conviction of the petitioner modified the sentence alone to that of discharge instead of dismissal.

Note: *Note: Section 73 of the Air Force Act, 1950 lists punishments which may be inflicted in respect of offences committed by persons subject to the Act. The list does not contain 'discharge' as punishment.*

Acquittal due to lack of evidence

The AFT Principal Bench New Delhi in the case of *Major S S Chillar v. Union of India*, TA No. 246 of 2009 [WP(C) No. 2649 of 1989, Delhi High Court], decided on 1 April 2010, considered a prayer against the punishment awarded by a General Court Martial (GCM).

The petitioner was commissioned in the Indian Army on 20 December 1970 in the Madras Regiment as a 2nd Lieutenant. The petitioner, before his commission in the Army, had served in the JAT Regiment in the ranks since 4 November 1963. He was, in due course, promoted to the rank of Major (Substantive).

On 22 September 1984 the petitioner was transferred on deputation, to Headquarters Establishment under the IG Headquarters SFF, a civil organisations and not part of Regular Army. On 14 October 1984 the petitioner was transferred to another project on probation for a period of three months and was posted at Sarsawa near Saharanpur, U.P. On 17 October 1984 some of the personnel belonging to the same project were detailed to undergo training at Sarsawa. The petitioner submitted that some misfortune incident happened at Muzaffarnagar Railway Station and in that two officers wanted petitioner's assistance and asked the petitioner to tell the police authorities that the officers were away on training, but, he did not do it. Therefore, a grievance was nursed against him by these officers.

In the first week of November, 1984, the complete contingent moved to Delhi and the contingent was assigned the task of VVIP security. The petitioner also moved to Delhi. The petitioner, unable to adjust with the growing animosity including threats to his life from these officers, made an application for an interview with IG, SFF. The petitioner was interviewed on or around 24th November, 1984, and he made a request for sending back to the Indian Army. The petitioner was asked to make a written request for reversion to Indian Army.

On 1 December 1984 the petitioner was informed that his posting to a new place had been ordered, but, he immediately moved an application for reversion to the Indian Army. When the petitioner went to the residence of Lt Col Pathak, Commander Project, he saw a dressing table in room. He thought it is a suitable place to keep the application. As soon as the petitioner lifted the books/magazines, to keep the application underneath, so that it does not fly off, there was a blast. The petitioner does not remember anything thereafter till he regained consciousness in the Intensive Care Unit of the Army Hospital, Delhi Cantt. As a result of the blast petitioner received the injuries Laceration of right hand and mutilation of fingers and palm; multiple puncture wounds over the face; puncture wounds over right shin; and injury to right eye. The petitioner remained in the Army Hospital till 9 July 1985.

After the grenade blast took-place at Lt Col Pathak's room, the petitioner's bedding was searched and in the tent, which was shared by him and another officer, a live primed hand grenade (marking: Lot No. 104 & F-77 detonator KF 10-77) was recovered under his pillow. A court of inquiry was also conducted by the Commandant, Headquarter Establishment No. 22. The petitioner contented that the whole inquiry was conducted in his absence and in that inquiry he was found blameworthy. The petitioner was charged before the GCM for an offence under s. 69 of the Army Act, read with s. 5 of the

Explosive Substance Act, 1908. The GCM awarded the sentence of dismissal from service, which was confirmed by the competent authority.

The respondents contended that during the make safe operation it was revealed that the explosion in Lt Col Pathak's room was caused by a High Explosive-36 hand grenade. Another High Explosive-36 hand grenade was recovered, which was lying underneath the pillow inside a cardboard bulb cover wrapped in petitioner's the night suit. The grenade was armed and primed. On 2 December 1984 another hand grenade was found lying in the kitchen garden, same was also live. The court of inquiry found that petitioner entered into the room of Lt Col KD Pathak with the intention of placing a primed and armed HE-36 hand grenade, a booby trap, which exploded while it was being placed, he left a Punjabi advertisement in the room to mislead the authorities and create and arouse anti communal feeling. He was found in illegal possession of stolen property that is one IAFT-1752, a blank signed and stamped railway warrant.

The petitioner contended that that the entire investigation was illegal as no physical search was taken in the tent where his bed was kept; no proper sealing was done, no independent witnesses were produced and the area was open and accessible to all. There was also a serious mistake regarding identification of the tent number. The items recovered were not kept in sealed condition in possession of the competent authority. Identity of the main grenade was also not established because the number of the grenade, which was recovered, and number of the grenade, which was produced in the court, did not tally.

The Tribunal observed that in the charge sheet the number of the Hand Grenade is mentioned as HE 36 Lot No. 610H KF-77. The charge relates to possession of Hand Grenade HE 36 Lot No. 610H KF-77, which is said to be explosive substance. However, in the finding, the GCM authorities have deleted the lot No. HE 36 Lot No. 610H KF-77. The net result is that when the accused was charged for a particular substance, which is said to be an explosive substance and finding recorded by the GCM deletes this number of hand grenade, meaning thereby, the basis on which the accused had been charged for possessing a particular explosive and reference of that particular explosive has been deleted from the final finding, then, nothing remains of the offence. If the reference of hand grenade is deleted from the charge, then the truncated charge will reads as under: "at Delhi Cantt, on 01 Dec 84, was in possession of Hand Grenade...., an explosive substance, under suspicious circumstances." The Tribunal was of the opinion that this does not make a sense at all. The net result was the finding is totally defective. That means, defective in the sense that when the accused is not found guilty for possession of the hand grenade HE 36 Lot NO. 610H KF-77, then no offence pertaining to this hand grenade is stand proved. The Tribunal held that the finding guilty of the accused by the GCM was totally illegal and unsustainable in law.

The Tribunal also made serious observation against the trial by court martial:

> "We have seen number of Court Martial cases, which have come before this Tribunal and we find that most of the elementary mistakes were committed in conduct of the criminal trials under Court Martial proceedings. Now a proper appeal lies against the court martial proceedings before this Tribunal, the Tribunal has to examine all the procedure as well as substance of the criminal trial like in Court of Appeal, including appreciation of the evidence, and our experience is that the trials in the Court Martial proceedings relating to civil offence like murder or other penal code offences or offences under the other acts are not properly conducted like a regular criminal trial. The result is that they will turn into acquittal.
>
> Therefore, now in changed situation, when the Court Martial proceedings are amenable to regular appeal under the Act, the authorities have to undertake the overall review of conducting Court Martial trials pertaining to offences under penal code or other civil offences by a competent prosecutor, who has experience of trial as well as the Presiding Officer should also be a trained person, who has seen the trials conducted by Sessions Court, so that they can appreciate the difference between the two and regulate the Court Martial proceedings as if they are conducting a criminal trial before sessions. Such Presiding Officers should be sent for training in a criminal court, where trials are conducted, likewise, the Prosecutors and the Judge Advocate. Therefore, the matter requires a serious consideration of overhauling of the procedure."

The Tribunal further highlighted that before presenting the matter for Court Martial three tier proceedings are taken, first, a preliminary enquiry, then, at the charge stage, and, thirdly summary of evidence, ultimately the matter goes to Court Martial. Therefore, this is a four tier exercise, which is also cumbersome, time consuming and totally unwarranted. Once the investigation is done, then, the case should be immediately taken before the Court and Court find prima facie charges, then, either Court may send it to session court for trial or if authorities want to try by Court Martial, then, it can apply before the Court.

The Tribunal acquitted the petitioner of all the charges and set aside the order of GCM as well as the confirmation order.

Review of decision

The AFT New Delhi Principal Bench, Court No. 2, in the case of *Ex Col A. K. Kadian v. Union of India*, RA No. 47 of 2011, in TA No. 245 of 2010 [WP (C) No. 830 of 2002 of Delhi High Court], decided on 4 May 2012, considered a prayer for review of its judgement and setting aside proceedings of GCM.

The applicant had requested for condonation of the delay and for the review of AFT judgement and order dated 24 May 2011 under Rule 18 of the Armed Forces Tribunal (Procedure) Rules, 2008 and prayed that the GCM proceedings against him be set aside with all consequential benefits. The applicant had contended that the GCM was time barred as the period of limitation commenced from the date when the Court of Inquiry was submitted i.e. on 14 Aug 1995 and GCM was convened as on 08 Sep 1998. Therefore, GCM was time barred as it was convened after 3 years. He further contended that this point was raised during the hearing of the case but that was not considered by the Tribunal. In support of his contention, the appellant also relied upon the judgment in the case of *J S Sekhon v. Union of India,* 2010 Vol. 8 SCALE and Civil Appeal No. 2107 of 2012 pertaining to *Rajvir Singh v. Secretary, Ministry of Defence* decided on 15 Feb 2012.

The Tribunal was of the view that the point of limitation has to be taken from the date when convening authority got the knowledge of the report which was stated as 26 Sep 1995, the date when show cause notice was issued to the applicant. The GCM was convened on 8 Sep 1998 and thus was convened within 3 years. The Tribunal referred to the decision of the Supreme Court in the case of *Union of India v. V N Singh* 2010 (5) SSC. The Tribunal also considered the issue regarding the seniority of the JAG in GCM. The JAG was changed, on administrative grounds, and a perusal of the GCM proceedings nowhere indicated that applicant had raised objections on this aspect during the trial by GCM. It held that the issue, therefore, does not merit mention and was no error in the judgment.

The Tribunal was of the opinion that the scope of review is limited and these objections cannot be re-heard. The scope of review is not at par with appeal. Referring to the decision of the Supreme Court in *Kerala State electricity Board v. Hitech Electrothermics & Hydropower Ltd* JT 2005 (7) SC page 485, the Tribunal commented:

> "In review petition it is not open to the court to re-appreciate the evidence and reach a different conclusion even if that be possible, permitting review petitioner would amount to converting a review petition into an appeal in disguise. Therefore, the review petition is not maintainable".

Dismissing the application the Tribunal held that the present review petition dated 2 Aug 2011 has also not been submitted within prescribed period of 30 days and is beyond the period of limitation since judgment is dated 24 May 2011.

Composition of court, petition dismissed

The AFT Principal Bench New Delhi in the case of *Commander Ravinder Singh v. Union of India*, OA No. 421 of 2010, decided on 29 May 2012, considered a prayer for quashing of finding and sentence of court martial.

The petitioner joined the Indian Navy in July, 1987 and was commissioned as a Sub Lt on 01 January 1989. He opted for aviation branch and joined the

Air Force Academy, Dundigal, Hyderabad in July 1989 for flying training. After successful flying training, he became a Naval helicopter pilot. At the material time, he was serving in the Indian Navy in the rank of Commander as a staff pilot. The petitioner got married in 1993 and had a son out of the said wedlock. The marriage ended in a divorce on 21 August 2008. During the divorce proceedings, the father-in-law of the petitioner filed a false criminal case against him and his family to pressurize them to withdraw the divorce case and demanded a huge sum of alimony. Petitioner paid Rs 10 lacs as full and final payment as alimony in addition to the regular maintenance of Rs 12,000/- per month. The criminal complaint was finally quashed by the High Court of Allahabad vide its order dated 12 November 2008.

During the month of November 2008, the petitioner was issued a show cause of notice for absenting without leave and other misconducts. After the record of summary of evidence, he was served with charge sheet containing nine charges under sections 51, 68, 48 (c), 47 (a), and (c) of the Navy Act, 1957. Out of 9 charges, the court martial found the petitioner guilty of charge Nos. 4, 6, 8 and 9. He was awarded the sentence of forfeiture of seniority of 12 calendar months and deduction of mulcts for 42 days. Further, his statutory petitions under sections 160, 161 and 162 of the Navy Act, 1957 were rejected by the Chief of Naval Staff. The petitioner contended that his trial was vitiated because (i) investigation was carried out in violation to para 149 of the Regulations for the Navy, (ii) the court martial was improperly constituted, (iii) he was not given the service of suitable officer to defend him during the court martial, (iv) verdict of court martial was unreasoned and non-speaking.

The Tribunal reconciled two provisions i.e. sections 97 (10) and 123 of the Navy Act, 1957, and observed that the complete procedure of court martial was given in Chapter XIII Procedure of Court Martial. Section 123 appears in this Chapter XIII whereas section 97(10) appears in Chapter XII i.e. Authorities Having Power to Award Punishment. Section 97 talks of Constitution of Court Martial under this Chapter. Therefore, two provisions appear in different chapter and it has different purpose. Section 123 will come into pay when trial begins. The constitution or reconstitution is pre-trial issue. The Tribunal held that in the present case, the contingency of numbers of the executive members was reduced then this is not the contingency which contemplated in section 123, therefore, it was open for the respondents to reconvene a fresh court martial.

After going through the evidence, the Tribunal was of the opinion that the act of the petitioner was totally unwarranted and unbecoming of an officer. While considering that the recording of reasons in the finding on charges would show proper application of mind, the Tribunal held that such requirement has been dispensed with in the Navy Act, and the respondents are not under obligation to pass a speaking order. The Tribunal dismissed the petition.

Punishment of dismissal converted to compulsory retirement

The AFT Principal Bench New Delhi, Court No. 2, in the case of *Col S K Jain v. Union of India*, OA No. 445 of 2010, decided on 1 June 2012, considered a petition for quashing and setting aside of the findings and sentence of the GCM.

The applicant was posted as the Commandant of Northern Command Vehicle Depot in 2006. On 18 December 2008, he was tried by a GCM on three charges under section 69 of the Army Act, relating to criminal misconduct contrary to section 5(2) of Prevention of Corruption Act, 2006 (J&K) and section 63 of the Army Act. The GCM concluded on 26 March 2009 and held the applicant guilty of first and second charges under section 69 of the Army Act, and not guilty of third charge. He was sentenced to dismissal from service. His pre-confirmation petition under section 164 of the Army Act was rejected on 04 June 2009. However, the outcome of his post confirmation petition dated 3 November 2009 was not known.

The Tribunal concluded that the charge of having demanded the alleged amount is not found proved beyond reasonable doubt. The burden of proving charge even in such type of cases of corruption always lies on the prosecution. The Tribunal referred to the judgement of the Supreme Court in *Subhash P. Sonvare v. State of Gujarat* (2002) 5 SCC 86 wherein their Lordships had held that the demand for illegal gratification should be established as mere possession of recovery of the illegal gratification cannot be grounds for conviction. In the instant case, the Tribunal was of the view that neither the demand has been proved nor the recovery of the said envelope containing the money has been proved beyond reasonable doubt. The Tribunal also relied upon the decisions of the Supreme Court in *Abdulla Mohammed Pagarkar v. State* (Union territory of Goa, Daman and Diu) (1980) 3 SCC 110 wherein the Court held that section 3 of the Evidence Act of 1972, clearly indicates that for any charge to be proved "suspicion, however, strong cannot be a substitute for proof". Further, under section 102 of the Evidence Act, onus of proof of existence of every ingredient of a charge always rests on the prosecution and never shifts on the accused.

Also, in *M.K. Harshan v. State of Kerala,* AIR 1995 SCC 2178, the Supreme Court observed that "acceptance of illegal gratification should be proved" and in a trap case, recovery of tainted money from the accused does not constitute corroborated evidence and could suffer from infirmities. Plea of the accused on the other hand that tainted money was planted without his knowledge appears to be probable and thus the accused was given the benefit of doubt. The Tribunal held that the facts of the present case are almost similar and therefore, the recovery of envelop with the said money cannot be taken as conclusive proof especially so, when the demand for illegal gratification has not been proved beyond doubt.

As regard the second charge, the Tribunal was of the opinion that the charge should have been framed under section 63 of the Army Act for not following the standing instructions as regards the disposal of surplus/old arms and ammunition. The Tribunal quashed the second charge and substituted it with charge under section 63 of the Army Act i.e. failing to obey standing orders in maintaining good order and discipline. The Tribunal held that since charge No. 2 has proved, ends of justice will be met by sending the applicant on compulsory retirement from the date of dismissal with all pensionary and retirement benefits. The Tribunal further directed that the order must be complied with within 120 days, failing which an interest @ 12% would be levied on the sum due, till the date of payment.

Note: *Section 71 of the Army Act, 1950, lists punishment which can be awarded by a court martial to an individual subject to the Act. The list does not include 'compulsory retirement' as punishment.*

Misappropriation of fund, no interference

The AFT Principal Bench New Delhi in the case of in the case of *Maj Gen KTG Nambiar v. Union of India*, TA No. 412 of 2010 [WP (C) No. 7867 of 2008], decided on 29 May 2012, considered a petition for quashing the findings and sentence of the GCM.

The petitioner while serving in Army was tried by GCM on 18 charges under sections 45, 52 (f), 54 (b), 63 and 69 of the Army Act. The GCM held the Petitioner guilty of seven charges and not guilty of the balance 11 charges. He was sentenced to forfeiture of three years past service for the purpose of pension and also severe reprimand.

The Tribunal observed that the petitioner had collected Rs. 76 lakhs in cash from civilians while functioning as a Chairman of a civilian club in an unauthorised manner and there was no resolution which permitted him to undertake this exercise. More so when he had already collected Rs. 37 lakhs by cheque, he ventured to collect Rs. 76 lakhs in cash. This very act of collecting such a huge amount from civilians without proper proceedings being drawn and seeking the permission from the committee does not behove the status and conduct of an Army Officer.

The Tribunal noted that the petitioner was charged correctly under the Army Act and the findings given by the GCM were based on proper evidence and were fully substantiated. The Tribunal did not find any merit in the case and dismissed the petition.

Insensitivity, callousness and delay

The Armed Forces Principal Bench New Delhi in the case of *Nb Sub Raju Thapa v. Union of India*, MA Nos. 166 of 2012 and 250 of 2011 in OA No. 453 of 2010; *Hav Vijay Kumar v. Union of India* MA Nos.172 of 2012 and 251 of 2011 in O.A. No. 454 of 2010; *Hav Pradhan Pandurang Wakoji v. Union of India* MA Nos.173 of 2012 and 252 of 2011 in OA No. 455 of 2010, decided on 3 September 2012, considered the insensitive handling of court martial cases by the Government.

In this case all the three petitioners faced Court Martial. They were found guilty and were awarded punishment of two years RI and dismissal from service for some criminal offence. They challenged the verdict of Court Martial by filing writ petition in the MP High Court. The Single Judge by the order dated 29 January 2008 set aside the Court Martial. Against that the Union of India went into appeal by filing Letters Patent Appeal (LPA). The Division Bench of MP High Court in the LPA modified the order of the Single Judge on 04 July 2008.

Thereafter, a review application was filed by the petitioners and in that the order was passed on 10 December 2009 and the direction was issued that the order in writ appeal was recalled and the order passed by the Single Judge was affirmed, inasmuch, as to fall out of the same would be to continuance of the Court Martial proceedings against the petitioners and at the time when the proceeding was in continuum these petitioners were in custody. It was also submitted that if the petitioners surrendered, the Court Martial shall continue under the Army Act. It was further submitted that the petitioners had absconded and they had taken law onto themselves and in order to do complete justice a condition precedent was that the petitioners shall surrender and the Court Martial shall continue as per order passed by the learned Single Judge from that stage.

The petitioners surrendered before the competent authority and the earlier concession order passed in the writ appeals was recalled and accordingly, the review application filed by the Union of India was allowed. Thereafter, the Union of India filed an application for modification of this order passed on 10 December 2009 by the Division Bench in LPA. That application for modification of the order was dismissed for want of prosecution. The Union of India again filed an application for restoration. Since it was barred by time, therefore, it was withdrawn and again an application for recall was being sought to be filed by the Union of India along with an application for condonation of delay.

The Tribunal shown concerned that the way things had been handled by the government was most unfortunate; and the whole sequence of events showed total insensitivity on their part. During this lengthy process of litigation, the petitioner Vijay Kumar had already expired. Another petitioner Nb Sub Raju Thapa had superannuated on completion of tenure in February 2007. He was again arrested and kept in custody for one year for completing the court martial. He was released and was without any pensionary benefits. The third petitioner Hav Pradhan Pandurang Wakoji was released, but was without pension and other benefits.

The Tribunal observed that the position in the case was same as the last order passed by the High Court on 10 December 2009. Neither the respondents had conducted the fresh court martial nor had they decided the benefits to be given to both the surviving petitioners.

The Tribunal directed that the pensionary benefits to Nb Sub Raju Thapa be released subject to the court martial proceedings. As regard Hav Pradhan Pandurang Wakoji, the Tribunal directed that he should be taken back in service and whatever salary due to him should be paid till the fresh court martial was undertaken. The Tribunal directed that these directions shall be final subject to the order passed by the MP High Court, in case the respondents file an application with the application for condonation of delay. Further, the order should be implemented within a period of 3 months subject to orders of the MP High Court.

Sentence of dismissal converted to discharge

The AFT Principal Bench New Delhi in the case of *Lt Cdr Alok Ambastha v. Union of India*, TA No. 84 of 2010 [WP(C) No. 6048 of 2003], decided on 21 December 2012, considered a prayer for quashing of the findings and recommendation of a court martial. The petitioner also prayed for directions to reinstate him back in service with all consequential benefits.

The petitioner was commissioned into the Navy on 01 January 1989 in the Executive Branch. In December 1999, while the petitioner was posted to INS Androth and working as Canteen Officer of the Ship, a board of inquiry (BOI) was ordered in which the evidence was recorded against him. On 19 June 2000, a court martial was convened and petitioner was tried for offence under sections 68 and 77(2) of the Navy Act 1957. The petitioner was found guilty of charge 1(a) by the court martial but after the judicial review, he was pronounced not guilty by the CNS. He was found guilty of charges 1(b) and 1(c), charge 2, charge 3(a), 3(c) and 3(d). The petitioner was sentenced "to be dismissed from Naval Service, to suffer a fine of Rs. 14,875/- and to suffer such other consequential penalties involved." This sentence was upheld by the CNS and also by the Central Government.

The petitioner contended that provisions of para 205 of the Regulations for the Navy were violated by BOI in that he was not allowed to sit in the BOI despite the fact that his military reputation and character was involved. In support of his contentions, the petitioner cited the case of AFT in *Lt Col Prasad Purohit v. Union of India* OA No. 485 of 2010, in which the requirement of invoking the clause under para 205 of the Navy Regulations (Army Rule 180) was held mandatory.

The petitioner also contended about the recommendations of the JAG on his judicial review. It was stated that certain documents were allowed by the court martial which were not produced earlier in the proceedings and therefore, it was incorrect for the court martial to base its decision on such documents and questions which were not tendered earlier. Further, the amount deposited by the petitioner to make good the alleged losses to the canteen was taken as confession, which was incorrect. The allegation against the trial judge advocate (TJA) was that he was biased and while going through the facts of the case he also dwelled on the issue which in a way influenced the members of the court martial. Further, under section113 of the Navy Act, 1957, the TJA was only required to "sum up in the open court by evidence for the prosecution and the defence and lay down the law by which the court is to be guided."

The respondents contested that the petitioner was given all the necessary opportunity to be present during the conduct of the BOI. Further, the petitioner was supplied with the charge-sheet, the copy of the BOI and all related documents. The TJA had dealt with the case in detail and complied with all the requirements and had shown no bias as alleged, by the petitioner.

After going through the evidence, the Tribunal was of the view the court martial was wrong in punishing the respondent under section 74 despite the charge being under section 68 of the Navy Act. The ingredients of section 68 are: neglect to obey, or contravention of any provisions of the Act or any regulation made under this Act, or any general or local order, unless other punishment is provided for in the Act for such act or omission, and the maximum permissible sentence is two years. While under section 74, the ingredients are entirely different, being to be guilty of an act, disorder, or neglect to the prejudice of good order and naval discipline, not hereinbefore specified, and then the maximum punishment prescribed is three years. Neglecting to obey or contravening of provision or regulation or any general or local order, cannot in any manner be even put at par with being guilty of an act, disorder or neglect to the prejudice of the good order and naval discipline. Failure to prove any of the ingredients of section 68 and proving all remaining ingredients does not make out an offence under section 74. Therefore, the petitioner could not be held guilty under section 74 with the aid of section 127. In order to set the things right, and to avoid all confusions, the Tribunal exercising its powers under section 15(6) of the AFT Act, and held the petitioner guilty of the offence under section 74 of the Navy Act.

The Tribunal also observed that the petitioner was subjected to double jeopardy in terms of money that was taken from him and yet he was charged with criminal breach of trust vide charge 2. Relying on the decision of the Supreme Court in the case of R. Venkatkrishnan v. Central Bureau of Investigation, where the Apex Court had held that the intention of criminal breach of trust has to be established; the Tribunal observed that the present case, there was no intention of criminal breach of trust. The petitioner had drawn the stores on credit and he immediately made good the amount on return from leave when he was told about his dues to the canteen stores that he had taken on credit. The items were not misappropriated for his personal use but were taken as legitimate purchase on credit for which he made good the payment. The Tribunal held that charge No. 2 therefore cannot sustain and must be set aside. The Tribunal upheld the findings guilty by the court martial for charge No. 3(a), 3(c) and 3(d).

The Tribunal, however, observed that the sentence of dismissal and fine of Rs. 14,875/- awarded to the petitioner was too harsh. The Tribunal set aside the sentence of dismissal and fine; and substituted as 'discharge' from the date of dismissal, with the order that the petitioner would be entitled to consequential benefits.

Note: *Section 81 of the Navy Act, 1957 lists punishments which can be inflicted under the Act. The Tribunal held that the petitioner was guilty of an offence under section 74 of the Navy Act. It could have awarded any punishment listed under section 81 of the Act. The list does not include 'discharge' as punishment.*

Prosecution based only confession: unlawful

The AFT Principal Bench New Delhi in the case of *Jai Prakash Rana v. Union of India*, TA No. 183 of 2010 [WP(C) No. 11192 of 2005], decided on 1 December 2010, considered a prayer for setting aside findings and sentence of a GCM.

The appellant served in the Army for about 29 years. On 10 August 2003, at about 0430 AM, an FIR was lodged before the Sadar Police alleging theft of Rs. 2.35 lakhs from Regimental Treasury Chest (RTC), wherein the said amount was kept in a plastic bag duly sealed. The police submitted final report stating that they could not find any clue. Subsequently, a GCM was convened for the trial of the petitioner in respect of the alleged offences. The appellant was charged under sections 52 (a) and 63 of the Army Act.

Based on the evidence, the GCM found the petitioner not guilty of the second charge, but held him guilty of the first charge with the variation that the words "from the Regimental Treasury Chest of Headquarters 50 (Independent) Parachute Brigade" shall be read as "from the Subedar Major's Office in 50 (Independent) Parachute Brigade Camp" and sentenced him to two years and six months of RI and dismissal from the service. His statutory complaint under section 164(2) of the Army Act was rejected.

The appellant contended that he was falsely implicated in the case and actually the offence was committed by certain other persons, with whom he was in no way connected. There was no evidence to fasten the culpability of the appellant since no there was no evidence of his involvement in the alleged offence. The appellant was held guilty on the basis of the confessional statement made by him at the time when he was under custody. The statement cannot be considered as a voluntary statement, since that was obtained under threat and coercion. Further, the trial was barred by the principle of stare decisis, as earlier on the report of theft, a crime was registered and a thorough investigation was made, wherein the police could not identify the accused. Subsequently, final report was submitted and the same was accepted by the concerned officer.

The respondents contested that in the court of inquiry, the appellant made a confession with regard to his involvement in the theft. On the basis of such court of inquiry, a summary of evidence was recorded and the petitioner was tried for the aforesaid offence. The petitioner made confession voluntarily and subsequently he retracted from his confessional statement. There was ample evidence to fix the culpability of the petitioner. Moreover, the trial of the petitioner was not barred by the principle of *stare decisis*.

The Tribunal observed that there was no inhibition under any statute from collecting evidence in a court of inquiry. However, Army Rule 180 makes it obligatory to afford an opportunity to a person whenever the inquiry affects his character or military reputation of being present throughout the inquiry and of making any statement and of giving any evidence and of cross examining any witness whose evidence, in his opinion, affects his character or military reputation and producing any witnesses in defence of his character or military reputation. The submission of final report by the police and its acceptance would not come in the way of holding of any court of inquiry.

The Tribunal observed that when the appellant was asked as to whether he had given the confession voluntarily, he stated that whatever confession he had made was not voluntary, because at that time he was under the influence of some drug which was administered on him in a cup of tea. It appeared from this evidence that the appellant retracted from his earlier confessional statement and stated that it was not made voluntarily. A person has, no doubt, a profound right not to be convicted of an offence which is not established by evidential standard of proof beyond reasonable doubt. A confession made by an accused person is irrelevant in criminal proceedings, if the making of the confession appears to the Court to have been caused by any inducement, threat or promise, having reference to the interrogation which continued for more than five hours. In this case, the Tribunal made observation that the appellant was kept constantly under threat and inducement by having the written statement from the appellant confessing his guilt. Where the statement is made as a result of harassment and continuous interrogation for several hours after the person is treated as an offender and accused, such statement must be regarded as involuntary. The Tribunal also referred the decision of the Supreme Court in *Bharat v. State of Uttar Pradesh* (1971(3) SCC 950, where the Apex Court observed:

> ".....confessions can be acted upon if the court is satisfied that they are voluntary and they are true. The voluntary nature of the confession depends upon whether there was any threat, inducement or promise and its truth is judged in the context of the entire prosecution case. The confession must fit into the proved facts and not run counter to them. When the voluntary character of the confession and its truth are accepted it is safe to rely on it. Indeed, a confession, if it is voluntary and true and not made under any inducement or threat or promise, is the most potent piece of evidence against the maker."

The Apex Court further observed that "a retracted confession must be looked upon with greater concern unless the reasons given for having made it in the first instance are on the face of them false."

The Tribunal rejected the prosecution case which was mainly based on the extra judicial confession which alone was not sufficient to hold the appellant guilty. The findings and sentence of GCM were set aside. The Tribunal held that the appellant shall be deemed to have been discharged from service from the date of the impugned order and he shall be entitled to all pensionary benefits from the date of his discharge.

Conviction without evidence

The AFT Principal Bench New Delhi in the case of *Maj KP Dutta v. Union of India*, TA No. 364 of 2009 [WP (C) No. 6373 of 2001 Delhi High Court], decided on 5 October 2010, considered a prayer challenging the GCM proceeding.

The appellant joined the Army on 20 March 1959 and was commissioned as a Special List Officer (Quarter Master) on 25 July 1977. He was promoted to the rank of Captain on 25 July 1983 and was posted to Indian Military Academy as Assistant Quarter Master on 1 June 1986 and remained there till 11 November 1989. On 25 August 1989, the appellant reported against his immediate superior officer and other principal staff officers to the Commandant about irregularities in drawing ration from contractors for the trainees of the Indian Military Academy (IMA) and in lieu thereof, receiving cash benefits. Subsequently, on account of the complaint, his superior officer started harassing and humiliating the appellant. He withdrew service benefits authorized to the appellant, therefore, the appellant wrote another letter to the then Commandant, to conduct an inquiry into the matter.

Instead of conducting inquiry, the Commandant transferred the appellant from IMA to another unit. The Commandant directed the appellant to hand over complete charge and documents pertaining to IMA furniture to his superior officer. Further, when JCO i/c Furniture, was posted out from IMA, deficiency was detected in the furniture stores while handing over charge to the newly posted JCO i/c. A Court of Inquiry was held to inquire into the circumstances under which some items of MES furniture were found deficient in the IMA. Alleging lack of supervision in carrying out the duties of Assistant Quarter Master and for accepting privately manufactured furniture in lieu of MES furniture, five courts of inquiry were held. As a consequence to the first court of inquiry, the appellant was awarded the punishment of 'severe displeasure' (to be recorded) by the Commandant. In the third court of inquiry, the appellant was ordered to pay Rs. 42,246/- towards cost of MES furniture. In the fourth court of inquiry, the appellant was exonerated of the alleged negligence on his part. And in the fifth court of inquiry, the GOC-in-Chief ordered deduction of Rs. 38,755/-, which was subsequently set aside by the Government of India.

On 15 September 1992, a charge sheet was issued to the appellant containing three charges under section 63 of the Army Act. He was tried by GCM and sentenced to take rank and precedence as if his appointment as substantive Major bore date 7 July 1993 and to forfeit 15 years past service for the purpose of pension. On appeal under section 164 (2) of the Army Act, the Chief of the Army Staff remitted the sentence "to forfeit 15 years of past service for the purpose of pension."

The appellant contended that he had been falsely implicated in this case. He was not the custodian of the furniture and was punished for the lapses noticed in the first court of inquiry. Successive courts of inquiry were illegal since they were conducted only to harass him. He was not accountable either for the shortage or replacement of furniture. The GCM arbitrarily held him guilty under the influence of his superior officers and the findings were based only on conjectures and surmises.

The respondents contested that there was ample evidence to prove the culpability of the appellant. He was liable since he was in charge of the store. The appellant cannot escape merely because there were other officials subordinate to him in whose custody the furniture were kept. He was a party to the replacement of the furniture. His intention was decipherable from the material evidence on record. The proceedings were not barred by limitation and there is no estoppel in initiating courts of inquiry in succession when new facts came to the notice of the concerned authorities.

The Tribunal examined the evidence and observed that the cumulative circumstances and the evidence leads to the conclusion that the appellant has not bought locally made furniture to make good the deficiencies as he had nothing to do with it and neither was he answerable for the deficiency nor for lack of supervision, though he had already been administratively punished. There was no evidence on record to show that statement of the appellant was false or leading to an act prejudicial to good order and military discipline. The statement by him before the COI, which could not otherwise be rebutted by evidence to be false, cannot be construed to be misconduct. The appellant had not committed any misconduct by violating any of the rules. Even if he countersigned the certificate, it can at the most be said to be misconduct or carelessness, for which he has already been punished. The word "misconduct" is defined in Black's Law Dictionary, 6th Edition at page 999 as "any unlawful behaviour by a public officer in relation to the duties of his office, wilful in character. The term embraces acts which the office holder had no right to perform, acts performed improperly, and failure to act in the face of an affirmative duty to act."

The Tribunal further observed that the fundamental principle of our criminal jurisprudence dictate that the accused is entitled to the benefit of any reasonable doubt. If two reasonably probable and evenly balanced views of the evidence are possible, one must necessarily concede the existence of a reasonable doubt. But, fanciful and remote possibilities must be left out of account. To entitle an accused person to the benefit of a doubt arising from the possibility of a duality of views, the possible view in favour of the accused must be as nearly reasonably probable as that against him. If the preponderance of probability is all one way, a bare possibility of another view will not entitle the accused to claim the benefit of any doubt. It is, therefore, essential that any view of the evidence in favour of the accused must be reasonable even as any doubt, the benefit of which an accused person may claim, must be reasonable.

The Tribunal held that the appellant was not guilty of any of the charges, and set aside the GCM findings and sentence.

Trial without evidence

The AFT Principal Bench New Delhi in *Brig PS Gill v. Union of India*, OA No. 147 of 2010, decided on 24 May 2011, considered a prayer for quashing of charge sheet against the petitioner.

A summary of evidence was recorded evidence against the petitioner on seven charges under sections 52(f) and 63 of the Army Act. The charges under section 63 were alternative to the first, third and fifth charges under section 52(f) of the Army Act. The seventh charge pertained to improper issue of a letter. It was alleged that the petitioner on 15 Mar 2005 (which came to the knowledge of the authority competent to initiate action on 25 Sep 2008), in the capacity of his being Chief Director of Purchase, Army Purchase Organisation, Ministry of Defence contrary to APO/MOD Consolidated Order No. 3 of 1987, with intent to defraud/improperly approved addition of two more tendering stations after issue of Acceptance of Tender on the last day of Delivery Period.

It was contended by the petitioner that even if the entire evidence collected during the course of inquiry was accepted on its face value, no offence was prima facie could be made out against him. The settled legal position was that if on the basis of material on record the court could form an opinion that the accused might have committed offence it can frame the charge, though for conviction the conclusion is required to be proved beyond reasonable doubt that the accused has committed the offence. At the time of framing of the charges the probative value of the material on record cannot be gone into, and the material brought on record by the prosecution has to be accepted as true. Before framing a charge the court must apply its judicial mind on the material placed on record and must be satisfied that the commission of offence by the accused was possible. Whether, in fact, the accused has committed the offence or not can be decided only during the trial. Charge may although be directed to be framed when there exists a strong suspicion but it is also trite that the Court must come to a prima facie finding that there exist some materials therefor. Suspicion alone, without anything more, cannot form the basis therefor or held to be sufficient for framing charge. (*Soma Chakravarty v. State through CBI*, 2007(5) SCC 403).

The petitioner further contended that six witnesses were examined in the Summary of Evidence and not even a single witness whispered about the culpability of the petitioner in the alleged offence. The evidence and other materials produced in the Summary of Evidence were silent, and do not remotely refer about any impropriety on the part of the petitioner or suggest that there was any illegality. It does not prima facie make out any offence for which above charges were framed against the petitioner. The petitioner continued to discharge his responsibility as being Senior Officer in a very honest and transparent manner but because of the mistakes of the Headquarter Western Command, the blame was attempted to be shifted against the petitioner without understanding the basic foundation of the case.

The Tribunal after the perusal of the exhibits observed that there was nothing to show that the addition of two tendering stations were not within the powers of the petitioner. Further the statement of six prosecution witness brought out the fact that no violation of the instructions/rules on the part of the petitioner was decipherable. The respondents, however, contested that in the case of risk purchase contracts, no relaxation of any kind to the terms and conditions of the original contract including specifications can be granted under any circumstances, as it would mean that stocks in RP contract are accepted on different terms and conditions compared to the original contract and in such case, the claim of RP loss will be held totally illegal and invalid by the Arbitrator and/or Courts of Law.

The Tribunal after scrutinizing the documents, was of the opinion that the entire evidence collected at the stage of recording of Summary of Evidence, does not show prima facie case against the petitioner to proceed with the trial against him. Even if the entire evidence produced from the side of the prosecution before the stage of summary of evidence was accepted to be true on its face value, no offence was said to have been committed by the petitioner and there was no ground to proceed with the trial against him. The Tribunal relied on the decision of the Supreme Court in the case of *State of Bihar v. Ramesh Singh* 1977(4) SCC 39, wherein the Court held:

> "....Strong suspicion against the accused, if the matter remains in the region of suspicion, cannot take the place of proof of his guilt at the conclusion of the trial. But at the initial stage if there is a strong suspicion which leads the court to think that there is ground for presuming that the accused has committed an offence then it is not open to the court to say that there is no sufficient ground for proceeding against the accused. The presumption of the guilt of the accused which is to be drawn at the initial stage is not in the sense of the law governing the trial of criminal cases in France where the accused is presumed to be guilty unless the contrary is proved. But it is only for the purpose of deciding prima facie whether the court should proceed with the trial or not. If the evidence which the prosecutor proposes to adduce to prove the guilt of the accused even if fully accepted before it is challenged in cross examination or rebutted by the defence evidence, if any, cannot show that the accused committed the offence, then there will be no sufficient ground for proceeding with the trial."

The Tribunal noted that the identical view was taken by the Supreme Court in the cases of *Union of India v. Prafulla Kumar Samal* 1979(3) SCC 4, *Niranjan Singh Karam Singh Punjabi v. Jitendra Bhimraj Bijjaya* 1990(4) SCC 76, and *P. Vijayan v. State of Kerala* 2010(2) SCC 398 as well. The Tribunal held that from the materials on record, no prima facie case was made against the petitioner and the charges framed against him were not sustainable. It quashed the charges against the petitioner.

Note: *The Union of India went in appeal against the decision of the Tribunal in this case. The Supreme Court did not discuss the controversy in the case but considered the provisions of sections 30 and 31 of the Armed Forces Tribunal Act, 2007. For the decision the Supreme Court, see under the heading 'Appeal to Supreme Court at page 68'.*

Excessive punishment

The AFT Regional Bench Lucknow in the case of *A K Bhardwaj (Ex Colonel) v. Union of India*, TA No. 429 of 2010, decided on 3 May 2011, considered challenges to the findings and punishment awarded by the GCM.

The applicant was tried by a GCM on 10 charges vide charge sheet dated 1 June 2006. The Court found him guilty on charges 1, 3, 4, 6, 9 and 10. The GCM gave special finding on charges 2 and 5. He was found not guilty of charges 7 and 8. The applicant/accused was awarded punishment of cashiering and RI for one year on 14 August 2007. The confirming officer by its order dated 22 December 2007 remitted unexpired portion of the RI. The post-confirmation petition was rejected by the Government on 22 September 2008.

The Tribunal substituted the punishment of 'forfeiture of 10 years of service for pension' against the punishment of 'cashiering' awarded by the GCM. The Tribunal further ordered that the appellant shall be deemed to have retired from service on 30 November 2010 but will not be entitled to pay and allowance for the period from 14 January 2008 (date of promulgation) till 30 November 2010. This period shall however, count for calculation of the pensionary benefits.

Offence under section 302 IPC, converted to 304 IPC

The AFT Principal Bench New Delhi in the case of *Ex Sep Balinder Pandey v. Union of India*, TA No. 432 of 2010 [WP (C) No. 3466 of 2007], decided 19 March 2012, considered a prayer for quashing the proceedings of a GCM.

The petitioner was enrolled in the Indian Army on 18 March 1983. He was subsequently posted in the hostile counter insurgency environment of Jammu & Kashmir. On 17 January 1994 at approximately 7.15 pm when liquor was being issued, the petitioner's loaded rifle Butt No. 95 accidentally fired a shot killing a Lance Naik. An FIR, No. 9 of 1994, was lodged in police station Punch under section 304 of the RPC by the company commander. After investigation the police authorities came to the conclusion that the crime was committed under section 304 of the Ranbir Penal Code (RPC). The petitioner was, however, charged under section 69 of the Army Act read with section 302 of the RPC. The charge read: "on 17 January 1994, by intentionally causing the death of XXXX of the same unit, committed murder." The petitioner was sentenced to suffer life imprisonment and to be dismissed from service.

In confirmation, the proceedings of the GCM were returned by the convening/confirming authority for revision. In the revision order, the convening authority commented:

> "While in no way intending to interfere with the discretion of the Court in arriving at their finding, I, as the Confirming officer, am of the view that the finding of Guilty arrived at by the Court on the charge is not supported by the reasons given by the Court, as Court has specifically mentioned in their reasons that the prosecution has failed to prove that the accused had intentionally caused the death of the deceased. The Court instead has said that the case was covered under the Fourth Clause of Section 300 of RPC, which means that the accused knew that his act of firing was so imminently dangerous that it would in all probability have caused the death of the deceased. In view of the above, the finding of the Court is perverse and to that extent is required to be reconsidered in the light of my following observations.
>
> In the particulars of the charge it is averred that the accused by intentionally causing death of XXXX of the same unit by committing murder. To find accused "Guilty" of this charge it was essential for the Court to have satisfied itself about intention to cause death, on the part of the accused. If Court was not satisfied of the proof of this essential ingredient but was satisfied that the accused while firing upon the deceased knew that his act of firing was so imminently dangerous that it must in all probability, cause death, the Court should have arrived at special finding as envisaged in Army Rule 62(4) & (5).

Notwithstanding such remarks by the confirming authority, the GCM on revision stuck by its earlier findings and sentence of guilty under section 302 of the RPC. The petitioner/accused's statutory complaint was rejected by the higher authorities.

The petitioner contended that investigation by the court of inquiry was not conducted properly and the mandatory provisions of Army Rule 180 were not applied correctly. Further, his statement was recorded as witness No. 1. He was not permitted to be present during the proceedings of the court of inquiry. Non-compliance of Army Rule 180 vitiated the entire proceedings and the consequent follow up action by the authorities. The petitioner also contended that he had no intention of killing the deceased and it had been purely accidental. For such accidental fire from his rifle he was very illegally and arbitrarily charged for an offence under section 302 of RPC. Instead, he should have been tried for an offence under section 304 of the RPC.

The Tribunal observed that while it had been established that the death of the deceased occurred by an act of the petitioner/accused, it has not been proved beyond reasonable doubt that the petitioner intentionally caused the death of the deceased. The intention to cause death has not been proved anywhere in the proceedings of the GCM. Not only this, at no stage has the prosecution been above to lead evidence of motive, mens rea, enmity or any other explanation for the death, and as accepted by the prosecution there is no eye-witness to the incident and conviction is based purely on circumstantial evidence.

Keeping in view the above, the Tribunal set aside the findings and sentence awarded by the GCM on 3 June 1995. It held the petitioner guilty of culpable homicide not amounting to murder as provided in section 304 of RPC read with section 69 of the Army Act and sentenced him to 10 years imprisonment. The Tribunal ordered that in case the petitioner/accused had already served this sentence, he would be set free, if not required in any other case.

Punishment of severe reprimand converted to reprimand

The AFT Principal Bench New Delhi in the case of *Gp Capt Ajit Singh, VSM v. Union of India* OA No. 117 of 2012, decided on 23 November 2011, considered a prayer to quash and set aside the findings and sentence of a GCM.

The petitioner was commissioned in the Indian Air Force as a Pilot (F) on 14 December 1979. On 26 December 1995, on a routine sortie, the petitioner had a mid air collision with another Aircraft resulting in crash of both the Aircrafts and causing a loss of Rs. 9.74 crore to the Government. The fall of debris of the crashed Aircrafts also resulted in the incidental death of two persons and injuries to one.

The petitioner was tried by the GCM during October-November 1998 and was found not guilty of all the charges. The confirming authority vide his order dated 27 August 1999 ordered a revision of findings and sentence by re-assembling the GCM on 08 November 1999. The GCM re-assembled accordingly and in the revised findings, found the petitioner guilty of first charge and not guilty of second and third charge. Thereby it imposed a sentence of "forfeiture of three months service for purpose of pay and pension and to be severely reprimanded." Aggrieved by this sentence, the petitioner filed a writ petition in the Delhi High Court which was transferred to the Armed Forces Tribunal as TA No. 343 of 2010. This TA was allowed by the AFT vide order dated 01 September 2010 in which the Bench directed:

> "10. In view of the aforesaid discussions, we are constrained to set aside the impugned order and remand the matter to the GCM for hearing the case from the stage it was remitted by the confirming authority. The GCM shall, however, be at liberty to take additional evidence and to afford audience to both the parties, if considered necessary, and to decide the case in accordance with law.
>
> 11. Since this case pertains to the year 1999 and there remains a possibility of availability of all the Members of the original GCM, the competent authority may substitute the members in the existing GCM, if not available or re-constitute the GCM for the purpose."

The petitioner was brought before the fresh GCM on 16 September 2011 and tried for three charges under ss. 62(a) and (d) of the Air Force Act, 1950. The

GCM found the petitioner guilty of first charge and not guilty of second and third charge and awarded sentence of severe reprimand. The petitioner, retired as Gp Capt, contended the punishment of severe reprimand awarded by the GCM.

The Tribunal observed that this was a one in a million chance that both the Aircrafts, though being separated widely in their flight paths, still managed to collide with each other. The Tribunal did not interfere with the findings of GCM. The Tribunal was of the opinion that considering the petitioner's length of service and his achievements both before the unfortunate collision and thereafter till the time he retired, was exemplary; the sentence of 'severe reprimand' was harsh. Further, the ends of justice will be met by substituting the sentence to that of 'Reprimand'. The Tribunal reduced the punishment from "Severe Reprimand" to "Reprimand".

Harsh sentence; acquittal with pensionary benefits

The AFT Principal Bench New Delhi in the case of *Wg Cdr M. S. Mander v. Union of India*, TA No. 14 of 2010, decided on 14 May 2010, considered a challenge to the disproportionate punishment awarded by the GCM.

Sep Garje (signalman) on 3 March 1998, alleged to have misbehaved with the wife of Flt Lt V, when he had gone to repair the telephone at his residence. Flt Lt V reported the matter to the petitioner, his commanding officer, who in turn reported it to the Station Commander on phone. The Station Commander directed the petitioner to further inquire into the matter before taking any action. The petitioner asked Flt Lt V to arrange the presence of Sep Garje. When Sep Garje did not turn up, he was forcibly brought in a vehicle driven by the petitioner personally. On questioning, Garje denied having done anything and gave an evasive reply. Thereupon, the petitioner ordered him to be kept in the guard room for further interrogation. While on way to the guard room in the Gypsy of the petitioner, in which three or four officers were also sitting, Garje jumped off the vehicle and started running on the kacha side. The officers, who were in the vehicle, followed him. While running, Garje fell into a ditch, his face down to the earth. He was taken to hospital for medical aid, where he died.

The petitioner and four other accused persons were tried by the GCM for offences punishable under Sections 302, 325 and 342 read with Section 149 of the Indian Penal Code. The petitioner/first accused was found guilty of Charge Nos. 3, 4 and 5 and the offence under section 304 Part II read with section 149 of the Indian Penal Code and sentenced to undergo rigorous imprisonment for five years and to be cashiered. On confirmation, the Chief of Air Staff (CAS) remitted the five years rigorous imprisonment to two years rigorous imprisonment and confirmed the sentence of cashiering. In respect of the other accused, the CAS remitted the sentence of RI and commuted the punishment of cashiering to forfeiture of two years past service for the purpose of promotion and two years service for the purpose of increased pay and pension and to be severely reprimanded. Against the punishment and sentence awarded by the GCM, the petitioner/accused filed an appeal in the High Court, which was transferred to the Tribunal.

The petitioner/accused contended that he felt humiliated for having been wrongly charged for an offence which he never committed and arbitrarily put to trial. He was given strikingly disproportionate and harsh sentence which was indicative of the biased attitude. The case was biased and the GCM appears to have been swayed by irrelevant considerations. The evidence has not been appreciated correctly by the GCM. It came to the conclusion merely on conjectures and surmises.

The respondents contested that the accused-appellant was found guilty of four charges for culpable homicide not amounting to murder under section 304 Part II read with section 149 IPC in conjunction with section 71 of the Air Force Act, for wrongly confining the deceased under s. 342 IPC read with section 71 of the Air Force Act, for behaving in a manner unbecoming the position and the character of an officer under section 45 of the Air Force Act and for an act prejudicial to good order and air force discipline by adopting improper method of investigation of alleged offence by deceased Garje. The accused appellant was convicted by the GCM after following due process of law. He was duly represented by counsel and neither had he objected to being tried by the GCM nor objected to any of the members at any stage, in spite of specific question put to him by the GCM to this effect. With regard to the misbehaviour of deceased Garje towards the wife of Flt Lt V, the GCM had gone in depth to ascertain the allegations, but no substantial evidence was found.

The respondents further contested that the petitioner was found guilty for adopting improper method of investigation for an offence alleged to have been committed by deceased Garje. The evidence on record suggested that some of the accused had picked up the deceased from his billet, taken him to the squadron Air Crew Rest Room (ACRR) and closed the ACRR shutters after he was taken inside. The appellant/accused brought the deceased in an unconscious state to the Station Sick Quarters. When he was medically examined, he was found to be in coma, suffering from severe head injury and multiple superficial injuries, including diffused swelling over scrotal sac. Though the deceased was operated upon on the same night, he succumbed to his injuries the next day. The sequence of events would itself show that the deceased was lifted by the accused-appellant and other accused. He was given fatal blows; resultantly he succumbed to his injuries. The materials and evidence on record substantiate the culpability of the accused-appellant. Even the inculpatory circumstances appearing against the accused-appellant also show his involvement in the crime.

The Tribunal observed that the appellant/accused gave his unworn statement in the GCM indicating how the unfortunate incident had taken place. The Tribunal opined, “This appears to be a natural statement of the appellant accused." The Tribunal concluded that in the absence of evidence, the case against the appellant/accused cannot stand. The findings and convictions were not sustainable. The Tribunal set aside the conviction and sentence awarded to the appellant/accused and ordered that the appellant/accused shall be deemed to be in service till the date of superannuation in the present rank and be entitled to pension thereafter.

Note: *The respondents have filed a SLP in the Supreme Court against the decision of the Tribunal.*

Reduction in punishment

The AFT Principal Bench New Delhi in the case of *Gautam Sanyal v. Union of India*, TA No. 484 of 2010 [WP (C) No. 1652 of 1990], decided on 19 April 2011, considered a petition for setting aside the proceedings of a GCM.

The petitioner was posted as Garrison Engineer at Gurdaspur in April 1982. Based on a complaint against the petitioner and his subordinates, an inquiry was instituted by his superiors. A charge sheet was drawn up against the petitioner on 25 March 1985, followed by recording of summary of evidence. The said charge sheet was cancelled and a modified charge sheet was issued to the petitioner on 19 May 1985 and a fresh summary of evidence was recorded. The petitioner was tried by a general court martial (GCM). Out of the six charges levelled against the petitioner under sections 52 (f), 57 (d) and 63 of the Army Act, the GCM found him guilty of five charges and sentenced him to undergo rigorous imprisonment for one year and to be cashiered. Both his pre- and post-confirmation petitions were rejected.

The petitioner contended that he was falsely implicated as a consequence of the conspiracy devised by his superiors and other officers. Further, he was not afforded a fair opportunity as contemplated under Army Rule 180 and also under Army Rules 22 to 24.

The Tribunal, due to lack of evidence, acquitted the petitioner for the offences under Charge Nos. 2, 3, 5 and 6, but upheld the conviction for the offence under Army Act Section 52(f) specified in Charge No. 1. The Tribunal converted the sentence of 'cashiering and the rigorous imprisonment for one year' into the sentence of imprisonment the petitioner had already undergone.

Note: *Note: The order of the Tribunal appears inappropriate as under section 74 of the Army Act, an officer shall be sentenced to be 'cashiered' before he is awarded punishment of imprisonment.*

***

The AFT Regional Bench Chennai in the case of *Lt (SDW) R.P. Sharma v. Union of India*, TA No.138 of 2010 [WP (C) No.19253 of 2000 High Court of Andhra Pradesh], decided on 19 November 2010, considered the challenges to a court martial.

The petitioner joined Indian Navy as Sailor in 1982 and was commissioned as Naval Officer on 01 April 1996. During the period 1996 to 1999, he was serving at Vishakhapatnam. In March 1999, a Board of Inquiry was ordered to investigate certain financial irregularities in the unit and the petitioner was also summoned as witness. The said Board submitted its report but the outcome of the inquiry was not known to the petitioner. Subsequently another Board of Inquiry was ordered in July 1999 for investigation into the circumstances leading to certain irregularities alleged to have been committed by certain officers of the unit.

A summary of evidence was subsequently ordered and the petitioner was tried by a Court Martial on 13 charges for falsification of documents, contravention of orders, negligence in performance of duties, cheating and acts prejudicial to good order and Naval discipline. The Court Martial had found the petitioner guilty of seven charges and awarded the punishment of forfeiture of thirty months seniority in rank of Lieutenant and forfeiture of thirty months time for promotion to next rank. Subsequently the Chief of Naval Staff (CNS) in judicial review set aside the findings in respect of three charged and reduced the punishment to forfeiture of seniority in rank for 24 months and a fine of Rs. 1000/- and severe reprimand. Not being satisfied with the verdict of CNS, the petitioner appealed to the Central Government against the said order which was rejected by the Government.

The petitioner contended that the Board of Inquiry held in March 1999 and July 1999 did not follow the mandatory procedure contained in para 205 of the Regulations of Navy Part II Chapter VII. Para 205 provides procedure to be adopted when character or conduct of a person in the Government service is involved. As per the said provisions in any enquiry in which the character or reputation of a person in Government Service is affected, he must be offered to be present throughout the inquiry enabling him to give his statement or evidence and must also be given an opportunity to cross examine any witness whose evidence is, in his opinion, affects him and also to produce defence witnesses.

The respondents denied the contention of the petitioner that his trial by Court Martial was based on the proceedings of the board of inquiry. The Court Martial trial was ordered based on an independent and de novo investigation by the Commanding Officer and also the evidence on record. Thereafter, in a trial by Court Martial, the accused was given every opportunity of putting up his defence before the Court. The Tribunal observed that Court Martial is an independent disciplinary process governed by separate and distinct provisions provided under Chapter V of Regulations of Navy Part II. The provisions of Board of Inquiry, provided under Chapter VII of the Regulations have no bearing on the trial by Court Martial.

After going through the evidence, the Tribunal set aside the conviction and sentence in respect of Charge No. 9. The Tribunal observed that when compared with the gravity of the offence, it cannot be said that the punishment imposed by the Court Martial was disproportionate. However, keeping in view the mental agony and anguish of the petitioner, the Tribunal ordered that the forfeiture of seniority in the rank of Lieutenant for a period of 24 calendar months to be reduced to nine calendar months and in other respects the conviction and sentence passed by the Chief of the Naval Staff will stand.

II. District Court Martial

Punishment of dismissal converted to discharge

The AFT Principal Bench New Delhi in the case of *Ex Cpl Nitish Kumar v. Union of India*, OA No. 184 of 2012, decided on 7 November 2012, considered challenge to the proceedings of and punishment awarded by the district court martial (DCM).

The petitioner, while serving at 13 BRD was granted leave of absence from 30 March 2010 to 20 May 2010. He overstayed the said leave without any sufficient cause from 21 May 2010 until he surrendered himself at 13 BRD on 03 August 2011. He was charged for the offence under section 39(b) of the Air Force Act, for overstaying leave without sufficient cause. During the trial by the DCM, the petitioner/accused gave unsworn statement under the Air Force Rule 66(2). The petitioner was questioned by the court and he also produced two witnesses in defence. The DCM found the petitioner/accused guilty and awarded the punishment of dismissal from service, reduction to ranks, and three months RI. The confirming officer remitted the unexpired portion of the imprisonment.

The Tribunal observed that the petitioner was ordered to be posted outside from Delhi to J&K on 16 February 2010 after having served at Delhi for about 3 years and 4 months. Then the petitioner had applied on 18 February 2010 for cancellation of this posting, which prayer was turned down on 22 March 2010. The Tribunal observed that the qualifying service of the petitioner/accused was less than ten years, and therefore, irrespective of whether the petitioner was discharged or dismissed, he would not be entitled to any pension. The Tribunal did not interfere with the finding of the DCM; however, in order to enable the petitioner to get himself rehabilitated by way of seeking other employment anywhere else, it converted the punishment of dismissal into discharge.

Note: *Note: Section 73 of the Air Force Act, 1950 does not include 'discharge' as punishment which could be awarded by a court martial. Since the Tribunal did not interfere with the finding of the DCM, which held the petitioner guilty, the conversion of punishment of 'dismissal' into discharge appears irregular.*

Opportunity to cross examination denied

The AFT Principal Bench in the case of *Ex Cpl Madan Kumar Singh v. Union of India*, OA No. 144 of 2009, decided on 11 April 2011, considered the legality of DCM.

The appellant was tried on thirty five charges, which pertained to (a) using insubordinate language to his superior officer; (b) disobeying a lawful command given by his superior officer by not parking the service vehicle at the road side and switching off the engine; (c) not following the instructions given to him by his superior officer at the parade ground; (d) over-speeding while driving the service vehicle; (e) not reporting to the Main Guard Room when ordered by his superior officer; (f) refusing to accept the leave cancellation certificate when ordered by the Unit Adjutant; (g) refusing to wait outside the office of his commanding officer when personally ordered by him; (h) failing to report for duty when ordered by the Unit Adjutant; (i) making false allegation against his superior officer while making a ROG complaint; and (j) assaulting his superior officer, etc. The applicant was tried by the DCM and was held guilty for 24 charges (out of 35 charges) and sentenced (a) to suffer rigorous imprisonment for one month; (b) to be dismissed from service; and (c) to be reduced to the ranks. The pre- and post-confirmation petition filed against the findings and sentence of the DCM were rejected.

The appellant pointed out that the findings arrived at by the DCM were illegal, mainly on the grounds that (a) the entire case was fabricated on account of enmity and the charges were framed with a mala fide intention to oust the appellant from service; (b) the DCM was convened against the provisions of Rule 43 of the Air Force Rules; (c) a fair opportunity to defend was not afforded to the appellant; (d) no documents were provided to the appellant; (e) the trial was not conducted in a fair and impartial manner; (f) proper legal assistance to the appellant was denied; (g) he was denied the opportunity to cross examine the witnesses and to examine defence witnesses; and (i) he was not provided a "friend of the accused" of choice.

The Tribunal considered the question whether the appellant was prejudiced by not testing the veracity of the witnesses for non-availability of a counsel of his choice. The Tribunal held that the prosecution witnesses were examined by the DCM in the absence of the defence lawyer, without giving the appellant an opportunity to cross examine any of them. Therefore, it cannot be said to be a fair trial. The Tribunal made reference to section 138 of the Indian Evidence Act, which stated that in the absence of cross examination, no reliance can be placed on the testimony of the witnesses examined in chief unless the accused chooses to do so.

The Tribunal placed its reliance on the decision of the Supreme Court in *Jayendra Vishnu Thakur v. State of Maharashtra* 2009(7) SCC 104, wherein the Apex Court has held:

> "24. A right to cross examine a witness, apart from being a natural right, is a statutory right. Section 137 of the Evidence Act provides for examination-in-chief, cross-examination and re-examination. Section 138 of the Evidence Act confers a right on the adverse party to cross-examine a witness who had been examined in chief, subject of course to expression of his desire to the said effect. But indisputably such an opportunity is to be granted. An accused has not only a valuable right to represent himself, he has also the right to be informed thereabout. If an exception is to be carved out, the statute must say so expressly or

the same must be capable of being inferred by necessary implication. There are statutes like the Extradition Act, 1962 which excludes taking of evidence vis-a-vis opinion (Sarabjit Rick Singh v. Union of India, 2008(2) SCC 417)."

The Tribunal held that the appellant has been denied the opportunity of cross examining the prosecution witnesses. It set aside the conviction and sentence awarded by the DCM and remanded the case to DCM only for affording the appellant an opportunity to cross examine the prosecution witnesses already examined. The DCM was directed to record a fresh finding on the basis of the evidence on record, including the cross examination part of the witnesses, after serving notice to the appellant. The appellant was reinstated in service but without back wages.

Lack of evidence

The AFT Regional Bench Chennai in the case of *Sep N. Baskaran v. Union of India*, TA No. 201 of 2010 [TA No. 898 of 2010, AFT, Regional Bench, Lucknow (WP No.11294 of 2007, Madhya Pradesh High Court at Jabalpur)] decided on 11 April 2011, considered an appeal against the verdict of the DCM.

The appellant was tried by a DCM under section 40(a) of the Army Act for having pushed and slapped his Adjutant on the face. He was awarded the punishment of reduction to ranks and to suffer three months RI. The confirming authority while confirming the findings and sentence on 24 May 2007 had directed the sentence of RI shall be carried out by 'confinement in military custody'. The findings and sentence of the DCM was promulgated to the appellant on 25 May 2007.

Since the appellant was sentenced to be reduced to the rank, he was reverted to the rank of a 'Sepoy'. The terms of engagement of Sepoy are prescribed in Regulations for the Army Para 134. As the appellant had already completed the terms of engagement of service prescribed for the rank of a Sepoy of 20 years (21 years 10 months) of service, he was liable to be discharged from service on completion of terms of engagement for his rank which he was presently holding. He was transferred to pension establishment i.e., Army Medical Corps Records, Lucknow, for completion of his pension documents and discharge. The applicant was discharged from Army Service with effect from 1 September 2007 (F/N) on completion of his terms of engagement.

The applicant alleged that during the recording of court of inquiry and his trail mandatory provisions of the Army Rules 180 and 23 were violated and he was not given opportunity to cross-examine the witnesses during trial.

The Tribunal observed that out of the eight witnesses examined on the side of the prosecution, no witness has corroborated the evidence of PW 1 as to the effect that at the time of occurrence, the appellant had uttered any filthy language against or any word as spoken to by PW1. Under such circumstances, the evidence of PW1 as narrated by him was considered highly doubtful. The Tribunal was of the view that the prosecution has not proved the guilt of the accused beyond any reasonable doubt. The Tribunal set aside the verdict of the DCM dated 28 March 2007 against the appellant. The Tribunal ordered that since the appellant has completed his tenure of service, he was entitled to all monetary benefits including pension in the rank he was holding at the time of DCM proceedings (Havildar).

III. Summary General Court Martial (SGCM)

Punishment reduced

The AFT New Delhi Principal Bench in the case of *Ex Sep/Dvr Rakesh Kumar v. Union of India*, OA No. 116 of 2010, decided on 25 February 2011, considered a prayer for quashing SGCM proceedings.

The appellant, while attached on temporary duty at Nagaland, was charge sheeted for having committed the offence under section 69 of the Army Act contrary to section 376 (1) of the Indian Penal Code. He was tried by SGCM on 28 July 2008. Having found him guilty, the SGCM sentenced him to RI for five years and to be dismissed from service. His pre- and post-confirmation petitions were rejected.

The appellant/accused contended that the trial by the SGCM was against the statutory provisions of law as it did not comply with Army Rule 180 by not giving him the opportunity to cross examine the witnesses. The sample sent to the Forensic Science Laboratory did not contain semen spermatozoa of the appellant, which was not taken into consideration by the SGCM while finding him guilty of the charge. The appellant further contended that he was charge-sheeted for an offence under section 354 of the IPC, whereas the trial was conducted under section 376(1) IPC, which was not informed to him. The findings arrived at by the SGCM were on conjectures and surmises and there was nothing on record to prove his guilt.

The Tribunal examined the evidence and came to conclusion that the case of "attempt to rape" has been well established. Further, the offence fell under section 69(b) of the Army Act, for which the maximum sentence was seven years and the appellant/accused had already undergone half of the sentence. The Tribunal reduced the sentence to the period already undergone by the appellant/accused.

Insufficient evidence, acquittal

The AFT Regional Bench Kochi in the case of *Gopi K v. Union of India*, TA No. 11 of 2009 [WP (C) No.19632 of 2003 of the Kerala High Court], decided on 30 July 2010, considered a prayer for challenges to the proceedings of a SGCM.

The petitioner on 2 February 2000, after doing escort duty for the Army bus to Jammu and back to his unit had taken his service rifle with 10 live rounds to his barracks at about 1830 hours. He had been detailed for subsequent night duty at the main gate. After dinner, while washing his plate outside the barrack, he threw dirty water from his plate on to the face of Sapper Mani who had also gone there to wash his plate. When questioned by Mani about his act, L/Nk Gopi caught him by the collar and threatened to kill him. Thereafter, while Mani was narrating the incident to Sapper Jose Cyriac inside the barrack, L/Nk Gopi went towards them cocking his rifle. Sapper Jose Cyriac pushed Sapper Mani away and held the rifle by the barrel pushing it upward when a round was fired by L/Nk Gopi. While trying to snatch the rifle away a second round was also fired. Meanwhile Hav Chandran and Nk Pradeep joined in the effort to disarm L/Nk Gopi and the rifle was snatched away. Then L/Nk Gopi picked up a stove lying nearby and hit Spr. Mani on his head. Others present then caught hold of L/Nk Gopi and took him outside and tied him to a tree. Meanwhile other officers of the unit reached the site. While being tied to the tree L/Nk Gopi continue shouting in Tamil that he would "kill ten more people." The Second-in-Command of the unit reached the place immediately and placed the accused in the unit quarter guard.

After initial inquiry, a summary of evidence was ordered which completed on 5 February 2000. The petitioner/accused was tried by a SGCM for the offence of attempt to murder Sapper Mani contrary to section 307 of Ranbir Penal Code (RPC). An Advocate of Jammu and Kashmir High Court was appointed as the prosecution counsel. One officer was detailed as defending officer and an Advocate of Jammu and Kashmir High Court as the defence counsel. The accused pleaded 'not guilty' to the charge. The petitioner was found "not guilty of attempt to murder but guilty of attempt to culpable homicide not amounting to murder contrary to section 308 of RPC." The petitioner/accused was sentenced to "suffer rigorous imprisonment for one year and to be dismissed from service".

The Tribunal made certain important observations of the evidence: (i) Two rounds were fired inside the barracks at about 2100 hours from the rifle which the accused was carrying, one of which hit the wall above the door and the other the leg of a charpoy and no one was injured. (ii) The Second-in-Command, spoke with the accused and then ordered that the accused be taken to quarter guard. The court failed to get valuable first hand input of the incident by not calling him as a witness. He had not deposed in the Summary of Evidence either. (iii) No medical checkup or psychiatric evaluation was carried out of the accused who had exhibited intoxicated, murderous behaviour and who had been manhandled by witnesses. (iv) Considering the events as averred by witnesses, a deeper probe into the "failure of leadership" in the Unit that night would have revealed a clearer picture of the events that night. (v) There was a reasonable doubt as to when and where the rifle was cocked.

The Tribunal was of the opinion that the SGCM had not done justice to the responsibility that has been placed on them. The SGCM had not considered the effect of contradictions in the evidence of eye witnesses or whether the version as spoken by the eye witnesses is probable or possible. It also did not consider the inherent improbabilities in the prosecution case. The Tribunal held that the prosecution failed to establish the guilt of the accused beyond doubt; hence he was entitled to an acquittal. The petitioner/accused was found 'not guilty' of the offences under section 308 of RPC also. The conviction and sentences imposed on the petitioner/accused was set aside.

Conviction based on confession, not corroborated

The AFT Principal Bench New Delhi in the case of *Ex Major YS Nagar v. Union of India*, TA No. 677 of 2009 [WP (C) No. 985 of 2001] , decided on 25 February 2011, considered a prayer for quashing the findings and sentence arrived at by the SGCM.

The appellant, on being commissioned in the Army on 19 December 1981, was chosen to carry out the intelligence duties in the troubled and terrorists infested valley of Srinagar in Jammu & Kashmir. During his service in Jammu & Kashmir, the appellant had tumbled upon a case relating to theft of large quantity of carpets from a factory in Srinagar, wherein the needle of suspicion pointed to certain Army officials also, which caused the fabrication of this case against him. The appellant was arrested on 24 February 1997 by the J&K police on the ground that three FIRs pertaining to robbery of cash and a vehicle had been registered and the appellant was a suspect. Taking notice of all the first information reports, the appellant was charge sheeted for having committed robbery contrary to section 392 of the Ranbir Penal Code (RPC) and for having possessed fire arms or ammunition without valid licence contrary to section 25(1)(a) of the Arms Act 1959. The SGCM found the appellant guilty of having committed the offence under section 392 RPC and not guilty of the offence under section 25(1)(a) of the Arms Act 1959. He was sentenced to be cashiered and to suffer rigorous imprisonment for seven years. While confirming the findings, the GOC-in-C, Northern Command remitted the sentence of seven years RI to three years RI. Both his pre- and post-confirmation petitions were rejected.

The appellant contended that the SGCM erred in relying upon the evidence of the accomplices viz. PW 2, PW 5 and PW 12. There was no evidence on record corroborating the evidence of the accomplices in material particulars. The appellant further contended that one tainted evidence cannot corroborate another.

The respondents contested that the appellant and the three accomplices had travelled in the same white Gypsy and committed the offence together. The respondents contested that the SGCM considered the entire evidence. Further, the appellant had made an extra judicial confession to his commanding officer on 14 March 1997 admitting his guilt. Under section 133 of the Indian Evidence Act, an accomplice shall be a competent witness against an accused person and conviction is not illegal merely because it proceeds upon the uncorroborated testimony of an accomplice. Therefore, the corroboration of evidence of the accomplice is not a requirement of law, but is merely the rule of prudence.

The Tribunal observed that two accomplices were not examined as prosecution witnesses, and third accomplice had not supported the prosecution case. It was categorically stated by him that he did not travel with the accomplices or the appellant on the alleged dates. Further, no test identification parade was conducted to establish the identity of the appellant or to link him with the commission of the alleged crime. Therefore, the SGCM arrived at the conclusion merely on conjectures and surmises and there was no evidence worth credence to prove the involvement of the appellant in the alleged offence. The amount was not recovered from the appellant and the material witnesses stated that they had not seen the appellant as they were blind folded.

The respondents also contested that PW 5 was tried by the SGCM separately for similar offences and was sentenced to be dismissed from service. As against PW 2 and PW 12, there was no evidence of their active participation in the commission of the offence as they were merely members of the protection party or driver of the vehicle used by the appellant. The evidence on record also proved that they were not aware of the intentions of the appellant or PW 5. They only obeyed the illegal orders of the appellant. Based on the information given by three complainants, police were detailed to keep watch and the Gypsy vehicle driven by the appellant was intercepted by them after a chase. One of the complainants recognised the vehicle and identified the appellant to be the person involved in the robbery. The appellant was given full opportunity to examine the prosecution witnesses, but he chose not to examine any of them. The extra judicial confession made by the appellant and its voluntary submission were proved before the SGCM through PW 20, who recorded the extra judicial confession. The appellant was afforded full opportunity to defend himself at the trial, wherein he was represented by a defending officer, two senior advocates and a friend of the accused.

The Tribunal observed that the Armed Forces (Jammu and Kashmir) Special Powers Act 1990 (Act 21 of 1990) was in force at the relevant time, which conferred certain special powers upon members of the Armed Forces in the disturbed areas in the State of Jammu and Kashmir. Under section 4 of the Act, any commissioned officer, for maintenance of public order, after giving such due warning as he may consider necessary, fire upon or otherwise use force, even to the causing of death, against any person who is acting in contravention of any law or order for the time being in force in the disturbed area or even arrest, without warrant, any person who has committed a cognizable offence or against whom a reasonable suspicion exists that he has committed or is about to commit a cognizable offence and may use such force as may be necessary to effect the arrest and to stop, search and seize any vehicle or vessel reasonably suspected to be carrying any person who is a proclaimed offender, or any person who has committed a non-cognizable offence. So, if any person was intercepted/interrogated by the Army officer within those powers conferred upon him by the Act 21 of 1990, no illegality or impropriety could be attached which may construe any offence.

The Tribunal also observed that from the materials on record, it appeared that the FIR with regard to the incident dated 19 February 1997 was lodged on 21 February 1997 at 1235h and with regard to the lodging of the FIR in respect of the incidents of 20 February 1997 and 21 February 1997 were concerned, there was reasonable delay, which would cast a cloud of suspicion on the credibility of the entire warp and woof of the prosecution story (*Ganesh Bhavan Patel v. State of Maharashtra* – AIR 1979 SC 135). In the absence of any identity of the persons who looted the complainants, the belated lodging of the reports would assume a circumstance that the complainants were deliberately creating time with a view to mould their case. There was no evidence to substantiate the plea. Both the material witnesses have not seen the appellant as they were sitting behind the driver seat and they were blind folded. Under such circumstances, test identification parade was necessary.

The Tribunal noted that in this case, the appellant was not known to two witnesses: PW 17 and PW 19, and, therefore, necessity to conduct a test identification parade was a must. No efforts seemed to have been taken in this case for conducting a test identification parade to prove the trustworthiness of the statement of the witnesses. The whole idea behind the test identification parade is that witnesses who claim to have seen the culprits at the time of occurrence are to identify them from the midst of other persons without any aid or any other source. The test is done to check upon their veracity. In other words, the main object of holding an identification parade, during the investigation stage, is to test the memory of the witnesses based upon first impression and also to enable the prosecution to decide whether all or any of them could be cited as eye witnesses of the crime (*Santokh Singh v. Izhar Hussain* - 1973(2) SCC 406). The identification proceedings are in the nature of tests and significantly, therefore, there is no provision for it in the Code and the Indian Evidence Act, 1872. It was desirable that a test identification parade should have been conducted as soon as possible after the arrest of the accused. This becomes necessary to eliminate the possibility of the accused being shown to the witnesses prior to the test identification parade.

As regard the confessional statement, the Tribunal observed the appellant had provided his official vehicle during the incidents which occurred from 19 February 1997 to 21 February 1997. The appellant had made it clear in his confessional statement that it was necessary for obliging a few surrendered militants and also to build up good rapport with them. There was no denial of the fact that the appellant as posted in the Intelligence Wing and such nature of duties was cast upon him. Even his name got changed for enabling him to mix up with the militants and to derive information from them. Even if the vehicle was made available by him, that is not the charge. However, the appellant is no where shown having participated in the incidents. As regards the total amount looted, he is simply attributing his knowledge and it cannot be inferred whether he looted the money or not.

The Tribunal after considering the evidence was of the view there was no trustworthy evidence by which the culpability of the appellant could be fastened for the aforesaid offences. The Tribunal set aside the findings and sentence of the SGCM and ordered that the appellant shall be deemed to have been discharged from service from the date he acquires pensionable service; and shall be entitled to all pensionary benefits from that date.

Prosecution based on extrajudicial confession

The AFT Principal Bench New Delhi, in the case of *Ex. Sepoy Gnr Amarjit Singh v. Union of India*, TA No. 189 of 2009 [WP(C) No. 1166 of 1996] decided on 27 August 2012, considered a prayer against the conviction and sentence by the SGCM.

The petitioner was enrolled in the Indian Army in the Field Regiment. He was jointly tried by a SGCM on two charges; the first charge under section 69 of the Army Act for murder, contrary to section 302 read with section 34 of the Ranbir Penal Code (RPC), and the second under section 69 of the Army Act for causing disappearance of evidence contrary to section 201 read with section 34 of the RPC.

The SGCM was conducted against the petitioner as well as other two other accused, L/Nk M Singh and Gunner R Singh, and were sentenced to life imprisonment and dismissal from service. Thereafter, matter was remitted back by confirming authority with regard to conviction of all accused under section 302 read with section 34 RPC and court revised their finding. The SGCM convicted the petitioner/accused Amarjit Singh under section 302 RPC and sentenced him to life imprisonment and dismissal from service. However, no separate sentence under section 201 read with section 34 RPC was passed. The SGCM deleted the charge of murder against accused M Singh and R Singh. They were charged under section 201 read with section 34 RPC. The Court convicted M Singh and R Singh under aforesaid section and sentence them to 6 years and 5 years imprisonment respectively and dismissal from service.

The petitioner made reference to the proceedings of the SGCM, court of inquiry and the summary of evidence and contended that there was no evidence to connect the petitioner with the commission of crime. The respondents, on the other hand, supported the proceedings of the SGCM.

The Tribunal observed that the order of the SGCM was non-speaking. The Tribunal scrutinized the evidence and observed that entire prosecution story had been enfolded by the evidence of Major B S Yadava (PW-1) of Field Regiment. After one of the soldiers of the unit went missing, a search for him was made and his body was found in a pond, about 200 meters away from the gun location. Few documents like identity card, driving licence and a fifty rupees currency note was recovered from the body. After completing the formalities, the body was taken away by the civil police to civil hospital, Rajouri on 22 April 1991. Before the body was taken away by the civil police, a military court of inquest was also held. Thereafter, on 23 April 1991, the post-mortem of the dead body was conducted and on 25 April 1991 the body was cremated.

During the investigation by Major Yadava on 29 July 1991 all the accused persons went to him and told that they wanted to inform something important relating to the incident of 14 April 1991. They were called one by one in his office. They first called M Singh (Accused No. 1). He said that he committed a mistake and wished to make a voluntary statement. Maj Yadava recorded his statement in English and the accused was also explained in Punjabi as well as Hindi and after having understood the statement he signed the same. Major Yadava also recorded the statement of Amarjit Singh (Accused No.2) who gave his version of the incident. Major Yadav further examined R Singh, (Accused No.3), who also by and large deposed same about the incident and supported the version that all three were drinking. Some more statements were also recorded. The Tribunal observed that the evidence which was reproduced, speaks volume that each one was trying to shift the blame on another. The question was that what would be the value of these statements, when they have been completely disowned during the trial by SGCM.

The petitioner contented that the evidence was inadmissible in law as so called extra-judicial confession had been retracted by the persons making them. The extra judicial confession couple with the last scene cannot clinch the evidence of the prosecution so as to uphold the conviction of the accused. The so called extra-judicial confessional evidence recorded by Major Yadava was also not consistent. The extra-judicial confession was very weak evidence and this confession alone cannot be sufficient to convict the accused for the crime. The Tribunal observed that, Courts have laid down that while considering the extra-judicial confession following factors should be kept in view namely, (i) to whom it is made; (ii) the time and place of making it; (iii) the circumstances & manner of narration creates a lot of doubt. It was very difficult in the background of unreliable extra-judicial confession to pin down petitioner/accused Amarjit Singh as responsible for death of L/Hav Amar Singh. The another difficulty in the present case, the Tribunal observed, was that so for as conviction of petitioner/accused Amarjit Singh under section 302 read with 34 RPC was concerned, it provided a benefit of doubt to the petitioner and accordingly, the Tribunal set aside the conviction under section 302 RPC.

On the question whether the petitioner/accused Amarjit can be convicted under section 201 read with section 34 RPC which had not been disturbed by the confirming authority. The Tribunal observed that there was no difficulty in accepting that all the three accused were responsible for disposal of the dead body of the deceased.

The Tribunal acquitted the petitioner/accused from the offence under section 302, but maintained the conviction under section 201 read with 34 and sentenced him to 5 years imprisonment and dismissal from service. Since the petitioner/accused had already undergone imprisonment for more than five years, the Tribunal ordered that he should not be sent back to jail, if not required in any other case and also confirmed his dismissal from the service.

Exceeding the right of private defence

The AFT New Delhi Principal Bench in the case of *Sep Raj Bahadur Singh v. Union of India,* TA No. 228 of 2009 [WP(C) No. 4018 of 2006 of Delhi High Court], decided on 27 January 2010, considered the trial of the petitioner under section 302 of the IPC by a SGCM.

In this case the petitioner was performing sentry duty alone at the main gate. He suddenly saw a man coming towards the gate with one hand in his pocket, which in those circumstances could be suspected to be having a hand grenade. As per procedure, the petitioner cautioned him not to advance to the gate but the individual did not stop. The petitioner assuming him to be a militant had no option but to open fire, aiming at lower portion of the body. The intruder died at the spot. The petitioner was tried by a SGCM under section 302 of the IPC. The Tribunal held that the petitioner has not been able to justify the opening of two rounds of fires causing fatal injury to intruder and by this he exceeded his right of private defence. He was found guilty under section 69 of the Army Act read with section 304 Part-I IPC and not under section 302 and sentenced to 10 years RI and a fine of Rs. 5,000.

Lack of evidence

The Armed Forces Tribunal Principal Bench New Delhi in the case of *Ex Hav Ashok M Rao v. Union of India*, TA No. 391 of 2010 [WP (C) No. 301 of 2008], decided on 25 March 2011, considered a prayer for quashing the proceedings of a SGCM.

The appellant was enrolled in the Army on 28 February 1990. On 7 March 2006, a surprise check was conducted in the unit of the appellant and a sum of Rs. 95,800/- was found from the box of the appellant. The said amount was seized. The appellant was tried under section 69 of the Army Act for committing a civil offence contrary to section 5(2) of the Prevention of Corruption Act, 2006. He was held guilty and sentenced (a) to be reduced to the ranks; (b) to be dismissed from service; and (c) to suffer rigorous imprisonment for three years in civil jail. His petition under section 164 (2) of the Army Act was rejected by the Chief of the Army Staff.

The appellant contended that (a) he was not afforded a chance to cross examine the witnesses, thereby Army Rule 22 was not complied with; (b) he was tried under section 69 of the Army Act, for which the respondents failed to take permission from the civil court under section 125 of the Army Act; (c) he was denied the right to engage a civil counsel to defend his case; (d) the charge levelled against him was very ambiguous as regards the amount alleged to have been found from his possession; (e) he should have been arraigned under the Prevention of Corruption Act and not under section 69 of the Army Act by the SGCM; and (e) the findings arrived at by the SGCM were merely on conjectures and surmises and there was no evidence worth credence to prove that the amount of Rs. 90,000/-, which was recovered from him, was disproportionate to his known source of income. The respondents claimed that the prosecution was based on the confession made by the appellant that he had obtained the money by selling military diesel to BPL drivers.

The Tribunal relied on the decision of the Supreme Court in *M. Krishna Reddy v. State Deputy Superintendent of Police, Hyderabad* 1992(4) SCC 45, wherein the apex Court enunciated the principles of law, which read:

> "7. To substantiate a charge under Section 5(1)(e) of the Act, the prosecution must prove the following ingredients, namely, (1) the prosecution must establish that the accused is a public servant, (2) the nature and extent of the pecuniary resources or property which were found in his possession, (3) it must be proved as to what were his known sources of income, i.e. known to the prosecution, and (4) it must prove, quite objectively, that such resources or property found in possession of the accused were disproportionate to his known sources of income. Once the above ingredients are satisfactorily established, the offence of criminal misconduct under Section 5(1)(e) is complete, unless the accused is able to account for such resources or property. In other words, only after the prosecution has proved the required ingredients, the burden of satisfactorily accounting for the possession of such resources or property shifts to the accused."

The Tribunal observed that except an extra judicial confession, there was no other substantive evidence in the case. The fact, situation and the surrounding circumstances of making confession cast a doubt on the veracity or voluntariness of the confession. Such a confessional statement cannot be relied upon. The Tribunal relied upon the decision of the Supreme Court in *Kuldeep Singh and another v. State of Punjab* 2002(6) SCC 757: "It is the settled legal position that extra judicial confession is evidence of weak nature."

The Tribunal held that the prosecution failed to prove that the appellant had amassed income disproportionate to his known sources of income and the charge under section 69 of the Army Act read with section 5(2) of the Prevention of Corruption Act 2006 (1949 AD)(J&K), which is pari materia to section 13(1)(e) of the 1988 was not established against the appellant. The Tribunal set aside the finding and sentence of SGCM and ordered that the appellant shall be deemed to have been discharged from service and would be entitled to all pensionary benefits from the deemed date of his discharge.

Note: *The respondents failed to execute the orders of the Tribunal in this case. On 19 November 2012, a cost of Rs. 20,000/- was imposed by the Tribunal and it directed that the amount should be recovered from the person concerned who was actually accountable for delay in execution of the order. On 31 January 2013, the case again came before the Tribunal in that the appellant alleged that order of the Tribunal dated 25 March 2011 was still not executed by the respondents. The*

Tribunal observed that the counsel for the respondents was not in a position to say whether order in question has been executed or not. The Tribunal commented that if the orders of the Tribunal are not executed for years, then there was no purpose for passing the orders; and gave a further time of four weeks for the execution.

IV. Summary Court Martial (SCM)

Violation of Army Rule 115

The AFT Regional Bench Lucknow, in the case of *Ex Naik Ravindra Kumar Kushwaha v. Union of India*, TA No. 146 of 2010, decided on 18 April 2011, considered a prayer for quashing the proceedings of a SCM.

The applicant was tried by a SCM on 15 July 1998 on three charges under the sections 52 (a), 56 (a) and 63 of the Army Act and awarded punishment of reduction in rank, dismissal from service and RI for six months. His petition under section 164 of the Army Act was rejected. His writ petition was transferred to the Tribunal.

The Tribunal observed that there were two sets of summary of evidence and in view of the plea of guilty recorded in the proceedings; no evidence was led by the parties. The petitioner contended that plea of guilty was wrongly recorded and he never signed against such plea. The respondents also failed to provide the original SCM proceedings to the Tribunal and the photocopy of the proceedings did not contain any certificate required under Army Rule 115. The Tribunal further observed that on account of conviction and sentence in unfair trial, the applicant's career has been damaged.

The Tribunal held that the applicant would be entitled to his salary from the date of dismissal i.e. 15 July 1998 till his date of engagement with interest @ 8% per annum. In addition the applicant would also be entitled to a compensation of Rs 2.0 lakhs.

***

The AFT Principle Bench New Delhi in the case of *Ex Gnr Ghan Shyam Singh v. Union of India*, TA No. 39 of 2010 [WP (C) No. 5888 of 2001], decided on 18 February 2013, considered a prayer for setting aside SCM proceedings.

The petitioner was enrolled in the Army on 10 August 1981. The petitioner while posted at Bikaner suffered mental break-down. He was downgraded to low medical category 'C' for psychiatry by a Medical Board held at Military Hospital, Delhi on 17 April 1990. After a month thereafter, he was again sent to Military Hospital, Delhi for re-evaluation of medical category with a view to discharge him from service on grounds of medical disability. In August 1990, the Petitioner was also operated in the Military Hospital for suspected case of cancer of the mouth.

The petitioner was granted 10 days casual leave from 21 to 30 September 90. While on leave at his home in Gorakhpur, he fell seriously sick. He was treated at Medical College Hospital, Gorakhpur and his family sent a telegram to his unit informing them of such sickness. In response, the unit instructed the petitioner to report of Military Hospital Gorakhpur and he accordingly reported to the Military Hospital, where he was advised to continue with his treatment at Gorakhpur Medical College Hospital. The petitioner remained under treatment at Gorakhpur Medical College Hospital till May 1991 as he was medically unfit to undertake any journey to join his unit. Once the petitioner was medically fit to undertake the journey, he reported to his unit at Bikaner on 11 May 1991. However, he was not allowed to join the duty and was told to go to the Artillery Centre at Nasik and join there, which he did on 15 May 1991. He was placed in military imprisonment which terminated with his trial on 12 September 1991 by the SCM for the offence under section 39 (b) of the Army Act for overstay of leave from 30 September 90 to 15 May 91. The SCM sentenced him to six months rigorous imprisonment and to be dismissed from service.

The petitioner contended that (i) he was not given a copy of the court of inquiry held to ascertain his absence under section 106 of the Army Act, wherein he was declared a deserter; (ii) he was not given a copy of the Summary of Evidence held in his case; (iii) he did not plead guilty to the charge as he did not sign the plea of guilty which was a mandatory requirement; (iv) no medical examination was conducted before the trial by SCM; and (v) a Junior Commissioned Officer (JCO) who had no knowledge of law was detailed as the friend of accused, and this JCO was of no assistance to him during the trial. Further, he remained in military imprisonment for a period of 79 days which was illegal and that he was illegally tried by the Commanding Officer of the Artillery Centre because it was only the Commanding Officer Field Regiment who could have tried him.

The respondents contested that a court of inquiry held under s. 106 of the Army Act was not required to be given to the petitioner as vide Army Rule 183(3), the authorities are merely required to make an entry of the findings of the inquiry in the unit Court Martial Book and destroy the original proceedings. The respondents also contested that a copy of summary of evidence as well as charge sheet was given to the petitioner on 05 September 1991, one week before his trial. The respondents also clarified that the petitioner had been sent for medical examination prior to the summary court martial and graded medical specialist diagnosed that there was no evidence of psychosis and the petitioner was fit to stand trial by court martial.

The Tribunal observed that the record of the proceedings showed that the plea of guilt was not signed by the petitioner. Therefore, it appeared that the petitioner might not have been informed about the general effect of the plea of guilt or about the difference in procedure which is involved in thc plea of guilt. Therefore, the finding based on the alleged plea of guilt would have no meaning at all. The Tribunal referred to the decision of the Delhi High Court in *L/Nk Gurdev Singh v. Union of India* (WP (C) No. 776 of 1995 dated 1 February 2008), which was followed by the Tribunal in *Ex Nk Subhash Chand v. Union of India* (TA No. 723 of 2009 dated 27 April 2010). The observations made by the Delhi High Court in L/Nk Gurdev Singh's case were:

> "Though the petitioner has allegedly admitted the charge by pleading guilty, his signatures nowhere appear on the purported plea of guilt. When an accused person pleads guilty, it would be necessary to obtain his signatures to lend authenticity to such proceedings. This basic requirement was not even adhered to, the absence whereof lends credence to the allegation of the petitioner that he was not even present at the time of recording of the summary court martial proceedings and he never pleaded guilty.
>
> In our recent judgment pronounced on 17 January 2008 in LPA No. 254 of 2001 entitled The *Chief of Army Staff v. Ex.14257273 K. Sigmn Trilochan Behera*, we have concluded that such court martial proceedings would be of no consequence and would not stand the judicial scrutiny. In forming this opinion, we had referred to the judgment of the Jammu & Kashmir High Court in the case of *Prithpal Singh v. Union of India*, 1984 (3) SLR 675 (J&K). We had also take note of the instructions issued by the respondents themselves in the year 1984, based on the aforesaid judgment of the Jammu & Kashmir High Court, mandating that signatures of the accused pleading guilty of charge be obtained and if there is an infraction of this procedural requirement, it would violate the mandatory procedural safeguard provided in Army Rule 115(2) and would also be violative of Article 14 of the Constitution of India.
>
> Faced with this, an innovative justification was sought to be given by the respondents, namely, the said guidelines were issued by Northern Command whereas the petitioner was tried by the unit in Eastern Command. We feel that the law of the land has uniform application across the country and there cannot be one law for a particular command and different law for another command under the Army. We may note that even this Court has taken similar view in *Lachhman (Ex Rect) v. Union of India*, 2003 II AD (Delhi) 103 wherein it was held as under:-
>
> > "The record of the proceedings shows that the plea of guilty has not been entered into by the accused nor has it been recorded as per Rule 115 in as much neither it has been recorded as finding of court nor was the accused informed about the general effect of plea of guilt nor about the difference in procedure which is involved in plea of guilt nor did he advise the petitioner to withdraw the plea if it appeared from the summary of evidence that the accused ought to plead not guilty nor is the factum of compliance of sub-rule (2) has been recorded by the Commanding Officer in the manner prescribed in sub rule 2(A). Thus the stand of the respondents that the petitioner had entered into the plea of guilt stands on highly feeble foundation."

The Tribunal commented that the legal position remains that the plea of guilt has necessarily got to be signed by the petitioner to give it authenticity. In this case, the signatures of the petitioner did not appear on the plea of guilt. It was, therefore, to be presumed that the petitioner did not plead guilty and the SCM proceedings should have been conducted on such premise. The Tribunal set aside the SCM proceedings and ordered that the petitioner will be deemed to be in service till he attains minimum pensionable service of 15 years. Based on the principle of "No Work No Pay", he would not be entitled to any salary for this period. However, he would be entitled to pension and other such retirement benefits from the date of the order.

No action against the instigator or co-accused

The AFT New Delhi Principal Bench in the case of *Ex L/Nk (DMT) Shyam Sunder Thakur, v. Union of India*, OA No. 87 of 2009, decided on 19 October 2010, considered a prayer for setting aside the proceedings of SCM.

The applicant was enrolled in the Army on 3 October 1998 as a Driver. He was charged under section 40 (a) of the Army Act for pointing his personal weapon rifle 5.56 mm INSAS at his superior (Naik) and moving threateningly towards him. He was tried by SCM and awarded the punishment of dismissal from the service on 3 October 2007.

The applicant contended that during the "face off" with Naik, while he was holding his own rifle, there was no magazine attached and the rifle was incapable of firing. Therefore, there was no threat to life of Naik. Further, it was not that the applicant had moved towards Naik with a view to assault him, the fact of the matter was that both the applicant and Naik moved towards each other in an aggressive manner. Therefore, it was not only the applicant who was at fault for supposedly assaulting Naik, the latter was equally culpable for assaulting his subordinate i.e. the applicant. The applicant also contended that he was tried by SCM in a most illegal and arbitrary manner, without application of mind or examination of evidence. He was dismissed from service, without giving any credit to his unblemished service of 13 years.

The respondents contested that the applicant was serving in an active border area in Jammu and Kashmir, wherein all personnel routinely moved with their personal weapon and ammunition. Therefore, any individual pointing his weapon against a colleague will be construed to be an act of assault and cannot be condoned. The aspect as to whether the magazine was attached with the rifle or whether the rifle was loaded was not relevant, because in that spur of the moment, when a threatening gesture is made, the person subjected to such threat cannot start analysing the efficacy of that threat and has to presume that the gesture was a genuine threat.

The Tribunal observed that there were no legal infirmities during the trial, which was conducted in accordance with the law. However, in view of the fact that there was provocation to the applicant and that he and Naik were placed in identical circumstances, while no action has been taken against Naik, it was inappropriate to single out the applicant for punishment. The Tribunal, therefore, set aside the proceedings of 3 October 2007, with the direction that the applicant to be reinstated within 90 days of the order.

Harsh and disproportionate punishment

The AFT Principal Bench New Delhi in the case of *Ex Gnr Krishan Kumar v. Union of India*, TA No. 312 of 2009 [WP (C) No. 7333 of 2009] decided on 19 October 2010, considered a prayer for setting aside his trial held by SCM.

The appellant was enrolled in the Army on 25 January 2002. On 10 September 2007, the appellant was posted to Field Regiment which was located in Assam. The appellant along with other personnel of his unit was assigned the specific task of carrying out surprise check of terrorists. They were required to establish "STOP" i.e. a military tactical post from where they could monitor the movement of terrorists. The appellant was detailed in one of these STOPs. The task was performed on the intervening night of 10/11 September 2007 and was completed by 0230 hrs on 11 September 2007. Thereafter, at 0545 hrs the same morning he was woken up and it was alleged that the appellant behaved in an intoxicated manner by running and shouting.

During the tactical manoeuvres in the night of 10/11 September 2007, the villagers had got agitated and initially 15 to 20 ladies assembled near the Army Camp at 0900 hrs on 11 September 2007 to complain about the manner in which the Army personnel had searched the village in the absence of the local police. This agitation by the locals increased and the village headman as well as the SHO of the local Police Station also arrived there. Thereafter, the media reached the site and because of all this intense pressure an FIR (No. 25/2007) was filed by the Police. Further, the Div HQ ordered a court of inquiry.

The petitioner was tried under section 36 (c) of the Army Act for "found highly intoxicated while deployed as stop on active service during Counter Terrorist Operations in operational area." He was awarded sentence of one year of RI and dismissal from the service on 12 November 2007. The Brigade Commander remitted the unexpired portion of the rigorous imprisonment on 25 January 2008.

The petitioner contended that the higher authorities in the Army had to show that they had taken some disciplinary action and found the appellant to be a very convenient scapegoat. He was not afforded adequate opportunities to defend himself during the trial or to put forth his case in accordance with the norms of natural justice. The appellant also contended the provisions of Army Rule 180 were not invoked. He was not allowed to be present throughout the inquiry and was not given the opportunity to cross examine any witness. Further, he was not even heard during the application of Army Rule 22 on 4 October 2007 wherein the commanding officer proceeded with the hearing as if Army Rule 180 had been invoked against the appellant during the court of inquiry, and therefore he could not produce any witnesses in defence. During the recording of summary of evidence which was held from 6 to 27 October 2007, he was pressurized to give a statement that he had consumed country liquor.

The appellant further contended that the timing of his SCM was wrongly entered. The fact remained that four personnel of the unit were tried by SCM by the commanding officer on the same day. None of them was heard in the manner as mandated by law and a common paper for compliance of Army Rule 115(2) was got signed from the appellant.

The respondents contested that appellant was deployed in a field area and was on active duty wherein a high degree of self conduct and discipline was expected. Therefore, for the appellant to illicitly procure and consume country liquor when operating with his weapon and ammunition was contrary to all norms of the Army discipline and in fact his conduct could have been dangerous to his colleagues and to the civil population at large. After consuming liquor, for approximately three hours, the appellant indulged in disturbing the civil population thereby drawing adverse public attention. The appellant was highly intoxicated, abusive in behaviour and compromised the ongoing Military operations. Therefore, it was not a trivial issue as was being made out by the appellant but one that ran contrary to all the functional norms and discipline of the Army.

The Tribunal observed that the appellant had put in six years of unblemished service and at the young age of 25 was proceeded against so harshly was injudicious. There was no evidence on record to suggest that the appellant's intoxication compromised the ongoing military operations by the Army. Neither was there any evidence that he consumed alcohol while on sentry duty nor did he commit any grievous offence after intoxication. Further, there was no evidence of the petitioner having used physical force against any soldier or civilian or being abusive against his superiors or of causing damage to any government property. Considering these facts, the Tribunal was of the opinion that the sentence awarded to the appellant was grossly disproportionate and harsh. For an offence of this nature, the appellant had already served 75 days in custody which meets the ends of justice. The Tribunal directed that the appellant be reinstated in service within 90 days of the order.

Punishment of dismissal: pensionary benefits

The AFT Regional Bench Kolkata in the case of *Gangeshwar Baitha (Ex-Havilder) v. Union of India*, TA No. 92 of 2010 [WP No. 18470 (W) of 2004], decided on 10 January 2011, considered a prayer for release of pensionary benefits.

The petitioner joined Indian Army in July 1971. He was absent without leave during the period from 11 March 1987 to 25 April 1987. The petitioner was tried by a SCM, which found him guilty on 6 May 1987 and awarded the sentenced of 'to be reduced in rank and dismissal from service'. The said punishment order was communicated to the wife of the petitioner at her native place at Bihar. The petitioner submitted a representation on 15 January 1991 praying for relief of pension and gratuity. However, respondents by their letter dated 11 March 1991 informed the petitioner that because of the punishment imposed upon him in the SCM, he was not eligible for service pension and gratuity. The petitioner again submitted a representation to the Chief of the Army Staffs on 1 September 2003 praying for release of pension and other benefits in his favour. The Record Officer, Bihar Regiment by their letter dated 27 December 2003 advised the petitioner to approach the President of India for such relief.

The petitioner contended that since in the punishment order there was no indication of denial of pensionary benefit the concerned authorities were wrong in withholding the pension and gratuity due to him.

The respondents contested that since the petitioner was dismissed from service under the Army Act he was not entitled to pension and gratuity under the Pension Regulation 1962. However, in an exceptional case the President of India may sanction such service pension in favour of the dismissed army personnel. Accordingly he was rightly advised to submit a representation with the President of India. However, the petitioner did not adhere to such suggestions. Further, in view of the decision of the Supreme Court in *Shiv Dass v. Union of India* 2007 AIR SCW 1487 the writ petition was not maintainable due to long delay.

The Tribunal observed that under sub-section (h) of s. 71 of the Army Act 1950 it has been provided that the Court Martial has the power of directing forfeiture of service for the purpose of increased pay, pension or any other prescribed purpose. Therefore, it was within the jurisdiction of the Court Martial to pass such sentence, but such sentence was not imposed upon the petitioner. As such, the authorities were not justified in not paying pensionary relief to the petitioner on the basis of sentence imposed upon him in the SCM. The Tribunal referred the decision of the Supreme Court in *Major G S Sodhi v. Union of India* 1992 (5) SLR 108; the Delhi High Court in *Brig A K Malhotra v. Union of India* 1997 (4) Service Law Reporter (Full Bench), wherein legal position was summarized as:

> "Under Regulations 3 and 4 so far as pension is concerned and Regulations 2A and 4 so far as gratuity is concerned, army personnel have normally a right to pension or gratuity if their service has been satisfactory. Even if they have been cashiered dismissed or removed by order of Court Martial, normally they are entitled to pension, gratuity and other benefits to the extent the Court Martial has not, as a measure of punishment for an offence, thought it fit to deprive them of. It is then in the discretion of the President acting under Regulation 16(a) to forfeit a part or whole of their pension. This discretion is not absolute. Merely because the punishment of cashiering, dismissal or removal has been imposed by the Court Martial, the pensionary benefits under Regulation 16(a) or other benefits do not stand forfeited. On the other hand , the fact that up to the date of the offences which were the subject matter of Court Martial proceedings, the service was satisfactory and the fact

> that the Court Martial had not thought it fit to forfeit the whole or part of pensionary or other benefits, ought to be taken into account by the Competent Authority under Regulation 16(a). while considering these later factors, the normal rule is that pensionary and other benefits are to be granted unless the Competent authority comes to the conclusion that the service of the officer taken as a whole was not satisfactory from the beginning or unless the offences which are proved and for which he has been sentenced are so extraordinarily grave that the entire previous satisfactory service is to be excluded from consideration. That would be a rare situation. Indeed if the offence committed was so extraordinarily grave, one would have expected the Court Martial itself to forfeit the pensionary or other benefits."

The Tribunal directed that the authority concerned should initiate an administrative proceeding by issuing a show cause notice to the petitioner as to why the pensionary benefit to which he was entitled, should not be forfeited.

Irregularities in court of inquiry and Army Rule 22

The AFT Principal Bench New Delhi in the case of *Sep Joga Singh v. Union of India*, TA No. 699 of 2009 [WP (C) No. 1917 of 2001] , decided on 24 February 2011, considered a prayer for quashing the findings and sentence arrived at by the SCM.

The appellant joined the Army on 01 January 1996 and was posted to the Sikh Regiment. His battalion was in Punjab till February 1999 and on 21 March 1999, he along with some other personnel of his unit reported to Rangiya (Near Guwahati) as part of the Advance Party of his unit to relieve another Battalion from their operational responsibility. On 25 March 1999, the appellant was detailed for Road Opening Duty along with a few other soldiers and the Army personnel were spread over an area of 2 to 3 kms. The appellant was deployed in an area opposite cinema hall and there was no separate spot/post earmarked for duty and all he was required to do was to dominate his stretch of the road tasked to him. While performing such duty, the appellant felt thirsty and went to drink water from a tap close to the cinema hall. He informed his 'buddy', and was away from the "Post" from 1345 hrs to 1400 hrs i.e. for a period of barely 15 minutes, during which period he was within the area of his responsibility and was fully capable of performing the assigned duty of road protection. During this period a complaint was made the lady operator of the STD booth located in the cinema hall complex that a soldier had misbehaved with her.

The commanding officer the appellant ordered a court of inquiry to investigate the circumstances under which the appellant misbehaved with lady in an STD booth at about 1400 hrs on 25 March 1999. It was followed by the summary of evidence. The appellant was tried by SCM under section 36 (d) (leaving his post without orders from his superior officer) of the Army Act and sentenced to dismissal from the service.

The petitioner contended that was implicated in a fabricated incident in a most harsh, illegal and mala fide manner, subjected to SCM and dismissed from the service. Further, the charge preferred by the Army authorities was that of absence from his post, the sentence was awarded to him was for misbehaviour with the lady operator. The summary of evidence as well as court of inquiry clearly established that the emphasis was on the fact that the appellant supposedly misbehaved with the lady operator. His absence from duty for this period of 15 minutes was a very secondary issue during the entire investigation.

The petitioner also brought out certain procedural illegalities in his trial:

(i) He was not given any time to prepare his defence. The Summary of Evidence was given to him on 28 April 1999 and his court martial was held on the same day. This was a gross violation of law and had denied him an opportunity to prepare his defence.

(ii) No hearing under Army Rule 22 was held. He was not been given any opportunity to explain his position/defence to the commanding officer.

(iii) The petitioner was called as Witness No 1 in the court of inquiry and forced to make self-incriminating statement. The court did not apply mandatory provisions of Army Rule 180.

(iv) The sentence awarded to him was harsh and shockingly disproportionate.

The respondents contested that the charge under section 36 (d) was preferred because of fact that victim was not forthcoming to lodge a complaint or to make a statement as it normally happens in our society where a social stigma is attached to the victims of sexual offences, thereby discouraging them to seek justice for themselves. The appellant had acted in a manner most unbecoming of a soldier in uniform by leaving his post in an operational area with the mala fide intention of misbehaving with a lady, and deserved severe punishment.

The Tribunal observed that the court of inquiry, the summary of evidence as well as counter affidavit proved that the authorities have linked both the offences i.e. misbehaviour with lady and leaving his post; but have formerly charged him only for leaving his post. The Army authorities were at liberty to investigate the charge of misbehaviour and punish him for the same. However, they have not charged him for such misbehaviour but have punished him for such misbehaviour, else why should a sepoy be dismissed from service for an absence of 15 minutes during which he went to quench his thirst? This amounted to vindictiveness, illegality and total arbitrariness. The Tribunal set aside the proceedings of the SCM and ordered that the appellant would be deemed to be in service till he attained his pensionable service after which he would be entitled to pension.

Records not available with the government

The AFT Principal Bench New Delhi in the case of *Ex Nk Jawar Singh Chauhan v. Union of India*, TA No. 475 of 2009 [WP (C) No. 144 of 1998, Delhi High Court], decided on 24 February 2011, considered the punishment awarded by the SCM.

The appellant was entrusted with the discipline and administration of recruits in a particular barrack. On 8 February 1987, when the appellant found that recruit D Singh not in his bed at the time of lights out, he had a search conducted for him and when the recruit came before him, there was an altercation and during such altercation, the appellant slapped him once. This one slap was projected by D Singh as being hit with a rifle sling on his hands and feet. The appellant was tried by a SCM on 27 February 1987 under section 45 of the Army Act, held guilty, and sentenced to dismissal from the service. His petition under s. 164 (2) of the Army Act was rejected in form of a non-speaking order dated 16 October 1987.

The appellant contended that he was not provided with the copy of the proceedings of the SCM or of the summary of evidence. He also contended to the 'plea of guilty' as recorded in the SCM, stating that he had never pleaded guilty during the summary of evidence or the court martial. Even the mandatory certificate under Army Rule 115(2) was not been signed by him. There was also non compliance of Army Rules 22, 115(2), 116 and 54, which deprived him of a just and fair trial. The appellant further contested the proportionality of the sentence as to whether a mere slap to an ill-disciplined recruit actually warranted his dismissal; especially when he had an excellent record of service, was an Instructor posted at the centre and tasked with the onerous responsibility of disciplining the recruits. The appellant also urged that he had put in 12 years and 128 days of meritorious service and to dismiss him in such high handed manner was uncalled for.

The respondents admitted that the original records of the SCM proceedings as well as the connected documents such as summary of evidence and the hearing under Army Rule 22 had been destroyed by the concerned department. In the absence of any records or evidence of the court martial, the Tribunal set aside the proceedings of SCM including the sentence of dismissal.

The Tribunal ordered that the appellant shall be deemed to be in service till he completes 15 years service and will be entitled to back wages from the date of his dismissal (27 February 1987) to the date he completes minimum pensionable service of 15 years, after which he will be entitled to pension in the rank of Naik.

Gross irregularities during trial

The AFT Principal Bench New Delhi in the case of *Ex Rfn Satbir Singh v. Union of India*, TA No. 454 of 2009 [WP (C) No. 1384 of 1999, Delhi High Court], decided on 24 February 2011, considered a prayer for quashing the punishment awarded by SCM.

The appellant was enrolled as a Sepoy in 1985. On account of Holi festival, 27 March 1994 was a holiday, and liquor was issued to jawans to celebrate the festival. It was alleged that the appellant, while not on duty committed offence under the Army Act and was charged under section 48 (intoxication), section 63 (an act prejudicial to military discipline in that he visited village Kupup violating the Battalion Routine Order, and section 46 (a) (disgraceful conduct). The SCM found the appellant guilty of the offences under sections 48 and 63 of the Army Act and sentenced him to dismissal from the service.

The appellant contended that the entire incident, investigation, recording of evidence and SCM was fabricated and illegal to dismiss him at the behest of some senior officers. The reasons were: (i) The timings of the three offences alleged to have been committed are most inconsistent and have been put there without any application of mind and were indicative of the casual manner in which the authorities have proceeded, (ii) In relation to the second charge, the Battalion Routine Order No. 158 of 1993 was never produced either during the initial hearing under AR 22 or at the recording of summary of evidence or at the trial; (iii) During the trial, the commanding officer (CO) decided not to proceed with the third charge merely because the appellant had pleaded not guilty to this charge and had pleaded guilty to the first two charges; (iv) The CO has erred with regard to the third charge, in that in the memorandum which he had signed after the court martial, he specifically stated that one of the reasons for the harsh punishment accorded to the petitioner was that "he was trying to have carnal intercourse with dog, however, the penetration could not be proved." It was inexplicable as to how after dropping the third charge the CO can still consider the third charge while giving such harsh punishment; (v) There was no commonality at all in any of the witnesses produced during Army Rule 22 and summary of evidence; (vi) The Commanding Officer ordered a summary of evidence to be recorded on 30 March 1994, but the summary of evidence was recorded on 6 January 1995, after a period of more than nine months, which has not been explained at any stage by the Commanding Officer; (vii) There were serious inconsistency in the SCM proceedings is that while the trial commenced at 1205h and concluded at 1230h, the promulgation has taken place at 1205h. This was grossly inconsistent and inexplicable and leads to the obvious conclusion that there was no factual trial and the appellant was only marched up to his CO and the formalities were completed in a very mechanical manner later.

The appellant also submitted that in a letter written to his wife (the next of kin) after the court martial on 28 January 1995, the CO informed that her husband had been dismissed from service for the following offences; in that he included the third charge, i.e. s. 46 (a) of the Army Act for disgraceful conduct of unnatural kind. The appellant further contended that if the third charge had been dropped, then how the CO could refer to it in the Memorandum of the SCM or inform the appellant's wife that he had been held guilty of this charge.

The Tribunal observed that the respondents had no real justification for the various legal inconsistencies that were brought out by the appellant. The Tribunal was of the opinion that this leads to a very definite conclusion that the entire proceedings of the SCM were a sham and had been completed after a period of almost nine months after the incident, in a most illegal and injudicious manner. The Tribunal set aside the proceedings of the SCM with the order that the appellant shall be deemed to be in service till such time that he earns pensionable service, after which he will be entitled to pension.

Violation of Rule 22

The AFT Principal Bench New Delhi in the case of *Ex Signalman Vijay Kumar v. Union of India*, TA No. 630 of 2009 [WP (C) No. 2123 of 2000, Delhi High Court], decided on 24 February 2011, considered a prayer for quashing the punishment awarded by SCM.

The appellant was enrolled in the Army on 5 July 1996. On 1 February 1998, the appellant along with a few other personnel of his unit was deployed on night guard duty at Military Cantonment. The appellant was on duty from 2100h to 2300h and was to be relieved by L/Nk Ramesh. Both L/Nk Ramesh and the appellant had consumed liquor on the night of the incident and at 2300h, the appellant went at least twice to wake up L/Nk Ramesh, so that he could relieve him from duties. Heated argument ensued between the appellant and L/Nk Ramesh, wherein L/Nk Ramesh alleged that the appellant pointed a loaded LMG towards him. There was a scuffle between these two individuals and Nb Sub Madan Mohan and L/Hav Ponnacha intervened. The appellant was taken into custody and a charge under section 63 of the Army Act. A summary of evidence was held, in which five witnesses were examined. He was subsequently tried by a SCM and sentenced to dismissal.

The appellant contended a court of inquiry was ordered into the incident but provisions of Army Rule 180 were not applied thereby depriving him of the opportunity of being present throughout the inquiry, of cross examining the witnesses, producing defence witnesses and making a statement. The court of inquiry, therefore, gave a one sided account of the incident, which was the basis on which the authorities proceeded against him. Further, no hearing under Army Rule 22 was held. Army Rule 22 has been further amplified by Army Order No. 24 of 1994, wherein it categorically states that non-compliance of the rule will vitiate any subsequent disciplinary proceedings. In addition, the plea of guilt endorsed in the SCM proceedings was not an unequivocal plea of guilty. In fact, he was induced to plead guilty with a promise that a lenient view would be taken against him. It was also contended by the appellant that the sentence awarded to him was harsh and shockingly disproportionate.

The respondents contested that the appellant had committed a very serious offence and the LMG was, in fact, loaded with 24 rounds of ammunition and could have resulted in loss of life. Further, both L/Nk Ramesh and the appellant had consumed some alcohol, they were not "intoxicated" and were capable of performing their normal functions and had a clear understanding of events. For an offence of this nature, the punishment meted out to the appellant was not harsh, especially considering that he had two red ink entries earlier in his career.

The Tribunal was of the view that since no hearing under AR 22 had been held and also that the plea of guilty was not in consonance with the summary of evidence wherein the appellant had repeatedly indicated that he was not guilty, it was incumbent on the Commanding Officer to convert the 'plea of guilty' to 'not guilty' under the provisions of AR 116(4). The Tribunal was of the opinion that there has been miscarriage of justice. It, therefore, set aside the proceedings of the SCM and directed that the appellant be deemed to be in service till he completes minimum pensionable service, after which he will be entitled to pension in accordance with the Rules.

Irregularity during trial

The AFT Principal Bench New Delhi in the case of *Satpal Singh v. Union of India*, TA No. 536 of 2009 [WP (C) No. 2161 of 1998] decided on 1 December 2010, considered a prayer for setting aside SCM proceedings.

The appellant was granted annual leave from 5 July to 4 September 1995. During the period of leave, the appellant had gone to his village in Delhi. His village was one of the worst affected during the floods in September 1995 and consequently, because his aged parents had to be assisted, he overstayed his leave. The appellant informed about the delay to his unit. He reported to Transit Camp at Jammu 15 days late. Because of the procedural formalities at the Transit Camp and the heavy rush of transients, he could not be sent to his unit within the desired time frame and he continued to stay at this Transit Camp for approximately 15 days. Thereafter, the commanding officer of the Transit Camp ordered him to go to the Army Medical Corps Centre and Training School, Lucknow where he reported on 27 October 1995. Immediately on reporting to the Centre, he had informed his Subedar Suresh Kumar about the floods at his village and also that he had reported to 213 Transit Camp. The appellant was tried by a SCM for two offences under sections 39(b) and 54(b) of the Army Act on 10 January 1996, and was sentenced to dismissal from service.

The appellant contended that the fact he reported to 213 Transit Camp was not taken into consideration by the SCM. Further, no effort was made by the respondents to ascertain whether the appellant, in fact, reported to 213 Transit Camp or not, in that the respondents had sent a query to the Transit Camp on 5 January 1996, response to which was sent by the Transit Camp on 16 January 1996 and in the interim, the appellant was tried by SCM and dismissed from service on 10 January 1996. It was, therefore, a mockery of justice that the respondents could not even wait for the reply from the Transit Camp before proceeding against him.

The appellant further contended that all necessary proof was submitted by him about the floods, in that newspaper clipping, certificate from the village elder, as well as from the local Bharat Kissan Union office of his village was submitted, which was not even enquired into by his commanding officer and was arbitrarily dismissed. The appellant also contended that his signatures do not appear on the 'plea of guilty' on the original record of the SCM proceedings which certifies to the compliance of Army Rule 115(2). In fact, his signature was obtained on a blank paper and the certificate typed on it after the trial and pasted onto the proceedings. This was in gross violation of the legal principles. Further, a gross illegality had been committed by the officer conducting the trial, in that at page "C" of the proceedings, the officer conducting the trial has changed the plea of "guilty" to "not guilty", supposedly in accordance with the provisions of Army Rule 116(4) and endorsed the following certificate: "The court having satisfied from the statement of the accused (or the Summary of Evidence) that the accused did not understood the effect of the plea of "Guilty" alters a plea of "Not Guilty". In accordance with this certificate, when the plea of "guilty" is changed to "not guilty", the summary of evidence has to be set aside and the testimony of all the witnesses recorded afresh during the proceedings. This was not done and in gross violation of the provisions of the Army Act and the Rules, the he was dismissed from the service.

The respondents admitted that during the summary of evidence, only two witnesses had been examined, the first of which Sub Suresh Kumar (PW 1) was performing the duties of JCO Adjutant at the Army Medical Corps Centre and School, Lucknow and had accepted the surrender of the appellant. He had also testified that the appellant had informed him of the flood in his house and also that he had reported to 213 Transit Camp only 15 days late from leave. PW 2 is a Clerk who has merely testified on the factual position of his leave certificate. The Tribunal observed that in the face of such sketchy evidence/ investigation, a fair and judicious trial cannot be expected. The Tribunal also observed that the record of the proceedings showed that the plea of guilt had been signed by the appellant on an overleaf annexed to the proceedings and it was recorded on the original proceeding.

The Tribunal relied on the decision of the Delhi High Court in *L/Nk Gurdev Singh v. Union of India* (WP (C) No. 776 of 1995 dated 1 February 2008), which was followed by the Tribunal in *Ex. Nk Subhash Chand v. Union of India* (TA No. 723 of 2009 dated 27 April 2010). The observations made by Delhi High Court in L/Nk Gurdev Singh's case were:

"Though the petitioner has allegedly admitted the charge by pleading guilty, his signatures nowhere appear on the purported plea of guilt. When an accused person pleads guilty, it would be necessary to obtain his signatures to lend authenticity to such proceedings. This basic requirement was not even adhered to, the absence whereof lends credence to the allegation of the petitioner that he was not even present at the time of recording of the summary court martial proceedings and he never pleaded guilty.

In our recent judgment pronounced on 17 January 2008 in LPA No.254 of 2001 entitled The *Chief of Army Staff v. Ex. 14257273 K. Sigmn Trilochan Behera*, we have concluded that such court martial proceedings would be of no consequence and would not stand the judicial scrutiny. In forming this opinion, we had referred to the judgment of the Jammu & Kashmir High Court in the case of *Prithpal Singh v. Union of India* 1984 (3) SLR 675 (J&K). We have also taken note of the instructions issued by the respondents themselves in the year 1984, based on the aforesaid judgment of the Jammu & Kashmir High Court, mandating that signatures of the accused pleading guilty of charge be obtained and if there is an infraction of this procedural requirement, it would violate the mandatory procedural safeguard provided in Rule 115(2) of the Army Rules and would also be violative of Article 14 of the Constitution of India.

Faced with this, an innovative justification was sought to be given by the respondents, namely, the said guidelines were issued by Northern Command whereas the petitioner was tried by the unit in Eastern Command. We feel that the law of the land has uniform application across the country and there cannot be one law for a particular command and different law for another command under the Army. We may note that even this Court has taken similar view in *Lachhman (Ex Rect) v. Union of India* 2003 II AD (Delhi) 103 wherein it was held as under:

> "The record of the proceedings shows that the plea of guilty has not been entered into by the accused nor has it been recorded as per Rule 115 in as much neither it has been recorded as finding of court nor was the accused informed about the general effect of plea of guilt nor about the difference in procedure which is involved in plea of guilt nor did he advise the petitioner to withdraw the plea if it appeared from the summary of evidence that the accused ought to plead not guilty nor is the factum of compliance of sub-rule (2) has been recorded by the Commanding Officer in the manner prescribed in sub rule 2(A). Thus the stand of the respondents that the petitioner had entered into the plea of guilt stands on highly feeble foundation."

The Tribunal set aside the SCM proceedings of 10 January 1996, with the order that the appellant shall be deemed to be in service without back wages and the interregnum period shall be counted towards the effective service rendered for all purposes.

Power to enhance punishment : not allowed

The AFT New Delhi Principal Bench in the case *Naik Yogendra Singh v. Union of India*, TA No. 543 of 2010, [WP (C), High Court Mumbai] decided on 16 September 2010, considered the trial by SCM.

The petitioner was initially tried by SCM on 11 February 2008. He was convicted for the offence committed on 11 January 2007 under section 69 of the Army Act read with section 354 of the IPC and sentenced reduction in rank. The petitioner alleged that while initiating disciplinary proceedings against him, a fair court of inquiry was not held and the relevant Rules were not adhered to. He was not even supplied copies of the court of inquiry and the summary of evidence so as to enable him to cross examine the witnesses.

The petitioner was subsequently served with the show cause notice by the Commander HQ Mumbai Sub Area, wherein reference to the incident of 11 January 2007 and his trial by SCM was also made. The other two instances with regard to over-stayal of leave were also referred to in the show cause notice issued under section 20 of the Army Act read with Army Rule 17. A subsequent dismissal order of 18 March 2009, referring to the incident of 11 January 2007, stated that taking into gravity of the charge further retention of the petitioner in the service was detrimental to the interest of maintenance of military discipline.

The Tribunal held that after the trial of the petitioner by SCM, and the exercise of powers by the competent authority under section 20 of the Army Act amounted to putting the accused in peril twice for the same offence. The Bench referring to the decision of the Supreme Court in *Union of India v. Harjeet Singh Sandhu* (AIR 2001 SC 1772), observed that the commanding officer has no power under section 20 of the Army Act to enhance the punishment awarded by the SCM. The Tribunal held that the petitioner shall be deemed to have been discharged from service from the date of his dismissal from service and shall be entitled to all pensionary benefits.

Harsh Punishment

The AFT Regional Bench Chennai in the case of *K Tirupathi v. The Chief of the Army Staff* , TA No. 40 of 2009 [WP No. 36700 of 2003], decided on 4 March 2010, considered a prayer for quashing the punishment awarded by the SCM.

The petitioner was recruited as a Gunner in the Indian Army. He was employed in the house of his commanding officer to work as orderly and entrusted with the house hold work such as to washing, to polish the shoes, taking care of the children by taking them to school and to bring them back, to purchase vegetables and other provisions, etc. The petitioner alleged that even though he had carried out the work entrusted to him without any protest, the said officer and his wife treated him like a slave and on one occasion their attitude towards him was intolerable which made him to burst his feelings. Since then the commanding officer and his wife made all kinds of attempts to victimize the petitioner in one way or other which prompted him to come out from the house and on his request he was posted as a sentry. To take revenge, the commanding officer charged the petitioner under (i) section 36 (d) of the Army Act – leaving his post without orders from his superior officer; (ii) section 38 (1) of the Army Act – deserting the service, (iii) section 52 of the Army Act – committing theft in respect of property belonging to the Government.

The petitioner was tried by SCM on 24 April 2001 and awarded the punishment of (i) to suffer rigorous imprisonment for one year in civil prison, and (ii) dismissal from service. The trial lasted merely for one hour from 0700 hrs to 0800 hrs. Immediately after the award of the punishment, the petitioner was sent to prison on the same day i.e., 24 April 2001 and was detained in district jail Sivasagar to undergo the RI. He was not allowed to file any appeal against the order of punishment and could not contact his mother. The petitioner's mother was making periodical representations to the authorities concerned and that in the reply of 30 July 2001, she was informed about the punishment. After the completion of one year imprisonment, the petitioner approached the civil court for his reinstatement and to set aside the impugned order of the summary court martial.

The petitioner contended that the matter was investigated by the commanding officer but he was not given any opportunity to cross examine any witness disposed against him. He was forced to sign in the places marked by the commanding officer and it was written as if he waived the right to cross examine the witnesses. The reply, the respondent contested that the petitioner was given sufficient opportunity to explain his case before the court of inquiry. He deserted the service with a weapon and live ammunition and was apprehended at Guwahati Railway station. When he was brought in front of the commanding officer, he pleaded guilty to the charges.

The Tribunal observed that the Daily Arms Issue Register produced by the respondent was highly doubtful because the signature of the petitioner contained in it did not tally with the signature of the petitioner in other documents. The Tribunal also pointed out that conduct of the SCM itself was questionable because it started at 0700 hours on 24 April 2001 and completed at 0800 hours on the same date. The Tribunal held that third charge framed against the petitioner was not proper because the arms and ammunition were issued to the petitioner and it cannot be said that the petitioner had committed theft of arms and ammunition under section 52(a) of the Army Act.

Tribunal referred the observation of the Supreme Court in *Sheel Kr. Roy v. Secretary, Ministry of Defence* (2008) I MLJ (Crl) 481 (SC): "Other relevant facts not taken into consideration. Merely because the appellant was in the Army, he is not deprived for human or Fundamental Rights. Fairness and reasonableness is the hallmark of Article 14 of the Constitution of India. Imposition of double punishment by Court Martial without giving reasons is wholly arbitrary. Impugned order is unsustainable. In the circumstance, the appellant must be deemed to have been discharged from service with effect from the date of the impugned order of dismissal."

The Tribunal modified the punishment of dismissal to that of discharge from service with effect from the normal date of petitioner's superannuation in the present rank as a Sepoy. The petitioner was deemed to be discharged with effect from the date of judgement with full pensionary benefits.

Conviction without evidence

The AFT Principal Bench New Delhi in the case of *Ex Signalman Rajesh Kumar v. Union of India*, TA No. 426 of 2010 [WP (C) No. 44 of 2008], decided 5 February 2010, considered a prayer for quashing the proceedings of SCM.

The petitioner was performing the duties as a Sahayak to an officer since the month of October 1997. The said officer was having a Maruti Car bearing registration No XXXX. The petitioner proceeded on leave on 26 November 1997 and had also given his contact number to the officer. On 28 November

1997, the said officer noticed that his care was not in the garage and the complaint to that effect was also lodged to the Police at PS Delhi Cantt. The officer called back the petitioner to assist in the investigations and he expressed his suspicion on Driver Ashok Kumar who in the past had enquired about that vehicle. His whereabouts were also disclosed by the petitioner and the vehicle was recovered from the possession of Ashok Kumar on 30 November1997 in Jhunjhunu, Rajasthan. Driver Ashok Kumar gave his confessional statement and also implicated the petitioner stating that the said vehicle was sold by the petitioner to him for consideration of Rs 50,000; out of which Rs 30,000/- were paid by him and the rest of the amount was assured to be paid after some time. On the basis of the confessional statement of Ashok Kumar, the petitioner was also tried by the SCM on 31 August 2000 for the offence under section 379 IPC read with section 52(a) of Army Act. The culpability of the petitioner was fixed on the so called confessional statement recorded by the civil police. The petitioner was awarded the sentence of six months RI and the dismissal from service.

The petitioner contended that the SCM awarded him punishment without any evidence merely on conjectures and surmises. Further, while recording his plea of guilty provisions of Army Rule 115(2) were not taken into consideration.

The Tribunal observed that the confession made before the civil police had no legal sanctity and could not be had in evidence. Moreover such confession of co-accused cannot be the sole basis of conviction as was held by the *Apex Court in the case of Sidharth v. State of Bihar*, 2006 (1) SCC. The Tribunal also observed that Driver Ashok Kumar thereafter absconded and no opportunity was given to the petitioner to cross examine him. Further there was no evidence with regard to the receipt of Rs. 30,000 by the petitioner from Ashok Kumar as a part of the consideration of that vehicle. In addition the complainant was never examined by the SCM. He was the person who could give the best evidence. The non production of the evidence has certainly prejudiced the fair trial of the appellant.

Relying on the decision of the Supreme Court in the case of *S. Harnam Singh v. State (Delhi Administration)* AIR 1976 SC 2140, the Tribunal observed that the petitioner was held guilty without recording the statement of any of the witness. Such plea of guilt alone is not sufficient unless there was evidence worth credence to fix the culpability of the petitioner. The Tribunal set aside the punishment awarded by SCM, with the order that the petitioner shall be deemed to have discharged from service on the date when he was dismissed and would be entitled for pensionary benefits.

Non-compliance of Army Rule 115

The AFT Regional Bench Lucknow in the case of *Hav Shiv Kumar Joshi v. Union of India*, OA No. 02 of 2009, decided on 16 March 2010, considered the challenge to the sentence awarded by a SCM.

The applicant was charged for (a) committing theft of HDFC Bank ATM Debit Card, the property belonging to Naik V Kumar of the same Regiment, and (b) with intent to cause wrongful loss to Naik V Kumar withdrawing Rs. 15,000/- from HDFC Bank Account by using ATM Debit Card. The petitioner, as stated in the SCM proceedings, had pleaded guilty to both the charges and was awarded punishment of dismissal from service and reduction to the ranks.

The Tribunal observed that Army Rule 115 has not been complied with in this case as the plea of 'guilty' or 'not guilty' has to be separately recorded in respect of each charge whereas the commanding officer has recorded the plea of guilty in a composite manner. The Tribunal further observed that the provisions of Rule 115 (1) appear to be mandatory in view of the word "shall" used therein. A further safeguard in sub-rule 2A of Rule 115 was inserted by amendment in the Army Rules in 1993. In a case the accused pleads guilty a certificate of the commanding officer is required to the effect that the accused has understood the nature of the charges and was informed of the general effect of the plea of guilty and about the difference in procedure which will be followed in consequence of the plea. Rule 116 contains further safeguards. Sub-rule 2 of Rule 116 provides that after the accused has pleaded guilty the court shall read the summary of evidence. Sub-rule 4 of Rule 116 casts a duty upon the court that if from the statement of the accused or from the summary of evidence or otherwise it appears to the court that the accused did not understand the effect of the plea of guilty it shall after the record and enter a plea of "not guilty" and proceed with the trial accordingly.

The plea of "guilty" or "not guilty" has a very serious effect upon the trial. If the accused pleads guilty the prosecution does not have to prove the charge by leading evidence to discharge the heavy burden which rests upon it. The accused also loses the right to lead evidence in defence. If the court accepts the plea, the accused is to be convicted. It is for this reason that courts have held even in respect of trials under the Cr. PC that the court is not bound to accept the plea of guilty unless it is satisfied that the accused has understood the effect of the plea.

The Tribunal was of the view that the use of the word "shall" in the Rules and the nature and effect of the plea of guilty, the Rules 111(2) and 115(1) are mandatory and they have not been complied with in the SCM. It is well settled that non- compliance of a mandatory provision will vitiate the entire proceeding [*Chief of Army Staff v. Ex. Sep Dvr (MT) M.Z.H. Khan* Mil LJ 2006 All DB 152 and *Devi Lal Sahu v. Union of India* 2009 (2) Service Cases Today 152 (Raj)]. The Tribunal held that the proceedings of SCM were not held in accordance with law. The Tribunal therefore quashed the proceedings of SCM and directed the respondents to hold re-trial from the stage of the arraignment of charges. The petitioner was free to seek the change of the "friend of the accused."

Trial of attached person

The AFT Regional Bench Lucknow in the case of *Sepoy/Chef (U) Raj Kumar v. Union of India*, TA No. 48 of 2009 [WP (C) No. 4963 of 2007], decided on

21 January 2010, considered a petitioner against the finding and punishment awarded by the SCM.

The petitioner was charged under section 39(b) of the Army Act for having been granted leave of absence from 08 August 2002 to 20 August 2002 to proceed home, but failed without sufficient cause to rejoin duty on expiry of said leave, till he surrendered voluntarily at the Rajput Regimental Centre on 14 December 2002 on his own accord. The petitioner pleaded "guilty" and was awarded punishment of dismissal from service and rigorous imprisonment for one year by his commanding officer.

The petitioner contested that the (i) commanding officer of administrative battalion, Rajput Regimental Centre, Fatehgarh had no jurisdiction to try him, since he belonged to another Unit i.e., 16 Rajput Regiment; (ii) trial was barred by limitation under section 122 of the Army Act; (iii) the Army Rules 22, 115, and 116(4) were not complied with; (iv) Subedar Om Prakash who was detailed as 'friend of the accused' was illiterate and was not competent to defend the petitioner; and (v) procedure provided in the aforesaid Rules was not complied thus violating Article 14 of the Constitution of India.

The Tribunal observed that there was no bar to attachment of an accused to another unit. If the accused can be legally attached to another unit there would be no hurdle created by section 116 in the accused being tried by the commanding officer of that unit because all that section 116 requires is that the accused must be tried by the commanding officer of "any corps, department or detachment of the regular army". The commanding officer of the unit to which the accused had been attached would be covered under that description. The definition of commanding officer in paragraph 9 of the Regulation for the Army includes within it the commanding officer of a unit to which the soldier may be attached. Further, Note 4 of section 120 also does not provide anything to the contrary. What Note 4 requires is that the accused must be under the command of the officer holding the SCM. The requirement appears to be that on the date of the trial the accused belongs to the unit the commanding officer of which is holding the trial. The Tribunal was of the view that no infirmity in the procedure adopted by the SCM had been demonstrated. The conviction recorded in the SCM was on the basis of the plea of "guilty" and was not be vitiated by any error. Considering the totality of the circumstances and the fact that the petitioner had already spent more than seven months imprisonment, the Tribunal ordered that the ends of justice would be met by reducing the sentence of imprisonment to what the petitioner has already undergone. The conviction and findings of the SCM were affirmed.

Violation of Army Rule 115(2) and Army HQ instructions

The AFT Principal Bench New Delhi in the case of *Naik Dinesh Chand Sharma v. Union of India*, TA No. 180 of 2010 [WP (C) No. 2537 of 1998], decided on 26 July 2010, considered challenges to the order passed by the SCM. The petitioner was charged under section 69 of the Army Act for committing a civil offence under section 354 of the IPC using criminal force to a woman with intent to outrage her modesty.

The petitioner contended that at the time of the incident, i.e. on 6 October 1997, he had completed 16 years of meritorious service during which there had been no complaint about his discipline or conduct. Further, in the evening of 6 October 1997 at 5.00 pm, the Adjutant of the Regiment, drove him to the house of the prosecutrix and in a most authoritarian manner, ordered him to stand at attention and asked the prosecutrix whether she identified him or not. The identification procedure was ad hoc and against all laid down norms. The petitioner also contended that he was not permitted to produce any defence witness in the summary of evidence neither was he permitted to cross examine the prosecution witnesses. It was also contended that since the commanding officer had visited the house of the prosecutrix and had supposedly taken part in the investigation of the incident, he was debarred from holding the trial under Army Rule 39.

The petitioner further contended that (i) the identification conducted by the authorities was against all norms of law and natural justice; (ii) he was not even asked as to whether he was 'guilty' or 'not guilty' and the 'plea of guilt' was written by his commanding officer; (iii) he has not signed against the 'plea of guilty' as was required in the SCM form; (iv) the commanding officer had himself made the certificate of compliance of Army Rule 115(2) and signed such certificate; and (v) the compliance certificate of Army Rule 115(2) was typed on a separate piece of paper and his signatures obtained in an underhand manner and this slip of paper was pasted to the SCM proceedings.

On the issue that the plea of guilty has not been signed by the petitioner, the Tribunal referred to the observations made by the Delhi High Court in *L/NK Gurdev Singh v. Union of India*, (WP (C) No. 776 of 1995 dated 1 February 2008), which read: "Though the petitioner has allegedly admitted the charge by pleading guilty, his signatures nowhere appear on the purported plea of guilt. When an accused person pleads guilty, it would be necessary to obtain his signatures to lend authenticity to such proceedings. This basic requirement was not even adhered to, the absence whereof lends credence to the allegation of the petitioner that he was not even present at the time of recording of the summary court martial proceedings and he never pleaded guilty."

The Tribunal also referred to judgment in the case of *The Chief of Army Staff v. Ex.14257273 K Trilochan Behera* LPA No. 254 of 2001, where in it was concluded that such court martial proceedings would be of no consequence and would not stand the judicial scrutiny. In forming this opinion, The Tribunal had referred to the judgment of the Jammu & Kashmir High Court in the case of *Prithpal Singh v. Union of India*, 1984 (3) SLR 675 (J&K). Based on this judgement of the Jammu & Kashmir High Court, the Army authorities had issued instructions that signatures of the accused pleading guilty of charge be obtained and if there is an infraction of this procedural requirement, it would violate the mandatory procedural safeguard provided in Army Rule 115(2) and would also be violative of Article 14 of the Constitution of India.

The Tribunal held that the legal position remains that the plea of guilt is necessarily required to be signed to give authenticity to it, which was not done in the present case. It referred to the decisions of higher courts in the following cases: (i) Delhi High Court in *L/NK Gurdev Singh v. Union of India* (WP (C) No. 776 of 1995 dated 1 February 2008); (ii) Allahabad High Court in *Uma Shanker Pathak v. Union of India*, 1989 (3) SLR 405.; and (iii) The Jammu & Kashmir High Court in *Sukanta Mitra v. Union of India*, 2007 (2) 197 (J&K).

In view of the above, the Tribunal set aside the impugned SCM proceedings. The sentence of dismissal was converted to discharge with the order that the petitioner shall be entitled to pension and other benefits as due.

Violation of section 116

The AFT Principal Bench New Delhi in the case of *Ex Hav Nancha Ram Jat v. Union of India*, TA No. 649 of 2009 [WP (C) No. 12353 of 2005], decided on 22 July 2010, considered a petition for quashing the SCM proceedings.

The appellant was enrolled in the Army as Gunner (GD) in the year 1980 and in the due course was promoted to the Rank of Havildar. The petitioner was alleged to have molested wife of a military person in the night intervening 24/25 November 99. The matter was investigated by a court of inquiry, followed by the recording of summary of evidence and additional summary of evidence. He was tried by SCM and dismissed from the service.

The petitioner contended that a false and frivolous complaint was made against him. It was a result of conspiracy hatched by his rivals to harm him. Further, in the court of inquiry, a number of witnesses were examined but no opportunity was given to him to cross examine them, despite the fact that his reputation was involved in these proceedings. Apart from it, on the basis of the recommendations made in the court of inquiry; summary of evidence and additional summary of evidence were recorded but the Commanding Officer of his Unit did not order for the initiation of disciplinary proceedings against him. Further, he was attached to another unit where he was tried by SCM and the said SCM had no jurisdiction under section 116 of Army Act.

The Tribunal, relying on the interpretation of the scope of section 116 of Army Act by Delhi High Court in the case of *Ex LN Vishav Priya Singh v. Union of India*, 147 (2008) Delhi Law Times 202 (DB), set aside the impugned findings along with order of SCM. It directed that the appellant shall be deemed to have been discharged from service and shall be entitled to pensionary and other benefits as due to him from the date he was dismissed.

***

The AFT Principal Bench New Delhi in the case of *Ex Hav Rakesh Dhaka v. Union of India*, TA No. 684 of 2009 [WP (C) No. 5325 of 2000], decided on 2 July 2010, considered a petition for quashing the SCM proceedings. The petitioner was charged under sections 47 and 63 of the Army Act.

The Tribunal observed that the record of SCM proceedings reveals that with regard to Charge No. 1 accused had pleaded guilty. But from the leaf affixed on the SCM proceedings, it was evident that it has not been signed by the accused. It simply conveyed that measures for explaining the outcome of 'plea of guilt' in pursuance to Army Rule 115(2) were taken by the commanding officer but the fact remains that appellant did not sign that overleaf affixed with that form and endorsement was given that the appellant refused to sign the 'plea of guilt'. With regard to the Charge No. 2, the SCM found the appellant 'not guilty', therefore, the punishment awarded to the appellant was on account of his being guilty of the First Charge, which was not sustainable.

The Tribunal, relying on the interpretation of the scope of section 116 of Army Act by Delhi High Court in the case of *Ex LN Vishav Priya Singh v. Union of India*, 147 (2008) Delhi Law Times 202 (DB), set aside the conviction and the sentence awarded by SCM to the appellant. The Tribunal ordered that the appellant shall be deemed to be in service till he reaches the minimum pensionable service. He shall not be entitled for back wages/salary for the interregnum period i.e. from the date of his dismissal till to the period he attained minimum pensionable benefits.

No irregularity in trial

The AFT Principal Bench New Delhi in the case of *Ex Nk N A. Mithilesh Kumar v. Union of India*, TA No. 747 of 2009 [WP (C) No. 5979 of 2008], decided on 22 July 2010, considered a petition for quashing the punishment of dismissal awarded by the SCM.

The petitioner was enrolled in 1988 as a Nursing Assistant in the Army Medical Corps and had served almost 19 years before his dismissal. The petitioner contended that his problems started while he was posted to Gorkha Rifles, wherein the commanding officer was annoyed with him because the petitioner was unable to do physical training exercise due to his low medical status. Consequently, the commanding officer implicated him in a false and fabricated case under section 64(e) of the Army Act, i.e. allegedly obtaining for himself a gratification as a reward for procuring an advantage for a person in the service. The petitioner contended that the in the court of inquiry provisions of Army Rule 180 were not followed. The petitioner also contested that while the convening order of the summary of evidence was personally signed by the commanding officer in his official capacity, the order convening the SCM, which was a far more important action on the part of the respondents, has not been signed by the commanding officer.. This order has been signed by an officer of the rank of Major detailing his own commanding officer for the SCM, which was a gross impropriety. In accordance with the Army Rules, the convening order also should have been signed by the commanding officer.

The petitioner further contended that there were a number of irregularities during his trial. The officer who recorded the summary of evidence, was also detailed to attend the SCM and another officer of the rank of Lieutenant, who was PW 5 in the summary of evidence, was also detailed to attend the trial. These two officers, who have been part of the summary of evidence, cannot be made to attend the trial and this was a gross illegality on the part of the respondents. The recovery of money from the appellant was done in a gross violation of the laid down Rules and no seizure memo was made and petitioner's signatures were not obtained to the effect that recovery was done in his presence. In addition the 'friend of the accused', who was detailed to defend him was not legally qualified and neither was he able to defend the appellant. He was thrust upon him and that he was not given any opportunity to select a person of his choice.

The appellant also contested that he did not plead guilty during SCM, and was threatened by the commanding officer to sign the proceedings on a 'plea of guilty' and was assured of a light sentence should he do so. The appellant contested that the entire trial finished in five minutes the respondents had not complied with the mandatory requirements of supplying the pre-trial documents 96 hours in advance, which was a statutory right as enshrined in the Army Act and the Army Rules. This prejudiced his defence. The punishment of reduction to the ranks, six months imprisonment and dismissal awarded to him was harsh considering his good conduct in the service.

It was contested by the respondents that holding of the court of inquiry in this case was not mandatory. Authorities were at full liberty to hear the case under Army Rule 22 and thereafter proceed with recording of the summary of evidence should it be so ordered. In this instance, no court of inquiry was ever conducted. The accused was given an opportunity to cross examine witness during the recording of summary of evidence, which he declined. Contrary to the plea taken by the appellant that the trial finished in five minutes, the original record of the SCM showed that the trial lasted from 1130 to 1300 hours, i.e. for a period of 90 minutes. The Tribunal did not find any merit in the appeal and dismissed the same.

Desertion converted into overstayal of leave, punishment reduced

The AFT New Delhi Principal Bench in the case of *Pradeep Kumar Singh v. The Chief of the Army Staff*, TA No. 545 of 2009 [WP (C) 8385 of 2009] decided on 3 April 2012, considered a prayer for quashing the SCM proceedings.

The petitioner was enrolled in the Army on 29 July 1998. He had put in 18 years and 117 days colour service. He was granted annual leave from 06 April 2005 to 06 June 2005 after expiry of which he had sought extension, but nothing was conveyed to him about the extension.

A court of inquiry was ordered by the petitioner's commanding officer vide order dated 29 October 2005 for declaring the petitioner as deserter. The petitioner surrendered voluntarily of on 05 May 2006 and was tired under sections 38 (1) and 54 (b) of the Army Act. The petitioner pleaded guilty to both the charges. The SCM awarded the sentence of dismissal from service. His petition under s. 164 of the Army Act was rejected by the Chief of Army Staff on 2 July 2008.

The petitioner contended that once he reported back on duty to the parent unit, he was not taken on strength and had to shuttle between his unit and ASC Centre. Further, he could not be charged under section 38(1) of the Army Act as he was not a deserter and so far as second charge was concerned, the amount has already been deposited, therefore, he could not have punished a second time. The petitioner also contended that he was not given sufficient opportunity to defend himself during the trial by the SCM.

The Tribunal observed that the petitioner proceeded on leave and he sought an extension but the extension was not been granted and the petitioner reported back on duty to the parent unit, but was not taken on strength. He was sent from one location to other location. If the petitioner had intended not to report back and absented himself voluntarily, then perhaps he would have fallen in the definition of desertion. In this case, the petitioner himself reported back to the unit but he was not taken on strength and he was going from pillar to post. Therefore, it was not a case which can strictly fall in the four corners of section 38(1) of desertion. More appropriately this was a case where a person has remained absented without leave and would come under section 39 of the Army Act, 1950. If the authorities, would have properly looked into the matter then they would have realised that this was a case of over staying of leave rather than desertion.

The Tribunal set aside the conviction and sentence of the petitioner under section 38 of the Army Act, 1950. However, the Tribunal convicted the petitioner under section 39 for absence without leave and awarded the punishment of the reduction to the ranks. The conviction of the petitioner for second charge was exonerated with the condition that this would not entitle him to be reinstated in service.

Prayer for pardon

The AFT Regional Bench Guwahati in the case of *Oinam Doren Singh v. Union of India* OA No. 01 of 2011, decided on 3 May 2011, considered a petition against the punishment of dismissal awarded by the SCM.

The appellant was serving in the LADMR and attached to Administrative Regiment AAD College. On the night of 13 October 2008 the appellant tried to outrage the modesty of the wife of a Sepoy. A complaint having been made against the appellant, a court of inquiry was conducted followed by recording of summary of evidence. The appellant was tried by a SCM on 19 May 2009 under section 69 of the Army Act, contrary to section 354 of the Indian Penal Code. During the trial, the appellant admitted the charge levelled against him and the witnesses produced on behalf of the prosecution proved the allegations. The appellant also admitted the allegations made against him by the PW 1 (Sepoy) and PW 2 (victim) supporting the prosecution case. The SCM having found the charge levelled against the appellant as proved, awarded the punishment of dismissal from service vide order dated 19 May 2009. Against the order, the appellant preferred an appeal on 16 June 2009, which was dismissed.

The appellant contended that proper and fair opportunity was not given to him in defending the case and the confessional statement was not recorded by following the procedure prescribed by law. It was further contended that the punishment of dismissal from service was disproportionate to the offence charged.

The Tribunal observed that there was no disclosure of mind of the authority to the effect that there were considerations of the gravity of the offence in awarding the punishment. The Tribunal was of the opinion that the records should have disclosed at least the minimal necessity of application of mind by the authority while inflicting the punishment of dismissal. The Tribunal allowed the appellant to file an application under section 179 of the Army Act before the appropriate authority praying for infliction of lesser punishment with sufficient reason in the facts and circumstances of the case. In the event of such application being filed within 30 days of the judgment, the respondent authority is to dispose of the same within a period of 45 days from the receipt of application.

Unjust punishment

The AFT Regional Bench Guwahati in the case of *Shri Shiv Murath Singh Yadav v. Union of India*, TA No. 18 of 2010 [WP (C) No. 5439 of 1999] decided on 10 November 2011, considered a prayer for quashing punishment awarded by the SCM.

Petitioner, after his recruitment in the Army, was initially posted at the Kumayun Regiment Centre. On 20 March 1998, while he was serving at Mokokchung, Nagaland, SCM proceedings were initiated against him for charges under sections 48 and 63 of the Army Act, 1950 for his being found in an intoxicated state on field on 06 August 1998 at 1400 hrs, while on 'active service', and for his carrying a cocked weapon in violent posture at the same time. The petitioner pleaded guilty for both the charges and the commanding officer, holding the SCM, imposed the punishment of dismissal from service on 16 August 1998. His application to the Chief of Army Staff under s. 164 of the Army Act was rejected.

The petitioner contended that there was nothing on record to show that on the date of the alleged offence, he was in 'active service' as defined by section 3(i) of the Army Act. The punishment imposed on the petitioner was severe and unfair. He further contended that the SCM proceedings were not properly conducted and the charges were not properly explained to him. He was directed to plead 'guilty' before the SCM, on a promise that only minor punishment would be imposed on him. The punishment of dismissal from service imposed for the minor offences was too harsh.

The Tribunal observed that neither the original charge sheet dated 14 August 1998 nor a Xerox copy was available in the SCM proceedings. In view of that the statement of the petitioner, in the affidavit, that no charge sheet was served on him during SCM proceedings and that it was sent to him along with the order of dismissal, has to be taken to be true more so because the said statement of the petitioner was not denied on oath by any officer, who had personal knowledge or who took part in the SCM proceedings. The Tribunal further observed that the certificate dated 16 August 1998, issued by the Medical Officer, found in the SCM proceedings shows that the petitioner was 'fit/unfit' to undergo trial by the SCM on 16 August 1998. As both the words, 'fit' and 'unfit' are found in the medical certificate, it is clear that there was no application of mind by the Medical Officer when he gave that certificate and that he mechanically or routinely affixed his signature to the certificate.

The Judicial Member partly allowed the petition and set aside the sentence of dismissal from service and the same was modified as forfeiture of pay and allowances for a period of two months. He ordered that the petitioner shall be reinstated into service without back wages, but will entitled to all the benefits, which he would have been entitled to, had he been in service from the date of his dismissal till the date of reinstatement. The Administrative member expressed the opinion that there was no merit in the contentions taken by the petitioner and the petition was liable to be dismissed.

As there was a difference of opinion between the Members of the Bench, the case was referred to the Chairperson for decision. The Third Member observed that Army Rule 34 provides that where the accused is in active service there must be an interval of not less than 24 hours between service of charge sheet and arraignment of the charges. In this case, the original charge sheet was dated 16 August 1998, and the arraignment of charges was also made on 16 August 1998, on which date the SCM proceedings commenced and concluded. It was thus quite clear that the interval of 24 hours between service of charge sheet and the arraignment was not there. The Member referred to the decision of the Supreme Court in *Union of India v Anil Kumar Pandey*, (2009) 10 SCC 552, and held that this fact was enough to demonstrate that the trial was not a fair trial and for setting aside the Court Martial proceedings. The Third Member observed that from the summary of evidence it does not appear that the applicant adopted any violent posture or that he had cocked the weapon himself. The appellant was no doubt in active service, but, considering the totality of the circumstances it appears that the punishment of dismissal was disproportionate and unjust. The Member held that the punishment of dismissal as deserter was unjust.

Double jeopardy

The AFT Regional Bench Guwahati in the case of *Rfn (Tailor) Bhupal Ram Okesa v. Union of India*, TA No. 49 of 2010 [WP (C) No. 6030 of 2007], decided on June 2011, considered a prayer for quashing SCM proceedings.

The appellant was recruited in the Assam Rifles as Sepoy on 09 September 1985. The unit of the petitioner wherein he was operationally deployed was under the Army and accordingly the petitioner was subjected to the Army Act in terms of SRO 318 dated 06 December 1962 as amended by SRO 325 dated 31 August 1977. While the appellant was discharging his duties, he was sent to 162 Military Hospital, Dinjan, Tinsukia for medical check up on 15 February 2000, but he did not return to his duty. On receipt of the information regarding his absence without leave he was considered as a deserter and an apprehension roll was issued on 16 May 2001 and subsequently a court of inquiry was held under section 106 of the Army Act. He was declared deserter with effect from 18 February 2000. The appellant remained absent from duties from 18 February 2000 to 07 May 2004.

The appellant contended that while he started from his working place to 162 Army Hospital, Dinjan on 16 February 2000 for medical treatment as per movement order, he suffered immense mental disturbance believing himself that he would die without seeing his family members and relatives who were residing at his home in Uttaranchal and he proceeded to Delhi wherefrom he was picked up by his relative from the street and with the aid and assistance of the family members the appellant was treated by a doctor at Azadpur, New Delhi. Further, after recovery from ailment, in the last part of May, 2003, he along with his wife proceeded to attend his duties and reached Lohitpur, Arunachal Pradesh on 23 May 2003 and found that his unit had already shifted to Kohima. The appellant and his wife then reached Kohima on 25 May 2003 and tried to meet the Unit Commander, but he was not allowed to do so. The appellant, therefore, by filing a representation dated 10 June 2003 addressed to the Director General, Assam Rifles, Shillong and subsequently by issuing a notice through his advocate on 10 March 2003 prayed for allowing him to join his duties. Upon receipt of the said legal notice, the appellant was intimated through his lawyer that his prayer would be considered once he rejoined the unit.

On such instructions, the appellant joined in his service on 08 May 2004 and on 17 January 2005 an order was issued that the appellant would be tried by a SCM for commission of offence under section 38(1) of the Army Act for remaining absent without leave from 18 February 2000 to 07 May 2004. The appellant was also informed that he can depute a person of his choice in the proceedings to assist him in the trial. In terms of the above decision, the appellant was issued charge sheet, summary of evidence and Special Part One Order No. S/01/2005 dated 18 January 2005 whereby he was informed that he would be tried by the SCM on 20 January 2005. The appellant was awarded the punishment of dismissal by the SCM. The appellant was also supplied with one set of SCM proceedings which indicated that he was dismissed from service with effect from 20 January 2004 on the ground of desertion from service and further intimating him that he may submit any appeal against the said order before the appellate authority. The appellant accordingly submitted an appeal before the appellate authority on 22 January 2005. Thereafter, vide letter dated 19 May 2005 the appellant was intimated that the SCM proceedings held against him has been set aside by the Commander Assam Rifles and he was directed to report back and join the unit forthwith. Accordingly, the appellant re-joined his unit, as directed.

Thereafter, vide another letter dated 20 September 2006 it was intimated that the appellant would again be tried by a SCM on 25 September 2006 and furnished him the copies of the charge sheet, summary of evidence and Special Battalion Routine Order Part-I Ser No. S/01/2005 dated 19 September 2008. In the SCM the charges levelled against the appellant was that he deserted the service and that on 18 February 2000 while he was on active service absconded himself without leave while proceeding to Military Hospital till he voluntarily rejoined at Battalion Headquarters on 08 May 2004. Accordingly, the SCM was held against the appellant and he was found guilty of the offences and awarded the punishment of dismissal from service with effect from 25 September 2006 vide impugned order dated 25 September 2006.

The appellant contended the order of dismissal as illegal, unjust, improper and without jurisdiction and that he could not be tried twice for the same offence. Further, the earlier proceedings of SCM having been set aside by the competent authority, the subsequent proceedings on the same charge was without jurisdiction. That apart, the charge sheet and other documents was issued only on 25 September 2006 and he was tried on the same day and the penalty of dismissal was also imposed on him on the same date in gross violation of the principles of natural justice and fair play. It was further submitted that in the meantime the appellant having crossed the age of superannuation, even if dismissal order was set aside, he would not be taken back to service at this stage.

The respondents contested that the appellant absented himself from service from 18 February 2000 till 8 May 2004 without leave and the same was found to be proved in the proceedings and accordingly he was awarded the punishment of dismissal from service. It was further contested that the earlier SCM was set aside by the reviewing authority on technical ground and thereafter the fresh proceeding was drawn up against the appellant on the same charge. In the SCM proceedings dated 25 September 2006, the appellant pleaded guilty of the offences and, complying with the provisions of s. 115 (2) of the Army Act, the appellant was found guilty and awarded the punishment of dismissal from service. It was further stated that at the stage of summary of evidence the appellant was given sufficient and full opportunity to defend his case and thereafter the charge sheet was served upon him for committing the offence under s. 38(1) of the Army Act for unauthorized absence from duty. The respondents further contested that the earlier proceedings SCM having been set aside on technical ground there was no bar in trying the appellant afresh by way of SCM even it was on the same charge and, that the appellant had pleaded guilty during his trial by the SCM.

The Tribunal observed that the appellant was earlier tried by a SCM in 2004 and the said proceeding was set aside by the higher authority on review.

It was no where found from the record that while setting aside the proceedings of the SCM in terms of section 162 of the Army Act, the authority reserved to proceed against the appellant afresh. The order dated 19 May 2005 clearly disclosed that the proceedings against the appellant were set aside and he was directed to re-join in his service forthwith, which he accordingly did and thereafter the subsequent proceedings started. The records further revealed that the charge sheet was drawn up on 20 September 2006 on the same set of allegations like the earlier one. The proceedings were conducted and concluded on the same date i.e. on 25 September 2006.

The Tribunal further observed that the trial commenced at 1100 hrs wherein the appellant allegedly pleaded guilty and ended at 1130 hrs. A certificate was also appended in the proceedings that before recording the plea of guilty, the Court also explained to the accused the meaning of the charge to which he pleaded guilty and ascertained that he understood the charge. It was also certified to the effect that the plea of guilty and difference in procedure which would follow consequent to the said plea, was also informed to the appellant and the Court was satisfied that the appellant admitted his guilt upon proper understanding of facts in issue. This certificate was appended in purported compliance of the Army Rules 115(2) and 115(2)(a). The proceedings before awarding sentence were also taken simultaneously. It was found that the appellant was under arrest while the proceedings against him continued. Finally, the trial closed at 1130 hrs and the promulgation of sentence was made on the same day at 1400 hrs.

The Tribunal was of the opinion that it was practically impossible to discharge all the functions by the SCM right from the stage of explaining the charges to the explanation of the effect of the plea of guilt within a short span of half an hour. The Tribunal was of the view that it was nothing but mechanical discharge of judicial function in a purported manner.

The Tribunal observed that section 121 of the Army Act prohibits such second trial providing that when any person subject to the Act has been acquitted or convicted of an offence by a court martial or by a criminal court, or has been dealt with under any of the sections 80, 83, 84 and 85, he shall not be liable to be tried again for the same offence by a court martial or dealt with under the said sections. That apart, Article 20(2) of the Constitution of India protects a person from double jeopardy. Article 20(2) of the Constitution bars prosecution and punishment after conclusion of earlier proceedings on the same ground on the doctrine of *autrefois acquit*. This fundamental right of the appellant, also recognized by statute in section 121 of the Army Act, was infringed by the action of the respondents by prosecuting and punishing the appellant subsequently for the same charge.

The Tribunal also observed that there was another gross violation in conducting the proceeding against the appellant inasmuch as the mandatory requirement of Army Rule 34 was not followed. Under the Rule 34, an accused before he is arraigned, shall be informed by the officer of every charge for which he is to be tried and also that on his giving the names of the witnesses or whom he desires to call in his defence, reasonable steps would be taken for procuring their attendance, and those steps shall be taken accordingly. The rule further provides the interval between his being so informed and his arraignment shall not be less than 96 hours or where the accused person is in active service less than 24 hours. The appellant was not called upon to give the names of his witnesses or whom he desires to call in his defence either in the notice dated 20 September 2006 or in the communication dated 25 September 2006 communicating the charge sheet. The provisions under Army Rule 34 were a mandatory requirement to be followed by the Court and it will not alter the situation even if the accused admits his guilt. The Tribunal referred the decision of the Supreme Court in the case of *Union of India v. A.K. Pandey* (2009) 10 SCC 552.

The Tribunal held that the conviction and sentence of the appellant inflicted by the impugned order dated 25 September 2006 discharging him from service on the ground of desertion was illegal and unsustainable and accordingly the same was set aside and quashed. Since the appellant had already crossed the age of superannuation, there was no question of reverting him back to his service. After setting aside the earlier SCM, the appellant, as directed rejoined his service on 20 June 2005 and the effect of these events would be that the appellant deemed to continue in his service till that date and in the process he completed 15 years of service and would be entitled to get his usual service pension as per rules; which was to be paid to him within a period of three months of the order.

V. Limitation of Trial

Section 122 Army Act 1950

The AFT Regional Bench Lucknow in the case of *Lt Col Ranjodh Singh v. Union of India*, OA No. 88 of 2012, decided on 16 March 2012, considered a prayer for limitation of trail under section 122 of the Army Act.

The applicant was charged for certain offences relating to illegal gratification and was tried by a GCM which convicted the applicant and awarded the sentence of RI for five years and cashiering from service. The charge sheet on the basis of which the trial was held was dated 28 April 2008. The conviction and sentence of the applicant was set aside by the Tribunal in TA No. 68 of 2010 on various grounds on 05 October 2010 but the Tribunal authorized retrial of the applicant in exercise of powers under section 16 of the Armed Forces Tribunal Act.

In consequence a convening order dated 29 June 2011 was issued for holding the trial of the applicant with effect from 12 July 2011. The GCM assembled on 12 July 2011. The applicant was arraigned on the basis of the earlier charge sheet dated 28 April 2008. Before the GCM the applicant raised a plea in bar advancing two contentions; (i) that the trial was barred by the provisions of section 121 of the Army Act, as this was a second trial and; (ii) that the trial was barred by the provisions of section 122 of the Army Act, which lays down a period of limitation of three years. The GCM overruled the plea in bar by its decision dated 06 January 2012. Aggrieved with the decision, the applicant has filed the petition in the Tribunal.

The applicant contended that in case the dates mentioned in clauses (a),(b) and (c) of s. 122 of the Army Act, would be anterior in point of time to the date of the charge sheet and, therefore, even if the limitation is treated as commencing from the date of the charge sheet, which was 28 April 2008 the present trial was barred by limitation as it commenced on 12 July 2011, the date when the GCM assembled. Further, from a combined reading of s. 122 of the Army Act and s. 16 of the AFT Act, it was apparent that the words 'retrial' and 'retried' used in s. 16 have not been used in s. 122 of the Army Act.

For considering the issue, the Tribunal referred to the scheme and purpose of section 122 of the Army Act. It was obvious that retrial can be ordered by the Tribunal after the accused has already undergone trial by a court martial in which he has been convicted for an offence. If the original trial of the accused was not commenced within the period of limitation provided under section 122, the original trial itself would be barred by limitation and would be illegal and if in such a case the conviction is quashed by the Tribunal, there would be no occasion to authorize retrial.

The Tribunal observed that the question of retrial would arise only in a case where the original trial was within the period of limitation. The commencement of the period of limitation under clauses (a), (b) and (c) of section 122 has been provided for in the context of the prosecuting authorities and is, therefore, relevant insofar as the original trial is concerned, which is instituted by the prosecution authorities without the intervention of the Tribunal. A retrial, however is authorized by the Tribunal in exercise of its judicial powers and that too when "it appears to the Tribunal that the interests of justice" so require.

In the opinion of the Tribunal, once the original trial has commenced within the period of limitation and a retrial has been ordered, recourse to clauses (a), (b) and (c) of section 122 of the Army Act would be of little relevance. On a plain reading of section 122 also it is evident that the word 'retrial' has not been used therein. A retrial is ordered in exercise of the appellate powers of the Tribunal and that an appeal is a continuation of trial is a settled proposition of law. The order of retrial in appeal is like a remand for the purpose of taking fresh evidence and is permissible under section 16 only where the evidence has either been received by the Tribunal or is available to be received. The Tribunal has also discretion of exercising power under section 17(c) of the AFT Act to receive evidence before itself.

The Tribunal was of the view that retrial is an alternative course for the Tribunal by which instead of receiving the evidence available, itself, it authorizes that the evidence be recorded by the court martial. As fresh evidence can be received by the Tribunal under section 17 without the bar of limitation under section 122, there was no reason why in the case of retrial where similar exercise was to be conducted by the court martial under authorization by the Tribunal the provisions of section 122 be read in such a manner as to come in as a bar. In the Tribunal's opinion, the expression 'no trial by Court Martial of any person subject to this Act for any offence shall be commenced' used in section 122 of the Army Act was with reference to the original trial and not to a retrial.

The Tribunal further opined that the limitation envisaged in clauses (a), (b) and (c) of section 122 of the Army Act was the same as in section 469 of the Code of Criminal Procedure, 1973. One difference between the scheme of the Cr PC and that of the Army Act on the point of limitation is that whereas under section 468 of the Cr PC the language used is "no court shall take cognizance of an offence ....after the expiry of the period of limitation", in section 122 the provision is that no trial by Court Martial shall be commenced after the period of three years limitation specified in the section. For the purpose of giving effect to the true import and purpose of section 468, the courts have given a purposive interpretation and not a strict literal interpretation to the expression 'no court shall take cognizance of an offence'.

Referring to the decision of the Supreme Court in the case of *Japani Sahoo v. Chandra Shekhar Mohanty* 2007 AIR SCW 4998 the Tribunal opined that decided cases have held that if the complaint or charge sheet has been filed within the period of limitation, the court can take cognizance of the offence even after the period of limitation. In many cases a retrial denovo may have to be authorized because of an error in procedure committed by the Court Martial and delay may have taken place on account of the pendency of the proceedings. A court martial commences when the members of the court assemble as held in the case of *Union of India v. Major General Madan Lal Yadav(Retd)*, AIR 1996 SC 1340. The Court is required under the Rules to satisfy itself that it is legally constituted. An erroneous decision on the point may vitiate all subsequent proceedings in the trial and a retrial may have to be ordered.

In cases where an accused has pleaded guilty in the original trial and has been convicted and sentenced by court martial but on appeal the Tribunal comes to the conclusion that the accused did not understand the effect of his plea of guilty. The Tribunal would have to set aside the conviction and may decide to authorize a retrial. In such a case there would be no evidence on the record, as the accused had pleaded guilty. However, evidence in the Summary of Evidence would be available to be received. The retrial authorized in such a case would be a denovo trial with fresh arraignment. Delay in such a case and examples can be multiplied would have occurred in the trial proceedings for no fault of the prosecution. Although the scheme of the Army Act provides for a speedy trial but there is no limitation of time for completion of the trial. In many cases the period of three years limitation may have run out during the course of the Court Martial proceedings or thereafter during the pendency of the Appeal before the Tribunal or shortly after the Tribunal's order before the retrial commences. A court martial is also a court and the principles laid down in Japani Sahoo's case that the prosecution ought not to suffer for delay caused by faulty trial on part of the Court Martial would be relevant for interpreting section 122 of the Army Act.

The applicant relied upon the decision of the Supreme Court in *Ex Havildar Ratan Singh v. Union of India*, AIR 1992 SC 415; and *Major Radha Krishan v. Union of India*, AIR 1996 SC 3091 in support of the contention that the period of limitation under section 122 cannot be extended and that section 122 is a complete code in itself.

In the opinion of the Tribunal, section 122 of the Army Act was applicable to the commencement of the original trial and not to a retrial. Further, the purpose of enacting the provision for limitation was essentially that after a long lapse of time the memory of the witnesses may fail and the accused cannot be kept in suspense for indefinite period with the sword of Damocles' hanging over his head. Section 16 of the AFT Act itself ensures safeguard of the interest of the accused as the power authorizing retrial can be exercised only when evidence has been received or is available to be received and that too only in the interest of justice. Sub Section 3 of s. 16 bars fresh investigation.

In the Tribunal's view as a retrial was a consequence of authorization by the Tribunal, there was no bar in the Tribunal itself fixing in its order the time limit for commencement of the proceedings to prevent misuse. The OA was thus dismissed.

Supreme Court's interpretation

The Supreme Court in the case of *Rajvir Singh v. The Secretary, Ministry of Defence*, Civil Appeal No. 2107 of 2012 [Arising out of SLP (Civil) No. 26892 of 2011], decided on 15 February 2012, interpreted the period of limitation under section 122 of the Army Act. This appeal was directed against the judgment and order of 19 August 2011 passed by the Armed Forces Tribunal, Regional Bench, Lucknow, by which it dismissed OA No. 116 of 2011 filed by the appellant.

Facts: A GCM was directed to be convened by order dated 23/26 August by the General Officer Commanding, Madhya Bharat Area, (GOC, MB Area) to try the appellant on different charges relating to gross financial irregularities punishable under section 52(f) of the Army Act. The charges against the appellant pertained to the periods 2005-2006 and 2006-2007 when he was posted as officiating Commandant, Central Ordnance Depot, Chheoki. According to the charges, in procurement of stores he violated and flouted the relevant rules and in making purchases worth about Rs. 2.2 crores, he caused wrongful loss of Rs. 60.18 lakhs to the Government.

The appellant challenged the convening order before the Armed Forces Tribunal (in OA No. 216 of 2010) on the plea that his trial by GCM was barred by limitation under section 122 of the Army Act. At that stage the Tribunal did not go into the merits of the appellant's challenge and dismissed the OA leaving it open for the appellant to raise his objections before the

GCM. In pursuance of the liberty given by the Tribunal, the appellant raised the objection before the GCM that his trial before it was barred by limitation. The GCM upheld the appellant's objection and by order dated 17 February 2011, allowed the "plea in bar" raised by the defence.

The confirming authority, *i.e.*, the Officiating GOC, MB Area, however, refused to confirm the order of the GCM and by order dated 29 March 2011 held that reckoning from the date on which the commission of the offence and the identity of the appellant as one of the offenders came within the knowledge of the competent authority, the order giving direction for convening the GCM was passed within a period of three years and, therefore, the bar of limitation did not come in the way of the trial of the appellant before the GCM. He directed the GCM to proceed with the trial of the appellant as if the "plea in bar" was found not proved.

The appellant challenged the order of the confirming authority once again before the Tribunal in OA No. 116 of 2011. The Tribunal, relying upon the decisions of the Supreme Court in *Union of India v. V. N. Singh* (2010) 5 SCC 579 and *J.S. Sekhon v. Union of India* (2010) 11 SCC 586, held that the GCM was convened within the period of limitation; and rejected the application and upheld the order passed by the confirming authority.

The Supreme Court considered its earlier decisions in *V.N. Singh* and *J.S. Sekhon,* dealing with the period of limitation for trial and interpreted section 122 of the Army Act. It held that in both these cases the real issue before the Court was that "who was the competent authority to initiate action against the delinquent officer and whose knowledge would be relevant for the purpose of section 122 of the Army Act." The Supreme Court held that the period of limitation under section 122 of the Army Act begins when the offence and the identity of the accused comes to the knowledge of the officer empowered to convene the court martial. It set aside the judgment and order passed by the Tribunal and quashed the direction by the GOC, MB Area, for reassembly of the GCM.

The Supreme Court observed that insofar as the appellant was concerned, the GOC-in-C, Central Command, was undeniably the competent authority to initiate proceeding against him and to convene a GCM to try him. Further, on the basis of the court of inquiry report and the recommendation of the GOC, MB Area; the GOC-in-C, had clearly formed the opinion that the culpability of the appellant was established and there was cogent and adequate material evidence regarding the cognizable acts of omission/commission committed by him. Nonetheless, on 7 May 2007, the GOC-in-C, did not direct for initiating proceeding against the appellant and to convene the GCM for his trial but clubbed his case with Major General S. P. Sinha in whose case the integrated headquarter of MoD Army was the competent authority and sent his recommendation to the integrated HQ to hold a Court of Inquiry to examine the role of the Major General in the irregularities committed at the Central Ordnance Depot, Chheoki, during his tenure there.

The Supreme Court observed that in both, *V.N. Singh and J.S. Sekhon*, the real issue before the Court was that who was the competent authority to initiate action against the delinquent officer and whose knowledge would be relevant for the purpose of s. 122 of the Act. In both cases, it was contended, on behalf of the delinquent officers, that the knowledge of "the person aggrieved" long preceded the knowledge of the competent authority and reckoning from the date of knowledge of "the aggrieved person", the order convening the GCM was barred by limitation. In *V.N. Singh*, it was submitted on behalf of the officer that one *Brigadier K.S. Bharucha* was the aggrieved person and in *J.S. Sekhon*, it was submitted that the Commander Works Engineer was the person aggrieved and if the period of limitation was computed from the date of their knowledge then the order convening the GCM was barred by limitation. In both cases, the Court held that that part of section 122 that referred to the knowledge of the person aggrieved had no application to the facts of the case and the relevant date for computing the period of limitation was the date of knowledge of the competent authority to initiate action against the delinquent officer.

The Supreme Court held that the GOC-in-C, Central Command was in knowledge of the offence and the identity of the appellant as one of the alleged offenders on 7 May 2007. Reckoning from that date, the order passed by the GOC, MB Area, to convene the GCM on 23/26 August 2010 was clearly beyond the period of three years and hence, barred in terms of section 122.

The Supreme Court also commented: "One feels sorry to see a trial on such serious charges being aborted on grounds of limitation but that is the mandate of the law. It is seen above that GOC-in-C, CC had come to know about the offence and the offender being the appellant on 7 May 2007. It took one year from that date for him to pass the order for initiating disciplinary action against him on 12 May 2008. There were still two years in hand, which is no little time but that too was spent in having more than one rounds of hearing of the charges in terms of Army Rule 22 with the result that by the time the order came to be passed to convene GCM, more than three years had lapsed from the date of the knowledge of the competent authority…Before concluding, we may also note that other officers who were allegedly involved in irregular purchases for the Central Ordnance Depot, Chheoki, also seem to have got away with very light, if at all, any punishment."

The Supreme Court set aside the judgment and order passed by the Tribunal, and quashed the direction by the GOC, MB Area, for reassembly of the GCM.

VI. Appeal to Tribunal

Interpretation of section 164

The AFT Regional Bench Jaipur in the case of *Ex Hav Suresh Kumar v. Union of India*, TA No. 99 of 2009 [SBCW No. 5302 of 2005 transferred to the

Tribunal vide order dated 16 November 2009] and *Ex Sep P. R. Yadav v. Union of India*, TA No. 22 of 2010 [SBCW No. 2215 of 2002 transferred to the Tribunal vide order dated 27 November 2009], decided on 2 July 2010, considered an important legal question: "Whether an army personnel convicted by a court marital, who had already availed the remedy of appeal by way of petition provided under section 164 of the Army Act, 1950 can still avail the remedy of appeal under section 15 of the Armed Forces Tribunal Act, 2007?"

Since an important legal question was involved, the Tribunal invited members of the bar to assist by way of advancing their arguments for and against the above referred legal question posed by the Tribunal.

Some of the views expressed before the Tribunal are as follows:

1. Prior to coming into existences of the Tribunal, there was no independent judicial forum available under the law. The only remedy available under the law against the findings and sentence recorded by the court martial was a petition under s. 164 of the Army Act, 1950. Against the order/ judgment passed by the competent authority under s. 164 of the Army Act, the only remedy available under the law was judicial review under Article 226 of the Constitution of India. However, after the coming into existence of the Tribunal, against the findings and sentence passed by the court marital, the appellate jurisdiction vests in the Tribunal under section 15 of the Act of 2007 and all pending suit or other proceedings inclusive of appeal pending before any court including a High Court stood transferred to this Tribunal.

   The person aggrieved by the findings and sentence recorded by the court martial may prefer a petition under s 164 of the Army Act before the competent authority but that petition cannot be termed as an appeal and as such, this Tribunal is having jurisdiction to decide the appeal under section 15 of the AFT Act against the findings and sentence passed by the court martial and confirmed by the competent authority under section 164 of the Army Act.

   While deciding the petition under section 164 of the Army Act, opportunity of hearing is not provided to the applicant and as such, the petition under section 164 cannot be termed as an appeal but it is in the form of administrative action of the competent authority. The appeal when filed before any court or Tribunal requires decision based on appreciation of facts, evidence and the law and such power is provided to the Tribunal under section 15 of the Act. For civil matters, application can be moved under s. 14 of the Act and for criminal matters, appeal can be moved under section 15 of the Act. Further section 21 of the AFT Act enumerates an embargo that application under section 14 of the Act, not to be admitted unless other remedies available under the Army Act are exhausted but section 21 is not applicable for appeal under section 15 of the Act.

   Since the Tribunal has been invested under section 15 of the Act with the power to entertain, hear and decide the appeal against the findings and sentence recorded by the court martial, the jurisdiction of the competent authority provided under section 164 of the Army Act cannot remain in existence. Moreover, section 35 of the Act is applicable to all pending or decided cases by the competent authority under section 164 of the Army Act also and an appeal still lies against the order/judgment passed on a petition by the competent authority under section 164 of the Army Act.

The provision of section 15 read with section 35 of the AFT Act provides a wider jurisdiction and power to the Tribunal to entertain, hear and decide the appeals filed against the findings and sentence recorded by the court martial. Section 39 of the Act provides that the provisions of the Act shall have effect notwithstanding anything inconsistent therewith contained in any other law for the time being in force or in any instrument having effect by virtue of any law other than the Act. Thus, there being inconsistency in the Army Act and the Armed Forces Tribunal Act, the later will prevail as it is a special law. Sections 34 and 35 of the AF Act clearly specifies and give a mandate to the Tribunal to decide the appeal under section 15 of the Act notwithstanding a petition has been decided by the competent authority under section 164 of the Act.

[View expressed by M/s. Sandeep Singh Hora and Jitendra Mitruka, the counsel appearing for the applicants.].

2. M/s S.B. Singh and R.S. Bhaduria also supported the views expressed by M/s Sandeep Singh Hora and further added that even if a petition has been decided by the competent authority under section 164 of the Army Act against the findings and sentence recorded by the court martial, the Tribunal has ample jurisdiction and power to entertain, hear and decide the appeal under section 15 of the Act, which stood transferred from High Court to the Tribunal. They further contended that sections 14 and 15 of the Act start with the words "Save as otherwise expressly provided in this Act" and there is no specific saving clause which deprives this Tribunal to entertain, hear and decide the appeal, which stood transferred from High Court, in spite of the fact that a petition under section 164 of the Army Act against the findings and sentence recorded by the court martial has already been decided by the competent authority.

   Section 15 of the Act specifically provides that any person aggrieved by an order, decision, finding or sentence passed by a court marital may prefer an appeal in such form, manner and within such time as may be prescribed. This clearly indicates that any person aggrieved by an order, decision, finding or sentence passed by a court martial may prefer an appeal before the Tribunal under section 15 of the Act.

   The word 'Appeal' means a statutory right of carrying a case from an inferior court to superior court or authority with a view to ascertain whether the judgment passed in favour or against is sustainable. An appeal is a creation of statute and only exists where expressly given and cannot be implied one. Before coming in to existence of the Tribunal, a right of appeal to the aggrieved person against the order, judgment, finding or sentence awarded by a court martial was available in the form of petition under section 164 of the Army Act to the authority provided therein and who, in turn, would exercise the powers enumerated under section 165 and 179 to 192 of the Army Act after going through the entire facts and the oral as well as documentary evidence. As the only remedy available was under s. 164 of the Army Act, the aggrieved person was having no right of appeal against the order passed by the competent authority under section 164 of the Army Act as he was having a remedy only under Article 226 of the Constitution of India in the form of judicial review.

Section 15 of the Act specifically provides that an appeal will lie before the Tribunal against the order, decision, finding or sentence passed by a court martial and if the competent authority has decided the petition against the order, decision, finding or sentence passed by the court martial under section 164 of the Army Act, then the order, decision, finding or sentence passed by the court martial will merge in to the order passed by the competent authority under section 164 of the Act and the order, decision, finding or sentence passed by the court martial will loose its identification. If a person has preferred a writ petition under Article 226 of the Constitution of India for judicial review challenging the order passed on a petition under s. 164 of the Army Act against the order, decision, findings and sentence recorded by the authority, then this Tribunal will have no right, power, authority or jurisdiction to entertain, hear and decide such an appeal under section 15 of the Act.

According to the Tribunal, a bare perusal of section 35 of the Act clearly reveals that this section is related to filing of an appeal before the Tribunal and transfer of appeals pending before any court inclusive of High Court. The word 'authority' is missing conspicuously in section 35 of the Act, although it has been used for the purposes of any order being made by the authority but in the later part, the word 'authority' has not been used. This clarifies that if any appeal or petition is pending before the competent authority under section 164 of the Act, that will not be transferred because this section does not mention the word 'authority' for transfer of pending appeals before the competent authority. Thus, if any matter is pending before the competent authority under section 164 of the Act against any order passed by a court martial, that will not stand transferred to this Tribunal as per the provisions of section 35 of the Act and for this reason, if any matter is decided by a competent authority under section 164 of the Act, an appeal cannot be filed before this Tribunal against the said order passed by the competent authority. As per section 35 of the Act, only those matters shall stand transferred to this Tribunal, which are pending before any court including High Court and not pending before any authority. For transfer, it must be established that only those cases shall stand transferred to this Tribunal over which the Tribunal has jurisdiction to decide in the form of appeal. In this view of the matter, appeals pending before the competent authority under section 164 of the Act against the order passed by the court martial cannot be transferred to the Tribunal.

The power and jurisdiction of the competent authority under section 164 of the Army Act were exercisable by the authority immediately before the enactment of the Armed Forces Tribunal Act, 2007. The Act so enacted nowhere has repealed the existing powers or jurisdiction of the authority deciding an appeal against the order of the court martial, though the powers of an authority under Army Act and that of the Tribunal under the Act of 2007 are concurrent one having no inconsistency but both operates in two different field, having their own umbrella under the different Act. The criminal jurisdiction of the respective courts and the authority have not been abrogated by the enactment of the Act of 2007, though in civil matter, the exclusion of jurisdiction has been enacted specially under section 33 of the Act of 2007, but such is not the case about criminal matters. Hence, if the litigant had prepared a petition under section 164 of the Army Act, the same should be decided by the authority itself and as per section 35 of the Act, the same cannot stand transferred to the Tribunal for adjudication.

Similarly, if the authority has decided the appeal/petition, against which a judicial review is pending before High Court under Article 226 of the Constitution, the same also cannot be transferred to the Tribunal because the Tribunal has been invested with power of appeal only under section 15 of the Act of 2007, not of the power to hear judicial review.

The Tribunal was of the view that it lacks jurisdiction to entertain, hear and decide the matter arising out of the order passed by the competent authority under s. 164 of the Army Act against the order passed by the court martial as the AFT Act has specifically invested power in the Tribunal to entertain, hear and decide the appeals against the order passed by the court martial and not by the competent authority under s. 164 of the Army Act.

The Bench held that an army personnel convicted by a court martial, who had already availed the remedy of appeal by way of petition provided under section 164 of the Army Act can neither avail the remedy of appeal under section 15 of the AFT Act nor the remedy of judicial review before the Tribunal.

Note: *In view of the author, this is not a correct interpretation of the provisions of section 164 of the Army Act. The correct interpretation of section 164 was done by the Kochi Bench in Capt Tony George v. Union of India, TA No. 164 of 2010 [WP (C) No. 6522 of 2001 of High Court Delhi and TA No. 736 of 2009 of AFT New Delhi], decided on 28 October 2010. The Kochi Bench did not agree with the above view taken by the Jaipur Bench.*

Appendix-A

The Armed Forces Tribunal Act, 2007[1] (Act No. 55 of 2007)

The Armed Forces Tribunal Act, 2007

An Act

To provide for the adjudication or trial by Armed Forces Tribunal of disputes and complaints with respect to commission, appointments, enrolment and conditions of service in respect of persons subject to the Army Act, 1950, the Navy Act, 1957 and the Air Force Act 1950 and also to provide for appeals arising out of orders, findings or sentences of court martial held under the said Acts and for matters connected therewith or incidental thereto.

BE it enacted by Parliament in the Fifty-eighth Year of the Republic of India as follows:

Chapter I
Preliminary

1. Short title and commencement: (1) This Act may be called the Armed Forces Tribunal Act, 2007.

(2) It shall come into force on such date as the Central Government may, by notification, appoint.

2. Applicability of the Act: (1) The provisions of this Act shall apply to all persons subject to the Army Act, 1950, (46 of 1950) the Navy Act, 1957 (62 of 1957) and the Air Force Act, 1950 (45 of 1950)

(2) This Act shall also apply to retired personnel subject to the Army Act, 1950 (46 of 1950) or the Navy Act, 1957 (62 of 1957) or the Air Force Act, 1950 (45 of 1950) including their dependants, heirs and successors, in so far as it relates to their service matters.

3. Definitions: In this Act, unless the context otherwise requires,—

(a) "Administrative Member" means a member of the Tribunal who is not a Judicial Member within the meaning of clause (g);

1. See Gazette of India, Part II, Section 1, No. 66, New Delhi, December 28, 2007.

(b) "application" means an application made under sub-section (2) of section 14;
(c) "appointed day" means the date with effect from which the Tribunal is established by notification under section 4;
(d) "Bench" means a Bench of the Tribunal;
(e) "Chairperson" means the Chairperson of the Tribunal;
(f) "court-martial" means a court-martial held under the Army Act, 1950 (46 of 1950) or the Navy Act, 1957 (62 of 1957) including the disciplinary courts constituted under the Act or the Air Force Act, 1950 (45 of 1950);
(g) "Judicial Member" means a member of the Tribunal appointed as such under this Act, and includes the Chairperson, who possesses any of the qualifications specified in sub-section (2) of section 6;
(h) "Member" means a member (whether Judicial or Administrative) of the Tribunal and includes the Chairperson;
(i) "military custody" means the arrest or confinement of a person according to the usages of the service and includes naval or air force custody;
(j) "notification" means a notification published in the Official Gazette;
(k) "prescribed" means prescribed by rules made under this Act;
(l) "president" means the President of India;
(m) "rules" means the rules made under this Act;
(n) "service" means the service within or outside India;
(o) "service matters", in relation to the persons subject to the Army Act, 1950 (46 of 1950) the Navy Act, 1957 (62 of 1957) and the Air Force Act, 1950 (45 of 1950) mean all matters relating to the conditions of their service and shall include:
    (i) remuneration (including allowances), pension and other retirement benefits;
    (ii) tenure, including commission, appointment, enrolment, probation, confirmation, seniority, training, promotion, reversion, premature retirement, superannuation, termination of service and penal deductions;
    (iii) summary disposal and trials where the punishment of dismissal is awarded;
    (iv) any other matter, whatsoever, but shall not include matters relating to:
        (i) orders issued under section 18 of the Army Act, 1950 (46 of 1950) sub-section (1) of section 15 of the Navy Act, 1957 (62 of 1957) and section 18 of the Air Force Act, 1950; (45 of 1950);
        (ii) transfers and postings including the change of place or unit on posting whether individually or as a part of unit,

formation or ship in relation to the persons subject to the Army Act, 1950 (46 of 1950) the Navy Act, 1957 (62 of 1957) and the Air Force Act, 1950 (45 of 1950);

(iii) leave of any kind;

(iv) summary court martial except where the punishment is of dismissal or imprisonment for more than three months;

(p) "summary disposals and trials" means summary disposals and trials held under the Army Act, 1950 (46 of 1950) the Navy Act, 1957 (62 of 1957) and the Air Force Act, 1950; (45 of 1950)

(q) "Tribunal': means the Armed Forces Tribunal established under section 4.

Chapter II

Establishment of Tribunal and Benches Thereof

4. Establishment of Armed Forces Tribunal: The Central Government shall, by notification, establish a Tribunal to be known as the Armed Forces Tribunal to exercise the jurisdiction, powers and authority conferred on it by or under this Act.

5. Composition of Tribunal and Benches thereof: (1) The Tribunal shall consist of a Chairperson, and such number of Judicial and Administrative Members as the Central Government may deem fit and, subject to the other provisions of this Act, the jurisdiction, powers and authority of the Tribunal may be exercised by Benches there of.

(2) Subject to the other provisions of this Act, a Bench shall consist of one Judicial Member and one Administrative Member.

(3) Notwithstanding anything contained in sub-section (1), the Chairperson:

(a) may, in addition to discharging the functions of a Judicial Member of the Bench to which he is appointed, discharge the functions of an Administrative Member of any other Bench;

(b) may transfer a Member from one Bench to another Bench;

(c) may, for the purpose of securing that any case or cases, which having regard to the nature of the questions involved, requires or require, in his opinion, or under the rules made under this Act, to be decided by a Bench composed of more than two members, issue such general or special orders, as he may deem fit:

Provided that every Bench constituted in pursuance of this clause shall include at least one Judicial Member and onc Administrative Member.

(4) Subject to the other provisions of this Act, the Benches of the Tribunal shall ordinarily sit at Delhi (which shall be known as the Principal Bench), and at such other places as the Central Government may, by notification, specify.

6. Qualifications for appointment of Chairperson and other Members: (1) A person shall not be qualified for appointment as the Chairperson unless he is a retired Judge of the Supreme Court or a retired Chief Justice of a High Court.

(2) A person shall not be qualified for appointment as a Judicial Member unless he is or has been a Judge of a High Court.

(3) A person shall not be qualified for appointment as an Administrative Member unless:

(a) he has held or has been holding the rank of Major General or above for a total period of at least three years in the Army or equivalent rank in the Navy or the Air Force; or[2]

(b) he has served for not less than one year as Judge Advocate General in the Army or the Navy or the Air Force, and is not below the rank of Major General, Commodore and Air Commodore respectively.

Explanation: When a serving person is appointed as an Administrative Member, he shall have retired from service prior to assuming such appointment.

7. Appointment of Chairperson and other Members: (1) Subject to the provisions of this section, the Chairperson and other Members of the Tribunal shall be appointed by the President:

Provided that no appointment under this sub-section shall be made except after consultation with the Chief Justice of India.

(2) The President may appoint one or more Members of the Tribunal to be the Vice-Chairperson, or, as the case may be, the Vice-Chairpersons, thereof.

8. Term of office: The Chairperson or a Member shall hold office for a term of four years from the date on which he enters upon his office and shall be eligible for re-appointment:

Provided that no Chairperson shall hold office as such after he has attained,

(a) in case he has been a Judge of the Supreme Court, the age of seventy years; and

(b) in case he has been the Chief Justice of a High Court, the age of sixty-five years:

Provided further that no other Member shall hold office as such Member after he has attained the age of sixty-five years.

9. Resignation and removal: (1) The Chairperson or a Member may, by notice in writing under his hand addressed to the President, resign his office:

Provided that the Chairperson or a Member shall, unless he is permitted by the President to relinquish his office sooner, continue to hold office until the expiry of three months from the date of receipt of such notice or until

---

2. Word 'or' substituted for the word 'and' vide The Armed Forces Tribunal Act (Removal of Difficulties) Order , 2008. SRO 18 (E) dated 21 July 2008. Published in the Gazette of India, Extraordinary, Part II, Section 4, dated 21 July 2008.

a person duly appointed as his successor enters upon his office or until the expiry of his term of office, whichever is the earliest.

(2) The Chairperson or a Member shall not be removed from his office except by an order made by the President on the ground of proved misbehaviour or incapacity after an inquiry made by a sitting Judge of the Supreme Court in which such Chairperson or other Member had been informed of the charges against him and given a reasonable opportunity of being heard in respect of those charges.

(3) The Central Government may, by rules, regulate the procedure for the investigation of misbehaviour or incapacity of the Chairperson or other Member referred to in sub-section (2).

10. Salaries, allowances and other terms and conditions of service of Chairperson and other Members: The salaries and allowances payable to, and the other terms and conditions of service (including pension, gratuity and other retirement benefits) of, the Chairperson and other Members shall be such as may be prescribed by the Central Government:

Provided that neither the salary and allowances nor the other terms and conditions of service of the Chairperson and other Members shall be varied to their disadvantage after their appointment.

11. Prohibitions as to holding of offices, *etc.*, by Chairperson or Member on ceasing to be such Chairperson or Member: On ceasing to hold office:

(a) the Chairperson shall be ineligible for further employment either under the Government of India or under the Government of a State;

(b) a Member other than the Chairperson shall, subject to the provisions of this Act, be eligible for appointment as a member of any other Tribunal but not for any other employment either under the Government of India or under the Government of a State; and

(c) the Chairperson or other Members shall not appear, act or plead before the Tribunal.

12. Financial and administrative powers of Chairperson: The Chairperson shall exercise such financial and administrative powers over the Benches as may be prescribed:

Provided that the Chairperson shall have the authority to delegate such of his financial and administrative powers as he may think fit to any other Member or any officer of the Tribunal, subject to the conditions that such Member or officer shall, while exercising such delegated powers, continue to act under the direction, control and supervision of the Chairperson.

13. Staff of the Tribunal: (1) The Central Government shall determine the nature and categories of the officers and other employees required to assist the Tribunal in the discharge of its functions and provide the Tribunal with such officers and other employees as it may think fit.

(2) The salaries and allowances payable to, and the other terms and conditions of service of the officers and other employees of the Tribunal shall be such as may be prescribed.

(3) The officers and other employees of the Tribunal shall discharge their functions under the general superintendence of the Chairperson.

Chapter III

Jurisdiction, Powers and Authority of the Tribunal

14. Jurisdiction, powers and authority in service matters: (1) Save as otherwise expressly provided in this Act, the Tribunal shall exercise, on and from the appointed day, all the jurisdiction, powers and authority, exercisable immediately before that day by all courts (except the Supreme Court or a High Court exercising jurisdiction under articles 226 and 227 of the Constitution) in relation to all service matters.

(2) Subject to the other provisions of this Act, a person aggrieved by an order pertaining to any service matter may make an application to the Tribunal in such form and accompanied by such documents or other evidence and on payment of such fee as may be prescribed.

(3) On receipt of an application relating to service matters, the Tribunal shall, if satisfied after due inquiry, as it may deem necessary, that it is fit for adjudication by it, admit such application; but where the Tribunal is not so satisfied, it may dismiss the application after recording its reasons in writing.

(4) For the purpose of adjudicating an application, the Tribunal shall have the same powers as are vested in a Civil Court under the Code of Civil Procedure, 1908, (5 of 1908) while trying a suit in respect of the following matters, namely:

- (a) summoning and enforcing the attendance of any person and examining him on oath;
- (b) requiring the discovery and production of documents;
- (c) receiving evidence on affidavits;
- (d) subject to the provisions of sections 123 and 124 of the Indian Evidence Act, 1872, (1 of 1872) requisitioning any public record or document or copy of such record or document from any office;
- (e) issuing commissions for the examination of witnesses or documents;
- (f) reviewing its decisions;
- (g) dismissing an application for default or deciding it exparte;
- (h) setting aside any order of dismissal of any application for default or any order passed by it ex-parte; and
- (i) any other matter which may be prescribed by the Central Government.

(5) The Tribunal shall decide both questions of law and facts that may be raised before it.

15. Jurisdiction powers and authority in matters of appeal against court martial:

(1) Save as otherwise expressly provided in this Act, the Tribunal shall exercise, on and from the appointed day, all the jurisdiction, powers and authority exercisable under this Act in relation to appeal against any order, decision, finding or sentence passed by a court martial or any matter connected therewith or incidental thereto.

(2) Any person aggrieved by an order, decision, finding or sentence passed by a court martial may prefer an appeal in such form, manner and within such time as may be prescribed.

(3) The Tribunal shall have power to grant bail to any person accused of an offence and in military custody, with or without any conditions which it considers necessary:

Provided that no accused person shall be so released if there appears reasonable ground for believing that he has been guilty of an offence punishable with death or imprisonment for life.

(4) The Tribunal shall allow an appeal against conviction by a court martial where

(a) the finding of the court martial is legally not sustainable due to any reason whatsoever; or

(b) the finding involves wrong decision on a question of law; or

(c) there was a material irregularity in the course of the trial resulting in miscarriage of justice, but, in any other case, may dismiss the appeal where the Tribunal considers that no miscarriage of justice is likely to be caused or has actually resulted to the appellant:

Provided that no order dismissing the appeal by the Tribunal shall be passed unless such order is made after recording reasons therefor in writing.

(5) The Tribunal may allow an appeal against conviction, and pass appropriate order thereon.

(6) Notwithstanding anything contained in the foregoing provisions of this section, the Tribunal shall have the power to—

(a) substitute for the findings of the court martial, a finding of guilty for any other offence for which the offender could have been lawfully found guilty by the court martial and pass a sentence afresh for the offence specified or involved in such findings under the provisions of the Army Act, 1950 (46 of 1950) or the Navy Act, 1957 (62 of 1957) or the Air Force Act, 1950, (45 of 1950) as the case may be; or

(b) if sentence is found to be excessive, illegal or unjust, the Tribunal may—

(i) remit the whole or any part of the sentence, with or without conditions; (ii) mitigate the punishment awarded;

(iii) commute such punishment to any lesser punishment or punishments mentioned in the Army Act, 1950, (46 of 1950) the Navy Act, 1957 (62 of 1957) and the Air Force Act, 1950, (45 of 1950) as the case may be;

(c) enhance the sentence awarded by a court martial:

Provided that no such sentence shall be enhanced unless the appellant has been given an opportunity of being heard;

(d) release the appellant, if sentenced to imprisonment, on parole with or without conditions;

(e) suspend a sentence of imprisonment;

(f) pass any other order as it may think appropriate.

(7) Notwithstanding any other provisions in this Act, for the purposes of this section, the Tribunal shall be deemed to be a criminal court for the purposes of sections 175, 178, 179, 180, 193, 195, 196 or 228 (45 of 1860) of the Indian Penal Code and Chapter XXVI of the Code of Criminal Procedure, 1973. (2 of 1974)

16. Re-trial:[3] (1) Except as provided by this Act, where the conviction of a person by court martial for an offence has been quashed, he shall not be liable to be tried again for that offence by a court martial or by any other Court.

(2) The Tribunal shall have the power of quashing a conviction, to make an order authorising the appellant to be retried by court martial, but shall only exercise this power when the appeal against conviction is allowed by reasons only of evidence received or available to be received by the Tribunal under this Act and it appears to the Tribunal that the interests of justice require that an order under this section should be made:

Provided that an appellant shall not be retried under this section for an offence other than—

(a) the offence for which he was convicted by the original court martial and in respect of which his appeal is allowed;

(b) any offence for which he could have been convicted at the original court martial on a charge of the first-mentioned offence;

(c) any offence charged in the alternative in respect of which the court martial recorded no finding in consequence of convicting him of the first-mentioned offence.

(3) A person who is to be retried under this section for an offence shall, if the Tribunal or the Supreme Court so directs, whether or not such person is being tried or retried on one or more of the original charges, no fresh investigation or other action shall be taken under the relevant provision of the Army Act, 1950 (46 of 1950) or the Navy Act, 1957 (62 of 1957) or the Air Force Act, 1950 (45of 1950) as the case may be, or rules and regulations made there under, in relation to the said charge or charges on which he is to be retried.

---

3. Section 16 (1) of the Act has been incorporated from section 18 of the British Court-Martial (Appeals) Act, 1968. Section 16 (2) and (3) have been incorporated from Section 19 of the British Act.

17. Powers of the Tribunal on appeal under section 15: The Tribunal, while hearing and deciding an appeal under section 15, shall have the power:

(a) to order production of documents or exhibits connected with the proceedings before the court martial;
(b) to order the attendance of the witnesses;
(c) to receive evidence;
(d) to obtain reports from Court martial;
(e) order reference of any question for enquiry;
(f) appoint a person with special expert knowledge to act as an assessor;[4] and
(g) to determine any question which is necessary to be determined in order to do justice in the case.[5]

18. Cost: While disposing of the application under section 14 or an appeal under section 15, the Tribunal shall have power to make such order as to costs as it may deem just.

19. Power to punish for contempt: (1) Any person who is guilty of contempt of the Tribunal by using any insulting or threatening language, or by causing any interruption or disturbance in the proceedings of such Tribunal shall, on conviction, be liable to suffer imprisonment for a term which may extend to three years.

(2) For the purposes of trying an offence under this section, the provisions of sections 14, 15, 17, 18 and 20 of the Contempt of courts Act, 1971 (70 of 1971) shall mutatis mutandis apply, as if a reference therein to:

(a) Supreme Court or High Court were a reference to the Tribunal;
(b) Chief Justice were a reference to the Chairperson;
(c) Judge were a reference to the Judicial or Administrative Member of the Tribunal;
(d) Advocate-General were a reference to the prosecutor; and
(e) Court were a reference to the Tribunal.

20. Distribution of business among the Benches: The Chairperson may make provisions as to the distribution of the business of the Tribunal among its Benches.

Chapter IV
Procedure

21. Application not to be admitted unless other remedies exhausted: (1) The Tribunal shall not ordinarily admit an application unless it is satisfied

---

4. An expert is one who has devoted his time and study to a special branch of learning, and thus is especially skilled on those points on which he is asked to state his opinion. The Indian Evidence Act, section 45 deals with opinions of expert. The Use of the term "special expert knowledge" appears superfluous. The sub-section (f) should have been "to appoint an expert to act as an assessor;"

5. This sub-section may be amended to read as "to determine any question in order to do justice in the case."

that the applicant had availed of the remedies available to him under the Army Act, 1950 (46 of 1950) or the Navy Act, 1957 (62 of 1957) or the Air Force Act, 1950 (45 of 1950) as the case may be, and respective rules and regulations made thereunder.

(2) For the purposes of sub-section (1), a person shall be deemed to have availed of all the remedies available to him under the Army Act, 1950 (46 of 1950) or the Navy Act, 1957 (62 of 1957) or the Air Force Act, 1950, (45 of 1950) and respective rules and regulations:

(a) if a final order has been made by the Central Government or other authority or officer or other person competent to pass such order under the said Acts, rules and regulations, rejecting any petition preferred or representation made by such person;

(b) where no final order has been made by the Central Government or other authority or officer or other person competent to pass such order with regard to the petition preferred or representation made by such person, if a period of six months from the date on which such petition was preferred or representation was made has expired.

22. Limitation:[6] The Tribunal shall not admit an application:

(a) in a case where a final order such as is mentioned in clause (a) of sub-section (2) of section 21 has been made unless the application is made within six months from the date on which such final order has been made;

(b) in a case where a petition or a representation such as is mentioned in clause (b) of sub-section (2) of section 21 has been made and the period of six months has expired thereafter without such final order having been made;

(c) in a case where the grievance in respect of which an application is made had arisen by reason of any order made at any time during the period of three years immediately preceding the date on which jurisdiction, powers and authority of the Tribunal became exercisable under this Act, in respect of the matter to which such order relates and no proceedings for the redressal of such grievance had been commenced before the said date before the High Court.

(2) Notwithstanding anything contained in sub-section (1), the Tribunal may admit an application after the period of six months referred to in clause (a) or clause (b) of sub-section (1), as the case may be, or prior to the period of three years specified in clause (c), if the Tribunal is satisfied that the applicant had sufficient cause for not making the application within such period.

23. Procedure and powers of the Tribunal: (1) The Tribunal shall not be bound by the procedure laid down in the Code of Civil Procedure, 1908 (5 of 1908) but shall be guided by the principles of natural justice and subject to the other provisions of this Act and any rules made thereunder, the Tribunal

6. This should have been 22. Limitation. (1) The Tribunal shall .....

shall have the power to lay down and regulate its own procedure including the fixing of place and time of its inquiry and deciding whether to sit in public or in camera.

(2) The Tribunal shall decide every application made to it as expeditiously as possible after a perusal of documents, affidavits and written representations and after hearing such oral arguments as may be advanced:

Provided that where the Tribunal deems it necessary, for reasons to be recorded in writing, it may allow oral evidence to be adduced.

(3) No adjournment shall be granted by the Tribunal without recording the reasons justifying the grant of such adjournment and cost shall be awarded, if a party requests for adjournment more than twice.

24. Term of sentence and its effect on appeal: (1) The term of any sentence passed by the Tribunal under clause (a) of subsection (6).of section 15 of this Act shall, unless the Tribunal otherwise directs, be reckoned to commence on the day on which it would have commenced under the Army Act, 1950, (46 of 1950) the Navy Act, 1957 (62 of 1957) or the Air Force Act, 1950 (45 of 1950) as the case may be, under which the court martial against which the appeal was filed, had. been held.

(2) Subject to the provisions of sub-section (3), any sentence passed on an appeal from the Tribunal to the Supreme Court in substitution for another sentence shall, unless the Supreme Court otherwise directs, be reckoned to commence on the day on which the original sentence would have commenced.

(3) Where a person who is undergoing sentence is granted stay of the operation of the said sentence, either by suspension or otherwise, pending an appeal, the period during which he is so released due to the sentence having been so stayed, shall be excluded in computing the term for which he is so sentenced by the Tribunal or the Supreme Court, as the case may be.

25. Right of applicant or of appellant to take assistance of a legal practitioner and of Government, *etc.*, to appoint counsel:

(1) A person making an application or preferring an appeal to the Tribunal may either. appear in person or take the assistance of a legal practitioner of his choice to present his case before the Tribunal.

(2) The Central Government or the competent authority, as may be prescribed, may authorise one or more legal practitioners or any of its law officers to act as counsel and every person so authorised by it may present its case with respect to any application or appeal, as the case may be, before the, Tribunal.

26. Condition as to making of interim order:

(1) Notwithstanding anything contained in any other provisions of this Act or in any other law for the time being in force, no interim order (whether by way of injunction or stay or in any other manner) shall be made on an application or appeal, or in any proceeding relating thereto, unless:

(a) copies of such application or appeal, as the case may be, and all documents in support of the plea for such interim order are furnished to the party against whom such application or appeal, as the case may be, is made or proposed to be made; and

(b) opportunity of being heard is given to the other party in the matter:

Provided that the Tribunal may dispense with the requirements of clauses (a) and (b) and make an interim order as an exceptional measure if it is satisfied, for reasons to be recorded in writing, that it is necessary so to do for preventing any loss being caused to the applicant or to the appellant, as the case may be.

(2) Where any party against whom an interim order, whether by way of injunction or stay or in any other manner, is made on an application or appeal or in any proceeding relating thereto under sub-section (i), without—

(a) furnishing to such party copies of such application or appeal, as the case may be, and all documents in support of the plea for such interim order; and

(b) giving such party an opportunity of being heard, and making an application to the Tribunal for the vacation of such order and furnishing a copy of such application or appeal, as the case may be, to the party in whose favour such order has been made or the counsel of such party, the Tribunal shall dispose of the application within a period of fourteen days from the date on which it is received or from the date on which the copy of such application is so furnished, whichever is later, or where the Tribunal is closed on the last day of that period, before the expiry of the next working day; and if the application is not so disposed of, the interim order shall, on the expiry of that period, or, as the case may be, the expiry of the said next working day, stand vacated.

27. Power of Chairperson to transfer cases from one Bench to another: On the application of any of the parties and after notice to the parties concerned, and after hearing such of them as he may desire to be heard, or on his own motion without such notice, the Chairperson may transfer any case pending before one Bench for disposal, to, any other Bench.

28. Decision to be by majority: If the Members of a Bench differ in opinion on any point, the point shall be decided according to the opinion of the majority, if there is a majority, but if the Members are equally divided, they shall state the point Or points on which they differ and make a reference to the Chairperson who shall either hear the point or points himself or refer the case for hearing on such point or points by one or more of the Members of the Tribunal and such point or points shall bc dccidcd according to the opinion of the majority of the Members of the Tribunal who have heard the case, including those who first heard it.

29. Execution of order of Tribunal: Subject to the other provisions of this Act, and the rules made thereunder, the order of the Tribunal disposing of an application shall be final and shall not be called in question in any Court and such order shall be executed accordingly.

Chapter V
Appeal

30. Appeal to Supreme Court: (1) Subject to the provisions of section 31, an appeal shall lie to the Supreme Court against the final decision or order of the Tribunal (other than an order passed under section 19):

Provided that such appeal is preferred within a period of ninety days of the said decision or order:

Provided further that there shall be no appeal against an interlocutory order of the Tribunal.

(2) An appeal shall lie to the Supreme Court as of right from any order or decision of the Tribunal in the exercise of its jurisdiction to punish for contempt: .

Provided that an appeal under this sub-section shall be filed in the Supreme Court within sixty days from the date of the order appealed against.

(3) Pending any appeal under sub-section (2), the Supreme Court may order that:

(a) the execution of the punishment or the order appealed against be suspended; or

(b) if the appellant is in confinement, he be released on bail:

Provided that where an appellant satisfies the Tribunal that he intends to prefer an appeal, the Tribunal may also exercise any of the powers conferred under clause (a) or clause (b), as the case may be.

31. Leave to appeal:[7] (1) An appeal to the Supreme Court shall lie with the leave of the Tribunal; and such leave shall not be granted unless it is certified by the Tribunal that a point of law of general public importance is involved in the decision, or it appears to the Supreme Court that the point is one which ought to be considered by that Court.

(2) An application to the Tribunal for leave to appeal to the Supreme Court shall be made within a period of thirty days beginning with the date of the decision of the Tribunal and an application to the Supreme Court for leave shall be made within a period of thirty days beginning with the date on which the application for leave is refused by the Tribunal.

(3) An appeal shall be treated as pending until any application for leave to appeal is disposed of and if leave to appeal is granted, until the appeal is disposed of; and an application for leave to appeal shall be treated as disposed of at the expiration of the time within which it might have been made, but it is not made within that time.

---

7. Section 31 of the Act has been incorporated from sections 39 (2) and 40 (1) and (3) of the British Court-Martial (Appeals) Act, 1968

32. Condonation: The Supreme Court may, upon an application made at any time by the appellant, extend the time within which an appeal may be preferred by him to that Court under section 30 or sub-section (2) of section 31.

Chapter VI
Miscellaneous

33. Exclusion of jurisdiction of civil courts: On and from the date from which any jurisdiction, powers and authority becomes exercisable by the Tribunal in relation-to service matters under this Act, no Civil Court shall have, or be entitled to exercise, such jurisdiction, power or authority in relation to those service matters.

34. Transfer of pending cases: (1) Every suit, or other proceeding pending before any court including a High Court or other authority immediately before the date of establishment of the Tribunal under this Act, being a suit or proceeding the cause of action whereon it is based, is such that it would have been within the jurisdiction of the Tribunal, if it had arisen after such establishment within the jurisdiction of such Tribunal, stand transferred on that date to such Tribunal.

(2) Where any suit, or other proceeding stands transferred from any court including a High Court or other authority to the Tribunal under sub-section (1):

(a) the court or other authority shall, as soon as may be, after such transfer, forward the records of such suit, or other proceeding to the Tribunal;

(b) the Tribunal may, on receipt of such records, proceed to deal with such suit, or other proceeding, so far as may be, in the same' manner as in the case of an application made under sub-section (2) of section 14, from the stage which was reached before such transfer or from any earlier stage or de novo as the Tribunal may deem fit.

35. Provision for filing of certain appeals: Where any decree or order has been made or passed by any court (other than a High Court) or any other authority in any suit or proceeding before the establishment of the Tribunal, being a suit or proceeding the cause of action whereon it is based, is such that it would have been, if it had arisen after such establishment, within the jurisdiction of the Tribunal, and no appeal has been preferred 'against such decree or order before such establishment or if preferred, the same is pending for disposal before any court including High Court and the time for preferring such appeal under any law for the time being in force had not expired before such establishment, such appeal shall lie to the Tribunal, within ninety days from the date on which the Tribunal is established, or within ninety days from the date of receipt of the copy of such decree or order, whichever is later.

36. Proceedings before Tribunal to be judicial proceedings: All proceedings before the Tribunal shall be deemed to be judicial proceedings within the meaning of sections 193, 219 and 228 (45 of 1860) of the Indian Penal Code.

37. Members and staff of Tribunal to be public servants: The Chairperson, other Members and the officers and other employees provided under section 13 to the Tribunal shall be deemed to be public servants within the meaning of section 21 (45 of 1860) of the Indian Penal Code.

38. Protection of action taken in good faith: No suit, prosecution or other legal proceeding shall lie against the Central Government or against the Chairperson or any other Member or any other person authorised by the Chairperson, for anything which is done in good faith or intended to be done in pursuance of this Act or any rule or order made thereunder in the discharge of official duties.

39. Act to have overriding effect: The provisions of this Act shall have effect notwithstanding anything inconsistent therewith contained, in any other law for the time being in force or in any instrument having effect by virtue of any law other than this Act.

40. Power to remove difficulties: (1) If any difficulty arises in giving effect to the provisions of this Act, the Central Government may, by order published in the Official Gazette, make such provisions, not inconsistent with the provisions of this Act as appear to it to be necessary or expedient for removing the difficulty:

Provided that no order shall be made under this section after the expiry of two years from the date of commencement of this Act.

(2) Every order made under this section shall, as soon as may be after it is made, be laid before each House of Parliament.

41. Power of Central Government to make rules: (1) The Central Government may, by notification, make rules for the purposes of carrying out the provisions of this Act.

(2) Without prejudice to the generality of the foregoing power, such rules may provide for all or any of the following matters, namely:

(a) the case or cases which shall be decided by a Bench composed of more than two Members under clause (c) of sub-section (3) of section 5;

(b) the procedure under sub-section (3) of section 9 for the investigation of misbehaviour or incapacity of Chairperson or other Member;

(c) the salaries and allowances payable to, and the other terms and conditions of service of the Chairperson and other Members under section 10;

(d) the financial and administrative powers which the Chairperson may exercise over the Benches of the Tribunal under section 12;

(e) the salaries and allowances payable to, and other terms and conditions of service of the officers and other employees of the Tribunal under sub-section (2) of section 13;

(f) the form in which an application may be made under sub-section (2) of section 14, the documents and other evidence by which such application shall be accompanied and the fee payable in respect of the filing of such application or for the service of execution of processes;

(g) the other matter which may be prescribed under clause (i) of sub-section (4) of section 14;

(h) the form and manner in which an appeal may be filed, the fee payable thereon and the time within which such appeal may be filed under sub-section (2) of section 15;

(i) the rules subject to which the Tribunal shall have power to regulate its own procedure under sub-section (1) of section 23;

(j) competent authority who may authorise legal practitioners or law officers to act as counsel under sub-section (2) of section 25;

(k) any other matter which may be prescribed or in respect of which rules are required to be made by the Central Government.

42. Power to make rules retrospectively: The powers to make rules under section 41 shall include the power to make such rules or any of them retrospectively from a date not earlier than the date on which this Act shall come into operation but no such retrospective effect shall be given to any such rule so as to prejudicially affect the interests of any person to whom such rule may be applicable.

43. Laying of rules: Every rule made under this Act shall be laid, as soon as may be after it is made, before each House of Parliament while it is in session, for a total period of thirty days which may be comprised in one session or in two or more successive sessions, and if, before the expiry of the session immediately following the session or the successive sessions aforesaid, both Houses agree in making any modification in the rule or both Houses agree that the rule should not be made, the rule shall thereafter have effect only in such modified form or be of no effect, as the case may be; so, however, that any such modification or annulment shall be without prejudice to the validity of anything previously done under that rule.

Appendix-B

The Armed Forces Tribunal (Procedure) Rules, 2008

Ministry of Defence, Notification

New Delhi, the 17th September, 2008

S.R.O. 26(E) – In exercise of the powers conferred by clauses (f), (g) and (k) of sub-section (2) of Section 41 of the Armed Forces Tribunal Act, 2007 (55 of 2007), the Central Government has made these rules.

1. Short title and commencement: (1) These Rules may be called the Armed Forces Tribunal (Procedure) Rules. 2008.

(2) They shall come into force from the date of publication in the Official Gazette.[1]

2. Defintion: (1) In these rules, unless the context otherwise requires,-

(i) "Act" means the Armed Forces Tribunal Act, 2007 (55 of 2007);

(ii) "agent" means a person duly authorized by a party to present an application, written reply, rejoinder or any other document on its behalf before the Tribunal;

(iii) "applicant" means a person making an application to the Tribunal under sub-section (2) of Section 14 or an appeal under sub-section (2) of Section 15 of the Act;

(iv) "application includes Original Application (O.A.), Review Application (R.A.), Transferred Application (T.A.), Miscellaneous Application (M.A.), Application for Transfer (A.T.) and Contempt Application (C.A.), filed before the Tribunal;

(v) "Code" means the Code of Civil Procedure, 1908 (5 of 1908);

(vi) "Court appealed from" includes a tribunal or any other judicial body or court-martial or authority against the decision of which an appeal is preferred to this Tribunal;

(vii) "Form" means the form set out in the appendices to threes rules;

---

1. Published in the GAZATTE OF INDIA: EXTRAORDINARY, PART II, SEC IV, Dated July 26, 2008.

(viii) "Judgment" includes decree, order, sentence or determination of any Court, Tribunal, Judge, Judicial Officer or authority;

(ix) "legal practitioner" shall have the same meaning as assigned to it in the Advocates Act, 1961 (25 of 2961) and includes a Standing Counsel authorized or appointed by the Central Government to accept the service for any Department or Organisation of Union of India;

(x) "Legal representative" means a person who in law represents the estate of a serving or deceased person and includes a person or persons in whom the right to receive pensionary, retirement, terminal, disability or other benefits or family pension vests;

(xi) "Officer of the Judge-Advocate General's Department" means an officer commissioned into the Judge-Advocate General's Department of the Army or an officer permanently transferred to that Department after qualifying at the Judge-Advocate General's Departmental examination and includes an officer of Judge-Advocate General's Department of Navy and Air Force;

(xii) "Pleadings" shall include original applications, reply statement, rejoinders and additional applications or statements supplementing the original applications and the reply statements, as may be permitted by the Tribunal;

(xiii) "Registrar" means Registrar of the Armed Forces Tribunal or its Benches and shall include Registrar-General, Principal, Additional, Joint and Deputy Registrars, authorized to discharge the functions of the Registrar;

(xiv) "Registry" mean the Registry of the Tribunal or any of its Benches as the case may be;

(xv) "Section" means a section of the Act;

(xvi) "Services" means the Army, Navy and Air Force, as applicable;

(xvii) "Standing Counsel" means as advocate authorized to act; represent and accept the service for the Army, Navy or Force or for the Union of India;

(xviii) "Transferred application" means the suit or other proceeding which has been transferred to the Tribunal under sub-section (1) or sub-section (2) of section 34;

(xix) "Vice-Chairperson" means a Vice-Chairperson of a Tribunal.

(2) The words and expressions used and not defined in these rules but defined in the Act, the Army Act, 1950 (46 of 1950), the Navy Act, 1957 (62 of 1957) and the Air Force Act, 1950 (45 of 1950) shall have the same meaning respectively assigned to them in those Acts and respective rules made there under.

3. Language of the Tribunal: 1. The language of the Tribunal shall be English;

Provided that the parties to a proceeding before the Tribunal may file documents drawn up in Hindi;

Provided further that:

(a) the Bench may, in its discretion permit the use of Hindi in the proceedings;

(b) The Bench hearing the matter may, in its discretion, direct English translation of pleadings and documents to be field.

(2) No document in a language other than English intended to be used in any proceeding shall be received by the Registrar unless it is accompanied by a translation in English certified to be a true translation.

(3) The Bench may, in it discretion, make final orders either in Hindi or in English;

Provided that where a final order is made in Hindi, an authenticated English translation there of shall simultaneously be prepared and kept on record.

4. Procedure for filing applications: (1) An application to the Tribunal shall be presented in Form I by the applicant in person or by an agent or by a duly authorized legal practitioner to the Registrar or any other officer authorized in writing by the Chairperson or Vice-Chairperson to receive the same or be sent by registered post or by courier with acknowledgment due addressed to the Registrar of the Bench concerned.

(2) (i) The application under sub-rule (1) shall be presented in triplicate in the following two compilations:-

(a) *Compilation No. 1* – application along with an attested true copy of the impugned order against which the application is filed;

(b) *Compilation No. 2* – all other documents and annexures relied upon by the applicant and referred to in the application in a paper book form.

(ii) All the documents filed in the tribunal shall be accompanied by an index in duplicate containing their details memo of the parties and a list of relevant dates. The amount of application fee affixed or paid on any such documents shall also be indicated in the index.

(3) where the number of respondents is more than one, as many extra copies of the application and all other documents and annexure referred thereto in paper-book form as are the number of respondents together with unused file size envelope bearing the full address of each respondent shall be furnished by the application;

Provided that where the number of respondents is more than five, the Registrar may permit the applicant to file extra copies of the application at the time of issue of notice to the respondents.

(4) The applicant may attach to and present with his application a receipt slip in ***Form II*** which shall be signed by the Registrar or the Officer receiving the application on behalf of the Registrar in acknowledgement of the receipt of the application.

(5) Notwithstanding anything contained in sub-rules (1) to (3), the Tribunal may permit more than one person, other than the person serving

in the regular Army, Navy or Air Force to join together and file a single application if it is satisfied, having regard to the cause of action and the nature of relief prayed for, that they have a common interest in the matter:

Provided that all affected persons are impleaded as parties and they join together to file such an application, when they are likely to be affected by the decision in the case.

5. Presentation and scrutiny of applications: (1) The Registrar or the officer authorized under rule 4 shall endorse the date of receipt on the application and also on the duplicate copy of the index and return the same to the party and in case of an application received by post, he shall endorse the date of this receipt and send the duplicate index to the applicant concerned.

(2) If, on scrutiny, the application is found to be in order, it shall be duly registered and given a serial number.

(3) If the application is found to be defective and the defect noticed is formal in nature, the Registrar may allow the applicant to rectify the same in his presence, and if the said defect is not formal in nature, the Registrar may for sufficient cause return the said application for rectification or amendment to the party filing the same, and for this purpose may allow the party concerned such reasonable time as he may consider necessary. Where an application is received by registered post, the applicant shall be informed of the defects, if any, and he shall be required to rectify the same within such time as may be stipulated by the Registrar.

(4) (i) If the applicant falls to rectify the defect within the time allowed under sub-rule (3), the Registrar may by order and for reasons to be recorded in writing, decline to register the application and place the matter before the Bench for appropriate orders. Such matter may be dealt with and disposed by the Bench in Chamber.

(ii) Any applicant aggrieved by any order made by the Registrar under this rule may, within fifteen days of the making of such order, appeal against it to the Chairperson in case the matter relates to Principal Bench and to the Vice-Chairperson concerned, in the case of any other Bench and such appeal may be dealt with and disposed of in chamber by the Chairperson or the Vice-Chairperson concerned or in their absence by any Member authorized by the Chairperson by special or general order, whose decision thereon shall be final.

6. Place of filing application: (1) An application shall ordinarily be filed by the applicant with the Registrar of the Bench within whose jurisdiction-

(i) the applicant is posted for the time being, or was last posted or attached; or

(ii) where the cause of action, wholly or in part, has arisen:
Provided that with the leave of the Chairperson the application may be filed with the Registrar of the Principal Bench and Subject to the orders under section 14 or section 15 of the Act, such

application shall be heard and disposed of by the Bench which has jurisdiction over the matter

(2) Notwithstanding anything contained in sub-rule (1), a person who has ceased to be in service by reason of his retirement, dismissal, discharge, cashiering, release, removal, resignation or termination of service may, at his option, file an application with the Registrar of the Bench within whose jurisdiction such person is ordinarily residing at the time of filling of the application.

7. Application fee : (1)[2] Every application filed with the Registrar shall be accompanied by a fee of rupees two hundred and fifty to be remitted either in the form of crossed demand draft on a nationalized bank in favour of the Registrar of the concerned Bench and payable at the main Branch of that bank at the station where the seat of the said Bench is situated, or remitted through a crossed Indian Postal Order drawn in favour of the Registrar of the concerned Bench and payable at the post office of the station where the said Bench is situated:

Provided that where the Tribunal permits a single application to be filed on behalf of more than one person, the fee payable shall be rupees five hundred:

Provided further that where the Tribunal is satisfied that an applicant is unable to pay the prescribed fee on ground of indigence, it may exempt such an applicant from the payment of application fee.

(2)[3] Notwithstanding anything contained in sub-rule (1), the application fee referred to in that sub-rue shall be payable only is respect of –

- (i) Original Application (OA);
- (ii) Review Application (RA);
- (iii) Contempt Application (CA);
- (iv) Application for restoration of Petition (MA); and
- (v) Application for transfer of case (from one bench to another or from one court to another in the same Bench (AT).

8. Contents of application: (1) Every application filed under section 14 or section 15 shall be fairly and legibly typed or printed in double spacing on one side of thick paper of good quality with an inner margin of about three cm width on top and on the left side.

(2) Paragraphs shall be divided into sub-paragraphs and numbered consecutively. Each paragraph shall contain, as nearly as may be a, separate accounts of events.

(3) Dates of Gregorian Calendar shall also be given where Saka or other dates are used.

---

2. Re-numbered as sub-rule 7 (1), vide the Armed Forces Tribunal (Procedure) Amendment Rules, 2011.
3. Sub-rule 7 (2), inserted vide the Armed Forces Tribunal (Procedure) Amendment Rules, 2011.

(4) At the foot of every application there shall appear the name and signature of the applicant or the agent or legal practitioner, if any, who has drawn and settled it.

(5) The particulars to be stated in address for service shall as far as possible contain the following:-

(i) the name of the road, street, lane of municipal or other number of the house;
(ii) the name of the town or village;
(iii) the post office or postal district together with pin code; and
(iv) any other particulars including personal number, rank appointment held, unit or office or pension payment order (PPO) number necessary to identify the addressee.

(6) Every interlineations, erasure or correction in any application shall be initialed by the applicant or his agent/legal practitioner presenting it.

(7) It shall not be necessary to present a separate application to seek an interim order or direction if the same is prayed for in original application.

(8) An applicant may, subsequent to the filing of an application made under the Act, may apply for an interim order or direction. Such an application shall, as far as possible, be in separate form.

(9) Where the applicant seeks condonation of delay, he shall file a separate application supported by an affidavit.

9. Documents to be annexed to the application: (1) The following documents shall be annexed to the application:

(i) an attested true copy of the order against which the application is filed;
(ii) copies of the documents relied upon by the applicant and referred to in the application; and
(iii) an index of the documents.

(2) The documents referred to in sub-rule (1) may be attested by a legal practitioner or by a Gazetted Officer and each document shall be marked serially as Annexure A-1, A-2, A-3 and so on.

(3) Where an application is filed by an agent, documents authorizing him to act as such shall also be appended to the application:

Provided that where an application is filed by a legal practitioner, it shall be accompanied by a duly executed "Vakalatnama".

10. Plural remedies: An application shall be based upon a single cause of action and may seek one or more relief, provided that they are consequential to one another.

11. Service of notices and processes issued by the Tribunal: (1) Notices to be issued by the Tribunal may be served to the party by any of the following modes:

(i) service by the party itself;
(ii) by hand delivery (dasti) through a process server;

(iii) by registered post or a courier agency 'with acknowledgment due'; or

(iv) through the concerned Head of office of the same Department:

Provided that if the Tribunal does not specify the mode of service, notice may be sent by registered post "with acknowledgment due" and the provision of Order V of First Schedule to the Code of Civil Procedure, 1908 (5 of 1908) shall apply to such mode of service.

(2) Where notice issued by the Tribunal is served by the party himself by 'hand delivery' (dasti), he shall file with the Registry of the Tribunal, the acknowledgment, together with an affidavit of service.

(3) Notwithstanding anything contained in sub-rule (1) the Tribunal may, taking into account the number of respondents and their places of residence or work and other circumstances, direct that notice of the application shall be served upon the respondents in any other manner, including any manner of substituted service, as it appears to the Tribunal just and proper. The Tribunal may also, in its discretion, having regard to the nature of the case, direct the service of the notice on the Standing Counsel, authorized to accept the service, for all the three service Headquarters, Army, Navy and Air Force and the Ministry of Defence.

(4) Every notice issued by the Tribunal shall unless otherwise ordered, be accompanied by a copy of the application and a copy of the impugned order.

(5) Every applicant shall pay the following fee for the service or execution of processes, in respect of an application where the number of respondents exceeds five:-

(i) a sum of rupees fifty for each respondent in excess of five respondents; or

(ii) where the service is in such a manner as the Tribunal may direct under sub-rule (3), such sum, not exceeding the actual charges incurred in effecting the service, as may be determined by the Tribunal.

(6) The fee for the service or execution of processes under sub-rule (3), shall be remitted in the manner prescribed in rule 4 within one week of the date of the order determining the fee or within such extended time as the Registrar may permit.

(7) Notwithstanding anything contained in sub-rules (1) to (3), if the Tribunal is satisfied that it is not reasonably practicable to serve notice of application upon all the respondents, it may, for reasons to be recorded in writing, direct that the application shall be heard notwithstanding that some of the respondents have not been served with notice of the application:

Provided that no application shall be heard unless:

(i) notice of the application has been served on the Central Government or the State Government if such Government is a respondent;

(ii) notice of the application has been served on the authority which passed the order against which the application has been filed; and

(iii) the Tribunal is satisfied that the interests of the respondents on whom notice of the application has not been served are adequately and sufficiently represented by the other respondents on whom notice of the application has been served.

(8) The office of the Department or Ministry receiving notices or documents from the Tribunal shall mention name and designation along with office stamp, date and time of receipt on the acknowledgement slip before the same are returned to the Tribunal.

12. Filing of reply and other documents by the respondents: (1) Each respondent intending to contest the application, shall file in triplicate the reply to the application and the documents relied upon in paper-book form with the Registry, within one month of the service of notice of the application on him.

(2) In the reply filed under sub-rule (1), the respondent shall specifically admit, deny or explain the facts stated by the applicant in his application and may also state such additional facts as may be found necessary for the just decision of the case. It shall be signed and verified as a written statement by the respondent or any other person duly authorized by him in writing in the same manner as provided for in Order VI, Rule 15 of the Code of Civil Procedure 1908 (5 of 1908).

(3) The documents referred to in sub-rule (2) shall also be filed along with the reply and the same shall be marked as R1, R2, R3 and so on.

(4) The respondent shall also serve a copy of the reply along with documents as mentioned in sub-rule (2) on the applicant or his legal practitioner, if any, and file proof of such service in the Registry. In the case of more than one applicant, a copy of the reply shall be sent to each one of them.

(5) The Tribunal may allow filing of the reply after the expiry of the prescribed period with the leave of the Tribunal, or where appropriate order imposition of costs or pass any other order.

(6) The Tribunal may permit the parties to amend the pleadings in the same manner as provided under Order 6, Rule 17 of the Code of Civil Procedure, 1908 (5 of 1908).

(7) An officer acquainted with the facts of the case but not below the rank of Commissioned Officer or a Group 'A' Officer or a Desk Officer in any Ministry or Department of the Union of India may verify the pleadings and other documents to be filed for and on behalf of the Union of India before the Tribunal.

12A. Every application under rule 8 and the reply under rule 1 shall be supported by an affidavit of the person verifying the application or reply, as the case may be.[4]

13. Filing of written statements before the Benches expeditiously: After the receipt of the notice from the Tribunal the respondents will file their statements/reply on the date fixed for hearing to enable the Tribunal to dispose of the application filed before it as expeditiously as possible. If for any reasons, the service Headquarter or the Department/Ministry is unable to file their statements on the date fixed, they will produce through a responsible official, the required records/documents before the Tribunal to enable it to proceed with the case further on the basis of the records/documents and written statements may be filed subsequently.

14. Date and place of hearing to be notified: The Tribunal shall notify to the parties the date and the place of hearing of the application in such manner as the Chairperson may by general or special order direct.

15. Calendar of cases: Each Bench shall draw up a calendar for the hearing of transferred cases and, as far as possible, hear and decide the cases according to the calendar.

16. Action on application for applicant's default: (1) Where on the date fixed for hearing of the application or on any other date to which such hearing may be adjourned, the applicant does not appear when the application is called for hearing; the Tribunal may, in its discretion, either dismiss the application for default or hear and decide it on merits.

(2) Where an application has been dismissed for default and the applicant files an application within thirty days from the date of dismissal and satisfies the Tribunal that there was sufficient cause for his non-appearance when the application was called for hearing, the Tribunal shall make an order setting aside the order dismissing the application and restore the same:

Provided that, where the case has been disposed of on merits the same shall not be reopened except by way of review.

17. *Ex parte* hearing and disposal of application: (1) Where on the date fixed for hearing the application or on any other date to which such hearing may be adjourned, the applicant appears and the respondent does not appear when the application is called for hearing, the Tribunal may, in its discretion adjourn the hearing or hear and decide the application ex parte.

(2) Where an application has been heard ex parte against a respondent or respondents, such respondent or respondents may apply within thirty days from the date of the order to the Tribunal for an order to set aside and if such respondent or respondents satisfy the Tribunal that the notice was not duly served, or that he or they were prevented by any sufficient cause from appearing when the application was called for hearing, the Tribunal shall make an order setting aside the ex parte hearing as against him or them upon such terms as it thinks fit, and shall appoint a day for proceeding with the application;

4. Sub-rule 12A, inserted vide the Armed Forces Tribunal (Procedure) Amendment Rules, 2011.

Provided that where the ex parte hearing of the application is of such nature that it cannot be set aside as against one respondent only, it may be set aside as against all or the other respondents also:

Provided further that in cases covered by sub-rule (7) of Rule 11, the Tribunal shall not set aside ex parte hearing of an application merely on the ground that such notice was not served upon a respondent or respondents.

18. Application for review: (1) No application for review shall be entertained unless it is filed within thirty days from the date of receipt of copy of the order sought to be reviewed.

(2) An application for review shall ordinarily be heard by the same Bench which has passed the order, unless the Chairperson may, for reasons to be recorded in writing, direct it to be heard by any other Bench.

(3) Unless otherwise ordered by the Bench concerned, an application for review shall be disposed of by circulation where the Bench may either dismiss the application or direct notice to be issued to the opposite party.

(4) Where an application for review for review of any judgment or order has been disposed of, thereafter no application for further review shall lie.

(5) No application for review shall be entertained unless it is supported by a duly sworn affidavit indicating therein the source of knowledge, personal or otherwise. The counter-affidavit in review application will also be a duly sworn affidavit wherever any averment of fact is disputed.

19. Substitution of legal representatives: (1) In the case of death of a party during the pendency of the proceedings before the Tribunal, the legal heir or representatives of the deceased party may apply within ninety days of the date of such death for being brought on record as a necessary party.

(2) Where no application is received from the legal heir or representative within the period specified in sub-rule (1), the proceedings against the deceased party shall abate:

Provided that for good and sufficient reasons the Tribunal, may on an application, set aside the order of abatement and substitute the legal heir or representatives.

20. Adjournment of hearing: (1) The Tribunal may if sufficient cause is shown at any stage of proceedings grant time to the parties or any of them, and adjourn the hearing of the application. The Tribunal may make such order as it deems fit with respect to the costs occasioned by the adjournment. All adjournments shall be to a day certain and no application or matter shall be adjourned sine die except for reasons recorded in writing.

(2) The Tribunal shall have the power to decline an adjournment and also to limit the time for oral arguments;

Provided that where the Tribunal deems it necessary, for reasons to be recorded in writing, it may allow oral evidence to be adduced.

21. Order to be signed and dated: Every order of the Tribunal shall be in writing and shall be signed by the Member or Members constituting the Bench, which pronounced the order. The orders shall be pronounced in open Court.

22. Publication of orders: Such of the orders of the Tribunal, as are deemed fit for publication in any authoritative report or Military Law Journal or the press, may be released for such publication on such terms and conditions as the Chairperson may specify by general or special order.

23. Communication of orders to the parties: (1) Every interim order, granting or refusing or modifying interim relief and final order shall be communicated to the applicant and to the concerned respondent or to their legal practitioner either by hand delivery or by post free of cost:

Provided that unless ordered otherwise by a Bench, a copy of the final order need not be sent to any respondent who has not entered appearance:

Provided further that when the applicants or the respondents are represented by a legal practitioner, under a single *Vakalatnama*, only one copy shall be supplied to such legal practitioner as named therein.

(2) If the applicant or the respondent to any proceeding requires a copy of any document or proceeding the same shall be supplied to him on such terms and conditions and on payment of such free as may be fixed by the Chairperson by general or special order.

24. Inspection of the Records: (1) Inspection of records of a pending or decided case before the Tribunal shall be allowed only under the orders of the Registrar.

(2) The parties to any case or their legal practitioner may be allowed to inspect the record of the case on making an application in writing to the Registrar.

(3) Subject to such terms and conditions as may be prescribed by the Chairperson by a general or special order, a person who is not a party to the proceedings, may also be allowed to inspect the record after obtaining the permission of the Registrar in writing.

25. Powers of the Tribunal with regard to certain orders and directions: Nothing in these rules shall be deemed to limit or otherwise affect the inherent powers of the Tribunal to make such orders or give such directions as may be necessary or expedient to give effect to its orders or to prevent abuse of its process or to secure the ends of justice.

26. Commission for local inquiry and accounts: (1) Whenever it becomes necessary in the course of proceedings before the Tribunal to appoint a commission to make a local inquiry or to examine documents or accounts, the Chairperson or the Vice-Chairperson may issue orders for such appointments, specifying therein:

(i) the precise matter of the inquiry; and

(ii) the reason asking why the evidence bearing on that matter could not reasonably have been taken in the usual way in the proceedings in the Tribunal.

(2) Commissioners to examine accounts may be selected from persons competent in the particular form of accounts.

(3) The Tribunal shall exercise great care in selecting persons for

appointment as commissioners for the purpose of making inquiries. The habitual employment of the same person should be avoided.

(4) The Tribunal shall for the said purpose, maintain a list of legal practitioner's whom the Chairperson or Vice-Chairperson may select, from time to time, as fit to be employed in such cases.

(5) The legal practitioner so appointed shall receive a fee of Rs. 800/- for the first effective hearing and Rs. 500/- for every subsequent effective hearing in the same or similar matters or for non-effective hearing. In criminal cases including murder appeals, the fee shall be Rs. 2000/- for preparation of the case, Rs. 12000/- per effective hearing and Rs. 500/- per non-effective hearing.

(6) The certificate for the hearing shall be signed by the Registrar and the payment shall be made by the Government on production of the said certificate.

27. Registration of legal practitioner's clerk: (1) No clerk-employed by a legal practitioner shall act as such in the Tribunal or be permitted to have access to the records and obtain copies of the orders of the Bench of the Tribunal in which the legal practitioner ordinarily practice unless his name is entered in the Register of Clerks maintained by the said Bench. Such clerk shall be known as a "Registered Clerk".

(2) No person shall be employed by a legal practitioner as his clerk unless such person has been a legal practitioner's clerk for three year, or is a qualified petition-writer or has passed the Graduation Examination of a recognized University:

Provided that no such person shall by employed as a Clerk:

(i) if he has been declared a tout; or

(ii) if he is an undischarged insolvent; or

(iii) if he has been convicted for an offence involving moral turpitude; or

(iv) if he has been dismissed from the service of Government, unless he can shows that his dismissal was not due to conduct showing him unfit to be legal practitioner's clerks, or

(vi) if he is unfit to be a legal practitioner's clerk for any other sufficient reason.

Explanation: "Tout" means a person who procures or attempts to procure for any consideration from any legal practitioner or from any person acting on his behalf, the employment of such legal practitioner in legal business, or who, for purposes of such procurement, frequents the precincts of the Tribunal.

(3) A legal practitioner desirous of registering his clerk shall make an application to the Registrar in ***Form III*** and pay a sum of one hundred rupees as one time Tribunal Fee. On such application being allowed by the Registrar, his name shall be entered in the Register of Clerks.

(4) The Registrar may, for reasons to be recorded in writing, decline

to register any clerk, who in his opinion suffers from any disqualification specified in Rule 27 or is otherwise unsuitable to be registered at such.

(5) The Registrar may, for reasons to be recorded in writing, cancel the registration of any clerk after giving him and his employer an opportunity to show cause against such cancellation.

(6) An appeal may be filed against the order of the Registrar made under sub-rule (4) and (5) within 30 days from the date of the order to the Chairperson or Vice-Chairperson.

(7) After registration of the clerk, the Registrar shall direct the issue of an identity card to him which shall be non-transferable and shall be produced by the holder upon request by an officer or other employees of the Tribunal authorized in this behalf. The identity card shall be issued under the signature of the Deputy Registrar of the Bench concerned.

(8) A register of all the clerks registered under sub-rule (2) shall be maintained in the office of the Registrar of each Bench.

(9) A legal practitioner shall have at a time not more than two registered clerks unless the Registrar by general or special order otherwise permits.

(10)Whenever a legal practitioner ceases to employ a registered clerk, he shall notify the fact at once to the Registrar by means of a letter enclosing therewith the identity card issued to his clerk by the Registry, and on receipt of such letter the name of the said registered clerk shall be struck off from the register.

(11)No legal practitioner shall employ as his clerk any person who is prohibited in the sub rule (2) above.

28. Working hours of the Tribunal: The offices of the Tribunal except on Saturday, Sundays and other public holidays, shall remain open daily from 9.30 A.M. to 5.30 P.M. subject to any general or special order made by the Chairperson. Any urgent matter filed before 12 noon shall be put before the Bench for hearing on the following working day. In exceptional cases, it may be received thereafter for hearing on the same day with the leave of the Chairperson or Vice-Chairperson, as the case may be.

29. Sitting hours of the Tribunal: Unless otherwise ordered by the Chairperson by any general or special order or by the Vice Chairperson concerned with the prior approval of the Chairperson, the Tribunal, including Vacation Bench shall hold its sitting on all working days from 10.00 A.M. to 1.00 P.M. and from 2.00 P.M. to 4.30 P.M.

30. Functions of the Registrar: (1) The Registrar shall have the custody of the records of the Tribunal and shall exercise such other functions as are assigned to him under these rules or by the Chairperson or the Vice-Chairperson of the Bench concerned by separate order.

(2) The Registrar may, with the approval of the Chairperson or of the Vice-Chairperson of the Bench concerned delegate to the Additional Registrar any function or power required by these rules to be performed or exercised by the Registrar.

(3) In the absence of the Registrar, the Additional Registrar or any other officer to whom the powers and functions of the Registrar are delegated by the Chairperson or Vice-Chairperson, may exercise the powers and functions of the Registrar.

(4) The Registrar may if the circumstances so require, or if so directed by the Bench, at any time adjourn any matter and lay he same before the concerned Bench.

31. Powers and duties of Registrar: The Registrar shall have the following powers and duties subject to any general or special order of the Chairperson or the Vice-Chairperson of the Bench concerned, namely:

(i) to receive all applications and other documents including transferred applications;

(ii) to decide all questions arising out of the scrutiny of the applications before they are registered;

(iii) to require any application presented to the Tribunal to be amended in accordance with the Act and the rules;

(iv) subject to the direction of the respective Benches, to fix the date of first hearing of the applications or other proceedings and issues notices thereof;

(v) to direct any formal amendment of records;

(vi) to order grant of copies of documents to parties to the proceedings;

(vii) to grant leave to inspect the records of the Tribunal;

(viii) to dispose of all matters relating to the service of notices or other processes, applications for the issue of fresh notices and for extending the time for filling such applications and to grant time, not exceeding 30 days, for filing a reply or rejoinder if any, and to place the matter before the Bench for appropriate orders after the expiry of the aforesaid period;

(ix) to requisition records from the custody of any Court, Service Headquarter, office, Department or other authority;

(x) to receive application within ninety days from the date of death for substitution of legal representatives of the deceased parties during the pendency of the application;

(xi) to receive and dispose of application for substitution, except where the substitution would involve setting aside an order of abatement;

(xii) to receive and dispose of application by parties for return of documents;

(xiii) registration of the legal practitioner's clerk;

(xiv) In case of the Principal Bench, to call for information and records and to inspect or cause to be inspected the Registry of the other Benches under general or special orders as may be issued by the Chairperson from time to time.

32. Seal and emblem: (1) The official seal and emblem of the Tribunal shall be such as the Chairperson may from time to time direct and shall be kept in the custody of the Registrar.

(2) Subject to any general or special direction by the Chairperson, the seal of the Tribunal shall not be affixed to any order, summons or other process save under the authority in writing of the Registrar or the Additional Registrar.

(3) The seal of the Tribunal shall not be affixed to any certified copy issued by the Tribunal save under the authority in writing of the Registrar or the Additional Registrar.

33. Dress of the Members and staff of the Tribunal: The dress for the Members of the Tribunal including Chairperson and Vice-Chairperson and the staff shall be such as the Chairperson may specify.

34. Dress of the parties: A legal practitioner or as the case may be, the Presenting Officer shall appear before the Tribunal in his professional dress, if any, and if there is no such dress-

(i) if a male, in shirt and trousers with or without tie or in a lounge suit;

(ii) if a female, in a saree or any other customary dress of a sober colour.

[F. No. 1(1) 2007-D(AFT Cell)]

AJAY TIRKEY, Jt. Secy.

Form I

[See rule 4]

Application Under Section 14 and 15 of the Armed Forces Tribunal Act, 2007

Title of the Case:

Index

Sl. No.	*Description of documents relied upon*	*Page No*
1.	Application along with true copy of the impugned order	
2.	All other documents and annexures	
3.		
4.		

Signature of the applicant

For use in Tribunals' Office Date of filling ____________________ or Date of receipt by Post ____________________ Registration No . ____________________ ***Signature*** ***For Registrar***

In The Armed Forces Tribunal____________________ Bench

A.B. (add description such as personal Number, Rank, Name, Unit or Formation, present address and place of posting or last posting)

Applicant

Versus

C.D. (add description and the residential or official address on which the service of notices is to be effected on the respondent or respondents. The details of each respondent are to be given in a chronological order.)

Respondent

Details of Application

1. **Particulars of the impugned order against which the application is made:** (Particulars of the order giving the details like the number, date and the authority which has passed the order, against which the application is made.)

2.Jurisdiction of the Tribunal:

The applicant will indicate that the subject matter of the impugned order against which he wants redressal is within the jurisdiction of the Tribunal.

3. Limitation:

The applicant further declares that the application is within the limitation period prescribed in Section 22 of the Armed Forces Tribunals Act, 2007.

4. Facts of the Case:

(Give here a concise statement of facts in a chronological order, each paragraph containing as nearly as possible a separate issue of fact.)

5. Grounds for relief with legal provisions:

6. Details of the remedies exhausted:

The applicant declares that he has availed of all the remedies available to him under the relevant service Act/Rules/Regulations.

(Give here chronologically the details of representations/complaints made and the outcome of such representations/complaints with reference to the number of Annexure to be given in support thereof.)

7. Matter not previously filed or pending with any other Court/Bench of Tribunal:

The applicant further declares that he had not previously filed any application, writ petition or suit regarding the matter, in respect of which this application is made, before any court or any other authority or any other Bench of the Tribunal nor any such application, write petition or suit is pending before any of them.

In case the applicants had previously filed any such application, writ petition or suit, the stage at which it is pending, and if decided, the list of the decisions should be given with reference to the number of Annexure to be given in support thereof.

8. Relief (s) Sought:

In view of the facts mentioned in para 4 above, the applicant prays for the following relief (s):

(Specify below the relief (s) sought explaining the grounds for such relief (s) and the legal provisions, if any, relied upon.)

9. Interim order, if any prayed for:

Pending final decision on the application, the applicant seeks the following interim relief:

(Give here the nature of the interim relief prayed for).

10. In the event of application being sent by registered post or by courier, it may be stated whether the applicant desires to have oral hearing at the admission stage and if so, he shall attach a self addressed Post-Card or Inland Letter, at which intimation regarding the date of hearing could be sent to him.

11. Particulars of Banks Draft/Postal order filed in respect of the application fee.

12. List of enclosures:

1.

2.

Verification

I, No _______________, Rank _____________, Name ___ _____________ S/o, W/o, D/o ____________ age __________ belonging to _______ name of the unit/ formation ___________ and resident of _____________ do hereby verify that the contents of paras ________ to _________ are true to my personal knowledge and paras __________ to _____________- believed to be true on legal advice and that I have not suppressed any material fact.

Date : ____________

Place: ____________

Signature of the applicant

To,

The Registrar

Armed Forces Tribunal

______________ Bench

______________ (Place)

Form II

[See rule 4(4)]

Reciept Slip

Receipt of the application filed in the Armed Forces Tribunal.......

..................................Bench..by
No..................................Rank .... Name..................................
.... in the Ministry/Department/Office of
.... residing at .... Is hereby acknowledged.

For Registrar,
Armed Forces Tribunal
.... Bench

Dated : ....
Seal : ....

Form III
(see rule 27)
Application for the Registration of a Clerk

1. Name of legal practitioner on whose behalf the clerk is to be registered
2. Particulars of the clerk to be registered
   (i) Full name (in capital):
   (ii) Father's name:
   (iii) Mother's name:
   (iv) Husband / Wife's name (if applicable)
   (v) Age and date of birth:
   (vi) Place of birth:
   (vii) Nationality:
   (viii) Educational qualifications with year of passing and a certified copy of graduation degree or mark sheet.
   (ix) Particulars of previous employment, if any:
   (x) Name of concerned legal practitioner:
   (x) Postal address:
   (xi) Telephone / Mobile Number
   (xii) Payment details:

Attested passport size photograph to be pasted

I, ... (Clerk above named) do hereby affirm that the particulars relating to me given above are true.

(Signature of Clerk)

3. Whether the legal practitioner has a clerk already registered in his employ and whether the clerk sought to be registered is in lieu of or in addition to the clerk already registered.

4. Whether the clerk sought to be registered is already registered as a clerk of any other legal practitioner and if so, the name of such practitioner.

I........................ (legal practitioner) certify that the particulars given above are true to the best of my information and belief and that I am not aware of any fact which would render unsuitable the registration of the said .... (name) as a clerk. Further, I enclose Postal Order for Rs. 10, being the cost of Identify Card along with two passport size photographs of the applicant duly attested by me.

Signature of the legal practitioner

Date: ______________

To
The Registrar,
.... Bench
Armed Forces Tribunal

Appendix-C

The Armed Forces Tribunal (Procedure for appointment of Vice-Chairperson and other Members) Rules, 2008

S.R.O. 65: In exercise of the powers conferred by clause (k) of sub-section (2) of Section 41 read with Section of the Armed Forces Tribunal Act, 2007 (55 of 2007), the Central Government hereby makes the following rules to regulate the procedure of appointment of Vice-Chairperson or other Members of the Armed Forces Tribunal, namely:

1. Short title and commencement: (1) These rules may be called the Armed Forces Tribunal (Procedure for appointment of Vice-Chairperson and other Members) Rules, 2008.

(2) They shall come into force on the date of their publication in the Official Gazette.[1]

2. Definitions: (1) In these rules, unless the context otherwise require:-

(a) "Act" means the Armed Forces Tribunal Act, 2007 (55 of 2007);

(b) "Chairperson" means the Chairperson of Selection Committee;

(c) "Tribunal" means the Armed Forces Tribunal established under section 4 of the Act.

(2) Words and expressions used in these rules and not defined but defined in the Armed Forces Tribunal Act, 2007 (55 of 2007) shall have the meaning respectively assigned to them in the Act.

3. Composition of Selection Committee: There shall be a Selection Committee for the purpose of the selection of the Vice-Chairperson and Members in the Tribunal consisting of the following:

(a) Sitting Judge of the Supreme Court nominated by the Chief Justice of India - Chairperson

(b) Chairperson, Armed Forces Tribunal - Member

(c) Secretary to the Government of India, Ministry of Defence - Member

1. Published in THE GAZETTE OF INDIA: JULY 26, 2008, Part II, Sec. 4.

(d) Secretary, Government of India,
Ministry of Law and Justice,
Department Legal Affairs - Member

4. Vacancies: (1) The anticipated vacancies of Vice-Chairpersons and Members shall be placed before the Selection Committee for a block of six months, i.e., January to June and July to December of each calendar year.

(2) The Chairperson of the Tribunal shall indicate the number of vacancies of the Vice-Chairperson and the Members to be filled from the judicial stream and the administrative stream respectively to the Central Government, whereupon the procedure to fill up the vacancies accordingly shall be initiated by that Government.

5. Procedure for inviting/processing of candidatures. (1) The Selection Committee shall devise its own procedure and lay down guidelines for inviting applications as also for the selection of the Vice-Chairperson and the members of the Tribunal.

(2) The Selection Committee shall recommend the names of persons for appointment as the Vice-Chairperson and Members from amongst the persons on the list of candidates prepared by the Central Government, after obtaining names from the various cadres controlling authorities.

(3) The Central Government shall, after taking into consideration the recommendations of the selection Committee, and in consultation with the Chief Justice of India in accordance with the provision contained in Section 6 and 7 of the Act, make a list of persons for appointment as the Vice-Chairperson and Members of the Tribunal.

6. Meetings of the Selection Committee.- (1) The Selection Committee shall normally hold its meetings at New Delhi or at such place or places, as may be authorized by the Chairperson by recording the reasons for the change of the venue of such meetings.

(2) The notice/agenda, as the case may be, for the meeting of the Selection Committee shall be issued in advance. The date and venue for the meeting shall be fixed with the convenience of the Chairperson.

(3) The minimum quorum for the meeting shall be the Chairperson and at least, one other member.

7. Criteria for selection: Merit in terms of suitability and not seniority shall be the sole criterion in the matter of filling up the post of the Vice-Chairperson from amongst Member of the Tribunal.

8. Consultation with the Chief of India: (1) The recommendations of the Selection Committee shall be placed before the Chief Justice of India for his views.

(2) The recommendations of the Selection Committee, together with the views of the Chief Justice of India shall be submitted to the competent authority for orders.

[F. No.8 (1)/2007-D(AFT (Cell]
SUMAN K. SHARMA, Under Secy.

Appendix-D

The Armed Forces Tribunal (Procedure for investigation of misbehaviour or incapacity of Chairperson and other Members) Rules, 2008

Ministry of Defence

New Delhi, the 21st July, 2008

S.R.O. 61: In exercise of the powers conferred by sub-section (3) of Section 9 read with sub-section (1) and clause (b) of sub-section (2) of Section 41 of the Armed Forces Tribunal Act, 2007 (55 of 2007), the Central Government hereby makes the following rules, namely:

1. Short title and commencement: (1) These rules may be called the Armed Force Tribunal (Procedure for investigation of misbehavior or incapacity of Chairperson and other Members) Rules, 2008.

(2) They shall come into force on the date of their publication in the Official Gazette.[1]

2. Extent of application: These rules shall be applicable to every Chairperson, Vice-Chairperson, Administrative Member and Judicial Member of the Armed Forces Tribunal.

3. Definition: (1) In these rules, unless the context otherwise requires,-

(a) "Act" means the Armed Forces Tribunal Act, 2007 (55 of 2007);

(b) "Administrative Member" means a Member of the Armed Forces Tribunal established under the Act who is not a Judicial Member within the meaning of clause (g) of Section 3;

(c) "Chairperson" means a Chairperson of a Tribunal and includes a Vice-Chairperson;

(d) "Committee" means the Committee referred to in sub-rule (2) of rule 4;

---

1. Published in THE GAZETTE OF INDIA: JULY 26, 2008, Part II, Sec. 4.

(e) "Judge" means a sitting Judge of the Supreme Court appointed by the President under sub-rule (2) of rule 5 to conduct the inquiry;

(f) "Judicial Member" means a Member of a Tribunal appointed as such under the Act, and includes the Chairperson or a Vice-Chairperson who possesses any of the qualifications specified in sub-section (2) of Section 6;

(g) "Member" means a Member (whether Judicial or Administrative) of the Tribunal, and includes a Chairperson and a Vice-Chairperson;

(h) "Section" means a Section of the Act;

(i) "Tribunal" means the Armed Forces Tribunal established under the Act;

(j) "Vice-Chairperson" means a Vice-Chairperson of the Tribunal.

(2) Words and expressions used in these rules and not defined but defined in the Armed Forces Tribunal Act, 2007 (55 of 2007) shall have the meaning respectively assigned to them in the Act.

4. Committee for investigation of complaints: (1) If a written complaint, alleging any definite charge of misbehaviour or incapacity to perform the functions of the office in respect of a Member is received by the Central Government, it shall make a preliminary scrutiny of such complaint.

(2) If, on preliminary scrutiny, the Central Government considers it necessary to investigate into the allegation, it shall place the complaint together with supporting material as may be available, before a Committee consisting of the following officers to investigate into the charges made in the complaint:

(i)	Cabinet Secretary	- Chairperson
(ii)	Secretary, Ministry of Defence	- Member
(iii)	Secretary, Department of Legal Affairs, Ministry of Law and Justice	- Member

(3) The Committee shall device its own procedure and method of investigation which may include recording of evidence of the complainant and collection of material relevant to the inquiry which may be conducted by a Judge of the Supreme Court under these rules.

(4) The Committee shall submit its findings to the President as early as possible within a period that may be specified by the President in this behalf.

5. Judge to conduct inquiry: (1) If on the receipt of the findings of the committee, the President is of the opinion that there are reasonable grounds for making in inquiry into the truth of any imputation of misbehaviour or incapacity of a Member, he shall make a reference to the Chief Justice of India requesting him to nominate a Judge of the Supreme Court to conduct the inquiry.

(2) The President shall, by order, appoint the Judge of the Supreme Court nominated by the Chief Justice of India for the purpose of conducting the inquiry.

(3) Notice of appointment of a Judge under sub-rule (2) shall be given to the Member concerned.

(4) The President shall forward to the Judge a copy of:

(i) the articles of charges against the Member concerned and the statement of imputations;

(ii) the statement of witnesses, if any, and

(iii) material documents relevant to the inquiry

(5) The Judge appointed under sub-rule (2) shall complete the inquiry within such time or further time as may be specified by the President.

(6) The Member concerned shall be given a reasonable opportunity of presenting a written statement of defence within such time as may be specified in this behalf by the Judge.

(7) Where it is alleged that the Member concerned is unable to discharge the duties of his office efficiently due to any physical or mental incapacity and the allegation is denied, the Judge may arrange for the medical examination of the Member by such Medical Board as may be appointed for the purpose by the President and the Member concerned shall submit himself to such medical examination within the time specified in this behalf by the Judge.

(8) The Medical Board shall undertake such medical examination of the Member as may be considered necessary and submit a report to the Judge stating therein whether the incapacity is such as to render the Member unfit to continue in office.

(9) If the Member refuses to undergo such medical examination as considered necessary by the Medical Board, the Board shall submit a report to the Judge stating therein the examination which the Member has refused to undergo, and the Judge may, on receipt of such report, presume that the Member suffers from such physical mental incapacity as is alleged against the Member.

(10) The Judge may, after considering the written statement of the Member and the Medical Report, if any, amend the charge referred to in clause (i) to sub-rule (4) and in such a case, the Member shall be given a reasonable opportunity of presenting a fresh written statement of defence.

(11) The Central Government shall appoint its officer or an advocate to present the case against the Member.

(12) Where the Central Government has appointed an advocate to present its case before the Judge, the Member concerned shall also be allowed to present his case by an advocate chosen by him.

6. Application of the Departmental Inquiries (Enforcement of Witness and Production of Documents) Act, 1972, to inquiries under these rules: The provisions of the Departmental Inquiries (Enforcement of Witness and Production of Documents) Act, 1972 (18 of 1972), shall apply to the inquiries made under these rules as they apply to departmental inquiries.

7. Powers of Judge: The Judge shall not be bound by the procedure laid down in the Code of Civil Procedure, 1908 (5 of 1908), but shall be guided by the principles of natural justice and shall have power to regulate his own procedure including the fixing places and times of his inquiry.

8. Suspension of Member: Notwithstanding anything contained in rule 6 and without any prejudice to any action being taken in accordance with the said rule, the President, keeping in view the gravity of charges, may suspend the Member of the Tribunal against whom a complaint is under investigation or inquiry.

9. Subsistence Allowance: The payment of subsistence allowance to a Member under suspension shall be regulated in accordance with the rules and orders for the time being applicable to a Secretary to the Government of India belonging to the Indian Administrative Service.

10. Inquiry Report: After the conclusion of the investigation, the Judge shall submit his report to the President stating therein his findings and the reasons thereof on each of the articles of charges separately with such observations on the whole case as he thins fit.

[F. No. 8 (1)/2007-D (AFT Cell)]
SUMAN K. SHARMA, Under Secy

Appendix-E

The Armed Forces Tribunal (Financial and Administrative Powers) Rules, 2008

Ministry of Defence
Notification

New Delhi, the 12th September, 2008

S.R.O.25 (E) - In exercise of the powers conferred by Section 41 read with Section 12 of the Armed Forces Tribunal Act, 2007, the Central Government hereby makes the following rules, namely:

1. Short title and commencement: (1) These rules may be called the Armed Forces Tribunal (Financial and Administrative Powers) Rules, 2008.

(2) They shall come into force on the date of their publication in Official Gazette.[1]

2. Definitions: In these rules the context otherwise requires,-

(a) 'Act' means the Armed Forces Tribunals Act, 2007 (55 of 2007);
(b) "Chairperson" means the Chairperson of the Tribunal;
(c) "Tribunal" means the Armed Forces Tribunal.

3. Sitting of an additional Bench at place other than the place where it shall ordinarily sit: If at any time the Vice-Chairperson of any additional Bench is satisfied that circumstances exist which render it necessary to have sitting of the said Bench at any place falling within its territorial jurisdiction, other than the place falling within its territorial jurisdiction, other than the place or places at which it ordinarily sits, he may with the previous consent of the Chairperson direct that the additional Bench shall hold its sittings as any such appropriate place.

4. Powers of Chairperson: The Chairperson shall have the same powers as are conferred on a Department of the Central Government in respect of the delegation of Financial Powers Rules, 1978, the General Financial Rules

1. Published in THE GAZETTE OF INDIA: EXTRAORDINARY, September 12, 2008, Part II, Sec. 4, No. 18.

1963, the Fundamental and Supplementary Rules, the Central Civil Services (Leave) Rules, 1972, the Central Civil Services (Joining Time) Rule 1979, the Central Civil Services (Conduct) Rules, 1964, the Central Civil Services (Classification, Control and Appeal) Rules, 1965 and the General Provident Fund (Central Services) Rules, 1960;

Provided that the exercise of the financial powers shall be subject to any procedural or other instructions issued from time to time by the Government and after obtaining the advice of the Financial Adviser and Chief Accounts Officer of the Tribunal.

Provided further that in respect of matters not within the competence of the Chairperson, concurrence of the Ministry of Finance or any other authority shall obtained by the Chairperson through the Ministry of Defence.

[F. No. 1(1)/2008-D (AFT Cell)]

AJAY TIRKEY, Jt. Secy

Appendix-F

The Armed Forces Tribunal (Salaries, Allowances and Conditions of Service of Chairperson and Members) Rules, 2009[1]

1. Short title and commencement: (1) These rules may be called the Armed Forces Tribunal (Salaries, Allowances and Conditions of Service of Chairperson and Members) Rules, 2009.

(2) They shall come into force from the date of publication in the official gazette.

2. Definition: (1) In these rules, unless the context otherwise requires,-

(a) "Act" means the Armed Forces Tribunal Act, 2007 (55 of 2007);

(b) "Tribunal" means the Armed Forces Tribunal established under Section 4 of the Act;

(c) "Chairperson" means the Chairperson of the Tribunal appointed under Section 7 (1) of the Act;

(d) "Member" means a member (whether Judicial or Administrative) of the Tribunal appointed under Section 7(1) of the Act;

(e) The words and expressions used herein and not defined but defined in the Act shall have the meaning respectively assigned to them in the Act.

3. Pay and Allowances, Leave, Pension, Provident Fund, Travelling Allowance, Leave Travel Concession, Accommodation etc., to the Chairperson and Members of the Armed Forces Tribunal: (a) When a Retired Judge of the Supreme Court is appointed as Chairperson of the Tribunal, he shall be entitled to salary, allowances and other perquisites as are available to the sitting judge of the Supreme Court, and as provided in the Supreme Court Judges (Salaries and Conditions of Services) Act, 1958 (51 of 1958), and these shall apply mutatis mutandis along with rules made

1. Made by the Central Government in the exercise of the powers conferred by Section 10 read with clause (c) of sub-section (2) of Section 41 of the Armed Forces Tribunal Act, 2007 (55 of 2007). Ministry of Defence, Notification, New Delhi, vide SRO 7(E) dated 18 May 2009.

thereunder as amended from time to time. The Chairperson shall be entitled to take his spouse with him while travelling within the country while on official visit to Benches.

(b) When a Retired Chief Justice of a High Court is appointed as Chairperson of the Tribunal, he shall be entitled to salary, allowances and other perquisites as are available to the sitting Chief Justice and as provided in the High Court Judges (Salaries and Conditions of Services) Act, 1954 (28 of 1958), and these shall apply mutatis mutandis along with rules made thereunder as amended from time to time:

Provided that in case the retired Judge of the Supreme Court or the retired Chief Justice of a High Court, is in receipt of, or has received or has become entitled to receive any retirement benefits by way of pension, gratuity, employer's contribution of the Contributory Provident Fund or other forms of retirement benefits, the pay of such Chairperson shall be reduced by the gross amount of pension or employer's contribution to the Contributory Provident Fund or any other form of retirement benefits, if any (except pension equivalent of retirement gratuity), drawn or to be drawn by him.

(c) When a serving or retired Judge of a High Court is appointed as Judicial member of the Tribunal or when any person from the three services is appointed as administrative Member of the Tribunal, he shall be entitled to salary, allowance and other perquisites as are available to the sitting Judge of a High Court and as provided in the High Court Judges (Salaries and Conditions of Services) Act, 1954 (28 of 1958), and these shall apply mutatis mutandis along with rules made thereunder as amended from time to time:

Provided that in case the retired Judge of a High Court, or a person from the three services, is in receipt of, or has received or has become entitled to receive any retirement benefits by way of pension, gratuity, employer's contribution of the Contributory Provident Fund or other forms of retirement benefits, the pay of such Member shall be reduced by the gross amount of pension or employer's contribution to the Contributory Provident Fund or any other form of retirement benefits, if any (except pension equivalent of retirement gratuity), drawn or to be drawn by him.

4. Residuary Provision - Matters relating to the terms and conditions of service of the Chairperson or Members of the Tribunal with respect to which no express provision has been made in these rules, shall be determined by the rules and orders or the time being applicable to a Secretary to the Government of India.

5. Powers to relax rules - The Central Government shall have the power to relax any provision of these rules in respect any class or category of persons.

F. No. 1 (4)/2008-D (AFT Cell)]

AJAY TIRKEY, Jt. Secy.

Appendix-G

The Armed Forces Tribunal (Practice) Rules, 2009[1]

The Armed Forces Tribunal (Practice) Rules, 2009

1. Short title and commencement–

(1) These rules may be called the Armed Forces Tribunal (Practice) Rules, 2009.

(2) They shall come into force from the date of publication in the official gazette.

2. Defintion. – (1) In these rules, unless the context otherwise requires-

(i) "Act" means the Armed Forces Tribunal Act, 2007 (55 of 2007);

(ii) "agent" means a person duly authorized by a party to present an application, written reply, rejoinder or any other document on its behalf before the Tribunal;

(iii) "applicant" means a person making an application to the Tribunal under sub-section (2) of Section 14 or an appeal under sub section (2) of Section 15 of the Act;

(iv) "Application" includes Original Application (OA), Review Application (RA), Transferred Application (TA), Miscellaneous Application (MA), Application for Transfer (AT) and Contempt Application (CA), filed before the Tribunal;

(v) "Code" means the Code of Civil Procedure, 1908 (5 of 1908);

(vi) "Court appealed from" includes a tribunal or any other judicial body or court-martial or authority against the decision of which an appeal is preferred to the Tribunal;

(vii) "Form" means the form set out in the appendices A and B to these rules;

---

1. Made by the Central Government in the exercise of the power conferred by clauses (f), (g) and (k) of sub-section 2 of section 41 of the Armed Forces Tribunal Act, 2007 (55 of 2007). Ministry of Defence, Notification, New Delhi, vide SRO 6(E) dated 11 May 2009.

(viii) "Full Bench" means a Bench duly constituted consisting of tree or more Members;

(ix) "Judgment" includes decree, order, sentence or determination of any Court, Tribunal, Judge, Judicial Officer or authority;

(x) "Legal practitioner" shall have the same meaning as assigned to it in the Advocates Act, 1961 (25 of 2961) and includes a Standing Counsel authorized or appointed by the Central Government to accept the service for any Department or Organization of the Union of India;

(xi) "Legal representative" means a person who represents the estate of a serving or deceased person and includes a person or persons in whom the right to receive pensionary, retirement, terminal, disability or other benefits or family pension vests under any law for the time being in force;

(xii) "Officer of the Judge-Advocate General's Department" means an officer commissioned into the Judge-Advocate General's Department of the Army or an officer permanently transferred to that Department after qualifying at the Judge-Advocate General's Departmental examination and includes an officer of Judge-Advocate General's Department of Navy and Air Force;

(xiii) "Procedure Rules" means the Armed Forces Tribunal (Procedure) Rules, 2008 under the Act;

(xiv) "Pleadings" shall include original applications, reply statement, rejoinders and additional applications or statements supplementing the original applications and the reply statements, as may be permitted by the Tribunal;

(xv) "Registrar" means Registrar of the Armed Forces Tribunal or its Benches and shall include Registrar-General, Principal, Additional, Joint and Deputy Registrars, authorized to discharge the functions of the Registrar;

(xvi) "Registry" mean the Registry of the Tribunal or any of its Benches as the case may be;

(xvii) "Section" means a section of the Act;

(xviii) "Services" means the Army, Navy and Air Force, as applicable;

(xix) "Standing Counsel" means as advocate authorized to act; represent and accept the service for the Army, Navy or Force or for the Union of India;

(xx) "Transferred application" means the suit or other proceeding which has been transferred to the Tribunal under sub-section (1) or sub-section (2) of section 34;

(xxi) "Vice-Chairperson" means a Vice-Chairperson of the Tribunal appointed under sub-section (2) of section 7 of the Act.

(2) The words and expressions used and not defined in these rules but defined in the Act, the Army Act, 1950 (46 of 1950), the Navy Act, 1957 (62 of 1957) and the Air Force Act, 1950 (45 of 1950) shall have the same meaning respectively assigned to them in those Acts and respective rules made there under.

PREPERATION AND PRESENTATION OF PLEADINGS AND OTHER PAPERS

3. Preparation of pleadings and other papers –

(1) All pleadings, affidavits, memoranda and other papers filed in the tribunal shall be fairly and legibly type written or printed in English or Hindi language on durable white full escape folio paper of metric A-4 size (30.5 cms long and 21.5 cms wide) on one side only in double space with a left margin of 5 cms and right margin of 2.5 cms duly paginated, indexed and stitched together in the paper book form.

(2) English translation of documents or pleadings shall be duly authenticated by any legal practitioner.

4. Date and Signature – A party required to affix his signature shall also state his name in capital letters near his signature and, initial or sign at the bottom of each page and shall also put date beneath his signature on the last page.

Explanation – The expression 'signature' or 'initials' includes thumb-mark.

5. Attestation – (1) The attestation contemplated in sub-rule (2) of rule 9 of the AFT (Procedure) Rules 2008, shall be made at the end of the document in the form given below:

"This Annexure........is the true copy of the original document."

(Signature)

Name and Designation of the Attestor with date

(2) Sub-rule (1) above shall also govern production of photocopies of the documents, provided they are clear and legible.

6. Production of Authorization for and on behalf of more than one person – where an application or pleading or other proceeding is purported to be filed by more than one person as sinle application under sub-rule (5) of Rule 4 of AFT (Procedure) Rules 2008, the person or persons who sign or verify the same shall produce along with such application, etc. for verification by the registry, a true copy of the authorization or Vakalatnama empowering such person(s) to do so:

Provided that the registrar may at any time call upon the party to produce such further materials as he deems fit for satisfying himself about due authorization.

7. Procedure on production of defaced, torn or damaged documents – When a document produced along with any pleading appears to be defaced, torn or in any way damaged or otherwise its condition or appearance requires special notice, a mention regarding its condition and appearance shall be made by the party producing the same in the index of such a pleading and the same shall be verified and initialed by the officer authorized to receive the same.

8. Receipt of papers – (1) All pleadings and papers shall be received in the Registry only during the office hours on the working days, provided they are presented or sent by post in the manner provided under Rule 4 of the AFT (Procedure) Rules 2008.

(2) All pleadings and papers received before 12 noon shall, ordinarily be processed immediately for being listed before the Bench on the next working day.

9. Date of stamping on papers and maintenance of Inward Register – (1) The receiving branch of the Registry shall immediately on receipt of any application or appeal or other pleadings or papers and in accordance with Rule 5 of the AFT (Procedure) Rules 2008, and affix the date-stamp of the tribunal in the following manner:

(i) Date-stamp shall be affixed on all pages of the main copy and on the first page of the each copy.

(ii) Receiving clerk shall affix his initials on the stamp affixed on the first page of the main application or appeal and on the first page of all other copies.

(2) Receiving branch of the Registry shall after affixing of the date-stamp, enter the details thereof in the inward register, register No. I and assign a diary number. The Index shall be in Form No. 1. The same diary number shall be entered immediately below the date-stamp on the first page of the main application or appeal and on the first page of all other copies.

SCRUTINY, REGISTRATION, NUMBER AND POSTING FOR ADMISSION OR ORDERS

10. Scrutiny of application or petition or other pleadings and papers – (1) The Scrutiny Branch of the registry shall, on receipt of the application or appeal or pleadings from the receiving branch, scrutinize the same as expeditiously as possible by not beyond two days from the date of receipt:

Provided that if, for any reason, the scrutiny is not completed within the said period, the same shall be immediately reported to the registrar, who shall take prompt steps to complete the scrutiny.

(2) The report of the scrutiny of the application shall be in Form No. 2 and of Contempt Application either civil or criminal in Form No. 3 and the scrutiny report shall be annexed to the application or appeal.

(3) Report of scrutiny of all other pleadings and papers shall be recorded on the reverse side of the last page of such pleadings or papers.

11. Maintenance of Order Sheet – (1) The Scrutiny Branch shall attach an order sheet to every OR or RA or TA or AT or CA in duplicate in Form No. 4.

(2) The column : Notes of the Registry" in the order sheet shall be used for the notings by the Registry and the column "Orders of the Tribunal" is meant for the use of the Bench.

(3) (a) The entries in the order sheet shall be in hand writing and the removal of the order sheet for typing should be avoided.

(b) Continuous page numbers should be given to the order sheet.

(c) Before any entry is made in the order sheet for the day, the date, month and year shall first be entered and underlined in the middle of the column.

(d) Brief orders may be written on the order sheet itself and initlalled by the members of the Bench.

(e) In the case of lengthy orders, only the operative portion of the order need be entered in the column "orders of the Tribunal" and initialled by the Tribunal Officer.

(f) The orders shall be annexed to the order sheet giving them continuous paging and reference to the order shall be made by mentioning only page number of the order annexed.

(g) The presence of the legal practitioner or party be indicated by their initials.

(h) No gaps shall be left between two entries in the order sheet and the gaps, if any, shall be covered by drawing a line across.

12. Classification of papers – (1) The papers received in the Registry in all application and Contempt applications except Miscellaneous applications, shall be classified and placed in files "A", "B" and "C" as provided in **Form No. 5.**

(2) (i) File "A" shall consist of two separate pars i.e. part I and Part II. Part I shall contain the order sheet and orders annexed thereto and Part II shall contain the application with annexures, reply with annexures and rejoinders with annexures and arrange as far as possible consecutively in the order of the partied.

(ii) File "B" shall contain the duplicate copy of the papers as in File "A".

(iii) File "C" shall contain the remaining papers including Vakalatnama, notices, postal acknowledgments, miscellaneous applications, replies and rejoinders thereto and Supreme Court orders, etc., if any.

13. Submission of case files to Registrar – On completion of scrutiny, the Scrutiny Branch shall place the case file duly classified as "A", "B" or "C" along with the report of scrutiny and the order sheet before the Registrar for his orders.

14. Registration and Numbering – (1) The Registrar on examining the application or appeal or pleadings and the scrutiny report shall, if they are in order, direct registration or acceptance.

(2) Applications under section 14 of the Act ordered to be registered shall be numbered as OA No.----------/20

(3) Cases received on transfer under section 27 or section 34 of the Act shall be numbered as AT/TA No.---------/20

(4) Applications received from the Supreme Court, High Courts and other Courts purporting to be by transfer but not covered by section 34 of the Act shall be numbered as Original Application of the year during which they are received.

(5) Applications for review of any order of the Tribunal and ordered to be registered, shall be numbered as RA No........./20 .

(6) Applications under the Contempt of Courts Act 1973 ordered to be registered, shall be numbered as CA (Civil/Criminal) No........./20 .

(7) Other applications of miscellaneous nature ordered to be registered shall be numbered as MA No........./20 .

(8) Applications referred to in this rule shall be entered in Register No. II.

(9) Separate registers shall be used for each category of applications referred to in this rule.

(10) The registers shall be maintained from 1 January to 31 December of each calendar year.

15. Maintenance of India Postal Orders or demand drafts register –

(1) Indian Postal Orders or Demand Drafts received in the registry shall be entered immediately on their receipt in the Judicial Branch in Register No. III.

(2) On every first working day of the week, the Indian Postal Orders or Demand Drafts received by the Judicial Branch during the previous weeks shall be transmitted along with the Indian Postal Orders or Demand Draft Register to the Section Officer in-charge of Judicial Branch, who after scrutiny shall affix his initials in the relevant column in the Register and transmit the same to the Cash Section.

(3) The Officer in-charge of Cash Section shall, after verifying the entries in the Register along with the Indian Postal Orders or Demand Drafts, put his initials in the relevant column in the Register in token of acknowledgement.

16. Rectification of defects – (1) If on scrutiny, any application or pleading filed in the Tribunal is found to be defective, the register shall notify in Form No. 6 on the notice board of the tribunal fixing the time for rectifying the same in the manner as provided under Rule 5 of the AFT (Procedure) Rules 2008.

(2) The Registrar may, for good and sufficient reasons, extend the time for rectifying the defects, provided the total period for rectification including the extended period does not exceed thirty days.

(3) If the party or his legal practitioner contests the office objection and the Registrar is not satisfied, the matter shall be placed before the Bench for appropriate orders.

(4) If the party or his legal practitioner rectifies the defects and submits the application or pleadings within the time granted, the Registrar on being satisfied, may order for its registration or acceptance and numbering as provided in sub-rule (2) of the Rule 2 of the AFT (Procedure) Rules 2008.

(5) The papers shall be returned to the party or his legal practitioner only after obtaining acknowledgement thereof in the Inward Register–Register No. I.

17. Posting of cases for admission or orders before the Bench – (1) Subject to the orders of the Chairperson or Vice-Chairperson of the concerned

Bench, all registered applications or appeals shall be posted for admission or orders before the appropriate Bench on the next working day.

(2) The notice of posting shall be given by notifying in the daily cause list for the day in such manner as the Chairperson may be general or special order direct.

(3) Before placing the records of the case for admission or order, the Registry shall state in brief in the column "Notes of the Registry" of the Order sheet, the date of presentation or registration, the subject matter of the application and the date of posting before the Bench and fill up the columns in file covers "A" and "B".

(4) The constitution of Benches and distribution of work shall be as per the orders as may be made by the Chairperson from time to time.

18. Posting of urgent cases – Notwithstanding anything contained in Rule 14 of the AFT (Procedure) Rules 2008, the Chairperson of Vice-Chairperson and in his absence the senior most Member of the Bench may order any case not included in the daily cause list to be listed on urgent basis for admission or orders. Such directions shall promptly be carried out by the registry after completing all formalities.

19. Matters to be attended to prior to commencement of sitting –

(1) Unless otherwise directed by the Members constituting the Bench, the Tribunal Officer shall ensure that records of the cases listed for admission or orders before the bench on the next working day are sent to the residence of the Members before the evening of the day on which the cause list is published.

(2) The Tribunal Officer shall ensure that the case records so sent to the residence of the Members are brought back to the concerned Court Hall before commencement of the Court sitting.

(3) The Tribunal Officer shall verify the case records listed for the day and arrange them in the serial order as given in the cause list well before the commencement of the sitting.

(4) The Tribunal Officer of the Bench concerned shall ensure that the Court Hall is ready for commencement of the sitting at the prescribed time for such sitting.

(5) If, for any reason, the Bench cannot sit or the sitting is delayed, the Registrar shall promptly obtain the orders of the Chairperson or Vice-Chairperson and notify the same on the Notice Board and in the Court Hall through the Tribunal Officer.

20. Maintenance of Tribunal Diary – (1) The Tribuna Officer of the Bench concerned shall maintain legibly a Tribunal Diary in Register No. IV, wherein he shall record the proceedings of the Tribunal for each sitting day with respect to the application listed in the daily cause list.

(2) The matters to be recorded in the Tribunal Diary shall include details as to whether the case is adjourned, or part-heard or heard and disposed of or head and orders reserved, as the case may be.

21. Statutes or Citations for reference – The parties or legal practitioners shall before the commencement of the proceedings for the day, furnish to the Tribunal Officer a list of law journals, reports, statutes and other citations, which may be cited for reference.

22. Calling of cases in Tribunal – The Tribunal Officer shall call the cases listed in the cause list in the serial order in accordance with rules 14 and 15 of the AFT (Procedure) Rules, 2008, and Orders of the Bench.

23. Regulation of Tribunal Work – (1) When the Bench is sitting, the Tribunal Officer shall ensure -

(a) that no inconvenience or wastage of time is caused to the Bench in making available the services of Tribunal Master, stenographer or peon;

(b) that perfect silence is maintained in and around the Tribunal Hall and no disturbance whatsoever is caused to the functioning of the Bench; and

(c) that proper care is taken to maintain dignity and decorum of the Tribunal.

(2) When the Bench passes an order or directions, the Tribunal Officer shall ensure that the records of the case along with proceedings or orders of the Bench are transmitted immediately to the Judicial Branch.

(3) The Judicial Branch shall verify the case records received from the Tribunal Officer with reference to the cause list and take immediate steps to communicate the directions or orders of the Bench to all concerned.

SERVICE OF NOTICE

24. Issue of Notice – (1) Unless otherwise ordered by the Tribunal, when a notice is ordered, the applicant shall, in cases governed by sub-rule (5) of the Rule 11 (6) of the AFT (Procedure) Rules 2008, pay the prescribed fee for service of notice accompanied by a memo in Form No. 7 within seven days from the date of order and in case of default, no notice shall be issued to any of the respondents and the matter shall be placed immediately before the Bench for appropriate orders.

(2) Where the notice is returned to the Tribunal with an endorsement of the postman regarding non-service owing to refusal of the same by the party concerned, the Registrar shall declare that the notice has been duly served on the respondent.

(3) Where the notice was properly addressed, pre-paid and duly sent by registered post, acknowledgement due, the declaration referred to in sub-rule (b) shall be made when for any reason the acknowledgement is not received by the Tribunal within thirty days from the date of the issue of the notice.

25. Steps for issue of fresh notice – (1) If any notice is returned unserved in the circumstances not specified in sub-rules (2) and (3) of Rule 24, that fact and the reason therefore shall be listed immediately on the notice board of the Registry.

(2) The applicant or his Legal Practitioner shall within seven days from the date of such notification take steps for service of fresh notice.

26. Consequence of failure to take steps for issue of fresh notice – If the applicant or his legal representative fails to take necessary steps in time for service of fresh notice on the respondent(s) and consequently, the service remains incomplete, the Registrar shall post the case before the Bench for further directions.

27. Service of notice, etc., on legal practitioners – A legal practitioner representing a party in any proceeding and any person authorized to accept notices on behalf of a party, shall receive notices, orders, directions, pleadings, etc., required to be served on such party in connection with such proceedings and such service shall be deemed to be proper service on the party.

28. Form of Notice – Notice to show cause regarding admission shall be in Form No. 8 and the notice ordered after admission shall be in Form No. 9.

29. Entries regarding service of notice or process – The Judicial Branch of the Registry shall record in the column in the order sheet "Notes of the Registry", the details regarding completion of service of notice on the respondents, such as date of issue of notice, date of service, date of return of notice if unreserved, steps taken for issuing fresh notice and date of completion of service, etc.

FILING OF REPLY STATEMENT OR REJOINDER

30. Filing of reply Statement – (1) Each respondent shall file the reply statement in the manner as provided under Rule 12 of the AFT (Procedure) Rules 2008.

(2) When all or any of the respondents(s) fail to file reply stamen in the form, manner and within the time as provided under Rule 12 of the AFT (Procedure) Rules 2008, the case shall be deemed to be ready for hearing and included in the ready list for final hearing.

31. Filing of rejoinder – (1) The applicant (s) intending to file rejoinder to the reply statement filed by all or any of the respondent(s) shall do so, with the leave of the Bench or Registrar within the time granted.

(2) The rejoinder shall be filed within the time granted, duly signed and verified in the manner prescribed for filing reply statement under Rule 12 of the AFT (Procedure) Rules 2008.

(3) After the expiry of the time granted for filing the rejoinder, the case shall be deemed to be ready for hearing and included in the ready list for final hearing.

32. Papers not to form part of the records – (1) Except with the leave of the Tribunal, the following shall not form part of the records of the case:-

(a) Reply statement filed after the expiry of the time granted for the purpose;

(b) Rejoinder filed without the leave of the Tribunal or filed after the expiry of the time granted; and

(c) Additional pleadings filed without the leave of the Tribunal or filed after the expiry of the time granted.

(2) The above papers treated as not forming part of the record shall be notified on the Notice Board of the Registry requiring the party to take them back within four weeks from the date of the Notification, failing which the Registry shall take steps to destroy the same.

33. Incorporation of amendments, filing of additional reply, etc. – (1) When the Tribunal allows an application for amendment of the pleadings or for addition of parties, the same shall be carried out in red ink indicating the date of the order and duly signed by the party or legal practitioner, who has obtained the order, within the time granted for the purpose by the order or if no time is granted, within 14 days from the date of the order.

(2) If, the Bench or the Tribunal has directed furnishing of a fresh copy incorporating the amendments or addition of parties, the same shall be filed in triplicate and after serving a copy of the amended pleading on the other party within the time granted by the Tribunal of if not time granted, within 14 days from the date of the order.

(3) In case of default under sub-rule (1) and (2), the Registry shall place the matter before the Bench for orders.

PROCEEDINGS BEFORE REGISTRAR'S COURT

34. Matters to be listed before the Registrar's Court – Once an application or appeal is admitted and notice ordered, the same shall be posted before the Registrar for completion of pleadings.

35. Cause List for Registrar's Court – Cases required to be dealt with by the Registrar shall be notified in a separate daily cause list and the cases so notified shall be taken up in the Registrar's Court in the serial order as indicated in the cause list.

36. Recording of proceedings – After hearing the parties or their legal practitioners and on perusing the records, the Registrar may record his decisions in the column "Notes of the Registry" in the order sheet and put his initials with date.

37. Inclusion of cases in the ready list when pleadings are complete – If the pleadings are complete or if the case is deemed to be ready for hearing, the Registrar shall record the same in the order sheet and order for inclusion in the list of cases ready for final hearing.

PREPARATION OF READY LIST, WARNING LIST, DAILY CAUSE LIST AND POSTING OF CASES

38. Maintenance of Ready List - (1) The Judicial Branch of the Registry shall maintain separate registers in Register No. 5 for each category of cases, which are ready for hearing.

(2) The registers shall contain separate sections for each year and inclusion of cases in the register shall be year-wise and in the order in which they become ready for hearing.

39. Preparation of Warning List – (1) The Registry shall prapare for each category of cases, a separate list called “Warning List” consisting of such number of cases as may be sufficient in the opinion of the Registrar, for being posted for hearing for a period of two weeks.

(2) Cases in the Warning List shall be arranged according to the year and number of registration and not on the basis of their serial number in the Ready List and oldest among the cases be included first followed by the next oldest and so on.

40. Publication of Warning List – (1) The Judicial Branch of the Registry shall publish the Warning list on the Notice Board of the Registry on the last working day previous to the 1st and 15th of every month.

(2) The total number of cases to be included in each Warning list as fixed by the Registrar shall, as far as possible, be maintained by adding at the bottom of the list, such number of case are required to make good the deficiency, having regard to the number of cases transferred to the Daily Cause List.

(3) From the Warning List so published, sufficient number of cases shall be taken for inclusion in the Daily Cause List in the order in which they appear in the Warning list, subject to the orders of the Chairperson or Vice-Chairperson or the Bench.

41. Preparation and Publication of Daily Cause List – (1) The Judicial Branch of the Registry shall prepare and publish on the notice board of the Registry before 5.30 p.m. on each working day the cause list for the next working day and where practicable on the internet.

(2) Subject to the directions of the Chairperson or Vice-Chairperson or the Bench, listing of cases in the Daily Cause List shall be in the following order:-

(i) Cases for “Pronouncement of Orders”,

(ii) Cases “For being spoken to”,

(iii) Cases for Admission”,

(iv) Cases for “Orders and Directions”,

(v) Contempt applications,

(vi) Part-heard cases, latest part-heard having precedence,

(vii) Cases posted as per directions of the Court, and

(viii) Cases from the “Warning list”.

(2) The title of the Daily Cause List shall consist of the name of the Bench, the day, date and time of the Bench sitting, Tribunal Hall number and the quorum indicating the names of the Chairperson or Vice-Chairperson or Member constituting the Bench with abbreviations in brackets (J) for Judicial and (A) for Administrative.

(3) In the Warning List and in the Daily Cause List, the following particulars shall be shown against the number of each case:-

(i) Names of legal practitioners appearing on both sides, giving in brackets the rank of the parties whom they represent.

(ii) Names of the parties, if unrepresented with their serial order in brackets.

(4) Office objections and special directions, if any, shall be briefly indicated in the Daily Cause List below the case number.

(5) The Daily Cause List and progress of the cases listed for the day before the Benches will be made available on the internet and hard copy will be available on the nominal payment as decided by the Chairperson, or Vice-Chairperson.

42. Carry forward of Cause List and adjournment of cases on account of non-sitting of a Bench – (1) If by reason of declaration of holiday or for any other reason, the Bench does not function for the day, the Daily Cause List for that day shall, unless otherwise directed, be treated as the Daily Cause List for the next working day in addition to the cases already posted for that day.

(2) When the sitting of a particular Bench is cancelled for the reason of absence of Member(s) of the Bench, the Registrar shall, unless otherwise directed, adjourn the cases posted before that Bench to a convenient date.

(3) The adjournment or posting or directions shall be notified on the notice board.

43. Supply of Cause List – (1) Two copies of fortnightly Warning list and Daily Cause list shall be furnished to the Bar Association of Armed Forces Tribunal for display on their notice board.

(2) Copies of the Daily Cause list or the warning list or both may be furnished to the legal practitioners on payment of fees at the rate specified below:

I. Daily Cause list:

Per Bench (consisting of two members) - Rs. 240 per annum.

II. Warning List:

Per Bench (consisting of two members) - Rs.100 per annum.

(3) Application for supply of Warning or Daily Cause list or both shall made in writing to the Registrar accompanied by one year's subscription by way of Demand Draft or Indian Postal Orders drawn in favour of the Registrar of the concerned Bench seven days before the date from which supply is to commence.

(4) The rates specified in sub-rule (2) shall be subject to such modifications as may be made by the Chairperson from time to time.

(5) The legal practitioners concerned shall be responsible to obtain copies of above lists from the delivery counter.

44. Request for Adjournments – Unless the Bench otherwise permits, request(s) for adjournments of the case(s) listed in the Daily Cause List shall be entertained only at the beginning of the session.

45. Early hearing of cases – (1) If early hearing of a case out of turn is required, the party or legal practitioner shall make an application stating the reasons thereof in Form No. 10, after serving copy thereof to the other party or parties.

(2) The application shall, if in order, be listed before the Bench headed by the Chairperson or in his absence the Vice-Chairperson nominated by him in the case of the Principal Bench and before the Vice-Chairperson and in his absence before the senior-most available member for orders in the case of other Benches.

45. Maintenance of Stage Register and Posting Register – (1) The Judicial Branch of the Registry shall maintain a Stage Register in Register No. VI for each category of applications or appeals from the stage of first posting till disposal.

(2) Posting Register shall be maintained in Form Register No. VII.

(3) All orders regarding clubbing at cases shall be entered in the order sheets of all the cases required to be clubbed together and posted accordingly.

(4) The Section Officer concerned shall ensure that the aforesaid registers are promptly and properly maintained and the directions of the Bench faithfully carried out.

47. Vacation Bench Sittings and Posting of cases – (1) When the Tribunal is closed for vacation, the Vacation Bench shall sit on such days as the Chairperson in the case of Principal Bench and Vice-Chairperson in the case of other Benches, and in his absence the senior-most Member available, may specify.

(2) During the vacation, only matters, which are required t to be immediately dealt with, shall be received in the Registry.

(3) The Registrar, on being satisfied about the urgency, shall order registration and posting of such cases.

(4) During the vacation, the Registrar may accept replies, rejoinders etc., provided a copy of the same has been served on all the other parties or legal practitioners.

(5) Inspection of records may be permitted during the vacation in accordance with these rules.

(6) Certified copies of the records may be supplied during the vacation according to these rules.

FULL BENCH MATTERS

48. Preparation and filing of paper books on reference to the Full Bench – When a Bench of the Tribunal makes an order referring the case or issues to a Full Bench, the applicant or such other party, as the Bench directs, shall furnish in Paper Book form duly indexed and continuously paginated three or five sets (depending upon the number of members of the Full Bench) for the use of the Bench and one set to each of the parties or their legal practitioner on the other side, within two weeks or such other period as the Bench may direct, arranging the papers in the following orders :-

(i) Index. Page No.

(ii) Written chronology of events or orders relevant to the case,

(iii) Order of Reference,

(iv) Memo of Parties,

(v) Application,

(vi) Annexures to the application,

(vii) Reply by each respondent in the order of their ranking,

(viii) Annexures at the end of reply of each respondent,

(ix) Rejoinder, if any,

(x) Annexures to rejoinder, if any, and

(xi) Other relevant papers with description and date:

Provided that if the same legal practitioner appears for more than one party, only one set of paper book need be furnished to him.

49. Circulation of order of reference to other Benches – The Registrar of the referring Bench shall send a copy of the Order of reference to all the other Benches of the Tribunal for information.

50. Seeking orders of Chairperson for constitution of Full Bench and fixing the date of hearing – The Registrar of the referring Bench shall forward a copy of the Order of Reference to the Registrar of the Principal Bench for securing orders of the Chairperson for constitution of the Full Bench and fixing the date of hearing.

51. Conveyance of the orders of the Chairperson – The Registrar of the Principal Bench shall, on receipt of the copy of the Order under Rule 50, obtain the orders of the Chairperson and convey the same to the Registrar of the referring Bench.

52. Notification regarding Full Bench hearing – The Registrar of the referring Bench shall, immediately on receipt of orders of the Chairperson, notify the parties or legal practitioners the date of hearing of the case by the Full Bench.

53. Circulation of Full Bench decision – The Registrar of the referring Bench shall circulate the decision rendered by the Full Bench to all other Benches of the Tribunal.

INSPECTION OF RECORDS

54. Grant of Inspection – (1) Inspection of records of a pending or decided case before the Tribunal shall be allowed only under the orders of the Registrar.

(2) The parties to any case or their legal practitioner may be allowed to insect the record of the case on making an application in writing to the registrar.

(3) Subject to such terms and conditions as may be specified by the Chairperson by a general or special order, a person who is not a party to the proceedings, may also be allowed to inspect the records after obtaining the permission of the Registrar in writing.

55. Application for grant of inspection – (1) The application for inspection of records as provided under Rule 54, shall be in Form No. 11 and presented at the filing counter of the Registry between 10 a.m. and 3 p.m. on any working day two days before the date on which inspection is sought, unless otherwise permitted by the Registrar.

(2) The Judicial Branch of the Registry shall submit the application with its remarks before the Registrar, who shall on consideration of the same pass appropriate orders.

(3) Inspection of records of a pending case shall not ordinarily be permitted on the date fixed for hearing of the case or on the preceding day.

56. Fee payable for Inspection – (1) No fee shall be charged for inspection of records of a pending case by a party to the case or his legal practitioner.

(2) A fee of twenty-five rupees shall be payable by way of demand draft or Indian Postal Order drawn in favour of the Registrar on any application for inspection of records of a decided case by a party to the case or his legal practitioner.

(3) A fee of one hundred reuppe shall be payable by way of demand draft or Indian Postal Order drawn in favour of the Registrar on any application for inspection of records of a pending or decided case by a person other than a party to the case.

57. Mode of Inspection – (1) On grant of application for inspection of the records, the Section Officer in-charge of the Judicial Branch shall arrange to procure the records of the case and allow inspection of such records on the date and time fixed by the Registrar between 10 a.m. and 12.30 p.m. and between 2.30 p.m. and 4.30 p.m. in the presence of an officer authorized in that behalf.

(2) The person inspecting the records shall not in any manner cause dislocation, mutilation, tampering or damage to the records in the course of inspection.

(3) The person inspecting the records shall not make any marking on any record or paper so inspected and copying, if any, of the documents or records inspected may be done only in pencil.

(d) The officer supervising the inspection, may at any time prohibit further inspection, if in his opinion, any of the records are likely to be damaged in the process of inspection or the person inspecting the records has violated or attempted to violate the provisions of these Rules and shall immediately make a report about the matter to the Registrar and shall make entry to that effect in column (8) of the Inspection Register and seek further orders of the Registrar, thereof.

58. Maintenance of Register of Inspection – The Section Officer in-charge of the Judicial Branch shall cause to maintain a register in Register No. VIII for the purpose of inspection of documents or records and shall obtain therein the signature of the person making such inspection.

LEGAL PRACTITIONER BEFORE THE TRIBUNAL

59. Appearance of legal practitioner – No legal practitioner shall be entitled to appear and act in any proceedings before the Tribunal unless he files into Tribunal a Vakalatnama in Form No. 12 duly executed by or on behalf of the party for whom he appears.

60. Appearance on behalf of Government, etc. – (1) Any legal practitioner appearing on behalf of the Central Government or its department or all the three services (Army, Navy and Air Force) or any Government servant sued or suing in his official capacity shall not be required to file a Vakalatnama but he shall file into Tribunal a Memo of Appearance in Form No. 13 duly signed by him.

61. Nomination or engagement of another legal practitioner – Where a legal practitioner who has filed the Vakalatnama engages or nominates another legal practitioner to appear and argue his client's case but not to act for the client, the Tribunal may permit such other legal practitioner to appear and argue.

62. Consent for engaging another legal practitioner – A legal practitioner proposing to file a Vakalatnama in any case or proceeding before the Tribunal in which there is already a legal practitioner on record, shall do so only with the written consent of legal practitioner on record or when such consent is refused, with the permission of the Tribunal.

63. Restrictions on appearance – A legal practitioner who has tendered advice in connection with the institution of any case or other proceeding before the Tribunal or has drawn pleadings in connection with any such matter or has during the progress of any such matter acted for a party, shall not, appear in any case or proceeding or other matter arising therefrom or in any matter connected therewith for any person whose interest is opposed to that of his format client, except with the prior permission of the Tribunal.

64. Access to information – A legal practitioner appearing for the party in any matter before the Tribunal shall be entitled to communicate personally with or receive any information regarding the said matter from any officer of the Tribunal subject to such conditions as may be specified by the Tribunal.

65. Execution of Vakalatnama – (1) Every Vakalatnama authorizing a legal practitioner to plead or act shall be dated at the time of its execution.

(2) In case the person is in custody, the Vakalatnama shall be attested by a Judicial Officer or Gazetted Officer serving in connection with the affairs of the Union or of any State in India.

(3) The authority attesting the Vakalatnama under sub-rule (2) shall certify that it has been duly executed in his presence and subscribe his

signature giving his name and designation and attestation shall be made only after the name of the legal practitioner is inserted in the Vakalatnama before its execution.

(4) When a Vakalatnama is executed by a party who appears to be illiterate, blind or unacquainted with the language of the Vakalatnama, the attestor shall certify that the Vakalatnama were read, translated and explained in his presence to the executant, that he signed or affixed his thumb mark in his presence.

(5) Every Vakalatnama shall contain an endorsement of acceptance by the legal practitioner in whose favour it is executed and shall also bear his address for service.

(6) If the Vakalatnama is in favour of more than one legal practitioner, it shall be signed and accepted by all of them, giving the address for service of any one of them.

REGISTERED CLERKS OF LEGAL PRACTITIONERS

66. Notifying registration and cancellation of clerks – The registration of a clerk or cancellation under Rule 27 of the AFT (Procedure) Rules 2008, shall be notified on the notice board of the Tribunal and a copy sent to the legal practitioners Bar Association.

67. Issue of Identity Card – (1) An Identity Card as referred to in sub-rule (7) of Rule 27 of the AFT (Procedure) Rules 2008, shall be issued in Form No. 14 to every registered clerk of the legal practitioner on his remitting a fee of fifteen repuues by way of Indian Postal Order or demand draft drawn in favour of the Registrar.

(b) The registered clerk shall carry with him the Identity Card and produce the same when required by any official of the registry for identification.

(2) An Identity Card once issued shall be in force for a period of five years unless cancelled under sub-rule (5) of the Rule 27 AFT (Procedure) Rules 2008.

68. Access to information by registered clerks – The registered clerks may communicate personally with any Sectional or Departmental Head not below the rank of a Section Officer for information regarding their respective legal practitioner (employers) pending in the Tribunal.

69. Carrying out corrections – (1) The Section officer in-charge of Judicial Branch may permit a registered clerk to correct any clerical or typographical mistake in any pleadings or other proceedings.

(2) The correction shall be made in the presence of the Section Officer and duly initialed by the maker as well as the Section Officer.

70. Discharge of duties of an absentee clerk – In case of illness or absence on leave of a registered clerk, the Deputy Registrar or the sectional head of the Judicial Branch may on the requisition of the legal practitioner under whom such registered clerk is engaged, permit the registered clerk of another legal practitioner to discharge the duties of absentee for a specified period, which will not exceed more than two months.

71. Presentation and return of papers – Registered clerk may present or take back papers on behalf of the legal practitioner whom he represents but he will not act at his own in any case unless permitted in writing by the Registrar or Sectional Head of Judicial Branch on the requisition of the legal practitioner as mentioned under Rule 70.

AFFIDAVITS

72. Title of affidavits – Every affidavit shall be ascribed "In the Armed Forces Tribunal,.........Branch at ...." followed by the cause title of the application or other proceeding in which the affidavit is sought to be used.

73. Form and contents of the affidavit – (1) Every affidavit shall be drawn up in Form No. 15 in the first person and divided into paragraph numbered consecutively.

(2) Every affidavit shall contain the full name, occupation, age, father's or mother's or husband's name, as the case may be, and address of the deponent.

(3) The deponent shall be identified with such other particulars as may be necessary to identify him and he shall affix his signature or mark on each page.

74. Corrections or erasures, etc. – Corrections, erasures and interlineations shall be initialed by the attestor and the number of corrections made on each page indicated.

75. Persons authorized to attest – Affidavits shall be sworn or affirmed before any Judicial Officer, Registrar, Joint Registrar and Deputy Registrar of the Tribunal, Notary, District Registrar or Sub-Registrar.

76. Affidavits of illiterate, blind etc. – Where an affidavit is sworn or affirmed by any person who appears to be illiterate, blind or unacquainted with the language in which the affidavit is written, the attestor shall certify that the affidavit was read, explained or translated by him or in his presence to the deponent and that the deponent has put his signature or mark in his (attestor) presence in Form No. 16.

77. Identification of deponent – If the deponent is not known to the attestor, his identity shall be testified by a person known to him and the identifying person shall affix his signature in token thereof.

78. Annexures to the affidavit – Document accompanying an affidavit shall be referred to therein as Annexure No........ and the attestor shall make the following endorsement thereon:

"This is the document marked as Annexure No......in the Affidavit of ....

(Signature)

Name & designation of the attestor with date"

DISCOVERY, PRODUCTION AND RETURN OF DOCUMENTS

79. Application for production of documents, form of summons – (1) Except otherwise provided, discovery, production and return of documents shall be regulated by the provisions of the Code of Civil Procedure, 1908 (5 of 1908).

(2) An application for summons to produce documents shall be in Form No. 17 setting out (i) the document(s) the production of which is sought, (ii) the relevancy of the document(s), and (iii) in case where the production of a certified copy would serve the purpose, whether application was made to the proper officer and the result thereof.

(3) A summon for production of documents in the custody of a public officer other than a Court shall be in Form No. 18 and shall be addressed to the concerned Head of the Department or such other authority as may be specified by the Tribunal.

80. Summoning of documents – Notwithstanding anything contained in these Rules, the Tribunal may, suo motu, issue summons for production of public documents or other documents in the custody of a public officer.

81. Marking of documents – (1) The documents when produced shall be marked as follows:-

(i) If relied upon by the applicant's side they shall be numbered as 'A' series.

(ii) If relied upon by the respondent's side they shall be marked as 'R' series.

(iii) The Tribunal exhibits shall be marked as 'C' series

(2) The Tribunal may direct the applicant to deposit in Tribunal by way of Indian Postal Order or demand draft drawn in favour of the Registrar a sum sufficient to defray the expenses for transmission of the records before the summons is issued.

(3) The transmission of the records shall ordinarily be by registered post or parcel.

82. Return and transmission of documents – (1) An application for return of the documents produced shall be in Form No. 17.

(2) No application referred in sub-rule (1) shall be entertained after the destruction of the records.

(b) The Tribunal may, at any time, direct return of documents produced subject to such conditions as it deems fit.

EXMAMINATION OF WITNESSES AND ISSUE OF COMMISSIONS

83. Procedure for examination of witnesses, issue of commissions, etc. – The provisions of Orders XVI and XXVI of the Code of Civil Procedure, 1908, (5 of 1908) shall mutatis mutandis apply in the matter of summoning and enforcing attendance of any person and examining him on oath and issuing commission for the examination of witnesses or for production of documents.

84. Examination in camera – The Tribunal may in its discretion examine any witness in camera and may also hold the entire or part of the proceedings in camera depending upon the sensitivity of the case.

85. Form of oath or affirmation to witness – An oath shall be administered to a witness in the following form:-

"I .... do swear in the name of God/solemnly affirm that what I shall state shall be truth, the whole truth and nothing but the truth."

86. Form of oath or affirmation to interpreter – An oath or solemn affirmation shall be administered to the interpreter, if any, in the following form before his assistance is taken for examining a witness:-

"I .... do swear in the name of God/Solemnly affirm that I will faithfully and truly interpret and explain all questions put to and evidence given by witness and translate correctly and accurately all documents given to me for translation by this Tribunal."

87. Officer to administer oath – The oath or affirmation shall be administered by the Tribunal Officer.

88. Recording of deposition – (1) The Deposition of witness shall be recorded in Form No. 19.

(2) Each page of the deposition shall be initialled by the Members constituting the Bench.

(3) Corrections, if any, pointed out by the witness may, if the Bench is satisfied, be carried out and duly initialed and in case corrections pointed out by the witness are not accepted by the Bench, a note to that effect be appended at the bottom of the deposition.

89. Numbering of witnesses – The witnesses called by the applicant or petitioner shall be numbered consecutively as PWs and those by the respondents as RWs.

90. Grant of discharge certificate – A witness discharged by the Tribunal may be granted a certificate to that effect in Form No. 20 by the Registrar.

91. Payment to the witness – (1) Where the Tribunal issues summons to a Government servant to give evidence or to produce documents, the person so summoned shall be paid travelling allowance (TA) and daily allowance (DA) admissible to him as per Rules.

(2) Where there is no provision for payment to TA and DA by the employer to the person, summoned to give evidence or to produce documents, he shall be entitled to be paid as 'bhatta', a sum assessed by the Registrar sufficient to defray the traveling and other expenses having regard to the status and position of the witness.

(3) The party applying for the summons shall deposit with the Registrar the amount of 'bhatta' as estimated by the Registrar before the summons is issued.

(4) If the witness is summoned as a Court witness, the amount estimated by the Registrar shall be paid as per the directions of the Tribunal.

(5) The provisions of sub-rule (1) to (4) would apply mutatis mutandis to the interpreter as well.

92. Records to the furnished to the Commissioner - (1) The Commissioner shall be furnished by the Tribunal with such of the records of the case as the Tribunal considers necessary for executing the Commission.

(2) Original documents will be furnished only if a copy will not serve the purpose or cannot be obtained without unreasonable expense or delay.

(3) The delivery and return of records shall be made under proper acknowledgement.

93. Taking of specimen handwriting, signature, etc – The Commissioner may, if necessary, take specimen of the handwriting, signature or finger print of any witness examined before him.

PRONOUNCEMENT OF ORDER

94. Order – The final decision of the Tribunal on an application or appeal before it shall be described as "Order".

95. Operative portion of the Order – All order and directions of the Bench shall be stated in clear and precise terms in the last paragraph of the order.

96. Corrections – The Member of the Bench who has prepared the order shall initial all corrections and affix his initials at the bottom of each page.

97. Pronouncement of order – (1) The Bench shall where possible pronounce the order immediately after the hearing is concluded.

(2) When the order are reserved, the date for pronouncement not later than 30 days shall be fixed and the date so fixed shall not be changed except due notice to all parties or legal practitioner.

(3) Reading of the operative portion of the order in the open court shall be deemed to be pronouncement of the order.

(4) Any order reserved by a Circuit Bench of the Tribunal may be pronounced at the principal place of sitting of the Bench.

98. Pronouncement of order by any one Member of the Bench – (1) Any one Member of the Bench may pronounce the order for and on behalf of the Bench.

(2) When an order is pronounced under this Rule, the Tribunal officer shall make a note in the order sheet, that the order of the Bench consisting of ....as members was pronounced in Open Court by ....(name of the member).

99. Authorising any Member to pronounce order – (1) If the Member of the Bench who heard the case are no readily available or have ceased to be Members of the Tribunal, the Chairperson or Vice-Chairperson, as the case may be, authorize any other Member to pronounce the order on his being satisfied that the order has been duly prepared and signed by all the Members who had heard the case.

(2) The order pronounced by the Member so authorized shall be deemed to be duly pronounced.

(3) The Member authorized under sub-rule (1) for pronouncement of the order shall affix his signature in the order sheet of the case stating that he has pronounced the order as provided in this rule.

(4) If the order has not been signed by reason of sickness, death, retirement or resignation or for any other reason by any one of the Members of the Bench who heard the case, it shall be deemed to have been released from part-heard and listed afresh for hearing.

100. Making of entries by Tribunal officer – The Tribunal Officer shall, immediately after pronouncement of an order by the Bench, make necessary endorsement on the case file regarding the date of such pronouncement, the nature of disposal and the constitution of the Bench pronouncing the order and he shall also make necessary entries in the Tribunal diary maintained by him.

101. Transmission of order by the Tribunal officer – (1) The Tribunal Officer shall immediately on pronouncement of the order, transmit it with the case file to the Principal Registrar or Registrar as the case may be.

(2) On receipt of the order from the Tribunal Officer, the Principal Registrar or Registrar as the case may be, shall after due scrutiny, satisfy himself that the provisions of these Rules have been duly complied with and in token thereof affix his initials, with date on the outer cover of the order.

(3) The Principal Registrar or Registrar as the case may be, shall thereafter cause to transmit the case file and the order to the Judicial Branch for taking expeditious steps to prepare copies and their communication to the parties.

102. Format of order of the Tribunal - (1) The format of order of the Tribunal shall be in Form No. 21.

(2) All orders shall be neatly and fairly typewritten in double space on one side only on durable foolscap folio paper of metric A-4 size (30.5 cms long and 21.5 cms wide) with left side margin of 5 cms and right side margin of 2.5 cms.

(3) The corrections, if any, in the order shall be carried out neatly .

(4) Sufficient space may be left both at the bottom and at the top of each page of the order to make its appearance elegant.

(5) Members constituting the Bench shall affix their signatures in the order of their seniority from right to left.

103. Costs – (1) Unless otherwise quantified by the Tribunal, when costs are awarded in a case, the same shall be determined as follows:-

(i) For applicant(s):

Legal Practitioner's fee	Rs. 5,000
Expenses	Rs. 500

(ii) For Respondent(s)

Legal Practitioner's fee	Rs. 5,000
Expenses	Rs 500

(2) Only one set of costs shall be awarded to the applicants as also when the same counsel appears for more than one respondent.

(3) When costs are awarded a Bill of Costs in Form No. 22 shall be prepared giving the details of the costs awarded to the parties and annexed to the order.

104. Compliance of urgent orders – (1) Whenever the Bench passes an order, final or inter-locator, requiring immediate compliance, the Tribunal Officer shall immediately transmit the case file and the order to the Principal Registrar or Registrar as the case may be, who shall ensure prompt action on the same day.

(2) Files with Dasti orders should be stapled with "To-day" flags and superscribed with OA, TA, RA, CA, MA or AT No. with the signature of the Tribunal Officer with date.

105. Placing copies of common orders – (1) When more than one case is disposed of by a common order, the Judicial Branch shall keep the original order in the main case and a certified copy in the other connected case files.

(2) In the order sheet of the connected case(s), the Section Officer in-charge of the Judicial Branch shall note that the original order is kept in the main case file (giving its number).

106. Indexing of case files disposal – After communication of the order to the parties or legal practitioners, the official concerned shall arrange the records with pagination and prepare the Index Sheet in Form No. 23 and he shall affix initials and then transmit the records with the index duly initialed, to the records room.

107. Transmission of files or records or orders – Transmission of files or records of the cases or orders shall be made only after obtaining acknowledgement in the movement register maintained at different sections or levels as per the directions of the Registrar.

108. Copies of orders in Library – (1) The Section Officer of the Judicial Branch shall send copies of every final order to the Library.

(2) Copies of all orders received in each month shall be kept at the Library in a separate folder, arranged in the order of date of pronouncement, duly indexed and stitched.

(3) A consolidated index shall also be prepared at the end of every year and kept in a separate file in the Library.

(4) The order folders and the indices may be made available for reference in the Library to the legal practitioners.

GRANT OF CERTIFIED COPIES AND FREE COPIES

109. Form and fee of application – (1) Every application for grant of certified copy shall be in Form No. 24 and accompanied with a non-refundable fee for Rs. 10 (Rupees Ten only), and in case of urgent copy a non-refundable fee of twenty five rupees in the form of Indian Postal Order or demand draft drawn in favour of the Registrar and payable at the place of the Bench of the Tribunal.

(2) If the certified copies applied for are for more than one document in the same cases, only one application shall be filed.

110. Right of the party to obtain certified copy – A party to an application or appeal or his legal practitioner shall be entitled to obtain certified copy of the record, preceding or original document filed in case on payment of fee specified in these rules.

111. Application for copies by stranger – (1) Applications for copies of documents (other than orders) by person not parties to the proceedings shall be allowed only by order of the Registrar obtained on a duly verified petition in Form No. 17, setting forth the purpose for which the copy is required on payment of fee specified under these rules.

(2) Copies of orders can, however, be granted to any person on payment of fees specified under these rules.

112. Register of copy application and requisition register – (1) A Register of copy application shall be maintained in Register No. IX and a Requisition Register in Register No. X with regard to request for the files in the copying branch.

(2) Entries in respect of urgent copy applications shall be underlined in red ink.

113. Copying fee – The copying fee payable for obtaining an ordinary copy shall be at the rate of rupees two per page and for urgent copy at the rate or rupees five per page irrespective of the number of word or lines in each page.

114. Scrutiny of copy application, requisitioning of case records and rectification of defects – (1) If the application is in order, necessary entries shall be made in the Register of Copy Application and the Requisition Register and the same sent to the official-in-charge of records. The officer-in-charge of the records shall as soon as possible transmit the records along with the application after making an entry in the application and initialling the same.

(2) If the application is found to be defective, the same shall be notified on the notice board of the Registry.

(3) If the defects are not rectified within three days from the date of such notice, the copy application shall be struck off.

(4) On removal of defects within three days, the application shall be deemed to have been made on the date of the application.

115. Determination of additional copying fee – (1) On receipt of the records, the officer-in-charge of copying section after satisfying that the records are completed shall determine the additional copying fee payable over and above the copying fee of ten or twenty-five rupees already paid and make an entry thereof in the application with his initials.

(2) Additional fee payable shall be notified on the notice board of the Registry.

116. Remittance of additional copying fee – (1) Additional copying fee shall be remitted by the applicant between 10.30 am and 4.30 pm in the form of Indian Postal Order or demand draft drawn in favour of the Registrar and payable at the place of the Bench within two days, in the case of urgent copy, and within seven days in the case of ordinary copy, from the date of notice.

(2) If the additional fee payable is not remitted within the time permitted under sub-rule (1), the application shall be struck off.

117. Order of preparation of certified copy – Certified copies shall be prepared in the order in which they become ready in all respects and the urgent applications shall take precedence over all ordinary applications.

118. Time-limit for issue of urgent or ordinary copy – Urgent copy shall be delivered to the applicant as far as possible within three days and ordinary copy within ten days from the date the application.

119. Notifying when copies are ready for delivery and consequence of not taking delivery – (1) On each working day before 11.30 am, the officer in-charge of the copying branch shall cause to prepare in duplicate in Form No. 25, a list of cases in which certified copies are ready for delivery and publish one copy of the same on the notice board of the Registry with his signature, and the other copy shall be retained for record.

(2) If the applicant fails to take delivery within three months, the certified copy prepared shall be destroyed and the copying fee paid forfeited to Government.

120. Proper accounting of copying fee received – The Officer in-charge shall ensure that the copying fee received in the registry is promptly accounted in the India Postal Order or demand draft Register and transmitted to the Cash Section for crediting them to the Government account.

121. Preparation and comparison of certified copy – (1) A certified copy shall be made by photocopying process or by typing.

(2) When the copy is so made, it shall be compared by the official in-charge of copying branch with the document of which the copy is made, aided by another official in the copying branch and he shall, after satisfying himself

that the copy prepared faithfully and legibly reproduces the document desired, appended a certificate as under and affix his initials:

"Certified that this is a true and accurate copy of the document or order as in the case file (OA, RA, TA, CA, MA, AT No....../20...) and that all the matter appearing therein have been legibly and faithfully copied with no modifications."

(3) The officer in-charge of copying branch shall affix an endorsement on the last page of the copy as under and put his initials:

(i) Serial No. of the copy of application:

(ii) Name of the applicant:

(iii) Date of presentation of application:

(iv) Number of pages:

(v) Copying fee charged, urgent or ordinary:

(vi) Date of preparation of copy:

(vii) Date on which copy is ready:

(viii) Date given for collection of copy:

(ix) Date of delivery:

(4) The certificate and the endorsement shall be made with the help of a rubber stamp and the entries however, shall be made in ink.

(5) The officer authorized to issue the copy shall affix his signature below the endorsement and cause to affix the seal of the Tribunal on all pages of the copy and also initial wherever there are corrections.

122. Re-transmission of case records – On completion of the preparation of the certified copy, the officer-in-charge of the copying section shall re-transmit the records of the case to the concerned branch, after making necessary entries in the Requisition Register and obtain acknowledgement of the official, who receives back the records, in the relevant column of the Register.

123. Mode of delivery of certified copy – At the time of the delivery of the certified copy, the official concerned shall obtain the signature of the applicant in the relevant column in the Register of Copy Applications, record the date of such delivery on the copy application and fill up relevant column regarding the date of delivery in the endorsement stamped on the certified copy.

124. Request for certified copy by post – (1) Where the applicant desires to heave the certified copy sent to him by post, he shall send an additional sum of twenty-five rupees by way of India Postal Order or demand draft drawn in favour of the Registrar and payable at the place of the Bench for defraying the postal charges, etc.

(2) If the amount sent is found to be inadequate, the applicant shall intimated to remit the balance amount within the time specified and on receipt of the intimation, the applicant shall remit the amount in the manner provided in sub-rule (1) and within the time specified.

125. Intimation of rejection – If for any reason the copy application is rejected, due intimation be given to the applicant and the refundable amount if any, returned to him.

126. Supply of free copy only once – Once free copy of the order is sent as provided in Rule 23 of the AFT (Procedure) Rules 2008, the Tribunal shall not be required to issue any more fee copies.

127. Certifying of free copies – Every free copy issued to a party or his legal practitioner in accordance with the rules shall be certified to be "True Copy" and shall be superscribed "FREE COPY UNDER RULE 23 OF THE AFT (PROCEDURE) RULES 2008" with a rubber stamp and signed by the officer authorized in that behalf and he shall also cause to enter the date and other details of furnishing of such free copy in the Register of Free Copies in Register No. XI.

128. Time for furnishing free copies – (1) Judicial Branch of the Registry shall issue free copies of the order to the parties or their legal practitioners as provided under Rule 23 of the AFT (Procedure) Rules 2008, as far as possible within seven days from the date of pronouncement of the order.

(2) If the free copy of the order is delivered by hand to parties or their legal practitioner, the officer in-charge shall obtain acknowledgement thereof in the relevant column in the Register of Free Copies.

129. Furnishing of free copy in a joint application – When joint application or appeal is made, only one free copy of the order contemplated by Rule 23 of the AFT (Procedure) Rules 2008, shall be issued, either to their legal practitioners or if they are appearing in person, to any one of the applicants.

130. Furnishing of corrected free copy of order – Whenever clerical or typographical errors or mistakes in an order are rectified subsequent to the issue of the free copy thereof, the Registrar shall cause to issue a corrected free copy of such order to the parties or their legal practitioners.

APPEAL TO SUPREME COURT

131. Manner of service of order notice issued by the Supreme Court – Service of orders or notices on respondents ordered by the Supreme Court in an appeal or application pending before that Court shall be effected in the manner provided by the Supreme Court Rule, 1966 as amended from time to time.

132. Steps to comply with Supreme Court directions – (1) Unless otherwise ordered by the Supreme Court, the appellant or his legal practitioner shall be notified to deposit the transmission charges and cost of preparation of record, if any, etc., within fifteen days of the receipt of the notice.

(2) When the party or legal practitioner fails to deposit the amount as aforesaid, the Registrar shall forthwith submit a report thereof to the Registrar of the Supreme Court.

133. Register of Special Leave Petitions or Appeals – (1) A Register in the form of Register No. XII shall be maintained in regard to Special Leave Petitions (SLPs) or Appeals against the orders of the Tribunal to the Supreme Court and necessary entries therein be made by the Judicial Branch.

(2) The register under sub-rule (1) shall be placed for scrutiny by the Chairperson or Vice-Chairperson in the first week of every month.

134. Placing of Supreme Court orders before Chairperson, etc., – Whenever an interim or final order passed by the Supreme Court in an appeal or other proceeding preferred against a decision of the Tribunal, is received, the same shall forthwith be placed before the Chairperson or Vice-Chairperson or Members for information and kept in the relevant case file and immediate attention of the Registrar shall be drawn to the directions requiring compliance.

135. Circulation of the orders of the Supreme Court – All orders of the Supreme Court including dismissal of SLPs shall be circulated to the Members of the Bench whose decision was challenged before the Supreme Court and kept in the relevant case file.

136. Registrar to ensure compliance of Supreme Court orders – It shall be the duty of the Registrar to take expeditious steps to comply with the directions of the Supreme Court.

RETENTION, PRESERVATION AND DESTRUCTION OF RECORDS

137. Procedure regarding retention, preservation and destruction of records – All the records, registers and files shall be retained and preserved in the record room from the date of completion till the period provided for their destruction in accordance with the rules made in this behalf.

138. Receipt, scrutiny and custody of records – The officer in-charge of the record room shall be the custodian and responsible for the records lodged in the record room and he shall receive the records sent to the record room and scrutinize the records within three days of the date of receipt of records in the record room.

139. Rectification of defects or securing of missing records – If on scrutiny under Rule 138, any defect or missing of documents is found in the records, the officer in-charge shall intimate the same and remit the records back to the branch or section from which the records were received and thereupon, the Section Officer in-charge of the concerned branch or section shall cause to take steps to rectify the defects or secure the missing records so pointed out, and after such rectification or securing the missing document, re-transmit the records to the record room within three days of its receipt from the record room.

140. Maintenance of Register of records received in the record room – The officer in-charge of record room shall maintain a register in Register No. XIII of records received in the Record Room.

141. Entry regarding destruction – Entries regarding destruction shall be made in the relevant columns of Register No. XIII.

142. Preservation of records requiring permanent retention – (1) Records required to be preserved permanently shall be stacked in bundles of convenient size, arranging them in chronological order.

(2) The bundle so prepared under sub-rule (1) shall be wrapped in 'Kora Cloth' on which shall be attached labels indicating in chronological order, registration numbers of the cases included in each bundle and such bundles shall be arranged serially and kept in the records room.

143. Retention of records beyond prescribed period – The Registrar may for reasons to be recorded in writing and with prior permission of the Chairperson order that record of any particular case be preserved beyond the prescribed period provided under the rules for destruction.

MISCELLANEOUS

144. Circuit Benches – The provisions of these Rules shall mutatis mutandis govern applications entertained by circuit benches subject to such adaptations as may by order be made by the concerned Vice-Chairperson on being satisfied that it is necessary to do so in the interest of justice.

145. Use of computers – (1) The Chairperson may issue such orders or directions as may be necessary for complying with the provisions of the relevant rules with the aid of the computer and for effective use of the computer facility as and when introduced.

(2) Compliance with such orders or directions issued by the Chairperson from time to time shall be deemed to be due compliance of the provisions of the relevant rules.

146. Classification of cases – (1) The scrutiny branch of the Registry shall, at the time of scrutiny, make classification of the cases as both department-wise (Army, Navy and Air Force) and subject-wise.

(2) The department-wise (Army, Navy and Air Force) classification shall be made in accordance with Form No. 26, as may be modified by the Chairperson from time to time.

(3) Subject-wise classification shall be made in accordance with Form No. 27, as may be modified by the Chairperson from time to time.

(4) The classification under this rule shall be entered in the relevant columns in the report of scrutiny in Form No. 2 or Form No. 3, Order Sheet in Form No. 4 and Facing Sheet of the final cover in Form No. 5.

147. Furnishing of weekly and monthly statement – (1) The Registrar of each Bench shall prepare a weekly progress report in Form No. 28 and circulate among all the Members of the Bench concerned.

(2) The Vice-Chairperson of the Bench concerned shall forward a consolidated monthly progress report in Form No. 28 to the Chairperson before the 7th day of each month.

(3) The Registrar of the concerned Bench shall prepare a monthly statement in two parts as in Form No. 29 regarding filing, disposal and pendency of cases and forward the same to the Principal Registrar of the Principal Bench before the 7th day of each month.

148. Inspection of Registry – (1) The Principal Registrar or the Registrar as the case may be, shall conduct inspection of the sections twice a year viz., for the period from 1st January to 30th June and 1st July to 31st December, on such date as maybe found convenient.

(2) The report of inspection of the Judicial Branch, Library, Administrative Branch and Record Room shall be as per Schedules I to IV to Appendix 'C', as may be modified by the Chairperson from time to time.

(3) The Section Officer concerned shall promptly comply with the directions of the Registrar and submit a report about due compliance to the Registrar within such time as the Registrar may grant.

(4) The Registrar shall submit a report to the Chairperson or Vice-Chairperson containing brief summary of his inspection of the Registry, directions given by him to the sections and branches and the steps taken for due compliance with such directions.

149. Due compliance with the provisions of the Act and the rules – The Registrar or any officer authorized by him may, for the purpose of satisfying himself that the provisions of the Act and the rules are duly complied with, make such enquiry as he deems fit and call upon such party, as he deems necessary to appear before him and pass such orders as he deems proper.

[F. No. 1(2)/2007/D(AFT Cell)]
AJAY TIRKEY, Jt Secy

Note:- For Forms under the Armed Force Tribunal (Practice) Rules, 2009 see page 417 onwards of the book.

Appendix-H

THE ARMED FORCES TRIBUNAL (AMENDMENT) BILL, 2012

A

BILL

To amend the Armed Forces Tribunal Act, 2007

BE it enacted by Parliament in the Sixty-third year of the Republic of India as follows:–

1. (1) This Act may be called the Armed Forces Tribunal (Amendment) Act, 2012.
   (2) It shall come into force on such date as the Central Government may, by notification in the Official Gazette, appoint.

2. For section 8 of the Armed Forces Tribunal Act, 2007 (hereinafter referred to as the principal Act), the following section shall be substituted, namely:-

Term of office of Chairperson or Member

"8. The Chairperson or a Member of the Tribunal shall hold officer as such for a term of five years from the date on which he enters upon his officer but they shall not be eligible for reappointment:

Provided that no Chairperson shall hold the officer after he has attained:-

(a) In case he has been a Judge of the Supreme Court, the age of seventy years; and

(b) In case he has been the Chief Justice of High Court, the age of sixty-seven years:

Provided further that no Judicial Member shall hold office as such Judicial Member after he has attained the age of sixty-seven years:

Provided also that no Administrative Member shall hold office as such Administrative Member after he has attained the age of sixty-five years."

3. For section 19 of the principal Act, the following section shall be substituted, namely:-

Power to Punish for Contempt

"19. The Tribunal shall have, and exercise, the same jurisdiction, powers and authority in respect of contempt of itself as a High Court has and may exercise and, for this purpose, the provisions of the Contempt of Courts Act, 1971 shall have effect subject to the modification that:-

(a) The references therein to a High Court shall be construed as including a reference to such Tribunal;

(b) The reference to the Advocate general in section 15 of the said Act shall be construed in relation to the Armed Forces tribunal, as a reference to the Attorney-General or the Solicitor-General or the Additional Solicitor-General."

Appendix-I

STANDING COMMITTEE ON DEFENCE 2012-2013 (FIFTEENTH LOK SABHA)

MINISTRY OF DEFENCE

THE ARMED FORCES TRIBUNAL (AMENDMENT) BILL, 2012

EIGHTEENTH REPORT

Presented to Lok Sabha on 20 March 2013

(Abstracts)

1.4 The Ministry of Defence has in their background note on the Armed Forces Tribunal (Amendment) Bill, 2012, given reasons for bringing forth two amendments to the Armed Forces Tribunal Act (AFT Act), 2007. In regard to first amendment concerning the enhancement of term of office from four to five years for the Chairperson or a Member of the Tribunal and age of Judicial Member in case he has been Chief Justice of High Court from Sixty five to Sixty Seven years, the provisions have been picked up from the National Green Tribunal Act, 2010. This would avoid repeated selection of Members for short tenures so as to provide the Tribunal with stability and continuity. In regard to the second amendment concerning conferment of powers of civil contempt, the Ministry has informed that the Armed Forces Tribunal, Principal Bench, had brought out that the AFT Act, 2007, in its present form did not contain any provision for the execution of the order finally passed by the Tribunal. Even the arrangements made in Section 29 of AFT Act, 2007 which stated that "subject to the other provisions of this Act and the rules made thereunder, the order of the Tribunal disposing of an application shall be final and shall not be called in question in any court and such order shall be executed accordingly" did not operate as a string of caution unless powers were conferred to get its orders enforced. Further, there was no other provision in the Act to get its order complied with, in case of failure to do so. As the existing power to punish for contempt covers only for criminal contempt, this provision could not be used to enforce its orders.

1.5 Under the existing provisions contained in section 8 of the Armed Forces Tribunal Act, the Chairperson or a Member of a Tribunal shall hold office for a period of four years from the date on which he enters upon his office and shall be eligible for reappointment. However, no Chairperson shall hold office as such after he has attained – (a) in case he has been a Judge of the Supreme Court, the age of seventy years; and (b) in case he has been the chief Justice of a High Court, the age of sixty-five years. It further provides that the Members, both judicial and Administrative, shall hold office until they attained the age of sixty-five years. The Judicial Members are not completing their term of office and thus vacancies are arising frequently on regular basis in the Tribunal.

1.6 It is, therefore, proposed to change the term of office of the Chairperson and Members from four years to five years from the date on which they enter upon their office and shall not be eligible for reappointment. It is further proposed to enhance the age limit of the Chairperson, in case he has been the Chief Justice of a High Court, from sixty-five years to sixty-seven years. In order to avoid repeated selection of Members for short tenures so as to provide the Tribunal with stability and continuity, it is also proposed to enhance the age limit of Judicial Member from sixty-five years to sixty-seven years.

1.7 Section 19 of the AFT Act, 2007 enables the Tribunal to punish for criminal contempt only and not for civil contempt. The aforesaid Act in its present form does not contain any provision for the execution of the orders finally passed by the Tribunal as a result of which cases involving serious questions of law of public importance are to be taken to the Supreme Court for appropriate directions. It is, therefore, proposed to confer powers of civil contempt to the said Tribunal in addition to the existing powers of criminal contempt. The proposed amendment would give the same jurisdiction, powers and authority to the said Tribunal in respect of contempt of itself as a High Court has and may exercise and, for this purpose, the provisions of the Contempt of Courts Act, 1971, shall have effect subject to certain modifications mentioned in the Bill.

Proposed Amendment to Section 8

2.1 Clause 2 of the Bill provides for substitution of new Section for Section 8. By virtue of this amendment, it has been proposed to amend the term of office of Chairperson or member from four to five years and upper age limit of Judicial Member in case he has been the judge of High Court from sixty-five to sixty-seven years. The Ministry has also proposed that Chairperson or a Member shall not be eligible for re-appointment.

2.3 As such, while the age of Chairperson and Judicial Member is proposed to be enhanced, there is no change in the age of an Administrative Member.

2.4 The information collected by the Committee in the form of Memorandum from various stakeholders and evidence tendered before them would, summarily reveal that there was near consensus on both these issues.

2.15 Other non-official experts/stakeholders were also of the same view. However, one of the expert who retired as Judge Advocate General (JAG), Major-Gen. Nilendra Kumar JAG (Retired), was of the opinion that increasing tenure from 4 to 5 years will bring in complacency in the members giving them security of tenure.

2.16 One Ex-Air Force Officer, Wing Commander U.C. Jha (Retired), also echoed the above view in his memoranda and stated that assured five years tenure to a retired personnel will lead to complacency and Chairperson may continue with four years but tenure of members should be reduced to 3 yrs.

2.21 The Committee find that the first amendments proposed in the Bill vide Clause – 2 is in regard to fixing of the tenure of the Chairperson or the Member of the Tribunal from four to five years and raising the age of Judicial members from sixty-five years to sixty-seven years. Nevertheless, it has also been added that the Members would not be eligible for re-appointment. During examination, the Committee pondered over the views expressed by the nodal Ministry i.e., Ministry of Defence and the Ministry in-charge of drafting the bill i.e., Ministry of Law and Justice in addition to the Administrative Members of the Armed Forces Tribunal, the three Vice-Chiefs of the Services and several un-official witnesses. A close scrutiny of the evidence and material submitted before the Committee reveals that near unanimity exists on this amendment. The Committee are not inclined to accept the views expressed by two non-official witnesses who have stated that such a move to enhance the tenure of members would lead to complacency, thus find that the views of almost all the major stake holders are in favour of this proposed amendment. The Committee are in no doubt that such a move as envisaged by the Ministry of Defence and concurred in by the representatives of the services and all other stake holders would bring stability and continuity in the functioning of the Armed Forces Tribunal. Once implemented, the larger benefits of it would definitely be passed on to the retired and serving Armed Forces Personnel. The Committee, therefore, in no uncertain words acquiesces with the proposed amendments in the two sub-clauses in Clause 2 of the Bill in totality.

Proposed amendment to Section 19

3.1 Clause 3 of the Bill seeks to substitute new section for Section 19. It has been proposed to confer power of civil contempt to the Armed Forces Tribunal. However, the power for criminal contempt already exists in the Act.

3.3 The Committee wanted to know the precise difference between the criminal and the civil contempt. Throwing light on the query, the Ministry of Defence in a written note informed as under:

'As of now Section 19 of the Armed Forces Tribunal Act has given powers of criminal contempt to AFT. As per this provision, any person who is guilty of contempt of the Tribunal by using any insulting or threatening language, or by causing any interruption or disturbance in the proceedings of such Tribunal shall, on conviction, be liable to suffer imprisonment for a term which may extend to three years.

Civil contempt as defined in Section 2 (b) of the Contempt of Courts Act, 1971 means wilful disobedience to any judgment, decree, direction, order, writ or other process of a Court or wilful breach of an undertaking given to a Court. Civil contempt would become applicable in AFT after proposed amendment in AFT Act. This will help AFT to charge a person who is disobeying AFT's order to implement AFT"s order or to face punishment.'

3.4 A close scrutiny of the examination of this amendment would reveal in the succeeding paragraphs that the views of the Defence Services were dichotomous with that of the Ministry and also other stakeholders.

3.5 The Defence Secretary while briefing the Committee on this amendment of the Bill stated:

"The MoD after seeking legal advice from the Ministry of Law, consulting the DoPT and taking all the issues in consideration, decided to move this proposal that the AFT should be given power of civil contempt."

3.6 Intimating the views of the Services, the Defence Secretary said:

"It is pertinent to mention that the views of Services were also sought on the proposed amendment. The Services while not agreeing with the proposed amendment have opined that the AFT Act was passed after having considered all the aspects including the functioning of the Armed Forces and there is need to let the system stabilize and review the matter after a reasonable period. The Chief of Staff Committee was of the view that some more time may be given to settle down the issue may be revisited after five years and a decision may be taken based on the inputs from the three Services and the serving/retired personnel."

3.13 When asked to give his views on this amendment, the Vice-Chief of Army Staff during evidence said:

"We are not in agreement with the second amendment. That is giving the powers of the civil contempt. The Chairman and Hon. Members will be aware that Armed Forces Tribunal has already got the powers of criminal contempt. By this amendment they want to now confer the powers of civil contempt, which is not in the interest of the service or in the overall interest of state due to the reasons that I will just mention.

Firstly, the proposed amendment seeks to confer powers of civil contempt to the Hon'ble Tribunal in addition to the existing powers of the criminal contempt. Section 19 of the AFT Act 2007 confers only the powers of criminal contempt. The Parliament in its wisdom and knowing fully well the implications of bestowing these powers, consciously decided not to arm

Hon'ble Tribunal with such powers. There is a difference between the other Tribunal and AFT, that the working conditions of Armed Forces, which the Parliament had kept in mind when they conferred AFT with powers of criminal contempt. The working conditions, in case of an Army, if one is posted in a forward area or in an operational area, the communications are not as good as in peace areas. It takes considerate time before the matter is conveyed to the concerned persons who are supposed to appear in the Court or to bring them there. Similarly, the ship is at sea for months. He cannot be expected to unload from the ship and come for the contempt. Thus, the working conditions of Armed Forces being operationally committed are totally different than in the civil society. That is the reason probably for the Parliament not earlier giving the civil contempt powers to AFT. However, I may also add in the same breath that ours is a very disciplined force."

3.14 He further apprised the Committee:

"Everything moves with the orders. We are used to obeying the orders of our superior authority and the court. It is our bounden duty and it is ensured by regulations within the Army that Court orders are duly complied with. There is not wilful negligence or contempt of court. The proposed amendment will put a lot of handicaps in the functioning of the Forces in view of their deployment in the forward areas and operational areas, AFT Act was formulated in 2009 with a very conscious decision by the Parliament. We need to give time for it to stabilize and see what the problems are coming out of it. We have not visualized any problems having come and the Act of this nature and proposed powers of civil contempt should not be given to the AFT in a hurry."

3.16 He further stated:

"....Army is operationally deployed either in the North East or in J&K. Most of these, so to say, civil contempt cases are cases by name against the Senior Commanders and Commanding Officers, who are responsible for all the administration and discipline in units and formations. Can you imagine a unit carrying out counter infiltration or counter terrorist operations without the Commanders or Commanding Officer who is missing frequently for such summons from the court? All our operations are at the battalion level and in our case the CO is virtually there in all the operations. We will have serious operational problems and it will jeopardize our operational efficiency. That is what I can say as the Vice-Chief. I am telling from the experience because bulk of my forty years service, I have spent in the forward areas. Most of such cases are against the commanders because they are supposed to implement the directions. It is, therefore, not advisable, to bestow civil contempt powers to AFT."

3.17 Elucidating his view-point, the Ministry through a written reply communicated the views of the services as under:

"The proposal of amendment of AFT Act 2007 has been examined. After the AFT Act was enacted in 2007, the Armed Forces Tribunal started functioning w.e.f. Aug 2009. AFT Act was passed after having considered all the aspects including the functioning of the Armed Forces. There is a need to let the system stabilize and review the matter after a reasonable period.

In the present circumstances, the COSC is of the view that some more time may be given to the system to settle down and the issue may be re-visited after five years and a decision may then be taken based on the inputs from the three Services and the serving/retired personnel."

3.18 During oral evidence on the amendments, the Vice-Chief of Naval Staff said:

"....Naval Headquarter views are not in agreement. The primary reason is that with regard to Sections 14, 15, 17, 18 and 20 of the Contempt of Courts Act, 1971, these are related to criminal contempt committed by a person. The amendment in Section 19 of the Act is primarily proposed to give powers of civil contempt, which were missing in the AFT Act. One of the reasons for not vesting the AFT with civil contempt powers was perhaps due to the fact that the AFT has been given powers of execution of their orders. Thus, it is apparent that it is not bestowing the AFT Act with powers of civil contempt which was a conscious move which was taken at that point in time. Hence the same was not incorporated under the AFT Act.

Another reason which requires consideration with regard to bestowing the power of contempt of the AFT, the possibility of AFT issuing contempt notices to the Commanding Officer, Commander in Chief and indeed to the Service Chief and also directing them to appear in person before the AFT cannot be ruled out. Such a direction would not be in the best interest of the Services and it may lower the morale of the Service personnel. It also needs to be mentioned that due to the disciplined nature of the Defence Forces, the Armed Forces personnel follow the orders and directions of the superiors including the AFT in letter and spirit. It is only in a few cases where the orders and directions of the AFT have not been complied with in a time-bound manner. This is due to the filing of appeal in the Apex court or due to the reason for awaiting the Ministry of Defence approval for implementation of the AFT directives. Under the circumstances, the contempt powers, if bestowed, could result in passing of directions to senior officials of the Armed Forces and the Ministry of Defence, senior officials also to appear before the AFT, which may not be desired. In any case, the AFT, as said by Lt. Gen. S.K. Singh, has been established recently. Therefore, a further view could be taken after a few years when the situation has stabilized. That is the view of the Naval Headquarters."

3.19 The views of the Vice-Chief of Air Staff were also on the similar lines. He stated before the Committee:

"On the second point on contempt of court, once again as has been stated by Vice-Chiefs of Army and Navy, criminal contempt powers are available to the Tribunal. In terms of civil powers for contempt, it was decided in 2009 for the reason that have been stated already, I would not repeat them, suffice it to say that the system should be allowed to settle down and reviewed after five years. Therefore, let the present system continue till 2014, and thereafter, take a decision."

3.20 The Committee thought it prudent to know about the stand of the one of the important stakeholders in this regard i.e. the Armed Forces Tribunal itself. Therefore, they decided to hear the views of the Administrative Member of the Principal Bench as well as one Administrative Member from a Bench (Chandigarh), where the maximum number of cases were pending for adjudication. When asked to put his arguments, the Administrative Member of the Principal Bench stated before the Committee as under:

"As regards the issue of civil contempt, as you are aware, we have the powers of criminal contempt but not of civil contempt. As of now we have a great number of cases which come up for execution. We call them execution petition and sometimes it takes the form of contempt application. As of now we have had 2172 cases for execution. These are cases, after having been disposed of by the Tribunal have not been implemented by the respondent and therefore the applicant has come up once again as an execution petition. Execution petition is also dealt with by the Tribunal. Firstly it is in fructuous work and secondly it is costly for the applicant and thirdly it amounts to further delays in execution for another couple of months. Most importantly, all Tribunals and courts have got this power of civil contempt. As per the mandate of the Supreme Court they have said that all courts tribunals must have the power to ensure that their orders are executed. Besides this, what is important is that the orders of the tribunal which are based on the existing laws and rules. We do not go beyond that. We are not framing any rules for ourselves. So, it is well within the ambit of reasonableness. In a case, where someone has approached the Supreme Court for execution, the Solicitor General had assured the Supreme Court that an ordinance to that effect for granting powers of contempt will be issued shortly. That was about a couple of months ago. So, I suppose this is one of the fall outs of that petition and also what the Solicitor General had told the Supreme Court."

3.21 On a query in regard to any probable misuse of powers once civil contempt is conferred to the Tribunal, the Administrative Member from Chandigarh Bench stated as under:

"....So, eventually if we ever have to use the powers of the civil contempt it would be in relation to the officers at the Service Headquarters and or in the Ministry of Defence. In most of the Service matters that is, matters concerning personnel, the execution lies with the Ministry of Defence, though they have delegated the powers to the Service Headquarters, yet the Service Headquarters do not have financial powers. Now, if a person has been granted the pension, final the approval has to be given by the Ministry of Defence. So, it is because of these reasons that the cases are pending. The power itself is rarely used because the tribunals have the ex-judges of the High Courts sitting there and the officers are reasonably senior, if at all it is ever used, it will be judiciously used. I do not think that anybody should have fears that it will abused by the Armed Forces Tribunal in any manner."

3.27 The Committee also obtained written memoranda from two non-official witnesses/experts in regard to the examination of the subject: Wing Commander U.C. Jha (Retd.) and Col. R. Balasubramanian (Retd.) Assistant Solicitor General of India were also of the view that conferment of civil contempt is necessary for execution of the decisions of the Tribunal by the concerned authorities.

3.29 The Ministry also informed the Committee through a written reply that Ministry of Law and Justice also endorsed the advice of the learned Attorney-General who in his opinion dated 14.07.2011 opined as under:

"I have carefully considered the matter. I fail to see any reason for drawing a distinction between conferring powers of criminal contempt and not conferring the powers of punishing civil contempt. A Tribunal which has power to issue binding orders, would be rendered effete if it does not have power to ensure that its orders are complied with. As a matter of constitutional law, the opinion of my learned predecessor is clear and I agree with it that there is no impediment. As a matter of policy, I see no reason why such power should not be conferred. On the contrary, it is clear that it should be so conferred."

3.32 During oral evidence, Secretary, Ministry of Law and Justice again endorsed his views and stated:

"....As far as the second amendment is concerned regarding civil contempt, I am in support of this amendment. It is needed. The Central Administrative Tribunal and other Administrative Tribunals created under the Administrative Tribunal Act already has this power."

3.33 He also clarified about the powers of AFT as under:

"This Tribunal is on par with the High Court and High Court has already the power to punish intentional disobedience of its orders. So, it is but natural that the Tribunal of this level and whose decisions are also declared to be final should have the power to punish for wilful disobedience of its orders. That is inherent in the judicial system which is needed."

3.34 After hearing the views of all the stakeholders and Ministries, including Ministry of Law and Justice, the Committee wanted to have explicit opinion of the Ministry of Defence as a summation to the proposed amendments in the Bill. On a specific query whether the Ministry of Defence had any objections, if the powers of civil contempt is given to the AFT, the Defence Secretary candidly stated as under:

"I have no objection because this is the proposal of the Ministry that the power should be given to it. This is our proposal. As to the compliance of the order, AFT is an Hon. court and has the powers equivalent to the High Court. So, the Ministry is committed to comply with the orders as long as a considered decision in consultation with a legal advice is not taken in that view should go in for an appeal. Otherwise, we have to comply with this order and we comply with the orders also."

3.35 Clarifying further on the role of the AFT in the light of the powers of civil contempt, the Defence Secretary while deposing before the Committee said :

"The AFT is not meant only for the retired people and it is also for the serving people. So, you have cases regarding service matters, like promotion, etc. Secondly, it is not that everything comes up to the Ministry level. There are different levels of decisions also. Some decisions are taken at the field level, some at the Corp Commander level and some at the Service Headquarters. I think the AFT is a step in the right direction. The object is to provide them a speedy justice through the mechanism of the AFT. Earlier, this redressal was being sought through the normal course, high courts and others. This is something which we do not deny. The AFT has a utility. Thirdly, challenging the authority of any authority is a fundamental right of every individual, whether he is in service or retired. We have to provide a reasonable opportunity to him and an institution where he can go and file his grievance. Coming to the compliance of the order, as I said, it is our earnest effort that we must respect the order of the AFT. As I said, it is equivalent, in terms of status, to the high courts. Therefore, we do that always. But there may be cases where we have difference of interpretation.

The Government may not agree or we feel that there is a scope for appeal, in that case, we go to appeal in Supreme Court or file writ in High Court. It is an institution which has a utility and we support that and that is why we have come for this amendment."

3.38 The Committee are not oblivious of the fact that the beneficiaries of the Armed Forces Tribunal Act are the retired or serving defence personnel. In this context, the views of the Vice-Chiefs of the services on the conferment of the powers of Civil Contempt on the Tribunal assume significance. A thorough examination reveals that the forces have opposed the conferment of the Civil Contempt mainly on the apprehension that it would impinge on operational requirements such as the absence of the summoned commanding officers jeopardising operational efficiency, difficulties in receiving summons in inaccessible terrains etc. The Committee are given to understand by the Services that AFT Act which is in nascent stage needs to be stabilised. The Defence Secretary has also shared the concerns of the forces with the Committee. The views of the three Vice-Chiefs as given before the Committee are on similar lines.

3.39 The Committee note that the Ministry of Defence, Ministry of Law and Justice and other stake holders including Administrative Members of the Armed Forces Tribunal etc. are in support of the conferment of powers of Civil Contempt mainly on the grounds of providing speedy justice to the aggrieved persons and obviating the longer and expensive processes of approaching higher courts.

3.40 After weighing all the pros and cons of the submissions made in regard to the conferment of powers of Civil Contempt to the Tribunal envisaged in the proposed bill, the Committee are compelled to tread cautious approach in this regard. While they are conscious about providing speedy justice to defence personnel (retired or serving), they do not want to disturb the highest standard of discipline prevalent among the forces. The Committee are of the view that if unfettered Civil Contempt powers are bestowed on AFTs, the discipline would be compromised to a great extent. This view of the Committee, is substantiated by the spate of recent judgements delivered by some of the AFTs with regard to issues concerning conflict of interest of Members of the Tribunal and impinging policy matters. Hence, the Committee are inclined to give Civil Contempt powers to AFTs with regard to the cases of retired defence personnel but conferment of such powers with regard to serving defence personnel is not acceptable till the justice delivery system through AFTs is stabilized. In other words, they want that no serving defence officer should be made to appear before the Tribunal for Civil Contempt. The Ministry could revisit this arrangement after sometime if it considers that the system has become matured enough. The Committee want the Ministry to bring necessary changes in the Bill. Armed Forces however, should develop a strong grievance redressal system so as to ensure speedy justice to serving defence personnel.

3.41 To give teeth to the Tribunal, the Committee recommend that the Civil Contempt powers proposed to be given to the Tribunal shall be applicable on the Ministry of Defence and all other civilian organizations as well as retired defence personnel.

4.13 The Armed Forces Tribunal Act, 2007 was enacted with a view to provide for quicker and less expensive justice to the members of the armed forces. The Committee however, find that as many as 4605 cases were pending before various benches of the Tribunal as on 30 November, 2012. Needless to say that such a large number of cases going to Armed Forces Tribunals reflects inadequacies in the grievance redressal system available in the Armed Forces. The Committee are of firm view that it is high time that Ministry of Defence took concerted steps to strengthen mechanism for redressal of grievances of members of the forces by stipulating that the higher/appellate authority in the three wings of the services should decide the representations of the aggrieved members by invariably issuing a speaking order in a time bound manner in each case. The Committee feel convinced that such a strengthened mechanism will go a long way in dispensations of quick and cheaper justice besides decreasing the burden of cases on the Armed Forces Tribunal.

FORM NO. 1

[See rule 9(2)]

FORM OF INDEX

THE ARMED FORCED TRIBUNAL ....BENCH

OA/RA/CA (Civil/Criminal)/MA/TA/ 20....

A..}

} Applicant/Petitioner

B... }

By Legal Practitioner Mr./Ms.

A..}

} Respondents

B... }

By Legal Practitioner

INDEX

Sl. No	Brief description of proceedings/ documents	Page No. From	Page No. To

Signature of the applicant
Legal Practitioner

FOR USE BY THE REGISTRY

Date of presentation/Filing

Date of Receipt by post

Registration (diary) No.

Signature
for Registrar

FORM NO. 2

[See rule 10 (2)]

THE ARMED FORCES TRIBUNAL, ...BENCH

Diary No ___________

Report on the scrutiny of Application

Presented by: ....Date of presentation ______________

Applicant (s) ....

Respondent (s) ....

Nature of grievance ....

No. of applicants .... No. of respondents: ....

CLASSIFICATION

Subject...........(No........)Department.................(No ....)

---

1. Is the application in the proper form?

   (Three complete sets in paper-book from in two compilations)
2. Whether name, together with personal number, rank, unit or formation etc as applicable, age description and address of all the parties have been furnished in the cause title?
3. (a) Has the application been duly signed and verified?

   (b) Have the copies been duly signed?

   (c) Have sufficient number of copies of the application been filed?
4. Whether all the necessary parties are imp leaded?
5. Whether English translation of documents in a language other than English or Hindi been filed?
6. Has the Vakalatnama/Memo of appearance/authorisation been filed?
7. Is the application maintainable? (u/s 2, 14, 15, 16, 19 or u/r 9 etc.).
8. Is the application accompanied by Indian Postal Order / Demand Draft for rupees two hundred fifty or as required? (vide rules 13 and 15.)
9. Has the Impugned order's original / duly attested legible copy been filed?

10. Have legible copies of the annexure been duly attested and filed?
11. Has the Index of documents been filed and pagination done properly?
12. Has the applicant exhausted all available remedies as provided under Section 21?
13. Does the application meet requirement of Section in time? (See Section 21)
14. Whether requirement of period of limitation indicated in Section 22 has been met.
15. Has the declaration as required by item 7 or Form I of AFT (Procedure) Rules 2008 has been made?
16. Have required number of envelopes (file size) bearing full address of the respondents been filed?
17. (a) Whether the relief's sought for arise out of single cause of action?

    (b) Whether any interim relief is prayed for?
18. In case Miscellaneous Application for condonation of delay is filed, is it supported by an affidavit or the applicant?
19. Any other point?
20. Result of the scrutiny with initial of the scrutiny clerk.

Section Officer

____

Deputy Registrar

____

REGISTRAR

FORM NO. 3

[See rule 10(2)]

ARMED FORCES TRIBUNAL,........BENCH

Diary No...........20...

C.P. (Civil/Criminal)......20...

Between

....Petitioner(s)

By

....

(Name of the Counsel, if any)

And

....Petitioner(s)

By

....

(Name of the Counsel, if any)

Subject: (No...........) Department: (No......)

REPORT OF THE SCRUTINY OF CONTEMPT OF COURT PETITION (CIVIL/CRIMINAL)

1. Whether the name (including as far as possible, the name of Father/ mother/husband), age, occupation and address of the respondent(s) are given?

Note: Together with personal number, rank, unit or formation, age, etc., as applicable.

2. Whether the parties impleaded as petitioner(s) and respondent(s) are proper?

Note :- (a) In case of civil contempt for disobeying the order of the Tribunal, it is the party in whose favour the direction is issued that can be impleaded as applicant and the party against whom the direction is issued can be impleaded as the respondent.

(b) In case of criminal contempt, the party who is alleged to have committed contempt, that can be impleaded as respondent.

3. Nature of the Contempt (Civil/Criminal) and the provisions of the Act invoked?

4. (a) Date of alleged Contempt?

(b) Date of filing of the Contempt Petition?

(c) Whether the petition is barred by limitation under section 20 of the Contempt of Courts Act, 1971?

5. (a) Whether the grounds and material facts constituting the alleged contempt are given?

(b) Whether the grounds and facts alleged in the petition are divided into paragraphs and numbered?

(c) Whether the petition is accompanied by supporting documents or certified/photostat (attested) copies of the original thereof?

(d) If the application relies upon any other document(s) in his possession, whether copy of such document(s) is/are filed along with the application?

(e) Whether the application and its annexures have been filed in a paper-book from and duly indexed and paginated?

(f) Whether three complete sets of the paper-books have been filed?

(g) Whether equal number of extra copies of paper-books have been filed in case there are more respondents than one?

6. Whether the nature of the order sought from the Tribunal is stated?

7. Whether the petition is supported by an affidavit sworn to by the applicant verifying the facts relied upon?

Note:- No affidavit is required if the Motion is by Attorney General/Solicitor General/Additional Solicitor General.

8. Whether the applicant or his legal practitioner have signed the petition indicating the place and date?

9. In case of Civil Contempt whether the petition is accompanied by a certified copy of the judgement/decree/order/undertaking alleged to have been disobeyed by the alleged contemner?

10. (a) In case of criminal contempt, not covered by section 14* of the Contempt of Courts Act, whether the petitioner has produced the consent obtained from the Attorney General/Solicitor General/Additional Solicitor General?

(b) If not, whether the petition contains the reasons thereof?

*Contempt committed in the presence or hearing of the Member(s).

11. Whether the petitioner had previously made a Contempt Petition on the same facts? If so, have the following been furnished:

(a) Number of the application?

(b) Whether the petition is pending?

(c) If disposed of, nature/result of the disposal with date?

12. Whether the draft charges are enclosed in a separate sheet?

FOR ATTENTION

Orders on the administration side have to be obtained from the Chairperson/ Vice Chairperson or Member designated in case of action for criminal contempt, as required by Rule 7 (ii) of the Contempt Rules before placing for preliminary hearing.

FORM NO. 7

[See rule 24 (1)]

THE ARMED FORCES TRIBUNAL,.................. BENCH

at.................................

No.................... of 20..........

Between

.... Applicant (s)

By Legal Practitioner Shri.................................

and

.... Respondent (s)

By Legal Practitioner Shri.................................

PROCESS MEMO

Please issue notice/process to the following parties and a sum of Rs ....is paid herewith by way of I.P.O./D.D. No............... of ....

Rank of the Party in the Proceedings 1	Name of the Party 2	Address for Services 3

Place: Legal Practitioner for the Applicant

Date: Central Government Standing Counsel

FORM NO. 8

[See rule 28]

ARMED FORCES TRIBUNAL, ...BENCH

Applicant (s)		Respondent (s)
	Versus	
Represented by		Represented by
Legal Practitioner Shri		Legal Practitioner Shri

To,

1. ....
2. ....
3. ....
4. ....

NOTICE TO SHOW CAUSE REGARDING ADMISSION

Whereas an application filed by the above named applicant (s) under Section 14 or 15 as applicable of the Armed Forces Tribunal Act 2007, as in the copy annexed hereuto has been registered and upon preliminary hearing the Tribunal has directed that you should be given an opportunity to show cause why the application should not be admitted.

Notice is hereby given to you to appear in this Bench of the Tribunal in person or through a Legal Practitioner in this matter at of the .... day of.........20.........to show cause, why the application should not be admitted. If you fail to appear, the application will be heard and decided in your absence.

Given under my hand and the seal of this Tribunal, this the ......day.......of...20...

By order of the Tribunal

Registrar

FORM No. 9

[See rule 28]

ARMED FORCES TRIBUNAL, ……….BENCH

Original Application No ……………………………….. / 20…………

………………………………………………………………………………

Applicant(s) (By Legal Practitioner/Govt. Legal Practitioner) Shri………)

To,

……………………………………………………………………..

…………………………………………………………………….

ORDER AFTER ADMISSION

Whereas an application filed by the above named applicant (s) under Section 14 or 15 as applicable of the Armed Forces Tribunal Act 2007, as in the copy annexed hereunto has been registered and upon preliminary hearing the Tribunal has admitted the application.

Notice is hereby given to you that if you with to contest the application, you may file your reply along with the documents in support thereof and after seeing copy of the same on the applicant or his legal practitioner within 30 days of receipt of the notice, before this Tribunal, either in person or through a legal practitioner appointed by you in this behalf. In default, the said application may be heard and decided in your absence on or after that date without any further notice.

Issued under my hand and the seal of the Tribunal this the ……day of……

By order of the Tribunal

Registrar

FORM NO. 10

[See rule 45 (1)]

IN THE ARMED FORCES TRIBUNAL, ...BENCH

APPLICATION FOR EARLY HEARING

Misc, Application No ....of..................in Original/Transferred Application No ....of 20...........Applicant/Petitioner.

Versus

.... Respondent(s) / Applicant(s)

Brief facts to justification for early hearing of the application.

Relief or Prayer:

Verification:

I,............(Name of the applicant) S/o, D/o, W/o.............. ....age.....................working..................in the office of..........................resident of..............................do hereby verify that the contents of para ....to.......................are true on legal advice and that I have not suppressed, any material fact.

Signature of the applicant

Place: ....

Signature of the Legal Practitioner

Dated: ....

FORM NO. 11

[See rule 55 (1)]

IN THE ARMED FORCES TRIBUNAL,.................. BENCH

OA/TA/RA/CA/AT/MA No. .... of ....20...........

....Applicant /s

Versus

....Respondent /s

APPLICATION FOR INSPECTION OF DOCUMENTS / RECORDS

I hereby apply for grant of permission to inspect the documents / records in the above case. The details are as follows: -

---

1. Name and address of the person seeking inspection:

---

2. Whether he is a party to the case/his legal practitioner and if so, his rank therein:

---

3. Details of the papers/documents sought to the inspected:

---

4. Reasons for seeking the inspection:

---

5. The date and duration of the inspection sought:

---

6. Whether any fee is payable and if so, the mode of payment:

Place:.........

Date:.........

Applicant

Office Use:

Granted inspection for .... hours on ....rejected.

Registrar AFT ....

FORM NO. 12

[See rule 59 and 65]

FORM OF VAKALATNAMA

ARMED FORCES TRIBUNAL, ...BENCH

OA/RA/CA/AT/MA/TA No.____________of 20....____________________

____Applicant/s

Versus

____Respondent/s

I,____________________in the above application do hereby appoint and retain Shri________________ Legal Practitioner to appear, plead and act for me/us in the above application and to conduct and prosecute all proceedings that may be taken in respect thereof including Contempt of Court Application and Review Applications arising there from and applications for return of documents, enter into compromise and to draw any moneys payable to me/us in the said proceeding.

Place: ....

Signature of the party

Date: ....

Executed in my presence.

"Accepted"

*Signature with date Signature with date

(Name and designation) (Name of the Legal Practitioner)

Name and address of the Legal Practitioner for service

*The following certification to be given when the party is unacquainted with the language of the *Vakalatnama* or is blind or illiterate:

The contents of the Vakalatnama were truly and audibly read over / translated into .... language known to the party executing the Vakalath and he seems to have understood the same.

(Signature with date)

(Name)

FORM NO. 13

[See rule 60]

IN THE ARMED FORCES TRIBUNAL,.................. BENCH

OA/TA/RA/CA (Civ/Cri)/AT/MA No. .... of ....20...........

....Applicant /s

Versus

....Respondent /s

MEMO OF APPEARANCE

I, ...having been authorized ....
....(here furnish the particulars of authority)
by the Central Government notified under Section 25(2) applicable of the Armed Forces Tribunal Act, 2007, hereby appear for Applicant No. ....Respondent No.....................and undertake to plead and act for them in all matters in the aforesaid case.

Place:.........

Signature and Designation of the Legal Practitioner

Date:..........

Address of the Legal Practitioner for service.

FORM NO. 15

[See rule 73 (1)]

ARMED FORCES TRIBUNAL, ...BENCH

O.A. / R.A. /T.A. /A.T. / C.A. / (Civil / Criminal) / No. .... of 20...

.... Applicant / s

Versus

.... Respondent / s

AFFIDAVIT

I, ... No .... Rank ....aged...................
...............years, son / daughter / wife / husband of..........................
.........name and occupation of the deponent, unit...............................
.................................residing at..
....
....do hereby swear in the name of God/solemnly affirm and state as follows:-

Para 1

Para 2

Para 3

....

....

....

Contents of paragraphs No(s)........................are within my personal knowledge and contents of paragraph No(s)............are based on information received by me which I believe the same to be true (state the source of information wherever possible and the grounds for belief, if any)

....

Signature of the Deponent

Name in Block Letters

Place: ....

Date: ....

No. of corrections on Page No(s).

Identified by: ....Sworn/solemnly affirmed before me on this the ....day of ....20.....

Signature

(Name and Designation of the Attesting authority with seal)

*To add endorsement in form No. 16 when necessary.

FORM NO. 16

[See rule 76]

ARMED FORCES TRIBUNAL, ………..BENCH

CERTIFICATION WHEN DEPONENT IS UNACQUAINTED WITH THE LANGUAGE OF THE AFFIDAVIT OR IS BLIND OR ILLITERATE

Contents of the affidavit were truly and audibly read over/translated into …………………...languagc known to thc dcponcnt and put his signaturc or mark in my presence.

(Signature)

Name and Designation with date

FORM NO. 17

[See rule 79(2) and 111(1)]

ARMED FORCES TRIBUNAL, ...BENCH

AN APPLICATION FOR SUMMONS TO PRODUCE DOCUMENTS OR FOR RETURN AND TRANSMISSION OF DOCUMENTS OR FOR OBTAINING COPIES BY STRANGERS

OA/RA/CA/AT/MA No ....of ....

....Applicant

Versus

....Respondent

(Brief facts leading to application)

It is therefore prayed that summons may please issued to the persons/ authorities/officials named and addressed as shown below for production of documents/exhibits for the reasons shown against each or the documents/ exhibits summoned earlier may be retuned and transmitted or copies of documents mentioned below may be supplied.

1. Name:...
2. Address: ....
3. Nature and description of exhibit or document: ....
4. Justification: ....

Verification

I,....................Name, No, Rank, unit ....Age, ... resident of .... do hereby verify that the contents of para 1 to.....above are true no legal advice and that I have not suppressed any material fact.

Place: ....

Signature of Applicant

Date: ....

Signature of Legal Practitioner

FORM NO. 18

[See rule 79 (3)]

ARMED FORCES TRIBUNAL, ...BENCH

OA/RA/CA/(Civil /Criminal) AT/MA No .... of 20...

SUMMONS FOR PRODUCTION OF DOCUMENTS OR EXHIBITS BY THE TRIBUNAL

Between

....Applicant/s

By Legal Practitioner Shri ....)

and

....Respondent/s

By Legal Practitioner Shri ....)

To

Whereas the Tribunal Suo Motu or on consideration of the request made by Shri........... ....(applicant/Respondent No.) having been justified that production of the following documents/records under your control/custody is necessary for proper decision of the above case, you are hereby directed to cause production of the said documents/records before this Tribunal / forward duly authenticated copies thereof on or before the ....day of........................20.....

(Enter description of documents requisitioned)

Date: ....

"By Order Tribunal"

Registrar

FORM NO.19

[See rule 88 (1)]

ARMED FORCES TRIBUNAL, ...BENCH

TA/OA/RA/CA/(Civil / Criminal) AT/MA No.................................of 2010

DEPOSITION OF PW / RW

1. Name:
2. Number and Rank:
3. Father's / Mother's / Husband's Name:
4. Unit / Formation:
5. Age:
6. Occupation:
7. Place of Residence and address:
8. Name of the officer administering the oath / affirmations:
9. Name of the interpreter if any, duly sworn / solemnly affirmed:

Examination-in-chief: By

....

....

Cross-examination: By

....

....

Re-examination, if any:

....

(Signature of the witness on each page)

Statement was read over / translated to the witness who admitted it to be correct.

Signature of the Member of the Bench with date

FORM NO. 20

[See rule 90]

ARMED FORCES TRIBUNAL, ...BENCH

CERTIFICATE OF DISCHARGE

Certified that .... Appeared before this Tribunal as a witness in OA / RA / TA / AT / CA (civil / criminal) / MA No................ of 2010 on behalf of the applicant / petitioner / respondent / as court witness on the .... day of .... 20....and that he was relieved at.................................. on ....
He was paid / not paid any TA and DA / Batta of Rs......................
....

Date: ....

Signature of Principal Registrar / Registrar

FORM NO. 22

[See rule 103 (3)]

ARMED FROCES TRIBUNAL,..........BENCH

BILL OF COSTS

(To be annexed to the order)

OA/ RA/ TA/AT/CA/MA/No .... of 20.....

Costs awarded to applicant No .... Respondent No ....and payable by applicant No .... Respondent No ....

(i) Legal Practitioner's fee .... Rs ....

(ii) Expenses .... Rs ....

Total Rs

Seal of the Tribunal

(Signature)

Principal Registrar / Registrar

Note. - No bill of costs need to be prepared or annexed, if costs not awarded.

FORM NO. 24

[See rule 109 (1)]

IN THE ARMED FORCES TRIBUNAL,................... BENCH

OA/TA/RA/CA (Civ/Cri)/AT/MA No............ of ....20...........

....Applicant/s

Versus

....Respondent/s

APPLICATION FOR GRANT OF CERTIFIED COPIES

1. Name and address of the applicant:
2. Whether the applicant is a party to the case, if not whether an application under rule 109 is filed:
3. Whether the case is pending or disposed of:
4. Description with date of the documents of which copy is applied for:
5. No. of copies required and nature of application (whether urgent or ordinary):
6. Details of the fee remitted along with the application:

Dated this the .... day of ....20......................

Signature of the Applicant

Legal Practitioner for the Applicant

FOR OFFICE USE

Granted / Rejected

Additional copying fee payable/paid and details thereof:

(Initials of the officer in-charge)

FORM NO. 25

[See rule 119 (1)]

IN THE ARMED FORCES TRIBUNAL, ………..BENCH

NOTIFICATION OF CERTIFIED COPIES READY FOR DELIVERY

Sl. No. 1	Copy Application No. 2	Name of the Applicant 3	Case No. 4	Date on which copy is ready for delivery 5

(Signature of the Officer in-charge with date)

FORM NO. 26

[See rule 146 (2)]

DEPARTMENT WISE CLASSIFICATION OF CASES

(A) ARMY

(B) NAVY

(C) AIR FORCE

(D) EX SERVICEMAN

(E) WIDOWS / DEPENDENTS

FORM NO. 27

[See rule 146 (3)]

SUBJECT WISE CLASSIFICATION OF CASES

1. Enrolment and grant of commission.
2. Ad hoc appointment / regularization.
3. Allotment/ Vacation/Eviction of Government Quarters/of Government hired accommodation matters.
4. Examination and courses.
5. Creation and abolition of posts.
6. Pay and allowances, pensionary benefits, compensation.
7. Disciplinary Cases –
   (a) Court Martial – SGCM, GCM, DCM, SCM.
   (b) Summary award/Summary Trial.
   (c) Adm Action including termination of service.
   (d) Award of censure.
   (e) Suspension.
   (f) Bails.
   (g) Wrongful confinement.
   (h) Disciplinary and Vigilance Ban.
8. Deputation / repatriation / absorption in Government / public sector.
9. Ration and uniform.
10. LTC.
11. Medical facilities.
12. Special provisions for Ex-serviceman / physically handicapped / casualty.
13. Retirement, dismissal, discharge, release and resignation.
14. Selection / Promotion / grant of substantive rank etc.
15. Seniority / Confirmation.
16. Claims of medical Reimbursement, Leave, Joining time etc.
17. Compassionate appointment / appointment of dependents dying in harness.
18. Crossing of efficiency bar.

19. Date of birth.
20. Entry in Character Rolls / confidential / Service Record.
21. Fixation of Pay.
22. Travel Regulations.
23. Grant of pension, family, family pension, other retirement benefits and interest on retirement benefits.
24. Grant of refusal to grant Advances / Loans.
25. Grant, refusal or recover of allowances.
26. Stagnation increment.
27. Annual Confidential Report.
28. Compulsory retirement.
29. Retrial benefits (other than pension).
30. Pension matters -
    (a) Disability pension
    (b) Family pension
    (c) Special family pension
31. Maintenance allowance
32. Contempt matters
33. Miscellaneous.

Index

Other Valuable Books

VOICE of CBI

M Narayanan
(Former Jt Director: CBI)

ISBN 978-81-7049-467-6
₹ 595.00 $ 35.00

Legal Guide *for* Police and Citizens

SP Kar, IPS
Former IGP-Assam

ISBN 978-81-7049-459-1
₹ 495.00 $ 30.00

The 21st Century Army
Strategies for Future

Lt Gen Gautam Banerjee
PVSM, AVSM, YSM

ISBN: 978-81-7049-414-0
Rs. 795.00 $ 45.00

Is It Police?
Confession of a Top Cop

VK Singh, IPS

ISBN: 978-81-7049-431-7
Rs. 595.00 $ 35.00

Legal Safeguards for Defence Personnel

Air Cmde.
Ranvir Kumar, AVSM
Former Judge Advocate General (Air)

ISBN: 81-7049-277-7
Rs. 495.00 $ 30.00

Leadership Failure in Police

Dr NC Asthana, IPS
Dr Anjali Nirmal

ISBN 978-81-7049-464-5
₹ 995.00 $ 55.00

The Sikh Detective

A Novel by
Col KS Rajamani

ISBN 978-81-7049-465-2
₹ 495.00 $ 30.00

Army Leadership

Department of the Army, USA

ISBN: 978-81-7049-445-4
Rs. 595.00 $ 40.00

Armed Forces Tribunal

Wg Cdr Dr. UC Jha

ISBN 978-81-7049-362-4
Rs. 495 $ 30.00

The Writing on the Wall: India Checkmates America 2017

General S. Padmanabhan, PVSM, AVSM, VSM (Retd.)
(Former Chief of the Army Staff, India)

ISBN: 81-7049-175-4
Rs. 595.00 $ 35.00

General Salute

Lt Col Arun Jha

ISBN: 978-81-7049-437-9
Rs. 495.00 $ 30.00

Human Rights: International Challenges

Dr. S. Subramanian, IPS
(Former DG: CRPF & NSG: Director: SPG & NPA: Minister: Embassy of India, Germany
Foreword by:
Justice Ranganath Mishra
(Former Chief Justice of India)

Two Volumes

ISBN: 81-7049-068-5
Rs. 2200.00 (Set) $ 30.00